BUILD A WEB SITE

The Programmer's Guide to Creating, Building, and Maintaining a Web Presence

net.Genesis
and
Devra Hall

PRIMA PUBLISHING

To Mom and Dad

P™ is a trademark of Prima Publishing, a division of Prima Communications, Inc.

Prima Publishing™ is a trademark of Prima Communications, Inc.

Prima Online™ is a trademark of Prima Publishing, Inc.

Prima Computer Books is an imprint of Prima Publishing, Rocklin, California 95677.

Project Editor: Stefan Grünwedel

ISBN: 0-7615-0064-2

Library of Congress Catalog Card Number: 94-74104

Printed in the United States of America

96 97 98 AA 10 9 8 7 6 5 4 3

Contents

Table of Listings

Foreword

It seems just a short time ago, and yet such a long time ago, that the World Wide Web was a new, struggling project. The Web spread from that obscurity to its later strength through efforts at the grass-roots level. Hardly any work on the Web was mandated by corporate management. In that unofficial, "alternative" USENET group alt.hypertext, people discussed in their spare time their dreams of what the Web could be.

Matthew Gray was an early supporter of this underground movement. Largely at his instigation, MIT's boringly named—but really quite interesting—"Student Information Processing Board" started an unofficial Web server, which was later to compete with the "official" MIT server. Across the globe people found that there was always room in hyperspace to plant their view of things.

As I write this, the now-widespread users of the Web are realizing that alongside this free expression one needs a sense of responsibility to portray the status of one's work accurately. The search is on for ways to test the accuracy of information, and security protocols are being proposed to allow one to conduct secure, bona fide commerce on the Web. Recently there was concern that a terrorist group used the Internet to communicate and express their extreme views on the Web. Along with the fear that schoolchildren will be misled and corrupted come demands for censorship by "trusted" parties.

Now that the Web has grown to the point where there is a need for books about it, let's remember that it is just an infrastructure. Like paper, the Web enables communication but does not constrain it. The existence and power of the Web relies on its generality. The decentralized nature of the Web is essential to its existence, and does not allow a single notion of what is "proper." Though later there may be more sophisticated ways of labeling hypertext and guiding the reader (the road markings of the information highway), there is no substitute for being streetwise. However, the more we write about what we believe, and link to that which we respect, the safer the Web becomes.

This book is intended for those who want to know how the Web works and how to build it. So welcome, gentle reader, and may you feel both freedom and the responsibility which it brings you. Have fun.

Tim Berners-Lee
Cambridge, Massachusetts
May, 1995

Acknowledgments

Thanks to Brad and Will for believing in us and for their continual support; to Devra Hall for putting up with the Boston weather—and all our quirks and personalities—in order to give us a voice to the rest of the world; to Sean for the being the danger boy and keeping the office fun by bringing Steph in; to D, Vicki, Julian, and Matt for helping us refine the content and work out all the bugs; to George for being there from the beginning; to Jenn for taking care of us and taking care of George; to Barry Friedman for giving us the chance; to Sherri Morningstar for being so incredibly forgiving, helpful, and wonderful; to Stefan Grünwedel, Barbara Archer, and Ben Dominitz for being so patient and giving us a helping hand through the project; to Nanette for helping us get our ideas out there; to our parents for always being there; to Chistopher Sawyer-Lucanno for teaching us how to write (and for Matt's thesis); to Dave and Roger from Net Info for helping us keep our network up so we could work on the book; to Taylor and Webster at WING for helping us keep the Tank on the Net; to Clockwork Design Group Inc. for making us look good; for Michael Neubarth at *Internet World* magazine for giving us a forum to express our ideas and a voice to the world; to Tom Hagopian and Dick Glover at ESPN for giving us our first chance; to Rob Hunter for being the inside man at ESPN; to John Kirby for the great sidebar; to Amy Batchelor for suffering through the beginning of the book with us; to the Student Information Processing

Board for bringing the Web to MIT and for all the years of experience and assistance; and to Dan Connolly, Simon Spero, and Tim Berners-Lee for helping us find the information we needed.

net.Genesis

Those of us who make a living writing about technology must keep up with all of its new developments—but that is easier said than done. And that is why the opportunity to work on this book was especially exciting for me. These young Web-masters from MIT live and breathe on the cutting edge of new technologies. They have razor-sharp minds, and their company, net.Genesis, is destined for great success. (Their clients already know this.) I'd like to thank Sherri Morningstar for recommending that I be the one to put their expertise and Web-savviness into book form so that others could benefit from their advice.

I'd also like to thank my favorite editorial team. The relationship between author and copyeditor can be touchy, but Peter Weverka has just the right touch. A project editor can make or break a book. Stefan Grünwedel is my all-time, favorite project editor. I suspect that his excellence and dedication are well nurtured by the rest of the Prima family.

Many bright minds and skilled hands contribute to the making and marketing of a book. Special thanks go to the President of Prima Publishing, Ben Dominitz, for believing in this book; Managing Editor Paula Munier Lee, for helping the editorial process flow smoothly; Barbara Archer in the publicity department for getting the word out; and Lynne Ford for helping the sales force get this book on the stores' shelves.

Finally, I'd like to acknowledge the efforts of Susan Glinert of BookMakers for her superb handling of design and production tasks; Paul Page Design for the cover; and indexer Mark Landerghini.

Devra Hall

Introduction

In the past year or two, the World Wide Web has gained tremendous notoriety and media attention. NCSA's Mosaic sparked much of the interest as the "killer app" which brought the vast resources of the Internet to the common user. Nearly a year later, Netscape Communications Corp. (formerly known as Mosaic Communications Corp.) recruited many of the Web's founders and gained the spotlight with its massive public relations engine. Behind this wave of attention came dozens of books which sought to ride the wave of attention and teach everyday users about the World Wide Web and its primary language—HTML.

However, nearly all these books left intermediate and advanced users wanting. The available books served as an introduction, but left readers wondering what more they could do. Most books only touched on the basics of HTML. They didn't delve into the more powerful, evolving HTML specifications.

Build a Web Site is aimed at taking users beyond simple HTML authoring and educating users about the technical details of the World Wide Web. It covers the protocols and standards that make up the information structure that is the Web. It covers HTML (2.0 and 3.0), URLs, CGI, and HTTP.

Specifically, the book provides information to help you think about the issues that need to be addressed before and after you set up a site, tips and hints on setting up a solid, reliable site, and advice on avoiding common mistakes. The book also includes many sample programs that will help you fully understand the specifications being described and realize how they can be used to your advantage.

I.1 What This Book Covers

This book is broken into four parts. Part I focuses on describing the World Wide Web and its evolution. Chapters 1 and 2 provide brief definitions of various elements of the Web and lay the foundation for understanding why the Web is the way it is. Chapter 3 gives the reader the instructions necessary to set up their own site. The chapter also talks about some of the issues and concepts of concern when setting up a site.

Part II is devoted to explaining and understanding the technical specifications and protocols which make up the Web. We discuss the Hypertext Transfer Protocol, Hypertext Markup Language, Uniform Resource Locator specification, and the Common Gateway Interface. For each of these standards we explain how the specifications are commonly used, in addition to what they say.

Part III focuses on the design and programming aspects of the Web. This portion of the book is intended for those users that want to get their hands into the inner workings of the Web so they can extend the functionality of their Web server, fully utilize the power of their site, or write their own client or server.

Part IV is designed to be used as a reference manual for all your technical questions. This section includes the actual specifications for the major protocols and standards of the Web. It should be noted that some of the specifications are still evolving and for the most recent versions the online copy should be consulted.

I.2 Helpful Code Samples

Throughout the book, we provide many samples of code which you can use to help understand the specifications being discussed. Each code sample includes the name of the file that it is saved under. You can download each file by using FTP. In order to download any piece of code used in the book, do the following:

1. FTP to ftp.netgen.com.
2. Log in as “anonymous” with your username as your password.

3. Change directories to /pub/book. Each listing in this book includes its own filename.
4. Type **get** and the name of the file you wish to download.

Here's how it might look for you to download a file called *filename.pl*:

```
> ftp ftp.netgen.com
Connected to netgen.com.
220 netgen FTP server (Version wu-2.4(1) Sun Jul 31 21:15:56 CDT 1994) ready.
Name (ftp.netgen.com:mkgray): anonymous
331 Guest login ok, send your complete e-mail address as password.
Password:
230 Guest login ok, access restrictions apply.

ftp> cd /pub/book
250 CWD command successful.

ftp> get filename.pl
200 PORT command successful.
```

Please let us know if you have any difficulties with this code.

I.3 Prerequisites for Reading This Book

Build a Web Site is aimed at intermediate and advanced Web users, although we encourage "ambitious beginners" to use this book to help them strive towards a more thorough understanding of the Web. Because of the current platform distribution of Web servers, this book is primarily aimed at users of UNIX machines who are running a Web server or who are interested in setting up a Web server. All code samples in the book are written in perl and are intended to run on UNIX platforms.

I.4 Conventions

Special typefaces are used throughout the book to denote different things. URLs are denoted as such: **http://www.netgen.com**.

Code is shown in a fixed-width font:

```
# Grep the index for the specified word
$results .=  $grep -i \'$pattern\

# Print out the results
print "<ul>\n";
foreach $result (split ("\n", $results))
{
  print "<li> $result\n";
}
```

Any code you should type appears in **boldface**. If something happens as a result, it appears below it, as shown:

```
> nifty.pl
Fulfilling http://www.netgen.com/...
Processing: http://www.netgen.com/...
URL: http://www.netgen.com/
Proto: http Siteport: www.netgen.com Path: /
creating socket to www.netgen.com:80...
binding...
connecting...
connected.
```

PART I

Web Basics

This introductory section provides you with an overview of the World Wide Web. Included are a discussion on interactivity, a historical timeline of Web developments, and projections about the future of the Web. This is followed by definitions of terms and concepts that are fundamental for developing an understanding of how the Web operates. This section concludes with key considerations that you must address before building your site, and instructions for configuring your server software.

CHAPTER 1

The What and Why of the Web

CHAPTER AT A GLANCE

This chapter provides a brief, nontechnical description of the World Wide Web and its relationship to the Internet. We talk about the types of information available on the Web, and the different levels of interactivity you can enjoy. We also provide a timeline of significant events detailing the history of the Web, describe how the Web evolved both technically and socially, and discuss the Web's possible future developments.

The Internet is a vast cyberspace where you can gather, disseminate, and exchange all types of information. The World Wide Web was conceived so that computer users could have a single, unified means of accessing hypermedia documents from anywhere on the Internet. However, the Web is a complex place, and accessing documents on the Web was quite difficult until the development of NCSA Mosaic, a WWW *browser* (a program that allows you to view documents on the Web and follow links from document to document). NCSA Mosaic presented the Web to users in a seamless interface that hid much of the Web's inherent complexity. Thanks to Mosaic and other GUI (graphical user interface) browsers, accessing sites throughout the world is as simple as "pointing and clicking." In this book, you will come to understand the Web's fundamental technology, appreciate the elegance of browsers like Mosaic, and be in a better position to exploit the Web's functionality.

Due in large part to the torrent of media attention that the Internet and the Web have received recently, many people mistakenly assume that the Web and the Internet are synonymous. This is not true. The Web is a collection of protocols and standards for accessing information on the Internet, and the Internet is the physical medium used to transport the data. Unlike other Internet standards and protocols (such as FTP and Gopher), Web standards and protocols (including HTTP and HTML) allow related information to be *hyperlinked*. Hyperlinking means that a document has pointers to related documents. This is one of the features that distinguishes the Web from other means of accessing information on the Internet.

So the Web is a medium for "distributed hypermedia." What does that phrase mean? "Distributed" describes the large number of computers all over the world that use the Internet as their mode of transit. When you traverse the Web, you are likely to be pointing and clicking your way around the entire globe. When you click on a link, you don't know whether the information you're retrieving is coming from Sweden, Bangkok, San Jose, or next door. You may think you know—after all, the Web page on your screen most likely has some type of identification—but the information you retrieve by clicking on links from that page may be coming from somewhere else.

For example, in this book you will find a lot of references to URLs. (A URL—the word stands for Uniform Resource Locator—is a sort of Web address, but we'll talk more about that later.) We've included these URLs in the figure so you can experience for yourself some examples of Web sites and their pages. If you examine these URLs, you will find that they all point to some page at netgen.com, our own site, which is physically located in Cambridge, Massachusetts. So how is it that the House of Representatives' Web site, a site

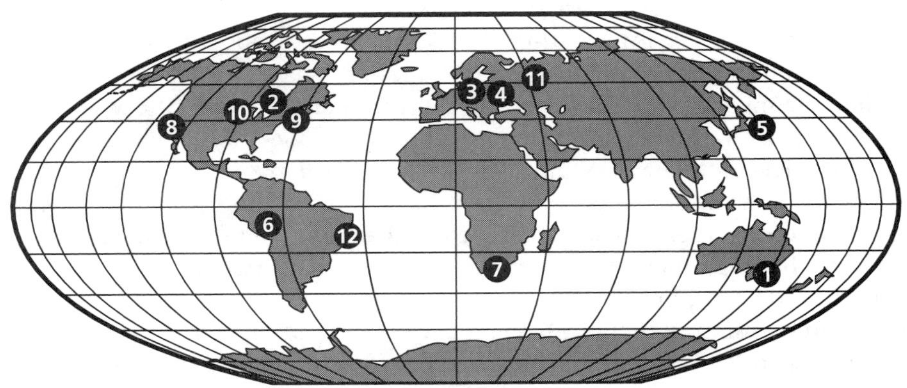

International URLs

URL	Location
1. **http://croom.syd.dah.csiro.au/**	Glebe, NSW, Australia
2. **http://www.cim.mcgill.ca/**	Montreal, Quebec, Canada
3. **http://www.embl-heidelberg.de/**	Heidelberg, Germany
4. **http://www.ens-lyon.fr/**	Lyon, France
5. **http://www.hiroshima-u.ac.jp/**	Hiroshima, Japan
6. **http://ulima.edu.pe/**	Lima, Peru
7. **http://www.ru.ac.za/**	Grahamstown, Eastern Cape, South Africa
8. **http://www.stanford.edu/**	Palo Alto, CA, USA
9. **http://www.netgen.com/**	Cambridge, MA, USA
10. **http://www.ncsa.uiuc.edu/**	Chicago, IL, USA
11. **http://www.novsu.ac.ru/**	Novgorod, Russia
12. **http://www.inf.ufsc.br/**	Santa Catarina, Brazil

Figure 1-1 The Web consists of information found throughout the world. Here is a tiny sample of sites accessible on the Web.

physically located in Washington, DC, has an address at netgen.com in Cambridge? It doesn't. When your browser points to the URL that we listed for the House of Representatives, you actually go to a page containing a description of the site and a link to the site. This is an example of hyperlinking. The reason we included the hyperlink is because sites can change locations. If we had listed the URL to the document and the site changed locations, the URL would no longer be valid. This way, we can change the URL on our site to keep up with sites that move, and no one has to worry about sites changing physical addresses.

The Web supports hypermedia and multimedia. Hypermedia is a combination of "hypertext" and "multimedia," where hypertext refers to the linking of related information and multimedia refers to using different types of data to represent information. For example, a data file that includes text, graphic images (drawings, photographs, etc.), audio (WAV and MIDI data), video and animation, as well as computer code or binary files, is a multimedia file.

Multimedia also refers to one type of medium inside another. For example, a text document with an *inline graphic* is a multimedia document. If not for the in-line graphic, you would have to use text to indicate where the graphic goes in the document and create a link from that text to an external file that contained the graphic image. Figures 1-2 and 1-3 show two versions of the net.Genesis home page. In Figure 1-2, our logo is an in-line graphic. In Figure 1-3, the text indicates "new logo" and there is a link to the external .GIF file containing the logo.

The Web supports multimedia, since it allows users to download all sorts of files—video clips, audio files, images, etc.—and view or play them on their computers. The Web supports hypermedia too, because all data types, including images and even portions of images, can be linked to other pieces of information.

NOTE

Video files are fun to download and play, but they are generally very large—hundreds of kilobytes, if not megabytes, in size. Downloading large video files can be time-consuming (even over a full T1), so be sure that you have lots of time to spare. Hiene Withagen maintains an archive of MPEG video clips at his site in The Netherlands, with a mirror site at Enterprise Integration Technologies in the United States. You can browse this archive from the net.Genesis site's book page.

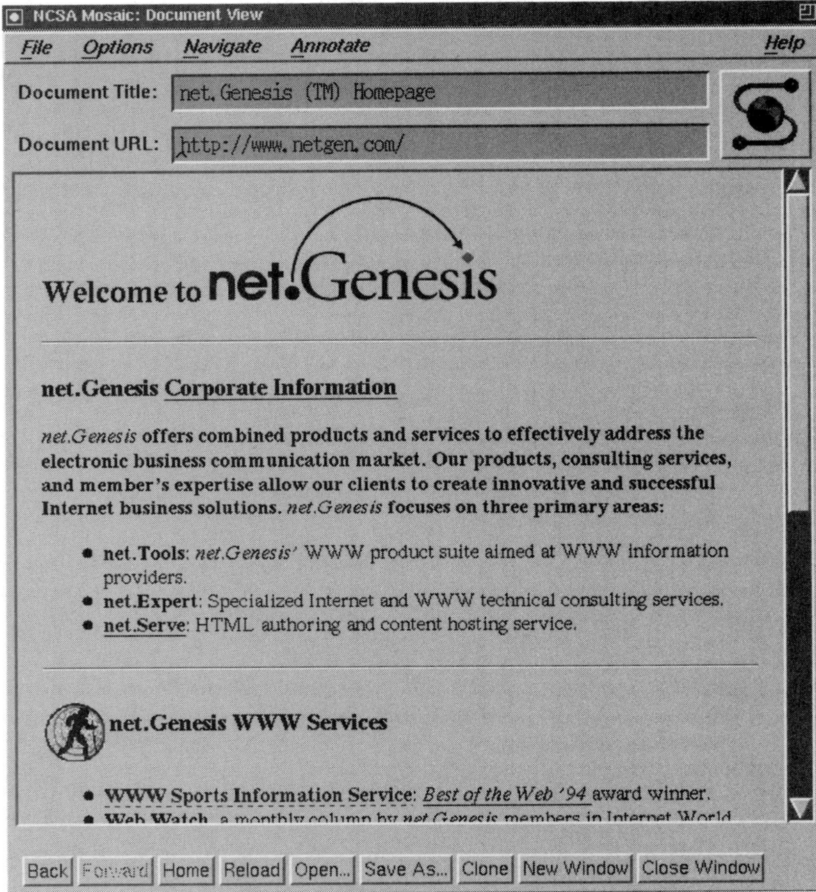

Figure 1-2 The net.Genesis home page, with the net.Genesis logo as an inline graphic

MPEG Video Clip Archive
http://www.netgen.com/book/mpeg_archive.html

With more and more people playing video games and using compact discs, multimedia doesn't seem like such a big deal. But it *is* a big deal. Not every machine can handle multimedia in all its variety. When you consider that the Web supports all types of data files, plus hyperlinking, and that the

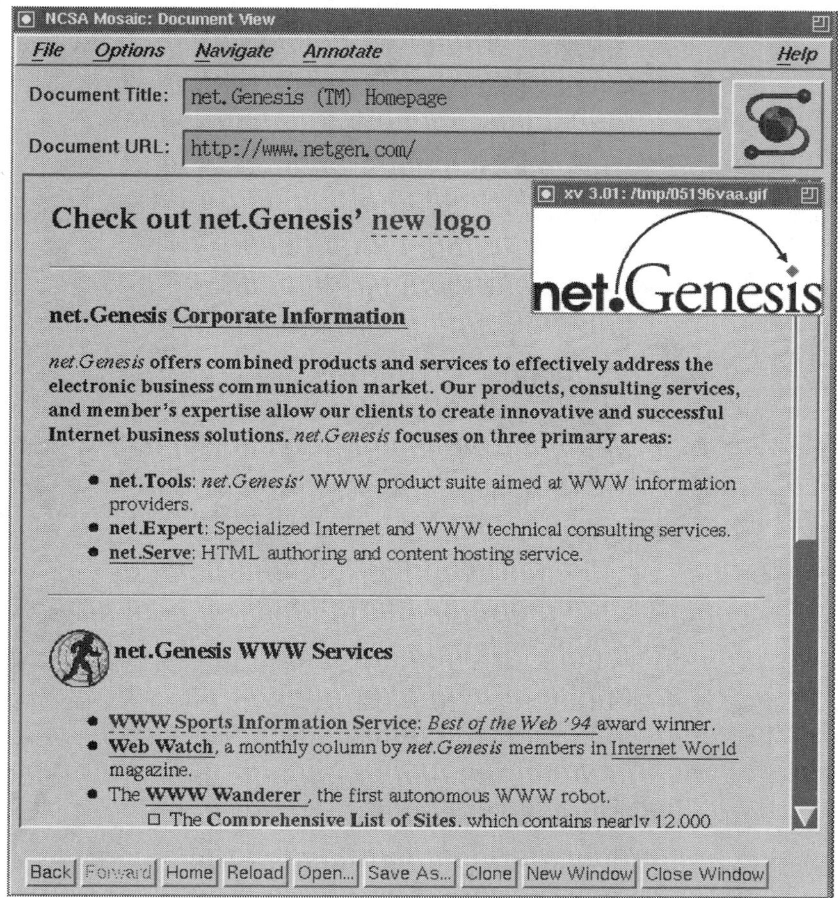

Figure 1–3 The net.Genesis home page, with a text indication for "new logo" and a link to the external .GIF file that contains the logo

people who access the Web use many different programs to create and access that data, the picture gets very complex. Compatibility issues alone can be a nightmare.

For starters, you can only hope that the browser a person uses to access Web data can interpret the data correctly. For example, many UNIX browsers won't know what to do with a QuickTime clip after they retrieve it, because QuickTime is primarily a Macintosh-based application. And that brings us full-circle to the standards and protocols that make the Web viable. But before we get into the mechanics of the Web, let's talk a little about hypertext and hypermedia.

1.1 The Web as a Repository of Information

People's thought and communication patterns are associative. We constantly link words, images, and sounds. (We also associate smells and tactile sensations, but where computers are concerned, that gets into the realm of virtual reality and is beyond the scope of the Web—at least for now.) Sometimes the associations are *tangential,* even arbitrary. For example, if you were requesting the latest NFL statistics but you suddenly remembered that your nephew had just finished playing his first college basketball game and you wanted to find out about the game, that association could be considered tangential.

At other times our associations are *supportive,* in that they provide additional details or a frame of reference. For example, when you read or watch a news report about the launch of the space shuttle, you usually see a photo or video clip of the launch as well. Visual images like these are supportive associations. If you wanted to know more, you might request the checklist NASA used before starting countdown. Such a list would provide more supporting data and yield greater depth of information.

Seeing the launch checklist could inspire a tangential association. For example, you might wonder how the checklist compares with an airline pilot's take-off checklist. Tangential links tend to provide breadth, while associative links go for depth. This distinction is not terribly useful except to illustrate the dimensional attributes that people ascribe to the Web. Perhaps you have already come across phrases such as "drilling down," which means to search out deeper levels of supporting data. Other words and phrases from the Web include "wandering," "browsing," "cruising," "navigating," and "surfing." All of these phrases refer to the notion that people access data on the Web by following *threads of information.*

Not everyone is interested in pursuing every level or tangent, and therein lies the beauty of the Web. You can publish *all* of your information (including the tiniest of details with links to the most obscure of supportive or tangential associations) and let the user choose what he or she wants to see. This is quite a luxury for both the information provider and consumer. In other media, especially print media—brochures, catalogs, and magazines—budget restrictions and production deadlines always seem to make

The Electronic Newsstand

Many magazines and newspapers have created their own Web sites. *Wired* has hit the Web big time. At its site, besides offering subscriptions and a library of back issues, *Wired* provides discussion forums, audio and video clips, news, and pointers to other hot sites on the Web. The Gate, a Web site for the *San Francisco Examiner* and the *San Francisco Chronicle,* features columns, sports stories, and classified ads—all the necessities of a newspaper. *Playboy* has a site where you can find quotes from back issues, playmate profiles, sex secrets, a comment form, and (of course) a subscription form. *PC Week* offers industry news bits, online columns, and a sampling of its lab reviews. These are just four of the many publications with a Web presence. You can find a good list of Web magazines at the Yahoo site.

Wired
http://www.hotwired.com

The Gate
http://www.sfgate.com

Playboy
http://www.playboy.com

PC Week
http://www.ziff.com/~pcweek

Yahoo Magazine List
http://akebono.stanford.edu/yahoo/entertainment/magazines/

including some of the data prohibitive. On the Web, color images aren't cost-prohibitive. You can add data whenever you want, and in the long run, server space is also less expensive.

Of course, there is a catch to offering a lot of information: You can't put up information in a chaotic, unorganized fashion and expect to make use of it. You have to structure the information in such a way that people can find what they are seeking. Designing a structure for the data is just as important as programming your server—perhaps it is more important, because unless information is accessible to users, even the slickest site doesn't have many visitors. We'll talk more about structuring data later in this chapter, and again in Chapter 10, where you'll get concrete design tips.

1.2 GUI Clients for Cruising the Net

For many years, the Internet has been a repository of vast amounts of information. But not until recently, with the advent of graphical user interface tools (browsers), did the Web become easy to access. Now people have really begun to get excited. The Web is currently being used very much as a presentation tool. Web standards and protocols, combined with browser technology, have made it possible to present information in an attractive manner, with in-line images and proportional fonts.

The most popular means of retrieving information from the Web is through GUI clients such as NCSA Mosaic. These clients allow users to "point and click" their way through the Web. GUI clients, by hiding much of the internal workings of the Web, provide a nearly seamless interface between users and data objects.

You don't need to know that your browser is issuing a series of commands and that, without your browser, you would have to type these commands at the prompt. For instance, you would have to type `cd` to change directories, `ls` to list the files, and `bin` to transfer binary files. You also would have to remember the host name and the path to the data object you wished to retrieve. Browsers handle all of this on your behalf.

Browsers are available for all the major platforms and for some of the minor ones as well. You can find browsers for UNIX, Macintosh, DOS, Windows, OS/2, X Windows, NeXT, Apple Newton, and SGI systems. Popular browsers include Mosaic, Netscape Navigator, Netcom NetCruiser, WinWeb, MacWeb, and Chameleon's WebSurfer, to name just a few. In addition, the major online services, such as America Online, Prodigy, and CompuServe, are beginning to offer Web access to complement their existing Internet features.

1.3 What Type of Information Should You Offer on the Net?

It's pretty safe to say that no matter what or how obscure your interests are, you can find information about them on the Internet. At the very least, you can find a relevant USENET newsgroup. With more and more Web sites appearing every day, chances are good that a Web site somewhere in the world is related to your interests. From the perspective of a Web site creator, you may even want to provide links from your site to related sites. Given the number of Internet users worldwide (estimates range from a few million to

The Keys to Success

Four factors have contributed to the tremendous success of the World Wide Web:

- **Critical mass**: At the time the Web was developed, enough people were using the Internet so that it became a general information distribution medium.
- **Hypermedia**: The Web's seamless integration of linked graphics, audio, and video, made creating Web sites and accessing the Web both fun and interesting.
- **General user knowledge**: Internet users had become familiar enough with distributed information systems. They were no longer intimidated by the complexity of these systems. The Web was an idea whose time had come.
- **NCSA Mosaic**: This flexible and easy-to-use browser substantially contributed to the popularity of the Web. Mosaic's functionality was not fundamentally different from that of other applications, but its attractive interface quickly established a devoted user-base. In addition, Mosaic could be used on UNIX, Windows, and Macintosh machines.

tens of millions), it is also a good bet that people will be interested in the site you want to build. How many people? That very important question will be the first of your key considerations when you get to Section 3.2 of this book.

Figure 1-4 shows the home page of the WWW Sports Information Service (SIS) that Eric Richard of net.Genesis created. Lots of sports fans and aficionados are on the Net. One of the great things about the Web is that any page can contain a link leading to any other Web page. For example, the TNS (Telemedia and Network Systems) site at the Laboratory for Computer Science has a link to the Sports site. Some sites, such as the Yahoo site, contain large pointer lists that link to scores of other sites, including the Sports Information Service.

WWW Sports Information Service
http://www.netgen.com/sis/sports.html

Yahoo
http://www.netgen.com/book/yahoo.html

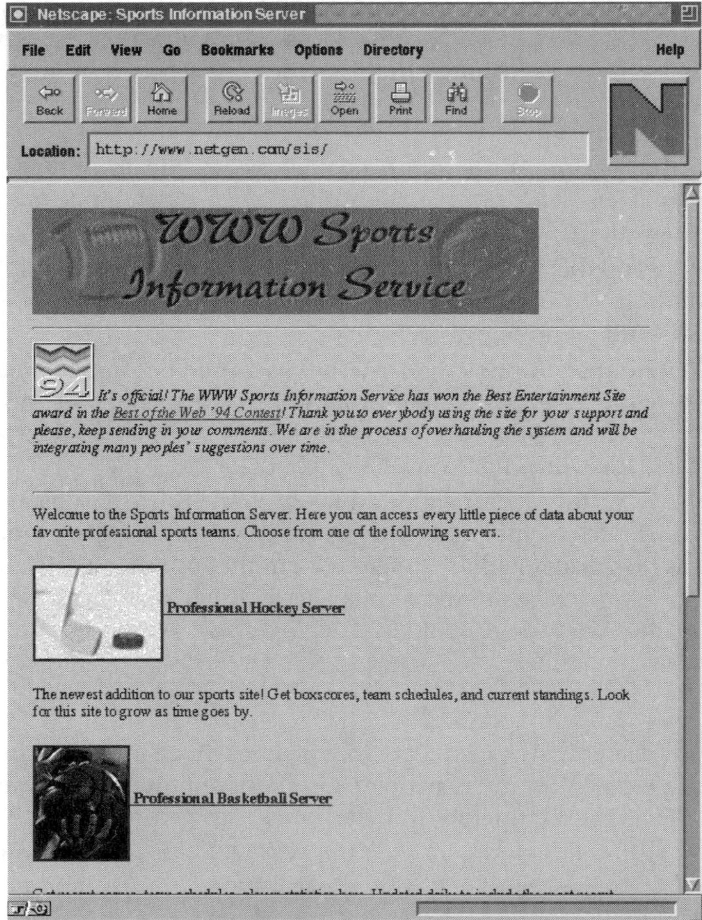

Figure 1–4 The home page of the WWW Sports Information Service

Many companies create Web sites as a means of getting information out to customers. It is easy to design a site so it communicates with both potential and existing customers. Company sites provide all kinds of information, including basic information on the company's services or products, and how to contact the company to ask questions, place orders, and even lodge complaints. Some sites post FAQs, which are documents with answers to "frequently asked questions." At company Web sites, you are likely to find corporate histories, copies of news releases, product specifications, and even product reviews (favorable ones, of course). Smart companies encourage users to comment on their products and services. They use the site as a means of obtaining information about customers. Using a Web site to interact with customers not only helps a company to be responsive, it is also a means of obtaining demographic data about customers that can be used to produce effective advertisements.

It is very important for new Web site builders to remember that the Web is meant to be a way of providing useful information. If your company is putting up tons and tons of in-your-face advertisements with little or no content, people are not going to be excited about you. Unless your ads are somewhat cool, or there is something really interesting about them, people won't come to your site in droves. If a company such as Nike that has terrific commercials put up a Web page with its hottest clips, it might be entertaining. But if some random company out there puts up a bunch of print ads, it's not going to work. Why? Because the Web is a very different medium in terms of how you generate interest. In-your-face hype works in the print and television media. On TV and in magazines, advertisers have thirty seconds or a one-page spread at most to present their ads, so they try to create lots of color, lots of splash, and lots of quick motion to catch the eye and attract attention.

RULE OF THUMB

While you might think of your Web site as your own personal television station, do not make the mistake of viewing the Web as a vehicle for one long commercial, because people will not stay tuned.

The way to make yourself stand out on the Web is by providing content. And that's one thing that a lot of sites, especially commercial sites, must realize. You have to provide information and services that are *useful* to people. If people find your site useful or interesting, if your product information does not get in the way and keep people from enjoying the other benefits your site has to offer, then people will visit (and revisit) your site. For example, the net.Genesis site offers services and resources in addition to corporate information. Usage logs of our site very clearly show that the useful information is what draws people. As the list below shows, only one percent of all hits were for net.Genesis corporate information. Most requests for corporate information come from users who came to the site for the other resources and then followed links to the corporate information. It's been our experience that people seek out sites that they like specifically to check out the product information and advertisements. The difference is that they do so because they want to, and this makes them potential customers who are motivated.

Total Hits (requests for data) at www.netgen.com: 161,879

Page Breakdown:

Sports Information Service: 38 percent

- NFL: 18 percent
- NBA: 35 percent
- NHL: 16 percent

The Wanderer's comprehensive list of Web sites: 23 percent

Wandex (a searchable index of the Web): 23 percent

Report of the growth of the Web: 2 percent

The net.Genesis home page: 1 percent

Other stuff: 4 percent

One of the most useful sites on the Web, and one that offers tasteful advertising along with entertaining content, is O'Reilly and Associates' Global Network Navigator (GNN). GNN presents a very effective blend of links between internally generated content and outside sites (each outside site is accompanied by a brief description). At the GNN site, you'll find columns and excerpts from O'Reilly publications, in addition to online catalogs. GNN designed the site to include graphics of a similar style. These graphics, which appear throughout the site, present a consistent look and feel.

By way of contrast, Prodigy's AstraNet is little more than a glorified hotlist. (A *hotlist* is a list in which each item is a hyperlink to other, related items.) Even though AstraNet is managed by Prodigy, one of the "Big 3" online services, very little effort was made to present real content on AstraNet. And the content that is available is only available for a fee. Most of the site is a list of links to outside resources. In spite of the fact that some effort went into organizing the site graphically and logically, very little effort was made to actually providing a service to Web users.

The Global Network Navigator
http://www.netgen.com/book/gnn.html

Prodigy's AstraNet
http://www.netgen.com/book/AstraNet.html

A Sampling of Web Sites

Individuals, companies, and government agencies set up Web sites for all sorts of reasons. Some sites, such as the Sports Information Service, appeal to a wide audience. Others are targeted at very specific audiences. Here are a few examples of sites to give you an idea of the variety of information that is found on the Web. None of these sites belong to net.Genesis, but we've created links on our site that will connect you with the sites shown here. The direct URL for each site is shown in parentheses.

The IBM Corporate Site
http://www.netgen.com/book/ibm.html

Contains lots of corporate information on products, services, technology and research, and more. (Their direct URL is **http://www.ibm.com** .)

The House of Representatives
http://www.netgen.com/book/housegov.html

Contains information about legislative processes, schedules of legislative activity, and the full text of all bills and resolutions. (Their direct URL is **http://www.house.gov** .)

The Monster Board
http://www.netgen.com/book/monster.html

This is an online job-placement service. You can submit your résumé search for job openings here. (Their direct URL is **http://www.monster.com/home.html** .)

***Paramount's Star Trek* Home Page**
http://www.netgen.com/book/paramount.html

Contains video and audio clips from the TV series, "Star Trek: Voyager." It previously had sneak clips for the movie, *Star Trek: Generations.* (Their direct URL is **http://www.paramount.com/** .)

International Association of Gay Square Dance Clubs
http://www.netgen.com/book/IAGSDC.html

Offers listings of IAGSDC conventions and member clubs, including a list of other gay and lesbian square dance resources. (Their direct URL is **http://hawg.stanford.edu/~sgreen/IAGSDC/html** .)

1.4 Interacting with the Web

Interactivity has various levels. The lowest level is when you are exploring the Web in search of information and you simply click on a button or select a menu option. Unlike television, where you can select a channel and watch it passively for hours on end, interacting with the Web is not a completely passive activity because you are continuously having to select information that's being presented to you. With each page, screen, or tidbit, you must make another choice, and to some extent your choices change the direction of what is happening on the other end (read on for one example).

One of the reasons that video and computer games are so popular is that they are interactive. Interactivity is engaging. An online version of the game Battleship is available on the Web, and the Yahoo site maintains a large list of interactive games and toys. You can find many interactive activities on the Web. For example, we have a link to an interactive frog dissection activity on the book page at the netgen.com site. First you see a picture of a frog. As you click on different parts of it, you see pictures of a virtual dissection. Each time you click on something, you get a new picture of the frog. By virtue of the choices you make, you control what information you get back.

Battleship
http://www.netgen.com/book/battleship.html

Game List
http://www.netgen.com/book/gamelist.html

Frog Dissection
http://www.netgen.com/book/frog-dissection.html

Up to this point we have talked about accessing static information in files. The only interaction that the user has with that kind of information is downloading it, looking at it, and possibly following a link to other information. (If you are confused by the use of the term "downloading" here, see the following sidebar, "I Didn't Ask for It.") At the downloading level, users don't really *interact* with the Web; nothing they do changes the content. They can't query the information or elicit responses from it that are specific to their needs.

To obtain the information you need, you sometimes have to provide data about yourself or data about the information you are seeking. This type of immediate input, which is achieved using Web forms, represents one of the highest levels of interactivity. For example, at the Monster Board, Adion uses

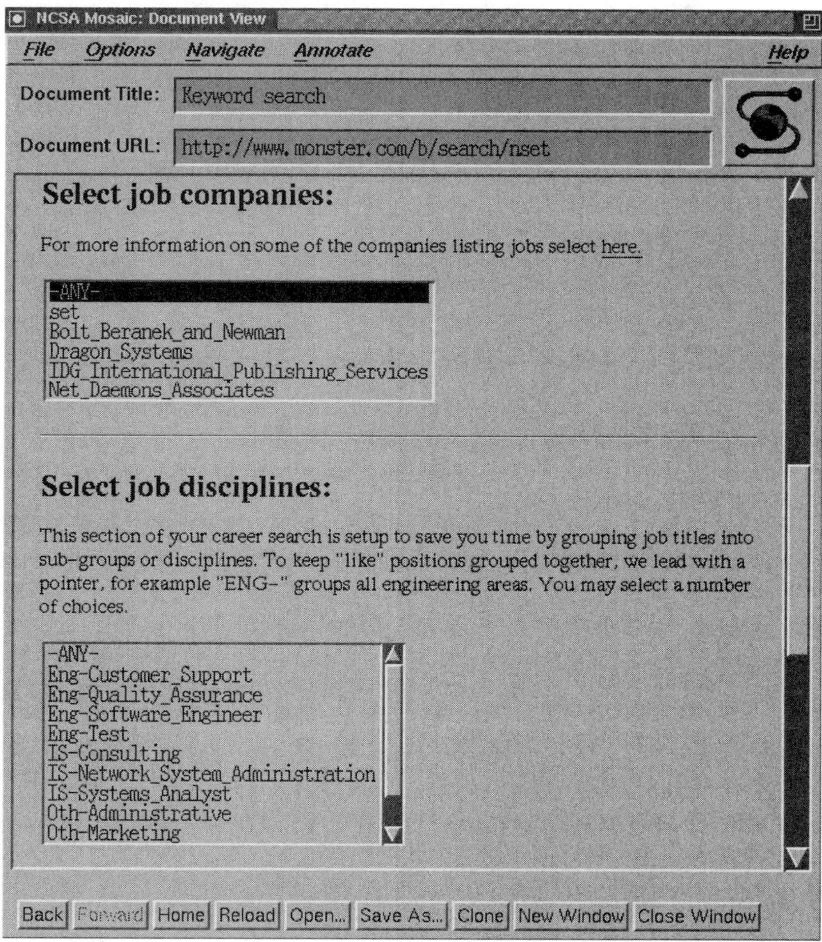

Figure 1-5 One of the data-input forms used on the Monster Board site

forms to focus user input (see Figure 1-5). With these forms, users search for job listings by state, company, industry, position, and other criteria.

Monster Site
http://www.netgen.com/book/monster-form.html

I Didn't Ask for It

Downloading a file means copying information from the server to your browser and transferring that information from there to your own system. Anyone who has ever retrieved a file from a remote system, or transferred an incoming e-mail message to the hard drive for later reading, has been downloading data. Downloading is a conscious activity on the part of the user.

Some commercial online services, such as America Online and Prodigy, download data to users' drives without requiring (or soliciting) any action on the part of users. This is typically done to provide new graphics and updated versions of service software. Usually, these downloads take up hard drive space on users' machines. Sometimes, however, the downloaded data is not written onto the hard drive, but is placed in memory instead, where it remains for as long as users maintain their connections with the online service.

Web page downloads are a hybrid of the copy-to-hard-disk and copy-to-memory scenarios. When you access a Web page (either by manually entering a URL or by selecting a link from another page), you automatically connect with that page's server and automatically request to see the specified page. The server gives you the requested page by passing it to your browser, and then it politely disconnects so as to be available to the next user. Your browser program downloads the page onto your system. In this case, the download is usually to a temporary file, but it remains there after the server disconnects. The page remains available on your system until your system cache clears.

Some browsers have the audacity to write directly to your hard drive, but this is not a good strategy for a browser. If you don't have much disk space on your drive, you might not be able to see the page. Then you'd be annoyed, you might blame it on the site, and you wouldn't ever visit that site again.

A form is a powerful tool. Web site creators should use them to facilitate and encourage communication from users. Companies often use sites for customer support by providing a Q&A bulletin board where customers can look for answers to their questions, but there must be a mechanism for submitting questions in the first place. Forms, feedback forms, comment forms, question forms, and order forms, if appropriate, provide this mechanism. You can also use forms to sponsor online discussions. In this case, the site becomes a "community database" where members of the community can express their opinions and see what others think.

Prime examples of sites as community databases include the Cardiff Movie Browser and the Ringo++ site. The Cardiff Movie Browser is a movie database. If you want to add a movie to the database or offer information about a movie already there, you can do so. You can also rate movies. Movie ratings from users are averaged to create an overall rating for each movie.

Ringo++ is a database of music ratings. Based on information in the database and a sample of your ratings, Ringo++ can recommend music it thinks you will like. You add to the music databases by using forms. You'll find all sorts of forms on the Web. In Chapter 11 we'll show you how to use CGI scripting to take the information from forms to do all kinds of interesting things.

Cardiff Movie Browser
http://www.netgen.com/book/movie-browser.html

Ringo++
http://www.netgen.com/book/ringo.html

Discussion Groups (with BBS-like Areas)
http://www.netgen.com/book/discussion-groups.html

1.5 A History of the Web

Tim Berners-Lee is the father of the World Wide Web. In March of 1989, when Berners-Lee was a physicist at CERN, he submitted his original proposal for the Web to the Electronics and Computing for Physics Division. Later, in 1990, Berners-Lee and colleague Robert Cailliau reviewed the responses to the original proposal and revised it. The introduction to the 1990 revision reads as follows:

> The current incompatibilities of the platforms and tools make it impossible to access existing information through a common interface, leading to waste of time, frustration, and obsolete answers to simple data lookup. There is a potential large benefit from the integration of a variety of systems in a way which allows a user to follow links pointing from one piece of information to another one. This forming of a web of information nodes rather than a hierarchical tree or an ordered list is the basic concept behind Hypertext.

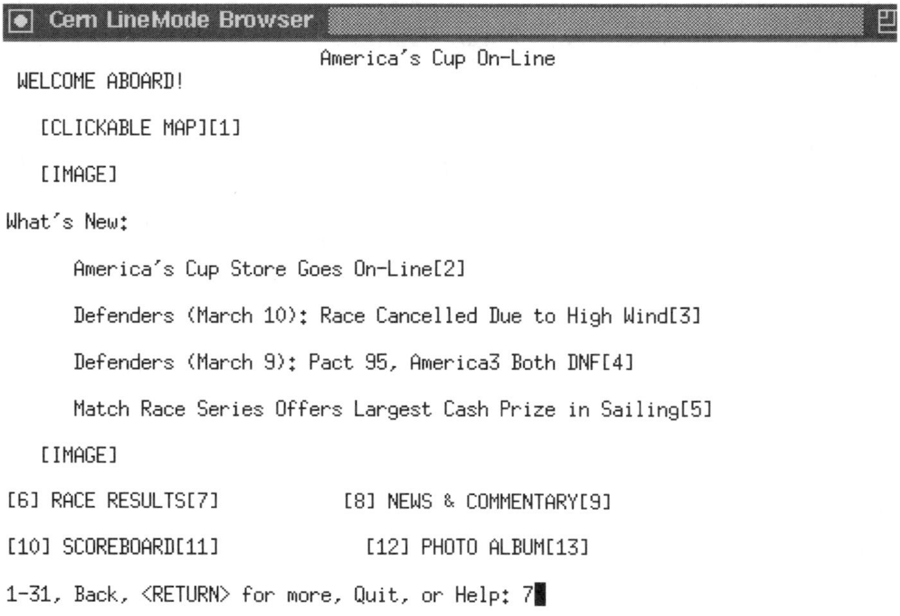

```
Cern LineMode Browser
                              America's Cup On-Line
 WELCOME ABOARD!

   [CLICKABLE MAP][1]

   [IMAGE]

What's New:

      America's Cup Store Goes On-Line[2]

      Defenders (March 10): Race Cancelled Due to High Wind[3]

      Defenders (March 9): Pact 95, America3 Both DNF[4]

      Match Race Series Offers Largest Cash Prize in Sailing[5]

   [IMAGE]

[6] RACE RESULTS[7]              [8] NEWS & COMMENTARY[9]

[10] SCOREBOARD[11]                [12] PHOTO ALBUM[13]

1-31, Back, <RETURN> for more, Quit, or Help: 7
```

Figure 1–6 The America's Cup On-Line Web site, viewed using the CERN LineMode Browser

The research proposal was accepted, and funding and resources were allocated. In the first year, experimentation was limited to CERN. Creating Web servers and sites was only half the battle; CERN members needed browsers to access data on the Web, so Nicola Pellow developed the Line Mode Browser. It wasn't very sophisticated (it had no mouse support or terminal recognition), but it did allow the CERN population to retrieve hypertext documents and indexes from Web servers. Figure 1-6 shows what the America's Cup On-Line Web site looks like from the CERN LineMode Browser. The LineMode Browser wasn't very user-friendly, but it was the first-ever Web client.

The LineMode Browser was made available to the public in March of 1991. The Web had gone public, so to speak. Early Web site creators included students at universities such as MIT, Stanford, and Carnegie Mellon. Computer companies, including Hewlett-Packard, IBM, Apple, DEC, and others, soon followed suit with sites of their own, as did the government. (These three

How the Web Was Started

Who: Tim Berners-Lee
What: The World Wide Web
Where: CERN
When: 1990
Why: To distribute theoretical physics research

Note: CERN (Conseil Européen pour la Recherche Nucléaire) is the European laboratory for particle physics located near Geneva in Switzerland and France. It is an international collaboration of member states, including Austria, Belgium, France, Germany, Greece, Spain, Sweden, Switzerland, and the United Kingdom.

user groups—educational institutions, companies, and government agencies—can often be identified by the suffixes .edu, .com, and .gov, respectively, in their Internet addresses.)

1.5.1 A Timeline of Noteworthy Events

This part of the chapter covers significant contributions to Web development and major entrants to the Web. From 1989 through the early 1990s, most of the work on the Web was done by CERN. But by 1993, the Web had begun gaining momentum and attracting users.

February, 1993: The alpha version of NCSA's Mosaic for X Windows provides a user-friendly GUI (graphical user interface) to the Web. There follows a substantial increase in Web interest.

March, 1993: Traffic on the Web accounts for one tenth of one percent of NSF backbone traffic. This raises people's awareness and more colleges, computer companies, and government offices begin setting up sites on the Web.

June, 1993: The WWW Wanderer, created by Matthew Gray of net.Genesis, makes a complete traversal of the Web. The Wanderer is the first-known autonomous Web agent, and at the time of traversal, the Web includes 134 reachable sites. (Other sites may have existed, but they were not connected or linked to the Web, so technically they were not yet Web sites.)

September, 1993: Web traffic measures one percent of NSF backbone traffic. This reflects a 1,000-percent growth in six months. This really gets people's attention. In the same month, the National Center for Supercomputing Application (NCSA) releases Mosaic for X Windows, Windows, and Macintosh, bringing a GUI to Web users across major platforms. Mosaic dominates the market for the next year.

October, 1993: The WWW Wanderer makes its last complete traversal of the Web. This time the Wanderer finds 623 sites, representing a 500-percent growth over a four-month period. Since that time, the Web has continued to grow so fast that the Wanderer has not been able to keep up. If this rate of growth continues, it is not reasonable to expect the Wanderer ever to complete a full traversal again. It is possible, however, for a successful traversal to be made once the Web's growth begins to slow down.

December, 1993: On December 8th, John Markov writes a one-and-a-half-page article in the business section of the *New York Times*. The article, titled "A Free and Simple Computer Link," is about Mosaic and the World Wide Web. The business world begins to recognize the viability of the Web as a commercial endeavor.

December, 1993: First Internet World Conference is held in New York City. Business and marketing professionals recognize the value of the Internet and MecklerMedia creates what it calls "North America's Largest Internet Conference and Exhibition."

March/April, 1994: Statistics from the National Science Foundation indicate that the Web finally surpasses Gopher in the sheer volume of data being sent across the backbone. This milestone serves as one more sign that the Web is becoming a very real phenomenon. (The following sidebar includes a graph of the usage statistics.)

April, 1994: CommerceNet becomes the first major commercial investment in the Web. CommerceNet is a nonprofit consortium of companies aimed at testing the Internet as a viable means for conducting commerce. Members of CommerceNet include Bank of America, Citibank, Enterprise Integration Technologies, IBM, Hewlett-Packard, General Electric, Intel, Lockheed, MCI, Sun Microsystems, Sybase, Symantec Corporation, Wells Fargo, and Xerox. Together these companies work to explore ways in which encryption and authentication can be used to make transactions on the Web more acceptable.

The Role of the NSF in the Internet and Web

The National Science Foundation funded the development of NSFNET, a high-speed network connecting universities and government agencies across the country in the late 1980s. The network was one of the first high-speed connections across the country and was used for much of the traffic across the Internet. The NSFNET Backbone Service—commonly referred to as simply "the backbone"—is maintained by the Merit Network Information Center (Merit NIC) in cooperation with MCI and IBM.

Merit maintains statistics on how the NSFNET backbone was used. It breaks down the usage by common services provided on the Internet (e.g., FTP, Gopher, and HTTP). These statistics are one gauge of the Web's tremendous growth. Figure 1-7 shows a graph that compares the use of Web and Gopher protocols in transmitting data across the NSFNET backbone.

In the past year, the government decided to stop funding the NSFNET backbone. This decision was primarily influenced by the fact that data was being carried on many high-speed commercial networks (UUNET, AlterNet, SprintLink, and MCI). Because the NSFNET was such an important part of the Internet's development, its termination has been an emotional issue for many long-time Net users.

The following is the formal announcement regarding the termination of the NSFNET:

```
From: Elise Gerich <epg@merit.edu>
Subject: 60 Day Termination Notice (fwd)
Date: Tue, 28 Feb 1995 12:59:18 -0500 (EST)
The following message has been sent to ANS to formally issue the 60 day
termination notice for the NSFNET Backbone Service. Many of you already
depend on an alternate network for your primary communication path, but
this is the final step in officially notifying ANS that the service will
cease.
It has been wonderful working with you all over the course of the NSFNET
award, and we hope that we will continue our fine working relationship in
the brave new world of post-NSFNET.
  --Elise
```

The Role of the NSF in the Internet and Web (Continued)

```
epg@merit.edu writes:
From epg@merit.edu Tue Feb 28 12:20:56 1995
From: epg@merit.edu
Date: Tue, 28 Feb 95 12:20:00 EST
Message-Id: <9502281720.AA03150@pepper.merit.edu>
To: becker@ans.net, dstaudt@nsf.gov, dvanbell@nsf.gov, phustone@nsf.gov
Subject: 60 Day Termination Notice
Cc: ema@merit.edu, epg@merit.edu, ittai@ans.net
Dear Jordan,
It is with mixed feelings that Merit sends this notification to ANS to
terminate the NSFNET Backbone Service at the following locations:
ENSS 128      Palo Alto       April 30, 1995  midnight PST
ENSS 129      Champaign       April 30, 1995  midnight CST
ENSS 130      Argonne         April 30, 1995  midnight CST
ENSS 131      Ann Arbor       April 30, 1995  midnight EST
ENSS 132      Pittsburgh      April 30, 1995  midnight EST
ENSS 133      Ithaca          April 30, 1995  midnight EST
ENSS 134      Cambridge       April 30, 1995  midnight EST
ENSS 135      San Diego       April 30, 1995  midnight PST
ENSS 136      College Park    April 30, 1995  midnight EST
ENSS 137      Princeton       April 30, 1995, midnight EST
ENSS 139      Houston         April 30, 1995, midnight CST
ENSS 140      Lincoln         April 30, 1995, midnight CST
ENSS 141      Boulder         April 30, 1995, midnight MST
ENSS 142      Salt Lake City  April 30, 1995, midnight MST
ENSS 143      Seattle         April 30, 1995, midnight PST
ENSS 144      Moffett Field   April 30, 1995, midnight PST
ENSS 145      College Park    April 30, 1995, midnight EST
ENSS 146      DC              April 30, 1995, midnight EST
ENSS 147      MFS             April 30, 1995, midnight EST
```

The Role of the NSF in the Internet and Web (Continued)

```
This notification also pertains to the cessation of NSFNET Backbone
Service at the Ameritech, MFS, PacBell, and Sprint Network Access Points.
A termination notice was issued previously for ENSS 138 (Atlanta) so that
node is not included in this termination notice.
It is sad to note that at midnight in each respective time zone, the
service that Merit, ANS, IBM, and MCI have collaborated to provide
over the last seven years will cease to exist. It is also with
pleasure that we complete this grand experiment on such a successful
note. I think that this partnership has succeeded beyond any of our
dreams. It has been fun!
   --Elise
```

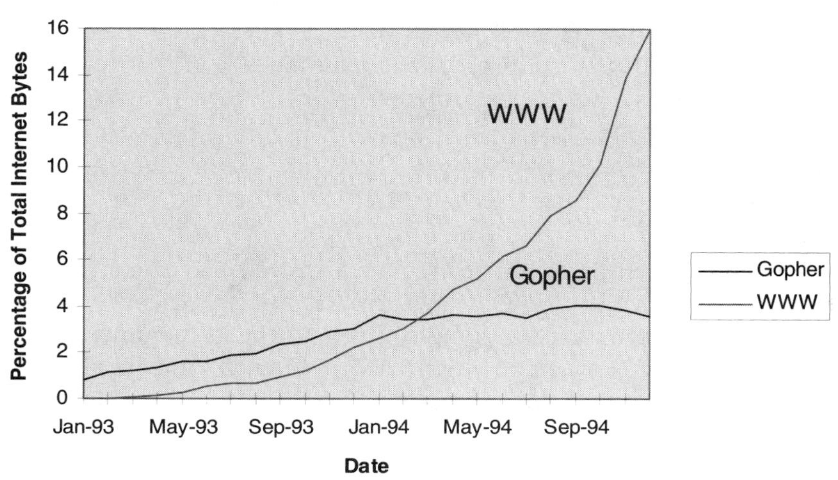

Figure 1–7 Merit statistics comparing Web and Gopher usage of the NSFNET backbone during 1993 and 1994

April/May, 1994: Best of the Web '94 Contest recognizes outstanding sites on the Web. The Best of the Web Contest is sponsored by Brandon Plewe. Entrants are nominated by users, who also vote for the winners. A total of 5,225 votes are cast, and the awards are announced at the WWW Conference in Geneva. (For a list of the 1994 winners, see the following sidebar.)

May, 1994: Sponsored by CERN, the First International WWW Conference is held in Geneva, Switzerland. The conference features 49 presentations and 11 workshops, with 380 participants.

June, 1994: The second Internet World Conference is held in San Jose, California.

July, 1994: MIT and CERN announce the formation of the Web Consortium, a group founded to organize and manage the progress of the Web.

October, 1994: Organized jointly by CERN and NCSA, the Second International WWW Conference: Mosaic and the Web is held in Chicago on October 17–19. This conference has over 1,300 participants.

November, 1994: The Wanderer finds more than 10,000 Web sites without completing a full traversal of the Web. Web growth is estimated at 50 to 100 new Web sites every day. More than 25 percent of the sites on the Web are commercial.

December, 1994: Third Internet World Conference is held in Washington, DC. It is attended by approximately 11,000 people and the Web is a hot topic of interest.

December, 1994: Netscape Communications Corp. releases version 1.0 of Netscape Navigator, the first major commercial browser. It soon begins to overtake Mosaic as the dominant browser in use.

February, 1995: CERN passes Web research to INRIA (the French National Institute for Research in Computer Science and Control), which played a significant role in the development of the Internet in France and Europe. INRIA intends to be involved in the evolution of Web component specifications, the development of reference code, and the promotion and dissemination of the Web in Europe. CERN intends to stay involved in the development process by concentrating on developments specifically related to its work. As the following quotation from INRIA

Winners of Best of the Web '94 Contest

The following people were winners in the Best of the Web '94 Contest:

Hall of Fame Inductees—Marc Andreessen, Eric Bina, Kevin Hughes, Rob Hartill, Lou Montulli

Best Overall Site—Winner: NCSA; Honorable mention: CERN, Global Network Navigator

Best Campus-Wide Information Service—Winner: Globewide Network Academy; Honorable mentions: Rensselaer Polytechnic Institute, University of Texas-Austin, Honolulu Community College, and University of Maryland-Baltimore County

Best Document Design—Winner: Travels with Samantha (Greenspun, MIT); Honorable mentions: *Wired*, GNN NetNews, and Principia Cybernetica Web

Most Important Service Concept—Winner: What's New on the WWW (from NCSA, winner of Best Overall Site); Honorable mentions: Global Network Navigator, Globewide Network Academy

Best Educational Site—Winner: Introduction to C++ (Marcus Speh); Honorable mentions: ArtServe, Expo, Museum of Paleontology, Views of the Solar System

Best Entertainment Site—Winner: Sports Information Service (Eric Richard, MIT); Honorable mentions: Movie Database, MTV, Doctor Fun, and *Wired*

Best Use of Interaction—Winner: Xerox Map Server (Steve Putz); Honorable mentions: Geometry Applications Gallery, Weather Map Requestor

Best Use of Multiple Media—Winner: Le Louvre (Nicola Pioch); Honorable mentions: Expo, TNS Technology Demos, USENET Image Gallery

Most Technical Merit—Winner: Xerox Map Server (Steve Putz); Honorable mentions: Interactive Genetic Art, Dutch Teletext Gateway

Best Commercial Site—Winner: O'Reilly and Associates; Honorable mentions: Hewlett-Packard, Sun Microsystems

Best Navigational Aid—Winner: World Wide Web Worm (Oliver McBrian); Honorable mentions: Internet Meta-Index, Virtual Tourist, Galaxy

Best Professional Service—Winner: OncoLink (Buhle & Goldwein); Honorable mentions: Unified CS Technical Report Index, Explorer, Virtual Hospital

demonstrates (available at the INRIA site), the current and future state of the Web has outgrown CERN's original mandate:

> As is well known, the World-Wide Web (WWW) originated at CERN with Tim Berners-Lee and his colleagues. It is now the information system which is largely driving the Internet, and which has a substantial global business potential for the near future. The World-Wide Web was conceived as a communication tool for the widely dispersed scientific community of High-Energy Physics. It is destined to become essential for the Global Information Infrastructure, and is thus a prime example of [an] important spin-off from pure scientific research.

April, 1995: Fourth Internet World Conference is held in San Jose, California. The conference features close to 200 exhibits and more than 60 sessions.

April, 1995: Third International WWW Conference: Technology, Tools, and Applications is held in Darmstadt, Germany, organized by the Fraunhofer Institute for Computer Graphics.

December, 1995: Fourth International WWW Conference '95 is scheduled in Boston, Massachusetts.

1.5.2 How the Web Has Progressed

Evolution is a cyclical process, and the Web is no stranger to the chicken-or-the-egg question. As more and more people use the Web, it becomes more useful because it connects more people and sites. Of course, the more useful the Web is, the more people participate. So which comes first?

A similar relationship exists between technical developments and increased participation. Most developers are afraid to spend time and money developing new products for small audiences. So the bigger the audience, the greater the development effort. On the other hand, new products that make the Web easier to use are to some extent responsible for the increase in the number of Web users. And of course, the more people use the Web, the more useful the Web is to those people.

On the technical side, many changes and enhancements have been made to the specifications of various protocols and standards. The changes and enhancements were made to increase the functionality and flexibility of the Web. New features were added to HTTP (Hypertext Transfer Protocol). HTML (Hypertext Markup Language) is now at version 3.0, and Netscape has added extensions to HTML 2.0. CGI scripting has emerged as a way to standardize scripts and make them useful with different servers, and a Common Log Format was established for user-access logs. The hottest new developments involve security measures. Security is crucial to the growth of commerce on the Web.

From a social perspective, the Web has grown by leaps and bounds. When it first began, only a few hundred people knew about it. That small community, which consisted primarily of scientists and the technologically savvy, was not daunted by the magic incantations (i.e., line commands) that were required to make use of the Web. John and Jane Q. Public, on the other hand, were not merely technophobic, they were excluded because they didn't know the magic words. And they didn't know the concepts either.

It wasn't long, however, before computer technology began to infiltrate the general populous. Newspapers and consumer magazines began publishing feature stories about computer technology, CD-ROMs, and the "information superhighway." Then the spotlight focused on the Internet and the Web. Magazines such as *Newsweek, Time,* and *U.S. News and World Report* have all published special editions devoted to cyberspace. Computer products and services are now advertised on television. One or two TV commercials even use a computer interface—complete with pull-down menus—to advertise products that have nothing to do with technology.

The concepts behind mouse clicking, drop-down menus, and graphical icons are now general knowledge. It has even become commonplace to ask people for their e-mail address, and it is no longer unusual to see Web addresses in the form of URLs. Even though URLs look and sound complicated, if you stop to think about it they are no more complex than standard three-line postal addresses. Developers have realized that they can create easy-to-use interfaces that hide the complexities and inner workings of the online world. Once John and Jane Q. Public got ahold of Mosaic, the Web became a wonderland. Suddenly, the Web was perceived as something that could be useful to ordinary people. Today, almost everyone has some knowledge about the online world, and many have heard about the Web.

The increasing number of people on the Web has changed the Web's "culture," too. The Web is no longer reserved for the technical elite. Now that the private club has become public, it has become an untapped resource for commercial enterprise. Just yesterday it was "cool" to include your e-mail address on your business card. Now your card is likely to include the URL to your own Web site. As more and more people continue to explore the Web, the greater the demand will become for better designs and more functionality—and the faster new developments will appear. This applies not only to new Web sites, but to new tools that make the Web ever easier to use. The workings of the Web remain fairly complicated, but this stays hidden behind the graphical user interfaces, so the Web becomes less intimidating.

Everybody on the Web is a consumer, and as the number of consumers increases, the variety of goods and services also proliferate, expanding the marketplace. All kinds of merchandise is available for purchase through the Web, and it is easy to stumble across something you want while browsing sites. The good part is that everybody on the Web can be a seller as well as a buyer. Not only has the Web become a place to do business, but it is recognized as a cost-effective medium for communication. If you are an entrepreneur or small business owner, you can afford to build your own Web site to promote and sell your products and services. You can compete directly with the big guys on the same cyberturf.

The Web promises to develop into an area of socialization as well. For example, the "Personal Technology" section of the *Seattle Times* on Sundays includes a regular feature, titled "The Electronic Neighborhood." In the March 12, 1995, issue, it listed the URLs to several Web sites, including two that would be celebrating St. Patrick's Day online. Other mentions included two sites that were offering online classes, several sites for children, and one for AIDS-related information. Also in the same issue was an article about computer bulletin boards becoming a means for social interaction.

Whether or not the Web becomes deeply integrated in our social lives remains to be seen. But clearly, the Web is a medium for communication, and the nature and content of that communication is limitless. Don't be surprised when print and broadcast advertisements begin to include URLs with tag lines such as "Check out the new rates at the First Card Savings Bank home page."

1.6 The Future of the Web

The emerging trends allow us to make some short-term predictions about the Web's ongoing evolution. We've only seen the beginning of the expansion of Web access across multiple platforms and the integration of software with Web tools. The commercialization of the Web has only just begun as well. Encryption will be the hot topic for the immediate future, and developers will continue to enhance Web standards and protocols.

Participation on the Web originally required knowing the UNIX operation system. Today, you can access the Web from just about any platform. Several major software manufacturers have announced that their products will provide Internet and Web access. For example, IBM's OS/2 Warp includes the Web Explorer. Novell and Oracle both came out with Internet Kits. Microsoft has announced that Windows 95 will include Spyglass' Mosaic Web browser and will be Internet-ready with a TCP/IP stack.

Access is only half of the story. Server software is also available for multiple platforms. Now you can create a Web server by using a Macintosh or IBM PC compatible. In Chapter 3, you'll find a list of servers that includes DOS and VMS as well. Of course, client access and server software isn't worth much if there is no content. People have become comfortable with word-processing and desktop publishing programs. These programs (along with third-party enhancements) are beginning to provide or soon will provide tools that convert plain documents into the HTML format. (The accompanying sidebar features some press release blurbs announcing new products.) All these developments help to increase the number of users on the Web significantly and make the Web an even more powerful medium for commercial enterprise.

Companies already realize that the Internet is something with which they must become involved if they are going to continue to conduct business. In order to remain competitive, they will have to do business online, and the Web is just the latest frontier in cyberspace. The only obstacle that has hampered the commercialization of the Web is the issue of security.

Soon, the major encryption, or security, wars will begin. A variety of different encryption methods and strategies will emerge, confusing consumers for a while as vendors vie for consumer patronage. The only benefit to this type of evolutionary process is that it promotes survival of the fittest, and the best software alternatives will ultimately win the greatest market share.

Browser software competition will also begin to heat up. HTML 3.0 has a lot of untapped power. The specification supports a lot of features, but until these features are supported by major browsers, they will remain obscure and rarely used. For example, HTML 3.0 has specifications for mathematical equations, but even the latest beta version of Netscape as of this writing (version 1.1b3) does not yet support these equations.

The World Wide Web is tremendously popular right now. It is growing at an absolutely astronomical rate. But at the same time there is a tremendous amount of uncertainty about what will happen in the future. Perhaps a new standard will come along to replace it, something with features that the Web doesn't have. It is even possible that the government or the academic world will develop another information highway solely for itself—an information "private road" free of the masses.

News Flash

Novell Adds Internet Access Tool Kit

SAN JOSE, CALIF. (BUSINESS WIRE, August 8, 1994)—In response to growing customer demand for easier access to resources on the worldwide Internet network, Novell Inc. Monday announced the availability of a free Internet Access Tool Kit, including free Internet connect time, with the purchase of its industry-leading LAN WorkPlace TCP/IP product.

SGI Introduces First Server Line with Built-in Authoring Tools

MOUNTAIN VIEW, CALIF. (Jan 24)—With a single announcement, Silicon Graphics has brought the power of Web publishing to the masses. The company, best known for manufacturing high-performance visual computing systems, unveiled WebFORCE, the first product line for creating and serving media-rich content for the World Wide Web.

Oracle's Internet Kit, Application Tools Allow Companies to Harness the Internet

SAN FRANCISCO, CALIF. (PRNewswire, Feb. 7)—Oracle Corp. (NASDAQ: ORCL) today expanded the reach of its interactive multimedia products and services for the evolving Information Superhighway with an initiative designed to enable corporations, small businesses, and individuals to take advantage of developing business opportunities on the Internet.

Oracle today announced the first phase of its Internet initiative, which consists of several components that link Internet-based World Wide Web servers to the wealth of information stored in Oracle7 databases worldwide. Leading database market research firm Dataquest estimates that more than 50 percent of corporate relational data resides in Oracle databases.

Frame Technology Announcement

SAN JOSE, CALIF. (BUSINESS WIRE, Jan. 3)—Frame Technology Corp. Tuesday announced that FrameMaker 4 users can easily publish their documents to the World Wide Web on the Internet—by converting FrameMaker files into HyperText Markup Language (HTML) with third-party products like Quadralay Corp.'s WebWorks Document Translator.

Whatever the future brings, the notion of distributed hypermedia is certain to have a strong influence on new developments. Most likely, the next protocol will build upon and extend the functionality of the current structure. A new protocol would surely not abandon any of the concepts that have evolved thus far; the concepts behind hypermedia and benefits of distributed hypermedia have really proven their worth.

CHAPTER 2

Introducing the Technical Side of the Web

CHAPTER AT A GLANCE

This introductory chapter defines and describes several fundamental concepts on which the Web relies. After defining a few basic terms, we describe the client-server model and discuss each of the Web standards and protocols. We also talk about the bodies that govern the evolution of these standards and specification documents.

Before you begin setting up a Web site, you should be familiar with some terms and concepts. The Web is based on a client-server model, with most client requests made using a GUI browser. The Web also follows various standards and protocols that are governed by a variety of boards and consortiums. If you are new to the Web and the world of hypermedia, and especially if you have never had any UNIX experience, you have to learn a few vocabulary words. Actually, the words will sound familiar; they have simply been given new meanings.

2.1 A Few Basic Terms

People always borrow old concepts to name new things. Computers and the Internet have given words such as "object," "document," and "page" new meanings, which, in turn, have evolved with the Web and trends in object-oriented programming and distributed processing.

An *object* on the Web is a piece of data in the form of a file. That file can contain any type of data, including text, graphic images, video, or audio. Or it could contain a combination of data types. Or it could be an executable program file. On the Web, there are many types of objects. Usually when you request data on the Web, you retrieve a *document object,* which can contain text, inline graphics, and links to other objects (e.g., different document objects, video clips, or program files).

On the Web, *page* is another word for a document object. It is one of those fuzzy words that some people equate with computer screens or windows. They think that whatever fits on a single screen or inside a window is a page. This definition of "page" tries to stretch the book analogy all the way into the electronic world. Online, a page is really one continuous piece of data. As such, it is more akin to a word-processing document in which you click the scroll bars to view what is not visible on the screen. Some people confuse a Web page with a Web *site.* A site is a set of conceptually related interlinked pages.

In order to retrieve and view Web documents and other objects, you need a *browser.* A browser is a software program that knows how to traverse the links in the Web, communicate with servers, and retrieve data. A *server* is a software program that manages data at a Web site. It responds to browsers requests. Browsers are also referred to as *clients,* and that explains the term "client-server." We'll talk about the client-server model in a moment.

The word *user* also has a variety of meanings. The most common definition refers to a human being who uses a machine to access information.

However, a user does not have to be a real person. In computer terms, a user is simply an account on a machine that has a name and a set of privileges (i.e., permission to access files and run programs). When we are talking about UNIX systems, every program on the system is "run as a user." This means that the program has the privileges associated with that account. When we start talking about Web servers, we will mention running the server as "root" or "nobody." These are just special users on UNIX systems.

2.2 The Client-Server Model

The World Wide Web is built on top of the client-server model. The client and server are programs that communicate with one another. The client contacts the server and requests a piece of information. Web browsers such as Mosaic are the clients that contact Web servers. The server's job is to wait around for connections from outside client machines, listen to their requests, and respond to—or "serve"—their requests. "Ask and ye shall receive" is the basic principle behind the client-server model. (See the "Transaction #1" sidebar.)

NOTE

While most servers just wait around for incoming requests, some protocols allow the server to take action without receiving a request from a client. For example, you could program a server to notify a client when it is 10 p.m. In this case, the server is seen as responding to some external influence (i.e., the fact that it is 10 p.m.) and issuing a response to the client. Because the server is responding to an external influence, it still fits the client-server model.

In order for the client and server to understand one another, both must observe the proper protocol. If the client makes a request in an unexpected way, the server is unlikely to respond appropriately. Similarly, if the server does not respond according to the protocol, the client will probably not understand the response. Which protocol is the best means of accomplishing a task is not of primary importance. What is most important is that the client and server observe the same one. Protocols exist to provide standardized guidelines. Of course, we would like protocols to be efficient, powerful, and robust, but if the client and server cannot even understand one another, all these qualities are useless. (See the "Transaction #2" sidebar.)

Client-Server Transaction #1 at Burger King

The client-server model isn't limited to computers. In the real world, there are people and companies whose sole job it is to wait for requests and respond appropriately. Here is an example of a simple client-server transaction in the real world. Joe is hungry and goes to Burger King. In computer terms, he's a "client." The cashier who stands behind the counter is ready to fill Joe's order. In computer terms, the cashier is a "server." So Joe walks up to the counter and says, "Hi. I'd like a whopper please." This is the "request." The server says, "Just a moment," goes off to get the burger, and gives it to the hungry Joe. This is the "response."

Client-Server Transaction #2 at Burger King

In the real world, people obey protocols. They allow us to understand what other people want so we can respond appropriately. Going back to our friend Joe at Burger King, we can see how protocols exist in our world.

Joe is hungry and goes to Burger King. The server is there waiting to fill his order. But instead of walking up to the cashier and placing his order, Joe sits down at an empty table and waits for someone to bring him his food. Obviously, nothing happens (after a couple of hours the manager may even throw Joe out).

There is a protocol for how to place a food order at Burger King. If you don't obey the protocol, the cashier will not understand your request.

2.3 The Influence of Pre-Web Protocols

FTP, Prospero, Archie, Gopher, and Veronica are a few of the Internet protocols that predate the Web. Each of these protocols provide a means for transferring information from one machine to another across the Internet. However, each is based on a different approach to finding and retrieving information. The design of the World Wide Web was heavily influenced by these protocols. And the Web was built upon these protocols so that information available through FTP and Gopher would be accessible on the Web. The primary Web protocol,

Service	Port	Rank	Packet Count	% Pkts	Rank	Byte Count	% Bytes
FTP-data	20	1	16465206600	18.758	1	5783759777700	30.251
WWW	80	2	11518306800	13.122	2	3382697720400	17.693
TELNET	23	3	9090741300	10.357	6	710204891700	3.715
NNTP	119	4	8770182550	9.992	3	2147622144350	11.233
SMTP	25	5	6455027600	7.354	4	1036881923950	5.423
DNS	53	6	4710381000	5.366	8	478697375750	2.504
IP	-4	7	3874094000	4.414	5	825896358700	4.320
IRC	6667	8	2347581400	2.675	9	265724401950	1.390
Gopher	70	9	2326624300	2.651	7	636782868350	3.331
FTP	21	10	1644507850	1.874	12	129223842350	0.676

Packet Total: 87,775,369,950
Byte Total: 19,119,019,090,700

Figure 2–1 NSFNET traffic distribution highlights for January, 1995

however, is HTTP (HyperText Transfer Protocol). It was designed specifically to transfer hypermedia documents. You could say that the Web, with its new protocols and standards, was built on top of the Internet.

2.3.1 FTP

Created in 1985, FTP (File Transfer Protocol) provides a standard means of accessing information on servers throughout the world. With this protocol, users can access files on remote machines without being concerned about remote file systems. Being able to do this is one of the most important aspects of the Web.

According to statistics from Merit Network Information Service about how the National Science Foundation Network (NSFNET) is used, FTP is the protocol most often used on the Internet (see Figure 2-1). HTTP, the protocol developed for the Web, is the second most-used protocol on the Internet. FTP provided for one of the first means of easily accessing data on remote machines.

The two most important characteristics of FTP are its dual connection and maintaining state. *Dual connection* refers to a two-port process. First the client connects to the server in order to request some data. Then the server connects to the client in order to deliver the data. These two tasks are not handled using the same connection. Instead, the server ends up talking on two separate ports, one for each part of the process. (We'll talk more about servers and connections in Chapter 5.)

One of the primary differences between FTP and HTTP is that FTP "remembers" the results from past client requests. This is often referred to as *maintaining state*. HTTP, on the other hand, doesn't remember anything from request to request. In FTP, you can issue a command to change directories. When you make your next request, the FTP server remembers what directory you were just in and interprets your request accordingly. Similarly, you might send a request to the server to switch into binary transfer mode. If you then send another request for a file, the server remembers that it is supposed to be in binary mode and transfers the file accordingly.

Maintaining state is a useful function, but it has its downside as well. Maintaining state is a powerful tool because it allows a client to make many simple requests, but it also requires the server to maintain a lot of information—the state of the connection—and maintain an open connection even when no request is being made. HTTP, the main protocol used for retrieving data on the Web, does not maintain state. It runs a little faster because it does not have to remember any information from the previous request.

From the Web's perspective, another weakness of FTP is that it does not specify what kind of file is being transmitted. When you use FTP to retrieve a graphic file—say, a photo of the space shuttle—FTP delivers the file without ever knowing or saying whether it is a bitmap, TIFF, compressed GIF, or some other file type. FTP doesn't even know or tell you that the file is an image. For all it knows, you just transferred a Microsoft Word document or an MPEG video. Worse, you may not know what format the file is in until you try to open it. When FTP delivers a file, it simply says, "Here's your file."

The FTP protocol is fine for passing files around, but it is not adequate for the Web by itself. The Web requires information about the type of each object to be sent along with the object. This is known as *content typing,* and it's one of the most powerful features of HTTP. Instead of saying, "Here's your file," HTTP says something more like, "Here's a GIF-encoded compressed file," when it delivers a file.

2.3.2 Gopher

The basic Internet Gopher protocol document was issued in 1991. The Gopher protocol is the one most closely related to the Web. Gopher does not support hypermedia documents, but it does support searches and links between menu items and files. Users of Gopher could search for a topic and then browse the resulting documents in a manner very similar to the way that people navigate the Web. However, one of the main weaknesses of the Gopher protocol is that it allows for a very limited set of document types. That is, Gopher users are not able to view images, PostScript files, and MPEG videos, but are limited to a very restricted set of file types.

Even though Gopher is very limited in its variety of content types, it has paved the way for the Web. People familiar with Gopher have caught on quickly to the concepts behind the Web. They understood how the Web works because they understand Gopher.

2.4 Web Standards and Protocols

The Web does not have a single standard or protocol. Instead, it encompasses many standards and protocols so that users may access information using any one of them. More importantly, the Web hides protocol layers from you. You see a standard interface and you don't have to know whether some information is coming from one protocol or another. In addition, the Web does not restrict the types of objects that can be sent. Although several standardized content types already exist (GIF images, MPEG video, HTML text, etc.), theoretically any content type can be transmitted over the Web.

The Web is primarily defined by four standards: URLs (Uniform Resource Locators), HTTP (Hypertext Transfer Protocol), HTML (Hypertext Markup Language), and CGI (Common Gateway Interface). Servers and clients on the Web use these standards as simple mechanisms for locating, accessing, and displaying information. Standards have also emerged for a Common Log Format, so that programs could be written to analyze the logs of any server. The latest issue under debate is security, but it will probably be a while before one encryption or authentication standard takes hold.

2.4.1 URL

By means of a standardized addressing scheme, Uniform Resource Locators can be used to locate and retrieve information anywhere on the Internet via a number of different protocols. URLs can specify FTP file retrieval, find newsgroups, define user e-mail addresses, and identify HTTP documents and other data objects.

A related standard, Uniform Resource Names (URNs), is also used to locate and retrieve data from the Web. The main difference between the two is that the URLs identify the exact location of the data, while the URN is just that, a name. It doesn't tell you where to find the data. Of course, the other big difference is that a URL appears to be more complex to the average user. URLs tell you the name of a resource on a server. For example **http://www.netgen.com/** is the URL for data that bears the URN of "net.Genesis home page."

To use URNs, a browser has to go somewhere to find the location that corresponds to the name. This seems like an extra step, but it has a very real benefit. URNs allow individual resources to be available at many locations. Copies of the same resource can be distributed across the Web, so that when a browser requests the resource, it finds the best location from which to retrieve it. URNs were designed to decrease the load on major servers and allow copies to exist and be retrieved from them. As of this writing, the exact format of URNs has not been defined. Therefore, the example presented above is only hypothetical. However, the debate between URLs and URNs is sure to go on for some time.

So far, URLs prevail, despite the fact that they are already too complicated to read. URNs could simplify matters, but only if the names resemble common language. For example, it would be pretty simple to retrieve a copy of the United States Constitution if you could point your browser to a resource identified as **URN://US_Constitution**. However, if URNs turn out to be as complicated as URLs, and you have to go to a place like **URN://doc/US/gov/Constitution/** to retrieve the Constitution, then the odds are against the adoption of URNs by the Web population.

2.4.2 HTTP

HTTP is the primary protocol for distributing information on the World Wide Web. It is a relatively simple, highly flexible protocol. To deliver requested information from a server to a client, HTTP defines a simple transaction that consists of four parts:

1. The client establishes a connection to the server.
2. The client issues a request to the server specifying a particular document to retrieve.
3. The server sends a response containing a status code and the text of the document, if it is available.
4. Either the client or the server disconnects.

One of the main goals of HTTP is to provide a simple algorithm that makes fast response times possible. To achieve this goal, HTTP is defined as a *stateless protocol* that does not retain information about a connection from one request to the next. By way of contrast, FTP maintains state. When you use FTP, you can change the directory you are working in, and the server remembers that directory when it gets your next request. With HTTP, on the other hand, the server does not remember the directory because the protocol does not allow the server to retain information from a previous connection.

NOTE

State can be maintained "outside" of the protocol. Many Web sites encode information in the URL that is used to maintain state. In addition, CGI scripts can be used to modify files or databases that save the user's state.

HTTP is limited to one request per connection. Unlike other protocols, such as FTP, the connection between server and client is broken after every request is made. Every time a client wants to fetch a document, it has to establish a new connection to the HTTP server. This is one of the main reasons why it takes so long to load HTML pages that have a lot of inline graphics. A separate connection must be established for each graphic. Establishing a connection is not usually time-consuming, but it can seriously affect performance at distant or heavily loaded sites.

Some clients, such as NCSA Mosaic, wait until a connection is closed before they open their next connection. However, many newer clients, such as Netscape Navigator, open multiple connections and receive documents in parallel. Unless bandwidth is an issue and creates a bottleneck when documents are being retrieved, this behavior results in a significant time savings, especially at sites that are loaded with inline images.

The primary difference between HTTP 0.9 and HTTP 1.0 is greater flexibility, which is made possible by two new enhancements. The first is the addition of transaction headers, and the second is the addition of several new methods. Headers make it possible to pass along information for facilitating authentication, encryption, and user identification. The new methods offer additional capabilities.

HTTP 1.0 adds headers to all transactions, whether they are client requests or server responses. When a client requests data, the request transaction header can include the name of the client software making the request (i.e., the browser type, whether it be Mosaic, Netscape Navigator, or another browser), which types of objects the client understands (i.e., data formats), and what languages the client understands (e.g., French, Japanese, or English).

NOTE

Similar to a header in word processing, an HTTP 1.0 header is a block of information that precedes the main data. Some people refer to the information in the header as *meta-information,* because it is, in essence, information about the information being requested or transmitted.

Similarly, when the server responds to a request, it can return a header along with the requested data. A response header can include information about the status of the request (whether it was successful or not), the length of the data being returned (i.e., the number of bytes transmitted, not including the header), the content type, the language of the content, and the date that the content was last modified.

Here is a sample header:

```
HTTP/1.0 200 Document follows
MIME-Version: 1.0
Server: CERN/3.0pre6
Date: Monday, 06-Mar-95 21:46:05 GMT
Content-Type: text/html
Content-Length: 2848
Last-Modified: Thursday, 02-Mar-95 23:05:33 GMT
```

When a client makes a request of a server, it uses certain methods of requesting information, depending on its purpose. Under HTTP 0.9, the only valid method was GET. HTTP 1.0 adds six new methods: POST, HEAD, PUT, DELETE, LINK, and UNLINK. We'll talk more about methods in Chapters 5 and 6.

2.4.3 HTML

The HyperText Markup Language, a language defined in SGML (Standard General Markup Language), is another major innovation associated with the World Wide Web. HTML is similar to many other *markup languages,* such as $\LaTeX$, RTF, and Frame. Markup languages define areas of text by "tagging" the specific formatting associated with those areas. In HTML, tags provide a functional description of a piece of text, not a description that specifies how that text is to be rendered.

There are no rendering restrictions on browsers, so a browser can render the tagged text as it sees fit. For example, you can use a tag in HTML to identify a piece of text as a first-level header (referred to as a *semantic markup*). Each browser is then free to render that text in whatever format it uses for first-level headers. For example, one browser might center first level headers, and another browser might underline them.

Some browsers allow you to define how a piece of semantic markup text should be represented. Other browsers have their own preset rendering instructions. But with or without your input, rendering decisions are controlled by the browser. For the most part, HTML itself does not support *physical markup*. For example, you cannot use HTML to specify an 18-point, bold, centered text segment. Of course, there are always exceptions to the rule, and we'll talk more about HTML in Chapters 7 and 8.

In addition to semantic markups, HTML provides the capability to create hypertext links between one document and another document or object, or even between locations in a single document. Using hypertext links, a user writing a document about high-energy physics, for example, could mark a piece of text to link it to another document. In the hypertext paradigm, a user can follow links arbitrarily from one topic to another. Links are the information threads that form the structure of the World Wide Web.

Evolving like a software program, features were added to HTML to meet needs that were not met under previous versions. HTML 1.0, the first version, was a basic document markup including links. HTML did not support forms until version 2.0. With version 3.0 comes support for tables and mathematical equations. Version 3.0 also offers much greater control over layout. Text can be wrapped around graphics and figures, with captions included.

Netscape enhanced the functionality to the already improved HTML 3.0 by adding extensions. New features gave the user even more control over the rendering of Web pages, and new tags allowed users to center text and specify font sizes. These new tags were not in the official HTML specification, but many have become de facto standards. HTML alone is a semantic, or functional, markup language, but the Netscape extensions add physical markup capabilities.

Figures 2-2 through 2-5 show the same America's Cup On-Line page viewed through four different browsers: Mosaic, Netscape Navigator, Arena, and Lynx. You can see how the different browsers render each Web page. For example, the Mosaic and Netscape browsers center the greeting "WELCOME ABOARD!," but Arena left-justifies it. The font in Netscape Navigator is also larger than the one in Mosaic.

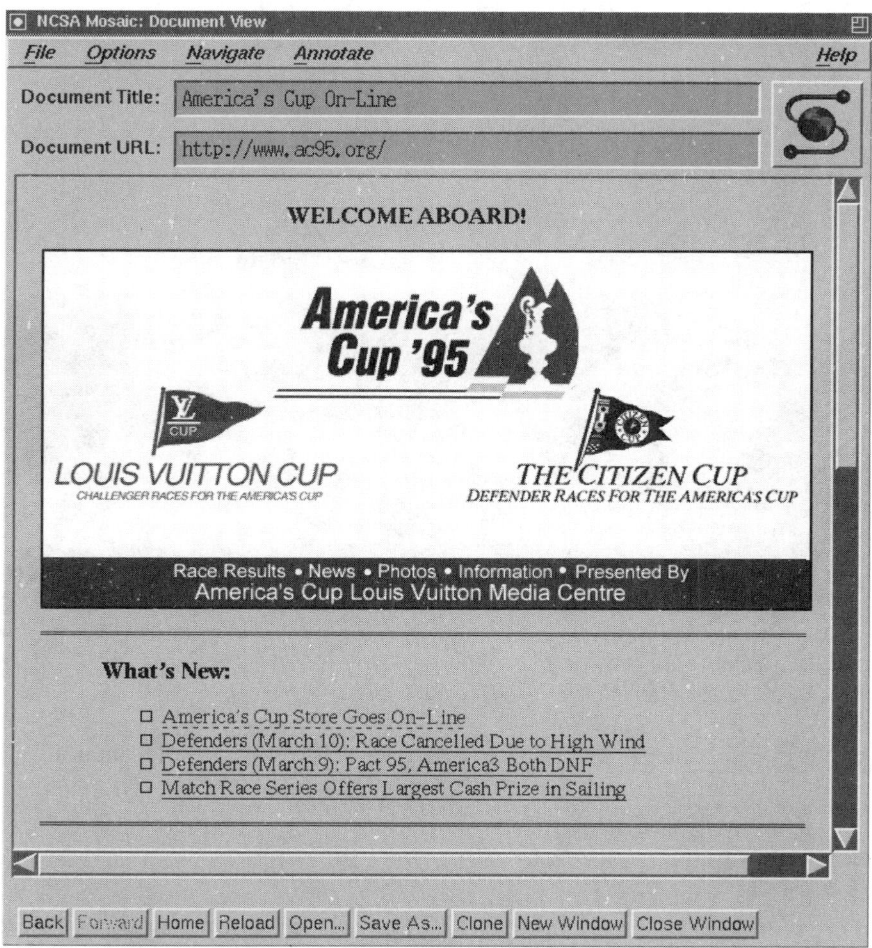

Figure 2-2 America's Cup On-Line page, viewed using Mosaic

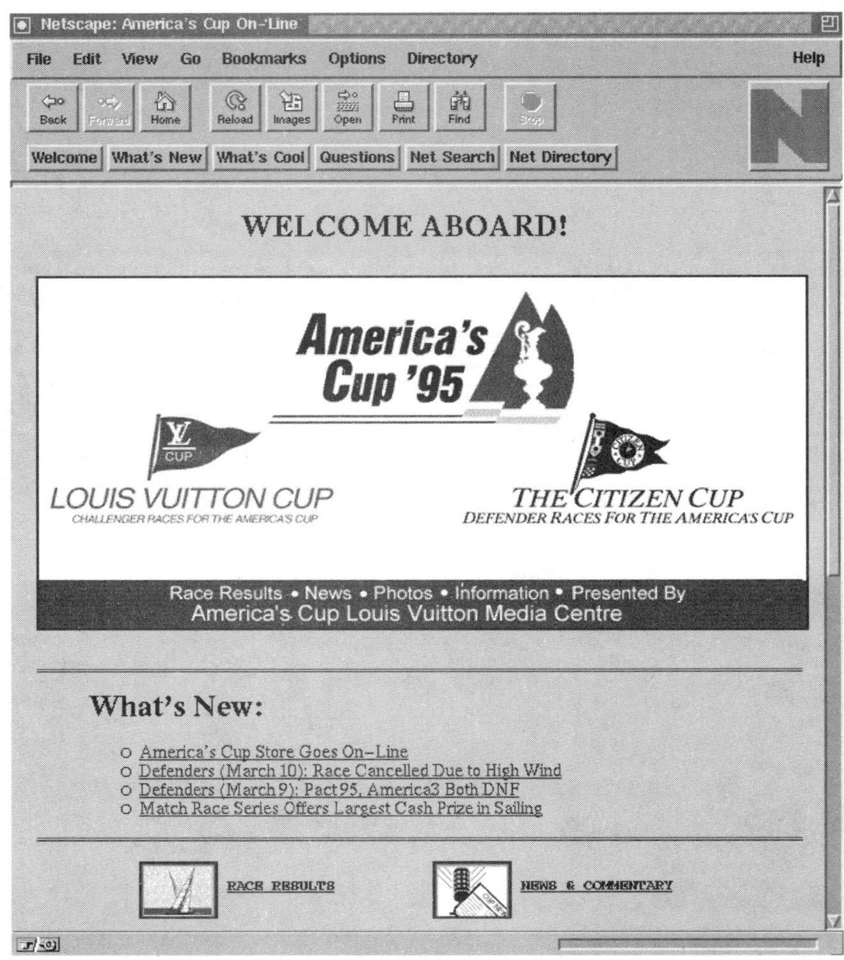

Figure 2-3 America's Cup On-Line page, viewed using Netscape Navigator

2.4.4 CGI

The tremendous amount and diversity of hyperlinked information available on the World Wide Web has led to the wide acclaim for it. However, most of the information on the Web is static and is served directly from HTML files. The information in these files only changes when the site administrator

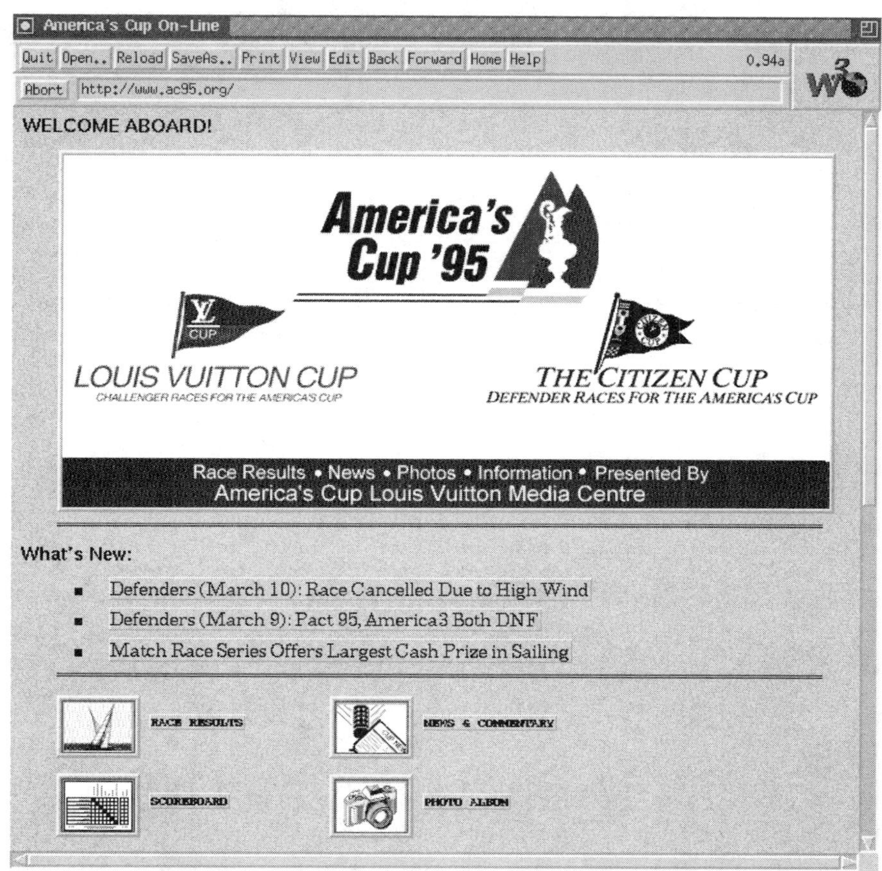

Figure 2-4 America's Cup On-Line page, viewed using Arena

intervenes and updates the content. Such static pages allow for little interactivity. They reduce much of Web exploring to a semi-passive activity.

While many sites do make their visitors semi-passive, the Web is usually lauded as an interactive medium. From online ordering to discussion groups and telerobotics, the most interesting Web sites depend on interactions between the user and the Web server. To make themselves more interactive, some sites generate HTML pages "on the fly," based on client input. Generally, this functionality is achieved through the CGI protocol. CGI "scripts," as CGI programs are commonly termed, make interactive features such as

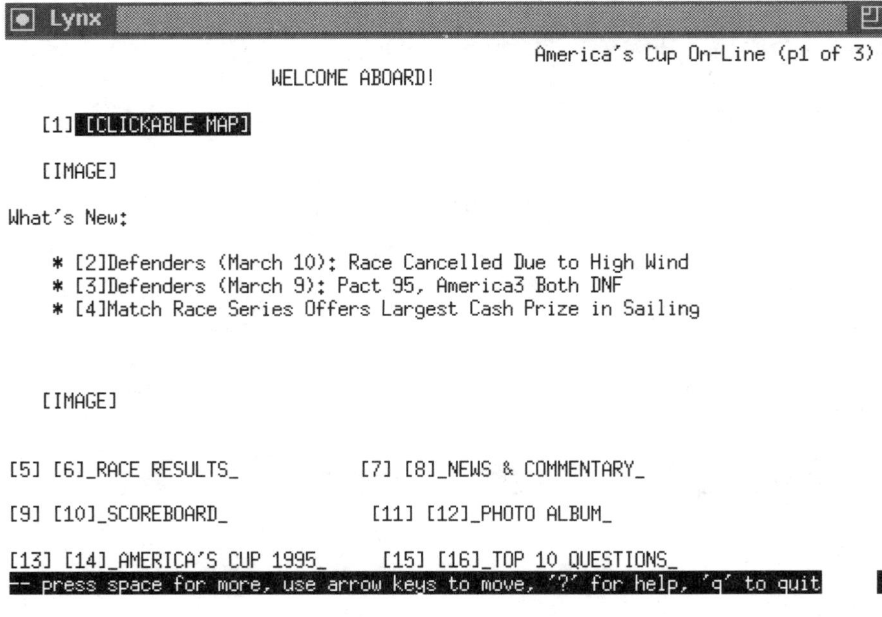

Figure 2–5 America's Cup On-Line page, viewed using Lynx

information gateways, feedback mechanisms, database access, ordering capabilities, personalized documents, and searching capabilities much more possible.

Common Gateway Interface scripting was developed as a standard for integrating custom programs with the server. Initially, each server had its own standards; without major modification, scripts written for one server could not be used on another server. But once the CGI standard was defined, it became possible to take a script or program written for one server and successfully run it on a different server. CGI is a good example of how standards can help bridge the incompatibilities inherent in systems with many participants who use lots of different software.

CGI is a standard for writing programs that can interact with a variety of Web servers. CGI defines an interface through which the server can pass information to the program, and the program can return information to the server. CGI is the main tool for creating truly interactive experiences on the Web.

2.4.5 Common Log Format

The Common Log Format, a standard format for access logs, was developed so that programs could be written to analyze the logs of any server. The Common Log Format specifies what information is logged and in what sequence the information appears. The standard also describes delimiters, such as square brackets and quotation marks, that are used to help identify the data. For example, the standard calls for date and time information to be placed inside square brackets, and requests to be enclosed by quotation marks.

The server automatically gathers the available data into the log. It lists which data was requested, when it was requested, what host the user was on when requesting the data, and whether the request was successful. The log might also record user names, but it does that only if you have modified your server software (we'll show you how in Chapter 14) or if the server automatically requires that requests for documents and objects be authenticated. Here's a sample log entry:

```
loki.netgen.com -- [03/Mar/1995:17:48:12 +0500] "GET http://www.netgen.com/
HTTP/1.0" 200 2848
```

Let's find out what each part means:

- `loki.netgen.com` is the hostname of client making the request, either the DNS name or IP number of the remote client.
- - (first hyphen) is information returned by Identd. A hyphen indicates no information returned.
- - (second hyphen) is UserName, if the user sent a UserID for authentication. A hyphen indicates no UserID sent.
- `03/Mar/1995:17:48:12 +0500` is the time and date of the request, according to the server machine.
- `GET http://www.netgen.com/ HTTP/1.0` is the actual request submitted, shown in quotation marks. The first word, GET, is the request method used. This is followed by the URL. The request ends with `HTTP/1.0`, specifying that the client would like the server to return a header along with the requested data.
- `200` is the status code returned by the server.
- `2848` is the number of bytes transferred from the server to the client, not including the HTTP/1.0 header.

All of these terms and concepts will be discussed in later chapters.

2.4.6 Security Measures

Both providers and customers on the Internet want to transfer credit card numbers and other private data securely. At the December, 1994, meeting of the IETF in San Jose, the Security Working Group was formed. The HTTPS working group is charged with developing requirements and specifications for providing security services to HTTP. Three of the protocols developed to meet the security needs of commercial providers on the Internet are Shen, S-HTTP (Secure HTTP), and SSL (Secure Sockets Layer). Each protocol works in a different way.

Shen was developed by Phillip M. Hallam-Baker at CERN. There is a server out there that supports Shen, but nobody uses it much. The Shen approach calls for three separate security-related mechanisms:

- Weak authentication with low maintenance overhead and without patent or export restrictions
- Strong authentication via public-key exchange
- Strong encryption of message content

Shen is built on top of the existing HTTP 1.0 specifications. It simply extends HTTP by defining new HTTP headers that can be used in the request or response to perform these functions.

The second security protocol, S-HTTP, was developed by Rescorla and Schiffman of Enterprises Integration Technologies (EIT). S-HTTP was designed to provide encryption and to authenticate the content, but it is not very popular yet. S-HTTP allows you to include extra information about the content—so you could say, for example, "This is encrypted," or "This requires authorization." And in the request you could say, "Here is my authorization," in addition to saying, "Here is my request."

Also in December, Netscape Communications Corporation released its Netsite Commerce Server. This server includes strong encryption and authentication features that address many of the Web's commercial needs. In order to create this product, Netscape came up with the specifications for the SSL (Secure Socket Layer). However, a lot of people were angry at Netscape because they felt it was not necessary to develop a new proprietary protocol. Why do that when the original version of HTTP provided a mechanism for a client and server to talk through an encrypted session? For Netscape to create its own standard just didn't seem like a reasonable thing to do. Since that time, Netscape has agreed to support other publicly available encryption schemes, such as S-HTTP.

It may seem strange that other developers haven't made much progress in creating new protocols for secure transmissions. They haven't largely because they would have to license the encryption algorithm. Netscape, the first company to produce commercial browser and server software licensed the RSA technology. (See the accompanying sidebar.)

2.5 Governing Bodies and How Specs Evolve

For a long time, the Web's user base was so small that users and developers determined the direction in which it developed. For the most part, developers at NCSA and CERN defined new servers and browsers, and thus determined how people used the Web. As for actual specifications that defined the Web, those specifications evolved in two ways.

2.5.1 Formal Standards Changes: IETF and Web Consortium

New specifications and changes to existing ones (i.e., from HTML 1.0 to 2.0, or HTTP 0.9 to 1.0) have to be approved by working groups of the Internet Engineering Task Force (IETF). Working groups are formal committees that meet to discuss and propose changes. They propose Internet Drafts, which the Secretariat announces and disseminates. The Secretariat maintains an Internet-Drafts index. HTML and HTTP, for example, are both Internet Drafts. They are currently under consideration and have not been formally approved. Internet Drafts are available via anonymous FTP at ds.internic.net in the /internet-drafts directory. They are deleted after six months.

In its next phase, an Internet Draft becomes an RFC (Request for Comment). RFCs are the official document series of the IAB (Internet Architecture Board), a body of the international organization known as the Internet Society. The RFC editor announces and disseminates new RFCs. All RFCs are archived permanently (i.e., they are never deleted, though they can be rendered obsolete by future RFCs). The IETF gathers public feedback on what changes should be implemented. Gopher is currently in the RFC stage. RFCs are available in the /rfc directory. Finally, a protocol specified in an RFC can become an Internet Standard. URLs have already achieved official Internet Standard status.

The other formal body that has plans to change the Web is the Web Consortium, formed as a cooperative effort between CERN and MIT. CERN is where the Web was founded and MIT is known around the world for its tech-

RSA History

RSA was the first public-key algorithm to support both encryption and authentication. Public-key algorithms use a pair of keys—a public key and a private key—to encrypt and decrypt messages. You share your public key with the world. Anyone can use your public key to encrypt data meant for your eyes only. When you receive the encrypted data, you use your private key to decrypt it. Your private key always remains secret. When you want to send confidential data to someone else, you use their public key to encrypt it, and they use their private key for decryption.

RSA was invented in 1977 by Ron Rivest, Adi Shamir, and Leonard Adleman. It is the most popular public-key algorithm. RSA is now one of the strongest algorithms commonly used.

The RSA algorithm is based on the idea that it is difficult to prime-factor a large number. (*Prime-factor* means to break a number down into its prime components.) RSA's public and private keys are based on a pair of 100 to 200–digit prime numbers.

The RSA algorithm is well known. It was described in a 1977 *Scientific American* article, titled "A New Kind of Cipher That Would Take Millions of Years to Break." However, despite its being well known, implementations of the algorithm are subject to export constraints. Believe it or not, products that implement RSA and other cryptographic algorithms are defined as "munitions" by the U.S. State Department and covered under the International Traffic in Arms Regulation Act.

nical prowess and ownership of the X Consortium, a project similar to the Web Consortium.

One of the goals of the Web Consortium is to work with all its members to propose intelligent specification standards to the IETF. The Consortium charges member companies an entrance fee. In return, it gives them access to the standards development process, allows them to get news of the standards more quickly than other commercial companies, and provides a means of participating in the formal change process.

A jumble of standards and protocols are already available. Multiple versions of various drafts and standards are available, each with a different set of features. Then you have commercial applications, such as Netscape's extensions, that do not even adhere to the specifications. However,

The Internet Engineering Task Force (IETF)

The following is an excerpt from the IETF home page:

> The Internet Engineering Task Force (IETF) is the protocol engineering and development arm of the Internet. The IETF is a large, open, international community of network designers, operators, vendors, and researchers who are concerned with the evolution of Internet architecture and the smooth operation of the Internet. The IETF is open to any interested individual.
>
> The IETF holds meetings three times a year. First-time attendees might find it helpful to read "The Tao of IETF." The actual technical work of the IETF is done in its working groups, which are organized by topic into several areas (e.g., routing, network management, security, etc.).

Relevant RFCs include:

- RFC 1630—Universal Resource Identifiers (Yes, the word should be "universal.")
- RFC 1737—Uniform Resource Names
- RFC 1738—Uniform Resource Locators

Important Internet Drafts include:

- draft-fielding-http-01
- draft-ietf-html-spec-01 (This is for HTML 2.0.)
- draft-ietf-html-specv3-00.txt
- draft-raggett-www-html-00

Netscape's extensions are supported by their popular browser, so they are likely to be successful and can become the de facto standard. The problem comes when everybody wants to create their own standard. The Web Consortium seems to be taking an active role in building a consensus between industry and users to make sure that standards are developed through a formal, controlled method.

2.5.2 Informal Social Changes

People are expressing their opinions on the Web, and that makes the Web change too. Sometimes a simple user interaction can be the impetus for informal social change. For example, users might tell developers what sorts of things they really want at a site. From this, the designers of the site can understand much better what is being expected of them and how to get it done.

The Netscape extensions to HTML were made to satisfy user demands for better ways to specify how the data being retrieved from the Web should be rendered. As we mentioned earlier, Netscape extensions allow text to be centered and wrapped around graphics. Neither of these enhancements went through a formal standardization process. Netscape simply announced the release of its product, including revisions to the original specification. Netscape did not go through formal procedures set up by the IETF before presenting these changes.

The result is that now you have a real standard (i.e., what the IETF is putting out in terms of HTML 2.0 or HTML 3.0 specifications) and Netscape's de facto standard. Netscape decided to do things its own way and users are jumping on the bandwagon. Netscape extensions are just one example of how social and market demand affect life on the Web. Some changes may never go through a formal procedure before they are implemented and become popular. Much to their credit, Netscape has since turned around and begun to support strongly the formal standards process, proposing extensions through formal routes and supporting existing proposals.

CHAPTER 3

Setting Up a Web Site

CHAPTER AT A GLANCE

This chapter rounds up the basic concepts every person needs to understand before setting up a Web site. In particular, we introduce the key issues that you should address before deciding on your Web requirements. We also talk about how to represent and structure your data. The chapter ends with detailed instructions for downloading server software and setting the configuration files for your site.

MORE DETAIL

Chapter 10 presents a detailed discussion of the issues and considerations involved in creating and maintaining a Web site.

Chapter 13 provides more information about HTTP servers: what the different models are and how to write your own server.

Establishing a World Wide Web (WWW) site and publishing information on the Internet is not especially difficult. Thousands of individuals, groups, and companies have already established a presence on the Web—and in doing so are contributing to the Web's popularity. In this chapter, you will become familiar with all the basic concepts that one should understand before setting up a Web site, especially key issues surrounding what the requirements for a Web site are. By the end of this chapter, you will be ready to create a simple site of your own. But before you can consider creating a site, you need to spend time considering the nature and/or purpose of your site.

3.1 Key Considerations

In order to determine the physical requirements of a Web site, you have to anticipate how much use you expect your site to experience. You must also consider your connection options and choose the hardware and software that will best meet your needs.

NOTE

If you have a shell account with an Internet Service Provider (ISP), and you want to create a Web site, you will have to use your ISP's hardware and software, as well as its Internet connection (you're already using its connection by virtue of your shell account). When you use your ISP's hardware and software, the ISP handles many of the tasks discussed in this chapter, including configuring, running, and maintaining the server software.

3.1.1 Anticipating Usage Patterns

One of the most important issues to consider before setting up a Web site is how much you expect the site to be browsed by others. Usage affects the network connection, software, and hardware needs of a system, so your estimate of usage cannot be a pie-in-the-sky guess, nor can it be based solely on the belief that your data is "way-cool" and will attract users. Different sites on the Web experience incredibly different loads. Some sites average hundreds of connections (or "hits") a day, while others average tens of thousands or even millions a day. There are ways to get a rough feel for how popular your site will be.

The first is to consider who your target audience is and how large it is. For example, information on an obscure sport like badminton may be as unique as information on an obscure medical disease. Nevertheless, although both types of content are unique, the medical paper is for a specific target audience, which in all likelihood is not very big. On the other hand, the sports information—even if it is about badminton—will likely appeal to a wider range of Internet users. After all, badminton is a popular backyard sport. One way of determining the potential size of an audience is to look at the readership of USENET newsgroups and online mailing lists that are similar in scope to your proposed site.

There is a particular USENET group—news.lists—which constantly sends out usage estimates for newsgroups. From that list you can see how many people are using a group. For example, when Eric Richard first thought of setting up the Sports Information Service, he checked out the newsgroups and found a dozen or so that focused on sports and related topics. Then he checked the news.lists newsgroup and evaluated the number of people visiting those newsgroups to get a feel for the popularity of different sports. He noticed, for example, that newsgroups related to professional sports had more users than groups that discussed the Olympics. Here's a sampling of the numbers Eric found:

```
rec.sport.hockey: 87,000 readers
rec.sport.football.pro: 81,000 readers
rec.sport.basketball.pro: 66,000 readers
rec.sport.olympics: 24,000 readers
```

This list is also available via anonymous FTP at rtfm.mit.edu in the file /pub/usenet/news.lists/USENET_READERSHIP.SURVEY.

Evaluate your findings carefully. Not only can you gauge potential usage, but you might come away with insights that will help when you design your site. There are many newsgroups on so many diverse topics, we'd be surprised if you couldn't find at least one that relates to your subject.

In addition to checking out related newsgroups, there are other ways to gauge potential usage of your planned site:

- Check out similar Web sites. (You can send e-mail to site administrators and ask for information.)
- Scan newsgroup archives. Some newsgroups maintain archives. Check a newsgroup's FAQ (file answering frequently asked questions) to find

references to archive lists and then scan the archive data to see if your topic is mentioned. For example, the FAQ for the newsgroup rec.sport.basketball.pro is available via FTP at ftp://rtfm.mit.edu/pub/usenet/rec.sport.basketball.pro/. Often FAQs contain references to mailing lists, which are yet another valuable resource. Based on the number of members on these lists and on the amount of discussion, you can often gauge how much demand there is for a particular type of information.

- Look at related sites to see if they ever receive regular requests for specific information. For example, if you were thinking of setting up a sports server devoted to the game of cricket, you could ask other sports servers if they ever receive requests for information about cricket.
- Ask around. Although perhaps a bit subjective, this is the best approach. Ask around by posting messages with active mailing lists and newsgroups. Ask those list users if they'd be interested in your proposed site, and find out more about their specific interests.

Another way to determine whether your site will get much use is to consider how unique your information is. If your site is one of only a handful that provide a type of information, your site will have more value. On the other hand, if your site is one among twenty or more that offer the same information, you will need a unique slant or way to make your site stand out from the others. One of the best examples of this is the "cybermall" phenomenon, which has become a major trend on the Web. Here you can shop for things ranging from flowers and books to CDs and computers. There are so many cybermalls online that none of them really provides a unique service—and no site has a monopoly on the service being provided. Each one must separate itself from the rest of the crowd by providing unique services or high-profile clients. For instance, if one cybermall is the only online store that sells Levi's, it will have something to distinguish itself from the rest.

The final, major factor in determining the usage of a site is how you intend to publicize it. Are you going to rely primarily on word of mouth? (See the "Get a Load of My Page" sidebar for suggestions.) It is quite clear that advertising a site on important lists like the NCSA "What's New Page" and Scott Yanoff's "List of Internet Services" has a very direct and immediate impact on how many people use a site. Listing a site on one of these lists can generate thousands of connections per week during the month that the site announcement is made. You can also post announcements to newsgroups. Another productive means of advertising a site is to find other sites on the Web that are related to yours and ask their administrators if they would mind providing a link to your site. Doing this, especially on a high-load site, can create a long-term stream of traffic.

There is no formula for determining how much use a site will receive, but considering the factors posed here will at least give you a reasonable idea of how much traffic your site will get.

Realistically, only a handful of sites in the world are currently getting millions of hits a day, and those include the NCSA and Netscape home pages. Mosaic users open on the NCSA page by default. Similarly, Netscape users automatically open the Netscape page. The fact that so many people use these two products accounts for the volume of usage at those sites. Anyhow, millions of hits a day is beyond the order of magnitude that you can expect for your own site, even if you're convinced that your site will be *the* site on the Web.

Your numbers will more likely be in the range of hundreds to hundreds of thousands of connections per day. If your home page tells about you as a person and nothing more, you may get a few hundred hits a day. Lots of people randomly browse the Web; they move from site to site, following links that seem interesting. Therefore, even if you run a small-scale site with only a few outside links pointing to it, your site may still get hundreds of connections a week from passersby who happen to see the link and check it out.

Likewise, if your site is interesting but not very well-advertised, you'll probably get a few hundred hits. On the other hand, if your site has a lot of information that's useful to people and people know it's there, you will easily get tens of thousands of hits a day. If you build it they will come—but only if they know it's there.

Other factors determining how much use a site gets include your network provider and how much effort you put into making others aware of your site. (See the sidebar titled "Ping" to learn how to gather performance statistics on a network provider.)

Whether you're anticipating hundreds, thousands, or tens of thousands of hits per day, you have to factor that number into all of the decisions you make. For example, if you're going to be getting a hundred hits a day, you can set up your site by using your PC or Mac at home on a 56K line, with little maintenance. A high volume of use might call for different machines and broader connections.

3.1.2 Network Connections

For a Web site to be accessible to the public, the host computer must have an Internet connection in the form of either a direct connection or one made

Get a Load of My Page

You can announce the arrival of a new Web site or page in several places. Here are four of the best to get you started:

- The NCSA "What's New Page" is available at **http://www.gnn.com/wn/whats-new.html**. Updates can be made via a forms interface at **http://www.gnn.com/wn/whats-new-form.html** or **http://www.digital.com/gnn/wn/whats-new-form.html**. Alternatively, you can send the NCSA e-mail at ncsa_wn@gnn.com.
- EINet Galaxy is available at **http://www.einet.net/**. Additions to the list can be submitted via a forms interface at **http://www.einet.net/annotate-help.html**.
- The Yahoo database is available at **http://akebono.stanford.edu/yahoo/form.html**. Additions to the list can be submitted via a forms interface at **http://akebono.stanford.edu/yahoo/bin/add**.
- Scott Yanoff's list of "Special Internet Connections" is accessible at **http://www.cs.uwm.edu/cgi-bin/finger?yanoff@alpha2.csd.uwm.edu**. Updates to the list are made by Scott Yanoff, who can be contacted via e-mail at yanoff@alpha2.csd.uwm.edu.

Don't forget, though, that as important as exposure is, presenting interesting and useful content is what makes a site successful in the long run.

through an Internet gateway on a local network. The first major consideration to take into account is continuous connectivity; users of the Web must be able to reach a site 24-hours a day, regardless of their location. For this reason, users who access the Web from behind a firewall usually are unable to provide Web sites. In addition, Web sites that use intermittent dial-up SLIP or PPP connections are only available sporadically. (A *firewall* is a device that separates a local network from the Internet for security purposes. The basic idea is to restrict all outgoing and incoming traffic through this one machine, which is really good at looking for dangerous connections and stopping them from getting through to your system.)

Another important factor in the performance of a Web site is deciding what size of a network connection is necessary. Network connections are measured in terms of *bandwidth,* or the speed at which the network transmits data to the Internet. In general, Internet connections range from 9.6-Kbps (kilobit per second) dial-up lines to 45-Mbps (T3) dedicated lines. A Web site can be run over a 9.6-Kbps connection, but data transfers are usually extremely slow, and multiple connections can easily overload the link. For most sites, a 56-Kbps line is the minimum bandwidth requirement. However, sites that experience heavy traffic or transmit image-intensive pages often require fractional T1 lines.

The bandwidth determines the amount of information that can flow through the network at any given time, so the size of the connection places a limit on the amount of data being transmitted from the server at one time. Sometimes, other factors besides the size of the connection determine whether the system can transmit the maximum amount of data. (The amount of data that gets through in a specific amount of time is called *throughput.*) A crucial problem of having a low bandwidth network connection is the lengthy period of time it takes to deliver documents to clients. This is called *latency.* For example, a 56-Kbps line takes a minimum of 15 seconds to transfer a 100K file (100 K = 800 Kbits = 56 Kbps sec.). On the other hand, it would take a minimum of half a second to send the same file across a 1.54-Mbps T1 line. Another critical measure of your site's performance is determined by your network's *packet lossage,* which happens when one or more *packets* (the unit that data is transmitted in) doesn't make it to its destination within the accepted amount of time and has to be resent. (For a more detailed description of the relationship between bandwidth, latency, throughput, and packet lossage, see the "Bandwidth, Latency, and the Post Office" sidebar.)

RULE OF THUMB

An average document takes several seconds to transfer over a 14.4-Kbps connection, about a second over a 56-Kbps line, and a fraction of a second over a T1. Obviously, these times get longer as the usage of the site goes up and users retrieve multiple documents at the same time.

While faster certainly is better in terms of network connectivity, faster is also substantially more expensive. People usually obtain an Internet connection from an Internet access provider. The bandwidth, cost, and terms vary widely among providers. Higher-bandwidth services are expensive. T1

Bandwidth, Latency, and the Post Office

When people talk about "getting a network," they tend to talk a lot about bandwidth. *Bandwidth* is the rate at which data is passed through a network. It's a measure of flow—how wide your pipe is and how much data you can push through it at one time. So people talk about connection lines in numbers. They talk about T1 lines, 1.54-Mbps (megabit per second) lines, 56-Kbps (kilobit per second) lines, and 14.4-lines.

Unfortunately, what no one really seems to talk about is the latency of the system. *Latency* is how long it takes to get data from one point to another. With regards to the Web, it is the amount of time it takes for a user to get a request from the browser to the server. The time it takes to get the data from the server back to the browser is also the latency.

Another important concept is throughput. *Throughput* is the total amount of data gets from one point to another in a certain period of time, and is defined by the following simple mathematical equation:

$$throughput = bandwidth \times latency$$

What people often fail to consider when they evaluate potential service providers is the provider's network latency (i.e., how long it takes for data to travel across your provider's network to get to the rest of the Internet). In addition, people tend to either underestimate or overestimate the bandwidth they're getting. For example, when you buy a T1, it's very possible that you'll share it with several other people, and that means you're not likely to get anywhere near full capacity.

Generally speaking, bandwidth is not going to be an issue. It only becomes an issue when you're transmitting large amounts of data, such as video files, or when you're transmitting a very large graphic or audio file on a slow line (below 56 Kbps). Even in those cases, bandwidth is only a mildly limiting factor. The place where you could really suffer is on latency and packet lossage. If your network service provider is very bad at getting packets from your location out to the rest of the world, every single request you make will be slowed down.

The Post Office is a good analogy when it comes to network delivery times. Think of a data packet as a letter and bandwidth as the number of letters that can pass through Boston's main office in a single day. In this analogy, latency is how long it takes to get a letter from Boston to its destination, throughput is the measure of how many letters leave Boston and arrive at their destinations, and packet lossage is the percentage of letters that end up in dead letter office.

Bandwidth, Latency, and the Post Office (Continued)

If we're concerned about sending a single letter to the West Coast and it takes a long time for the letter to get there (a high latency), then bandwidth really doesn't matter. What difference does it make if the Post Office can process 10 million letters on a single day (a high bandwidth) if *your* letter takes two weeks to get to its destination (lousy latency)?

On the other hand, if we're concerned about sending ten letters (multiple packets), we are concerned about both latency and bandwidth. If the Post Office is only capable of sending one letter through its system per day (a low bandwidth), it will take ten days to process the ten letters—and that's only if no one else mails anything on those days. Similarly, if it takes ten days for each letter to reach its destination (a high latency) but the letters can be processed on the same day (a high bandwidth), it will still take at least ten days to get all the letters delivered.

lines typically are priced at $2,000 to $5,000 per month, plus a $3,000 to $8,000 installation charge. A 56-Kbps connection is about $300 to $400 per month, plus a $500 startup fee. The average price for dial-up SLIP and PPP connections is only $35 to $40 per month, plus a $40 startup charge—but these are not dedicated (continuous) connections. Most major metropolitan areas are covered by local providers. National Internet access providers include AlterNet, MCI, NEARnet, Netcom, PSI, and Sprint.

CommerceNet Directory of Internet Service Providers
http://www.commerce.net/directories/products/inet.prov.dir.html

Besides considering the bandwidth and cost of a network connection, it is also important to examine network service providers' performance statistics. Whether a T1 has the potential to carry 1.54 megabits per second is meaningless if the network is being slowed down by large amounts of packet lossage or long delivery times. It is completely possible for the performance of a network service provider to become the bottleneck on a system and hamper its performance, no matter what the computer's speed or the network bandwidth. When you are evaluating network providers, make sure to look at the following criteria:

Performance/reliability: One of the simplest ways of evaluating a network service provider is to *ping* several hosts on the network and evaluate the statistics that are returned. A ping generally returns four important numbers: the minimum, average, and maximum latencies, and the percentage of packets that were lost. Between 1 and 4 percent is an acceptable packet lossage range (ideally, lossage should stay much closer to 1 percent). Depending on how far away the remote host is, latency times should not be more than one or two hundred milliseconds (ms). Good network service providers that are relatively close should have latencies significantly lower than this (less than 50 ms). By checking these statistics at various points during the day and over the course of a few days, you can obtain a reasonable profile of what kind of service you would be getting from this provider. Good providers have very low latency times and low packet lossage. In addition, high latencies and packet lossages are corrected very quickly (within one to two hours). Poor service providers have high latencies and packet lossage, and they are not good at correcting these problems (if they even fix them!). We pinged two sites to give you a comparative sample. See the "Using Ping" sidebar to learn the results.)

RULE OF THUMB

Packet lossage should almost never exceed 10 percent.

Customer references: Talk to a few of the service providers to check out the quality of the service. Ask if they have had problems with network outages, how quickly the network service provider responded, how receptive the service provider is to customer questions and problems, and if they have noticed any lag times in their connections. Performance statistics explains a lot, but a customer can give you a much better feel for how a provider has performed in the long term.

Available bandwidth: Ask network service providers how they are connected to the rest of the Internet. Most have substantially more bandwidth to the rest of the Net than a single T1. If they only have one T1 line and they are trying to sell you a T1, you will have to share that T1 with their other customers. Sharing a T1 line really shouldn't be a problem with the major, national network service providers (PSI, AlterNet, NearNet, etc.), but it can be a very real problem with small Internet service providers.

You can make an informed decision by appropriately dealing with the two major issues—requirements and cost—when you determine the size of the connection. Also, evaluating the requirements carefully helps to determine the upgrade path, if one should become necessary.

TIP

Consider the possibility of future upgrades when you obtain network service for the first time. It usually doesn't cost much to upgrade from a fractional T1 to a greater fraction of a T1, but going from a 56Kbps line to a fractional T1 costs a lot, because you have to pay the full cost of installation over again. Get terms for upgrade options from the network service provider. And also consider how quickly upgrades can be made. Some kinds of lines, fractional T1s in particular, take one or two days to upgrade, but other upgrades involve installing new lines and can take weeks or months.

Using Ping

Here is a sample of using a ping to evaluate a network connection. In order to provide a gauge of what a good and bad connection look like, we pinged Stanford and a site in Lithuania. If your Internet Service Provider (ISP) returns better statistics than the Stanford site (which it probably should, since we were pinging all the way across the U.S. from Boston), this is a good sign. If your ISP returns worse statistics or even statistics comparable to those of the Lithuania site, this is a very bad sign. The output of a ping varies from machine to machine, but all pings should return the same general information.

To see how to interpret a sample ping line, look at this line:

```
64 bytes from 36.56.0.151: icmp_seq=0 ttl=245 time=87.4 ms
```

Let's dissect it to find the hidden meanings:

- `64 bytes` is the amount of data sent
- `36.56.0.151` is the IP Address of the site you are pinging
- `icmp_seq=0` tells you which packet number in the sequence this ping is referring to
- `ttl=245` is how long ping will wait before giving up on this packet
- `time=87.4 ms` shows how long it took for this packet

Using Ping (Continued)

The only really important pieces of information from this line are the time it took for the packet to get to its destination (the latency for the packet) and the sequence number. (Sequence numbers should appear sequentially, without gaps. A gap indicates that a packet was lost.) This is just an example of the kind of information ping will generally return. Different pings output information in different formats.

A summary of the ping line looks like this:

```
15 packets transmitted, 15 packets received, 0% packet loss
round-trip min/avg/max = 82.2/85.3/98.4 ms
```

This tells you what percentage of packets were lost and how long it took the packets to get there (the minimum, maximum, and average latencies):

```
> ping stanford.edu
PING stanford.edu (36.56.0.151): 56 data bytes
64 bytes from 36.56.0.151: icmp_seq=0 ttl=245 time=87.4 ms
64 bytes from 36.56.0.151: icmp_seq=1 ttl=245 time=87.4 ms
64 bytes from 36.56.0.151: icmp_seq=2 ttl=245 time=82.4 ms
64 bytes from 36.56.0.151: icmp_seq=3 ttl=245 time=84.5 ms
64 bytes from 36.56.0.151: icmp_seq=4 ttl=245 time=98.4 ms
64 bytes from 36.56.0.151: icmp_seq=5 ttl=245 time=84.2 ms
64 bytes from 36.56.0.151: icmp_seq=6 ttl=245 time=85.4 ms
64 bytes from 36.56.0.151: icmp_seq=7 ttl=245 time=82.8 ms
64 bytes from 36.56.0.151: icmp_seq=8 ttl=245 time=87.9 ms
64 bytes from 36.56.0.151: icmp_seq=9 ttl=245 time=82.2 ms
64 bytes from 36.56.0.151: icmp_seq=10 ttl=245 time=82.7 ms
64 bytes from 36.56.0.151: icmp_seq=11 ttl=245 time=84.7 ms
64 bytes from 36.56.0.151: icmp_seq=12 ttl=245 time=84.2 ms
64 bytes from 36.56.0.151: icmp_seq=13 ttl=245 time=84.1 ms
64 bytes from 36.56.0.151: icmp_seq=14 ttl=245 time=82.4 ms
--- stanford.edu ping statistics ---
15 packets transmitted, 15 packets received, 0% packet loss
round-trip min/avg/max = 82.2/85.3/98.4 ms
```

Using Ping (Continued)

This looks like a *very* good connection. (It just so happens that this data is traveling from the East Coast to West Coast on a 45-Mbps line.) There is little variation between the minimum, average, and maximum latencies, which indicates that the service is pretty consistent. The 0 percent packet lossage is outstanding.

The results from the Lithuanian ping are much worse than those from Stanford, although we have to allow for the fact that the site we are pinging is in Lithuania. These statistics would be considered terrible if they were drawn from a site closer to us than Lithuania is:

```
> ping neris.mii.lt
PING neris.mii.lt (193.219.50.10): 56 data bytes
64 bytes from 193.219.50.10: icmp_seq=2 ttl=242 time=779.6 ms
64 bytes from 193.219.50.10: icmp_seq=3 ttl=242 time=799.6 ms
64 bytes from 193.219.50.10: icmp_seq=4 ttl=242 time=801.4 ms
64 bytes from 193.219.50.10: icmp_seq=5 ttl=242 time=774.7 ms
64 bytes from 193.219.50.10: icmp_seq=7 ttl=242 time=766.6 ms
64 bytes from 193.219.50.10: icmp_seq=8 ttl=242 time=777.0 ms
64 bytes from 193.219.50.10: icmp_seq=9 ttl=242 time=782.9 ms
64 bytes from 193.219.50.10: icmp_seq=10 ttl=242 time=800.7 ms
64 bytes from 193.219.50.10: icmp_seq=11 ttl=242 time=772.7 ms
64 bytes from 193.219.50.10: icmp_seq=12 ttl=242 time=762.4 ms
64 bytes from 193.219.50.10: icmp_seq=14 ttl=242 time=820.7 ms
--- neris.mii.lt ping statistics ---
15 packets transmitted, 11 packets received, 26% packet loss
round-trip min/avg/max = 762.4/785.3/820.7 ms
```

While the latencies are all reasonably close, they are still very bad. Latencies of more than about 100 milliseconds should be viewed with caution.

The packet lossage of 26 percent is also very difficult to work with. It means that one of every four packets sent is not received in the maximum time allowed and has to be resent. Not only does the high latency hurt, but it also means that a lot of time is spent waiting for the time-out (i.e., waiting to learn that the packet did not get to its destination).

To get an accurate perspective on the statistics, here are several tips:

Using Ping (Continued)

- Send a large number of packets each time you do a test. In other words, wait until a ping has sent 50 packets or so before stopping it and collecting statistics. This will smooth out local spikes in the statistics.
- Collect the statistics over a period of several days (i.e., collect them each day for a week). This will give you an idea of how consistently good or bad the connection is.
- Try to collect statistics at different times during the day. Statistics can vary significantly over the course of a day. By collecting at different times, you will get a good idea of the peaks and valleys of the statistics.

When you evaluate your statistics, you will most likely find that the minimum latency does not change significantly throughout the day. However, the average and maximum latencies and packet lossage are both likely to rise during the main part of the day and fall during the morning and evening.

It is important to realize that the average and maximum statistics are much more important to the service you receive than the minimum statistics. Regardless of how good the net connection *can* be, what is really important is how it really *is*. In addition, if you are going to use your net during the daytime only, it really doesn't matter how good the statistics are at night.

3.1.3 Host Computer Hardware

The chief hardware component of a Web site is the host computer, which houses the site's content. The software program that runs on the host is called a *Web server* or *HTTP server.* It interprets incoming requests and returns documents, objects, or other files. Server programs are available for most major operating systems, including UNIX, VMS, VM, Macintosh System 7, Windows (3.1, NT, and 95), and even Lisp machines. The question comes down to whether you want a PC-, Macintosh-, or UNIX-based system. (When we say PC-based here, we mean DOS. Although you can actually run Linux on a PC, we consider that to be UNIX-based.)

The major considerations in choosing a Web host computer are platform stability, performance, and RAM (random access memory). Platform stability is most important. If the operating system routinely crashes under normal loads, the Web site often will be inaccessible. In general, UNIX computers have the most stable and robust operating systems, but they also cost more and have more technical requirements. Macintosh and Windows machines are usually good for handling light loads, but are not recommended for heavy loads.

"Load" is not so much a measure of how many users there are, but of how many processes the machine is trying to do at one time. Of course, if a lot of users make requests at the same time, that also affects the load.

To provide a fully functional Web server that can handle a reasonable load and provide all the features that users expect from a professional site, the only real option is a UNIX-based machine. Windows NT may become an option at some point, but that has yet to be proven. If all you want to do is serve Web documents and you don't need a full, robust system, a Macintosh will suffice.

Most of today's business hardware—including 486-based PCs, 68040-based Macintoshes, and nearly every UNIX workstation—can handle the processing and I/O (input/output) demands of all but the most heavily trafficked Web servers. You can have a PC- or Mac-based server, but DOS, Windows, and System 7 were not built with networking in mind. These operating systems were designed to be personal computer interfaces. They have enough power to support networking, but that doesn't mean that they're necessarily stable.

Moreover, high volume loads often push a PC or Macintosh to its limits and hit obscure bugs in the system that haven't been fleshed out. UNIX systems, on the other hand, were intended for use as network servers in a multiuser environment. They were designed with protected memory and the ability to support preemptive multitasking. UNIX systems have served in this capacity for a lot longer than other system platforms, so more of the bugs have been fixed.

Once you've decided which system platform you want, the next factors to consider are memory capacity, CPU speed, and disk speed. Secondary issues are the memory and swap speeds. These two are tangential and don't have nearly as much importance as the first three.

A Web server is not processor-intensive, so CPU speed has little to do with bottlenecks. Unless you have very power-hungry scripts running on the back end, you aren't really going to drive your computer hard. What you do need, though, is a lot of memory. In fact, you can very easily run a Web server on a 386 or 486 with a reasonable CPU speed, as long as you have a lot of memory. A Web server should really have a minimum of 8MB of RAM. Sixteen megabytes is very good, but 32MB is even better. For a really intensive server, you should have 64MB of RAM.

Why do you need so much memory? Because having the server in memory makes the server work that much more quickly than it would if you had to swap out to read from disk. *Swapping out* means copying data from memory into a space on disk. Swapping takes on the order of microseconds, while accessing memory takes only nanoseconds. So you really have a difference of three orders of magnitude (a factor of 1,000). But a server couldn't take up that much memory, could it? Well, yes and no. Most servers work such that each time a connection is made to the server (that is, each time it receives a request), the server makes a copy of itself to handle the request. This is called *forking*. The more requests or connections there are, the more that copies of the server will be vying for memory space.

If there is not enough memory to go around, the system starts using temporary space on the hard drive. In other words, it "swaps out." Swapping out refers to the process of copying things from memory into a space on disk called the *swap space*. "Swapping in" is the process of moving information back from the swap space into memory. Swapping takes time. During peak loads, a system might have to swap, but until that time the system slows down tremendously if it doesn't have enough memory to handle all the server clones—the copies the server makes of itself. If you are wondering why this is such a big deal, it's because memory access is on the order of a hundred thousand times faster than disk access.

RULE OF THUMB

The server process should never have to swap out of memory, except perhaps during peak loads.

Web servers are not inherently load-intensive, so your machine does not have to be a high-powered workstation in order to serve Web documents. A desktop Macintosh can handle typical loads, which amount to a few thousand connections per week. Windows systems, however, don't fare as well because they create a heavy load on the machine itself. A Web server on a Windows machine runs much more slowly. A Pentium box running Linux or another *x*86-based UNIX operating system is the equivalent of a high-end workstation in terms of performance. The most highly trafficked sites (like NCSA) have to split their load between many machines. NCSA runs its server on four dedicated HP 7000s in order to handle the millions of connections a day that it receives.

To support heavy loads, the host computer should be a dedicated World Wide Web machine—one that is used exclusively for the Web site. Under low loads, a host can be used for tasks in addition to its Web server duties. By "low loads," we mean an average connection rate on the order of 750 connections per hour, with peak usage below 1,500 connections per hour. (It is very reasonable to assume that peak usage is roughly double average usage.)

Rule of Thumb for Selecting Servers

At net.Genesis we came up with a method to help us select the right server system. This is not a tried-and-true law, but a useful place to start. Table 3-1 shows six levels of hardware systems and memory. If you follow the steps listed below, you will arrive at a final number that tells you the level of machine you should use for your Web site. If a system has more memory than is shown for its level, consider the system as if it were in a category between one-half and one level higher. For example, a DEC DS5000 (level-3 machine) becomes a level-3.5 machine if it has 40MB of memory.

Here are the steps for determining the level of machine you should use for your Web site:

1. Start with a score of 1 if you want a Web server.
2. Add 1 if you will be transferring a typical balance of images and HTML documents (average document size about 10K); or add 2 if you will be transferring unusually large files (average above 25K), such as audio, graphics, or video.
3. Subtract 1 if your connection is greater than a half-T1.
4. Add 1 if you will be serving a substantial number of processor-intensive functions.

Table 3–1. Quickie Server Levels, Based on Machines and Memory

Level	Machine	Memory
1	Mid-level PCs (486 up to about 50MHz) or mid-level Macs	4–8MB
2	High-end PCs (high-end 486 or Pentium) or high-end Macs	8–16MB
3	Mid-level UNIX workstations (DS5000, SparcIPX, etc.)	8–24MB
4	Higher-end UNIX workstations (Sparc5, Pentium/486 UNIX box)	16–40MB
5	Very powerful UNIX workstations (Sparc20, DEC Alpha, HP9000)	32–64MB
6	Parallel processing workstations (multiprocessor machine, or multiple machines)	40–80MB

5. Subtract 1 if, on average, you will be handling fewer than 150 connections per hour (with peak usage at about 300 connections per hour); or add 1 if you will be handling more than 500 connections per hour (with peak usage at about 1,000 connections per hour); or add 2 if you will be handling more than 1,500 connections per hour (with peak usage at about 3,000 connections per hour); or add 3 if you will be handling more than 4,000 connections per hour (with peak usage at about 8,000 connections per hour); or add 4 if you will be handling more than 10,000 connections per hour (with peak usage at about 20,000 connections per hour).

Now let's look at two examples. The MIT SIPB Web server (1) processes a typical balance of documents (+1) on a T1 (–1), and handles more than 4,000 connections per hour (+3). These factors yield a total of 4, and in fact the MIT SIPB Web server is a Sparc5. In the second example, a Web server (1) is transferring mostly HTML, including some audio and video, so a typical average (+1) is only connected via a 56Kbps line (0) and expects about 1,000 connections per hour (+1), yielding a level-3 machine. If you anticipate growth to more than 1,500 connections per hour, a level-4 would be appropriate.

3.1.4 Server Software

Once you select a platform, you must download and configure your Web server software. After you retrieve the server software, you must decompress it with a decompression utility, review the documentation, and proceed with the installation. When you install server software, you often have to modify the configuration file to include information such as the name of the server, the server port, and the top-level directory or folder from which files are to be served.

A Complete List of Available Servers
http://www.netgen.com/book/server_list.html

The widest variety of stable World Wide Web server programs are for UNIX platforms. The two most popular are from CERN and NCSA. The NCSA server is relatively small and fast. The CERN server offers a wider array of features, including the ability to run as a proxy server (on a firewall host) with caching. Both servers support most UNIX platforms. Each includes features for server-side executable scripts, image maps (clickable images), and some degree of access control. Both servers are discussed in detail later in this chapter.

CERN
http://www.netgen.com/book/cern_httpd.html

NCSA
http://www.netgen.com/book/ncsa_httpd.html

Both the CERN and NCSA servers are public domain software. Netscape provides another UNIX option with its Netsite Commerce and Netsite Communications servers. Netscape's servers are not in the public domain, so they cost money, but they provide features that the CERN and NCSA public domain servers do not.

For Macintosh systems, MacHTTP is the only Web server currently available. It includes tools for file searches, handling log statistics, and scripting. Scripts can be written in HyperCard, AppleScript, and even MacPerl.

There are also two server programs for Windows systems: NCSA httpd for Windows (frequently called Win-httpd) and SerWeb. Win-httpd includes most features of the UNIX NCSA httpd server and is generally considered superior to SerWeb (even on SerWeb's home page). For Windows NT, the full-featured and relatively new HTTPS supports Intel *x*86 and DEC Alpha-based Windows NT systems. Now commercial servers are being developed on nearly all of these platforms.

MacHTTP Server
http://www.netgen.com/book/mac_httpd.html

Win-httpd Server
http://www.netgen.com/book/win-httpd.html

SerWeb Server
http://www.netgen.com/book/serweb.html

HTTPS Server
http://www.netgen.com/book/https.html

From the UNIX point of view, the choice is between NCSA, CERN, and Netscape. When making your choice, consider four things: speed, features, cost, and support. Of course, the cost of the NCSA and CERN servers is zero, because both are free. Netsite Communications costs over a thousand dollars, and Netsite Commerce runs a few thousand dollars more. The Netsite Commerce server provides encryption, hence the higher price tag. As more and more companies explore the potential of selling products online, encryption becomes increasingly important. Consumers appear eager to make online purchases but are unwilling to use their credit card numbers online without some protection.

All four servers support server-side executable scripts, image maps, and all the other standard features. The only extra value you get with the Netsite Communications server is customer support. If you don't need customer support, you might as well use one of the free servers. If service is important to you, then paying the price may be worth it.

The NCSA server is slightly smaller than CERN's. Designed to be a simple server, it runs faster and takes up less memory. On the other hand, the CERN server offers more features and functionality, and it allows you to customize things a little better. Netscape's two servers are designed to handle heavy loads and are also very fast. If you're going for speed and you need something that's can handle a lot of connections, the NCSA and Netsite servers are the way to go.

The CERN server makes a great *proxy server,* which acts as an intermediary. Its sole purpose is to ask another server for the document being requested and then pass on the document to the user. Instead of contacting the main server, a user actually contacts the proxy server, which in turn contacts the main server, gets the response, and sends it back to the user. Now, this may seem silly until you realize that a lot of people out there are behind firewalls and can't talk directly to the outside world. The only way connections can come in and out of their networks is through proxy servers.

The CERN server software also supports document caching. When a user requests a document from a CERN proxy server, the document gets written to the server's own disk, where it remains for an amount of time specified by the server. This way, the document is already available on the server's disk; in case a user requests the document again the server does not have to re-retrieve the document from the network. Using the server's disk in this fashion obviously speeds up server processing quite a bit, because the documents being requested most often are in the disk cache most of the time.

Another difference between the CERN and NCSA servers is that CERN's documentation is slightly better and available online. You can print out the CERN documentation if you like working with hard copy. In early March, 1995, we surveyed over 8,000 servers and found that approximately 58 percent used the NCSA server software, while just over 17 percent used the CERN software. Both Netsite software products combined accounted for less than 1 percent. (See Table 3-2.)

Table 3–2. Server Software Breakdown

Software	Sites Found	Percent of Total
NCSA	1,596	57.99
CERN	469	17.04
MacHTTP	90	3.27
GN	54	1.96
HTTPS	48	1.74
plexus	24	0.87
WinHttpd	20	0.73
Netsite Communications	11	0.39
Netsite Commerce	10	0.36

Notes: Based on our March 6, 1995, survey of 2,750 Web sites.
HTTPS is a server for Windows NT.
GN is an integrated HTTP-Gopher server for UNIX platforms.
Plexus is an HTTP server written in Perl for UNIX platforms.

3.2 Information Architecture

Information architecture refers to the actual content, how the data is represented, and how those representations are organized (hierarchical document structure). Because of the interactive nature of the World Wide Web, a site's information architecture has a lot to do with its quality. In general, navigational pages (as opposed to content pages) should be made as brief as possible. Ideally, they should present all relevant information on a single screen. A site's overall structure should be rational. The interface should be intuitive to make navigation easy for the user. To make site navigation simpler, include a site "map" and search functions. A site's content will be better received if it is nicely formatted and properly organized.

3.2.1 Data Representation

Information on the Web can include formatted text, images, audio, video, and other data types and files. Documents (as opposed to files) transmitted on the Web must be written in HTML (Hypertext Markup Language). HTML is a relatively simple language and a number of programs are available to assist in HTML generation and document conversion.

As a general rule, though, document-conversion tools do a poor job. Often the output ends up looking quite different from what you intended. Be sure to check the output of the converters you use and clean up documents before making them available. (If you make a bad impression, people may never come back to your site!)

We found a pretty good list of HTML editors. The list includes brief descriptions of editors as well as links to sites where you can download public-domain HTML editor software and order commercial programs.

List of HTML Editors
http://www.netgen.com/book/html_editors_list.html

Establishing the content of your site is far more important that any of the other issues discussed so far in this chapter. Content is what brings people to a site and keeps them there. If you can't attract people, all the other issues are irrelevant. There are several factors to consider when establishing a Web site's contents. The World Wide Web is a literal web of documents and other objects that are interconnected and accessible by way of hyperlinks. Thus, providing content for a Web site means completing two related tasks: converting content into HTML documents and objects, and linking those documents and objects into a coherent WWW structure.

The onscreen presentation of Web documents is controlled by two factors: the quality of the document's HTML and the manner in which browsers display that HTML to users. Compatibility is an issue. What you intend is not always interpreted the way you intended by users' browser software, because browsers on different platforms interpret HTML differently. For example, a Web page that appears one way on the NCSA Mosaic browser for UNIX X-Window platforms might appear another way on the MacWeb browser for Macintosh computers. However, most of the popular browsers conform to the standard specification for proper HTML authoring. Therefore, if a page's HTML is correct with respect to the specification, the page should appear uniformly over a wide range of browsers. (We'll talk more about HTML in Chapters 7 and 8, and in Appendix C, which provides an annotated copy of the complete specification.)

3.2.2 Structure

If you had all of your content on a single page, and that page was tens and tens of physical pages long, people would get very annoyed. It would be difficult to find the information they wanted. One of the things that you have to think about is how to create a somewhat hierarchical structure. Put yourself in the user's shoes. When you visit a site, you want a top-level overview of everything that is there so you can quickly decide where you want to go. That first link should lead to more specific information, and from there the links should continue to branch out.

Earlier in this chapter we talked a bit about the spatial nature of the Web. When you are designing a structure, be sure that some of the branches move side to side as well as up and down. You don't want a system where you walk down one path, get to the end, and have to come all the way back to the top in order to find more information on a different path. Paths should "cross-link." Not only does cross-linking make a site easier to navigate, it also makes a site more robust and gives it breadth as well as depth.

RULE OF THUMB

Do not force your users up a tree.

If your site offers a lot of good information, you may reasonably expect other Webmasters to make links to your top-level page. But you can't depend on anyone to make a pointer to a piece of information that's hidden way down in your site. You have to create a structure that makes it very easy for people to find the information they want. There are a couple of ways of doing this. One way is to create a hierarchical structure with the information organized into logical, progressive units so that people can figure out what they want and where to find it. A second way is to provide a search function, perhaps one that involves keywords. When someone comes to your site looking for a particular topic, they just type in keyword(s) describing the information they're looking for, and the information instantly appears.

However, you need to provide users with some assistance by giving them ideas about what they can search for. Too often, the search function consists of a page that says "Enter your keywords here," and the rest of the page is a big blank space. At a site like this, if they are not familiar with the content, most users just sit there wondering what to do. Then they might try entering a keyword or two. They might even get lucky and find exactly what they're looking for, but more often blind attempts don't come up with anything. Users then get bored, annoyed, and frustrated. They leave and head for some other site that provides a more satisfying experience.

To keep this from happening at your site, you need to provide some example searches, or even a list of frequently used keywords. You don't have to come up with a list of every imaginable keyword. Even if a popular keyword on the list isn't exactly what a user is looking for, the list will give the user a jump-start and provide him or her with a better feel for the content available at the site.

3.3 Setting Up the NCSA httpd

Follow the instructions in this section to set up a minimally functional World Wide Web server. The server setup presented here is based on a UNIX implementation using NCSA httpd. The NCSA Web server was designed to be simple and fast at the expense of additional functionality. Therefore, it makes for an ideal learning tool.

3.3.1 Downloading the NCSA Software

The first step is to decide which directory you want to be the root directory for your server. If it doesn't exist yet, create it. Then move into it. For this sample implementation, we use /usr/local as our root directory. Next, you need to transfer the software to your machine by using anonymous FTP. Finally, change directories to NCSA's current directory, use the ls command to list the files, and prepare for a binary transfer using the bin command.

NOTE

The /usr/local directory is normally a protected directory. If you cannot write to it, you will have to choose a different directory, such as /tmp. If you use a different directory, be sure to substitute your directory name for /usr/local wherever you see it in our sample implementation.

Your session will look something like the following:

```
cd /usr/local
ftp ftp.ncsa.uiuc.edu
Connected to ftp.ncsa.uiuc.edu.
220 larry FTP server (Version wu-2.4(25) Thu Aug 25 13:14:21 CDT 1994)
ready.
Name (ftp.ncsa.uiuc.edu:erichard): anonymous
331 Guest login ok, send your complete e-mail address as password.
Password: erichard@netgen.com
230-Please read the file README
230- it was last modified on Tue Jan 3 18:54:35 1995 - 26 days ago
230-Please read the file README.FIRST
230- it was last modified on Thu Jan 12 17:53:58 1995 - 17 days ago
```

```
230 Guest login ok, access restrictions apply.
Remote system type is UNIX.
Using binary mode to transfer files.
ftp> cd Web/httpd/Unix/ncsa_httpd/current
250 CWD command successful.
ftp> ls
200 PORT command successful.
150 Opening ASCII mode data connection for /bin/ls.
total 5930
drwxr-xr-x  2 12873  wheel    2048 Aug 22 12:23 .
drwxr-xr-x 11 12873  wheel    2048 Aug 22 12:23 ..
-rw-r--r--  1 12873  other     379 Aug 22 12:20 .index
-rw-r--r--  1 12873  wheel  331089 Jul 7 1994 httpd_decaxp.tar.Z
-rw-r--r--  1 12873  wheel  304886 Jul 7 1994 httpd_decmips.tar.Z
-rw-r--r--  1 12873  wheel  900323 Jul 7 1994 httpd_docs.tar.Z
-rw-r--r--  1 12873  wheel  425722 Jul 7 1994 httpd_hp.tar.Z
-rw-r--r--  1 12873  wheel  320585 Jul 7 1994 httpd_rs6000.tar.Z
-rw-r--r--  1 12873  wheel  422186 Jul 7 1994 httpd_sgi.tar.Z
-rw-r--r--  1 12873  wheel  108589 Jul 7 1994 httpd_source.tar.Z
-rw-r--r--  1 12873  wheel  211981 Jul 7 1994 httpd_sun4.tar.Z
226 Transfer complete.
ftp> bin
200 Type set to I.
```

Once you are in this directory, you need to download the correct file for your machine. Refer to Table 3-3 to select the appropriate file for your operating system. If your machine type is not listed, download the source file (httpd_source.tar.Z) and read the instructions on compiling it into a binary.

Table 3–3. NCSA Files for Various Operating Systems

File	Operating System
httpd_decaxp.tar.Z	Digital Equipment Corp. OSF/1 1.3
httpd_decmips.tar.Z	Digital Equipment Corp. Ultrix 4.2 Rev. 96
httpd_hp.tar.Z	Hewlett-Packard HP-UX 9.01
httpd_rs6000.tar.Z	IBM AIX 3.2.4
httpd_sgi.tar.Z	Silicon Graphics IRIX 4.0.5.C
httpd_sun.tar.Z	Sun Microsystems SunOS 4.1.3

(A *binary* is an executable file.) For this example, we will assume that we are using a Sun.

Use the get command to download the file to your system, and then quit, as follows:

```
ftp> get httpd_sun4.tar.Z
200 PORT command successful.
150 Opening BINARY mode data connection for httpd_sun4.tar.Z (211981 bytes).
226 Transfer complete.
211981 bytes received in 6.29 secs (33 Kbytes/sec)
ftp> quit
221 Goodbye.
```

Once you have downloaded the file, uncompress it and use the tar command to unarchive the file so that you can edit the configuration files:

```
> uncompress httpd_sun4.tar.Z
> tar -xvf httpd_sun4.tar
```

3.3.2 Editing the Configuration Files

In the process of unarchiving the files, the tar command also created the httpd_1.3/conf subdirectory. If you downloaded a different server version, the new directory name will be different—for example, httpd_1.2/conf. The directory name will always be of the form "httpd_*version#*/conf." Move to that subdirectory (using the cd command) and use the ls command to list the files located there.

Of the four files shown, httpd.conf-dist and srm.conf-dist are the two files you need to modify. Httpd.conf-dist is the main configuration file for the server, and srm.conf-dist maps user requests to files on the server. Access.conf-dist is the configuration file that handles access control, and mime.types maps file extensions to content types. You do not need to modify these last two files because the default settings are fine for a basic site. Make copies (using the cp command) of the distribution files for use with your server. Distribution file names end in *dist*:

```
> cd httpd_1.3/conf
> ls
access.conf-dist httpd.conf-dist  mime.types   srm.conf-dist
```

```
> cp access.conf-dist access.conf
> cp httpd.conf-dist httpd.conf
> cp srm.conf-dist srm.conf
```

Modifying httpd.conf

The following is the complete sample Sun httpd configuration file that we downloaded in our sample implementation. If you downloaded a configuration file for a different platform, it will not be exactly the same as this one:

```
# This is the main server configuration file. It is best to
# leave the directives in this file in the order they are in, or
# things may not go the way you'd like. See URL http://hoohoo.ncsa.uiuc.edu/
# for instructions.

# Do NOT simply read the instructions in here without understanding
# what they do, if you are unsure consult the online docs. You have been
# warned.

# Rob McCool (comments, questions to httpd@ncsa.uiuc.edu)

# ServerType is either inetd, or standalone.

ServerType standalone

# If you are running from inetd, go to "ServerAdmin".

# Port: The port the standalone listens to. For ports < 1023, you will
# need httpd to be run as root initially.

Port 80

# If you wish httpd to run as a different user or group, you must run
# httpd as root initially and it will switch.
```

```
# User/Group: The name (or #number) of the user/group to run httpd as.

User nobody
Group #-1

# ServerAdmin: Your address, where problems with the server should be
# e-mailed.

ServerAdmin you@your.address

# ServerRoot: The directory the server's config, error, and log files
# are kept in

ServerRoot /usr/local/etc/httpd

# ErrorLog: The location of the error log file. If this does not start
# with /, ServerRoot is prepended to it.

ErrorLog logs/error_log

# TransferLog: The location of the transfer log file. If this does not
# start with /, ServerRoot is prepended to it.

TransferLog logs/access_log

# PidFile: The file the server should log its pid to
PidFile logs/httpd.pid

# ServerName allows you to set a host name which is sent back to clients for
# your server if it's different than the one the program would get (i.e. use
# "www" instead of the host's real name).
#
# Note: You cannot just invent host names and hope they work. The name you
# define here must be a valid DNS name for your host. If you don't understand
# this, ask your network administrator.

#ServerName new.host.name
```

Now that you've seen the sample configuration file, you will need to make a decision about the following settings:

- ServerType
- Port
- Username, Group
- ServerAdmin
- ServerRoot

If these are not set properly, the server will not run. There are other settings that you may modify, but those are optional, and the default values are perfectly acceptable unless you are trying to do something fancy. These options include the following:

- TimeOut
- ErrorLog
- TransferLog
- PidFile
- ServerName
- AccessConfig, ResourceConfig, and TypesConfig
- IdentityCheck

Of these options, three do *not* appear in the default server configuration file:

- TimeOut
- AccessConfig, ResourceConfig, TypesConfig
- IdentityCheck

If you want to set any of these, you must put in the lines yourself.

Now that you know what's available, it's time to modify your configuration settings.

ServerType The ServerType option determines whether you run your server in standalone mode or through the inetd system process. *Inetd* is a standard UNIX process that acts as a *super daemon.* It listens for requests for many Internet services and then launches the correct daemon. Inetd is commonly used to handle other servers, such as the FTP and finger daemons.

However, for Web server services, it really doesn't make sense to run a server under inetd. Therefore, the recommended setup is:

```
Server standalone
```

Port The server uses a specific port to listen for clients, and this line specifies that port number. The standard port for http connections is port 80. However, because you have to run the server as root in order to listen to ports below 1024, many sites run their servers on port 8001.

The two common settings are:

```
Port 80
Port 8001
```

Username and Group These two options are used to set the server's user and group identification. If you have root access to the machine on which the Web server will be run, leave the defaults as follows:

```
User nobody
Group #-1
```

If you do not have root access, set the User option to your own username, for example:

```
User erichard
Group #-1
```

ServerAdmin The ServerAdmin setting specifies the address that is sent when the NCSA httpd reports errors to users of the system. It should be set to the e-mail address of your Web server administrator:

```
ServerAdmin webmaster@your.site.com
```

ServerRoot The ServerRoot option specifies the root directory of your server. The root directory is the directory in which the configuration files and access logs are stored. Remember that this setting will depend on the root directory and server version you are using. With the server in /usr/local, this setting should be as follows:

```
ServerRoot /usr/local/httpd_1.3
```

Port 8001

In order to make a connection to a machine on a network, you need two pieces of information: the machine's hostname (or IP address) and the port on the machine to which you want to connect. Every connection to the machine is made through a port (which is identified by a number) and a machine has thousands of available ports (65,535 to be exact). On UNIX machines, all ports below 1024 are reserved. This means that the only user that can use these ports is root. Therefore, any server (such as FTP, Gopher, or HTTP) that accepts connections via one of the reserved ports must be started as root.

Root—also known as the *superuser*—is a very powerful user in terms of its privileges. Root can read or delete any file on a machine, add or delete users, and change a user's password. Because root is such a powerful user, you want to run programs as root only when necessary, and only when you trust the program you are running. (If you don't know what a program is doing and you don't have any reason to trust it, you definitely should not be running that program, especially as root!) Once you start a program as root, UNIX fortunately allows you to relinquish root's privileges.

In late spring of 1993, Matthew Gray was setting up one of the first Web servers at MIT (the SIPB Web server) and he had to decide on which port to run the server. At that time, little was known about the security of Web server software. Plexus, the server program he decided to use, did go through the procedure of relinquishing its root privileges after it had established itself on port 80, but Matthew was not sure it did so completely. While the original servers claimed to be secure—and they probably were—Matthew didn't want to depend on their untested claims. Because of these concerns, he decided to run the MIT SIPB server on port 8001 so that he could run the server as a user other than root.

The MIT SIPB Site
http://www.mit.edu:8001

Today's servers have had time for more testing and presumably are more secure than the initial programs. Therefore, there is no real reason not to run an HTTP server on its default, port 80. Of course, nothing is impenetrable. Recently a bug was discovered in the NCSA server that allowed users to do pretty much anything they wanted to on the server. (Don't worry, it's been fixed.)

TimeOut TimeOut is the option that specifies the number of seconds that the server waits for a client to make a request or to read the server's response. After this time has passed, the server closes the connection:

```
TimeOut 1200
```

ErrorLog and TransferLog The ErrorLog and TransferLog options specify the locations of the server's error file and access logs. If the values do not begin with a slash (/), they are taken to be relative to ServerRoot:

```
>ErrorLog logs/error_log
>TransferLog logs/access_log
```

PidFile The PidFile option sets the location of the file in which the server logs its PID. PID stands for *process ID,* and every process has one, including your server. If you ever need to kill your server, you need to know its PID, which is stored in this file:

```
PidFile logs/httpd.pid
```

ServerName Whenever the server doesn't return the object requested, but returns a URL instead, this is called *redirection.* The ServerName option, used only in the case of self-redirection, lets you specify the name that is returned to the browser as part of the new URL. The browser automatically requests the object at the new URL, so you may never be aware that redirection has occurred. If you do not set this option, the system provides the hostname of the server. The most common use of this option is to return a name such as www.netgen.com, as opposed to the machine's canonical (official) name, which for our site is netgen.com. (The ServerName you use must be a valid hostname for that machine.)

```
>ServerName www.netgen.com
```

AccessConfig, ResourceConfig, and TypesConfig These options specify the locations of the global access configuration file, the resource configuration file, and the MIME typing configuration file, respectively. If the values do not begin with a slash (/), they are taken to be relative to ServerRoot. If no values are provided, the following default settings prevail:

```
>AccessConfig conf/access.conf
>ResourceConfig conf/srm.conf
TypesConfig conf/mime.types
```

IdentityCheck IdentityCheck is the option that specifies whether the server should attempt to obtain the usernames of users making requests. If this option is turned on, the apparent identities of the users are stored in the access log file along with the log of the request. We say "apparent" because the server relies on the Authentication Server Protocol (ASP) for this information, and ASP often lies. The bottom line is that most values returned by ASP are not valid, and we suggest that you set it to IdentityCheck to Off, as follows:

```
   IdentityCheck off
```

Modifying srm.conf

The following is the sample srm configuration file:

```
# With this document, you define the name space that users see of your http
# server.

# See the tutorials at http://hoohoo.ncsa.uiuc.edu/docs/tutorials/ for
# more information.

# Rob (robm@ncsa.uiuc.edu)

# DocumentRoot: The directory out of which you will serve your
# documents. By default, all requests are taken from this directory, but
# symbolic links and aliases may be used to point to other locations.
DocumentRoot /netgen/www/root

# UserDir: The name of the directory which is appended onto a user's home
# directory if a ~user request is recieved.
UserDir public_html
```

```
# DirectoryIndex: Name of the file to use as a prewritten HTML
# directory index
DirectoryIndex index.html

# FancyIndexing is whether you want fancy directory indexing or standard
FancyIndexing on

# AddIcon tells the server which icon to show for different files or file
name
# extensions
AddIconByType (TXT,/icons/text.xbm) text/*
AddIconByType (IMG,/icons/image.xbm) image/*
AddIconByType (SND,/icons/sound.xbm) audio/*
AddIcon /icons/movie.xbm .mpg .qt
AddIcon /icons/binary.xbm .bin
AddIcon /icons/back.xbm ..
AddIcon /icons/menu.xbm ^^DIRECTORY^^
AddIcon /icons/blank.xbm ^^BLANKICON^^

# DefaultIcon is which icon to show for files that do not have an icon
# explicitly set.
DefaultIcon /icons/unknown.xbm

# AddDescription allows you to place a short description after a file in
# server-generated indexes.
# Format: AddDescription "description" filename

# ReadmeName is the name of the README file the server will look for by
# default. Format: ReadmeName name
#
# The server will first look for name.html, include it if found, and it will
# then look for name and include it as plaintext if found.
#
```

```
# HeaderName is the name of a file which should be prepended to
# directory indexes.
ReadmeName README
HeaderName HEADER

# IndexIgnore is a set of file names that directory indexing should ignore
# Format: IndexIgnore name1 name2...
IndexIgnore */.??* *~ *# */HEADER* */README*

# AccessFileName: The name of the file to look for in each directory
# for access control information.
AccessFileName .htaccess

# DefaultType is the default MIME type for documents that the server
# cannot find the type of from filename extensions.
DefaultType text/plain

# AddType allows you to tweak mime.types without actually editing it, or to
# make certain files to be certain types.
# Format: AddType type/subtype ext1

# AddEncoding allows you to have certain browsers (Mosaic/X 2.1+) uncompress
# information on the fly. Note: Not all browsers support this.
#AddEncoding x-compress Z
#AddEncoding x-gzip gz

# Redirect allows you to tell clients about documents that used to exist in
# your server's namespace, but do not anymore. This allows you to tell the
# clients where to look for the relocated document.
# Format: Redirect fakename url

# Aliases: Add here as many aliases as you need, up to 20. The format is
# Alias fakename realname
Alias /icons/ /usr/local/etc/httpd/icons/
```

```
# ScriptAlias: This controls which directories contain server scripts.
# Format: ScriptAlias fakename realname
ScriptAlias /cgi-bin/ /usr/local/etc/httpd/cgi-bin/

# If you want to use server side includes, or CGI outside
# ScriptAliased directories, uncomment the following lines.
#AddType text/x-server-parsed-html .shtml
#AddType application/x-httpd-cgi .cgi
```

Now that you've seen this sample configuration file, you will need to set the DocumentRoot option, or else your server won't run properly.

There are other settings that you may modify, but those are optional, and the default values are perfectly acceptable unless you are trying to do something fancy. These options include the following:

- UserDir
- DirectoryIndex
- FancyIndexing

Now that you know what's available, it's time to modify your configuration settings.

DocumentRoot The DocumentRoot setting allows you to specify the root directory from which documents will be served:

```
DocumentRoot /usr/local/html
```

UserDir On occasion, you see URLs that contain a tilde (~). (Tildes are occasionally referred to by hackers as "twiddles.") Usually, tildes appear in association with a username. For example, **http://www.netgen.com/~devra/home.html.~devra** indicates that the file(s) reside inside Devra's home directory. The UserDir option provides a measure of protection by mapping the request to a subdirectory of the directory being referenced. For example, the following setting would map to /home/devra/html/home.html:

```
UserDir html
```

DirectoryIndex DirectoryIndex is the option that tells the server which file should be displayed when a directory is requested. If the file is present in the requested directory, the file is returned. If the file is not available, the system generates an index of the directory:

```
DirectoryIndex directory.html
```

FancyIndexing The FancyIndexing option specifies whether directories should be returned along with inline icons for each of the files. When set to Off, only a plain directory is returned:

```
FancyIndexing off
```

3.3.3 Running NCSA httpd

At this point, your configuration files are squared away, and you are ready to start your httpd server. If you are running your server in standalone mode, you need only execute the binary. Some systems don't automatically look into your current directory, so it is always safest to provide a full path (remember to use *your* current directory):

```
> /usr/local/httpd_1.3/httpd
```

If you are using a ServerRoot other than /usr/local/etc/httpd, be sure to use the -d option to specify this directory, as follows:

```
> /usr/local/httpd_1.3/httpd -d /usr/local/httpd_1.3
```

WARNING

If you left the User configuration option set to Nobody, or if your server is listening on a port lower than 1024 (i.e., you set Port to something less than 1024), you must be logged in as Root before you can run this command.

After running the server, you can kill it (that's a UNIX word for terminating your server) by typing the following command in the server's root directory:

```
> kill 'cat logs/httpd.pid'
```

If you make changes to the configuration, you can then restart the server with the new configuration options by typing the following command in the server's root directory:

```
> kill -HUP 'cat logs/httpd.pid'
```

3.4 Setting Up the CERN httpd

In this section we walk you through a basic installation of the CERN httpd. The CERN World Wide Web server was designed to be slightly more flexible and functional than the NCSA server. Besides providing a full-featured HTTP server, the CERN httpd can be run as a caching proxy server. These features will not be discussed here, but they make the CERN httpd an attractive server for users who are behind firewalls and need a proxy server.

3.4.1 Downloading the CERN httpd

The first step is to decide which directory you want to be the root directory for your server. If it doesn't exist yet, create it. Then move into it. For this sample implementation, we use /usr/local as the root directory. Next, you need to transfer the software to your machine by using anonymous FTP. Finally, change directories as shown, prepare for binary transfer using the bin command, and use the ls command to list the files.

NOTE

The /usr/local directory is normally a protected directory. If you cannot write to it, you will have to choose a different directory, such as /tmp. If you use a different directory, be sure to substitute your directory name for /usr/local wherever you see it in our sample implementation.

Your session will look something like the following:

```
> cd /usr/local
> ftp ftp.w3.org
Connected to www0.cern.ch.
220 www0 FTP server (Version wu-2.4(32) Wed Oct 5 20:14:59 MET 1994) ready.
Name (ftp.w3.org:erichard): anonymous
331 Guest login ok, send your complete e-mail address as password.
```

```
Password: erichard@netgen.com
230-
230-        Welcome to World Wide Web
230-
230 Guest login ok, access restrictions apply.
Remote system type is UNIX.
Using binary mode to transfer files.
ftp> cd /pub/www/bin
250 CWD command successful.
ftp> bin
200 Type set to I.
ftp> ls
200 PORT command successful.
150 Opening ASCII mode data connection for /bin/ls.
total 50
drwxrwxr-x 21 314   69      512 Jan 20 13:52 .
drwxrwxr-x 11 314   69      512 Jan 16 16:44 ..
drwxrwxr-x  3 12023 69      512 Oct 13 17:22 Dec-Alpha-AXP
drwxrwxr-x  3 13449 69      512 Jan 14 11:17 clipper
lrwxrwxrwx  1 12516 69      4 Jul 14 1994 dec-osf1 -> osf1
drwxrwxr-x  3 314   69      512 Jan 20 13:53 decstation
lrwxrwxrwx  1 314   69      5 Jul 14 1994 hp -> snake
drwxrwxr-x  3 12516 69      512 Oct 11 15:57 linux
drwxrwxr-x  3 314   69      512 Oct 13 17:03 mac
drwxrwxr-x  4 314   69      512 Sep 27 11:08 next
drwxrwxr-x  3 12516 69      512 Sep 27 11:08 next-386
drwxrwxr-x  2 314   69      512 Jul 14 1994 next-fat
drwxrwxr-x  3 12516 69      512 Sep 27 10:52 osf1
drwxrwxr-x  2 314   69      512 Jul 14 1994 pc-nfs
drwxrwxr-x  2 314   69      512 Jul 14 1994 pc-windows
drwxrwxr-x  3 314   69      512 Sep 27 10:54 rs6000
drwxrwxr-x  3 13449 69      512 Jan 19 09:52 sco
drwxrwxr-x  3 314   69      512 Sep 27 10:58 sgi
drwxrwxr-x  4 314   69      512 Sep 27 10:56 snake
```

```
drwxrwxr-x  3 12516 69      512 Sep 29 13:55 solaris
drwxrwxr-x  3 314   69      512 Nov 18 12:12 sun4
lrwxrwxrwx  1 12516 69      7 Jul 14 1994 sun4-sol2 -> solaris
lrwxrwxrwx  1 13449 69      10 Jan 20 13:52 ultrix -> decstation
drwxrwxr-x  2 314   69      512 Jul 29 1994 vm
drwxrwxr-x  3 314   69      512 Jan 11 09:07 vms
226 Transfer complete.
```

At this point, use the cd command to get into the directory for the platform that your machine is running. We are using a Sun for this example. Use Table 3-4 to select the appropriate files for your operating system.

Once in the directory, use the get command to download the file, and then quit, as follows:

```
ftp> cd sun4
250 CWD command successful.
ftp> get cern_httpd_3.0.tar.Z
200 PORT command successful.
150 Opening BINARY mode data connection for cern_httpd_3.0.tar.Z (762401
bytes).
226 Transfer complete.
762401 bytes received in 76.7 secs (9.7 Kbytes/sec)
ftp> quit
221 Goodbye.
```

Once you have downloaded the file, uncompress and use tar to unarchive the file so that you can edit the configuration files:

```
> uncompress cern_httpd_3.0.tar.Z
> tar -xvf cern_httpd_3.0.tar
```

3.4.2 Editing the Configuration Files

In the process of unarchiving the files, the tar command also created the cern_httpd_3.0/config/ subdirectory. If you downloaded a different version of the server, the new directory name will be different—for example, cern_httpd_2.0/config. The directory name will always be of the form "cern_httpd_*version#*/config." Move to that subdirectory (using the cd command) and use the ls command to list the files located there.

Table 3–4. CERN Directories for Various Operating Systems

Directory	Operating Systems
clipper	Intergraph Clipper C300/C400
dec-osf1	Digital Equipment Corp. OSF 2.0/3.0
decstation	Digital Equipment Corp. Ultrix 4.3
snake	Hewlett-Packard HP-UX 9.0
linux	Linux (x86) 1.1.29
next	NeXT NeXTSTEP (Black Hardware)
next-386	NeXT NeXTSTEP (White Hardware)
next-fat	NeXT NeXTSTEP (Black or White Hardware)
rs6000	IBM AIX 3.2
sco	SCO UNIX 3.0/3.2
sgi	Silicon Graphics IRIX 5.2
solaris	Sun Microsystems Solaris 2.3
sun4	Sun Microsystems SunOS 4.1.3
vms	Digital Equipment Corp. VMS

Of the five files shown, httpd.conf is the most generic configuration file and is the one most often used. It is the one you will modify now. The other four configuration files are samples that provide different types of server functionality. For example, proxy.conf is a sample configuration file for setting up a basic proxy server. You may wish to use these configuration samples at another time, so it wouldn't hurt to make backup copies of all five files now.

```
> cd cern_httpd_3.0/config/
> ls
all.conf   caching.conf httpd.conf    prot.conf   proxy.conf
> cp all.conf all.conf-dist
> cp caching.conf caching.conf-dist
> cp httpd.conf httpd.conf-dist
> cp prot.conf prot.conf-dist
> cp proxy.conf proxy.conf-dist
```

Modifying httpd.conf

The following is the complete sample Sun httpd configuration file that we downloaded in our sample implementation. If you downloaded a configuration file for a different platform, it will not be exactly the same as this one:

```
#
#    Sample configuration file for cern_httpd for running it
#    as a normal HTTP server.
#
# See:
#    <http://www.w3.org/hypertext/WWW/Daemon/User/Config/Overview.html>
#
# for more information.
#
# Written by:
#    Ari Luotonen April 1994 <luotonen@dxcern.cern.ch>
#

#
#    Set this to point to the directory where you unpacked this
#    distribution, or wherever you want httpd to have its "home"
#
ServerRoot/afs/sipb/project/www/cern-httpd/server_root

#
#    The default port for HTTP is 80; if you are not root you have
#    to use a port above 1024; good defaults are 8000, 8001, 8080
#
Port 8001

#
#    General setup; on some systems, like HP, nobody is defined so
#    that setuid() fails; in those cases use a different UserId.
#
UserIdnobody
#GroupIdnogroup

#
#    Logging; if you want logging uncomment these lines and specify
#    locations for your access and error logs
```

```
#
# AccessLog/where/ever/httpd-log
# ErrorLog/where/ever/httpd-errors
LogFormatCommon
LogTime    LocalTime

#
#    User-supported directories under ~/public_html
#
UserDirpublic_html

#
#    Scripts; URLs starting with /cgi-bin/ will be understood as
#    script calls in the directory /your/script/directory
#
#Exec /cgi/*/your/script/directory/*

#
#    URL translation rules; If your documents are under /local/Web
#    then this single rule does the job:
#
Pass /*    /*
```

Now that you've seen the sample configuration file, you will need to make a decision about the following settings:

- ServerRoot
- Port
- UserID
- GroupID

If these are not set properly, the server will not run.

Now that you know what's available, it's time to modify your configuration settings.

ServerRoot The ServerRoot option specifies the home directory of your server. The home directory is the directory in which the configuration files and access logs are stored. Remember that this setting will depend on the root directory and server version you are using. Because our sample server is in /usr/local, the setting should be as follows:

```
ServerRoot /usr/local/httpd_1.3
```

ServerType The ServerType option determines whether you will run your server in standalone mode or through the inetd system process. Inetd is a standard UNIX process that acts as a *super daemon.* It listens for requests for many Internet services and then launches the correct daemon. Inetd is commonly used to handle other servers, such as the FTP and finger daemons. However, for Web server services, it really doesn't make sense to run a server under inetd. Therefore, the recommended setup is:

```
Server standalone
```

HostName Whenever the server doesn't return the object requested but instead returns a URL, this is called *redirection.* The HostName option, when used for self-redirection, lets you specify the name that is returned to the browser as part of the new URL. The browser automatically requests the object at the new URL, so you may never be aware that redirection has occurred. If you do not set this option, the system provides the hostname of the server. The most common use of this option is to return a name such as www.netgen.com, as opposed to the machine's canonical (official) name, which for our site is netgen.com. (The HostName you use must be a valid hostname for that machine.)

```
HostName www.netgen.com
```

Port The server uses a specific port to listen for clients, and this line specifies that port number. The standard port for HTTP connections is port 80. However, because you have to run the server as root in order to listen to ports below 1024, many sites chose to run their servers on port 8001.

The two common settings are:

```
Port 80
Port 8001
```

PidFile The PidFile option sets the location of the file in which the server logs its PID. PID stands for *process ID,* and every process has one, including your server. If you ever need to kill your server, you need to know its PID, which is stored in this file:

```
PidFile logs/httpd.pid
```

UserId and GroupId The UserId and GroupId options specify the user and group names that the server uses when answering requests. Neither of these options should be changed. Unless you have a specific account set up to run the server, use your own username:

```
UserIdnobody
GroupIdnogroup
```

AccessLog, LogFormat, and LogTime The AccessLog, LogFormat, and LogTime options are used to configure the location and format of the access log. This file contains a history of all requests made to the server. The AccessLog option specifies the absolute pathname of the log file. The LogFormat option determines whether the log should use the "Old" format or the "Common" format. The common format is shared between the NCSA httpd and CERN httpd and should always be used. The LogTime directive specifies whether the times in the log file should be local time or GMT (Greenwich Mean Time):

```
AccessLog /tmp/httpd/logs/httpd-log
LogFormat Common
LogTime LocalTime
```

ErrorLog The ErrorLog option specifies the absolute pathname for the error log:

```
ErrorLog /tmp/httpd/logs/httpd-errors
```

UserDir On occasion, you see URLs that contain a tilde (~). (Tildes are occasionally referred to by hackers as "twiddles.") Tildes usually appear in association with a username. For example **http://www.netgen.com/~devra/**

home.html.~devra indicates that the file(s) reside inside Devra's home directory. The UserDir option provides a measure of protection by mapping the request to a subdirectory of the directory referenced. For example, the following setting would map to /home/devra/html/home.html:

```
UserDir html
```

3.4.3 Running CERN httpd

Once you have edited the configuration file, you can start the server by typing the following:

```
/usr/local/etc/cern_httpd_3.0/bin/httpd -r /usr/local/etc/
cern_httpd_3.0/config/httpd.config
```

Some systems don't automatically look into your current directory, so it is always safest to provide a full path. Remember to use *your* current directory. In the above example /usr/local is the current directory. Also notice that we have specified the location of the configuration file.

If you have any problems, you can run the server in verbose mode by using the -v option. In verbose mode, the server provides a detailed, step-by-step account of all of its actions so you can better determine where an error is occurring.

WARNING

If you left the User configuration option set to Nobody, or you set Port to something less than 1024, you must be logged in as Root before you can run this command.

3.4.4 Testing Your Server

Now that you have the server up and running, you can test it by using your browser to retrieve the URL. The syntax is as follows:

```
http://ServerName:Port
```

where *ServerName* and *Port* are the values you set in the configuration file, as in this example:

```
http://www.netgen.com:80
```

If you see your home page and can maneuver around, you have probably been successful. You might want to test you server from other machine locations as well.

3.5 About the Netsite Server

The Netsite Communications server doesn't provide any functionality that is not provided by NCSA and CERN, but it claims to be faster, more efficient, and easier to use. Netsite Communications does not include proxy or caching support. The Netsite Commerce server, on the other hand, does provide an additional feature: RSA encryption of all data it transfers. Both are CGI-compliant and use the Common Log Format.

Netsite does appear to be faster, and it may also be somewhat easier to use. You set it up by means of an easy-to-use online setup utility, so we cannot provide you with a printout of the files.

3.6 Introducing Advanced Features

True World Wide Web user interactivity is achieved through forms support. Forms allow users to transmit information back to a Web server. For a server to handle the incoming information, a Common Gateway Interface program must be present and properly written. Unfortunately, CGI scripts are technically complex, and each form typically requires a custom script. As site interactivity increases, the amount of technical resources required to support the site increases dramatically. An HTML form, and the requisite CGI script, must be written and tested. You can also write scripts to perform large database searches, send mail to individuals, add comments to a document, automatically generate custom HTML pages, and do much more besides.

With proper scripting, a site can offer a search capability for its contents. A robust search function gives users easy access to relevant information. You can also use scripts to control image maps so that the server can respond precisely to the position of a mouse-click on an image. For example, the U.S. Weather Map site displays a map of the continental United States; when you click on Boston, the server registers the position of the mouse-click and returns the day's weather forecast for the Boston metropolitan area.

U.S. Weather Map
http://www.netgen.com/book/weather-map.html

By systematically addressing all of the areas discussed in these first three chapters, you can transform yourself into a Webmaster. As you become familiar with the basics of site maintenance, you can implement more advanced script-based features—features that will, when applied creatively, greatly improve your Web site.

PART II

Understanding the Specifications

These chapters contain a thorough explanation of the following Web specifications:

- URL—Uniform Resource Locator
- HTTP—Hypertext Transfer Protocol
- HTML—Hypertext Markup Language
- CGI—Common Gateway Interface

A *specification* defines the rules that govern Internet or Web operations, and *standards* are those rules that have been approved by the Internet Engineering Task Force (IETF) or adopted for common use. It is important to realize that not everything set forth in an approved specification has been implemented.

There are always some differences between the specification documents and the way in which people have chosen to implement them.

The actual specifications (see Appendixes A–C) describe how things are supposed to work. Here we will explain how the specifications are currently implemented in real life. This section is designed to give you all the information you may need to understand the workings of each specification and standard, and how you might want to make them work for you.

CHAPTER 4

Uniform Resource Locators

CHAPTER AT A GLANCE

This chapter provides an in-depth discussion and interpretation of the specification governing Uniform Resource Locators (URLs). We discuss the practical application of URLs, how they address many different protocols, the strengths and weakness of the specification, and what you need to know in order to use it to your best advantage. We also explain the difference between URLs and URNs, and why this is important to know.

REQUISITES

A basic understanding of the Web and URLs as described in Chapter 2.

MORE DETAIL

Related to RFC 1738: Uniform Resource Locators (see Appendix A). Use this document for the exact specifications and a more detailed analysis of the syntax of URLs.

Related to RFC 1630: Uniform Resource Identifiers in WWW (available at **http://www.netgen.com/book**). Use this document to understand the overall design goals of URIs.

Related to RFC 1737: Functional Requirements for Universal Resource Names (available at **http://www.netgen.com/book**). See this document for more information on the design goals and descriptions of URNs.

Uniform Resource Locators (URLs) provide a means of identifying the location of resources on the Internet, and this chapter is devoted to understanding the specification that governs them. We'll talk about the strengths and weaknesses of the specification and give you some hints and tips for using URLs effectively. By the end of the chapter, you will be able to decipher complex-looking URLs and understand how they function.

4.1 Understanding URLs

In order to retrieve a resource from the Internet, you need to know how to find it. Similarly, if you are looking for a resource in the real world—say, the local supermarket—you need some means of figuring out where it is. There may be many of ways of getting there, and a lot of ways of describing where it is. For example, you could describe the location by providing the street address, by giving directions, or by describing its location relative to different landmarks. When you specify the directions to a location, you probably also include some information about the actual means of getting there (i.e. bus, car, walking, etc.). Similarly, identifying a resource on the Internet requires not only specifying its physical location, but the protocol which should be used to retrieve the data. URLs provide a single means of describing the locations of resources on the Internet.

NOTE

URLs were designed and implemented for use on the Web, but URLs are not restricted just to the Web. URLs are simply one more way of addressing information. There is no reason why a mail program or an FTP client could not be made to understand URLs.

In order to determine which naming scheme you should use to identify a resource, you need to know what type of resource it is and which protocol is the most appropriate for retrieving that type. For example, if you wanted a copy of an ASCII text file from the Gutenberg Library, you could use the FTP protocol. But if you wanted to access an HTML document on the Web, you would probably use HTTP, because HTTP is the most common means of accessing information on the Web. (In Chapter 7, you'll find out that HTML is the standard that supports hypertext links across the Web.) Besides needing the HTTP protocol, you need to know where the resource is located (i.e., the name of the host machine) and the name of the resource.

While the format of all URLs depend on the protocol used to access a resource, many protocols share a common URL format known as the Common Internet Scheme Syntax (CISS). This general format looks like this:

```
schemename://username:password@host:port/path
```

A *scheme* is URL format for a particular protocol. In general, schemes correspond to the various protocols used to access data. For example, FTP, HTTP, and Gopher are three protocols that have schemes defined in the URL specification document. (See Table 4-2 for a list of all defined URL schemes.) The scheme name is followed by a colon and two forward slashes (://). This portion alone indicates that the format adheres to the Common Internet Scheme Syntax (CISS). Schemes for several protocols—FTP, HTTP, Gopher, WAIS, Prospero, and file access—adhere to CISS; others, such as Mailto and News, do not. The format for the balance of the URL string depends on the scheme. Certain fields may be omitted and the default values vary. Finally, it is important to understand that *path* identifies the resource. It does not necessarily reflect a hierarchical structure or physical location as it does in DOS or UNIX.

NOTE

URLs that follow the CISS format are a subset of the general format for all URLs. The general format consists of the name of the scheme, a colon, and then a string that is specific to the scheme being used. The most general form of a URL is: *scheme:scheme-specific-string.* For more information on CISS, see Section 3.1 of Appendix A.

RFC 1739: Uniform Resource Locators
http://www.netgen.com/book/appendix/rfc1738.txt

The biggest advantage to using URLs is that they provide a single, uniform method of identifying resources that are available via many different protocols, including Gopher, WAIS, FTP, telnet, and HTTP. In the original specification, the *U* in URL stood for "Universal." Occasionally you hear people call them "Universal Resource Locators" instead of Uniform Resource Locators.

The ability of URLs to identify resources was a requirement of the specification for Uniform Resource Identifiers (URIs). Uniform Resource Locators are a type of URI, as are the Uniform Resource Names we talked about in

Chapter 2. The URI specifications documented in RFC 1630 defined URIs as a concept. Six months later, that concept came to fruition in the URL specification. But it was the URI specification that stated the overall design goal behind all URIs In particular, the URI specification made it a goal for URIs to provide a complete way of addressing information. In order to do that, a format had to be devised that could be used to encode any naming scheme without making any assumptions about that scheme. A format that does not have to take into account any assumptions about schemes is called an *extensible format*. Extensible formats allow you to add new naming schemes without requiring changes at a later date.

In addition, the URI specifications say that arbitrary but registered strings must be used as a prefix to meet the extensibility requirement. As an example, Microsoft could come up with a new URL scheme that uses a protocol specific to Windows NT if a new Windows NT file system becomes a popular way of distributing information.

Not all existing protocols have an established URL scheme, but it is reasonable to expect such schemes to evolve in the future. AFS and NFS are good examples of this potential. Both file systems are used throughout the world. If you wanted to address files within the AFS or NFS file systems using a URL, you would have to come up with a new scheme.

NOTE

Experimental naming schemes for AFS (Andrew File System), and NFS (Network File System) already exist.

Coming up with new URL schemes is fairly straightforward. According to the URL specifications, you need to demonstrate the "utility and operability" of a new URL scheme. In addition, the new scheme should be similar to URL formats already in place. New prefixes need to be defined and agreed to by the Internet Assigned Numbers Authority (IANA), but anybody can come up with new URL schemes and suggest them to IANA. You have to submit the protocol and explain how it works. The URL specifications must allow for experimental schemes, beginning with the string *x-*.

Another URI design goal is to be able to express a URI using seven-bit ASCII (i.e., U.S. ASCII) text. The idea here is for people to be able to transmit URIs through writing. Besides alphanumeric characters, the following characters are permitted in a URL: dollar signs ($), hyphens (–), underscores (_), periods (.), plus signs (+), exclamation points (!), asterisks (*), quote marks ('), commas (,), left parentheses, and right parentheses. The aim is extensibility, but this list sounds rather limiting—and it would be if not for the use of escape-code sequences.

If you want to use special characters in a URL, you need to substitute escape sequences for those characters. For example, spaces are not permitted in URLs, but you can include a space in a URL name by entering a percent sign (%) followed by the number 20. The string "Rajat Bhargava" would be "escaped" like so:

```
Rajat%20Bhargava
```

The percent sign tells you that the following number is an escape sequence. The number, meanwhile, must be the hexadecimal representation of the character's ASCII code. The ASCII value for a space is 32 and the hexadecimal representation of ASCII 32 is 20. Table 4-1 shows the meaning for several of the common escape-code sequences used in URLs and includes example for each.

When we cover CGI scripting in Chapter 11, we'll show you a script that handles the encoding and decoding of escape sequences.

NOTE

Before forms support was added in HTML 2.0, ISINDEX provided simple search capabilities. The user entered a series of keywords separated from one another by space characters, after which ISINDEX encoded the search string into the URL and replaced the spaces with plus signs. Plus signs for spaces was a logical substitution, because a plus sign is often used to represent the Boolean AND, and AND is exactly what ISINDEX interpreted it to mean.

Table 4–1. Escape-Code Sequences

String	Example	Meaning
%09	Column1%09Column2	The encoded value for a tab
%0a	Line1%0aLine2	The encoded value for a new-line character
%20	Eric%20Richard	The encoded value for a space
%40	erichard%40netgen.com	The encoded value for an at sign (@)
%26	dogs%26cats	The encoded value for an ampersand (&)
%3f	How%20are%20you%3f	The encoded value for a question mark (?)

Table 4–2. Common Default Values and Formats for Each URL Scheme

Scheme	URL Format	Defaults
FTP	ftp://user:password@host:port/path	Username = anonymous Password = user's e-mail address Port = 21
HTTP	http://host:port/path?searchpart	Port =80
Gopher	gopher://host:port/path	Port = 70
Mailto	mailto:local-address@host	none
News	news:newsgroup-name	none
	news:message_id	none
NNTP	nntp://host/newsgroup-name/article-number	Port = 119
Telnet	telnet://user:password@host:port	Port = 23 If omitted, user prompted for username and password
WAIS	wais://host:port/database wais://host:port/database wais://host:port/database	Port = 210
File	file://host/path	none
Prospero	prospero://host:port/hsoname;field=value	Port = 1525

Note: News and mailto do not use the Common Internet Scheme Syntax (CISS).

4.1.1 URL Formats

This section provides details on all the defined URL schemes. Table 4-2 shows the standard format (i.e., the format most commonly used) and the defaults associated with each scheme.

4.1.2 FTP

FTP URLs follow the syntax of CISS completely. The complete scheme for FTP is as follows:

```
ftp://user:password@host:port/path
```

However, standard usage omits the *user, password,* and *port* segments, leaving you with:

```
ftp://host/path
```

When specified, *user* is the username give during login, and *password* is the corresponding password for the log-in account. Both the username and password are usually omitted, and when they are, *anonymous* is the assumed value for the user, and the user's e-mail address takes the place of the missing password.

Host specifies the server machine's domain name or IP address, and *port* is the port number on the machine through which the connection is made. When the port number is omitted, Port 21 (the standard FTP default conversation port) is used as the default.

The *path* identifies the specific resource. FTP takes the *path* to be a series of commands separated by slashes (/) for change working directories and downloading a file.

For example, if you wanted to retrieve the net.Genesis Corporate Summary using FTP, you would use the following URL:

```
ftp://ftp.netgen.com/pub/summary
```

Because this URL does not provide user or password values, FTP substitutes the default values. *Anonymous* is the user and the requester's e-mail address is the password. Even though a port has not been specified, FTP establishes a connection to port 21 of the machine ftp.netgen.com. Once the connection has been made, FTP requests to change directories and move to the pub subdirectory. From there, it requests the file known as summary.

The next examples show two URLs that Eric Richard could use to identify the biosheet resource that is available via anonymous FTP at ftp.netgen.com. The first URL assumes the default values. The second includes all parts of the FTP scheme and includes an escape sequence. In both cases, the connection will be made on port 21 (the standard FTP data port), and the user and password values are *anonymous* and *erichard@netgen.com,* Eric Richard's e-mail address. Once the connection has been established, the URL specifies that the client should move to the pub directory and retrieve the biosheet file.

```
ftp://ftp.netgen.com/pub/biosheet
ftp://anonymous:erichard%40netgen.com@ftp.netgen.com:21/pub/biosheet
```

On the second line, we used the escape sequence %40 to place an @ character after *erichard,* but we left the @ character intact before *ftp.netgen.com.* The second @ character is part of the FTP URL syntax. It marks the end of the user/password and the beginning of the hostname. That's why we did not use the escape-code sequence there. However, the @ character would not be valid *inside* the username or password, so there we had to provide the escape-code sequence.

4.1.3 HTTP

HTTP URLs follow CISS, with one major exception: the HTTP specification states that no user or password can be used in an HTTP URL. So the complete scheme for HTTP is as follows:

```
http://host:port/path?searchpart
```

Host specifies the server machine's domain name or IP address, and *port* is the port number on that machine through which the connection is made. When the port number is omitted, port 80 (the standard HTTP port) is used as the default.

Path identifies the resource. *Searchpart* offers additional information about the resource. Both *path* and *searchpart* are optional. If *searchpart* is not provided, the preceding question mark is not needed. Similarly, if neither *path* nor *searchpart* is provided, the slash (/) before path becomes optional.

The following example makes an HTTP connection to www.netgen.com on port 80 (the default), and requests the resource /:

```
http://www.netgen.com/
```

NOTE

Slash (/) is a resource name just like any other name, and it happens that most sites use the slash as the top level, or home page, on their site.

If you wanted to use the Wandex resource to obtain a list of Web sites relating to computers, you could use the following HTTP URL:

```
http://www.netgen.com/cgi/wandex?words=computers
```

where `/cgi/wandex` is *path* and `words=computers` is *searchpart*. This URL makes an HTTP connection to www.netgen.com on port 80. It requests the CGI script for Wandex to create a listing of sites based upon the input provided in *searchpart* .

When an HTML form is submitted via the GET method, all of the information in the form is encoded in the URL that is requested. For each of the field values, the URL contains a string in the form *fieldname=fieldvalue*. Each of these field-value pairs is separated by an ampersand (&). Consider this example:

```
http://www.netgen.com/cgi/wandex?words=computers&domain=ch
```

This URL contains two field-value pairs: `words=computers` and `domain=ch`. These pairs could have been the result of submitting a form with two fields (*words* and *domain*) and their respective values (*computers* and *ch*).

4.1.4 Gopher

Gopher URLs follow CISS, with one major exception: the Gopher specification states that no user or password can be used in a Gopher URL. The complete scheme for Gopher is as follows:

```
gopher://host:port/path
```

Host specifies the server machine as it is identified by the site's domain name or IP address, and *port* is the port number on that machine through which the connection is made. When the port number is omitted, port 70 (the standard Gopher port) is used as the default. *Path* identifies the resource.

If you wanted to retrieve a Gopher document of Amtrak train schedules available from the host gwis.circ.gwu.edu at port 70, you would use the following URL:

```
gopher://gwis.circ.gwu.edu:70/11/General%20Information/
Train%20Schedules/Amtrak%20Train%20Schedules
```

The document path is /11/General%20Information/Train%20Schedules/. The name of the resource is Amtrak%20Train%20Schedules. Gopher URLs are a little less hideous looking when you remember that every %20 is a space in escape-code parlance. In other words, the path is really an escaped version of "/11/General Information/Train Schedules."

4.1.5 Mailto

Mailto is one of the URL schemes that does not use the CISS format. The syntax for a Mailto is as follows:

```
mailto:local-address@host
```

Local-address@host is the recipient's e-mail address, where *local-address* is typically the username and *host* is the machine on which the user's account resides. For example, you can send mail to Devra Hall by using the following Mailto URL:

```
mailto:devra@netgen.com
```

This specifies that mail should be sent to the address devra@netgen.com.

There are no defaults for Mailto.

4.1.6 News and NNTP

The News scheme is used to retrieve USENET news articles. Two formats exist for News URLs:

```
news:newsgroup-name
news:message_id
```

Newsgroup-name is the name of one or more newsgroups, and *message_id* is the identifier for a particular message. Because newsgroup names can be lengthy and you can specify a list of newsgroups, this format often results in long character strings.

The following example identifies the comp.infosystems.www.misc newsgroup:

```
news:comp.infosystems.www.misc
```

When you read newsgroups, your newsreader either reads the news in from a file on the local machine or uses a protocol called NNTP. An additional scheme has been defined to refer to documents available directly via NNTP.

NNTP URLs follow CISS with one major exception: the NNTP specification states that no username or password can be used in an NNTP URL. The complete scheme for NNTP is as follows:

```
nntp://host:port/newsgroup-name/article-number
```

Host specifies the server machine's domain name or IP address, and *port* is the port number on that machine through which the connection is made. When the port is omitted, port 119 (the standard NNTP port) is used as the default.

Newsgroup-name is the name of the USENET newsgroup, and *article-number* is the identification number assigned to the article in the newsgroup.

Let's consider the comp.infosystems.www.misc newsgroup that is available on the news.wing.net host machine. If you wanted to retrieve message #2347 from that newsgroup, you would use the following URL:

```
nntp://news.wing.net/comp.infosystems.www.misc/2347
```

NOTE

Most NNTP servers are configured to accept connections from a list of known clients. Therefore, don't expect that you will be able to use NNTP URLs which refer to remote NNTP servers.

4.1.7 Telnet

Unlike the other protocols that identify resources, the purpose of a Telnet URL is to identify an interactive service on a remote machine.

The complete scheme for telnet URLs is as follows:

```
telnet://user:password@host:port
```

In standard usage, however, the *user* and *password* segments are omitted, leaving you with:

```
telnet://host:port
```

When a user is specified, *user* is the username employed during login and *password* is the password for that log-in account. When these arguments are omitted, the user is prompted for a username and password when a connection is made to the remote machine.

Host specifies the server machine's domain name or IP address, and *port* is the port number on that machine through which the connection is made.

When the port number is omitted, port 23 (the standard Telnet port) is used as the default.

The following telnet URL specifies a telnet connection to the tech.mit.edu site using the username "www":

```
telnet://www:@the-tech.mit.edu
```

4.1.8 WAIS

WAIS (Wide Area Information System) URLs identify database resources. WAIS URLs follow CISS with one major exception: the WAIS specification states that no username or password can be used in a WAIS URL. The format for a URL using WAIS is:

```
wais://host:port/database
```

Host specifies the server machine's domain name or IP address, and *port* is the port number on that machine through which the connection is made. When the port is omitted, port 210 (the standard WAIS port) is used as the default. *Database* is the name of the database residing on the host machine that you wish to use.

To search a WAIS database, use the following WAIS URL format:

```
wais://host:port/database?search
```

where *search* is the criteria for searching the database. If you want to find a certain object in the database, you can use yet another WAIS format:

```
wais://host:port/database/wtype/wpath
```

where *wtype* is the object type and *wpath* is the object's document identifier in the WAIS index.

4.1.9 File

The File scheme is used to retrieve a document locally. If a File scheme fails, however, an attempt is made to retrieve the document via FTP. File URLs follow CISS with one major exception: the FILE specification states that no username, password, or port number can be used in a File URL. The standard format for the file URL is:

```
file://host/path
```

Host specifies the machine's domain name or IP address. To refer to the same machine as the one interpreting the URL, use the special value *localhost*. In the case of File URLs, *path* indicates the actual filename of the resource.

Suppose Matthew wanted to access Eric's homepage.txt file and both were using the same machine. Matthew would use the following URL:

```
file://localhost/home/erichard/homepage.txt
```

However, if Devra wanted to access that same file from her system in California, her URL line would look like this:

```
file://netgen.com/home/erichard/homepage.txt
```

This is because Devra has to access a remote host.

4.1.10 Prospero

We haven't seen any Web clients that implement the Prospero scheme directly. However, Archie is a Prospero client and it allows you to search databases of Prospero objects. According to the specification, Prospero URLs follow CISS with one major exception: no username or password can be used in a Prospero URL. The format for the Prospero URL is as follows:

```
prospero://host:port/hsoname;field=value
```

Host specifies the server machine's domain name or IP address, and *port* is the port number on that machine through which the connection is made. When the port is omitted, port 1525 (the standard Prospero port) is used as the default. *Hsoname* is the name of the Prospero object to be retrieved. *Field* and *value* help identify the object.

4.2 Using URLs

We spent the first part of this chapter discussing the theoretical foundations of Uniform Resource Locators. In this part of the chapter, we'll talk a bit about the practical application of URLs. We'll provide some hints and tips for using them.

4.2.1 The Power of Relative URLs

Normally, a URL tells you the absolute position of a resource. Wherever you are in the world, you can go to the host machine and follow the path from there to the document or object you wish to retrieve.

A *relative* URL is one that specifies the location of a resource relative to the document in which it was referenced. A relative URL says, "From where you are, follow these directions and you will find the resource." Relative URLs are very powerful and allow for a lot of flexibility in a site. If you consistently use relative URLs throughout your entire site, it's very easy to change your machine name, the port your server is listening on, or the path used to reference resources. There are two types of relative URLs: those that are relative to the server (i.e., they specify the full path to the resource, but not the protocol, serve name, or port) and those that only specify a path relative to the document that they are in.

If you use the first type of relative URL, it is possible to change the server name or the port that your server is listing without having to modify the text of any of your documents. If you use the second type of relative link, you can move entire subsections of your site to another machine or location within the site.

4.2.2 Capabilities and Limitations of URLs

The URL design has its strengths and its weaknesses. To begin with, the schemes used in URLs are case-sensitive. When you type **HTTP:**, the specification states that you should type lowercase letters: **http:**. However, the specifications also suggest that clients interpreting URLs should treat uppercase and lowercase letters in scheme names the same way. In other words, they should allow for *HTTP* in uppercase but automatically treat the letters as *http* in lowercase. However, not all browsers follow this suggestion. Case sensitivity is something that you should keep in mind when you are using URLs.

Earlier in this chapter we talked about the U.S. ASCII character set and escape-code sequences. What we did not mention is that certain characters have specific meanings when they are used in a URL. For example, open curly braces and closed curly braces, carets, tildes, brackets, slashes, question marks, colons, and ampersands all have special meanings.

You can use these characters for purposes of your own by substituting their escape-code sequences. Using escape sequences is important because they keep client programs from getting confused and interpreting URLs according to the specification. See Table 4-3 for a list of commonly used characters and their meanings inside URLs.

Throughout this chapter, we've touched on most of the strengths of the URL specification. We've talked about its flexibility and extensibility. Not only can you specify a variety of different protocols, but mechanisms allow you to add new schemes. Using escape characters, you can include special characters such as carriage returns and blank spaces within a URL.

Table 4–3. Common Characters in URL Strings

Character	Sample String	Meaning
//	http://www.netgen.com	When this string follows the scheme, it indicates that the URL obeys CISS
:	www.netgen.com:80	This is used to separate the hostname and the port number URLs
/	netgen.com:80/sis	This character is generally used to separate the hostname and port from the path.
	/sis/NHL/NHL.html	This is also commonly used within the URL path to denote a directory structure or hierarchy
?	/cgi/wais.pl?keyword	Within the URL path for an HTTP URL, a question mark denotes the beginning of the "query string"; all the text after it is not interpreted as the name of the file, but instead as user-submitted data
+	wais.pl?cats+dogs	Within the query string of an HTTP URL, a plus sign signifies a Boolean AND of words
=	/cgi/ wandex?keyword=computers	Within the query string of an HTTP URL, an equals sign serves as the delimiter between the key and the value for a field
&	/cgi/ register?name=Eric&company=net	Within the query string of an HTTP URL, an ampersand delimits sets of key-value pairs
~	http://www.netgen.com/ ~erichard	At the beginning of the path, a tilde indicates that the resource is in the specified user's home directory

Note: Open and closed curly braces, carets, and square brackets are all reserved but not yet used.

The fact that URLs are somewhat complex and obscure-looking is probably their biggest weakness. It is hard to remember a URL, let alone effectively communicate it to another person without tripping over your tongue. Take the Gopher URL for the Amtrak train schedule we looked at earlier in this chapter. It's a mouthful:

```
gopher://gwis.circ.gwu.edu:70/11/General%20Information/
Train%20Schedules/Amtrak%20Train%20Schedules
```

To a newcomer, even the URL for Matthew's home page is a little difficult to remember:

```
http://www.mit.edu:8001/people/mkgray/www/home_page.html
```

Some believe that remembering "www.mit.edu" is a lot easier than remembering "18.181.0.21" (the IP address). But to most people, both names are equally obscure. And escape sequences only compound the problem, since they make URLs seem even more complex and obscure.

With complexity, however, comes greater flexibility. And once you get used to them, URLs aren't so terribly awkward. Besides, think what how strange a postal address must be to someone who has never seen one. Or how strange a phone number must look to someone who has never seen a long string of digits like (617) 577-9800. The address and phone number would look pretty odd and probably would seem random to people who didn't know what they meant. Similarly, as you come to understand what all the parts of a URL are, URLs become less and less cumbersome.

Besides their complexity, another weakness of URLs is that they are meant to identify static resources such as documents and other objects. URLs are not well suited for identifying interactive resources such as Telnet and IRC (Internet Relay Chat) sessions. As you saw earlier in this chapter, there is a Telnet URL, and there has been discussion on an IRC URL, but both stretch the bounds of what makes sense for a URL. It's sort of like trying to create a postal address for an event in time. The address takes you to the place where the event occurs, but whether you get there at the right time is a matter of luck. It would be more realistic to identify an event with both an address *and* a time.

4.2.3 Hints and Tips for Working with URLs

What happens if you don't know the entire URL for the resource you seek? URLs are information addresses, and it is often possible to guess the address of information you want. You can start constructing a URL by guessing the site or domain name. Begin by making an educated guess—perhaps something along the lines of *www.domain*. For example, if you were interested in information about Xerox Corp., you could probably guess the hostname and construct a URL to get started. If you used:

```
http://www.xerox.com
```

you could be well on your way to finding the information you want.

If *http://www.domain* doesn't work, try *http://web.domain, gopher://gopher.domain,* or *ftp://ftp.domain.* And if that strategy doesn't work, start looking on large server lists, such as the comprehensive list of servers located at the net.Genesis site.

net.Genesis Comprehensive Server List
http://www.netgen.com/cgi/comprehensive

Another way to find a domain name is to use the whois command, as follows:

```
whois name
```

Whois is the Internet command for checking a database of domain names to see if there is a match. For example, if you wanted to find out if rajat.com is a registered domain name, you would use this whois command:

```
whois rajat.com
```

If rajat.com exists as a domain name, you get a listing with the name of the company or person who has that name and its, his, or her IP address. You can do this anytime you want to check whether a domain name is taken, or if you want a little more information about the domain name's holder.

Here are two examples of how to use the whois command to look for sites to see if they exist:

```
> whois netgen.com
[rs0.internic.net]
[No name] (NETGEN-HST)      NETGEN.COM      204.57.36.200
net.Genesis Corp. (NETGEN-DOM)      NETGEN.COM
```

```
The InterNIC Registration Services Host contains ONLY Internet Information
(Networks, ASN's, Domains, and POC's).
Please use the whois server at nic.ddn.mil for MILNET Information.

> whois devra.com
[rs0.internic.net]
No match for "DEVRA.COM".

The InterNIC Registration Services Host contains ONLY Internet Information.
(Networks, ASN's, Domains, and POC's).
Please use the whois server at nic.ddn.mil for MILNET Information.
```

Once you find the host or domain name, you can get to the root of the site, where most sites have a root-level document. The root of the site is generally the home page, and the URL is usually something like *http://hostname/index.html*, *http://hostname/Overview.html*, or *http://hostname/Welcome.html*. Once you find the root document, you can traverse the other links at the site.

To avoid common mistakes, follow these tips when you use URLs:

- Never capitalize the string that identifies the protocol. For example, the URL for the HTTP protocol should always begin with **http://**, not **HTTP://**. Clients such as Netscape recognize capitalization errors, but others such as NCSA Mosaic and Lynx do not.
- The server name is case-insensitive. Therefore, you can use the hostname WWW.W3.ORG or www.w3.org. Lowercase strings are easier to read, however.
- The server name can be a hostname or IP address. However, the use of IP addresses is discouraged because they make addresses less flexible. If you use an IP address in your URL, you are hard-coding the address. If the IP address of the site changes you need to go and change every URL to the new URL. However, if the site name is used and the address is changed, there is no change to the URLs. They still work. The change becomes transparent to the user.
- The port number and its preceding colon can be omitted for any of these protocols. If the port number is not present, the default port for the given protocol is used.

- The specifications permit the trailing slash on an HTTP URL to be omitted if no path is specified, but leaving in the slash is a good practice. For example, use **http://www.netgen.com/** instead of **http://www.netgen.com**. While the specs say that the trailing slash is optional, many browsers, including Mosaic, don't function properly without the trailing slash. Mosaic and the others do not *always* function incorrectly, but it's best to include the slash to be on the safe side.
- In URLs, a number of characters are considered special and have to be handled with escape sequences. Special characters include spaces, tabs, carriage returns, pound signs (#), and question marks. These characters are represented by a percent sign (%) followed by the character's hexadecimal ASCII value. For example, a space (hexadecimal ASCII 20) is represented as follows: `%20`.

4.2.4 State-Encoded URLs

State provides information about the prior actions of the user. In order for users to know what information has changed at a site since they were last there, state information must be maintained. In Chapter 2 we said that the FTP protocol maintains state, but HTTP does not. Therefore, if you want to maintain information from HTTP transactions, you have to store that information outside the protocol. One solution is to encode the information within a URL (i.e., use the format of a URL to hide information that can be used by the server).

You can use URLs to remember the history of previous requests to a server. This can be very useful for games or systems where users log in and track their movements through the site. Here is a URL for a hangman game that stores information about what the player has done so far:

```
http://www.cm.cf.ac.uk/htbin/RobH/hangman
```

When users start the game, they retrieve the URL of the form:

```
http://www.cm.cf.ac.uk/htbin/RobH/hangman?yqeosozqzt|0||
```

The search part of the URL—the part after the question mark—contains three parts, each delimited by a vertical bar (|). (This delimiter is by no means intrinsic to the URL protocol; but it was defined by the authors of the program being used to interpret the string.) The first part represents an encrypted (substitution-ciphered) version of the hangman word that the user must guess. The second part is a number representing how many hangman body parts to draw—that is, how many wrong guesses have occurred so far. The last part is a list of letters that have been guessed.

In the previous URL, the information after the question mark tells the script the word that is being guessed and that no guesses have been made. After choosing the letters *e*, *s*, *a*, *t*, and *z*, we reach the following URL:

```
http://www.cm.cf.ac.uk/htbin/RobH/hangman?yqeosozqzt|1|esatz|
```

Here is an excerpt from the HTML code being used on this page:

```
Pick a letter<p><h1>
<a href=http:hangman?yqeosozqzt|2|esatzb|>b</a> ,
<a href=http:hangman?yqeosozqzt|2|esatzc|>c</a> ,
<a href=http:hangman?yqeosozqzt|2|esatzd|>d</a> ,
<a href=http:hangman?yqeosozqzt|2|esatzf|>f</a> ,
...
</h1>
```

As you can see, each link goes to a slightly different URL, depending on the choice that the user makes by following the link.

The game script does not have to remember any information from request to request. All of the information that the script needs is being passed to it from the URL.

4.2.5 URL Mapping

One of the most common misconceptions people have about URLs is that the path specified in the URL matches up to a specific file in a directory structure. This is not necessarily true.

A whole URL is meant to identify a resource, not necessarily a file. It is not uncommon for the path to map to a file system, but you cannot assume that this is always the case. It is equally possible that the path corresponds to a query in a database or a call to a script.

NOTE

In Chapter 5, you'll see that it is possible for a URL to return one of many files based on other information. It is also possible for the server to return different files based on information in the search part of the URL. Finally, a server is also capable of generating an object on-the-fly, meaning that no actual file exists on disk.

The fact that many people use URLs as if they were implicitly mapping to a specific file is one of the biggest differences between the URL specification and its standard use. Take a look at the following URL:

```
http://www.mit.edu:8001/people/mkgray/home.html
```

You can tell a few things about this URL just by looking at it. For instance, you know that www.mit.edu is the host system. Some people would assume that there really is a "people" directory structure and that the home.html file is found in the "mkgray" subdirectory. However, that may or may not be true. You can't tell, and, more importantly, it doesn't really matter. What matters is that /people/mkgray/home.html identifies a resource.

An offshoot of the mistaken assumption that resources must be files is the notion that all resources pre-exist as files on disk, and that if the same resource is retrieved over and over again, it will continue to contain the same exact piece of data. This is also not an absolute. A lot of URLs actually map to things that are generated by a program on the server. A server could interpret a request and generate that data on-the-fly by finding the resource in a file or by looking it up in a database. Whichever mechanism it uses, the server then produces the information based on user input.

You can make an educated guess as to whether a resource is mapped to a file or an executable script. If "cgi" is part of the URL string, that's a good hint that the page is being generated dynamically. If several URLs have slightly different path elements in them but otherwise look the same—as was the case with the hangman example mentioned in Section 4.2.4—the path elements are likely being treated as query options, and that indicates a CGI script.

In a URL with a question mark followed by character strings, the character strings are typically queries on a CGI script. In fact, if anything after the question mark affects the output, you can be pretty sure that the output is being generated by a custom script.

4.2.6 Proxy Servers and Gateways

The URL specification defines schemes for most of the common protocols, but that does not mean that your browser supports all of these protocols. Most Web browsers support HTTP, FTP, Gopher, and Telnet. Some of them support mailto and WAIS. When it comes to schemes for new protocols, what matters is not whether the scheme is included in the specification, but whether or not browsers support it. For example, suppose "Psychic" became a valid protocol scheme. You might think that the following URL identifies the biography resource in Eric Richard's brain:

```
psychic://ericrichard/brain/biography
```

According to the hypothetical new scheme, this URL specifies that the resource is available by psychically connecting to Eric's brain and getting his life's story. But if your browser didn't yet support the new "Psychic" scheme, the command would not work. (Okay, that was a bizarre example, but we like to mess with Eric's mind.)

On a serious note, the same logic applies to potential schemes such as a Windows NT distributed file system or Lotus Notes server. Theoretically, the specification can support the design, but the implementation and support for schemes in real life is browser-specific.

Wide Area Information System (WAIS) is a good example of a scheme that is often not supported. The URL specification includes a scheme for WAIS, but not all browsers support it. If you need to use the WAIS scheme but your browser does not support it, you can configure your browser to use a specified WAIS proxy server whenever it encounters a WAIS URL. Instead of contacting a real WAIS server, your browser contacts the proxy server, and the proxy server fulfills your request.

Besides getting around the WAIS problem, you might use a proxy server because either it can handle the task better or for some reason you are prevented from making direct contact. Let's use a Burger King analogy. Suppose Eric is hungry and wants a Whopper from Burger King. In the first scenario, Eric is in a hurry and it would take too long to walk, so he asks Julian to bicycle over to Burger King and pick up a Whopper for him. In the second scenario, Eric is not in a hurry; he's immobilized. He can't go out, so he asks Julian to go to Burger King for him. In either case, Julian is Eric's proxy food orderer and places the order on his behalf.

What does this have to do with the Internet? Suppose that your browser does support WAIS but your direct connection to the WAIS server is a slow one. You would do better if you connected to a proxy server with a faster connection to the WAIS server. In other words, you would do better to get Julian to ride his bicycle to Burger King.

You can also use a proxy server when you are prevented from making a request directly, perhaps because you are behind a firewall or your user account does not have the necessary permissions to accomplish the task. In

1. Client sends request for document to proxy server.
2. Proxy server sends server request for document.
3. Server returns document to proxy server.
4. Proxy server returns document to client.

Figure 4–1 Client-server communication interchange using a proxy server

this case—and pardon us for stretching analogies—you would have Julian get the Whopper because you're immobilized.

The typical flow of requests using a proxy server is shown in Figure 4-1.

Another common use for proxy servers is to do something called *caching*. (We talked briefly about caching servers in Section 3.1.4 of the last chapter.) Caching produces a modified flow, as shown in Figure 4-2, and is often useful when the connection between A and B is very fast but the connection between B and C is very slow.

1. Client sends request for document to proxy server.
2. Proxy server checks whether it has a stored copy of document. If so, skip to step 6.
3. Proxy server sends server request for document.
4. Server returns document to proxy server.
5. Proxy server stores copy of document.
6. Proxy server returns document to client.

Figure 4–2 Client-server communication interchange using a proxy cache server

Because the proxy server is retrieving the object and then returning it to you, nothing prevents the proxy from modifying the object that it returns. Several such proxy servers take objects that they retrieve and modify them in humorous ways. One example is the Swedish Chef proxy server. It modifies documents that it reads as though they are being spoken by the infamous Swedish Chef from *The Muppet Show*. We show how to write a basic proxy server in Chapter 15.

Proxy servers do have practical uses. For example, a proxy server can automatically convert images from one format to another or translate documents from one language to another.

Some people confuse proxy servers with *gateways*. They do fulfill similar needs, but they are not the same thing. Browsers have to request proxy servers to act on their behalf, but users never know when requests are being made unless they are aware of their browsers' configuration settings. By way of contrast, a gateway is something that masquerades as something else. You don't request the use of a gateway. Gateways are disguised so well you never know when you are interacting with one.

It's probably better to explain these concepts by way of analogy. Suppose you receive a letter from a new French pen pal. Your pen pal doesn't speak English and the letter is written in French. That's no problem for you because your best friend studied abroad and speaks fluent French. You give your friend the letter and she translates it for you. In this case, your friend is acting like a proxy server. She is an intermediary acting on your behalf.

Now suppose you want to read Victor Hugo's *Les Misérables*, which was written in French. If you go to the library, borrow the original French edition, and ask your friend to translate it, she is once again acting as a proxy. On the other hand, if you go to the library and borrow the English translation, that's more like a gateway. It's true that a translation was done somehow, sometime, by someone or something, but it was done behind the scenes and not at your behest.

If your browser is communicating via the HTTP protocol, it assumes that it is communicating with an HTTP server. But if the server is in fact a WAIS server acting or masquerading as an HTTP server, and if the server responds to the http request, then that WAIS server is really what we call a gateway.

In the next chapter, we'll discuss the specification for HTTP (Hypertext Transport Protocol). HTTP servers can be written to act as go-betweens and make requests on behalf of clients. The CERN server (httpd) is one example of a server that offers proxy capabilities. You can download the CERN server and configure it to act as a proxy server, or use the proxy.conf configuration file with preconfigured default values for proxy service. The CERN server also offers caching capabilities. You can edit the configuration settings or use the cache.conf configuration file with preconfigured default values for cache service.

CHAPTER 5

Understanding the HTTP Specification

CHAPTER AT A GLANCE

This chapter provides an in-depth discussion and interpretation of the specification governing Hypertext Transfer Protocol (HTTP). We explain the communication interchange between client and server, and discuss why HTTP is integral to the Web. We describe the request methods, headers, and server responses—including status codes, header information, and MIME types. The chapter concludes with a discussion of S-HTTP extensions.

REQUISITES

A basic understanding of the Web and HTTP, as well as the client-server model as described in Chapter 2.

MORE DETAIL

Chapter 7 provides detailed examples of how the specification is implemented, what actual HTTP requests and responses look like, and code samples to perform HTTP requests and use the HTTP Header Information.

Chapter 12 provides an actual example of using this knowledge to write an HTTP client that will allow you to retrieve documents and analyze their content.

Chapter 13 provides an example of using this knowledge to write an HTTP server.

HTTP/1.0 Internet Draft specifications (see Appendix B) provide an in-depth definition of the standard and its features.

The Internet Draft on S-HTTP (available at **http://www.netgen.com/book**) provides an in-depth description of the security proposal by EIT.

In this chapter we discuss the specification governing the Hypertext Transfer Protocol (HTTP). You'll learn about the communication interchange between a client and server and understand why HTTP is integral to the Web. HTTP is, in fact, *the* communication protocol of the Web.

The Web was conceived with many goals in mind. Among them, providing:

- A distributed information system
- A unified common interface to multiple protocols
- Hypermedia support
- Extensibility, so that any and all data formats would be supported

The existing protocols could not fully support these goals, so a new and separate protocol was created. The HTTP specification called for:

> A protocol designed with the lightness and speed necessary for distributed, collaborative, hypermedia information systems. It is a generic, stateless, object-oriented protocol which can be used for many tasks, such as name servers and distributed object management.

NOTE

HTTP (Hypertext Transfer Protocol) is in some ways a misnomer because it implies that HTTP is only capable of transporting hypertext. This is not true. You can use HTTP to transport objects regardless of data type.

The first version of the HTTP specs, known as HTTP/0.9, fell short of achieving all of these goals. Version 0.9 only supported the GET method; it did not allow for meta-information in the request or the response, and it did not provide content-typing. (We'll define meta-information and content-typing in a moment.) In truth, it was no more powerful than other existing, established protocols like FTP. However, the second version of the specification, known as HTTP/1.0, extended the functionality of version 0.9. Indeed, several key attributes of version 1.0 met the goals of the World Wide Web.

5.1 How HTTP Satisfies Its Mandate

HTTP has six key attributes. Because HTTP was designed to be simple and flexible, it is stateless and connectionless. It is based on the client-server model and supports meta-information and content-typing.

5.1.1 Client-server model

We talked briefly about the client-server model in Chapter 2. HTTP is designed to support communication between clients and servers regarding the transfer of hypertext data. A single server can serve information to large number of clients all across the world.

5.1.2 Simplicity

HTTP is designed to be a very simple protocol and allow HTTP servers to handle large number of requests efficiently. When a client connects to an HTTP server, the only information that the client must send is the request method and the path information from the URL. The HTTP specifications define several request methods, but only three methods are commonly used: GET, HEAD, and POST. Each allows a client to communicate a different class of messages to the HTTP server. For this reason, HTTP servers can be small, simple programs. Because HTTP is a simple protocol, communication via HTTP is fast and incurs very low overhead compared to other protocols, such as FTP.

5.1.3 Flexibility and Content-Typing

HTTP allows for the transmission of arbitrarily typed data, so it's possible to transfer any kind of object using HTTP and have the client act appropriately on it. Content-typing identifies the type of data being transmitted. If data were tin cans, the Content-Types would be the labels on the cans telling you whether they contain Hunt's whole tomatoes or Campbell's tomato soup.

5.1.4 Connectionless

HTTP is a connectionless protocol, which means there is a limit of one request per connection. The client connects, makes its request, gets a response, and then disconnects. This is very efficient. With a connectionless protocol, the server wastes no idle time when there are no requests to fill, nor does it use up precious resources by keeping old requests on hand.

Using a connectionless protocol is sort of like writing a letter. Once you mail it, you are done. If you have more to say, you have to send a new letter. Protocols such as FTP that maintain a connection are like telephone calls. When you are on the telephone, you don't have to hang up and call the other party back after every sentence. That would be pretty annoying. Anyway, the point here is that a connectionless protocol is easier on the server because it only has to maintain connections that are active and it doesn't have to waste time between requests.

5.1.5 Stateless

The fact that HTTP is stateless is both a strength and a weakness. On one hand, without state, the protocol has no memory of the transaction, and the memory of any information that is needed for a subsequent transaction has to be maintained outside the protocol. (In the last chapter we mentioned maintaining state by encoding the information in a URL.) The lack of state also means having to transfer greater amounts of information with each connection, because information needed from the prior transaction has to be repeated. On the other hand, the lack of state makes HTTP a faster running protocol. The server can respond much more quickly because it does not have to maintain all the extra information.

5.1.6 Meta-information

With HTTP/0.9, a client receiving data had to make a lot of assumptions about what the server was sending. It had no idea how much data to expect, and thus could not tell whether it successfully received all the data or whether there was an error in the middle of the transmission. Nor could the client tell the language of the data or the type of object being transmitted. HTTP/1.0 solved these problems by supporting the inclusion of meta-information.

Meta-information is defined as information about information (see the sidebar, "Pizza, Anyone?"). In the case of HTTP/1.0, meta-information allows the server to provide information about the data being sent. For example, HTTP can provide information about the language or type of the object being sent. You can also use meta-information to make conditional requests and report the successful completion of a transaction. Meta-information makes it possible to do much more with the HTTP protocol than could be done without it.

Support for meta-information goes both ways. When servers respond to a client, they can send meta-information as part of the response. And clients

Pizza, Anyone?

Here's another one of our food analogies. If we handed you a piece of paper with the words *pepperoni, mushrooms,* and *onions* on it, you would have no idea how to interpret it. You'd be able to read the words, but you would wonder why we gave you the piece of paper. However, if we told you that the note was a list of the three toppings we wanted on our pizza or the three foods to which Matthew is allergic, you would have a context in which to understand the words. Without this information, you have no idea what the list means or even if the list is complete. The extra information that tells you how to interpret the data is the meta-information.

can send meta-information to help the HTTP server fill a request. These pieces of information are optional, but they can often prove very useful for the server. Because HTTP is stateless, you have to tell everything up front, and that makes the ability to send meta-information crucial.

Some Web clients, including MacMosaic, Netscape 0.9, and Lynx, use the optional From request field to identify the user of the client. This information can provide a weak means of authentication and can be used for user logging purposes. Lynx, Netscape, and some versions of Mosaic are also beginning to use the Referer field to identify which document contained the link that was followed. The From or Referer field can be logged to determine how many sites have links to a particular page. This information is useful to server administrators and advertisers who want to know how users are finding their sites. (We'll talk more about each field and its use in a moment.)

Other optional request fields allow the client to specify the preferred languages for the response or the accepted formats for the response. While these fields are rarely used, they provide a powerful means of requesting particular types of information, when available. HTTP supports four categories of meta-information, separated by their functional use. Each of these categories contains specific fields. The four categories are:

- General message
- Request header
- Response header
- Entity header

The Response and Request headers are specific to the request and response processes. We'll describe each Request and Response header in Sections 5.2.2 and 5.2.3, respectively. General and Entity headers are more general in nature. We discuss the General and Entity header fields in this section.

All of these meta-information bits can be thought of like Post-it Notes attached to a document. For example, suppose I gave you a report and said, "I got this from Fred." Whom the report came from would not be part of the content of the report, but it would tell you where I got it. Or suppose I gave you a floppy disk that contained this report and I put a Post-it on the disk that told you that the information on the disk was formatted as a Word-Perfect file. That Post-it would be providing you with information about the information on the disk. In other words, the Post-it would be providing meta-information.

All four types of HTTP header fields (Request header, Response header, General header, and Entity header) conform to the specifications in RFC 822 for header fields. The specifications state that a header should be the field's name followed by a colon and the field's value. Text that appears after the colon and is wrapped in parentheses is interpreted as a comment and ignored.

General Message Headers

General message headers can be used in both the request and response to provide information that is not directly about the request, response, or object being transmitted. The General message header fields are as follows:

- **Date** refers to the date and time in which the message originated.
- **Forwarded** is used by proxy servers to indicate the path that was taken from the client to the final server. You can use this information to diagnose problems in the transmission of the request or response.
- **Message-ID** contains an identification number for each message.
- **MIME-Version** specifies the version of MIME used in the message being sent. The default value is MIME version 1.0. (We'll be talking more about MIME very shortly.)

Entity Headers

Entity header fields provide information about the object that is being returned. Information in these fields explains how to interpret the object being submitted.

- **Allow** lists the standard HTTP methods that are valid for use with the object being transmitted. For example, if the header lists GET but does not list DELETE, then the object may be retrieved but not deleted.
- **Content-Length** specifies the size of the Entity-Body in bytes. Without this field, the client would not know how much to read and when to stop. HTTP 0.9 did not include this feature and was seen as a major drawback.
- **Content-Type** refers to the MIME Internet Type for the object returned. (See the "MIME" sidebar.) By identifying the object's data type (text, video, etc.), the client can act upon the object appropriately. HTTP 0.9 did not include this feature either and was seen as a major drawback. Table 5-2 lists the acceptable values for this field.
- **Content-Encoding** specifies the compression, encryption, or packetization mechanism used to encode the object. For example, if the object is a compressed GIF image, the Content-Type of the object would be image/gif and the Content-Encoding would specify that the file had been compressed. Two acceptable values include *gzip* and *compress*.
- **Content-Transfer-Encoding** is used to specify any encoding mechanisms used to transfer data to the client. Acceptable values include *7bit, 8bit, binary, quoted-printable,* and *base64*.
- **Content-Language** identifies the language of the object. It may surprise you to know that language applies not only to text-based documents, but to audio and other data types as well. The goal of this field is to allow objects to be identified by their language. That way, users can request the English, Swahili, or French version of a resource, for example. This ability becomes valuable in content negotiation. (See the sidebar "HTTP Negotiation Algorithm" in Section 5.2.2 for more information.)
- **Expires** contains the date on which the data becomes invalid. The value of this field is a standard UNIX time-date stamp.
- **Last-Modified** contains the date and time when the specified object was last modified. This is generally used to indicate whether a cached value of a resource should be considered state.
- **URI** is used to return the new URI for the object, if an object has been moved—sort of like a forwarding address field. This field can take an additional parameter, *vary,* which specifies that the resource in question refers to multiple versions of the same object that differ by language, content type, encoding, version, or character set. This field has replaced the Location header.

- **Location** is used to return a URI for an object that has moved. This header field has been replaced by the URI header field.
- **Version** specifies the version number of the document being returned.
- **Derived From** contains the version number of the document prior to any modifications made by the request.
- **Title** specifies the title of the object. The meaning of the field is equivalent to the <title> tag in HTML.
- **Link** specifies one or more link relationships between the object being sent and other objects. The use of the word *Link* may be misleading because, unlike the hypertext links that you follow, the values in the Link header field do not lead anywhere. The values are simple identifications. Currently, there are no defined link relationships.

5.2 The Client-Server Communication Interchange

This section contains an in-depth discussion of the communication interchange between client and server as provided for by the HTTP specification. Figure 5-1 shows a single HTTP server accepting connections from multiple remote clients in port 80.

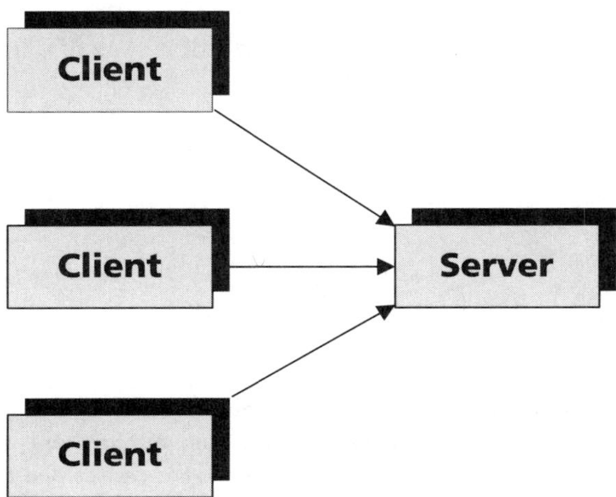

Figure 5-1 A single HTTP server accepting connections from multiple remote clients

MIME (Multipurpose Internet Mail Extensions)

MIME, defined in RFCs 1521 and 1522 (see netgen.com site), is a standard designed to support the inclusion of multiple typed objects in a single object. The protocol was conceived originally to allow for mail messages to include multiple parts. In addition, each of these parts could be *typed* (i.e., identified by their data type) so that users, for example, could include an image as an attachment to a mail message.

To do this, MIME defined a Content-Type header field based on a previous standard defined in RFC 1049. The specification states that this field comes before the actual content of the mail message and should "describe the data contained in the body fully enough that the receiving user agent can pick an appropriate agent or mechanism to present the data to the user, or otherwise deal with the data in an appropriate manner."

HTTP uses MIME to support content-typing, so the flexibility of MIME is what allows any data format to be transmitted across HTTP. MIME's flexibility is one of its strong points. Table 5-1 shows the seven general MIME Content-Types as defined in RFC 1521.

The Content-Type field is used as an object header. It includes a type and a subtype, as well as additional parameters that are required by certain types. The syntax of a MIME Content-Type is as follows:

```
type/subtype; parameter; parameter;...parameter
```

where *subtype* specifies a specific format for that type of data. Here are some examples:

text/html
video/mpeg
image/gif
audio/basic

Table 5-2 lists several commonly used subtypes.

NOTE

Many Content-Types begin with the letter *x* and a hyphen. These Content-Types are "experimental" and have not yet been officially adopted as MIME Content-Types. When Netscape decided to provide dynamic document capabilities via a multipart message where each part replaces the previously sent part, Netscape used the multipart/x-mixed-replace Content-Type.

MIME (Multipurpose Internet Mail Extensions) (Continued)

Table 5–1. MIME Content-Type

Content-Type	Meaning
text	The object contains textual information, regardless of the character set or formatting language
multipart	The object contains multiple parts
application	The object contains application or binary data (i.e., data that can be executed or is intended for another application)
message	The object is a mail message
image	The object is a picture
audio	The object is audio data
video	The object contains video data

Table 5–2. MIME Content-Types and Corresponding Subtypes

Type	Subtype	Meaning
application	msword	Microsoft Word document
	pdf	Adobe Acrobat document
	postscript	PostScript document
	rtf	Rich Text Format (RTF) document
	wordperfect5.1	WordPerfect 5.1 document
	x-dvi	device-independent file
	x-latex	$\LaTeX$ document
	zip	A file that has been compressed using PKZIP
	x-tar	A file that has been archived using Tar
audio	basic	8-bit ISDN mu-law encoded audio file
image	gif	CompuServe Graphic Interchange Format (GIF)
	jpeg	Joint Pictures Expert Group (JPEG)
	x-portable-bitmap	Portable bitmap
	x-xbitmap	X-bitmap
message	rfc822	Standard Mail Message
multipart	mixed	A message containing multiple parts of different types
	parallel	A message containing multiple parts in which the ordering of the parts is not significant
	x-mixed-replace	A message containing multiple parts in which each part is replaced by the next
text	html	HTML
	plain	Unformatted text
video	mpeg	Motion Pictures Expert Group (MPEG) video files
	quicktime	Apple QuickTime video files
	x-msvideo	Microsoft Video files

MIME (Multipurpose Internet Mail Extensions) (Continued)

Some Content-Types have optional or required parameters that specify more about the type of data being sent. During HTTP transaction, *charset, version,* and *boundary* are three of the standard parameters commonly passed along with the text/plain, text/html, and multipart Content-Type fields, respectively.

The *charset* parameter is used with the text type to identify the character of the object. Accepted values for the *charset* parameter are US ASCII (the 7-bit, standard American, ASCII character set) and International Standards Organization (ISO) approved character sets, ISO-8859-1 through ISO-8859-9. The default value for the parameter, if a value is not provided, is `charset=us-ascii`. Here's an example:

```
Content-Type: text/plain; charset=iso-8859-1
```

The version parameter is used with the text/html type to specify which version of HTML was used to create the document, as in this example:

```
Content-Type: text/html; version=3.0
```

This indicates that the document being sent it an HTML document that conforms to HTML 3.0.

Multipart Content-Type fields require a boundary parameter to identify the string that separates the parts of the object. RFC 1521 defines the syntax for the value of a boundary parameter as follows:

```
boundary := 0*69<bchars> bcharsnospace
```

where `0*69` means that the boundary can consist of 0 to 69 characters.

In English, this means that the boundary value can consist of 1 to 70 characters, from a set of acceptable characters, and cannot end in a space. Acceptable characters include all letters and digits, spaces, and the following special characters:

' ( ) + _ , - . / : = ?

MIME (Multipurpose Internet Mail Extensions) (Continued)

Here's an example of a MIME Content-Type for a multipart type:

```
multipart/multiple; boundary=my_boundary_string
```

Once the *boundary* value is defined in the Content-Type header, you can use the *boundary* value in conjunction with the two hyphen characters to denote the beginning of a new object, separate each of the parts, and mark the end of the object. In the next chapter, we'll show you specific examples of how boundary values are used.

Unlike some protocols, the client makes a single request in HTTP and that request *must* have all the necessary information. The client and server do not negotiate. Once the client makes a request, the server can't clarify it or ask for additional information. Figure 5-2 shows the flow of a client-server communication request, as follows: you open a connection, you make a request, the server responds, and the connection is closed.

5.2.1 Open a Connection

When an HTTP server is running, it is listening on a port (generally port 80) and waiting for a connection to occur. Opening a connection is like picking up the telephone and dialing someone's phone number. Technically speaking, the client opens a socket and binds that socket to a port. In UNIX everything is files, and that makes the implementation of network transfers easier and consistent with the rest of UNIX. Therefore, a socket is a special type of file that allows for network I/O. When you open a socket from the client's point of view, you are creating a virtual file. When you write to that file, you are really sending the data across the network (it just looks as though it is writing to a file from the computer's perspective).

Once that is done, the connection has been established and it's time to make a request.

5.2.2 Make a Request

Once the connection is open, the client may make a request by sending the request data string to the server on whichever port the HTTP server resides. An HTTP 1.0 request string is made up of one or more lines, followed by two carriage-return line-feeds (CRLFs). The first line is the request line. It includes a

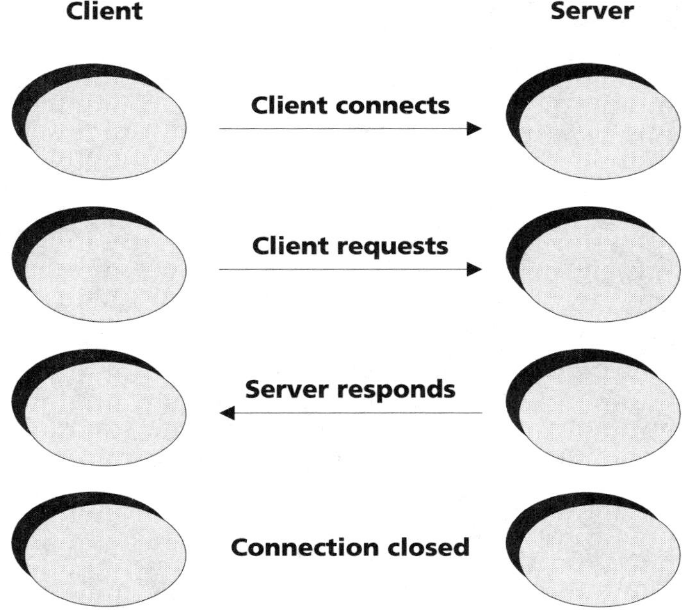

Figure 5–2 Client-server communication interchange—a four step transaction

method, the URI, and the protocol. The rest of the lines are headers of one type or another—first the General headers, then the Request headers, and finally the Entity headers. (HTTP 0.9 does not support header lines.) The two CRLFs signal the end of the request.

HTTP/0.9 only supported very simple client requests. In fact, an HTTP/0.9 request is referred to as a "simple request," in contrast to the "full request" added by HTTP/1.0. Simple requests take the following form:

```
GET URI
```

URI is either a full or partial Unique Resource Identifier (as defined by RFC 1630—see netgen.com site). It can be either a URL or a URN. Unless the server is being used as a proxy server, the URI provided in the request should not include the scheme name, hostname, or port of the URI. Because the connection has already been established to an HTTP server, the scheme name is implicitly assumed to be HTTP, and the server name and port number are set to the location of the server to which the connection is made. For example, once a connection has been established to the HTTP server at the site www.netgen.com, the request for **http://www.netgen.com/sis/** should be abbreviated as simply **/sis/**.

The following example is a valid request under HTTP/0.9. It uses the GET method to request the object /home.html:

```
GET /home.html
```

HTTP/1.0 added a much fuller syntax for requests. HTTP/1.0 allows for many new methods, as well as header information. The format of a full request is as follows:

```
Method URI HTTP-Version
General-Header
Request-Header
Entity-Header

Entity-Body
```

General headers, Request headers, and Entity headers contain the request's meta-information and are optional. In addition, the length of Entity-Body is determined by Entity-Header. If no length is provided, Entity-Body is assumed to be zero bytes long.

The blank line serves as a delimiter between the headers and Entity-Body. This line may not be omitted, even if no headers or Entity-Body are provided. For example, the simplest HTTP/1.0 request does not have any of the additional headers or Entity-Body. It might look like this:

```
GET / HTTP/1.0
```

The only difference between this request and the sample HTTP/0.9 request shown earlier is that this one includes a blank line and the version number. The HTTP version number must be included in full requests (i.e., using versions 1.0 or above). If the version number is not included, version 0.9 is assumed, and that makes it impossible to use the new features supported by the later version of HTTP. These two differences may appear minor, but the important thing to realize is that the simplest HTTP/1.0 example is as complex as the most complicated HTTP/0.9 request.

Methods

A *method* describes the action that should be performed on the specified resource. Under HTTP/1.0, the following methods are valid in a request: GET, HEAD, POST, PUT, DELETE, LINK, and UNLINK. In order to be considered HTTP/1.0 compliant, however, servers only have to support the GET and HEAD methods:

- **GET** is used to request an object identified by the URI from a server. If the object is a document or file, GET requests its contents; but if the object is a program or script, GET requests the results of executing the program or the output of the script. And if the object is a database query, GET requests the results of the query. Each time you follow a link on the Web, your browser uses the GET method to retrieve the document you requested.
- **HEAD** is used to ask the server for the object's meta-information (perhaps you want to know its size or the date it was last modified) but not the object itself. The HEAD method makes for a much quicker request, because the entire document does not need to be transferred. Clients that use caching often use a HEAD request to retrieve a document's Last-Modified-Date without retrieving the complete document.

TIP

The HEAD method is particularly useful for testing link validity and accessibility.

- **POST** is used when you need to transfer data from the client to the server so that the server can then do something with the data. The POST method is often used to submit the contents of an HTML form to an HTTP server for processing. For example, Chapter 1 we mentioned an online job placement service (the Monster Board) to which you can submit your résumé search for job openings. When you fill out a Web page form such as that one, your browser generally submits the data you input to the server by using the POST method.
- **PUT** is used when you want to create a new resource or update an existing one. The PUT method submits data to the server so that it will

be available via a specified URI. If data already exists at the specified URI, the data is used as a newer version. If no data already exists, the server tries to create a new resource at the specified URI.

- **DELETE** is used to tell the server to remove the specified resource.
- **LINK** is the method you use to tell the server to add *link relationships* to the object specified by the URI. Link relationships can indicate that one resource is a continuation of another, the predecessor to another, the parent of another in a hierarchy, or the creator of another. (See Section 5.1.6, "Meta-information," for more information on link relationships.)
- **UNLINK** is the method you use to tell the server to remove link relationships from the object specified by the URI.

NOTE

GET and HEAD requests produce identical responses, except that a HEAD request does not return `Entity-Body` **in the response. POST was originally meant to be thought of in terms of an attachment—for example, USENET posting where the posted data is attached to the UseNet object. Now, however, posting typically means that the posted data is to be handled by the object and not necessarily associated with the object in the future.**

Request Headers

Request headers qualify the request being made by telling the server how to interpret the request:

- **User-Agent** identifies the client program in use (e.g., NCSA Mosaic). In general, this field is the name of the browser. In the case of an autonomous agent, such as a robot or spider, the User-Agent field contains a string that identifies the program being run. The syntax of the User-Agent field is:

  ```
  User-Agent: product_list
  ```

  where *product_list* is a list of strings in the form product_name or product_name/product_version. It is considered common courtesy for browsers and agents to send the User-Agent field on all requests they make. The User-Agent field is usually used for statistical purposes (i.e., keeping track of which browsers are being used to access the site the most). However, you could actually use the User-Agent field to modify the response being returned to the user. (In Chapter 7 we'll show you the code to do this.)

- **If-Modified-Since** is the header field used in conjunction with the GET method to produce a conditional request. The server only returns the specified object if it has been modified since the given date. If the object was not modified after the given date, the server is instructed to return status code 304. (We'll talk more about status codes in the next section, which covers server responses. In addition, we will show examples of using this field in the next chapter.)
- **Pragma** is the header field by which a client can request the server receiving the request to behave in a certain way. The only value for this field specified under HTTP/1.0 is "no-cache." This value specifies that any caching servers that receive the request should actually request the document, whether or not it is cached.
- **Authorization** is the field that contains the authentication information that is to be sent along with the request. The server can use this information to determine whether the client has the appropriate permissions to make the request. The HTTP/1.0 specification provides for a simple authentication scheme that encodes the username and password. The Basic Access Authentication Scheme provides only a minimal level of authentication and should be considered insecure.
- **Referer** is the field that identifies the object containing the link that is the current request. In other words, if you were browsing the net.Genesis page and you wanted to follow a link from there to the Sports Information Service, your browser would issue a request to get the Sports Information Service object, and the Referer field in that request would contain the URI of the net.Genesis home page. The Referer field is usually used for statistical and maintenance purposes. If it is logged, the server administrator can determine how the site is being used and where people are finding information about the site's location.
- **From** contains the e-mail address of the user making the request. This field is usually used for logging purposes or as a default e-mail address to use in feedback forms. We'll show you a script using the From field for this purpose in the next chapter.
- **Accept** specifies a list of Content-Types or sets of Content-Types that the client will accept in the response. For each Content-Type or set of Content-Types, the client can provide a *quality factor* that reflects the

client's preference for various Content-Types. In addition, the client can provide a maximum accepted size for each of the types or sets of types. The HTTP server can then use this information and the HTTP Negotiation Algorithm (see the sidebar) to determine which object to return in response to the request.

- **Accept-Charset** is used to specify the character sets that the client can accept.
- **Accept-Encoding** specifies a list of content-encoding types, or sets of content-encoding types, that the client will accept in the response. For each content-encoding type or set of content-encoding types, the client can provide a quality factor that reflects the client's preference for various encoding methods. The HTTP server can then use this information and the HTTP Negotiation Algorithm (again, see the sidebar) to determine which object to return in response to the request.
- **Accept-Language** contains a list of languages, or sets of natural languages, that the client will accept in the response. For each language or set of languages, the client can provide a quality factor that reflects the client's preference for various languages.

5.2.3 Server Responds

Once the client makes the request, the server responds. An HTTP/1.0 response string is made up of one or more lines, followed by a blank line and the Entity-Body. The first line is the response line. It includes the server's protocol and status code. The rest of the lines are headers of one type or another. First come the General headers, then the Response headers, and finally the Entity headers. (HTTP 0.9 does not support header lines.) Then there's a blank line to separate the headers from the object data.

HTTP/0.9 only supported very simple server responses. In fact, an HTTP/0.9 response is referred to as a "simple response," in contrast to HTTP/1.0's "full-response." Simple responses, which do not have headers, take the following form:

```
Entity-Body
```

HTTP/1.0 added a much fuller syntax to the response; it allows for header information. The format of a full request is on the next page.

HTTP Negotiation Algorithm

One of the most powerful features of HTTP is that is allows the server to fill the client's request based on the Accept, Accept-Encoding, and Accept-Language header fields. In other words, when the server receives a request for a resource, it can decide exactly what to send back based on what the client says it can accept and on the size of each resource variant.

One of the main goals of content negotiation is to give clients an opportunity to receive data in the way they can handle it best and, preferably, to give it to them in small chunks. For example, your client (browser) could request the netgen.logo resource from the server at www.netgen.com. If multiple variations of this resource existed with different content types (i.e., a GIF version, a JPEG version, and a PostScript version), the server could make a decision as to which version to return to the client. In addition, if the server were capable of converting one of the versions to another type—say a TIFF—it could choose to make that conversion and return the result.

When clients provide Accept, Accept-Encoding, or Accept-Language headers, they are allowed to provide a *quality factor* with each type that they accept. A quality factor of 1 means that the client accepts the specified type perfectly. A quality factor of zero means that the client cannot handle the object type. Quality factors in between indicate various preference levels for the object type.

Other possible applications include returning objects of different languages based on the client's Accept-Language header, or returning objects that have been encoded differently based on the client's Accept-Encoding header.

```
HTTP-Version Status-Code Reason-Phrase
General-Header
Response-Header
Entity-Header
Entity-Body
```

General headers, Response headers, and Entity headers contain the response's meta-information and are optional. The length of Entity-Body is determined by Entity-Header. If no length is provided, Entity-Body is assumed to be zero bytes long.

The blank line serves as a delimiter between the headers and Entity-Body. It may not be omitted, even if no headers or Entity-Body are provided. The General header fields used in responses are exactly the same as the ones used in requests (see Section 5.1.6).

Here's a sample HEAD request and response using HTTP 1.0:

```
HEAD / HTTP/1.0


HTTP/1.0 200 OK
Date: Wednesday, 08-Mar-95 22:45:02 GMT
Server: NCSA/1.3
MIME-version: 1.0
Content-type: text/html
Last-modified: Sunday, 05-Mar-95 09:25:02 GMT
Content-length: 4778
```

Had the request been for GET / HTTP/1.0 instead of HEAD, the last blank line in the response would have been followed by 4,778 bytes of data (content-length) in the text/html format (Content-Type). This we know from the meta-information.

Status Codes

Status codes indicate whether the server was able to fulfill a request successfully. A status code is a three-digit number followed by a text phrase that explains what the code means. For example, the response line from the response sample above is:

```
HTTP/1.0 200 OK
```

where 200 is the three-digit code that means "okay."

Status codes all begin with the number 1, 2, 3, 4, or 5. Category 1 is not used, but is reserved for future use. Category 2 status codes indicate success—the server understood the client's request and was able to respond without problem. Category 3 codes usually indicate that a redirection occurred—the server understood and was able to retrieve the resource, but found it in a location other than the one specified in the request. Category 4 codes indicate a client error. Status codes beginning with the number 5 indicate a server error.

Table 5-3 shows the status codes and explanations as defined in the specification document (HTTP 1.0 Internet Draft, see Appendix B).

Table 5–3. Status Codes as Defined in the HTTP 1.0 Internet Draft

Code	Definition	Explanation
200	Okay	Used with GET, HEAD, and POST. No meta-information is required to be sent by the server. Entity-Header is always returned to the client. With GET, Entity-Body also needs to be returned.
201	Created	Used with POST and PUT. The URI header is requiring meta-information from the server. This code tells the client that an object was created with the following URI.
202	Accepted	Used with GET, HEAD, PUT, POST, and DELETE. No meta-information is required to be sent by the server. This code basically says, "I have accepted your information for processing, but the processing has not been completed."
203	Provisional information	Used with GET, HEAD, and POST. No meta-information needs to be sent by the server. This code indicates that the HTTP header that was returned came from a source other than the server to which the request was sent.
204	No content	Used to indicate that the specified request did not yield any content. This code should be used when the request is used by an executable, but no output is generated.
300	Multiple choices	Used to indicate that requested resource is available at multiple locations and that the client should choose from one of them. No headers are required for this response code.
301	Moved permanently	Used with GET, HEAD, POST, and PUT. The meta-information that needs to be provided by the server is the URI header and location. This code basically says, "Hey, this object has been moved permanently to this URI."
302	Moved temporarily	Used with GET, HEAD, POST, and PUT. The meta-information that the server needs to provide is the URI header and location. This code essentially says that the object has been moved temporarily to the following URI.
303	Method	Obsolete.
304	Not modified	Used with conditional GET. No meta-information is necessary.
400	Bad request	No meta-information required. The request the client sent was unusable.

Table 5–3. Status Codes as Defined in the HTTP 1.0 Internet Draft (Continued)

Code	Definition	Explanation
401	Unauthorized	Used to tell the client that their authentication failed and that they should try again.
402	Payment required	"Not currently supported but reserved for future use."
403	Forbidden	No meta-information required. Regardless of authorization, this request is not acceptable and will not be handled. The client shouldn't bother to try again.
404	Not found	No meta-information required. The object requested by the client could not be found.
405	Method not allowed	Server needs to allow meta-information back to the client. This code tells the client that the submission method is not allowed for the object being asked for.
406	None acceptable	Required meta-information that needs to be sent by the server is the Content-Type, content-encoding, and content-language. This code tells the client that the server did find something that matched the URI being requested, but that "something" didn't match any of the Accept, Accept-Encoding, and Accept-Language request headers. Because it wasn't acceptable, no part of the Entity-Body is included in the server's response.
407	Proxy authentication required	Required meta-information is Proxy-Authenticate. This code is very similar to 401, but the client "must first authenticate itself with the proxy." Basically, the server will tell the client what acceptable authentication scheme it is using. The client needs to try and authenticate itself.
408	Request timeout	No meta-information required. This code tells the client that it didn't generate a request for an object quick enough.
409	Conflict	Used to indicate that the request could not be fulfilled because of the state of the specified resource. No headers are required for this response code; however, the entity returned should clearly identify the source of the problem.
410	Gone	Used to indicate that the specified resource is unavailable and that no new address is known.
500	Internal server error	Something went wrong inside the server, so the request didn't work.

Table 5–3. Status Codes as Defined in the HTTP 1.0 Internet Draft (Continued)

Code	Definition	Explanation
501	Not implemented	Can't honor this request because the server doesn't know how to handle the functionality.
502	Bad gateway	Same as 500, except the server is a gateway or proxy server.
503	Service unavailable	Required meta-information for this is Retry-After. This code usually appears as the result of an overload of the system or downtime for maintenance, etc. This is a temporary condition, so the client should try to reconnect after the delay indicated in Retry-After.
504	Gateway timeout	Similar to 500, except the request didn't work because of a gateway or proxy.

In general, users do not see the status codes that are returned by the server (only your browser knows for sure). In addition, the user generally does not see redirections or authentication attempts. Typically, an unsuccessful requests receives a response with a status code that says the requested resource was not found, that the request was malformed, or that authentication is required to access the resource.

Of all these codes, you need only become familiar with a few. The one we hope you experience most often is 200 (Okay), but you'll probably hit your share of 400s (Bad request) and 404s (Not found), along with the occasional 500 (Internal server error). Codes 301 (Moved permanently) and 302 (Moved temporarily) are especially useful if you want to redirect the server to the new location instead of just returning a document with a link to the object's new location.

Response Header Information

Header lines make up the second portion of the server's response. The specification defines four Response header fields that may be used to qualify the response being sent:

- **Server** identifies the server software. The syntax of the Server field is:

  ```
  Server: product_list
  ```

  where *product_list* is a list of strings in the form of *product_name* or *product_name/product_version*.

- **WWW-Authenticate** informs the client that the requested URI is protected and that authentication is necessary. The header also states which scheme is being used to perform the authentication.
- **Retry-After** specifies how long it will be until the requested resource is available again.
- **Public** allows the server to specify a list of all nonstandard methods supported by the server.

Entity-Body

The final portion of the server response contains the object itself. Because HTTP is liberal about sending documents in any format, it is ideal for transmitting multimedia objects such as graphics, audio, and video files. The complete freedom to transmit data in any format is one of the most significant advantages afforded by HTTP and the Web.

5.2.4 Close Connection

When either the client or the server closes the connection, the request is terminated regardless of whether the transaction has been successful or was completed.

5.3 Evolution of HTTP

One of the hottest topics right now is being able to provide authentication and encryption via HTTP. The topic is so important because commercial services want to conduct online sales without having to worry about the security of the information being sent. Three proposals currently exist to provide authentication and encryption functionality: S-HTTP (Secure HTTP), Shen, and the Secure Sockets Layer (SSL). Meanwhile, work is also underway to define a brand-new version of HTTP, called HTTP-NG.

5.3.1 S-HTTP Extensions

Both the S-HTTP and Shen protocols are built on top of HTTP for the purposes of providing authentication and encryption for HTTP transactions. Both are simple extensions of the protocol. SSL is built at a level lower than HTTP and can be used for other socket-based protocols, such as FTP, Gopher, etc. Following is a description of the major changes proposed under S-HTTP.

S-HTTP is defined as a wrapper around the current specifications for HTTP. By "wrapper" we mean that the entire HTTP request (or response) is encrypted and used as the Entity-Body for an S-HTTP request or response. The S-HTTP request or response provides the information necessary for the other party to decrypt the Entity-Body and thus recover the original HTTP request or response.

New S-HTTP Request-Method and Request-Line Format

S-HTTP has defined a new method and request line for use in all S-HTTP requests. The proposed request line for all secure transactions is:

```
Secure * Secure-HTTP/1.1.
```

Notice that, unlike the HTTP 1.0 request line, this one does not specify a URI. In order to prevent a "cracker" (malicious hacker) from gaining additional information about the request being made, all the information is hidden in the encrypted portion of the message. While it may not seem like the URI you are requesting could provide information to an attacker, it can. Therefore, this request line is used to keep very little information about the request from being exposed.

New S-HTTP Response Line

S-HTTP also specifies that all server responses use the following Response header:

```
Secure-HTTP/1.1 200 OK
```

As stated before, this header is designed to prevent a malicious attacker from getting any information about the requested resource. The actual response to the request is hidden within the body of the response.

New S-HTTP Request Header Lines

S-HTTP has defined that the following new Request header lines is to be used in S-HTTP requests:

- **Content-Privacy-Domain** indicates the object's message format. The valid values for this field are PEM, PKCS-7, and PGP. PEM is used for the standard Privacy Enhanced Mail format defined in RFC 1421. PKCS-7 is a message format defined in the S-HTTP specification. PGP is used to denote the message format used by Pretty Good Privacy 2.6.

- **Content-Transfer-Encoding** defines how data in the object is represented. Depending on the Content-Privacy-Domain, acceptable values are 8BIT, 7BIT, and BASE64. The PKCS-7 can only use 8BIT or BASE64 encoding. PEM only accepts 7BIT encoding. PGP allows for all three types.
- **Content-Type** is not a new header field, but in S-HTTP the value returned should be `application/http`.
- **Prearranged-Key-Info** identifies the key that is to be used for the session. The key is selected from a lists of keys that the server and client share.
- **MAC-Info** (Method Authenticity Check) provides a checksum used to authenticate the server, ensure that the message is not a copy of an older message, and guarantee that the data in the message is not tampered with during delivery.

These are the major extensions to HTTP, as proposed by the S-HTTP Internet Draft. The specification also defines the format of the object's content. However, this formatting information is dependent on the privacy Domain and Transfer Encoding values. Also defined are additional HTML tags for embedding security-related information in HTML documents. Finally, the S-HTTP specification proposes a new scheme for URLs to indicate that the resource is available via a server that understands S-HTTP. S-HTTP URLs begin with the "shttp" scheme name.

5.3.2 HTTP-NG

HTTP-NG is a proposal for the next generation of HTTP. It was developed by Simon Spero of the University of North Carolina at Chapel Hill, Sunsite and Enterprise Integration Technologies. An obvious question is why didn't they just call it "HTTP/2.0"? The primary reason is that HTTP-NG is a complete reworking of HTTP and barely identifiable as the same protocol.

HTTP-NG attempts to eliminate many of the speed problems of the current version of HTTP. Substantial changes include binary encoding for much of the information currently in headers, multiple requests per connection, and asynchronous transmission of requests and responses.

Whether HTTP-NG gets adopted remains to be seen, but something like HTTP-NG needs to be adopted in order to accommodate the incredible growth of the Web.

Additional HTTP-NG Information
http:// www.netgen.com/book/http-ng.html

C H A P T E R 6

Using HTTP

CHAPTER AT A GLANCE

This chapter focuses on the practical application of the HTTP specification. We discuss what really happens during the communication interchange between client and server, and provide ways to work around the limitations in the HTTP specification. We describe how to simulate and debug a Web client using HTTP and explain why this would be meaningful. Also included are samples of program code to utilize header information, as well as code for a simple server, command-line HTTP client, and GET subroutine.

REQUISITES

A thorough understanding of HTTP as well as the client-server model as described in Chapters 2 and 5.

MORE DETAIL

Chapter 5 provides explanations of the HTTP specs in detail.

Chapter 12 provides an actual example of using this knowledge to write an HTTP client, which will allow you to retrieve documents an analyze their content.

Chapter 13 provides an example of using this knowledge to write an HTTP server.

The HTTP/1.0 Internet Draft (see Appendix B) provides an in-depth definition of the standard and its features.

In this chapter we talk about putting the HTTP specification to use. In many cases, not all the functionality defined in the specification has been implemented. On the other hand, some elements have been put to use for purposes well beyond the intentions of the original design. We also suggest ways in which to apply the power of this protocol, and toward that end you will find CGI scripts that you can use in this chapter. The examples of HTTP implementation in this chapter are included to help you understand the protocol. We cover subjects such as the intricacies of CGI and how to create a server later in the book (in Chapters 9, 11, and 13, respectively). In this chapter, the focus remains on HTTP and how you can use it to your advantage.

6.1 The Protocol as Implemented

In previous chapters, we talked about the communication interchange between client and server, and we described the HTTP specification. In this chapter, we'll show you the details of how things are used somewhat differently than they are in the HTTP specification.

Many methods defined in the HTTP specification have never been implemented. That is, the popular clients and servers either do not use them or do so infrequently. On the other hand, a couple of methods are now being used in ways that have evolved beyond the intent of the original specification. The same is true of many of the header fields. In this section, we show you what is and isn't being put to use, explain why, show you examples of how these things really work when implemented, and suggest ways to work around the limitations of the specification.

6.1.1 Request Methods

Even though the HTTP specification defines seven methods, only three—GET, HEAD, and POST—are used frequently. We like to call these three methods "major methods" because they are used extensively. We call the other four methods "minor methods" because they are used so rarely.

GET

According to the specifications, the purpose of the GET method is to retrieve the resource specified by the accompanying URL. The primary application of the GET method is to retrieve documents that are specified via a link. For example, when you select an HTTP link in your browser, the browser retrieves the document via the GET method, as shown on the next page.

```
GET /sis/sports.html
```

By appending search criteria, GET can also be used to specify searches:

```
GET /cgi-bin/wais.pl?dogs+cats
```

Here, GET uses the keywords *dogs* and *cats* to search the WAIS database. Data obtained by a search is a subset of a larger data set. And that subset has its own identity; i.e., it is defined by search criteria. So a URL with an appended query string is actually identifying a new resource.

In addition to the simple use of GET to retrieve documents that are linked to, GET (along with POST) is also commonly used to submit the contents of HTML forms. Since GET requests are supposed to be used to request the contents of a particular URL, and are not meant to include any object, the contents of the form are encoded in the URL used in the request. In Chapter 4 we mentioned that a question mark in a HTTP URL signifies the beginning of the search part of the URL, and all data from the form is encoded in this portion of the URL. Figure 6-1 shows the simple form corresponding to the following HTML:

```
<form action="http://www.netgen.com/cgi-bin/test-cgi" method="GET">
Field 1: <input type="text" name ="field1"><br>
Field 2: <input type="text" name ="field2"><br>
<input type="submit" value = "Submit the form">
</form>
```

As you can see from the METHOD attribute to the FORM element, the contents of this form would be submitted via the GET method.

If the user enters **Strawberry** in field1 and **Briggs** in field2, the client accesses the following URL:

```
http://www.netgen.com/cgi-bin/test-cgi?field1=Strawberry&field2=Briggs
```

which translates into the following request to the server at the site www.netgen.com:

```
GET /cgi-bin/test-cgi?field1=Strawberry&field2=Briggs HTTP/1.0
```

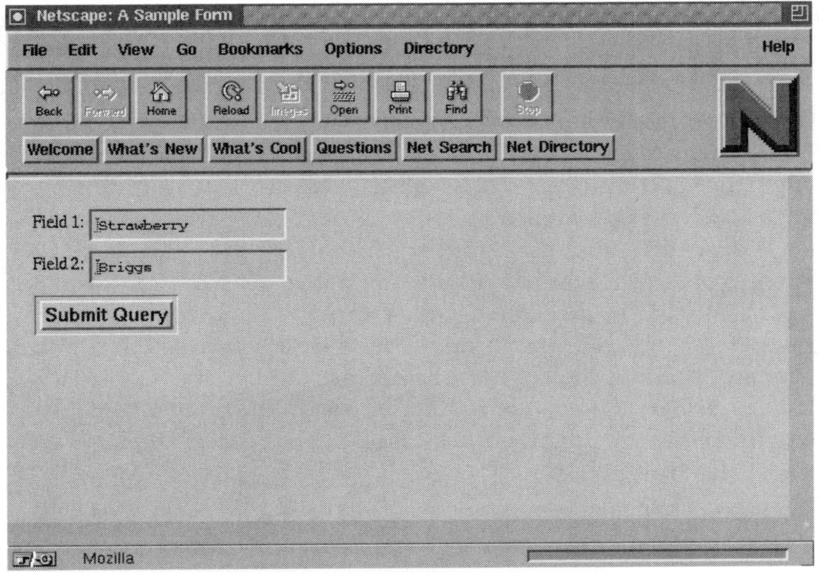

Figure 6–1 A simple input form with two fields

If you can use GET to perform a search, can you use GET to submit form data that does not represent search criteria? The answer is yes. It is not a very big stretch to go from submitting multiple field values for a search to submitting information to be used for other purposes. It explains how the original purpose of the GET method quickly surpassed its original intent.

Because people use GET to submit information from forms, it is not unusual for requests to contain hundreds of characters in the query string. However, each server has a built-in maximum number of characters it can accept in the URL part of the Request-Line. For example, the NCSA httpd can accept no more than 8,192 characters in the entire Request-Line. That is certainly a long string, but it still can present a problem when users submit arbitrarily long forms through the Request-Line.

Don't think of these huge URLs with multiple fields as identifying a resource. Think of them as submitting information to a resource (the program that is running on the server) so that the resource can process the data from the form and return a result. This is exactly what POST is meant to do.

POST

The POST method has also changed somewhat over time. Originally, it was meant to submit data that was related to a specific resource—something akin to posting a message to a USENET newsgroup or making an annotation to a document.

In fact, the CERN httpd provides a mechanism for server administrators to support a general POST method handler to do exactly this, but the primary use for POST is to submit data from a form to a script. The script then processes the form's fields. When the POST method is used in this way, the contents of the form are URL-encoded (using escape code sequences, as described in Chapter 4). The Content-Type for URL-encoded data sent with the request is application/x-www-form-urlencoded. The Content-Length header tells the server how much data to expect in the body. Using this information, the server can dynamically allocate the right amount of space before reading in the Entity-Body.

When you change the previous example to use POST, the HTML code looks like this:

```
<form action="http://www.netgen.com/cgi-bin/test-cgi" method="POST">
Field 1: <input type="text" name ="field1"><br>
Field 2: <input type="text" name ="field2"><br>
<input type="submit" value = "Submit the form">
</form>
```

Entering **Briggs** and **Strawberry** in field1 and field2 produces a request that looks like this:

```
POST /cgi-bin/test-cgi HTTP/1.0
Content-type: application/x-www-form-urlencoded
Content-length: 31

field1=Strawberry&field2=Briggs
```

The current problem with using POST for its intended purpose is that clients don't allow you to post an arbitrary object—an HTML page, an image, etc.—to a URI. However, CERN does provide a mechanism for general posting. Someday clients may allow you to post an arbitrary object to a resource as an annotation or addition to a page.

Following is a sample request that shows what it would look like to post a piece of plain text to a hypothetical resource called /test_post. The purpose of this sample request is to annotate the test_post resource with a new message concerning Microsoft Windows:

```
POST /test_post HTTP/1.0
Content-type: text/plain
Content-length: 58

A computer without Windows is like a fish without a bicycle
```

Different servers give different errors when you try to post to something that can't be posted to (like a normal HTML page). Following are the reactions of CERN, NCSA, and Netsite to general posts as they are currently set up.

CERN httpd actually does allow for a mechanism that would allow for general posting. However, almost nobody uses this mechanism. When this option is not used, CERN returns an error 500:

```
POST / HTTP/1.0

HTTP/1.0 500 This server is not configured to handle POST
MIME-Version: 1.0
Server: CERN/3.0pre6
Date: Thursday, 16-Mar-95 17:43:51 GMT
Content-Type: text/html
Content-Length: 222

...
```

The NCSA server returns an error 501:

```
POST / HTTP/1.0

HTTP/1.0 501 Not Implemented
Date: Thursday, 16-Mar-95 17:52:59 GMT
Server: NCSA/1.3
MIME-version: 1.0
Content-type: text/html

...
```

Netsite also returns error 500:

```
POST / HTTP/1.0

HTTP/1.0 500 Server Error
Server: Netsite-Communications/1.0
Date: Thursday, 16-Mar-95 17:54:41 GMT
Content-type: text/html
Content-length: 305

...
```

HEAD

The purpose of the HEAD method is to retrieve a resource's header or meta-information without retrieving the resource itself. At the beginning of the chapter, we showed you a sample GET command for retrieving the Sports Information Service home page. Using the HEAD command to retrieve only the header information for that resource yields the following:

```
HEAD /sis/sports.html HTTP/1.0

HTTP/1.0 200 Document follows
MIME-Version: 1.0
Server: CERN/3.0pre6
Date: Friday, 24-Mar-95 15:52:27 GMT
Content-Type: text/html
Content-Length: 2070
Last-Modified: Thursday, 02-Mar-95 07:27:44 GMT
```

Being able to retrieve meta-information, such as type, length, and date modified, without having to retrieve the object itself is very useful, so the HEAD method is implemented by all the major servers. In the example above, the Server header field identifies the server as the CERN httpd. The following two code blocks show a HEAD request and server response for the other two major servers, NCSA and Netsite Communications, respectively:

```
HEAD /home-pages.html HTTP/1.0

HTTP/1.0 200 OK
Date: Thursday, 16-Mar-95 17:31:11 GMT
Server: NCSA/1.3
MIME-version: 1.0
Content-Type: text/html
Last-modified: Tuesday, 14-Mar-95 14:22:34 GMT
Content-length: 91975

HEAD /images/bunny_square.gif HTTP/1.0

HTTP/1.0 200 OK
Server: Netsite-Communications/1.0
Date: Thursday, 16-Mar-95 17:36:52 GMT
Last-modified: Monday, 19-Sep-94 23:42:59 GMT
Content-Length: 639
Content-Type: image/gif
```

PUT

PUT is a "minor method" because it is rarely supported and almost never used. The CERN httpd provides a mechanism for using a general PUT script to handle PUT requests. However, this feature is disabled by default because of the security implications of allowing users to add arbitrary data to a site. The current version of NCSA httpd has not fully implemented the PUT method.

Here is a hypothetical request that shows what it would look like to post a piece of plain text to a resource called /unix_quotes. This request asks the server to attempt to make the Entity-Body available at the URI /unix_quotes:

```
PUT /unix_quotes HTTP/1.0
Content-Type: text/plain
Content-Length: 110

There are two major products popularized by Berkeley: LSD and UNIX. We don't
believe this to be a coincidence.
```

CERN httpd actually does support a mechanism that allows for general uses of PUT. The mechanism, a configuration option, allows server administrators to specify the name of a program to be called whenever people try to put things to their servers. However, almost nobody uses this mechanism. When it is disabled (the default), CERN returns a status code 403:

```
PUT / HTTP/1.0

HTTP/1.0 403 Method PUT is disabled on this server
MIME-Version: 1.0
Server: CERN/3.0
Date: Friday, 17-Mar-95 04:47:20 GMT
Content-Type: text/html
Content-Length: 211

...
```

NCSA Returns an error 501:

```
PUT / HTTP/1.0

HTTP/1.0 501 Not Implemented
Date: Friday, 17-Mar-95 05:06:21 GMT
Server: NCSA/1.3
MIME-version: 1.0
Content-Type: text/html

...
```

Netsite returns an error 500:

```
PUT / HTTP/1.0

HTTP/1.0 500 Server Error
Server: Netsite-Communications/1.0
Date: Friday, 17-Mar-95 05:06:57 GMT
Content-Type: text/html
Content-Length: 305

...
```

DELETE

DELETE is another "minor method." It is rarely supported and almost never used. The CERN httpd provides a mechanism so that users can use a general DELETE script to handle DELETE requests. However, this feature is disabled by default because of the security implications of allowing users to delete data from a site. The current version of NCSA httpd has not fully implemented the DELETE method. The NCSA server does recognize the DELETE method when it is submitted, but it is not programmed to take any action (i.e., it doesn't delete the resource).

Following are three sample requests, one for each major server. They show what it would look like to try to delete the contents of a hypothetical resource called "/". This request asks the server to attempt to delete the object referred to by the URI /.

When it is disabled, DELETE returns an error 403:

```
DELETE / HTTP/1.0

HTTP/1.0 403 Method DELETE is disabled on this server
MIME-Version: 1.0
Server: CERN/3.0pre6
Date: Friday, 17-Mar-95 05:35:05 GMT
Content-Type: text/html
Content-Length: 218

...
```

```
DELETE / HTTP/1.0

HTTP/1.0 501 Not Implemented
Date: Friday, 17-Mar-95 05:37:52 GMT
Server: NCSA/1.3
MIME-version: 1.0
Content-Type: text/html

...
```

```
DELETE / HTTP/1.0

HTTP/1.0 500 Server Error
Server: Netsite-Communications/1.0
Date: Friday, 17-Mar-95 05:38:33 GMT
Content-Type: text/html
Content-Length: 305

...
```

LINK and UNLINK

Neither the LINK nor the UNLINK method is currently supported by any client or server.

6.1.2 Request Fields

Now let's take a look at the Request header fields to see which meta-information is and isn't used. Like methods, not all Request header fields are implemented according to the specification. In this section we examine all but three of the Request header fields. Not much can be said about Authorization and Pragma. The Authorization fields do not really provide much security, so they are used infrequently. When they are used, they conform to the specification described in Chapter 5.

User-Agent

Nearly all browsers today send the User-Agent field to identify themselves to the server. Here is a list of values sent by the popular browsers:

- Mozilla
- NCSA Mosaic for the X Windows System
- Lynx
- IBM WebExplorer
- NCSA Mosaic for Windows
- WinMosaic
- MacWeb
- NetCruiser
- Enhanced NCSA Mosaic
- CERN-LineMode

NOTE

Netscape Navigator sends the `Mozilla` User-Agent field. According to the documentation, "it's spelled N-e-t-s-c-a-p-e, but it's pronounced 'Mozilla.'"

In addition, many Web spiders and robots use the User-Agent field to identify themselves:

- `WebCrawler`
- `Lycos`
- `MOMspider`
- `EIT Link Verifier Robot`

Some browsers do not conform to the User-Agent field syntax defined in the HTTP specifications. According to the specifications, the format should be:

`Product Name/Version Number`

Here are some examples of product names used by the nonconformist browsers:

- `MacMosaic 2.0.0 a17`
- `NCSA Mosaic Version 2.0.0a9 for Windows`
- `NetManage Chameleon Mosaic+ 4.03`

Because these browsers include their version numbers in the product name portion of the value, every new version of the software appears to be a completely new product. Beware of these anomalies. They can screw up statistical analyses that are based on the standard format of User-Agent fields.

Some browsers don't send the User-Agent field. Unfortunately, it's difficult to tell you which they are, because—well, you guessed it, they don't send their names. However, on rare occasions you'll find clues that identify these browsers (see "A Prodigy Anecdote" sidebar).

Besides using the User-Agent field for statistical purposes, it can also be used to return different responses based on the values in that field. The sample CGI script in Listing 6-1 returns an HTML document, the contents of which are based on the value of the User-Agent field. For now, try not to get embroiled in the perl code itself. Chapter 9 is devoted to CGI, and the script

A Prodigy Anecdote

Prodigy began offering its users access to the World Wide Web in February, 1995, when it provided them with a Web browser. We were curious whether our site would experience an influx of traffic from Prodigy users, and were surprised to find no requests showing `Prodigy` as the User-Agent. It turns out that for the first month that the browser was available, it did not provide a User-Agent field when making requests. However, we were still able to determine which connections were being made from the Prodigy browser. How? Due to Prodigy's unique interface to the Internet, all requests from Prodigy users came from a limited number of machines, all of which were located in the prodigy.com domain. When we looked at the access logs, we noticed requests coming from machines with hostnames ending in *prodigy.com*. We couldn't use the User-Agent field to determine whether Prodigy users hit our site, but the remote hostname was a dead giveaway.

contains plenty of comments that explain exactly what is happening (comment lines are preceded by a #).

Listing 6–1. **A sample User-Agent CGI script. This script returns an HTML document based on the value of the User-Agent field.**

```
#!/usr/bin/perl
# File Name: user_agent.pl

# Grab the User-Agent field from the environment
$client = $ENV{'HTTP_USER_AGENT'};

# Print out the Content-Type of the following document. It will
# be an HTML document.
print( "Content-type: text/html\n" );

# End the Header Fields information and begin the Content-Body
print( "\n" );
```

```
# Send the <html> and <head> tags
print( "<html>\n" );
print( "<head>\n" );

# Send a <title> tag.
print( "<title> Sample User-Agent CGI Script </title>\n" );

# Close the <head> tag and open the <body> tag
print( "</head>\n" );
print( "<body>\n" );

# Print out an <h1> line at the begin for the document.
print( "<h1>Greetings!</h1>\n" );

# Break the User-Agent field into its two parts.
($product_name, $version_number) = split ("/", $client);

# Check and see if it is Netscape (Mozilla is the User-Agent field
# that Netscape uses)
if ($product_name =~ /Mozilla/)
{
   # The client is Netscape
   print( "Congratulations, you are running Netscape.<br>\n" );

   # Check the version number to see if the user has an older version
   if ( ($version_number =~ /0\.9/) ||
        ($version_number =~ /1\.0/) )
   {
      # They are using an older version.
     print( "You should upgrade to the newer, more fun version though<br>\n" );
   }
}
```

```
# Check and see if they are running a version of Mosaic
elsif ($product_name =~ /Mosaic/i)
{
   # See if they are using NCSA Mosaic
   if ($product_name =~ /NCSA/i)
   {
     # Yup, they are.
     print( "Ah, good old Mosaic.  Still good enough for you?<br>\n" );
   }
   else
   {
     # They must be running an derived version of Mosaic
     print( "How many different Mosaic spin-offs are there?<br>\n" );
   }
}

# Check and see if they are running Lynx
elsif ($product_name =~ /Lynx/)
{
   print( "I guess this cruises along a lot faster than those hideous\n" );
   print( "Motif hogs, but alas, no images<br>\n");
}

# Check if they are running WebExplorer
elsif ($product_name =~ /WebExplorer/)
{
   print( "Cool Nuns in that commercial, eh?\n" );
   print( "At least it's better than Windows.<br>\n");
}

# Check if they are running Arena
elsif ($product_name =~ /Arena/)
{
   print( "HTML 3.0 is so cool! And Arena is funky-looking.\n" );
}
```

```
# Unknown browser type
else
{
   print( "Hm.  That's an unusual client.\n" );
   print( "Less than 1% of users use whatever the heck it is...<br>\n");
}

# Close the <body> tag
print( "</body>\n" );
```

Referer

More and more browsers have begun to send the Referer field. Here is a list of clients that currently use this field:

Netscape
Lynx
Spyglass Enhanced Mosaic
MacMosaic
AIR Mosaic
OmniWeb
O'Reilly Mosaic
Emacs-W3
internetMCI
Ventana Mosaic
CERN LineMode
PipeWeb
MidasWWW
Charlotte
Digital Mosaic
NEC MosaicView
AT&T Enhanced Mosaic
NOV*IX Mosaic
Internet Commander
Quarterdeck Mosaic
WebExplorer
MacWeb
IWENG (America Online)

NOTE

Referer. Hmm. Even though spell-checkers and dictionaries tell us it's r-e-f-e-r-r-e-r, this HTTP specification only uses one *r* in the middle. Incorrect as it may be, you must conform to the specification, or else the servers won't understand. (Either this is the revenge of a programmer who flunked spelling, or just the result of his ignorance.)

Based on this information—as well as some access log hacks that we will explain in Chapter 10—you can determine which pages are generating the most links to your site. For example, the following list identifies which pages at which sites accounted for the ten highest number of hits to **http://www.netgen.com/sis** during a six-hour period.

Top-10 Pages

1. **http://www.mit.edu:8001/services/sis/sports.html**
2. **http://www.yahoo.com/Entertainment/Sports/Basketball/NBA/**
3. **http://www.mit.edu:8001/services/sis/NBA/NBA.html**
4. **http://www.mit.edu:8001/services/sis/NFL/NFL.html**
5. **http://akebono.stanford.edu/yahoo/Entertainment/Sports/Basketball/NBA**
6. **http://www.mit.edu:8001/afs/athena/user/e/r/ericolaf/sports/sports.html**
7. **http://nearnet.gnn.com/gnn/wic/sports.10.html**
8. **http://gnn.com/gnn/wic/sports.10.html**
9. **http://wizard.spry.com/hotlists/SPORTS.HTML**
10. **http://www.medio.net/Sports/general.html**

From

More and more browsers are supporting the From field. Here are the latest browsers that currently support the From field:

MacMosaic	NetCruiser	CERN LineMode Browser
Lynx	AIR Mosaic	Mac Netscape

Versions of Netscape prior to version 1.0 sent the From header as well, but current versions do not. The original Netscape beta (version 0.9) was one of the first browsers to send the From field. Most people didn't know that the browser was sending this information and there was a brouhaha over allegations of privacy invasion. People wanted to be anonymous; they didn't like the browser sending their e-mail addresses and identifying them. By the next release, this feature was removed.

Here is an example of a request from Lynx that uses the From header field:

```
GET / HTTP/1.0
Accept: text/html
User-Agent:  Lynx/2.0.12  libwww/2.09
From:  erichard@netgen.com
```

Accept

Many browsers use the Accept header field, but few of them actually use the Accept header to send relevant information. Table 6-1 shows examples of values that various browsers send in their Accept fields.

Table 6–1. Sample Accept Headers for the Lynx, Mosaic, and Netscape Browsers

Browser	Accept Headers
Lynx	Accept: */*
	Accept: application/x-wais-source
	Accept: application/html
	Accept: text/plain
	Accept: text/html
	Accept: www/mime
Mosaic	Accept: */*
	Accept: text/plain
	Accept: application/html
	Accept: text/html
	Accept: audio/basic
	Accept: image/gif
	Accept: image/jpeg
	Accept: image/tiff
	Accept: video/mpeg
	Accept: application/postscript
Netscape	Accept: */*
	Accept: image/gif
	Accept: image/x-xbitmap
	Accept: image/jpeg

The values in Table 6-1 seem quite relevant, and you may wonder why we said they were not very useful. Unfortunately, nearly all browsers claim that they accept all Content-Types (that is what `Accept: */*` means). And they actually do accept all types, but that does not mean they know how to handle all types. When one of these browsers encounters a type that it doesn't know how to deal with, it asks the user if he or she would like to save the file to disk. For this reason, the Accept field really isn't useful for determining which types of data to send. In addition, none of the major browsers send quality factors for the types they do list. That makes it impossible to even prioritize between different Content-Types.

Of course, there is a workaround. If you ignore the */* Accept field value, you can use the Accept fields to do things that are at least somewhat useful.

Listing 6-2 shows a sample CGI script that returns either a GIF or a JPEG, depending on the value in the Accept header field of the browser. This script must be put in the CGI directory of your server. For example, if you name the script **images**, and the URLs beginning with *cgi-bin* are for your CGI directory, the URL for an image named *picture* would be:

```
http://your.server.name/cgi-bin/images/picture
```

The specification provides an algorithm for servers to handle this type of content negotiation themselves, but none of the major servers have been programmed to do this yet. They simply ignore the Accept header fields. For now, we use perl code to handle these negotiations, and you can too. If you want to use the code in Listing 6-2, be sure to change the line that defines `$images_dir` to reflect the location of stored images on your own server. The sample code fully implements the HTTP Negotiation Algorithm. After you take a look at the script itself, we'll show you ways you might use it.

Listing 6–2. **A sample Accept CGI script. It returns either a GIF or JPEG Accept field of the browser. This code fully implements the HTTP Negotiation Algorithm.**

```
#!/usr/bin/perl
# File Name: accept_image.pl

# This is the name of the directory where all the images should
# be retrieved from.
$images_dir = "/usr/local/etc/httpd/root/images";
```

```
# This is the name of the graphic which should be retrieved
# This file is assumed to be located under the directory
# specified in imagesdir.
$graphic_name = $ENV{'PATH_INFO'};

# Get the Accept header from the environment.  It is a comma-
# delimited list of Content-Types.  Separate this into its
# elements.
@accept  = (split ("," , $ENV{'HTTP_ACCEPT'}));

# Initialize variables
$accept_gif = 0;
$accept_jpeg = 0;

# Check to see if the client accepts GIFs or JPEGs and if they
# have a quality value associated with them.
foreach $type (@accept)
{
   if ($type =~ /image\/gif/)
   {
     # Grab the quality factor if it is available
     if ($type =~ /;\s*q\s*=\s*([\d\.]+)/)
     {
        $accept_gif = $1;
     }
     # Otherwise, default to 1
     else
     {
        $accept_gif = 1;
     }

     # Grab the maximum accepted size if it is available
     if ($type =~ /;\s*mxb\s*=\s*([\d]+)/)
```

```
            {
               $max_gif_size = $1;
            }
            # Otherwise, default to infinity
            else
            {
               $max_gif_size = -1;
            }

         }
         elsif ($type =~ /image\/jpeg/)
         {
            # Grab the quality factor if it is available
            if ($type =~ /;\s*q\s*=\s*([\d\.]+)/)
            {
               $accept_jpeg = $1;
            }
            # Otherwise, default to 1
            else
            {
               $accept_jpeg = 1;
            }
            # Grab the maximum accepted size if it is available
            if ($type =~ /;\s*mxb\s*=\s*([\d]+)/)
            {
               $max_jpeg_size = $1;
            }
            # Otherwise, default to infinity
            else
            {
               $max_jpeg_size = -1;
            }
         }
      }
```

```
# Check to see whether there is a GIF version of the file available
if (-r "$images_dir/$graphic_name.gif")
{
   # The file exists.  Make sure its size isn't larger than the
   # maximum acceptable size
   $gif_size = (stat ("$images_dir/$graphic_name.gif"))[7];

   if (($max_gif_size < 0) || ($gif_size <= $max_gif_size))
   {
      $gif_available = 1;
   }
   else
   {
      $gif_available = 0;
   }
}
else
{
   $gif_available = 0;
}

# Check to see whether a JPEG version of the file is available
if (-r "$images_dir/$graphic_name.jpeg")
{
   # The file exists.  Make sure its size isn't larger than the
   # maximum acceptable size
   $jpeg_size = (stat ("$images_dir/$graphic_name.jpeg"))[7];

   if (($max_jpeg_size < 0) || ($jpeg_size <= $max_jpeg_size))
   {
      $jpeg_available = 1;
   }
   else
```

```
        {
           $jpeg_available = 0;
        }
     }
     else
     {
        $jpeg_available = 0;
     }

     # If neither type of file is available or if the client
     # only accepts one type and it isn't available, return an
     # error message.

     $file_not_available = 0;
     if (($jpeg_available == 0) && ($gif_available == 0))
     {
     #  Neither format available.
       $file_not_available = 1;
     }
     elsif (($accept_jpeg == 0) && ($accept_gif == 0))
     {
     # Neither format accepted.
       $file_not_available = 1;
     }
     elsif ($accept_jpeg && ($accept_gif == 0) && ($jpeg_available == 0))
     {
     #  JPEG not available.
       $file_not_available = 1;
     }
     elsif ($accept_gif && ($accept_jpeg == 0) && ($gif_available == 0))
     {
     # GIF not available
       $file_not_available = 1;
     }
```

```
if ($file_not_available)
{
   print "Content-Type: text/html\n\n";
   print "<html>\n";
   print "<head>\n";
   print "<title>File Not Available</title>\n";
   print "</head>\n";
   print "<body>\n";
   print "<hr>\n";
   print "No acceptable image was available.\n";
   print "</body>\n";
   exit;
}

# Check to see if the client prefers one type and it's available
if (($accept_gif > $accept_jpeg) && $gif_available)
{
   $send_gif = 1;
}
elsif (($accept_jpeg > $accept_gif) && $jpeg_available)
{
   $send_jpeg = 1;
}
# OK, the client has no preferences over what is available
else
{
    # The client wants both types and both are available.
    # All else being equal, send the smaller file.
     if (($jpeg_available && $gif_available) &&
          ($accept_jpeg && $accept_gif))
    {
         # The JPEG is smaller.  Send it.
         if ($jpeg_size < $gif_size)
```

```
            {
               $send_jpeg = 1;
            }
            # The GIF is smaller. Send it.
            elsif ($gif_size < $jpeg_size)
            {
               $send_gif = 1;
            }
            # They are the same size.  Just send the JPEG
            else
            {
               $send_jpeg = 1;
            }
         }elsif ($jpeg_available)
      {
         $send_jpeg = 1;
      }
      else
      {
         $send_gif = 1;
      }
   }

   if ($send_jpeg)
   {
      # The client wants a JPEG, so let's give it to them
      print "Content-Type: image\/jpeg\n\n";
      $image_file = "$images_dir/$graphic_name.jpeg";
   }
   else
   {
      # The client wants a GIF, so let's give it to them
      print "Content-Type: image\/gif\n\n";
      $image_file = "$images_dir/$graphic_name.gif";
   }
```

```
# Send the file
undef $/;
open(IMG, $image_file);
while(<IMG>)
{
  print;
}
```

To show how this script uses the Accept header, let's assume that there are two files on www.netgen.com with the following names and sizes:

/netgen/httpd/root/images/netgen.logo.gif	2,130 bytes
/netgen/httpd/root/images/netgen.logo.jpeg	3,096 bytes

If you make a request for netgen.logo using the CGI script, and you only send an `Accept: image/gif` field, the server will respond by returning the GIF file:

```
GET /cgi/accept-image.pl/netgen.logo HTTP/1.0
Accept: image/gif

HTTP/1.0 200 Document follows
MIME-Version: 1.0
Server: CERN/3.0pre6
Date: Saturday, 18-Mar-95 00:18:21 GMT
Content-Type: image/gif
Content-Length: 2130

...
```

If you make a request through the CGI script for netgen.logo and send only an `Accept: image/jpeg` field, the server will respond by returning the JPEG file:

```
GET /cgi/accept-image.pl/netgen.logo HTTP/1.0
Accept: image/jpeg

HTTP/1.0 200 Document follows
MIME-Version: 1.0
Server: CERN/3.0pre6
```

```
Date: Saturday, 18-Mar-95 00:22:01 GMT
Content-Type: image/jpeg
Content-Length: 3096

...
```

If you send two Accept headers, one for image/gif and one for image/jpeg, it will default to sending a GIF, because the GIF is smaller.

```
GET /cgi/accept-image.pl/netgen.logo HTTP/1.0
Accept: image/gif
Accept: image/jpeg

HTTP/1.0 200 Document follows
MIME-Version: 1.0
Server: CERN/3.0pre6
Date: Saturday, 18-Mar-95 00:16:43 GMT
Content-Type: image/gif
Content-Length: 2130

...
```

If you send two Accept headers, one for image/gif and one for image/jpeg, but you provide a quality factor of 0.9 for the JPEG Content-Type, it will send the GIF instead of the JPEG, because the GIF quality factor defaults to 1 when no other factor value is provided.

```
GET /cgi/accept-image.pl/netgen.logo HTTP/1.0
Accept: image/gif
Accept: image/jpeg; q=.9

HTTP/1.0 200 Document follows
MIME-Version: 1.0
Server: CERN/3.0pre6
Date: Saturday, 18-Mar-95 00:23:54 GMT
Content-Type: image/gif
Content-Length: 2130

...
```

If you send two Accept headers, one for image/gif and one for image/jpeg, but you specify a maximum file size of 100 bytes for the JPEG Content-Type, it will send a GIF instead of the JPEG, because the GIF's maximum file size defaults to infinity when no other maximum value is provided and the JPEG that is available is more than 100 bytes long.

```
GET /cgi/accept-image.pl/netgen.logo HTTP/1.0
Accept: image/gif
Accept: image/jpeg; mxb=100

HTTP/1.0 200 Document follows
MIME-Version: 1.0
Server: CERN/3.0pre6
Date: Saturday, 18-Mar-95 00:24:47 GMT
Content-Type: image/gif
Content-Length: 2130

...
```

Accept-Encoding and Accept-Language

The specification includes two standard values for the Accept-Encoding header: *compress* and *gzip*. These values correspond to the compress and GNU zip methods. The idea behind these fields is very similar to the Accept header field. You could use the Accept-Encoding field to indicate that the client understands certain compression mechanisms.

Based on the Accept-Encoding field, a server could compress files before it sends them, because the server would know whether the client could decompress the files. Compressing files means a lot of work for the server, but it saves time when transferring graphics, text, and other files that compress well. On the other end, the client decompresses the files automatically.

At this time, however, none of the major browsers use the Accept-Encoding field because no major servers are programmed to pay any attention to the values in this field.

The Accept-Language field could be used to notify the server that the client understands certain languages. Based on this information, the server could determine what to send in the response. However, as is the case with the other Accept header fields, none of the major browsers use the Accept-

Language field because no major servers are programmed to pay any attention to its values.

Because the Internet is a global network, it would not be unreasonable for sites to provide versions of the same resource in different languages. In Chapter 4 we explained how you might guess the URL for each resource, but it would be infinitely easier for the user if browsers indicated a language preference. Then the script could select the appropriate resource automatically.

The code shown in Listing 6-2 could be modified to support content negotiation based on the Accept-Encoding or Accept-Language field. To do this, you would have to substitute the name of the header field on which the negotiation is based with acceptable values appropriate to the field, and delete the code that checks for maximum file size because it is not applicable to the Accept-Encoding or Accept-Language field.

If-Modified-Since

The If-Modified-Since header field is very useful for caching applications that only want to retrieve a document if it has changed since it was last stored in the cache. Following are two examples that show how to use the If-Modified-Since field.

The first example shows a conditional request in which the resource has not been modified since the given date, so the CERN server returns a `Not Modified` response. The Last-Modified header is also included in the response:

```
GET /sis/sports.html HTTP/1.0
If-Modified-Since: Fri Mar 24 21:00:00 1995

HTTP/1.0 304 Not modified
MIME-Version: 1.0
Server: CERN/3.0pre6
Date: Saturday, 25-Mar-95 02:04:24 GMT
Content-Type: text/html
Content-Length: 2070
Last-Modified: Thursday, 02-Mar-95 07:27:44 GMT

Connection closed by foreign host.
```

In the second example, the resource was modified after the If-Modified-Since date and the document is successfully returned.

```
GET /sis/sports.html HTTP/1.0
If-Modified-Since: Wed Mar 01 21:00:00 1995

HTTP/1.0 200 Document follows
MIME-Version: 1.0
Server: CERN/3.0pre6
Date: Saturday, 25-Mar-95 02:05:15 GMT
Content-Type: text/html
Content-Length: 2070
Last-Modified: Thursday, 02-Mar-95 07:27:44 GMT

<title>Sports Information Server</title>
<img src = "banner.gif" alt = "WWW Sports Information Service"><br>
<hr>
. . .
<hr>
<h5>Copyright 1995 net.Genesis Corporation.  All rights reserved.  Any
duplication or redistribution is prohibited.</h5>

Connection closed by foreign host.
```

When the NCSA server responds with a `Not Modified` status, it does not include the Content-Type, Content-Length, or Last-Modified header fields:

```
HTTP/1.0 304 Not modified
Date: Saturday, 18-Mar-95 07:57:06 GMT
Server: NCSA/1.3
MIME-version: 1.0
```

The same is true for the Netsite Commerce server, which has a slightly different explanation for status code 304 and doesn't include the MIME-version header field either:

```
HTTP/1.0 304 Use local copy
Server: Netsite-Commerce/1.0
Date: Saturday, 18-Mar-95 07:57:55 GMT
```

6.1.3 The Response: Status Codes

We covered the status codes and their meanings in Chapter 5 (Section 5.2.3) and, practically speaking, there isn't a lot you can do with them. However, a couple of status codes are worth mentioning. Here is an example of how HTTP authentication looks when you request a document without authorization:

```
GET /Wired/ HTTP/1.0


HTTP/1.0 401 Unauthorized
Date: Thursday, 16-Mar-95 19:03:06 GMT
Server: HotWired's Master Blaster 1.3
MIME-version: 1.0
Content-type: text/html
WWW-Authenticate: Basic realm="HotWired!"

....
```

When browsers see a 401 status code, they usually prompt the user for authentication. When the user submits this information, the browser attempts to make the request again, and this time it includes the Authorization header field. Currently, the Basic Access Authentication Scheme is the only means of providing authentication information via HTTP, and it should not be considered a means of securing data. The username and password are not sent in the clear, but they are minimally encrypted and can be decrypted easily.

Here is an example of accessing the same information using the Authorization header:

```
GET /Wired/ HTTP/1.0
Authorization: Basic ZXJpY2hhcmQ6VGVzdA==
```

Every time you try to access a page that requires authentication, the server returns a 401 status code. In general, your browser recognizes this status code and prompts you for your name and password. It then re-requests the same document, using this information in the Authorization header. Once you provide your name and password, most browsers cache this information—that is, they remember your name and password and automatically try them the next time the server returns a 401 status code. Only if the name and password fail will the client prompt the user again. By using this mechanism, browsers hide most of the repeat requests actually made to handle authentication.

The two redirection status codes (301–Permanent and 302–Temporary) are also used frequently. Redirection codes let the client know that a resource has moved and that it is now available at a specified URI. Redirection status codes are often used in CGI scripts. As you will see in Chapter 9, CGI scripts are allowed to return a redirection.

6.1.4 Object: Content-Type

Generally, the Content-Type of the Entity-Body is determined by the server. Most servers use the file extension to determine what the Content-Type of the Entity-Body is. For example, a server can tell that a file ending in .gif belongs to the image/gif Content-Type. Table 6-2 shows the default translation table used by NCSA Mosaic.

Each of the major servers allow you to select the default Content-Type to be used if the extension is unknown or there is no extension. Most servers default to either text/plain or text/html, but any values can be used. To prevent any ambiguity about what Content-Type header value should be sent with an object, it is wise to include an extension with files.

Table 6–2. The Default Translation Table Used by NCSA Mosaic

Extensions	Content-Type
ai, eps, ps	application/postscript
rtf	application/rtf
tex	application/x-tex
zip	application/zip
tar	application/x-tar
au snd	audio/basic
wav	audio/x-wav
gif	image/gif
jpeg, jpg, jpe	image/jpeg
tiff, tif	image/tiff
html, htm	text/html
txt	text/plain
mpeg, mpg, mpe	video/mpeg
avi	video/x-msvideo

Most Content-Types are pretty uninteresting in terms of their application, but a few can be used to do really interesting things.

Multipart Content-Types allow you to send multiple objects in response to a single HTTP request. As discussed in Chapter 5 ("Entity Headers" in Section 5.1.6), all multipart Content-Types have a required *boundary* parameter that specifies the delimiter between each part of the object.

Using the *multipart/mixed* Content-Type, you can send multiple, separate objects, each of which is handled by the client. Currently, no browsers support this Content-Type. However, the Netscape Navigator 1.1 beta supports the experimental multipart/x-mixed-replace Content-Type. Like the other multipart Content-Types, it can send multiple objects in a single response. However, the meaning of this experimental type is that each object replaces the previous one, the idea being that you can use this Content-Type to generate documents that are updated dynamically. This way, you could provide a resource—sports scores, for example—that updates itself automatically. Each time the page changes, a new version can be sent that replaces the previous version.

Listing 6-3 shows an example of a response from a server using this experimental multipart/x-mixed-replace Content-Type. In this example, a series of HTML documents are sent in turn, and each replaces the previous one. Viewed in Netscape 1.1b1, the process creates an HTML document that changes over time. Listing 6-3 shows the HTTP response as received by the client (browser). The browser renders the data from this response to create three documents, each replacing the last. Figure 6-2 shows the first two of three documents generated by this script.

NOTE

In this example, the *boundary* parameter "To-err-is-human-to-moo-bovine" is used as an example and is not inherent in the Content-Type.

Listing 6–3. **Response from a server using the multipart/x-mixed-replace Content-Type**

```
HTTP/1.0 200 OK
Content-type: multipart/x-mixed-replace; boundary=To-err-is-human-to-moo-
bovine

--To-err-is-human-to-moo-bovine
```

```
Content-Type: text/html

<h1>Quote of the moment...</h1>
<hr>
When aiming for the common denominator,
be prepared for the occasional division by zero.

<hr>

--To-err-is-human-to-moo-bovine
Content-type: text/html

<h1>Quote of the moment...</h1>
<hr>
If you're not part of the solution, then you're part of the precipitate.

<hr>

--To-err-is-human-to-moo-bovine
Content-type: text/html

<h1>Quote of the moment...</h1>
<hr>
Artificial Intelligence is the study of how to make real computers act like
the ones in movies.

<hr>

--To-err-is-human-to-moo-bovine--
```

Another interesting Content-Type is specified in RFC 1437. It defines the MIME encoding for matter-transport/sentient-life-form. (No kidding, get RFC 1437 from **http://www.netgen.com/book**.) No browser currently supports this Content-Type, but we mention it here to show the full flexibility of HTTP and MIME.

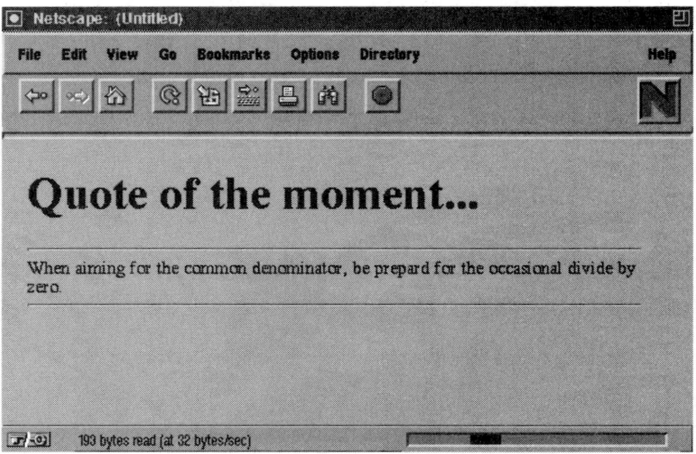

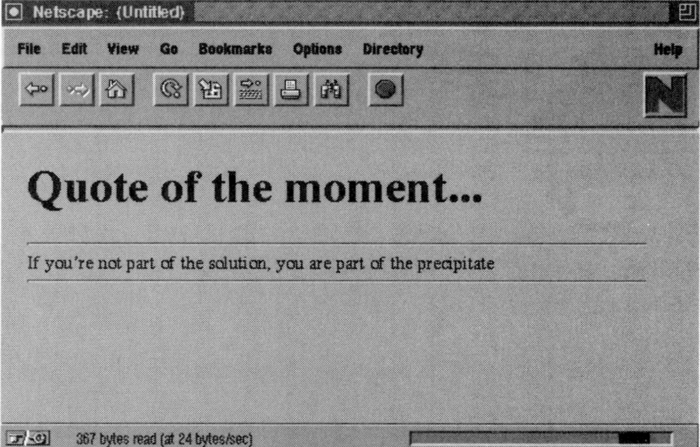

Figure 6–2 "Quote of the Moment," the first two of three documents returned from the server using the multipart/x-mixed-replace Content-Type. This is the rendering of what is shown in Listing 6-3.

6.2 Simulating a Web Client via Telnet

One of the most useful mechanisms for learning about HTTP is by acting as a client and sending requests to an HTTP server manually. To do this, you write a bunch of code that uses sockets to connect to the server, lets you send a request, gets the response, and closes the connection. Or you could use telnet to do the grunge work.

Telnet, a standard UNIX program, allows you to connect to and communicate with a remote machine. Generally, the program is used to log on to a remote machine and send commands to it. However, because you can specify the port number through which you communicate, you can use telnet as your interface to remote HTTP servers.

For example, suppose you want to retrieve the resource specified by **http://www.netgen.com/**. Let's go over the four steps of the HTTP transaction and see how to do them through telnet.

Step 1 is to connect to the server. This is done by running telnet and specifying the hostname and port number of the machine you are connecting to. In our example, the hostname is www.netgen.com and the port is 80 (remember, 80 is the default port for HTTP servers).

This opens a connection to the remote machine:

```
> telnet www.netgen.com 80
Trying 204.57.36.200...
Connected to www.netgen.com.
Escape character is '^]'.
```

Step 2 is to send a request. Looking back at the format of a request, the first line has to be a Request-Line of one of the following types:

- Simple request: METHOD URI
- Full request: METHOD URI HTTP-VERSION

Let's start out simple and use a simple request. Since you are trying to get the contents of a resource, you should use the GET method. The partial URI you should send is just "/". You would type in the following line:

```
GET /
```

When you hit Enter, the server processes your request, recognizes that it is a simple request, and returns the data.

Moving on to a full request, the method and URI don't change. Let's use "HTTP/1.0" for the version number. You would type the following line:

```
GET / HTTP/1.0
```

When you press Enter this time, nothing should happen because the server knows you might be sending header information and it is still waiting for you to end your request. For this example, we won't include any header information, so just press Enter again to send a blank line. The server will process your request.

Step 3 is to send a response. As soon as you end your request (by hitting Enter in a simple request or sending a blank line in a full request), the server processes your request and sends back a response. The response appears on your screen. In the case of a full request, the server sends a response header first. It contains many of the header fields that have been mentioned.

For both request types, the server next begins to send the Entity-Body. It, too, appears on the screen. Remember that any binary objects you request—images, videos, etc.—appear on the screen as well (that can be a mess!).

Step 4 is to close the connection. After the response is sent, the server generally kills the connection.

NOTE

Doing this via telnet is no different from what a client such as Mosaic, WebExplorer, or Netscape does. Your browser sends exactly this kind of information every time you follow a link. After you've entered these commands manually a few times, you'll come to appreciate all the work your browser does for you.

Let's look at some examples. We'll use telnet to access three sites, each of which runs a different server. In the first example, you'll telnet into www.netgen.com, where a CERN server is running, and request the / resource:

```
> telnet www.netgen.com 80
Trying 204.57.36.200...
Connected to www.netgen.com.
Escape character is '^]'.
HEAD / HTTP/1.0
```

```
HTTP/1.0 200 Document follows
MIME-Version: 1.0
Server: CERN/3.0pre6
Date: Thursday, 16-Mar-95 17:27:11 GMT
Content-Type: text/html
Content-Length: 2848
Last-Modified: Thursday, 02-Mar-95 23:05:33 GMT
Connection closed by foreign host.
```

In the second example, you'll telnet into www.mit.edu, where an NCSA server is running, and request the /home-pages.html resource:

```
> telnet www.mit.edu 8001
Trying 18.181.0.21...
Connected to ANXIETY-CLOSET.MIT.EDU.
Escape character is '^]'.
HEAD /home-pages.html HTTP/1.0

HTTP/1.0 200 OK
Date: Thursday, 16-Mar-95 17:31:11 GMT
Server: NCSA/1.3
MIME-version: 1.0
Content-Type: text/html
Last-modified: Tuesday, 14-Mar-95 14:22:34 GMT
Content-Length: 91975
Connection closed by foreign host.
```

In the third and last example, you'll telnet into www.playboy.com, where a Netsite Communications server is running, and request the /image/ bunny_square.gif resource:

```
> telnet www.playboy.com 80
Trying 204.71.64.65...
Connected to www.playboy.com.
Escape character is '^]'.
HEAD /images/bunny_square.gif HTTP/1.0
```

```
HTTP/1.0 200 OK
Server: Netsite-Communications/1.0
Date: Thursday, 16-Mar-95 17:36:52 GMT
Last-modified: Monday, 19-Sep-94 23:42:59 GMT
Content-Length: 639
Content-Type: image/gif

Connection closed by foreign host.
```

6.3 Sample Code for Creating a Full Request

Listing 6-4 shows you some sample code for creating a full request using the GET method. The response is included so that you can see the whole flow of the connection. Making an HTTP connection in perl is very straightforward. The library distributed with perl, called chat2.pl, makes TCP connections very simple. If you want to make an HTTP request from some other perl program, you can call this subroutine. We'll show you an example of how that's done in the next section. (We will use this code in Chapter 12 to implement a more fully functional client.)

Listing 6–4. **An HTTP GET subroutine. Given a host, port, and path, it retrieves the specified resource.**

```
# File Name: http_get.pl
# Require that the code for the chat2.pl package is used
require 'chat2.pl';

sub HTTP_get
{
  # This subroutine should be called with arguments of the host, the
  # port and the path.  Another routine would split a URL into these
  # parts.  For example, to retrieve http://www.netgen.com/
  # one would call:  &HTTP_get("www.netgen.com", 80, "/");
  local( $host, $port, $path ) = @_;

  # Open the connection to the server
```

```
if (!&chat'open_port( $host, $port ))
{
   print $!;
}

# Send the Request-Line
&chat'print( "GET $path HTTP/1.0\r\n" );

# Send the Header fields.
&chat'print( "User-Agent: net.Genesis perl HTTP_GET/0.5\r\n" );

# Send the CR LF line to indicate the end of the request
&chat'print( "\r\n" );

# Repeatedly listen to the connection until either the connection
# closes or it is quiet for 5 seconds.  Put the whole response in
# the variable, $response
while ( length( $tmp = &chat'expect( 5, '(.|\n)+', '$&') ) )
{
  $response .= $tmp;
}

# If the response contains two blank lines (either just newlines or
# newlines and carriage returns, depending on the server) then
# split it into headers and the body of the document

if( $response =~ /\r?\n\r?\n/ )
{
   $headers = $';
   $document = $';
}

# Otherwise, assume it's responding as a HTTP/0.9 request and treat
# the whole response as the document
```

```
  else
  {
     $headers = '';
     $document = $response;
  }

  # Return the headers and document
  ($headers, $document);
}
```

Using this code, you could build a very simple command-line HTTP client which could make HTTP requests and retrieve the actual text of the responses. This way, you could analyze the results of sending GET requests to servers.

6.4 A Simple HTTP Client

Listing 6-5 shows you one way to code the simple command-line HTTP client we just mentioned. This client makes a request by using the GET method, and the response is displayed. This is a *very* simple client with a limited purpose. Later, in Chapter 12, you will learn how to create a much more versatile client.

Listing 6–5. A simple command-line HTTP client

```
#!/usr/bin/perl
# File Name: simple_client.pl

# Use the file containing the HTTP_get subroutine
require "http_get.pl";

# Get the parameters of the connection from the command line
( $hostname, $port, $url ) = @ARGV;

# Tell the user what we are doing
print "Contacting host: $hostname\n";
print "Connecting to port: $port\n";
print "Retrieving resource: $url\n";
```

```
# Actually perform the request
( $headers, $body ) = &HTTP_get( $hostname, $port, $url );

print "\n";
# Display the headers if there are any
if ( $headers )
{
  print "Retrieved the Response-Headers\n";
  print "--------- --- ----------------\n";
  print $headers;
  print "\n";
}
else
{
  print "No Response Headers Received.\n";
}

print "\n";
#Display the returned object, if any
if ($body)
{
  print "Retrieved the Object-Body\n";
  print "--------- --- -----------\n";
  print $body;
  print "\n";
}
else
{
  print "No Object-Body Received.\n";
}
```

Following are two examples of what might be returned. The first example retrieves the Sports Information Service at the net.Genesis site:

```
> simple-client.pl www.netgen.com 80 /sis/

Contacting host: www.netgen.com
Connecting to port: 80
Retrieving resource: /sis/

Retrieved the Response-Headers
--------- --- ----------------
HTTP/1.0 200 Document follows
MIME-Version: 1.0
Server: CERN/3.0pre6
Date: Saturday, 18-Mar-95 21:00:15 GMT
Content-Type: text/html
Content-Length: 2070
Last-Modified: Thursday, 02-Mar-95 07:27:44 GMT

Retrieved the Object-Body
--------- --- -----------
<title>Sports Information Server</title>
...
```

The second example shows what an error in the request looks like:

```
> simple-client.pl www.netgen.com 80 /gimme-an-error

Contacting host: www.netgen.com
Connecting to port: 80
Retrieving resource: /gimme-an-error

Retrieved the Response-Headers
--------- --- ----------------
HTTP/1.0 404 Not found - file doesn't exist or is read protected [even tried
multi]
MIME-Version: 1.0
Server: CERN/3.0pre6
```

```
Date: Saturday, 18-Mar-95 21:00:56 GMT
Content-Type: text/html
Content-Length: 248

Retrieved the Object-Body
--------- --- -----------
<HTML>
<HEAD>
<TITLE>Error</TITLE>
</HEAD>
<BODY>
<H1>Error 404</H1>

Not found - file doesn't exist or is read-protected [even tried multi]

<P><HR><ADDRESS><A HREF="http://info.cern.ch/httpd_3.0/">CERN httpd
3.0pre6</A></ADDRESS>
</BODY>
</HTML>
```

6.5 A Simple HTTP Server

Listing 6-6 shows you the perl code for a very simple HTTP server with which to view the contents of all incoming requests. It does not actually serve documents, but it is very useful for viewing the complete text of requests being submitted by clients. This code is meant more as a utility than as a programming exercise. Do not get confused by the programming details. Instead, use the program as a tool to see the HTTP requests being made. Following the listing is the output generated by the server when it is contacted. We will get into more details of writing a server in Chapter 13.

Listing 6–6. A simple HTTP server that allows you to view the contents of all incoming requests

```
#!/usr/bin/perl
#File Name: simple-httpd.pl
# This is a standard perl library which is required to do socket
# communication.
require 'sys/socket.ph';
```

```
# Allow the user to specify the port to listen on via the command
# line.  If no value is provided, default to port 2345.
($port) = @ARGV;
$port = 2345 unless $port;

# Who is the program running as
$uid = $<;

# Ports numbers under 1024 are reserved and can only be connected
# to by root.
if (($port < 1024) && ($uid != 0))
{
    print "\n";
    print "Sorry, but you must run this program as root to use ports\n";
    print "less than 1024.\n";
    print "\n";
    exit;
}

# Define the packing format for a socket (don't worry about it)
$sockaddr = 'S n a4 x8';

# Get the system local protocol number for TCP
($name, $aliases, $proto) = getprotobyname('tcp');

# Get the port number by name if it is specified by name
if ($port !~ /^\d+$/) {
    ($name, $aliases, $port) = getservbyport($port, 'tcp');
}

# Report the port to the user
print "Port = $port\n";
```

```
# Generate the packed socket
$this = pack($sockaddr, &AF_INET, $port, "\0\0\0\0");

# Make the filehandle NS unbuffered
select(NS);
$| = 1;
select(stdout);

# Make a socket, bind to it, and listen for connections
socket(S, &AF_INET, &SOCK_STREAM, $proto) || die "socket: $!";
bind(S,$this) || die "bind: $!";
listen(S,5) || die "connect: $!";

# Make the socket unbuffered
select(S); $| = 1; select(stdout);

$con = 0;
print "Listening for connection 1....\n";

for(;;) {
    # Accept incoming connections and attach them to filehandle NS
    ($addr = accept(NS,S)) || die $!;

    # Keep track of how many connections you've had.
    $con++;

    # Fork a server to handle the request
    if (($child[$con] = fork()) == 0)
    {
     # Keep track of the current connection number.
     $child_connection = $con;

        print "Child accepts connection $child_connection.\n";
```

```
    # Figure out who the client is.
    ($af,$port,$inetaddr) = unpack($sockaddr,$addr);
    @inetaddr = unpack('C4',$inetaddr);
    print "$af $port @inetaddr\n";

    # Read in the header line from the connection
    $request_line = <NS>;

# Check the Request-Line to determine if it is a simple request
    # or a full request.  Ignore the regexp behind the curtain. :-)
if ($request_line =~ /^([A-Z]+)\s+([\S]+)\s+HTTP\/([\d\.]+)\s*$/)
    {
        # Looks like a full request
      $method = $1;
        $uri = $2;
        $version = $3;

      print "Received a full request\n";
      print "-------- - ------------\n";
      print $request_line;
      print "\n";
    }
elsif ($request_line =~ /^([A-Z]+)\s+([\S]+)\s*$/)
{
        # Looks like a simple request
      $method = $1;
        $uri = $2;

      # Default to HTTP/0.9 for simple requests
        $version = "0.9";

      print "Received a simple request\n";
      print "-------- - --------------\n";
      print $request_line;
}
```

```
else
{
    &status_code(400, "Bad Request");
  }

# Check to make sure it is a valid method
if ($method !~ /(GET|POST|HEAD|PUT|DELETE|LINK|UNLINK)/)
{
    &status_code(400, "Bad Request: Unknown Method $method\n");
}

# Initialize the Content-Length to 0;
$header_field{'content-length'} = 0;

# If the version is anything other than 0.9, watch the
# header-information and wait for a blank line. Then read in
# the Object-Body.
if ($version ne "0.9")
{
    print "Reading Header Fields\n";
       print "------- ------ ------\n";
    while ($header_line = <NS>)
    {
     # Strip off the newline character.
     chop($header_line);

     # A line with just a carriage return indicates the end
     # of the header information.
     if ($header_line eq "\r")
     {
         last;
     }
     # Check to makes sure the line is a valid header
     elsif ($header_line =~ /^\s*([^\:]+)\s*\:\s*(.+)\s*$/)
```

```
    {
        # Grab the field name and value
        $field_name = $1;
        $field_value = $2;

        # Convert the field name to all lowercase so there
        # are no case-sensitivity issues.
        $field_name =~ tr/A-Z/a-z/;

        # Save the value for later
        $header_field{$field_name} = $field_value;

        # Valid header format
        print "$header_line\n";
    }
    else
    {
        # Invalid header format.  Ignore it.
    }

}

print "\n";

# Now read in the body of the message.
$content_length = sprintf("%d", $header_field{'content-length'});

print "Reading Object Body: $content_length Bytes\n";
print "------- ------ ----- ";
print "-" x length($content_length);
print " -----\n";

# Read in $content_length bytes of data.
read (NS, $object_body, $content_length);
```

```
            # Print out the Object-Body
            print "$object_body\n";
            print "\n";
        }

        # Send a Response Header
        &status_code(204, "No Response");

    }

    printf("Listening for connection %d\n",$con+1);
}

sub status_code
{
  local ($code, $message) = @_;

  print "Sending Response-Line\n";
  print "------- -------------\n";

  # Form the Response-Line
  $response_line = "HTTP/1.0 $code $message\n";

  # Send the Response-Line
  print NS $response_line;

  # Send a CR LF string to indicate the end of the headers
  print NS "\r\n";

  print $response_line;
  print "\n";

  print "Closing Connection $child_connection.\n";
```

```
  print "\n";
  close(NS);

  exit
}
```

Here's what happens when you contact the simple server created with the code shown in Listing 6-6:

```
> simple-server.pl

Port = 2345
Listening for connection 1....
Listening for connection 2
Child accepts connection 1.
2 1118 127 0 0 1
Received a full request
-------- - ------------
GET /homepage.html HTTP/1.0

Reading Header Fields
------- ------ ------
User-Agent: Mozilla/1.1b1 (X11; international; Linux 1.1.54 I586)
Pragma: no-cache
Accept: */*
Accept: image/gif
Accept: image/x-xbitma
Accept: image/jpeg

Reading Object-Body: 0 Bytes
------- ------ ----- - -----

Sending Response-Line
------- -------------
HTTP/1.0 401 Unauthorized
```

```
Closing Connection 1.

Listening for connection 3
Child accepts connection 2.
2 1119 10 1 0 1
Received a Full-Request
-------- - ------------
GET /sis/NHL/NHL.html HTTP/1.0

Reading Header Fields
------- ------ ------
Accept: */*
Accept: application/x-wais-source
Accept: application/html
Accept: text/plain
Accept: text/html
Accept: www/mime
Accept: video/mpeg
Accept: image/jpeg
Accept: image/x-tiff
Accept: image/x-rgb
Accept: image/x-xbm
Accept: image/gif
Accept: application/postscript
User-Agent:  Lynx/2.3.7 BETA  libwww/2.14

Reading Object Body: 0 Bytes
------- ------ ----- - -----

Sending Response-Line
------- -------------
HTTP/1.0 401 Unauthorized

Closing Connection 2.
```

HTTP is a powerful protocol which provides you with a tremendous amount of flexibility. Current clients and servers are only tapping into a small portion of the features already described by the specifications, and extensions to HTTP are being proposed regularly to provide more functionality.

CHAPTER 7

An HTML Primer

CHAPTER AT A GLANCE

This chapter is a primer on the basics of HTML coding. After explaining the differences between semantic and literal markup, we cover in detail the HTML 2.0 and 3.0 elements and their respective attributes. We tell what each element and attribute does, and show you the syntax for their use. We also discuss why and when you might use each element or attribute, and list the elements in which another element may appear. It should be noted here that the HTML 3.0 specification is still evolving, so what we provide here is taken from the latest accessible version.

REQUISITES

A basic understanding of the Web and HTML described in Chapter 2.

MORE DETAIL

Chapter 8 provides a basis for understanding HTML design as well as guidelines for its effective use.

Chapter 10 provides hints and tips for designing the structure and HTML for your site.

Chapter 12 provides an actual example of using this knowledge to write an HTTP client which analyzes the content of HTML documents.

The HTML 2.0 Internet Draft (see Appendix C) provides an in-depth definition of the standard and its features.

HTML, the Hypertext Markup Language, is the lifeblood of the World Wide Web. Nearly every page on the Web relies entirely upon HTML to define its appearance. While HTML is efficient and relatively simple to learn, its lack of precise layout control can be confounding to "image-conscious" content providers.

With the advent of new browsers such as Mosaic 2.5, Netscape Navigator 1.1, and the Web Consortium's Arena—all of which support subsets of the HTML 3.0 specification—HTML use is poised to make the leap from HTML 2.0 to 3.0. HTML 2.0 was the first to define forms, while HTML 3.0 focuses on improved layout control. With it, you can create tables and equations, and you get greater flexibility with text flow and formatting. After HTML 3.0 becomes widely implemented, understanding the inherent concepts behind HTML, as well as its subtleties, will be extremely important if you want to become a proficient HTML author.

According to the HTML 3.0 specifications, HTML was guided by the following principles:

- It was meant to be a common language that could be used to "tie together information from widely different sources."
- It was meant to be simple for both HTML authors and programmers to use.
- It was meant to accommodate technological and social changes in the way people use the Web.
- It was meant to provide platform-independent viewing. It is "designed to allow rendering on a very wide range of devices from clunky teletypes to terminals, DOS, Windows, Macs, and high-end workstations, as well as nonvisual media such as speech and Braille."

HTML is currently the most widely publicized of the semantic markup languages. On the Web, browsers such as NSCA Mosaic, Lynx, and the Netscape Navigator render HTML by interpreting the HTML tags and displaying the results to the user. It is important to note that no precise definitions exist for displaying HTML tags. For instance, elements such as Strong and Emphasis appear in the Netscape browser (see Figure 7-1) much differently than they do in the Lynx browser (see Figure 7-2).

As the current draft of the HTML 3.0 specification says, "The Web has acted as a huge exercise in user testing, and we have been able to glean lots of information from the ways people abuse HTML in trying to get a particular effect; as well as from explicit demand for new features. HTML 3.0, as a result,

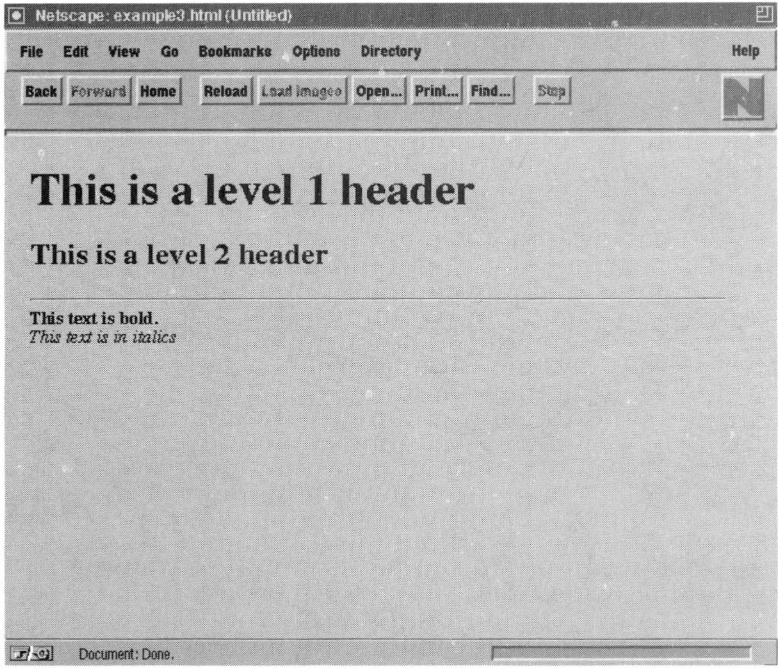

Figure 7–1 A sample page showing two header levels plus some bold (Strong) and italic (Emphasis) body text as rendered by the Netscape browser

includes support for customized lists; fine positioning control with entities like ace; [and] horizontal tabs and horizontal alignment of headers and paragraph text."

To accommodate the Web's widespread, cross-platform use, HTML is intended to be completely browser-independent. Currently, the majority of Web accesses come from graphical browsers such as Mosaic and Netscape. For these browsers, specifying particular fonts would be perfectly valid. Even though graphical browsers seem to receive all the media attention, a significant portion of Web accesses comes from Lynx, a text-only browser (see the "Browser Usage Breakdown" sidebar). Font specifications are useless with text-only browsers like Lynx, since they have very limited control over how they display text.

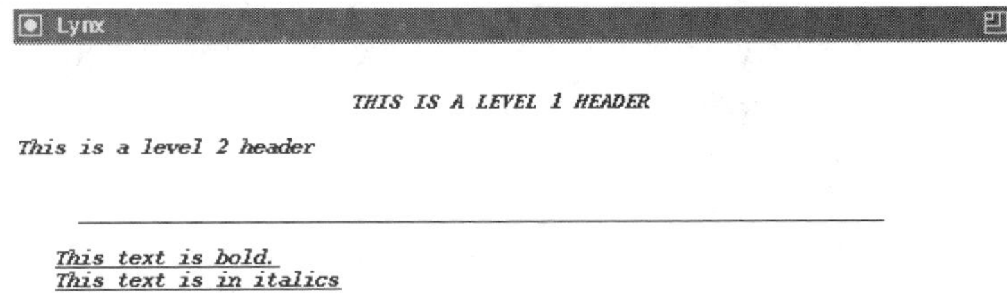

Figure 7–2 Sample page showing two heading levels plus some bold (Strong) and italic (Emphasis) body text as rendered by the Lynx browser.

Browser Usage Breakdown

The percentages shown below are based on a sample size of 260,000 requests registered at the net.Genesis Web site (**http://www.netgen.com**). The data was gathered on April 28, 1995.

Browser	Percentage of Hits (%)
Netscape (all platforms)	66
NCSA Mosaic (all platforms)	10
Lynx	5
WebExplorer	3
Air Mosaic	2
Other	13

A significant portion of Web requests are the result of image downloads. Because the Lynx browser is text-based and does not download images, the five-percent figure shown for Lynx is artificially low.

7.1 Semantic vs. Literal

Markup languages are a method of document layout description. When you use a markup language, page elements are described, or *tagged,* with different layout attributes. Using a markup language, you can define, or *tag,* a piece of text so it appears underlined or in boldface. Many markup language layout controls, or *tags,* appear within documents, such that page-description information is intermixed with actual document text.

In Section 2.4.3, we mentioned the differences between semantic and literal (or physical) markup languages. Literal markup languages contain exact, quantitative information that controls the size, position, line spacing, font, and style of elements on the page. A literal markup language might define a paragraph so it is centered on the page in 18-point Courier bold. Text output to this paragraph from within any program would appear, in theory, in 18-point Courier bold. PostScript is probably the most prolific literal markup language.

PostScript is an incredibly robust and precise document description language, but it has two major shortcomings: its size and complexity. Because PostScript offers such complete layout control, it must be very precise in describing how pages look, and its high level of precision requires daunting amounts of code. That's why PostScript files are so large. Moreover, PostScript is very complicated. A PostScript conversion program is required to generate valid code—most people can't tag PostScript by hand.

On the other hand, semantic markup languages are largely qualitative. Document description is based on the functional definition of the markup rather than precise physical descriptions. A semantic markup language might specify that a particular paragraph be *emphasized,* rather than define it as 18-point Helvetica bold. How that paragraph appears depends entirely on the viewing program's interpretation of the *emphasized* tag.

HTML is a semantic language. If the goal is to tag some text as 18-point Helvetica bold, then HTML most likely fails. But if the goal is for the user to understand how important a particular section is, then HTML does an incredible job. With just a few characters, HTML describes what needs to be done to the text without the tremendous overhead of a literal language.

Ironically, HTML's two main strengths, its simplicity and compactness, can also be considered its two main weaknesses. HTML is a very simple markup language with a small number of easily understood tags to control page layout. That makes HTML very easy to learn, and no specialized converters are required to generate valid HTML code. Most people can begin creating well-formatted HTML documents with no more than one hour of training and a simple text editor. And due to HTML's compactness (most tags are under ten characters in length), the file size of documents with full HTML markup are not much larger than the size of files with plain text alone. The formatting information of an HTML document occupies very little bandwidth "overhead," which is very advantageous given the most users' bandwidth limitations.

Unfortunately, HTML's simplicity and compactness cut down on layout control and flexibility. HTML 2.0, the currently accepted implementation, provides no means of controlling fonts, font sizes, image placement, and text flow, among other things. That ensures document consistency, but it also forces documents to look alike. For some users this is not a concern. They just want the information and don't care what it looks like. Other users and information providers, however, consider graphic presentations crucial. Obviously, the publishers of a conservative business journal would not want their content to look like that of a tabloid newspaper.

7.2 Why Follow Conventions?

Semantic markup languages make for consistent designs, but that doesn't keep people from using the semantic markup to produce the literal effects they want. For example, even though a piece of text is not meant to be a heading, some users mark it as a heading because they know that Netscape makes headings appear in a certain font and point size. The problem with this approach is that HTML rendering depends entirely on the user's browser, and what works with Netscape may not work with Mosaic or dozens of other browsers.

Most of the major browsers behave similarly, but real differences exist in how they handle HTML. If you use browser-specific tricks to achieve effects, you do so at your peril, because browsers that are completely specification-compliant may render your work incorrectly or even incompletely. For example, if you look back at Figure 7-1 and 7-2, you'll see that the Netscape browser renders all H1 elements in a large bold font and left-justifies the text, whereas the Lynx browser centers and capitalizes H1 elements. Unexpected behavior like this is why experienced HTML authors avoid clever *hacks* when they want to produce specific design effects.

NOTE

According to the *Hacker's Dictionary,* a *hack* is "a quick job that produces what is needed, but not well." It's like a *kludge,* "something that works for the wrong reason." Matthew's definition of a *hack* is "a rubber-band solution used when industrial-strength bungee cord would have been better; i.e., a quick and dirty solution to the problem."

At present, at least a dozen Web browsers have a significant user base. What's more, as Netscape's predominance over Mosaic has demonstrated, the "Top Browser" title is highly contestable. Less than a year ago, Mosaic was the "one true browser." Today, Mosaic accounts for less than 20 percent of all accesses. Based on how fast the current breakdown has developed, the coming year could see profound shifts in the browser marketplace. The moral of the story is that writing HTML geared toward the strengths of one browser is not prudent in the long run. The best way to be compatible with tomorrow's browsers is to adhere to common HTML specifications.

By conforming to the word and meaning of the specifications, you will be more likely to produce HTML pages that look good through a variety of browsers and remain stable as specifications and browsers evolve. On the other hand, if you depend on the behavior of today's browsers and abuse HTML elements to make pages look good, your site won't be a reliable one. Your page will likely look bad in some browsers and could be affected dramatically when browsers and the standards evolve.

An *element* in HTML is an identifier for a certain part of an object. An element can specify any number of things, including how a portion of an object is rendered, how the object is linked to different objects, etc. HTML elements have three parts:

- **A beginning tag**. In HTML, beginning tags indicate the element type. They start with an open angle bracket (<) and end with a close angle bracket (>). Between the two brackets is the element name followed by any attributes. For example:

```
<html version="-//IETF//DTD HTML//EN//2.0">
```

- **The content**. Whatever appears between the beginning and ending tags for an element is defined by that element (i.e., marked up). The content of an element may be made up of both text and other HTML elements.
- **An ending tag**. Ending tags start with an open angle bracket followed by a forward slash (</) and end with a close angle bracket (>). For example, the close tag for an HTML element is:

```
</html>
```

Some elements depart from this convention and either have one tag, such as the <P> tag, or have the same beginning and end tag, such as <MARK>.

Most tags have optional or required *attributes* so you can specify the exact meaning of the content. Element attributes allow you to tailor an element to your particular needs. For example, they can be used to specify the alignment of an element. Attributes in HTML are much like parameters for MIME Content-Types, which were discussed in Section 5.1.6. The value of an attribute provides more data about the characteristics of the element with which it is used.

NOTE

The element and attribute names within tags are always case-insensitive. This means that the following tags are considered equivalent: <HTML>, <html>, and <HtMl>. In addition, there is no requirement that the case of the opening and closing tags be the same. Therefore, the following pair of tags is completely valid: <EM>...</eM>. However, it is important to note that while the element and attribute *names* are case-insensitive, the same is not necessarily true of attribute *values.* In particular, the following are *not* equivalent: `<form method="POST">` **and** `<form method="post">`**.**

Every HTML document should begin with an HTML element which specifies that the content of the element should be interpreted as HTML.

Inside the HTML element, the document is divided into two main sections, the head and the body, denoted by the Head and Body elements. The Head element contains all of the meta-information about the actual content of the body. The Body element contains the main content of the document.

These three elements—HTML, Head, and Body—are called *document structure elements*. The remaining elements can be grouped into these categories: anchor (or link) elements, block formatting elements, information type elements, character formatting elements, image elements, list elements, and form elements.

HTML documents that are *written to spec* (i.e., that adhere to the definitions set forth in the specification document) have an HTML element, and within the HTML element are the Head and Body elements, within which are the actual contents of the HTML document.

NOTE

In HTML, the string `<!--` **is seen as the beginning of a comment and** `-->` **is seen as the end of the comment. All text between these strings should be ignored by any browser. This allows users to add**

comments to a document without affecting how it is rendered. For example, these comments might include a description of why certain information was included or omitted, notes about who authored the document and when, or what the document's filename is.

7.3 HTML 2.0 Elements with 3.0 Attribute Extensions

An HTML document is a plain-text document that consists of many formatting elements. As we just discussed, an element is a block of text that is marked with tags that describe the meaning of the text. For example, the Body element identifies the body of an HTML document.

In this section, we define the elements used in creating HTML documents, explain each element's function, and list the attributes that may be used with each element. Attributes that may be used with more than one element are described in the "Common HTML Element Attributes" sidebar so we don't have to repeat the definitions more than once. (You'll find that sidebar at the end of Section 7.3.1.)

HTML 2.0 and HTML 3.0 are currently both *Internet Drafts*. An Internet Draft is a working document of the IETF. Once it has been formalized, it can be accepted as an RFC within six months; otherwise it expires. HTML 3.0, besides introducing a number of new elements, introduces several new attributes for existing elements to extend the scope of the markup language. In this section we cover the elements defined in HTML 2.0 and point out corresponding new attributes defined in HTML 3.0 as extensions to those 2.0 elements. (We talk about elements that are new with HTML 3.0 in Section 7.4.) It should be noted that the HTML 3.0 specification was designed to be backward-compatible with the 2.0 specification.

7.3.1 Document Structure Elements

As mentioned earlier, the HTML Head and Body elements are known as document structure elements. They break the HTML document up into its major parts. Figure 7-3 shows the top-level structure of an HTML document.

HTML

You are not absolutely required to use the HTML element in an HTML document, but it is considered good practice to place the beginning and ending

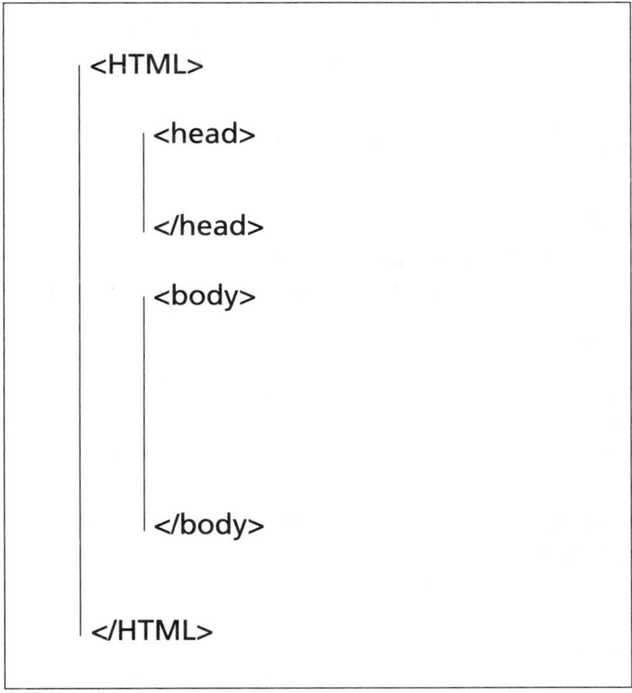

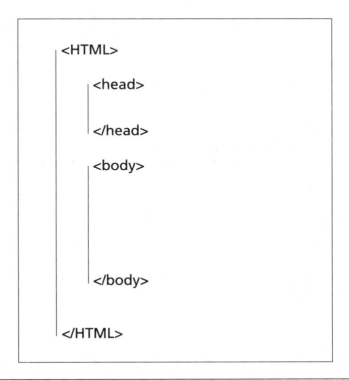

Figure 7–3 The document structure elements of an HTML document

HTML tags at the beginning and end of each document. This way, the browser knows that the document is using HTML. The tags that define the beginning and end of the element appear as follows:

```
<HTML> . . . </HTML>
```

The only elements that are allowed within an HTML element are the Body and Head elements. The HTML element cannot appear within any other elements.

In HTML 2.0, the opening HTML tag may also include the VERSION attribute, as follows:

```
<HTML VERSION=". . .">
```

VERSION is used to identify the exact version of the HTML specifications to which the document conforms. The version 2.0 specification is identified by a specific value, as follows:

```
<HTML VERSION="-//ietf//dtd html//en//2.0">
```

NOTE

Remember, element and attribute names may be either upper- or lowercase, but attribute values are case-sensitive.

In HTML 3.0, the opening tag may include the URN and ROLE attributes in addition to VERSION, as follows:

```
<HTML VERSION=". . ." URN=". . ." ROLE=". . .">
```

The version 3.0 specification is identified by a specific value, as follows (this attribute is rarely used):

```
<HTML VERSION="-//w3o//dtd w3 html 3.0//en">
```

The URN attribute specifies the URN for the document. Since URNs are not formally defined as yet, this field does not have any acceptable values. The ROLE attribute is a list of words that describe the functional uses of the document (e.g., table of contents, index, glossary, etc.). Currently, valid values for this attribute are not defined.

Head

The Head element defines the head portion of the document. It does not have any attributes. This section of the document is used to provide information about the document itself. The Head element is not required, but it is considered good practice to include the beginning and ending Head tags because some browsers are extremely rigorous about the specification and may not correctly render a page without the Head element. Also, some browsers may look for the Head element to find information about the document.

The tags that define the beginning and ending of the element are:

```
<HEAD> . . . </HEAD>
```

The Title, Isindex, Base, Meta, Nextid, and Link elements are all allowed with a Head element under both HTML 2.0 and 3.0. We discuss these elements in Section 7.3.2.

The Head element itself may only appear within the HTML element under both HTML 2.0 and 3.0.

Body

The beginning and ending Body tags mark the beginning and ending of the body section in an HTML document. The Body element is not required, but it is considered good practice to include the beginning and ending Body tags because some browsers are extremely rigorous about the specification and may not correctly render a page without a Body element.

The tags that define the beginning and ending of the element are:

```
<BODY> . . . </BODY>
```

In HTML 2.0, the Body element does not have any attributes. However, in HTML 3.0, the Body element may include the ID, LANG and CLASS attributes (see the "Common HTML Element Attributes" sidebar), as well as the BACKGROUND attribute. The value of the BACKGROUND attribute is the URI for an image that is to be used as the background for the document. Some browsers ignore this attribute.

In HTML 2.0, the following elements (listed alphabetically) may appear within the Body element: Address, Anchor, Blockquote, Bold, Citation, Code, Directory List, Definition List, Emphasis, Form, Headings 1–6, Horizontal Rule, Image, Isindex, Italic, Keyboard, Line Break, Menu, Ordered List, Paragraph, Preformatted Text, Sample, Strong, Teletype, Unordered List, and Variable. HTML 3.0 specifies an additional four elements that may appear within the Body element: Division, Figure, Math, and Table. We discuss these elements in Sections 7.2 and 7.3. The Body element itself may only appear within an HTML element.

NOTE

A *checksum* is a number associated with a block of data and is used to determine whether any of the data changed from the time the checksum was computed to the time the data was read. A very simple checksum is the length of the data. With this checksum, you can determine whether any characters were added or deleted

(because the checksum would change), but you cannot tell whether an equal number of characters were added *and* deleted, or if any characters changed. A *cryptographic checksum,* on the other hand, changes no matter what change is made to the data.

Common HTML Element Attributes

Ten attributes are commonly allowed within HTML elements. In alphabetical order, they are ALIGN, CLASS, CLEAR, HREF, ID, LANG, MD, NEEDS, NOWRAP, and SRC. Some of these are only valid under HTML 3.0, and we will note them as such.

- **ALIGN** is used to specify the alignment of an element. Generally, valid values for this attribute are "left," "right," "center," and "justify." (Some elements allow extra values for this attribute.)
- **CLASS** (HTML 3.0 only) is used to provide subclasses for tags. It is primarily used with style sheets to display a tag differently, based on the class type. If you created a style for programming languages such as C and perl, for example, you could use <CODE CLASS=perl> or <CODE CLASS=C>. You would use CLASS in conjunction with a style sheet, so that you could specify how certain parts of your document should look.
- **CLEAR** (HTML 3.0 only) is used to make text flow around an image that has been placed either flush left or flush right. Valid values in this attribute are right, left, and all. These values tell the browser to wait until the right or left (or both) margins are clear and then start the next tag there.
- **HREF** specifies a hypertext reference. Its value specifies the URI of the resource to which to link.
- **ID** (HTML 3.0 only) is similar to the NAME tag used in HTML 2.0. It provides an identifier for the start tag within the document, so that the specific location in the document can be referenced. It also provides a means of naming elements in a document for use with a style sheet.

  For example, if you had a List element halfway down an HTML document, you could use the ID attribute to provide a hypertext link to that element. This allows for hypertext links to specific locations within a document, as opposed to the whole document.

Common HTML Element Attributes (Continued)

- **LANG** (HTML 3.0 only) specifies the language to be used for an element. This value can be used by the client to determine how to render the element properly. For example, the value could be used to determine how to hyphenate the contents of an element. The value for this attribute is a standard ISO language abbreviation as defined by ISO 639 and ISO 3166.
- **MD** (HTML 3.0 only) is used to provide a message digest (a cryptographic *checksum*—see previous Note) and is valid for all elements that support links. It is used to specify a checksum for the object being linked to, so the user can be sure that the retrieved object is indeed the one that the author of the HTML page wanted the user to retrieve.
- **NOWRAP** (HTML 3.0 only) turns off the wrapping of lines within an element. Inside the element you can make explicit line breaks by using the BR tag.
- **SRC value** specifies the URI of a graphic image to be used with the element. For example, when used with a List element, the value specifies the URI for an image to be used as the bullet for the list. When used with the Image element, it specifies the URI of an inline image. In HTML 3.0, the SRC attribute may be used in conjunction with the MD attribute.

7.3.2 Head Elements

The following elements are valid only within the Head element of a document and are used to provide information about the document itself: Title, Base, Isindex, Meta, Nextid, and Link.

Title

The Title element is used to define the title of a document—that is, it gives a description of the document contents that is independent of the content itself. Generally, browsers display the title separately from the text of a document. Frequently they display the title in the title bar of the browser's window. For a document to be considered HTML 3.0–compliant, it must have at least a Title element.

The tags that define the beginning and ending of the element are:

```
<TITLE> . . . </TITLE>
```

In both HTML 2.0 and 3.0, the Title element does not have any attributes. Here is a sample Title element:

```
<TITLE>net.Genesis Home Page</TITLE>
```

The Title element itself may only appear within a Head element.

Base

The Base element is used to specify a URI from which all relative links in the document are to be interpreted. Both HTML versions 2.0 and 3.0 require the Base tag to have an HREF attribute, the value of which is the URI to be used as the base. Generally, this element is used only if a document can be referenced by different names (i.e., the same resource is available via two servers or can be reached via two paths). In cases where the document is available via two addresses, all of the relative links in the document have to be available via both paths. The Base element solves this problem by making all links relative to a single path. The Base element has no closing tag. The open tag is <BASE>. For example, if you retrieve the document at the URL

http://www.netgen.com/people/mkgray.html

and it contains this tag in the head of the document:

```
<BASE HREF="http://www.netgen.com/~mkgray/mkgray.html">
```

then all relative links will be taken from that location. To clarify, let's say the document retrieved above in its full content is as follows:

```
<html>
<head>
<title>Matthew's home page</title>
<base href="http://www.netgen.com/~mkgray/mkgray.html">
</head>
<body>
<h1>This is my home page!</h1>
This is my <a href="biography.html">biography</a>. I have an exciting life.
</body>
</html>
```

If we had not included the Base element in the document, the browser would have thought the relative link to biography.html was a link to **http://www.netgen.com/people/biography.html**. The Base element, however, indicates that a different URL should be taken as the base URL for relative links. So in this case the link should be to **http://www.netgen.com/~mkgray/biography.html**.

The Base element does not have an ending tag. It may only appear within a Head element.

Isindex

The Isindex element is used to indicate that the document is an index that users may search. It should be noted that this element is only used to inform the browser that the document may be searched; if search functionality is not already provided by the server, the Isindex element does not change this. You cannot add the Isindex element to an HTML document and expect the document to become searchable. For that you need to add a search engine or similar functionality.

In HTML 2.0, the Isindex element does not have any attributes; none are required in HTML 3.0. The Isindex element does not have an ending tag. The tag that defines the element is:

```
<ISINDEX>
```

In addition, HTML 3.0 supports the use of the HREF and PROMPT attributes. The value of the HREF attribute specifies the URI to which the query should be submitted for processing. The default value for this attribute is the URI of the document itself. The value of the PROMPT attribute is a string that should be used by the browser as the prompt for the query, as in this example:

```
<ISINDEX HREF="processor.pl" PROMPT="Search the net.Genesis Site:">
```

It specifies that the current document is searchable and that the query should be sent to processor.pl.

Officially, the Isindex element is only supposed to occur within a Head element, but most browsers accept it within the Body element as well.

Meta

The Meta element is used to provide meta-information about a document that is not otherwise specified within the Head element. In particular, the content field can be used to specify information that would have been provided had the document been retrieved via HTTP. In other words, the Meta element allows you to provide HTTP Response headers within the HTML. HTTP servers can scan the head of an HTML document for HTTP-EQUIV fields before they send a response, so they can include these values in the header.

The Meta element has no closing tag. The open tag is `<META>`.

Why would you want to simulate these headers? Because adding a specific header within the HTML document may be easier than modifying the server to send the appropriate header. Also, you will not always receive an HTML document via HTTP. You may get it by e-mail, floppy disk, FTP, etc. So by providing the meta-information, you can obtain the same information as though you received the object through HTTP.

Both HTML 2.0 and 3.0 allow the Meta tag to include the CONTENT attribute, as follows:

```
<META CONTENT="case-sensitive value">
```

In addition, both versions support the optional use of the HTTP-EQUIV and NAME attributes. The value of HTTP-EQUIV specifies the name of the HTTP Response header for which the value is being provided. And the value of the NAME attribute specifies the name of the property for which the value is being provided. Only use the NAME attribute if the meta-information being provided is *not* a valid HTTP Response header.

The value of the CONTENT attribute is the value that should be set for the NAME or HTTP-EQUIV field. For example, Refresh is a Response header, proposed and implemented by Netscape, that tells your browser to reload the page after a certain number of seconds. If the server scanned the file before sending it and sent this field in the header of the file, it would inform the client to re-request the file every ten seconds, for example:

```
<META HTTP-EQUIV="Refresh" Content="10">
```

This example tells the browser that the document is no longer valid after 2 p.m. on May 6, 1994:

```
<META HTTP-EQUIV="Expires" Content="Fri, 06 May 1994 14:00:00 EST">
```

The Meta element does not need an ending tag, and it may appear only within a Head element.

Nextid

The Nextid tag is only used by text editors to keep track of the next value to use when assigning ID numbers to elements. It ensures that ID numbers are not repeated. Nextid elements should be ignored by browsers.

The Nextid tag for HTML 2.0 and 3.0 is as follows:

```
<NEXTID N="lower-case value">
```

Suppose the Head element of your document contains the following Nextid element:

```
<NEXTID N=NETGEN1>
```

When you create a new element, its ID would be NETGEN1.

The Nextid element requires the use of an attribute (N), does not need an ending tag, and may only appear within the Head element of a document.

Link

The Link element is used to define relationships between the current document and other objects. No browser currently uses this information, but the idea is for browsers to use the information in this element to generate standard buttons that take you, for example, to a document's table of contents. These kinds of relationships could be very powerful, because it is not always clear how to find the information you need when you search the Web. The Link element specifies many of the most common relationships between documents, however. Link can make it easier to find things.

Here are the currently defined Link relationship values:

- **Home:** the specified object is the home page for this object
- **TOC:** the specified object is a table of contents for this object
- **Index:** the specified object is an index for this object
- **Glossary:** the specified object is a glossary of terms related to this object

- **Copyright:** the specified object is the copyright notice for this object
- **Up:** the specified object is the parent of this object in a hierarchy of objects
- **Next:** the specified object is the next object in a series of objects
- **Previous:** the specified object is the previous object in a series of objects
- **Help:** the specified object provides help in using the current object
- **Bookmark:** the specified object is at a particular location in this object

The Link tag for HTML versions 2.0 and 3.0 requires the use of the HREF attribute, as follows:

```
<LINK HREF="case-senstive URI value">
```

The value of the HREF attribute specifies the URI of the document to which the current document is related.

In addition, both HTML versions also support the use of the REV, URN, TITLE, and METHODS attributes, as follows:

```
<LINK HREF=". . ." REL=". . ." REV=". . ." URN=". . ." TITLE=". . ."
METHODS=". . .">
```

The value of the REL attribute specifies the type of relationship that the current document has to the resource specified in HREF, as in this example:

```
<LINK REL=Home HREF=home.html>
```

It indicates that home.html is the home page for the document in which this element appears.

In addition to the standard link relationships, HTML 3.0 allows two special values for the REL attribute. The "Banner" value specifies that the contents of the given URI be used as the banner for the current document. (See Section 7.4.1 on the Banner element for more information.) The "StyleSheet" value can be used to specify a link to the style sheet that should be used to format the document.

The value of the REV attribute specifies the type of relationship that the resource specified in HREF has with the current document. The values of the URN and TITLE attributes specify the URN and title of the object identified by the value of HREF. The value in the TITLE attribute can be used by the browser to tell the user the title of the document that the user was linking to. And, finally, the value of the METHODS attribute indicates the acceptable methods that may be used on the specified resource.

The Link element does not need an ending tag and it may appear only with a Head element.

7.3.3 Anchor Elements

Anchor elements are the fundamental building blocks of the Web. You use an Anchor element when you want to specify a link between a specific image or piece of text and another document or resource.

Anchors can be used to specify either the source or the destination of the link. The tags that define the beginning and ending of an Anchor element are:

```
<A> . . . </A>
```

Neither HTML 2.0 nor 3.0 require the use of attributes with the Anchor tag, but they do support various optional attributes. The Anchor element is very similar to the Link element described earlier, and uses many of the same attributes. The biggest difference between the two is that the Link element may be used only in the Head section of a document, but the Anchor element is designed for use within the Body section.

In HTML 2.0, the following attributes are supported for use with an Anchor tag: HREF, METHODS, NAME, REL, REV, TITLE, and URN. (In HTML 3.0, however, the METHODS and URN attributes are not supported.) HTML 3.0 supports the use of these additional attributes with the Anchor element: CLASS, ID, LANG, MD, and SHAPE.

NOTE

The HREF, CLASS, ID, LANG, and MD attributes were discussed in the "Common HTML Element Attributes" sidebar found earlier in this chapter.

The METHODS attribute specifies which methods may be used with the corresponding object. When you use the NAME attribute, you make it possible for other links to connect directly to specific locations within your document by specifying the NAME value. The value of NAME is a unique text string used to identify the anchor. In HTML 3.0, this attribute is superseded by the ID attribute, because the ID attribute provides the same functionality, but for all element types.

The value for the REL attribute specifies the type of relationship that the current document has to the resource specified in the HREF. Conversely, the value of the REV attribute specifies the type of relationship that the resource specified in HREF has with the current document.

The values of the TITLE and URN attributes specify the title and URN of the object identified by the value of HREF. A browser can use the value in the TITLE attribute to tell the user the title of the document to which the link leads before the link is actually made.

The SHAPE attribute is used to create links from regions of figures to other resources. Functionally, this attribute is replaces server-side, clickable image map support, since it allows such information to be encoded in the HTML itself. You could provide multiple anchors for a figure, each of which specified a link from a portion of the figure to a resource. This way, instead of having to pass the coordinates of a user's selection to the server to be processed, the browser could interpret the selection itself and retrieve the appropriate resource.

The acceptable values for the SHAPE attribute are as follows:

```
<A SHAPE="default">
<A SHAPE="circle x, y, r">
<A SHAPE="rect x, y, w, h">
<A SHAPE="polygon x1, y1, x2, y2, . . .">
```

Each value defines a particular region of the figure as a link. The "circle" value defines a circle centered at the coordinates *x,y* with radius *r.* The "rect" value defines a rectangular area with a width *w,* a height *h,* and with its upper-left corner positioned at *x,y.* The "polygon" value creates a polygon-shaped link defined by a series of points (each of the *x,y* pairs). The first pair of *x,y* coordinates should be the same as the last in order to close the polygon. The "default" value is used to define a link when the selection does not fit any of the other shapes.

In both HTML 2.0 and 3.0, the following elements (listed alphabetically) may appear within an Anchor element: Bold, Line Break, Citation, Code, Emphasis, Headings 1–6, Italic, Image, Keyboard, Sample, Strong, Teletype, and Variable. In addition, the following elements may appear within an

Anchor element when using HTML 3.0: Abbreviation, Acronym, Author, Big Print, Definition, Deleted Text, Horizontal Tab, Inserted Text, Italic, Language, Line Break, Math, Person, Short Quotation, Small Print, Strikethrough, Subscript, Superscript, and Underline.

The Anchor element itself may only appear with the following elements: Abbreviation., Acronym, Author, Bold, Big Print, Citation, Code, Definition Term, Deleted Text, Definition, Emphasis, Form, Headings 1–6, Italic, Inserted Text, Keyboard, Language, List Item, Math, Paragraph, Person, Preformatted Text, Quotation, Strikethrough, Sample, Small Print, Strong, Subscript, Superscript, Tab, Teletype, Underline, and Variable.

7.3.4 Block Formatting Elements

Block formatting elements are used to denote a segment of text that has a functional meaning separate from the rest of the document. Each block formatting element automatically places implicit paragraph breaks before and after itself.

Address

The Address element is used to declare that the content of the element is an address or signature. The element acts like a paragraph and automatically puts breaks before and after itself. The tags that define the beginning and end of an Address element are `<ADDRESS>. . .</ADDRESS>`. Here is a sample Address element:

```
<ADDRESS>
net.Genesis Corp.<BR>
56 Rogers St.<BR>
Cambridge, MA 02142<BR>
Tel: 617-577-9800
</ADDRESS>
```

Notice the Line Break elements after the first three address lines, but not after the line with the telephone number. The Address element takes care of the last line break automatically.

While HTML 2.0 does not support the use of any attributes with the Address tag, HTML 3.0 does support the use of the following attributes: CLASS, CLEAR, ID, LANG, and NOWRAP (see the "Common HTML Element Attributes" sidebar earlier in this chapter).

In both HTML 2.0 and 3.0, the following elements (listed alphabetically) may appear within an Address element: Anchor, Bold, Line Break, Citation, Code, Emphasis, Italic, Image, Keyboard, Paragraph, Sample, Strong, Teletype, and Variable. The following elements are allowed within an Address element in HTML 3.0: Abbreviation, Acronym, Author, Big Print, Definition, Deleted Text, Inserted Text, Language, Math, Person, Quotation, Small Print, Strikethrough, Subscript, Superscript, Tab, and Underline.

Under HTML 2.0, the Address elements is only allowed within the content of the Blockquote, Body, and Form elements.

In HTML 3.0, the Address element is allowed within the following elements: Anchor, Abbreviation, Acronym, Address, Admonishment, Author, Bold, Big Print, Blockquote, Line Break, Citation, Code, Definition List, Deleted Text, Definition, Division, Emphasis, Figure, Footnote, Form, Headings 1–6, Horizontal Rule, Italic, Image, Inserted Text, Isindex, Keyboard, Language, Math, Ordered List, Person, Preformatted Text, Quotation, Strikethrough, Sample, Small Print, Strong, Subscript, Superscript, Tab, Table, Teletype, Underline, Unordered List, and Variable.

Blockquote

The Blockquote element is used to quote sections of text from other resources. The tags that define the beginning and end of a Blockquote element under HTML 2.0 are `<BLOCKQUOTE> . . . </BLOCKQUOTE>`. In HTML 3.0 these tags are `<BQ> . . . </BQ>`. Here's a sample Blockquote element using HTML 2.0:

```
<BLOCKQUOTE>
Science is emphatically an important part of culture today, as scientific
knowledge and its applications continue to transform the world and condition
every aspect of the relations between men and nations.
</BLOCKQUOTE>
```

HTML 2.0 does not support the use of any attributes with the Blockquote element, but HTML 3.0 does support the use of the following attributes: CLASS, CLEAR, ID, LANG, and NOWRAP (see the "Common HTML Element Attributes" sidebar earlier in this chapter). Here's a sample Blockquote element using HTML 3.0:

```
<BQ LANG="de">
Ich bin ein Berliner.
<CREDIT>John Fitzgerald Kennedy, June 26, 1963</CREDIT>
</BQ>
```

In both HTML 2.0 and 3.0, the following elements (listed alphabetically) may appear within a Blockquote element: Address, Anchor, Blockquote, Bold, Citation, Code, Directory List, Definition List, Emphasis, Form, Heading 1–6, Horizontal Rule, Image, Isindex, Keyboard, Line Break, Menu, Ordered List, Paragraph, Preformatted Text, Sample, Strong, Teletype, Unordered List, and Variable.

In addition, the following elements may appear within a Blockquote element using HTML 3.0: Abbreviation, Acronym, Admonishment, Author, Big, Credit, Definition, Deleted Text, Division, Figure, Footnote, Inserted Text, Language, Math, Person, Quotation, Small, Strikethrough, Subscript, Superscript, Tab, Table, and Underline.

In HTML 2.0, the Blockquote element may appear within the following elements: Blockquote, Body, Definition, Form, and List Item. The Blockquote element may appear within the following elements in HTML 3.0: Abbreviation, Acronym, Address, Admonishment, Anchor, Author, Big, Bold, Citation, Code, Definition, Definition List, Deleted Text, Division, Emphasis, Figure, Footnote, Form, Headings 1–6, Horizontal Rule, Image, Inserted Text, Isindex, Italic, Keyboard, Language, Line Break, Math, Ordered List, Person, Preformatted Text, Quotation, Sample, Small, Strikethrough, Strong, Subscript, Superscript, Tab, Table, Teletype, Underline, Unordered List, and Variable.

Heading Elements (H1–H6)

Heading elements (H1, H2, H3, H4, H5, and H6) are used to denote heading levels. They might be used for chapter titles, section headers, and subsection headers. The H1 heading element is used for the highest level headers, and H6 heading is used for the lowest level headers. You should never skip heading levels. For example, it is acceptable to have an <h2> and then an <h3>, but it is not acceptable to have an <h2> and then an <h4>.

The tags that define the beginning and end of the Heading elements are:

```
<H1>. . .</H1>
<H2>. . .</H2>
<H3>. . .</H3>
<H4>. . .</H4>
<H5>. . .</H5>
<H6>. . .</H6>
```

HTML 3.0 added the ability to associate a sequence number with each heading level (for example, the section number). This sequence number is incremented by each subsequent heading element of the same level, and the sequence number for all lower level headings is reset to 1. Sequence numbers can be used to keep track of section and subsection numbering (i.e., "Section 3" or "Section 3.1.2"). It is up to the browser and the current style sheet to determine how the numbers are displayed.

While HTML 2.0 does not support the use of any attributes with heading tags, HTML 3.0 does support the use of the following attributes: ALIGN, CLASS, CLEAR, ID, LANG, MD, NOWRAP, and SRC (all of which are described in the "Common HTML Element Attributes" sidebar earlier in this chapter), plus DINGBAT, SEQNUM, and SKIP.

The DINGBAT attribute is used to specify a standard icon that precedes the header. If you need to advance the sequence number artificially in order to account for headers that have been left out, use the SKIP attribute to indicate how many headers to skip over. You can use the SEQNUM attribute to set the heading level sequence number to a specific value. Sequence numbers are initialized and incremented automatically, but the DINGBAT attribute allows you to override this process and change the sequence number.

In both HTML 2.0 and 3.0, the following elements (listed alphabetically) may appear within a Heading element: Anchor, Bold, Citation, Code, Emphasis, Italic, Image, Keyboard, Line Break, Sample, Strong, Teletype, and Variable.

The following elements are allowed within a Heading element in HTML 3.0: Abbreviation, Acronym, Author, Big Print, Definition, Deleted Text, Image, Inserted Text, Language, Math, Person, Quotation, Small Print, Strikethrough, Subscript, Superscript, Tab, Underline.

Under HTML 2.0, the Heading elements are only allowed within the content of the Anchor, Blockquote, Body, and Form elements.

In HTML 3.0, the Heading element may only appear within the following elements: Abbreviation, Acronym, Address, Admonishment, Anchor, Author, Big, Blockquote, Bold, Citation, Code, Definition, Definition List, Deleted Text, Division, Emphasis, Figure, Footnote, Form, Headings 1–6, Horizontal Rule, Image, Inserted Text, Isindex, Italic, Keyboard, Language, Line Break, Math, Ordered List, Person, Preformatted Text, Quotation, Sample, Small, Strikethrough, Strong, Subscript, Superscript, Tab, Table, Teletype, Underline, Unordered List, and Variable.

Horizontal Rule

The Horizontal Rule element produces horizontal lines for use as section dividers. Many document creators using HTML 2.0 ignored this element because it did not support the use of graphical rules. Their solution was to use Image elements instead. For users of text-only browsers, of course, this did not serve the same function.

The Horizontal Rule element has no closing tag. The open tag is <HR>.

HTML 3.0 extends the functionality of the Horizontal Rule element by supporting the use of six attributes. Two of them, SRC and CLASS, make it possible for the rendering of Horizontal Rule elements to be dependent on the browser and the values in these two attributes. The SRC attribute is used to provide an image to use for the horizontal rule, and CLASS specifies an associated style sheet. This means that document creators can use graphics for horizontal rules and still adhere to the use of functional tags that can be interpreted by all kinds of browsers.

The other attributes used with the Horizontal Rule element are CLEAR, ID, and MD. All six attributes are described in the "Common HTML Element Attributes" sidebar earlier in this chapter. The Horizontal Rule element does not need an ending tag.

Under HTML 2.0, the Horizontal Rule element is only allowed within the content of the Blockquote, Body, Form, and Preformatted Text elements.

In HTML 3.0, it may appear only within the following additional elements: Abbreviation, Acronym, Address, Admonishment, Anchor, Author, Big, Bold, Citation, Code, Definition, Definition List, Deleted Text, Division, Emphasis, Figure, Footnote, Headings 1–6, Image, Inserted Text, Isindex, Italic, Keyboard, Language, Line Break, Math, Ordered List, Person, Quotation, Sample, Small, Strikethrough, Strong, Subscript, Superscript, Tab, Table, Teletype, Underline, Unordered List, and Variable.

Line Break

The Line Break element is used to tell the browser to insert a line break at a point in the document. This element does not support the use of any attributes under HTML 2.0, and it does not allow an ending tag. The Line Break element has no closing tag. The open tag is <BR>.

Here's a snippet of sample HTML 2.0 code:

```
<BODY>
This is line 1. <BR> This is line 2. <BR> This is line 3.
</BODY>
```

When rendered, it looks something like this:

```
This is line 1.
This is line 2.
This is line 3.
```

HTML 3.0 supports the use of following attributes with the Line Break element: CLASS, CLEAR, ID, and LANG (see the "Common HTML Element Attributes" sidebar earlier in this chapter).

Under HTML 2.0, the Line Break element is only allowed within the content of the Anchor, Address, Blockquote, Body, Bold, Citation, Code, Definition, Definition Term, Emphasis, Form, Headings 1–6, Italic, Keyboard, List Item, Paragraph, Preformatted Text, Sample, Strong, Teletype, and Variable elements.

In HTML 3.0, Line Break elements may only appear with the following additional elements: Abbreviation, Acronym, Author, Big, Deleted Text, Image, Inserted Text, Language, Math, Person, Quotation, Small, Strikethrough, Subscript, Superscript, Tab, and Underline.

Paragraph

The Paragraph element is used to indicate that the content between the beginning and ending tags is a paragraph. The tags that define the beginning and end of a Paragraph element are `<P>. . .</P>`. However, no ending tag is actually required because the browser assumes that the paragraph extends to the next beginning Paragraph tag.

HTML 2.0 does not support the use of any attributes with Paragraph tags. HTML 3.0 supports the use of the following attributes: ALIGN, CLASS, CLEAR, ID, and LANG (see the "Common HTML Element Attributes" sidebar earlier in this chapter).

In both HTML 2.0 and 3.0, the following elements (listed alphabetically) may appear within a Paragraph element: Anchor, Bold, Citation, Code, Emphasis, Italic, Image, Keyboard, Line Break, Sample, Strong, Teletype, and Variable.

In addition, the following elements may also appear within a Paragraph element when using HTML 3.0: Abbreviation, Acronym, Author, Big, Definition, Deleted Text, Inserted Text, Italic, Language, Math, Person, Quotation, Small, Strikethrough, Subscript, Superscript, Tab, and Underline.

The Paragraph element itself may only appear within the following elements: Abbreviation, Acronym, Address, Admonishment, Anchor, Author, Big, Blockquote, Body, Bold, Citation, Code, Definition, Definition List, Deleted Text, Division, Emphasis, Figure, Figure, Footnote, Footnote, Form, Form, Headings 1–6, Horizontal Rule, Image, Inserted Text, Isindex, Isindex,

Italic, Keyboard, Language, Line Break, Math, Ordered List, Person, Preformatted Text, Quotation, Sample, Small, Strikethrough, Strong, Subscript, Superscript, Tab, Table, Table, Teletype, Underline, Unordered List, Variable

Preformatted Text

PRE tags indicate the beginning and ending of Preformatted Text blocks. These blocks are used to indicate that the content of the element should be rendered in a fixed-width font. Inside this element, newlines, tabs, and multiple spaces are rendered normally and not combined into a single character of white space. The tags that define the beginning and ending of the element are:

```
<PRE> . . . </PRE>
```

HTML 2.0 and 3.0 both support the use of the WIDTH attribute with the Preformatted Text element. The WIDTH attribute is used to specify the maximum number of characters that should appear on a line. In addition, HTML 3.0 supports the use of the following attributes with the Preformatted Text element: CLASS, CLEAR, ID, and LANG (see the "Common HTML Element Attributes" sidebar earlier in this chapter).

The following is an example of how you might want to use the Preformatted Text element:

```
<PRE>
          April 1995
S    M    T    W    T    F    S
                              1
2    3    4    5    6    7    8
9    10   11   12   13   14   15
16   17   18   19   20   21   22
23   24   25   26   27   28   29
30
</PRE>
```

If this had not been a Preformatted Text element, multiple spaces would have been treated as a single space, and newlines would have been ignored. In other words, this calendar would have been completely trashed upon rendering. All formatting—centering, alignment, etc.—was accomplished using spaces. The lines are separated with newline characters (hard returns).

In both HTML 2.0 and 3.0, the following elements (listed alphabetically) may appear within a Preformatted Text element: Anchor, Bold, Citation, Code, Emphasis, Horizontal Rule, Italic, Keyboard, Line Break, Sample, Strong, Teletype, and Variable.

In addition, the following elements are allowed within the Preformatted Text element when using HTML 3.0: Abbreviation, Acronym, Author, Big, Definition, Deleted Text, Image, Inserted Text, Language, Line Break, Math, Person, Quotation, Small, Strikethrough, Subscript, Superscript, Tab, Underline.

The Preformatted Text element itself may only appear with the following elements: Abbreviation, Acronym, Address, Admonishment, Anchor, Author, Big Print, Blockquote, Body, Bold, Bold, Citation, Code, Definition, Definition List, Deleted Text, Division, Emphasis, Figure, Footnote, Form, Headings 1–6, Horizontal Rule, Image, Inserted Text, Isindex, Italic, Keyboard, Language, Line Break, Math, Ordered List, Person, Quotation, Sample, Small, Strikethrough, Strong, Subscript, Superscript, Tab, Table, Teletype, Underline, Unordered List, and Variable.

7.3.5 List Elements

The elements described here are used to define various types of lists.

Definition List

The Definition List element is used for lists of terms and definitions (for example, glossaries and dictionaries). The tags that define the beginning and ending of the element are:

```
<DL> . . . </DL>
```

HTML 2.0 and 3.0 both support the use of the COMPACT attribute with the Definition List element. When the COMPACT attribute is provided, the client saves space by displaying the list either by reducing the vertical spacing between the items on the list or by using a smaller font size. In addition, HTML 3.0 supports the use of the following attributes with the Definition List element: CLASS, CLEAR, ID, and LANG (see the "Common HTML Element Attributes" sidebar earlier in this chapter).

Under HTML 2.0, the Definition List element is only allowed within the content of the Blockquote, Body, Definition Form, and List Item elements.

In HTML 3.0, the Definition List element may only appear within the following elements: Abbreviation, Acronym, Address, Admonishment, Anchor, Author, Big, Blockquote, Bold, Citation, Code, Definition, Deleted Text, Division, Emphasis, Figure, Footnote, Form, Headings 1–6, Horizontal Rule, Image, Inserted Text, Isindex, Italic, Keyboard, Language, Line Break, Math, Ordered List, Person, Preformatted Text, Quotation, Sample, Small, Strikethrough, Strong, Subscript, Superscript, Tab, Table, Teletype, Underline, Unordered List, and Variable.

In both HTML 2.0 and 3.0, the Definition and Definition Term elements may appear within a Definition List element. In HTML 3.0, the List Header element may also appear within a Definition List element.

Definition Term

The Definition Term element is used to specify a term within a definition list. The tags that define the beginning and ending of the element are:

```
<DT> . . . </DT>
```

The </DT> ending tag is not required, because the end of the element is assumed to occur at the beginning of the next Definition Term element. HTML 2.0 does not support the use of any attributes with the Definition Term element. HTML 3.0 supports the CLASS, CLEAR, ID, and LANG attributes.

In both HTML 2.0 and 3.0, the following elements (listed alphabetically) may appear within a Definition Term element: Anchor, Bold, Citation, Code, Emphasis, Italic, Image, Keyboard, Line Break, Sample, Strong, Teletype, and Variable.

In addition, the following elements may appear within the Term element when using HTML 3.0: Abbreviation, Acronym, Author, Big, Definition, Deleted Text, Inserted Text, Language, Math, Person, Quotation, Small, Strikethrough, Subscript, Superscript, Tab, and Underline.

The Definition Term element itself may only appear within a Definition List element.

Definition

The Definition element is used to provide a definition for a term within a definition list. The tags that define the beginning and ending of the element are:

```
<DD> . . . </DD>
```

The </DD> ending tag is not required, because the end of the element is assumed to occur at the beginning of the next DT element. HTML 2.0 does not support the use of any attributes with the Definition element. HTML 3.0 supports the use of the following attributes: CLASS, CLEAR, ID, and LANG.

In both HTML 2.0 and 3.0, the following elements (listed alphabetically) may appear within a Definition element: Anchor, Blockquote, Bold, Citation, Code, Directory List, Definition List, Emphasis, Form, Image, Isindex, Italic, Keyboard, Line Break, Menu, Ordered List, Paragraph, Preformatted Text, Sample, Strong, Teletype, Unordered List, and Variable.

In addition, the following elements may appear within a Definition element when using HTML 3.0: Abbreviation, Acronym, Admonishment, Author, Big, Deleted Text, Figure, Footnote, Inserted Text, Language, Math, Person, Quotation, Small, Strikethrough, Subscript, Superscript, Tab, Table, and Underline.

The Definition element itself may only appear within a Definition List element.

Figure 7-4 shows a sample page containing a Definition List with two items. The HTML for that page uses DL, DT, and DD elements, as follows:

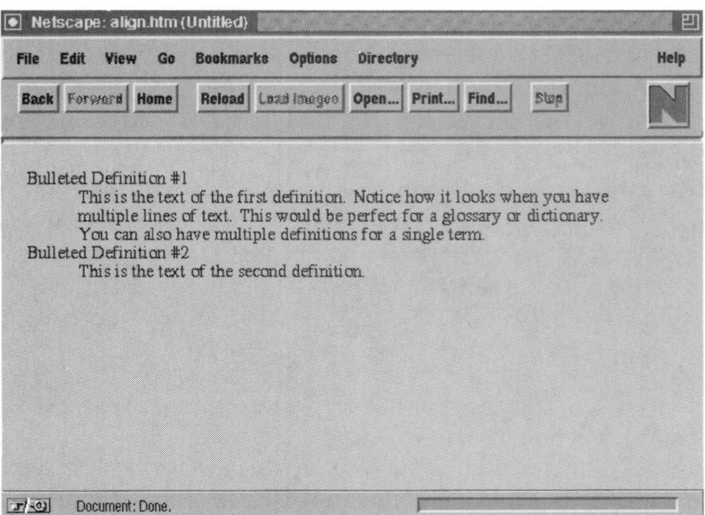

Figure 7-4 A sample page containing a Definition List with two items

```
<DL>
<DT>Bulleted Definition #1<DD>This is the text of the first definition.
Notice how it looks when you have multiple lines of text. This would be
perfect for a glossary or dictionary. You can also have multiple definitions
for a single term.
<DT>Bulleted Definition #2<DD>This is the text of the second definition.
</DL>
```

Directory List

The Directory List element is used in HTML 2.0 to display items in columns. This element cannot be found in the HTML 3.0 specification, because its functionality has been replaced by the Unordered List element using the PLAIN attribute and the WRAP attribute set to HORIZ. Browsers are asked to support the directory list functionality to maintain backwards compatibility.

Each list item is limited to 20 characters of information. The tags that define the beginning and ending of the element are:

```
<DIR> . . . </DIR>
```

HTML 2.0 does not support the use of any attributes with the Directory List element. The only element that may appear within a Directory List element is a List Item element. The Directory List element itself may only be used within Blockquote, Body, Definition, Form, or List Item elements.

List Item

The List Item element is used to specify an element in a Directory List, Menu List, Ordered List, or Unordered List. The tags that define the beginning and ending of the element are:

```
<LI> . . . </LI>
```

HTML 2.0 does not support the use of any attributes with the List Item element, but the following attributes are supported for use with HTML 3.0: CLASS, CLEAR, ID, LANG, MD and SRC (see the "Common HTML Element Attributes" sidebar earlier in this chapter), plus DINGBAT and SKIP.

When using HTML 2.0, the Directory List and Definition List elements may appear within a List Item element. Using either HTML 2.0 or 3.0, the following elements may appear within a List Item element: Anchor, Blockquote, Bold, Citation, Code, Definition List, Directory List, Emphasis, Form, Italic, Image, Isindex, Keyboard, Line Break, Menu, Ordered List, Paragraph, Preformatted Text, Sample, Strong, Teletype, Unordered List, and Variable.

In addition, the following elements may appear within a List Item element when using HTML 3.0: Abbreviation, Acronym, Admonishment, Author, Big, Definition, Definition List, Deleted Text, Figure, Footnote, Inserted Text, Language, Math, Person, Quotation, Small, Strikethrough, Subscript, Superscript, Tab, Table, and Underline.

The List Item element itself may only be used within Unordered List, Ordered List, Directory List (HTML 2.0 only), and Menu (HTML 2.0 only) elements.

The following is a sample directory listing with several List Item elements:

```
<DIR>
<LI> Macintosh<LI> Windows
<LI> UNIX  <LI> Windows NT
</DIR>
```

If you are using HTML 3.0, you could also use the List Header element, as follows:

```
<DIR>
<LH> COMPUTER PLATFORMS </LH>
<LI> Macintosh<LI> Windows
<LI> UNIX  <LI> Windows NT
</DIR>
```

Menu List

The Menu List element is used for menu lists. This element cannot be found in the HTML 3.0 specification, because its functionality has been replaced by the Unordered List element using the PLAIN attribute. However, browsers are supposed to support the menu list functionality in order to maintain backwards compatibility.

Menu lists are very similar to unordered lists, except they do not have bullets. The tags that define the beginning and ending of the element are:

```
<MENU> . . . </MENU>
```

HTML 2.0 does not support the use of any attributes with the Menu List element. The only element that may appear within a Menu List element is a List Item element. And the Menu List element itself may only be used within Blockquote, Body, Definition, Form, and List Item elements.

The following is a sample menu list with list items:

```
<MENU>
<LI> Item #1
<LI> Item #2
<LI> Item #3
</MENU>
```

Ordered List

The Ordered List element defines an ordered list, which is a numbered list of items. Just like Header elements, Ordered List elements maintain sequence numbers that browsers use for rendering purposes.

The tags that define the beginning and end of a Ordered List element are:

```
<OL> . . . </OL>
```

While HTML 2.0 does not support the use of any attributes with the Ordered List element, HTML 3.0 does support the use of the following attributes: CLASS, CLEAR, ID, and LANG (all of which are described in the "Common HTML Element Attributes" sidebar), plus COMPACT, SEQNUM, and CONTINUE.

The COMPACT attribute indicates that the browser should try to save space, either by reducing the vertical spacing, the font size, or something else. You use the SEQNUM attribute to set the sequence number of the first element to the specified value. For example, the following example would show a list of three elements, numbered from 100 to 102:

```
<OL SEQNUM=100>
<LI> Bulleted Item #1
<LI> Bulleted Item #2
<LI> Bulleted Item #3
</OL>
```

The CONTINUE attribute allows you to continue with a previously defined ordered list, and continue the sequence numbering from where you left off as well. Here is an example:

```
<OL>
<LI> Bulleted Item #1
<LI> Bulleted Item #2
<LI> Bulleted Item #3
</OL>
<OL CONTINUE>
<LI> Bulleted Item #4
<LI> Bulleted Item #5
<LI> Bulleted Item #6
</OL>
```

In both HTML 2.0 and 3.0, List Item elements appear within the Ordered List element. In HTML 3.0, the List Header element may also appear with the Ordered List element.

In HTML 2.0, the Ordered List element itself may appear only within the following elements: Blockquote, Body, Definition, Form, and List Item.

In HTML 3.0, the Ordered List element may also appear within the following elements: Abbreviation, Acronym, Address, Admonishment, Anchor, Author, Big, Blockquote, Bold, Citation, Code, Definition, Definition List, Deleted Text, Division, Emphasis, Figure, Footnote, Form, Headings 1–6, Horizontal Rule, Image, Inserted Text, Isindex, Italic, Keyboard, Language, Line Break, Math, Person, Preformatted Text, Quotation, Sample, Small, Strikethrough, Strong, Subscript, Superscript, Tab, Table, Teletype, Underline, Unordered List, and Variable.

Unordered List

The Unordered List element is used to define an unordered list of items (like a shopping list). Generally, an unordered list is presented as a list of bulleted items. HTML 3.0 gives you the ability to customize the bullets (by using the SRC attribute) and also provides features for multicolumn lists (with the WRAP attribute).

The tags that define the beginning and ending of the element are:

```
<UL> . . . </UL>
```

HTML 2.0 does not support the use of any attributes with the Unordered List element, but the following attributes are supported for use with the Unordered List element when using HTML 3.0: CLASS, CLEAR, ID, LANG, MD, and SRC (see the "Common HTML Element Attributes" sidebar earlier in this chapter), plus COMPACT, DINGBAT, PLAIN and WRAP.

The PLAIN attribute indicates that bullets should not appear before each item. This functionality is provided so that the Unordered List element can also be used to replace the Menu List element from HTML 2.0. If you want the bullets to appear, simply omit this attribute. On the other hand, if you want to replace the bullets with a thumbnail icon, use the DINGBAT attribute.

The WRAP attribute allows you to create multicolumn lists. The two valid values for this attribute are "horiz" and "vert," indicating that the list items should be wrapped either horizontally or vertically before jumping to the next column. If you want to make the list appear as small as possible, use the COMPACT attribute. It tells the browser to save space by reducing the vertical spacing, the font size, or something else.

The following is a sample Unordered List defined using HTML 2.0:

```
<UL>
<LI> Bulleted Item #1
<LI> Bulleted Item #2
<LI> Bulleted Item #3
</UL>
```

NOTE

We wanted to show you some pages illustrating the HTML 3.0 wrapping and dingbat attributes, but we haven't come across any browsers that support these items yet.

In both HTML 2.0 and 3.0, List Item elements appear within the Unordered List element. In HTML 3.0, the List Header element may also appear with the Unordered List element.

In HTML 2.0, the Unordered List element may appear only within the following elements: Blockquote, Body, Definition, Form, and List Item.

In HTML 3.0, the Unordered List element may appear only within the following elements: Abbreviation, Acronym, Address, Admonishment, Anchor,

Author, Big Print, Blockquote, Bold, Citation, Code, Definition, Definition List, Deleted Text, Division, Emphasis, Figure, Footnote, Form, Headings 1–6, Horizontal Rule, Image, Inserted Text, Isindex, Italic, Keyboard, Language, Line Break, Math, Ordered List, Person, Preformatted Text, Quotation, Sample, Small Print, Strikethrough, Strong, Subscript, Superscript, Tab, Table, Teletype, Underline, and Variable.

7.3.6 Information Type Elements

Information type elements describe how a piece of text is used. They designate a block of text that has a functional meaning. None of these elements produces line breaks before or after its content. The basic notion behind many of these attributes (especially the HTML 3.0–only elements) is to provide additional information to the browser about the meaning of the text.

Citation

The Citation element is used to identify a citation, such as a quote from a book, a magazine, and the like. The Citation element does not use any attributes. The tags that define the beginning and ending of the element are:

```
<CITE> . . . </CITE>
```

In both HTML 2.0 and 3.0, the following elements (listed alphabetically) may appear within a Citation element: Anchor, Bold, Line Break, Citation, Code, Emphasis, Italic, Image, Keyboard, Sample, Strong, Teletype, and Variable. In addition, the following elements may appear within a Citation element using HTML 3.0: Abbreviation, Acronym, Anchor, Author, Big Print, Bold, Code, Definition, Deleted Text, Emphasis, Image, Inserted Text, Italic, Keyboard, Language, Line Break, Math, Person, Quotation, Sample, Small Print, Strikethrough, Strong, Subscript, Superscript, Tab, Teletype, Underline, and Variable.

When using HTML 2.0, the Citation element itself may appear only within the following elements: Address, Anchor, Blockquote, Body, Bold, Citation, Code, Definition, Emphasis, Headers, Italic, Keyboard, List Item, Paragraph, Preformatted Text, Sample, Strong, Teletype, Term, and Variable.

The Citation element may also appear within the following elements when using HTML 3.0: Abbreviation, Acronym, Author, Big Print, Deleted Text, Image, Inserted Text, Italic, Keyboard, Language, Line Break, Math, Person, Quotation, Sample, Small Print, Strikethrough, Subscript, Superscript, Tab, and Underline.

Code

The Code element is used to define a block of code. Generally, the block is rendered in a fixed-width font. The Code element does not use any attributes. The tags that define the beginning and ending of the element are:

```
<CODE> . . . </CODE>
```

In both HTML 2.0 and 3.0, the following elements (listed alphabetically) may appear within a Code element: Anchor, Bold, Line Break, Citation, Code, Emphasis, Italic, Image, Keyboard, Sample, Strong, Teletype, and Variable. In addition, the following elements may also appear within the Code element when using HTML 3.0: Abbreviation, Acronym, Author, Big Print, Definition, Deleted Text, Image, Inserted Text, Language, Line Break, Math, Person, Quotation, Small Print, Strikethrough, Subscript, Superscript, Tab, and Underline.

When using HTML 2.0, the Code element itself may appear only within the following elements: Address, Anchor, Blockquote, Body, Bold, Citation, Code, Definition, Emphasis, Headers, Italic, Keyboard, List Item, Paragraph, Preformatted Text, Sample, Strong, Teletype, Term, and Variable.

The Code element may also appear within the following elements when using HTML 3.0: Abbreviation, Acronym, Author, Big Print, Deleted Text, Image, Inserted Text, Italic, Keyboard, Language, Line Break, Math, Person, Quotation, Sample, Small Print, Strikethrough, Subscript, Superscript, Tab, and Underline.

Keyboard

The Keyboard element is used to indicate text (usually commands) that users should enter. Generally, this element is rendered in a fixed-width font. The Keyboard element does not use any attributes. The tags that define the beginning and ending of the element are:

```
<KBD> . . . </KBD>
```

In both HTML 2.0 and 3.0, the following elements (listed alphabetically) may appear within a Keyboard element: Anchor, Bold, Citation, Code, Emphasis, Image, Italic, Keyboard, Line Break, Sample, Strong, Teletype, and Variable. In addition, the following elements may also appear within the Keyboard element when using HTML 3.0: Abbreviation, Acronym, Author, Big

Print, Definition, Deleted Text, Inserted Text, Language, Math, Person, Quotation, Small Print, Strikethrough, Subscript, Superscript, Tab, and Underline.

When using HTML 2.0, the Keyboard element itself may appear only within the following elements: Address, Anchor, Blockquote, Body, Bold, Citation, Code, Definition, Emphasis, Headers, Italic, Keyboard, List Item, Paragraph, Preformatted Text, Sample, Strong, Teletype, Term, and Variable.

In HTML 3.0, the Keyboard element may also appear within the following elements: Abbreviation, Acronym, Author, Big Print, Deleted Text, Image, Inserted Text, Italic, Language, Line Break, Math, Person, Quotation, Sample, Small Print, Strikethrough, Subscript, Superscript, Tab, and Underline.

Sample

The Sample element is used to identify a sequence of literal characters. Generally, browsers render the contents of this element in a fixed-width font. The Sample element does not use any attributes. The tags that define the beginning and ending of the element are:

```
<SAMP> . . . </SAMP>
```

In both HTML 2.0 and 3.0, the following elements (listed alphabetically) may appear within a Sample element: Anchor, Bold, Citation, Code, Emphasis, Image, Italic, Keyboard, Line Break, Sample, Strong, Teletype, and Variable. In HTML 3.0, the following elements may also appear within the Sample element: Abbreviation, Acronym, Author, Big Print, Definition, Deleted Text, Inserted Text, Language, Math, Person, Quotation, Small Print, Strikethrough, Subscript, Superscript, Tab, and Underline.

When using HTML 2.0, the Sample element itself may appear only within the following elements: Address, Anchor, Blockquote, Body, Bold, Citation, Code, Definition, Emphasis, Headers, Italic, Keyboard, List Item, Paragraph, Preformatted Text, Strong, Teletype, Term, and Variable.

The Sample element may also appear within the following elements when using HTML 3.0: Abbreviation, Acronym, Author, Big Print, Deleted Text, Image, Inserted Text, Italic, Keyboard, Language, Line Break, Math, Person, Quotation, Small Print, Strikethrough, Subscript, Superscript, Tab, and Underline.

Variable

The Variable element is used to specify variable names. The Variable element does not use any attributes. The tags that define the beginning and ending of the element are:

```
<VAR> . . . </VAR>
```

This style could apply to mathematical or programming variables, as in this example:

```
as far as I know, <var>x</var> plus <var>y</var> equals <var>z</var>.
```

In both HTML 2.0 and 3.0, the following elements (listed alphabetically) may appear within a Variable element: Anchor, Blockquote, Body, Bold, Citation, Code, Emphasis, Image, Italic, Keyboard, Line Break, Sample, Strong, Teletype, and Variable. In HTML 3.0, the following elements may also appear within the Variable element: Abbreviation, Acronym, Author, Big Print, Definition, Deleted Text, Inserted Text, Language, Math, Person, Quotation, Small Print, Strikethrough, Subscript, Superscript, Tab, and Underline.

When using HTML 2.0, the Variable element itself may appear only within the following elements: Address, Anchor, Bold, Citation, Code, Definition, Emphasis, Headers, Italic, Keyboard, List Item, Paragraph, Preformatted Text, Sample, Strong, Teletype, and Term.

The Variable element may also appear within the following elements when using HTML 3.0: Abbreviation, Acronym, Author, Big Print, Deleted Text, Image, Inserted Text, Italic, Keyboard, Language, Line Break, Math, Person, Quotation, Sample, Small Print, Strikethrough, Subscript, Superscript, Tab, and Underline.

Strong

The Strong element is used to indicate pieces of text that should be rendered with strong emphasis. Browsers generally render this element by making the contents bold. The Strong element does not use any attributes. The tags that define the beginning and ending of the element are:

```
<STRONG> . . . </STRONG>
```

In both HTML 2.0 and 3.0, the following elements (listed alphabetically) may appear within a Strong element: Anchor, Bold, Citation, Code, Emphasis, Image, Italic, Keyboard, Line Break, Sample, Strong, Teletype, Variable. In HTML 3.0, the following elements may also appear within the Strong element: Abbreviation, Acronym, Author, Big Print, Definition, Deleted Text, Inserted Text, Language, Math, Person, Quotation, Small Print, Strikethrough, Subscript, Superscript, Tab, and Underline.

When using HTML 2.0, the Strong element itself may appear only within the following elements: Address, Anchor, Blockquote, Body, Bold, Citation, Code, Definition, Emphasis, Headers, Italic, Keyboard, List Item, Paragraph, Preformatted Text, Sample, Strong, Teletype, Term, and Variable.

The Strong element may also appear within the following elements when using HTML 3.0: Abbreviation, Acronym, Author, Big Print, Deleted Text, Image, Inserted Text, Italic, Keyboard, Language, Line Break, Math, Person, Quotation, Sample, Small Print, Strikethrough, Subscript, Superscript, Tab, and Underline.

Emphasis

The Emphasis element is used for text that should be emphasized. Graphical browsers generally render Emphasis elements in italics. The Emphasis element does not use any attributes. The tags that define the beginning and ending of the element are:

```
<EM> . . . </EM>
```

In both HTML 2.0 and 3.0, the following elements (listed alphabetically) may appear within an Emphasis element: Anchor, Bold, Citation, Code, Emphasis, Image, Italic, Keyboard, Line Break, Sample, Strong, Teletype, and Variable. In HTML 3.0, the following elements may also appear within the Emphasis element: Abbreviation, Acronym, Author, Big Print, Definition, Deleted Text, Inserted Text, Language, Math, Person, Quotation, Small Print, Strikethrough, Subscript, Superscript, Tab, and Underline.

When using HTML 2.0, the Emphasis element itself may appear only within the following elements: Address, Anchor, Blockquote, Body, Bold, Citation, Code, Definition, Headers, Italic, Keyboard, List Item, Paragraph, Preformatted Text, Sample, Strong, Teletype, Term, and Variable.

The Emphasis element may also appear within the following elements when using HTML 3.0: Abbreviation, Acronym, Author, Big Print, Deleted Text, Image, Inserted Text, Italic, Keyboard, Language, Line Break, Math, Person, Quotation, Sample, Small Print, Strikethrough, Subscript, Superscript, Tab, and Underline.

7.3.7 Character Formatting Elements

Character formatting elements are used to specify the character format of their contents, such as bold, teletype, italic, and underline.

WARNING

Because these are physical (as opposed to semantic) markups, we advise you strongly not to use them. By sticking to semantic markups, your pages are more likely to be compatible with a wide variety of browsers, because browsers are more likely to support semantic tags than they are to support specific character styles.

Bold

The Bold tag specifically asks the browser to use a boldface font. If the browser cannot render text in boldface, it defaults to another format that it supports. The Bold element does not use any attributes. The tags that define the beginning and ending of the element are:

```
<B> . . . </B>
```

In both HTML 2.0 and 3.0, the following elements (listed alphabetically) may appear within a Bold element: Anchor, Bold, Citation, Code, Emphasis, Image, Italic, Keyboard, Line Break, Sample, Strong, Teletype, and Variable.

In HTML 3.0, the following elements are also allowed within the Bold element: Abbreviation, Acronym, Author, Big Print, Definition, Deleted Text, Inserted Text, Language, Math, Person, Quotation, Small Print, Strikethrough, Subscript, Superscript, Tab, and Underline.

In HTML 2.0, the Bold element may appear only within the following elements: Address, Anchor, Blockquote, Body, Bold, Citation, Code, Definition, Emphasis, Form, Headers, Italic, Keyboard, List Item, Paragraph, Preformatted Text, Sample, Strong, Teletype, Term, and Variable.

In HTML 3.0, the Bold element may also appear within the following elements: Abbreviation, Acronym, Author, Big, Deleted Text, Image, Inserted Text, Language, Line Break, Math, Person, Quotation, Small, Strikethrough, Subscript, Superscript, Tab, and Underline.

Teletype

The Teletype element specifies that the content be rendered to look like it came from an old teletype machine: i.e., in a fixed-width font. The Teletype element does not use any attributes. The tags that define the beginning and ending of the element are:

```
<TT> . . . </TT>
```

In both HTML 2.0 and 3.0, the following elements (listed alphabetically) may appear within a Teletype element: Anchor, Bold, Line Break, Citation, Code, Emphasis, Italic, Image, Keyboard, Sample, Strong, Teletype, and Variable.

In HTML 3.0, the following elements are also allowed within the Teletype element: Abbreviation, Acronym, Author, Big Print, Definition, Deleted Text, Inserted Text, Language, Math, Person, Quotation, Small Print, Strikethrough, Subscript, Superscript, Tab, and Underline.

In HTML 2.0, the Teletype element may appear only within the following elements: Address, Anchor, Blockquote, Body, Bold, Citation, Code, Definition, Emphasis, Headers, Italic, Keyboard, List Item, Paragraph, Preformatted Text, Sample, Strong, Teletype, Term, and Variable.

In HTML 3.0, the Teletype element may also appear within the following elements: Abbreviation, Acronym, Author, Big, Deleted Text, Image, Inserted Text, Language, Line Break, Math, Person, Quotation, Small, Strikethrough, Subscript, Superscript, Tab, and Underline.

Italic

The Italic element tells the browser should to render the element's content in an italic font. If the browser cannot render text in italics, it defaults to another format it supports. The Italic element does not use any attributes. The tags that define the beginning and ending of the element are:

```
<I> . . . </I>
```

In both HTML 2.0 and 3.0, the following elements (listed alphabetically) may appear within an Italic element: Anchor, Bold, Line Break, Citation, Code, Emphasis, Italic, Image, Keyboard, Sample, Strong, Teletype, and Variable.

In HTML 3.0, the following elements are also allowed within the Italic element: Abbreviation, Acronym, Author, Big Print, Definition, Deleted Text, Inserted Text, Language, Math, Person, Quotation, Small Print, Strikethrough, Subscript, Superscript, Tab, and Underline.

In HTML 2.0, the Italic element may appear only within the following elements: Address, Anchor, Blockquote, Body, Bold, Citation, Code, Definition, Emphasis, Headers, Italic, Keyboard, List Item, Paragraph, Preformatted Text, Sample, Strong, Teletype, Term, and Variable.

In HTML 3.0, the Italic element may also appear within the following elements: Abbreviation, Acronym, Author, Big, Deleted Text, Image, Inserted

Text, Language, Line Break, Math, Person, Quotation, Small, Strikethrough, Subscript, Superscript, Tab, and Underline.

Underline

The Underline element tells the browser to render an underline font. If the browser cannot render underlined text, it defaults to another format it supports. The Underline element does not use any attributes. The tags that define the beginning and ending of the element are:

```
<U> . . . </U>
```

In both HTML 2.0 and 3.0, the following elements (listed alphabetically) may appear within an Underline element: Anchor, Bold, Line Break, Citation, Code, Emphasis, Italic, Image, Keyboard, Sample, Strong, Teletype, and Variable.

In HTML 3.0, the following elements are also allowed within the Underline element: Abbreviation, Acronym, Author, Big Print, Definition, Deleted Text, Inserted Text, Language, Math, Person, Quotation, Small Print, Strikethrough, Subscript, Superscript, and Tab.

In HTML 2.0, the Underline element may appear only within the following elements: Address, Anchor, Blockquote, Body, Bold, Citation, Code, Definition, Emphasis, Headers, Italic, Keyboard, List Item, Paragraph, Preformatted Text, Sample, Strong, Teletype, Term, and Variable.

In HTML 3.0, the Underline element may also appear within the following elements: Abbreviation, Acronym, Author, Big, Deleted Text, Image, Inserted Text, Language, Line Break, Math, Person, Quotation, Small, Strikethrough, Subscript, Superscript, and Tab.

7.3.8 Image Element

The Image element is used to place inline images in an HTML document. It must be used in conjunction with the SRC attribute to identify the image file. Both HTML 2.0 and 3.0 support the use of the ALIGN, ALT, and ISMAP attributes. In HTML 3.0, the following attributes are also supported: CLASS, ID, LANG, MD, plus WIDTH, HEIGHT, and UNITS.

The Image element has no closing tag. The open tag is `<IMG>`.

NOTE

The following attributes were all defined in the "Common HTML Element Attributes" sidebar earlier in this chapter: SRC, ALIGN, CLASS, ID, LANG, and MD.

The ALT attribute tells what value a nongraphical browser should display instead of the image. By providing an ALT tag, a graphic can be summed up in words so that users still get a message of some kind. To indicate that the inline image is an image map, use the ISMAP attribute. When the ISMAP attribute is present and the Image element is contained within a hypertext link, the browser should allow the user to select a portion of the graphic and pass the location coordinates along to the server.

The values for the WIDTH and HEIGHT attributes suggest to the browser the width and height of the image display. By default, this value is measured in pixels. The UNITS attribute is used in conjunction with WIDTH and HEIGHT. The valid values for this attribute are "en" and "pixels" to indicate that the values for the HEIGHT and WIDTH attributes should be measured in en-units or pixels, respectively.

The ALIGN attribute is used to specify how text aligns with the baseline of an accompanying image. When used with the Image element, the only valid alignments are "TOP," "MIDDLE," or "BOTTOM." These values specify that the baseline of the text should be aligned with the top, middle, or bottom of the image. For example, when rendered, the following HTML code looks like the screen shown in Figure 7-5:

```
<IMG SRC="netgen.gif" ALIGN=TOP>This text should be even with the top of the
image.<p>
<HR>
<IMG SRC="netgen.gif" ALIGN=MIDDLE>This text is centered on the image.
<HR>
<IMG SRC="netgen.gif" ALIGN=BOTTOM>This text should share the same baseline
as the image.
```

No elements may appear within an Image element.

Under HTML 2.0, the Image element is only allowed within the content of the Anchor, Address, Blockquote, Body, Bold, Citation, Code, Definition, Term, Emphasis, Form, Headings 1–6, Italic, Keyboard, List Item, Paragraph, Sample, Strong, Teletype, and Variable elements.

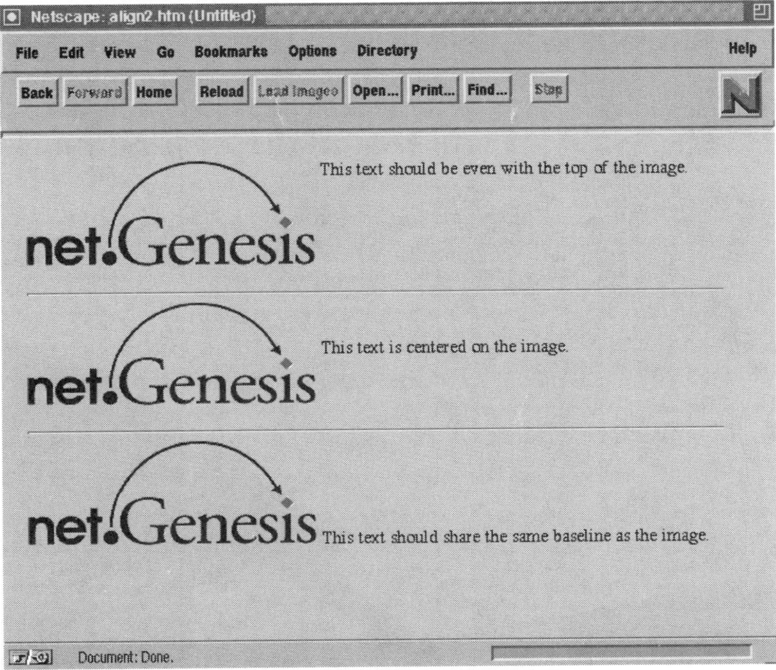

Figure 7–5 This page illustrates a TOP, MIDDLE, and BOTTOM alignment of text and an image

In HTML 3.0, the Image element itself may appear within the following elements: Abbreviation, Acronym, Author, Big, Deleted Text, Inserted Text, Language, Line Break, Math, Person, Quotation, Small, Strikethrough, Subscript, Superscript, Tab, and Underline.

7.3.9 Form Elements

Forms support is what makes a Web site truly interactive. Forms allow users to transmit information back to the Web server. Two things are necessary for form support to be functional. The first is a correctly written HTML document that contains the right form tags. Second is a CGI script to process forms when they are submitted. The CGI script is beyond the scope of this chapter, but we cover it in Chapter 9. In this section we describe the HTML elements used to define input forms and fields.

Form

The Form element is used to define a form. Both HTML 2.0 and 3.0 support the ACTION, METHOD, and ENCTYPE attributes. Only HTML 3.0 supports the SCRIPT attribute.

The tags that define the beginning and end of a Form element are `<FORM>. . . </FORM>`.

The value of the ACTION attribute specifies the URI of the resource to which the form's contents should be submitted. It defines the protocol that should be used when submitting the data. Currently, browsers are only required to support HTTP for submitting forms. If no value is provided for the ACTION attribute, the URI of the current document is assumed.

The value of the METHOD attribute specifies the method that should be used when submitting the data. This method must be valid for the protocol specified in ACTION. For example, if the value of the ACTION attribute specifies that the form should be submitted using HTTP, valid values for METHOD are "GET," "POST," and "PUT."

NOTE

Because the valid values for the METHOD attribute depend on the protocol being used, these values are not always case-insensitive. It depends on the protocol being used. In particular, HTTP methods are case-sensitive, which means that "get" and "Get" are *not* valid values for the METHOD attribute when HTTP is the protocol being used.

The ENCTYPE attribute specifies the format of the data to be submitted. Valid values for this field depend on the protocol and method being used. If HTTP is being used as the protocol with the POST method, for example, then the value of this attribute corresponds to the Content-Type sent in the request. If no ENCTYPE is provided in this situation, the value defaults to "application/x-www-form-urlencoded."

Finally, the SCRIPT attribute is used to provide a URL for a script that should be read in by the browser and used to process the form. No scripting language has been specified as yet.

In HTML 2.0, the following elements (listed alphabetically) may appear within the Form element: Address, Anchor, Blockquote, Bold, Citation, Code, Directory List, Definition List, Emphasis, Headings 1–6, Horizontal Rule, Image, Input, Isindex, Italic, Keyboard, Line Break, Menu, Ordered List,

Paragraph, Preformatted Text, Sample, Select, Strong, Teletype, Textarea, Unordered List, and Variable.

In HTML 3.0, the following elements may also appear within the Form element: Abbreviation, Acronym, Admonishment, Author, Big, Definition, Deleted Text, Division, Figure, Footnote, Inserted Text, Language, Math, Person, Quotation, Select (No Form), Small, Strikethrough, Subscript, Superscript, Tab, Table, and Underline.

Under HTML 2.0, the Form element is only allowed within the content of the Blockquote, Body, Definition, and List Item elements.

In HTML 3.0, the Form element itself may only appear within the following elements: Abbreviation, Acronym, Address, Admonishment, Anchor, Author, Big, Blockquote, Bold, Citation, Code, Definition, Definition List, Deleted Text, Division, Emphasis, Figure, Footnote, Headings 1–6, Horizontal Rule, Image, Inserted Text, Isindex, Italic, Keyboard, Language, Line Break, Math, Ordered List, Person, Preformatted Text, Quotation, Sample, Small, Strikethrough, Strong, Subscript, Superscript, Tab, Table, Teletype, Underline, Unordered List, and Variable.

Input

The Input element is used to create input fields on the form—that is, fields in which the user can input or modify values. The Input element uses only a beginning tag:

```
<INPUT>
```

Both HTML 2.0 and 3.0 support the use of the following attributes with the INPUT element: TYPE, NAME, VALUE, SRC, CHECKED SIZE, MAXLENGTH, and ALIGN. HTML 3.0 also supports the use of the ID, LANG, CLASS, DISABLED, ERROR, MIN, MAX, and ACCEPT attributes. (See the "Common HTML Element Attributes" sidebar earlier in this chapter for descriptions of the SRC, ALIGN, ID, LANG, and CLASS attributes.)

The value of the TYPE attribute specifies the type of input area that should be used. When using HTML 2.0, valid values for TYPE are: "CHECKBOX," "HIDDEN," "IMAGE," "PASSWORD," "RADIO," "RESET," "SUBMIT," and "TEXT." HTML 3.0 added support for three more TYPE values: "RANGE," "FILE," and "SCRIBBLE." If no type is provided, the value defaults to "TEXT." The TEXT type is used for a single line of user input. TEXT input fields can use the SIZE and MAXLENGTH attributes.

The PASSWORD type is used just like the TEXT type, except that when the user fills in the field, the text is not displayed by the browser. The HIDDEN type is similar in functionality, but not in purpose. The HIDDEN type is used to send content in the form without presenting it to the user. The HIDDEN type is commonly used to store information in a field that is used for processing and shouldn't be changed.

The CHECKBOX type is used to provide the user multiple values to choose from. The user can select more than one choice. If the field is selected when the form is submitted, the name and value for the field are submitted. If the field is not selected, no value is returned for the field. The default value for CHECKBOX fields is "ON."

The RADIO type gives users a series of choices from which they can only select a single value. In addition to the RADIO type, an explicit VALUE attribute must be included.

The RESET type is used to reset the form's fields to their initial values when selected. The VALUE attribute is used as a label for the submit field.

The IMAGE type value is no longer valid under HTML 3.0. However, in HTML 2.0 the IMAGE type is a combination of the SUBMIT type and an image map. When a user selects an IMAGE type, the form is automatically submitted along with the coordinates of the click in the image.

The SUBMIT type is used to submit the contents of the form when it is selected. The VALUE attribute is used as a label for the submit field. Unless it is explicitly included on the form, the submit button does not contribute a name and value pair to the string sent to the server. Under HTML 3.0, you can use the SRC attribute to specify an image to be used as the button.

The RANGE type is used to specify a range of values. Typically, it is rendered as a slider or knob. The MIN and MAX attributes are used to specify upper and lower bounds for the range. The VALUE attribute can be used to set the default value within the range.

The SCRIBBLE type is used to send images made by writing on another image. The value of the SRC attribute specifies the URI of the base image to provide to the user. The FILE type is used to send files to the server within the form. The ACCEPT attribute is used to specify a list of acceptable MIME Content-Types that can be sent with the form.

Getting back to the Input element attributes, the ALIGN attribute can be used only when TYPE equals "IMAGE," "SCRIBBLE," "SUBMIT," or "RESET," and it tells the browser how to align the image. Valid attribute values are the same as the ones for the ALIGN attribute of the Image element.

The CHECKED attribute is only valid when the value of the TYPE attribute equals "CHECKBOX" or "RADIO." In these cases, it indicates that the field should default to being selected.

The MAXLENGTH attribute is only valid when the value of the TYPE attribute equals TEXT. In these cases, MAXLENGTH limits the number of characters that the user may input.

The value of the NAME attribute is used as an identifier when the data is submitted.

The SIZE attribute is only valid when the value of the TYPE attribute equals "TEXT." In this case, it tells the browser how big the physical box should be.

The VALUE attribute is required for Input elements where TYPE equals "RADIO." In general, the value of this attribute will be sent when the field within the form is selected.

The DISABLED attribute specifies that the input field should be rendered but that the value should not be modifiable by the user. The ERROR attribute specifies a reason why the input field's value is incorrect. The INPUT element itself may only appear within a Form element or within another Input element.

No elements are allowed within the contents of the Input element under either HTML 2.0 or 3.0. Under HTML 2.0 and 3.0, the Input elements may appear only within the Form element.

Select

The Select element allows the user to select from a set of one or more Option elements. The Select element generally is rendered by browsers as a pull-down menu (or as a pop-up list with Lynx). HTML 3.0 allows you to define graphical menus by using the SRC attribute and the SHAPE attribute in each option element. By doing this, you can define a menu-like selection field that both text and graphical viewers can use. The beginning and ending tags for this element are:

```
<SELECT NAME="lowercase name value"> . . . </SELECT>
```

Both HTML 2.0 and 3.0 support the use of the ALIGN, NAME, SIZE, and MULTIPLE attributes. In addition, HTML 3.0 supports the use of CLASS, ID, LANG, SRC (see the "Common HTML Element Attributes" sidebar earlier in this chapter), plus MULTIPLE, NAME, HEIGHT, WIDTH, and UNITS.

If the MULTIPLE attribute is provided, it specifies that multiple values may be selected. The required NAME attribute provides the name part of the name/value pair that is sent when the data is submitted to the server. The SIZE attribute specifies the number of options that should be initially visible to the user.

The values for the WIDTH and HEIGHT attributes suggest to the browser the width and height of the image display. By default, this value is measured in pixels. The UNITS attribute is used in conjunction with WIDTH and HEIGHT. The valid values for the UNITS attribute are "en" and "pixels," which tell whether the values for the HEIGHT and WIDTH attributes should be measured in en-units or pixels, respectively.

Only the Option element may appear within a Select element under HTML 2.0 or 3.0. Under HTML 2.0, the Select element is only allowed within the content of the Form element.

In HTML 3.0, the Select element itself may only appear within the following elements: Abbreviation, Acronym, Address, Admonishment, Anchor, Author, Big, Blockquote, Bold, Citation, Code, Definition, Definition List, Deleted Text, Division, Emphasis, Figure, Footnote, Form, Headings 1–6, Horizontal Rule, Image, Inserted Text, Isindex, Italic, Keyboard, Language, Line Break (within a form), Math, Ordered List, Person, Preformatted Text, Quotation, Sample, Small, Strikethrough, Strong, Subscript, Superscript, Tab, Table, Teletype, Underline, Unordered List, and Variable.

Option

The Option element is only allowed in conjunction with the Select element. It is used to specify one of the options that the user may select. The beginning and ending tags for the element are:

```
<OPTION> . . . </OPTION>
```

The ending tag is not required, because the end of one option is assumed when the browser encounters a new beginning tag.

Both HTML 2.0 and 3.0 support the use of the SELECTED and VALUE attributes with the Option element. In addition, HTML 3.0 supports the CLASS, ID, and LANG attributes (see the "Common HTML Element Attributes" sidebar earlier in this chapter), plus ERROR, SHAPE, and DISABLED.

When the DISABLED attribute is present, it indicates that the option should be shown but not be selectable. Its functionality is similar to a "grayed-out" (or "ghosted") menu item. You might want to let the user know that a certain functionality exists but isn't available in the current form. The DISABLED attribute is only proposed and may not be supported by most browsers.

When the SELECTED attribute is present, it indicates that the option should be selected by default. And the VALUE attribute is used to specify the value that is returned to the server if the field is selected when the form is submitted. If the VALUE attribute is not specified, the contents of the Option element are used as the value that is sent.

The ERROR attribute specifies a reason why the input field's value is incorrect.

The SHAPE attribute is used for graphical menus. It is used to create links from regions of figures to other resources. Functionally, the SHAPE attribute replaces server-side, clickable image map support by allowing such information to be encoded in the HTML itself. For a figure, you could provide multiple anchors, each of which specified a link from a portion of the figure to a resource. Therefore, instead of having to pass the coordinates of a user's selection to the server for processing, the browser could interpret the selection itself and retrieve the appropriate resource.

The acceptable values for the SHAPE attribute are as follows:

```
<OPTION SHAPE="default">
<OPTION SHAPE="circle x, y, r">
<OPTION SHAPE="rect x, y, w, h">
<OPTION SHAPE="polygon x1, y1, x2, y2, . . .">
```

Each of these defines a region of the figure as a link. The "circle" value defines a circle centered at the coordinates *x,y* with radius *r.* The "rect" value defines a rectangular area with a width *w,* a height *h,* and its upper-left corner positioned at *x,y.* The "polygon" value creates a polygon-shaped link defined by a series of points (each of the *x,y* pairs). The first pair of *x,y* coordinates should be the same as the last in order to close the polygon. The "default" value is used to define a link when the selection does not fit any of the other shapes.

In HTML 2.0, no other elements may appear within an Option element. However, the following elements may appear with an Option element in HTML 3.0: Anchor, Address, Blockquote, Definition List, Directory List, Division, Emphasis, Figure, Form, Headings 1–6, Horizontal Rule, Image, Isindex, Math, Menu, Ordered List, Paragraph, Preformatted Text, Table, and Unordered List.

The Option element itself may only appear within a Select element under HTML 2.0 or 3.0.

Textarea

If you want to allow users to enter more than one line of input data, use the Textarea element. The beginning and ending tags are:

```
<TEXTAREA> . . . </TEXTAREA>
```

Both HTML 2.0 and 3.0 require the use of the NAME, ROWS, and COLS attributes. In addition, HTML 3.0 supports the use of the CLASS, ID, and LANG attributes (see the "Common HTML Element Attributes" sidebar earlier in this chapter), plus ALIGN, DISABLED, and ERROR.

The NAME attribute specifies the name of the field that will be used when the contents of the form are submitted. ROWS and COLS specify the number of row and columns that the input area should span.

The ALIGN attribute is used to specify the baseline alignment of text to the Textarea. When used with the Textarea element, the only valid alignments are "TOP," "MIDDLE," "LEFT," and "BOTTOM." These values specify that the baseline of the text should be aligned with the top, middle, left, or bottom of the image.

When the DISABLED attribute is present, it indicates that the option should be shown but not be selectable. Functionally, it is similar to a "grayed-out" (or "ghosted") menu item. You might want to let the user know that a certain functionality exists but isn't available in the current form. This attribute is only proposed and may not be supported by most browsers.

The ERROR attribute specifies a reason why the input field's value is incorrect.

No elements may appear within a Textarea element. In HTML 3.0, the Textarea element itself may appear only within a Form element.

7.4 HTML Level 3.0–Only Elements

HTML 3.0 adds many extensions to HTML 2.0. These extensions provide much more flexibility for formatting text and typing data so that text and data are rendered appropriately. This version of HTML also adds figures to give HTML more functionality.

7.4.1 Head Elements

HTML 3.0 allows for the following additional head elements.

Banner

The Banner element is used to define a special section of a document whose contents should always be visible (i.e., should not scroll with the rest of the page). The beginning and ending tags are:

```
<BANNER> . . . </BANNER>
```

Banner accepts the following attributes: ID, LANG, and CLASS.

Under HTML 3.0, the Banner elements may appear only at the beginning of the Body element.

In HTML 3.0, the following elements may appear within the Banner element: Abbreviation, Acronym, Address, Admonishment, Anchor, Author, Big Print, Blockquote, Bold, Citation, Code, Definition, Definition List, Deleted Text, Division, Emphasis, Figure, Footnote, Form, Headings 1–6, Horizontal Rule, Image, Inserted Text, Isindex, Italic, Keyboard, Language, Line Break., Math, Ordered List, Person, Preformatted Text, Quotation, Sample, Small Print, Strikethrough, Strong, Subscript, Superscript, Tab, Table, Teletype, Underline, Unordered List, and Variable.

Style

Authors can gain greater control over the way pages look by using the Style element. This one tells the browser to bypass its standard defaults and look elsewhere for its rendering information. The Style element has not yet been implemented and none of the browsers currently support it. However, we expect it to be used quite often in the near future. The amount of control it gives to the information provider is irresistible.

The beginning and ending tags for the Style element are:

```
<STYLE NOTATION="stylename"> . . . </STYLE>
```

The content of a Style element is interpreted according to style specifications corresponding to the value of the NOTATION attribute. This value must be the name of a recognized style notation. The only currently defined names are “w3-style” and “dsssl-lite.” DSSSL (Document Style Semantic Specification Language) is an ISO standard for SGML presentation semantics. As a whole, DSSSL is too complex for use on the Web, but DSSSL Lite (a subset of DSSSL created by James Clark) has potential.

Range

Another element that has been added to HTML 3.0 is the Range element. This lets you mark a section of content, such as something that recently changed or the results of a search. The kinds of marks that can be made are determined by the style sheets.

The current attributes are FROM, CLASS, ID, and UNTIL. The CLASS and ID attributes were defined earlier. The values of the FROM and UNTIL attributes are of the ID attribute used within other elements. Here is an example:

```
<RANGE CLASS=" . . . " FROM=" . . . " UNTIL=" . . . ">
```

Because the Range element allows you to specify the identifiers for the beginning and end of the range, ranges can overlap. As you can see in the next example, the first range (of the ABSTRACT type) extends from the identifiers MARK1 to MARK3. This overlaps the second range (of the CHANGED type) which goes from the identifiers MARK2 to MARK4:

```
<RANGE CLASS=ABSTRACT FROM=MARK1 UNTIL=MARK3>
<RANGE CLASS=CHANGED FROM=MARK2 UNTIL=MARK4>
<SPOT ID=MARK1>
<en>net.Genesis</en> is a high-end provider of Internet-based business
communications software and services. The assembled team of professionals,
with strong ties to the Massachusetts Institute of Technology (MIT) and the
Massachusetts high-tech community, has experience and technical competence
with developing software products for the Internet and the WWW.
<SPOT ID=MARK2>
The four founders have combined their technical and business acumen to
create a world-class, technology-advanced organization with a proven track
record.
<SPOT ID=MARK3>
Rajat Bhargava, President and CEO
Eric Richard, Director of Product Development
Matthew Cutler, Director of Business Development
Matthew Gray, Chief Technologist
<SPOT ID=MARK4>
```

7.4.2 Block Formatting Elements

HTML 3.0 allows for the following additional block formatting elements.

Division

The Division element is used to define standard sections of a document that are not otherwise supported (e.g., appendix, abstract, etc.). The tags that define the beginning and end of a Division element are:

```
<DIV> . . . </DIV>
```

No attributes are required, but the following attributes are supported for use with the Division element: ALIGN, CLASS, ID, LANG, and NOWRAP, all of which are defined in the "Common HTML Element Attributes" sidebar earlier in this chapter.

In HTML 3.0, the following elements may appear within the Division element: Abbreviation, Acronym, Address, Admonishment, Anchor, Author, Big, Blockquote, Bold, Citation, Code, Definition, Definition List, Deleted Text, Division, Emphasis, Figure, Footnote, Form, Headings 1–6, Horizontal Rule, Image, Inserted Text, Isindex, Italic, Keyboard, Language, Line Break., Math, Ordered List, Person, Preformatted Text, Quotation, Sample, Small, Strikethrough, Strong, Subscript, Superscript, Tab, Table, Teletype, Underline, Unordered List, and Variable.

In HTML 3.0, the Division element may appear only within the following elements: Abbreviation, Acronym, Address, Admonishment, Anchor, Author, Big, Blockquote, Bold, Citation, Code, Definition, Definition List, Deleted Text, Emphasis, Figure, Footnote, Form, Headings 1–6, Horizontal Rule, Image, Inserted Text, Isindex, Italic, Keyboard, Language, Line Break, Math, Ordered List, Person, Preformatted Text, Quotation, Sample, Small, Strikethrough, Strong, Subscript, Superscript, Tab, Table, Teletype, Underline, Unordered List, and Variable.

Horizontal Tabs

If you want to provide formatted, horizontal tabs in a document, use the Tab element. This element's two main uses are defining new tab stops and moving to defined tab stops. The Tab element has no closing tag. The open tag is `<TAB>`.

The ID attribute is used to define a new tab stop with the specified name at the current position. The value of this attribute should be unique within the document. The TO attribute is used to move to a previously defined tab stop. The value of this attribute should be the name of a tab stop.

The INDENT attribute is used to specify the number of en units to move horizontally. Basically, it functions as a means of manually specifying the location to move to.

In HTML 3.0, the Tab element may appear within the following elements: Abbreviation, Acronym, Anchor, Author, Big, Bold, Citation, Code, Definition, Deleted Text, Emphasis, Image, Inserted Text, Italic, Keyboard, Language, Line Break, Math, Person, Quotation, Sample, Small, Strikethrough, Strong, Subscript, Superscript, Teletype, Underline, and Variable.

7.4.3 List Elements

HTML 3.0 allows for the following additional list element.

List Header

The List Header element specifies the header for the list. The tags that define the beginning and ending of the element are:

```
<LH> . . . </LH>
```

HTML 3.0 supports the use of the following attributes with the List Header element: CLASS, ID, and LANG (see the "Common HTML Element Attributes" sidebar earlier in this chapter).

The following elements may appear within a List Header element: Abbreviation, Acronym, Anchor, Author, Big, Bold, Citation, Code, Definition, Deleted Text, Emphasis, Image, Inserted Text, Italic, Keyboard, Language, Line Break, Math, Person, Quotation, Sample, Small, Strikethrough, Strong, Subscript, Superscript, Tab, Teletype, Underline, and Variable.

The List Header element itself may only be used within the Unordered List, Ordered List, and Definition List element.

7.4.4 Information Type Elements

HTML 3.0 allows for the following additional information type elements.

Definition

The Definition element indicates that the element's content is the first use of a term and is defined here. The Definition element does not use any attributes. The tags that define the beginning and ending of the element are:

```
<DFN> . . . </DFN>
```

Here is an example:

```
<DFN>Hacks</DFN> -- technically oriented practical jokes -- are common
occurrences at MIT.
```

When using HTML 3.0, the following elements (listed alphabetically) may appear within a Definition element: Abbreviation, Acronym, Anchor, Author, Big Print, Bold, Citation, Code, Deleted Text, Emphasis, Image, Inserted Text, Italic, Keyboard, Language, Line Break, Math, Person, Quotation, Sample, Small Print, Strikethrough, Strong, Subscript, Superscript, Tab, Teletype, Underline, and Variable.

In HTML 3.0, the Definition element itself may appear within the following elements: Abbreviation, Acronym, Anchor, Author, Big Print, Bold, Citation, Code, Deleted Text, Emphasis, Image, Inserted Text, Italic, Keyboard, Language, Line Break, Math, Person, Quotation, Sample, Small Print, Strikethrough, Strong, Subscript, Superscript, Tab, Underline, and Variable.

Quotation

The Quotation element indicates that the text is a short quotation. The use of the LANG attribute is optional (see the "Common HTML Element Attributes" sidebar earlier in this chapter). The tags that define the beginning and ending of the element are:

```
<Q> . . . </Q>
```

In HTML 3.0, the following elements (listed alphabetically) may appear within a Quotation element: Abbreviation, Acronym, Anchor, Author, Big Print, Bold, Citation, Code, Definition, Deleted Text, Emphasis, Image, Inserted Text, Italic, Keyboard, Language, Line Break, Math, Person, Sample, Small Print, Strikethrough, Strong, Subscript, Superscript, Tab, Teletype, Underline, and Variable.

In HTML 3.0, the Quotation element itself may appear within the following elements: Abbreviation, Acronym, Anchor, Author, Big Print, Bold, Citation, Code, Definition, Deleted Text, Emphasis, Image, Inserted Text, Italic, Keyboard, Language, Line Break, Math, Person, Sample, Small Print, Strikethrough, Strong, Subscript, Superscript, Tab, Underline, and Variable.

Language

The Language element is used to specify the language of its content. The difference between the Language element and the LANG attribute used with other elements is that the Language element does not specify any other markup. For example, if you don't want the characters to also be bold, emphasized, italics, etc., you can just use the Language element. The tags that define the beginning and ending of the element are:

```
<LANG> . . . </LANG>
```

In HTML 3.0, the following elements (listed alphabetically) may appear within a Language element: Abbreviation, Acronym, Anchor, Author, Big Print, Bold, Citation, Code, Definition, Deleted Text, Emphasis, Image, Inserted Text, Italic, Keyboard, Line Break, Math, Person, Quotation, Sample, Small Print, Strikethrough, Strong, Subscript, Superscript, Tab, Teletype, Underline, and Variable.

HTML 3.0, the Language element itself may appear within the following elements: Abbreviation, Acronym, Anchor, Author, Big Print, Bold, Citation, Code, Definition, Deleted Text, Emphasis, Image, Inserted Text, Italic, Keyboard, Line Break, Math, Person, Quotation, Sample, Small Print, Strikethrough, Strong, Subscript, Superscript, Tab, Underline, and Variable.

Author

The Author element specifies the name of an author. It does not use any attributes. The tags that define the beginning and ending of the element are:

```
<AU> . . . </AU>
```

In HTML 3.0, the following elements (listed alphabetically) may appear within an Author element: Abbreviation, Acronym, Anchor, Big Print, Bold, Citation, Code, Definition, Deleted Text, Emphasis, Image, Inserted Text, Italic, Keyboard, Language, Line Break, Math, Person, Quotation, Sample, Small Print, Strikethrough, Strong, Subscript, Superscript, Tab, Teletype, Underline, and Variable.

In HTML 3.0, the Author element itself may appear within the following elements: Abbreviation, Acronym, Anchor, Big Print, Bold, Citation, Code, Definition, Deleted Text, Emphasis, Image, Inserted Text, Italic, Keyboard, Language, Line Break, Math, Person, Quotation, Sample, Small Print, Strikethrough, Strong, Subscript, Superscript, Tab, Underline, and Variable.

Person

The Person element specifies the name of a person. It does not use any attributes. The tags that define the beginning and ending of the element are:

```
<PERSON> . . . </PERSON>
```

This is another one of those elements that might be of some use to someone at some time. For example, it is not inconceivable for a robot to roam the Web and create an index of all the People elements. Who knows what that might lead to. It could create a treasure trove of information about a person or interest, or it could create something like this:

```
My favorite actors are <PERSON>Robin Williams</PERSON>, <PERSON>Steve
Martin</PERSON> and <PERSON>Billy Crystal</PERSON>. I am a real SNL
kinda guy.
```

In HTML 3.0, the following elements (listed alphabetically) may appear within a Person element: Abbreviation, Acronym, Anchor, Author, Big Print, Bold, Citation, Code, Definition, Deleted Text, Emphasis, Image, Inserted Text, Italic, Keyboard, Language, Line Break, Math, Quotation, Sample, Small Print, Strikethrough, Strong, Subscript, Superscript, Tab, Teletype, Underline, and Variable.

In HTML 3.0, the Person element itself may appear within the following elements: Abbreviation, Acronym, Anchor, Author, Big Print, Bold, Citation, Code, Definition, Deleted Text, Emphasis, Image, Inserted Text, Italic, Keyboard, Language, Line Break, Math, Quotation, Sample, Small Print, Strikethrough, Strong, Subscript, Superscript, Tab, Underline, and Variable.

Acronym

The Acronym element specifies that the element's content is an acronym. It does not use any attributes. The tags that define the beginning and ending of the element are:

```
<ACRONYM> . . . </ACRONYM>
```

This is another one of those elements that may be useful to someone for some reasons. Here's one potential example:

```
I am a member of the <acronym>Y.M.C.A.</acronym> and really don't like
<acronym>S.D.I.</acronym>
```

In HTML 3.0, the following elements (listed alphabetically) may appear within an Acronym element: Abbreviation, Anchor, Author, Big Print, Bold, Citation, Code, Definition, Deleted Text, Emphasis, Image, Inserted Text, Italic, Keyboard, Language, Line Break, Math, Person, Quotation, Sample, Small Print, Strikethrough, Strong, Subscript, Superscript, Tab, Teletype, Underline, and Variable.

In HTML 3.0, the Acronym element itself may appear within the following elements: Abbreviation, Anchor, Author, Big Print, Bold, Citation, Code, Definition, Deleted Text, Emphasis, Image, Inserted Text, Italic, Keyboard, Language, Line Break, Math, Person, Quotation, Sample, Small Print, Strikethrough, Strong, Subscript, Superscript, Tab, Underline, and Variable.

Abbreviation

The Abbreviation element specifies that the element's content is an abbreviation. It does not use any attributes. The tags that define the beginning and ending of the element are:

```
<ABBREV> . . . </ABBREV>
```

Here is an example:

```
I was born in <abbrev>Oct.</abbrev>, 1973.
```

In HTML 3.0, the following elements (listed alphabetically) may appear within an Abbreviation element: Acronym, Anchor, Author, Big Print, Bold, Citation, Code, Definition, Deleted Text, Emphasis, Image, Inserted Text, Italic, Keyboard, Language, Line Break, Math, Person, Quotation, Sample, Small Print, Strikethrough, Strong, Subscript, Superscript, Tab, Teletype, Underline, and Variable.

In HTML 3.0, the Abbreviation element itself may appear within the following elements: Acronym, Anchor, Author, Big Print, Bold, Citation, Code, Definition, Deleted Text, Emphasis, Image, Inserted Text, Italic, Keyboard, Language, Line Break, Math, Person, Quotation, Sample, Small Print, Strikethrough, Strong, Subscript, Superscript, Tab, Underline, and Variable.

Inserted Text

The Inserted Text element indicates text that has been inserted since a previous version of the document. Browser should render such elements in much the same way as a word-processing program displays ~~edits~~ revision marks. The Inserted Text element does not use any attributes. The tags that define the beginning and ending of the element are:

```
<INS> . . . </INS>
```

In HTML 3.0, the following elements (listed alphabetically) may appear within an Inserted Text element: Abbreviation, Acronym, Anchor, Author, Big Print, Bold, Citation, Code, Definition, Deleted Text, Emphasis, Image, Italic, Keyboard, Language, Line Break, Math, Person, Quotation, Sample, Small Print, Strikethrough, Strong, Subscript, Superscript, Tab, Teletype, Underline, and Variable.

In HTML 3.0, the Inserted Text element itself may appear within the following elements: Abbreviation, Acronym, Anchor, Author, Big Print, Bold, Citation, Code, Definition, Deleted Text, Emphasis, Image, Italic, Keyboard, Language, Line Break, Math, Person, Quotation, Sample, Small Print, Strikethrough, Strong, Subscript, Superscript, Tab, Underline, and Variable.

Deleted Text

The Deleted Text element indicates text that has been deleted since a previous version of the document. Browsers should render such elements in much the same way as a word-processing program displays ~~edits~~ revision marks. The Deleted Text element does not use any attributes. The tags that define the beginning and ending of the element are:

```
<DEL> . . . </DEL>
```

In HTML 3.0, the following elements (listed alphabetically) may appear within a Deleted Text element: Abbreviation, Acronym, Anchor, Author, Big Print, Bold, Citation, Code, Definition, Emphasis, Image, Inserted Text, Italic, Keyboard, Language, Line Break, Math, Person, Quotation, Sample, Small Print, Strikethrough, Strong, Subscript, Superscript, Tab, Teletype, Underline, and Variable.

In HTML 3.0, the Deleted Text element itself may appear within the following elements: Abbreviation, Acronym, Anchor, Author, Big Print, Bold,

Citation, Code, Definition, Emphasis, Image, Inserted Text, Italic, Keyboard, Language, Line Break, Math, Person, Quotation, Sample, Small Print, Strikethrough, Strong, Subscript, Superscript, Tab, Underline, and Variable.

Admonishment

The Admonishment element is used to add asides or warnings to a document. The tags that define the beginning and ending of an Admonishment element are:

```
<NOTE> . . . </NOTE>
```

No attributes are required, but the following attributes are supported: CLASS, CLEAR, ID, LANG, MD, and SRC (see the "Common HTML Element Attributes" sidebar earlier in this chapter).

The following elements may appear within the Admonishment element: Abbreviation, Acronym, Address, Anchor, Author, Big, Blockquote, Bold, Citation, Code, Definition, Definition List, Deleted Text, Division, Emphasis, Figure, Footnote, Form, Headings 1–6, Horizontal Rule, Image, Inserted Text, Isindex, Italic, Keyboard, Language, Line Break, Math, Ordered List, Person, Preformatted Text, Quotation, Sample, Small, Strikethrough, Strong, Subscript, Superscript, Tab, Table, Teletype, Underline, Unordered List, and Variable.

The Admonishment element itself may appear only within the following elements: Abbreviation, Acronym, Address, Anchor, Author, Big Print, Blockquote, Bold, Citation, Code, Definition, Definition List, Deleted Text, Division, Emphasis, Figure, Footnote, Form, Headings 1–6, Horizontal Rule, Image, Inserted Text, Isindex, Italic, Keyboard, Language, Line Break, Math, Ordered List, Person, Preformatted Text, Quotation, Sample, Small, Strikethrough, Strong, Subscript, Superscript, Tab, Table, Teletype, Underline, Unordered List, and Variable.

Footnote

The Footnote element is used to indicate that the element's content is a footnote. The tags that define the beginning and end of a Footnote element are:

```
<FN> . . . </FN>
```

No attributes are required, but the following attributes are supported for use with the Footnote element: CLASS, ID, and LANG (see the "Common HTML Element Attributes" sidebar earlier in this chapter.)

The following elements may appear within the Footnote element: Abbreviation, Acronym, Address, Admonishment, Anchor, Author, Big, Blockquote, Bold, Citation, Code, Definition, Definition List, Deleted Text, Division, Emphasis, Figure, Form, Headings 1–6, Horizontal Rule, Image, Inserted Text, Isindex, Italic, Keyboard, Language, Line Break., Math, Ordered List, Person, Preformatted Text, Quotation, Sample, Small, Strikethrough, Strong, Subscript, Superscript, Tab, Table, Teletype, Underline, Unordered List, and Variable.

The Footnote element itself may appear only within the following elements: Abbreviation, Acronym, Address, Admonishment, Anchor, Author, Big Print, Blockquote, Bold, Citation, Code, Definition, Definition List, Deleted Text, Division, Emphasis, Figure, Form, Headings 1–6, Horizontal Rule, Image, Inserted Text, Isindex, Italic, Keyboard, Language, Line Break, Math, Ordered List, Person, Preformatted Text, Quotation, Sample, Small Print, Strikethrough, Strong, Subscript, Superscript, Tab, Table, Teletype, Underline, Unordered List, Variable.

7.4.5 Character Formatting Elements

HTML 3.0 allows for the following additional character formatting elements.

Strikethrough

The Strikethrough element specifies that the browser should render in a ~~strikethrough~~ font (by drawing a line through the text). If the browser cannot render such a font, it defaults to another format supported by the browser. The Strikethrough element does not use any attributes. The tags that define the beginning and ending of the element are:

```
<S> . . . </S>
```

In HTML 3.0, the following elements (listed alphabetically) may appear within a Strikethrough element: Abbreviation, Acronym, Anchor, Author, Big, Bold, Citation, Code, Definition, Deleted Text, Emphasis, Image, Inserted Text, Italic, Keyboard, Language, Line Break, Math, Person, Quotation, Sample, Small, Strong, Subscript, Superscript, Tab, Teletype, Underline, and Variable.

In HTML 3.0, the Strikethrough element may appear within the following elements: Abbreviation, Acronym, Anchor, Author, Big, Bold, Citation, Code, Definition, Deleted Text, Emphasis, Image, Inserted Text, Italic, Keyboard, Language, Line Break, Math, Person, Quotation, Sample, Small, Strong, Subscript, Superscript, Tab, Teletype, Underline, and Variable.

Big Print

The Big Print element specifies that the browser should render text in a large font. If the browser cannot render in a large font, it defaults to another format supported by the browser. The Big Print element does not use any attributes. The tags that define the beginning and ending of the element are:

```
<BIG> . . . </BIG>
```

In HTML 3.0, the following elements (listed alphabetically) may appear within a Big Print element: Abbreviation, Acronym, Anchor, Author, Bold, Citation, Code, Definition, Deleted Text, Emphasis, Image, Inserted Text, Italic, Keyboard, Language, Line Break, Math, Person, Quotation, Sample, Small, Strikethrough, Strong, Subscript, Superscript, Tab, Teletype, Underline, and Variable.

In HTML 3.0, the Big Print element may also appear within the following elements: Abbreviation, Acronym, Anchor, Author, Bold, Citation, Code, Definition, Deleted Text, Emphasis, Image, Inserted Text, Italic, Keyboard, Language, Line Break, Math, Person, Quotation, Sample, Small, Strikethrough, Strong, Subscript, Superscript, Tab, Teletype, Underline, and Variable.

Small Print

The Small Print element specifies that the browser should render text in a small font. If the browser cannot render text in a small font, it defaults to another format supported by the browser. The Small Print element does not use any attributes. The tags that define the beginning and ending of the element are:

```
<SMALL> . . . </SMALL>
```

In HTML 3.0, the following elements (listed alphabetically) may appear within a Small Print element: Abbreviation, Acronym, Anchor, Author, Big, Bold, Citation, Code, Definition, Deleted Text, Emphasis, Image, Inserted

Text, Italic, Keyboard, Language, Line Break, Math, Person, Quotation, Sample, Strikethrough, Strong, Subscript, Superscript, Tab, Teletype, Underline, and Variable.

In HTML 3.0, the Small Print element may also appear within the following elements: Abbreviation, Acronym, Anchor, Author, Big, Bold, Citation, Code, Definition, Deleted Text, Emphasis, Image, Inserted Text, Italic, Keyboard, Language, Line Break, Math, Person, Quotation, Sample, Strikethrough, Strong, Subscript, Superscript, Tab, Teletype, Underline, and Variable.

Subscript

The Subscript element tells the browser to render the element's content in a subscript font. If the browser cannot render the content in subscript, another format supported by the browser is used by default. The Subscript element does not use any attributes. The tags that define the beginning and ending of the element are:

```
<SUB> . . . </SUB>
```

In HTML 3.0, the following elements (listed alphabetically) may appear within a Subscript element: Abbreviation, Acronym, Anchor, Author, Big, Bold, Citation, Code, Definition, Deleted Text, Emphasis, Image, Inserted Text, Italic, Keyboard, Language, Line Break, Math, Person, Quotation, Sample, Small, Strikethrough, Strong, Superscript, Tab, Teletype, Underline, and Variable.

In HTML 3.0, the Subscript element may also appear within the following elements: Abbreviation, Acronym, Anchor, Author, Big, Bold, Citation, Code, Definition, Deleted Text, Emphasis, Image, Inserted Text, Italic, Keyboard, Language, Line Break, Math, Person, Quotation, Sample, Small, Strikethrough, Strong, Superscript, Tab, Teletype, Underline, and Variable.

Superscript

The Superscript element tells the browser to render the element's content in a superscript font. If the browser cannot render text in superscript font, another format supported by the browser is used by default. The Superscript element does not use any attributes. The tags that define the beginning and ending of the element are:

```
<SUP> . . . </SUP>
```

In HTML 3.0, the following elements (listed alphabetically) may appear within a Superscript element: Abbreviation, Acronym, Anchor, Author, Big, Bold, Citation, Code, Definition, Deleted Text, Emphasis, Image, Inserted Text, Italic, Keyboard, Language, Line Break, Math, Person, Quotation, Sample, Small, Strikethrough, Strong, Subscript, Tab, Teletype, Underline, and Variable.

In HTML 3.0, the Superscript element may also appear within the following elements: Abbreviation, Acronym, Anchor, Author, Big, Bold, Citation, Code, Definition, Deleted Text, Emphasis, Image, Inserted Text, Italic, Keyboard, Language, Line Break, Math, Person, Quotation, Sample, Small, Strikethrough, Strong, Subscript, Tab, Teletype, Underline, and Variable.

7.4.6 Figure Elements

HTML 3.0 allows for the following new figure elements.

Figure

The Figure element provides a more robust and efficient means of placing inline images in a document than was possible using the original Image element. The Figure element allows images to be placed inline with text flowing around them. It also allows the image to have a credit and caption to go along with it.

The beginning and ending tags for the Figure element are:

```
<FIG SRC="URI case-sensitive value"> . . . </FIG>
```

The content of the Figure element is expected to describe the content of the figure, much like an ALT attribute for an Image element. However, the content of the Figure element allows for HTML markup, something that was not permitted with the ALT attribute.

According to the HTML 3.0 specification, the Figure element will "help to combat the tendency for authors to forget about the people limited to terminal access or the visually impaired relying on text to speech [i.e., voice synthesizers], as the new element forces you to write description text to define the graphical hypertext links."

The SRC attribute must be used with the Figure element, and the additional attributes supported for use with Figure element are as follows: ALIGN, CLASS, CLEAR, ID, LANG, MD, (all of which are described in the "Common

HTML Element Attributes" sidebar earlier in this chapter), plus NOFLOW, WIDTH, HEIGHT, UNITS, and IMAGEMAP.

The values for the WIDTH and HEIGHT attributes suggest to the browser the width and height of the image display. By default, this value is measured in pixels. The UNITS attribute is used in conjunction with WIDTH and HEIGHT. The valid values for this attribute are "en" and "pixels," which indicate whether the values for the HEIGHT and WIDTH attributes should be measures in en-units or pixels, respectively. In addition, the Figure element can be used in conjunction with the Figure Overlay element to reduce the amount of data that has to be sent in order to update an image.

The IMAGEMAP attribute specifies a URI for the clickable image map script support. This option is only used if no *hot zones* are defined within the figure or no overlays are used. (Hot zones produce graphical and textual hypertext links.)

As noted in the description of the Anchor element, the Figure element can be used in conjunction with the SHAPE attribute of the Anchor element to define hot zones in the image.

ALIGN tells the browser where to align the graphic on the page. When this attribute is used with the Figure element, a number of different values are possible: "BLEEDLEFT," "LEFT," "CENTER," "RIGHT," "BLEEDRIGHT," and "JUSTIFY." "BLEEDLEFT" is flush with the browser's window. "LEFT" is the left margin. "RIGHT" and "BLEEDRIGHT" are analogous. "CENTER" places the image between the text margins, so no text can flow around the figure. "JUSTIFY" sizes the image to meet the right and left margins, so no text can flow around it either.

The NOFLOW attribute specifies that the browser should not flow text around the figure.

In HTML 3.0, the following elements may appear within the Figure element: Abbreviation, Acronym, Address, Admonishment, Anchor, Author, Big, Blockquote, Bold, Caption, Citation, Code, Credit, Definition, Definition List, Deleted Text, Division, Emphasis, Footnote, Form, Headings 1–6, Horizontal Rule, Image, Inserted Text, Isindex, Italic, Keyboard, Language, Line Break, Math, Ordered List, Figure Overlay, Person, Preformatted Text, Quotation, Sample, Small, Strikethrough, Strong, Subscript, Superscript, Tab, Table, Teletype, Underline, Unordered List, and Variable.

In HTML 3.0, the Figure element may appear only within the following elements: Abbreviation, Acronym, Address, Admonishment, Anchor, Author, Big Print, Blockquote, Bold, Citation, Code, Definition, Definition List, Deleted Text, Division, Emphasis, Footnote, Form, Headings 1–6, Horizontal Rule, Image, Text, Isindex, Italic, Keyboard, Language, Line Break, Math, Ordered List, Person, Preformatted Text, Quotation, Sample, Small Print, Strikethrough, Strong, Subscript, Superscript, Tab, Table, Teletype, Underline, Unordered List, and Variable.

Figure Overlay

When you want to superimpose an image on a figure, use the Figure Overlay element. The Figure Overlay element has no closing tag. The open tag is `<OVERLAY>`.

This element does not require the use of any attributes, but these attributes are supported: SRC and MD (see the "Common HTML Element Attributes" sidebar earlier in this chapter) as well as WIDTH, HEIGHT, UNITS, X, Y, and IMAGEMAP.

The values for the WIDTH and HEIGHT attributes suggest to the browser the width and height of the image display. By default, this value is measured in pixels. The UNITS attribute is used in conjunction with WIDTH and HEIGHT. Valid values for this attribute are "en" and "pixels," which indicate whether the values for the HEIGHT and WIDTH attributes should be measures in en-units or pixels, respectively. In addition, the Figure element can be used in conjunction with the Figure Overlay element to reduce the amount of data that has to be sent in order to update an image.

The X attribute is the horizontal offset from the left corner of the base image, and the Y attribute is the vertical offset from the left corner of the base image. The IMAGEMAP attribute specifies a URI for the clickable image map script support. This option is only used if no hot zones are defined within the figure or no overlays are used.

No elements may appear within an Figure Overlay element, and the Figure Overlay element itself may appear only within a Figure element.

Caption

The Caption element is used as a descriptive label for a table or figure. The beginning and ending tags are:

```
<CAPTION> . . . </CAPTION>
```

The ALIGN attribute is used with the Caption element to specify the position relative to the table or figure. This element also supports the use of the ALIGN, CLASS, ID, and LANG attributes (see the "Common HTML Element Attributes" sidebar earlier in this chapter).

In HTML 3.0, the following elements may appear within the Caption element: Abbreviation, Acronym, Anchor, Author, Big Print, Bold, Citation, Code, Definition, Deleted Text, Emphasis, Image, Inserted Text, Italic, Keyboard, Language, Line Break, Math, Person, Quotation, Sample, Small, Strikethrough, Strong, Subscript, Superscript, Tab, Teletype, Underline, and Variable.

The Caption element itself may appear only within Table and Figure elements.

Credit

The Credit element is used to attribute a figure or quote to someone. The beginning and ending tags are:

```
<CREDIT> . . . </CREDIT>
```

The Credit element might be used for giving credit for a quote or picture to a newspaper or news agency. Ultimately, greater user control will be achieved by defining specific elements such as this one. For example, Credit may seem quite a bit like Citation, but having distinct elements allows for the possibility of formatting the two differently.

No attribute is required, but the CLASS, ID, and LANG attributes (see the "Common HTML Element Attributes" sidebar earlier in this chapter) may be used with the Credit element.

In HTML 3.0, the following elements may appear within a Credit element: Abbreviation, Acronym, Anchor, Author, Big, Bold, Citation, Code, Definition, Deleted Text, Emphasis, Image, Inserted Text, Italic, Keyboard, Language, Line Break, Math, Person, Quotation, Sample, Small, Strikethrough, Strong, Subscript, Superscript, Tab, Teletype, Underline, and Variable.

The Credit element itself may only appear within the Blockquote and Figure element.

7.4.7 Table Elements

HTML 3.0 allows for the following new table elements. According to the HTML 3.0 specifications, "The HTML table model was chosen for its simplicity and flexibility."

Table

The Table element allows users to define tables within an HTML document. By default, the size of an HTML table is generated automatically based upon the table's contents and the size of the window in which it is being displayed. However, you can override the default with the COLSPEC or WIDTH attribute.

The tags that define the beginning and end of a Table element are:

```
<TABLE> . . . </TABLE>
```

Tables have two types of cells: header and data. The header cells are centered automatically; the data cells are flush left. (This can be overridden with the ALIGN attribute). A table is defined by a set of Table Row elements and an optional Caption element.

The Table element does not require the use of any attributes. However, the following attributes are supported for use with the Table element: ALIGN, CLASS, CLEAR, ID, LANG, NEEDS, and NOWRAP (see the "Common HTML Element Attributes" sidebar earlier in this chapter), plus UNITS, COLSPEC, WIDTH, and BORDER.

The UNIT attribute specifies the type of units for the COLSPEC attribute. There are three possible values: "en," "pixels," and "relative"—the last of which is used to define the widths of columns relative to the total width of the entire table.

The COLSPEC attribute is used to specify the column widths and alignment for each column. The value is a space-delimited list of column entries corresponding to each of the columns, from right to left. Each column entry has the alignment of the column and a number that specifies the width of the column in whatever units are specified by the UNITS attribute. The possible values for the alignment are "L" (left), "C" (center), "R" (right), and "J" (justified).

For example, suppose you had five columns and the first two needed to be left-justified, the third centered, and the last two right-justified. Moreover, each column had to be 25 UNITS wide except for the center one, which had to be 50. You would use the following attribute:

```
COLSPEC="L25 L25 C50 R25 R25"
```

The COLSPEC attribute tells the browser how wide the table should be in UNITS. If the value in UNITS is relative, then the value is taken as a percentage between the right and left margins. The BORDER attribute tells the browser to create a border around the table. The exact type of border can be specified by the STYLE element.

The only elements that may appear within a Table element are an optional caption, and then one or more Table Row elements. (See the accompanying sidebar on tables.)

In HTML 3.0, the Table element itself may appear only within the following elements: Abbreviation, Acronym, Address, Admonishment, Anchor, Author, Big Print, Blockquote, Bold, Citation, Code, Definition, Definition List, Deleted Text, Division, Emphasis, Figure, Footnote, Form, Headings 1–6, Horizontal Rule, Image, Inserted Text, Isindex, Italic, Keyboard, Language, Line Break, Math, Ordered List, Person, Preformatted Text, Quotation, Sample, Small Print, Strikethrough, Strong, Subscript, Superscript, Tab, Teletype, Underline, Unordered List, and Variable.

Table Row

The Table Row element is used to specify a row of a table. The tags that define the beginning and end of a Table Row element are:

```
<TR> . . . </TR>
```

The closing Table Row tag is not necessary because a TR ending is assumed whenever a new TR element is encountered.

The Table Row element does not require the use of attributes. Nevertheless, the following attributes may be used with the Table Row element: ALIGN,

A Quick Introduction to Tables

HTML 3.0 tables basically look like this:

```
<table>
<tr>  <td>1,1</td>  <td>1,2</td>  <td>1,3</td>  </tr>
<tr>  <td>2,1</td>  <td>2,2</td>  <td>2,3</td>  </tr>
</table>
```

TR stands for Table Row and TD stands for Table Data. Figures 7-6, 7-7, and 7-8 provide you with an illustrated, quick introduction to the world of tables in HTML 3.0.

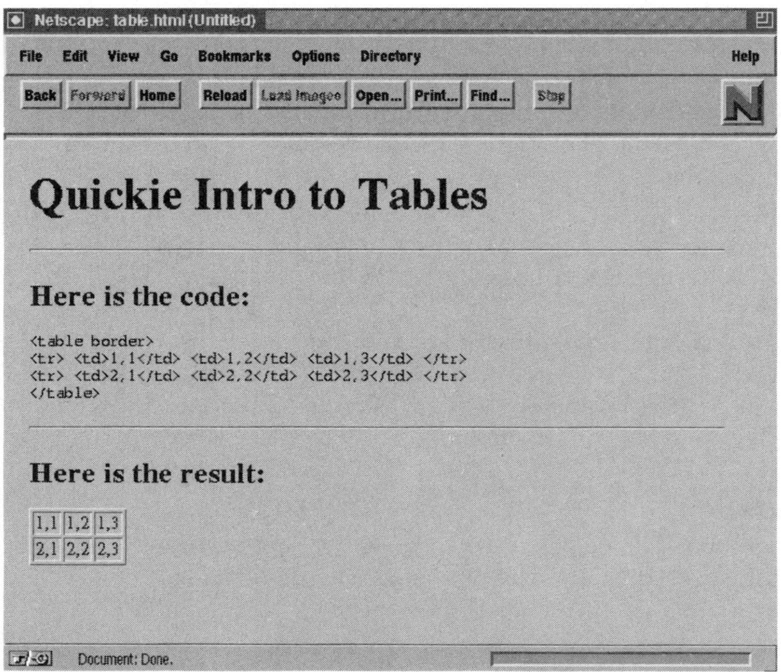

Figure 7–6 Quickie intro to tables—the basics

CLASS, ID, LANG, NOWRAP (see the "Common HTML Element Attributes sidebar earlier in this chapter). ALIGN supports an extra value, "decimal," which specifies that lines should be vertically aligned on their decimal point. DP specifies the character to be used as the decimal point. VALIGN specifies the vertical alignment within the table row. Acceptable values are "top," "middle," "bottom," and "baseline."

The Table Header and Table Data elements may appear within a Table Row element. The Table Row element itself may be used within a Table element.

Table Header and Table Data

The Table Header and Table Data elements are used to specify the table headers and table data within a table. The tags that define the beginning and end of a Table Header element are:

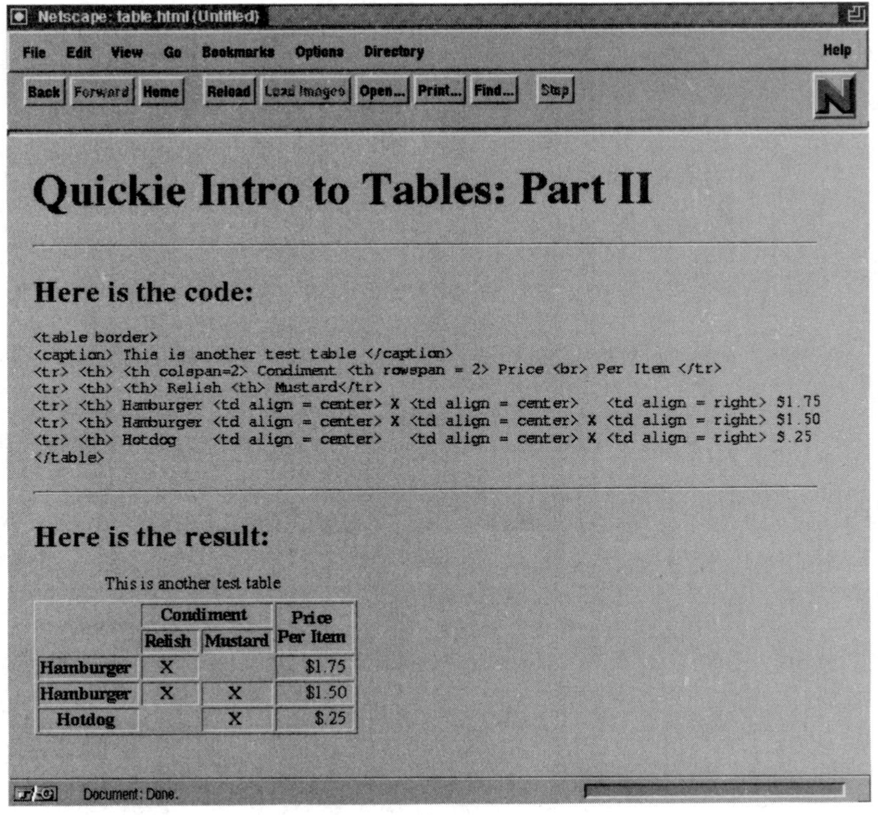

Figure 7-7 Quickie intro to tables—using the Caption and Table Header elements

```
<TH> . . . </TH>
```

while the tags that define the beginning and end of a Table Data element are:

```
<TD> . . . </TD>
```

No attributes are required for either element, but the following attributes are supported for use with these elements: ALIGN, CLASS, ID, LANG, and

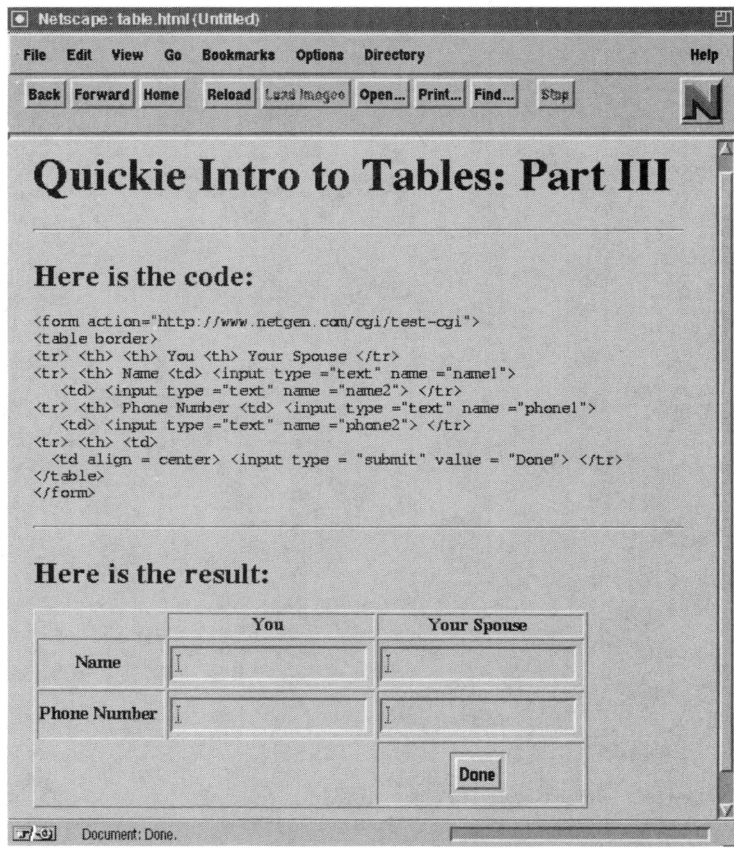

Figure 7–8 Quickie intro to tables—using Input elements

NOWRAP (see the "Common HTML Element Attributes" sidebar earlier in this chapter), in addition to COLSPAN, ROWSPAN, DP, VALIGN, AXIS, and AXES.

The COLSPAN attribute lets you span the cell across multiple columns. By default, only one column is spanned. This is quite useful for row headers. Similarly, the ROWSPAN attribute lets you span the cell across multiple rows. By default only one column is spanned. This is quite useful for row headers. The AXIS attribute defines an abbreviated version of a header for a cell. The AXES attribute contains a list of abbreviated names for the cell's row and column headers.

The following elements may appear within a Table Header element: Anchor, Abbreviation, Acronym, Address, Author, Bold, Big, Blockquote, Line Break, Code, Deleted Text, Definition, Division, Emphasis, Figure, Footnote, Form, Headers 1–6, Horizontal Rule, Italic, Image, Inserted Text, Isindex, Keyboard, Language, Math, Note, Person, Preformatted Text, Ordered List, Quotation, Strikethrough, Sample, Site, Small, Strong, Subscript, Superscript, Tab, Table, Teletype, Underline, Unordered List, and Variable.

In HTML 3.0, the following elements may appear within the Table Header and Table Data elements: Abbreviation, Acronym, Address, Admonishment, Anchor, Author, Big, Blockquote, Bold, Citation, Code, Definition, Definition List, Deleted Text, Division, Emphasis, Figure, Footnote, Form, Headings 1–6, Horizontal Rule, Image, Inserted Text, Isindex, Italic, Keyboard, Language, Line Break, Math, Ordered List, Person, Preformatted Text, Quotation, Sample, Small, Strikethrough, Strong, Subscript, Superscript, Tab, Table, Teletype, Underline, Unordered List, and Variable.

The Table Header and Table Data elements themselves may appear with Table Row elements.

7.4.8 Mathematical Equations

HTML 3.0 introduces the ability to create mathematical equations. HTML math functionality is based upon the LaTeX math mode. Equations are rendered through the use of various attributes and tags. Furthermore, specific markup tags are used for the mathematical equations. As this book goes to print, however, most of these new elements are undefined in their syntax.

CHAPTER 8

Using HTML

CHAPTER AT A GLANCE

This chapter provides an in-depth discussion and interpretation on the specification governing Hypertext Markup Language (HTML). We show you how to take advantage of its strengths and provide tips to work around its weaknesses. In particular, we suggest the use of various design elements and point out the pitfalls of using HTML in certain ways. We include pictures of pages depicting both good and bad design elements, and also talk specifically about using HTML for forms and tables.

REQUISITES

Enough familiarity with HTML 2.0 or 3.0 to write HTML documents as described in Chapter 7.

MORE DETAIL

Chapter 10 provides hints and tips for designing the structure and HTML for your site.

Chapter 12 provides an actual example of using this knowledge to write an HTTP client which analyzes the content of HTML documents.

The HTML 2.0 Internet Draft (see Appendix C) provides an in-depth definition of the standard and its features.

The best way to learn HTML is to start creating pages. Now that you've learned the fundamental tags that are used within the language, the best way to master HTML is to just start experimenting. Try things many different ways. For example, there are a number of ways to display lists, and it is a worthwhile exercise to display a list as menu, definition, ordered, unordered, etc., to see what the renderings look like. The same applies to many of the formatting tags.

8.1 Writing HTML

Because the HTML language is based entirely on plain ASCII text, you can use a word processor or text editor to write and edit HTML documents (see the "Emacs HTML Mode" sidebar). Each document should be in a separate file and saved as a text file. Many common PC-based word processors include HTML conversion tools. With these word processors, you can save a normal document (for example, a Microsoft Word document) as an HTML document. This way, you don't actually have to write any of the HTML yourself. However, most of these programs don't give you full control over what the HTML looks like after it is converted. Usually, you can do a lot more if you write the HTML yourself.

The common extensions for HTML files are .html and .htm. The .htm extension is for DOS-based systems that only recognize three-character extensions.

Emacs HTML Mode

Editing HTML is one of those things that a lot of people complain about because they don't like the markup concept. Many HTML editor programs exist, but very few make the process any simpler than it already is. A lot of techie types use the Emacs text editor, and it's probably one of the best. There exists a mode for Emacs called HTML mode, but this tends to make writing HTML more of an effort. Matthew has written a modified HTML mode that doesn't actually do anything except mark the different HTML tags in different colors. Matthew's code only works with Emacs19, which doesn't actually help in writing HTML code but does make it easier to figure out what your HTML is supposed to be doing.

Add the following code to your .emacs file:

Emacs HTML Mode (Continued)

```
(require 'hilit19)
(defun html-mode ()
  "Matthew's html mode"
  (interactive)
  (setq major-mode 'html-mode)
  (setq mode-name "HTML")
  (run-hooks 'fundamental-mode-hook))
(setq auto-mode-alist
      (append '(("\\.html$" . html-mode)
                ("\\.htm$" . html-mode))
              auto-mode-alist))
; HTML stuff
    (hilit-add-pattern "&[^;]+;" "" 'green 'html-mode nil)
   (hilit-add-pattern "<[Ii][mM][Gg] *[^>]+>" "" 'yellow 'html-mode nil)
    (hilit-add-pattern "<[hH][1-6]>" "" 'red 'html-mode nil)
    (hilit-add-pattern "</[hH][1-6]>" "" 'hex-c44 'html-mode nil)
    (hilit-add-pattern "[hH][Rr][Ee][Ff] *= *\"[^\"]+\"^\"]+\"" "" 'hex-
        28c 'html-mode nil)
    (hilit-add-pattern "<[aA][^>]+>" "" 'hex-55e 'html-mode nil)
    (hilit-add-pattern "</[Aa]>" "" 'hex-33c 'html-mode nil)
    (hilit-add-pattern "</[^>]+>" "" 'hex-c7c 'html-mode nil)
    (hilit-add-pattern "<[^>]+>" "" 'hex-b3b 'html-mode nil)
```

Now every time you load an HTML file, it will be in lots of pretty colors.

8.2 HTML, Head, and Body Elements

The HTML, Head, and Body elements are not absolutely required for correct rendering, but including them is a good practice if you want to conform to the specifications in this matter. A completely "correct" document sticks to the following format:

```
<html>
<head>
<!-- Head elements, such as Title go here -->
</head>

<body>
<!-- Body elements, such as paragraphs, text, etc., go here -->
</body>
</html>
```

Every HTML document should begin with a <HTML> tag and ends with a </HTML> tag. (See the "Writing Your Own HTML Page" sidebar.) The HTML element informs the viewer that this portion of the text should be interpreted as HTML. This way, the browser can interpret the text as HTML on its own without having to depend on an outside mechanism (such as a value in the Content-Type header provided by the server) to instruct it to do so. In addition, the HTML element allows for the possibility of including HTML within another document in the future.

Currently, most browsers accept HTML pages that do not use the Head and Body elements. However, according to the specifications, the Head and Body elements are required for separating different sections of a document. You can get away with it now, but not putting these elements in puts you at the mercy of the browser. As the specs evolve, browsers may expect Head and Body elements in the future. And they may use this information to do more interesting things. By not putting these elements in, you are setting yourself up for trouble in the future.

Writing Your Own HTML Page

Rajat Bhargava wanted to create his own home page. He wanted to include a picture of himself, some personal information, and links to the things that are of interest to him. When you create a page, you have to think about the stuff you want to include. The next consideration is whether to create a page that works in HTML 2.0 or a page that uses features supported only by HTML 3.0. For his home page, Rajat wanted to include some cool things that required HTML 3.0, but he also wanted a page that would run under HTML 2.0 specifications. In the end, he opted for two separate pages, one for each HTML version.

Writing Your Own HTML Page (Continued)

Once you've decided on the HTML version, the next task is to think about how the page will look. Rajat wanted his picture to be in the top-left corner with his name next to it. This is where the 2.0 versus 3.0 considerations begin. Rajat wanted his name to be right-justified, but that is not possible in HTML 2.0.

After his picture and his name, Rajat wanted a *divider* or horizontal rule. Version 2.0 does not allow this to be a graphic from within the Horizontal Rule element, so he could not use a graphic image. For the 3.0-compliant page, however, he could use a graphic image. After the divider, he wanted some text about himself that described his personal history. Then he wanted to list the sites of his main interests.

He wanted the net.Genesis home page to be the first site, and after that the MIT home page because MIT is his alma mater. He also put a link to his former employer, Intel. Rajat's other interests include Internet technology (hence the links to NCSA and the Web Consortium). Finally, because he wanted a fairly short home page, he decided to leave the user with a bit of contact information so the user could get in touch with him. In fact, he included a link to a simple form that we will show you in the sidebar in Section 8.6. Listing 8-1 shows the HTML code for Rajat's home page. Figure 8-1 shows what that home page looks like online.

Listing 8–1. Rajat Bhargava's home page

```
<HTML>
<HEAD>
<TITLE>Rajat Bhargava's Home Page</TITLE>
</HEAD>

<BODY>
<H1><IMG SRC="rajat.gif" ALIGN=TOP>Rajat Bhargava's Home Page</H1>
<HR>
My name is Rajat Bhargava and I am currently President and CEO of
<EM>net.Genesis Corp.</EM>, a company that I helped found in January of
1994.  Currently the company is located in Cambridge, MA, very close to
MIT, where I graduated with a degree in Electrical Engineering and Com-
puter Science.  Prior to starting <EM>net.Genesis</EM>, I worked for Intel
Corp. at a number of locations, including Arizona, California, and New
Jersey.  I worked in a number of different areas, including software
development, chip design, and microprocessor architecture.
```

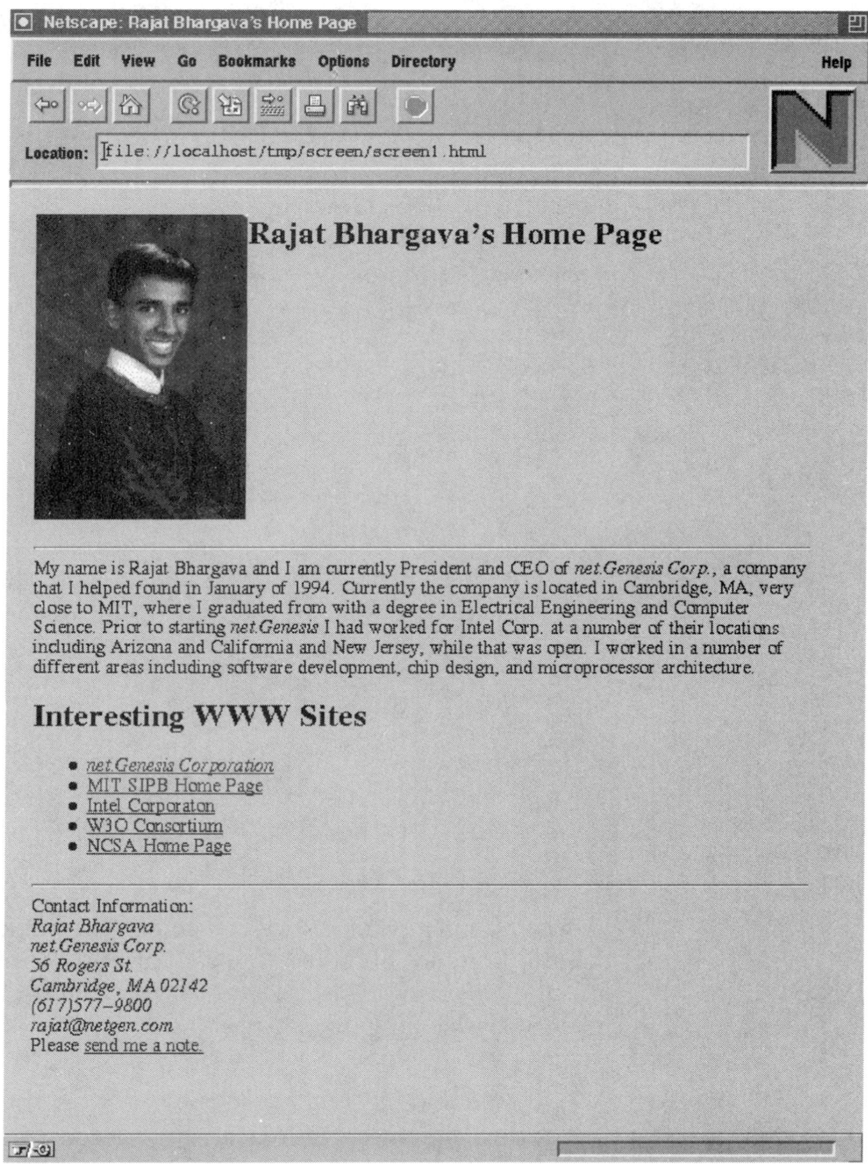

Figure 8–1 Rajat Bhargava's home page

Writing Your Own HTML Page (Continued)

```
<H2>Interesting WWW Sites</H2>
<UL>
<LI><A HREF="http://www.netgen.com"><EM>net.Genesis Corporation</EM></A>
<LI><A HREF="http://www.mit.edu:8001">MIT SIPB Home Page</A>
<LI><A HREF="http://www.intel.com">Intel Corporation</A>
<LI><A HREF="http://www.w3.org">W3 Consortium</A>
<LI><A HREF="http://www.ncsa.edu">NCSA Home Page</A>
</UL>
<HR>
Contact Information:
<ADDRESS>
Rajat Bhargava<BR>
net.Genesis Corp.<BR>
56 Rogers St.<BR>
Cambridge, MA 02142<BR>
(617)577-9800<BR>
rajat@netgen.com<BR>
</ADDRESS>
Please <A HREF="/feedback.html">send me a note.</A><P>
</BODY>
</HTML>
```

8.3 General HTML Style

HTML puts a lot of limits on how much you can do when you lay out a document, but an author can still put a lot of "style" into a document. To do this, you must conform to the standards as strictly and as well as possible and still manage to include your own "personal touches."

8.3.1 Using the ALT attribute

An easy way to improve vastly the appearance of a page is to consider carefully how you use the ALT attribute with images. As we mentioned earlier in this chapter, many people use text-only browsers. For their sake, you should include alternative text values when you place inline images. Whenever possible, give the alternative values the same function as the picture instead of merely having the alternative values describe the picture. For example, if you use a fancy graphic instead of a horizontal rule, do something like this:

```
<img src="fancy-hrule.gif" alt="----------------------">
```

NOTE

While it is certainly better to use the ALT attribute here, an even better answer would be to use the IMG attribute with the Horizontal Rule element (see Section 7.3.4 for more information about this). This way, nongraphical browsers will still be able to render the element as it is functionally intended. Of course, the IMG attribute is only supported for HTML 3.0.

If you wanted to put a logo at the top of the page, along with the name of your company, you could do the following:

```
<img src="logo.gif">XYZ Communications, Inc.
```

However, through a text-only viewer, this would look like:

```
[IMAGE] XYZ Communications, Inc.
```

which is somewhat unpleasant. You might try to rectify the situation by using the ALT attribute, as follows:

```
<img src="logo.gif" alt="Company Logo">XYZ Communications, Inc.
```

However, this is an example of how good intentions can get in the way of good results. When viewed through a text-only browser, the above code would look like this:

```
Company Logo XYZ Communications, Inc.
```

One of the reasons why this didn't work out is because the logo is not serving a functional purpose and the value for the ALT attribute is descriptive, not functional. It would be much better to include an empty string for the value:

```
<img src="logo.gif" alt="">XYZ Communications, Inc.
```

Now a text-only browsers would see it this way:

```
XYZ Communications, Inc.
```

On the other hand, if you are using an image with text in it—for example, if you have a graphical menu of buttons with labels—you should include an ALT attribute for each button. If you don't, your image will look terrible through text-only browsers. For example, the following HTML would be useless:

```
<img src = "corp_info.gif"> <img src="people.gif"><br>
<img src="services.gif"> <img src="clients.gif"><br>
```

Using a text-only browser, this is what you'd see:

```
[IMAGE] [IMAGE]
[IMAGE] [IMAGE]
```

Of course, each of these images would be represented as a link. However, the user has no idea what any of these links point to.

In this case, each graphic serves a functional purpose: it is being used to display text to the user. Therefore, the ALT attribute should be used to accomplish this, as in the following HTML:

```
<img src = "corp_info.gif" alt="Info"> <img src="people.gif"
alt="People"><br>
<img src="services.gif" alt="Services"> <img src="clients.gif"
alt="Clients"><br>
```

This results in greater functionality for users with text-based browsers, who would see:

```
Info      People
Services  Clients
```

Again, each piece of text would represent links to other pages. But this time, users can see what they are linking to.

8.3.2 The "Click Here" Syndrome

"Click here" is a common phrase on many Web pages—too many in our opinion. "For more information about our services, click here," where the phrase "here" or "click here" is the link, is not an imaginative use of a link. It diminishes the power of hypertext by making it little more than a means to provide menu-like selections (see Figure 8-2). As a user browses the Web, what catches his or her eye is the text of a link, not the words "click here." Those words do not convey much information. It makes more sense to have something like:

```
More information about <a href="services.html">our services</a> is
available.
```

instead of

```
For information about our services, <a href="services.html">
click here</a>.
```

Besides giving users real information about a link, creating meaningful links has another benefit. Many robots and spiders that index the Web use the text of a link to provide information about the document to which the link points. The text is an additional piece of information. It can be used to deduce the meaning or content of the page being pointed to. "Click here" does not provide useful data to robots and spiders.

Another argument against using the words "click here" is that users with text-only browsers are not actually "clicking." The whole notion of hypertext is rooted in the idea that pieces of data are linked to other related pieces of data. For text-based links to work, the text of the link should be meaningful to users and tell them what the link is pointing to. In and of themselves, the words "click here" don't say anything about where the link leads.

8.3.3 Dangling Spaces in Links

Whenever you create a link, you should be careful about white space. Some graphical browsers represent links by underlining. Therefore, if extra white space is put within within the body of a Link element, ugly little underscores appear on either side of the link. In effect, this extends the underlining, as Figure 8-3 shows.

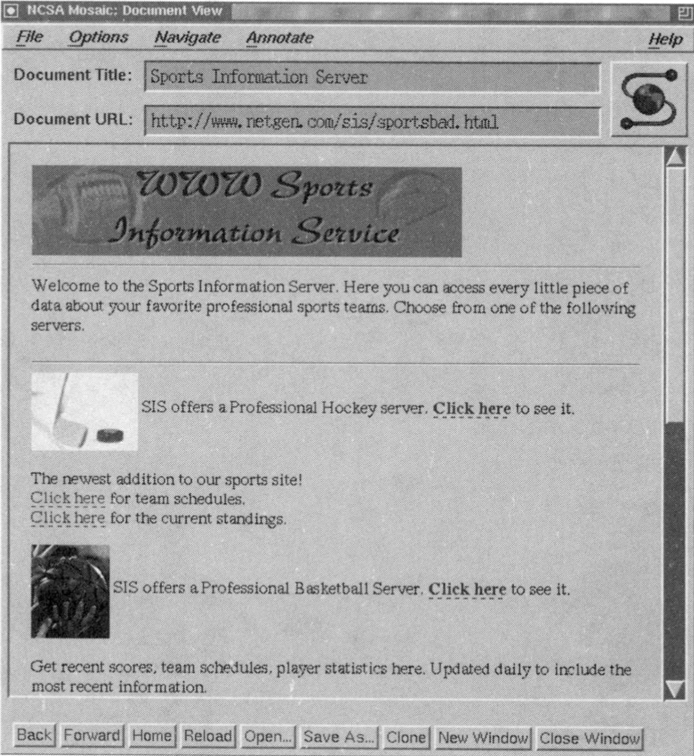

Figure 8–2a The left screen shows what the Sports Information Service page would look like if we used a lot of "click here" links. The right screen shows the real version of the Sports Information Service page, where

Sloppy underscores really stand out when images are used as links. In this case, the extra portion of the link will be very obvious. We know it's tempting to code this way, since it's easier to read code like the following:

```
<a href="foo.html"> <img src="foo.gif"> </a>
```

But when your browser gets ahold of it, your easy-to-read HTML code becomes a design faux pas with ugly little underscores that appear around the image, as Figure 8-3 shows.

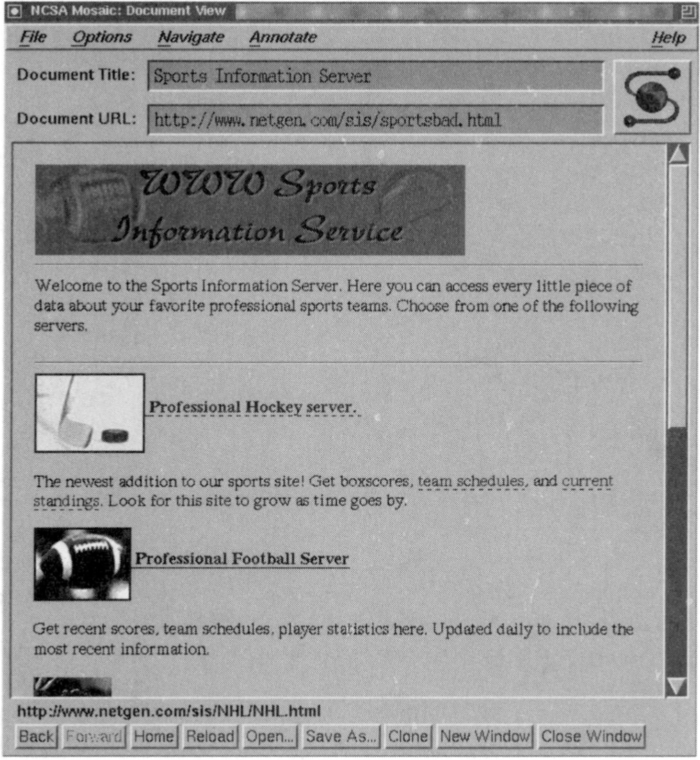

Figure 8–2b the underlined words are the links. This looks much more professional.

In HTML, any number of tabs, spaces, or carriage returns are equivalent to a single space. So you can't even get around the underscore problem with the following code:

```
<a href="foo.html">
<img src="foo.gif">
</a>
```

Only the following code eliminates these ugly underscores:

```
<a href="foo.html"><img src="foo.gif"></a>
```

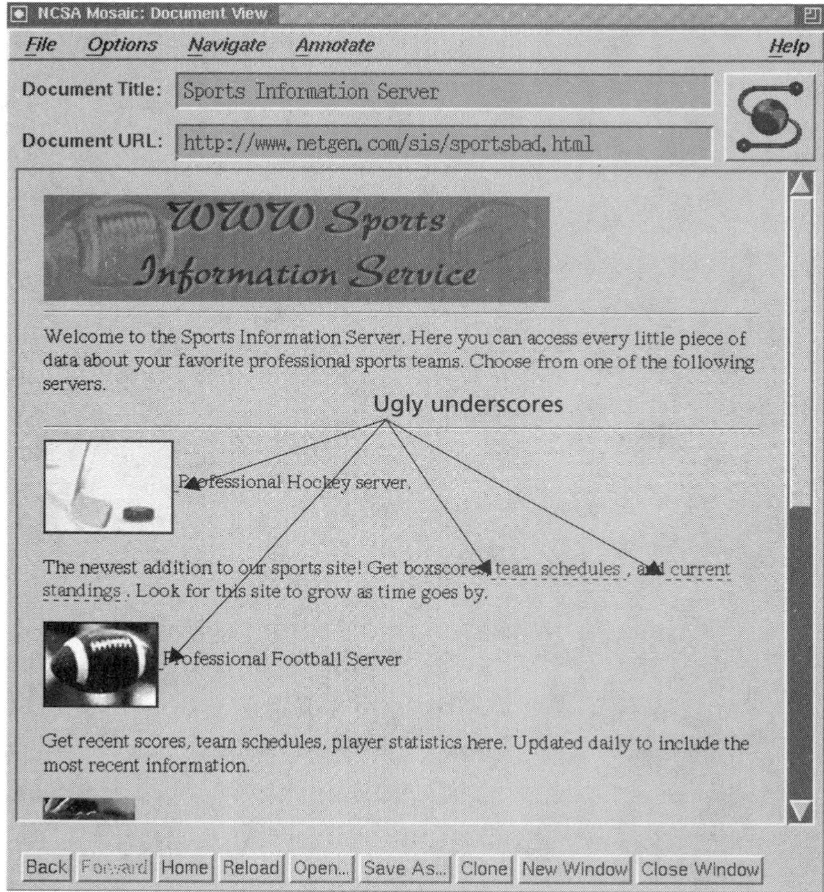

Figure 8–3 The Sports Information Service page with ugly little underscores where white space appears around text and graphic links. Functionally, the underscores create no problems, but they look sloppy.

If you want to put a little space between an image and some text, the following is also acceptable:

```
<a href="foo.html"><img src="foo.gif"> Here is some text</a>
```

But whatever you do, don't leave space at the beginning or end of a link.

8.3.4 Sign and Date Your Documents

It is always a good idea to "sign" pages with your e-mail address or link them to a feedback form so that users can provide comments. In addition, it is useful to put a "Last Updated" or "Last Modified" date on each page so that users know how up-to-date the information is. Many servers send a Last-Modified header when they know what the date is, but this information is not usually made available to users.

The NHL Standings page from the Sports Information Service (see Figure 8-4) is signed and dated. The next page shows an excerpt from the HTML.

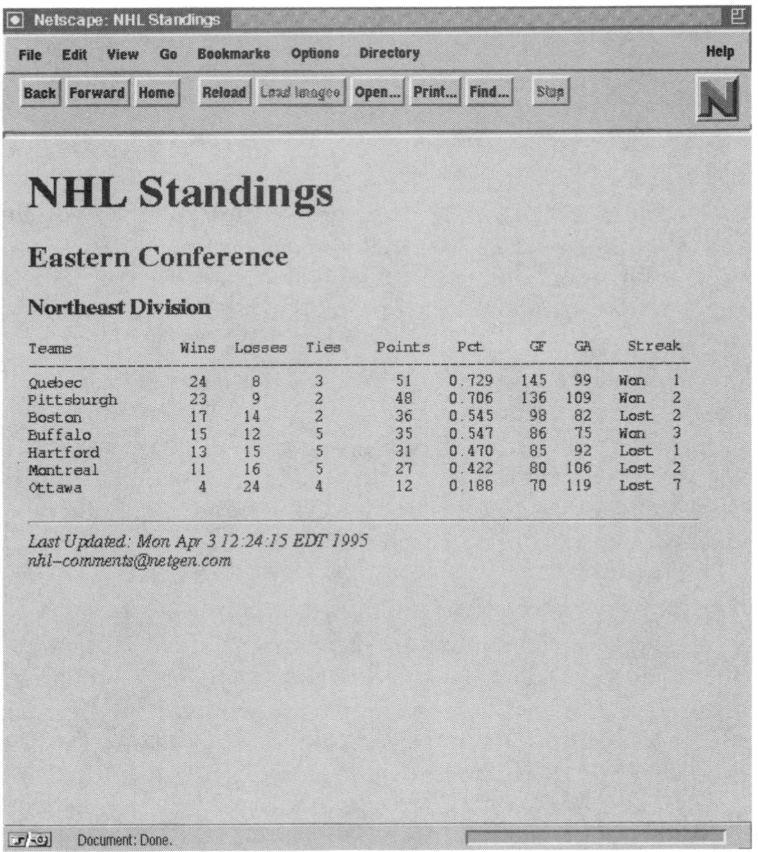

NHL Standings

Eastern Conference

Northeast Division

Teams	Wins	Losses	Ties	Points	Pct	GF	GA	Streak
Quebec	24	8	3	51	0.729	145	99	Won 1
Pittsburgh	23	9	2	48	0.706	136	109	Won 2
Boston	17	14	2	36	0.545	98	82	Lost 2
Buffalo	15	12	5	35	0.547	86	75	Won 3
Hartford	13	15	5	31	0.470	85	92	Lost 1
Montreal	11	16	5	27	0.422	80	106	Lost 2
Ottawa	4	24	4	12	0.188	70	119	Lost 7

Last Updated: Mon Apr 3 12:24:15 EDT 1995
nhl-comments@netgen.com

Document: Done.

Figure 8–4 The NHL Standings page from the Sports Information Service is signed and dated.

```
<html>
<head>
<title>NHL Standings</title>
</head>
<body>
...
<hr>
Last Updated: 03-Apr-1995 12:24:15 EDT
<address> nhl-comments@netgen.com</address>
</body>
</html>
```

8.3.5 Clickable Image Maps

Clickable image maps are great and can make a site look very attractive, but they must be used with caution. As we've noted before, many users out there have text-based browsers like Lynx that can't display images. These browsers generally just print something like [ISMAP] or [IMAGE] for the entire image map. Users who have slow connections often turn off image loading so they won't see the image.

Image maps do not allow users to see the URL that they are going to link to when they click on an image map. Users who are used to monitoring this information often find image maps annoying. Also, image maps place an extra level of overhead on the server. The server must execute a program to determine which URL to access based on the submitted coordinates. For a heavily loaded machine, this overhead may be a cause for concern. However, as we mentioned in Chapter 7, HTML 3.0 has added a means of defining image maps that takes care of this problem.

Image maps are certainly useful in general, but you should always question whether a particular use is necessary. One frequent but unnecessary use of image maps is to use a single graphic-image toolbar to direct users to different locations. This functionality could just as easily be achieved without incurring the image map's overhead by using adjacent graphics.

Therefore, whenever you use a clickable image map, you should supplement it with a text-based means of going to those same locations. There are two good ways to handle this. One way is to offer both capabilities on the same page, as Hewlett Packard does on its home page (see Figure 8-5).

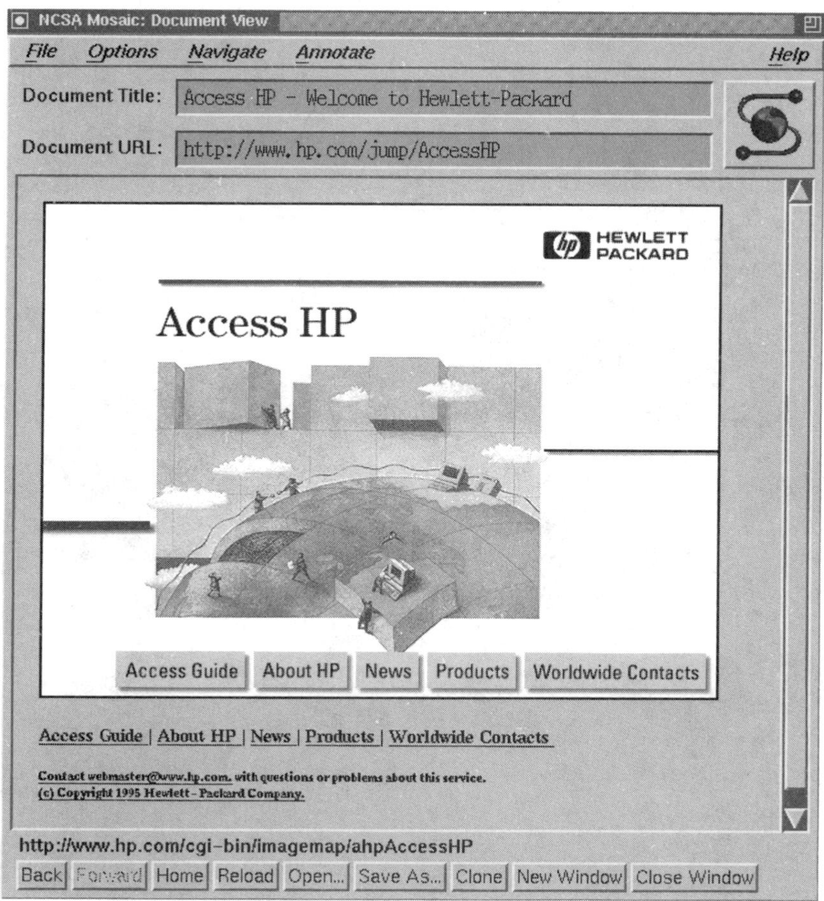

Figure 8–5 Hewlett Packard's home page offers both a clickable image map and text-based links.

Compaq displays a clickable image map on its home page with a text link at the bottom that allows users to continue without graphics (see Figure 8-6).

8.3.6 Blink

One of the Netscape extension tags is <BLINK>. This tag makes text blink. Some people think this is cute, but many find it very annoying. We suggest not using the Blink element in your documents.

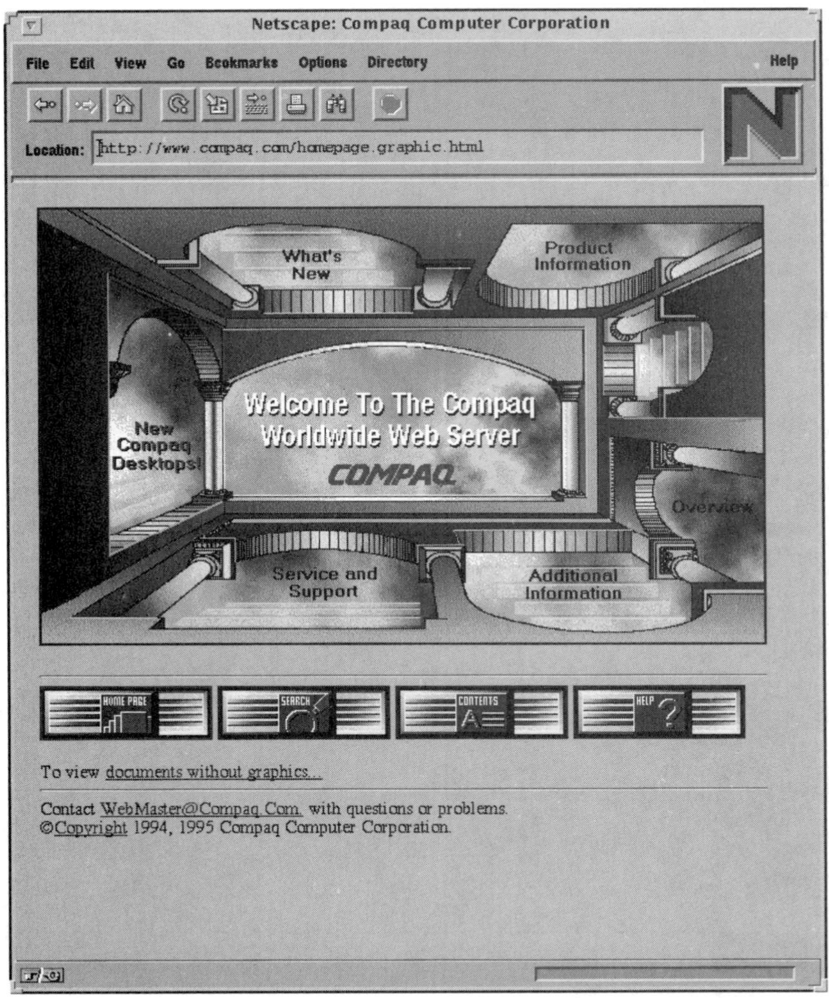

Figure 8–6 Compaq's home page offers a clickable image map and a text option at the bottom so users can continue without any graphics.

8.4 Common Errors

Learning to write HTML code is by no means difficult (as many elementary school students can attest), but understanding HTML's intricacies can be difficult and is vital to becoming a proficient HTML author. By understanding HTML's inherent limitations and why those limitations exist, an HTML author can make informed decisions when attempting to achieve "special effects" with HTML tags. As new HTML specifications become widely implemented, HTML authors who know how to use the specifications will be better able to exploit new standards.

Debugging HTML can often be a pain. Subtle errors in markup often produce peculiar effects in the actual rendering. Certain kinds of typos seem to occur a lot. Knowing what problems to look out for can save you lots of frustration and keep you from having to spend hours poring over the HTML.

Common errors include missing the closing quote mark, closing the wrong tag, invalid nesting of elements, misinterpreted comment strings, use of unknown elements, and the misuse of paragraph elements.

8.4.1 Missing the Closing Quote

One common error is to leave out the trailing quote on an attribute, as in this sample code:

```
<a href="http://www.netgen.com/>The net.Genesis Homepage</a>
```

missing quote

Leaving out the trailing quote confuses most clients terribly and is a very hard error from which to recover. Mosaic simply does not understand the URI, so when you click on the link, it simply brings you back to the same page (in other words, it creates a link back to itself). Netscape is a little more intelligent. It recovers when it sees the >, but this doesn't help if you have other attributes in the element—as in this example, which, in Netscape, creates a link to the resource "foo name":

```
<img src="foo name="bar">
```

This certainly isn't something that any browser should be expected to recover from. There is no way that Netscape, or any other browser, could figure out what you intended to do.

8.4.2 Closing the Wrong Tag

Another regular mistake is to mismatch opening and closing tags, i.e., closing a different tag than was opened. The following example is not uncommon:

```
<h2>Introduction to this Section</h3>
```

Many browsers choke on this because an <h2> tag is opened and then an <h3> tag is closed. Some browsers attempt to recover by guessing that you meant to close the <h2> tag. Others ignore the closed <h3> because there was no open <h3> and then continue waiting for the <h2> close tag.

8.4.3 Invalid Nesting of Elements

Another regular HTML error is to nest elements in inappropriate ways. You can place one element inside another, but it must be wholly contained and may not overlap. Below are examples of HTML code lines. The first one will not work because the two tags overlap:

```
<strong>This is some <em>very strong</strong> text</em>
```

The second one shows the same line properly constructed so that the tags do not overlap:

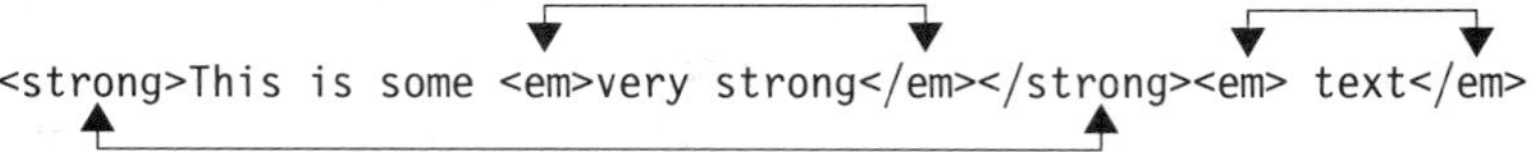
<strong>This is some <em>very strong</em></strong><em> text</em>

In the second case there are three tag sets, one of which is inside of the other. (It's like nesting parentheses in mathematical equations.)

Also, with the exception of most of the character formatting elements, most elements may be nested within themselves. For example, the behavior of multiple anchored text, such as the following, is not predictable:

```
<a href="home.html">This is <a href="matthew.html">Matthew</a>'s
homepage</a>
```

Sometimes, the browser simply ignores illegally embedded elements, but you can't count on it. Do not depend on the browser to be nice and understanding.

8.4.4 HTML Comment Strings

Even though the specifications define <!-- as the beginning of a comment string and --> as the end, many browsers get confused when a markup appears inside of a comment.

For example, consider the following piece of HTML:

```
This is <em>only a test</em>, please ignore.
```

If you wanted to comment this out, you would think all you have to do is add the beginning and ending comment tags to either end of the line, as follows:

```
<!-- This is <em>only a test</em>, please ignore. -->
```

Unfortunately, all too often this does not work. Instead of commenting out the whole line, most browsers get confused and misinterpret the line in one of two ways.

The first misinterpretation is shown in Table 8-1. Here, the opening comment tag (<!--) is ignored because the browser sees the < symbol and expects a tag, then it sees !-- and doesn't recognize it as a valid tag. The browser then recognizes the beginning and ending emphasized tags, and emphasizes the phrase, "only a test." The browser also displays the next text phrase, beginning with the comma and ending with the two dashes. Notice that once again the browser does not recognize the comment tag, so it treats the two dashes as regular text characters. Because the > symbol is not preceded by a tag name it recognizes, the browser treats it as a random character and is likely to display it as such.

The second misinterpretation is shown in Table 8-2. (Here the browser recognizes neither the opening comment tag (<!--) nor the opening emphasized tag, so it ignores both tags and the text in between.) It does display the "only a test" text phrase. When it sees the closing emphasized tag, it recognizes it but deems it spurious because it didn't recognize the corresponding open tag. The browser also displays the next text phrase that begins with the comma and ends with the two dashes. Notice that once again the browser does not recognize the comment tag, so it treats the two dashes as regular text characters. Because the > symbol is not preceded by a tag name it recognizes, the browser treats it as a random character and is likely to display it as such.

These are, of course, not the desired effect at all, so be careful when commenting out HTML.

Table 8–1. HTML Comment String Misinterpretation #1

Comment String	Misinterpretation
`<!-- This is`	`!--` is an unknown tag and is thus ignored
`<em>`	An open <em> tag is seen and recognized
`only a test`	This text is emphasized
`</em>`	A close <em> tag is seen and recognized
`, please ignore. --`	This text is displayed
`>`	A spurious close angle bracket, probably displayed

Table 8–2. HTML Comment String Misinterpretation #2

Comment String	Misinterpretation
`<!-- This is <em>`	An unknown tag, ignored
`only a test`	This text is displayed
`</em>`	A spurious close emphasis, ignored
`, please ignore. --`	Text, displayed
`>`	A spurious close angle bracket, probably displayed

8.4.5 Unknown Tags

Random tags—for example <FNORD>—are completely ignored by most browsers for a few reasons. First, when a browser encounters HTML with typos, it doesn't want to have to completely bail out. In such a case, it is often safer just to ignore unrecognized tags. Second, ignoring random tags helps browsers be more forward-compatible. If new tags are introduced, it is generally safer to ignore them than to complain about them. However, this does not mean all browsers are *required* to ignore unrecognized tags, so don't assume that they will ignore them. The comment tag `<!-- comment -->` is the only tag that you can assume is ignored.

NOTE

Fnord, a word from the *Illuminatus Trilogy,* cannot be seen or heard. It can be harmlessly inserted in the middle of text fnord without anybody noticing. If you ever hear someone say the word *fnord,* the proper response is, "Why were your lips moving when I didn't hear anything?" *Fnord* is a source of techie humor and fnord appropriate to this example because ignoring them completely fnord is exactly what browsers are supposed to do with <FNORD> tags.

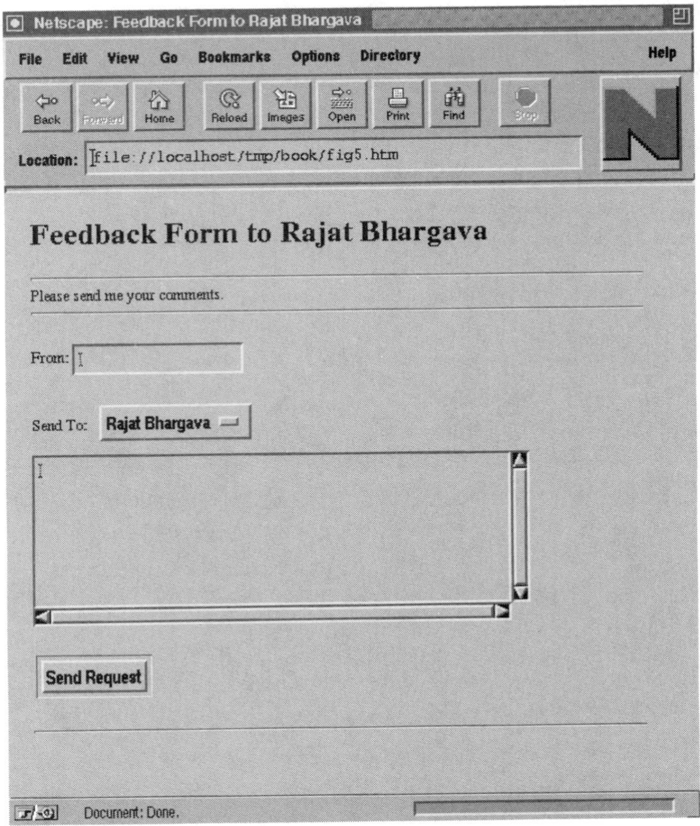

Figure 8–7 A sample feedback form

8.4.6 Vertical Space

In some browsers, using one or more paragraph tags to create vertical white space may produce bizarre effects. This is an HTML no-no. The following is never correct:

```
<P>
<P>
```

Not only is this considered a misuse of the <P> tag, but two repeated tags of any type are never correct.

If you need vertical white space, try using <BR>, the line-break tag. It works, although perhaps not as well as you might like, because it only signifies a line break. Two <BR> line-break tags do not specify a blank line of any particular height at all.

Remember, HTML is a semantic language, not a layout language. Admittedly, some of the elements have attributes with which you can specify physical parts of the layout, but you cannot ignore the functional meaning of the elements to make something look good.

8.5 Forms

HTML forms have problems with case-sensitivity, so you should be extra careful when writing them. Here are the areas you should be especially concerned about: method case-sensitivity, submit case-sensitivity, checkbox case-sensitivity, misplaced submit elements, stealth-mode submissions, and linking forms to other services.

The sidebar on the FORM template offers some sample HTML code that you can use as a template to create your own forms. You might also find this code handy to look at as we talk about forms.

8.5.1 Method Case-Sensitivity

The name of the method used to submit a form is case-sensitive. When you begin a form, you may want to specify a method, as in this example:

```
<form method="POST">
```

You do not have to specify the method (GET is the default), but if you do include it, it is critical for the value to be in all capital letters. Lowercasing the letters or initial-casing the word (entering **Get**) will not work. For example, this will not work:

```
<form method="post">
```

Nor will this code work:

```
<form method="Post">
```

A FORM Template: Some Sample Code

The following HTML code was used to create the page shown in Figure 8-7. You can use this sample form as a template to create your own forms:

```
<html>
<head>
<title>Feedback Form to Rajat Bhargava</title>
</head>
<body>
<h1>Feedback Form to Rajat Bhargava</h1>
<hr>
Please send me your comments.
<hr>
<form method=POST action="myURL">
From:<input name="from"> <p>

Send To:<select name="send_to">
<option value="rajat@netgen.com"> Rajat Bhargava
<option value="netgen@netgen.com"> net.Genesis
</select>

<br>
<input type="hidden" name="subject" value="Home Sample Feedback Form">
<textarea rows=10 cols=60 name="comments">
</textarea>
<p>
<!-- A "submit" button is required in order to submit any form-->
<input type="submit" value="Send Request"><p>
</form>
<hr>
</body>
</html>
```

In both of these examples, the POST method is not recognized, so the default method (GET) is assumed. As a result, errors can occur in the script that the data is sent to, since the script expects the data in one format but receives it in another.

8.5.2 Submit Case-Sensitivity

A key input type in forms is the submission button. It allows the user to instruct the browser to transmit the form's contents back to the server. The proper format for the submission element is lowercase, as follows:

```
<input type="submit">
```

Current versions of NCSA Mosaic do not interpret the submission element correctly if you use uppercase letters (i.e., entering **SUBMIT**). They do not understand the type attribute's value and therefore default to a "text" type. The submit button is critical to being able to use a form, so using uppercase letters can cause a lot of frustration.

NOTE

Not being able to interpret an uppercase submission element is the result of a bug in NCSA Mosaic. Most other browsers can accept uppercase. However, NCSA is currently the second most-used browser, so form authors must be careful not to fall into the uppercase trap!

8.5.3 Checkbox Case-Sensitivity

NCSA Mosaic exhibits similar buggy behavior in the case of entering **<input type = "checkbox"...>**. If you use **<input type="CHECKBOX">**, some versions of Mosaic will not understand the type attribute and will default to a "text" type. Make sure that the value *checkbox* appears in lowercase.

In the following example, the first field will be correctly interpreted as a checkbox, but the second will not:

```
<form>
<input type="checkbox" name = "good_field">
<input type="CHECKBOX" name="bad_field">
</form>
```

8.5.4 Misplaced Submit Element

Another important detail to keep in mind when writing forms is this: all forms elements must appear between the open and close form tag. A form with the following structure is not correct:

```
<form action="...">
[insert stuff here]
</form>
<input type="submit">
```

The correct structure for this form is:

```
<form action="...">
<input type="submit">
[insert stuff here]
</form>
```

Some browsers can handle this correctly, but others do not render the submit button, which makes the form pretty useless.

8.5.5 Stealth Mode Submissions

If you have been browsing forms on the Web with a graphical browser, you may have noticed that some forms do not have a submit button. For most browsers, the form is submitted when you hit the Enter key in a form with only one text-entry field. This kind of form submission is called "stealth mode" because the browser implicitly assumes that it is supposed to submit the form when you hit Enter. Because of this, some form designers leave out the submit button because they think it is unnecessary. But leaving it out is not a good practice. Some browsers—most notably Lynx, which a lot of people use—require a submit button. In such cases, there is no way of sending the information on a form back to the server without a submit button, and that can be very frustrating.

8.5.6 Linking Forms to Other Services

Putting links to other servers on a page is a common practice, but most people never think about including forms that access some other service. You can even include multiple forms on one page. For example, you could include a search form for Wandex at the bottom of a page. Your HTML for the page would look something like this:

```
<html>
<head>
<title> Sample page with a form at the bottom</title>
</head>
<body>
<h1>A page</h1>
So much of the time, web search pages are search pages and search pages
alone, and there will be a link at the bottom to a search engine. Why not
just have the search engine entry area at the bottom of the page anyway?
<hr>
<form action="http://www.netgen.com/cgi/wandex/index">
Search Wandex: <input name="words">
<input type="submit" value="Wandex">
</form>
</body>
</html>
```

Figure 8-8 shows the page that is rendered from this HTML code.

TIP

Whenever you include someone else's service on your page, be sure to give credit to that service.

8.6 Tables

The ability to define tables was one of the new features introduced in HTML 3.0. It gives you a lot of control over the layout of a piece of text. You can use it to format data in ways that weren't possible before.

8.6.1 Dynamic Column Widths

HTML offers convenient ways to make tables look good on users' screens. However, you can't presume to know precisely how a table will be rendered when it appears on users' screens.

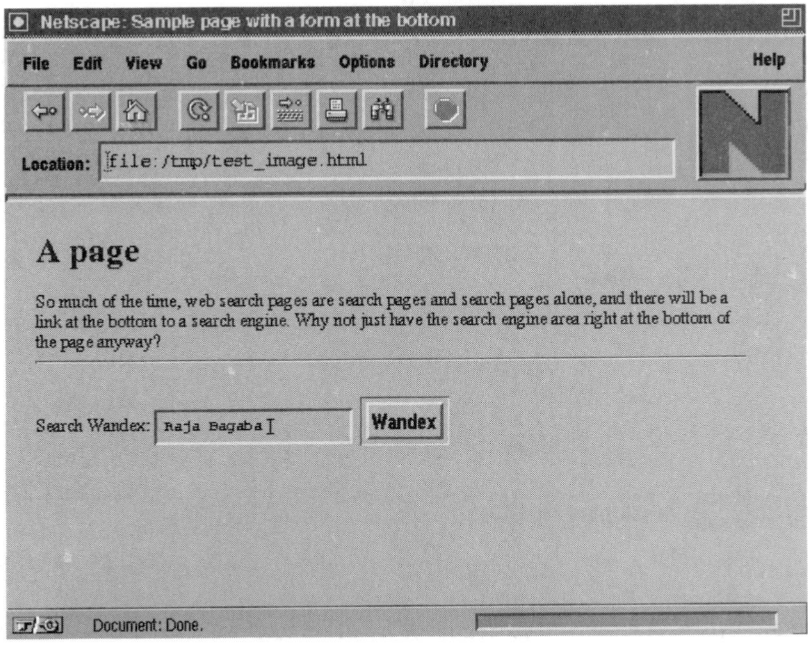

Figure 8–8 A sample page that includes an input form for the Wandex service

For example, you might assume that the following table would produce five columns of equal width:

```
<table>
<tr><td>

One might guess that this text would appear in a narrow column down the left
side, because it is in the first column, then there are four blank columns
to its right.
</td>  <td></td>  <td></td>  <td></td>  <td></td> </tr>
</table>
```

That guess would be wrong, because browsers are allowed to change a table's width and size to make it as easy to read as possible. Typically, empty columns are squished so more text can fit on the screen.

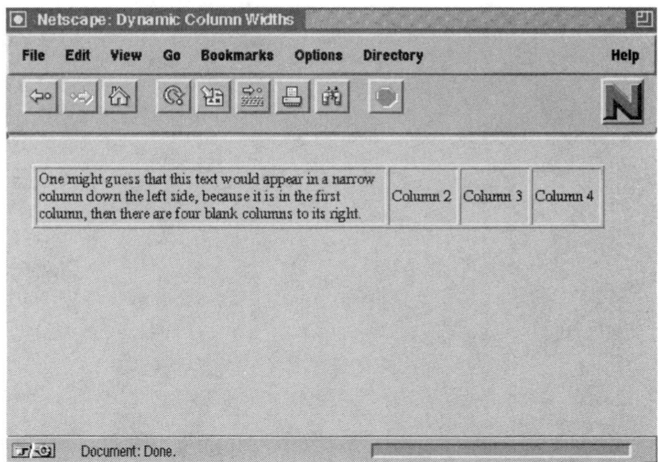

Figure 8–9 A sample page illustrating dynamic column widths

If you look at Figure 8-9, you will see a column on the left that is not equal in size to the other three empty columns. A browser can dynamically generate tables. Generally, they make empty columns only one or two characters wide.

8.6.2 Using Tables to Control Layout

Authors have more flexibility than ever before when it comes to laying out tables. In magazines and newspapers, text is usually laid out in columns, with objects such as photographs and headlines spanning multiple columns or rows. With the new functionality offered by HTML 3.0, such layout is now possible.

Figure 8-10 shows a sample newspaper-style page rendered from the following HTML code:

```
<table>
<tr><td valign=top colspan=5 align=center><h1>Newspaper</h1></tr>
<tr><td valign=top>"Our Slogan here!"</td valign=top>
<td valign=top colspan=3></td valign=top>
<td valign=top>March 19, 1995</td valign=top>
</tr>
```

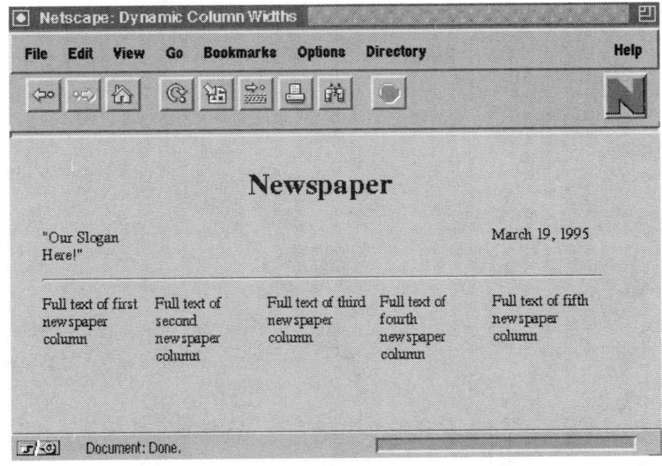

Figure 8–10 A sample page illustrating dynamic column widths

```
<tr><td valign=top colspan=5><hr></td valign=top></tr>
<tr>
<td width=160 valign=top>Full text of first newspaper column</td>
<td width=160 valign=top>Full text of second newspaper column</td>
<td width=160 valign=top>Full text of third newspaper column</td>
<td width=160 valign=top>Full text of fourth newspaper column</td>
<td width=160 valign=top>Full text of fifth newspaper column</td>
</tr>
```

There is more to writing HTML than what the specifications say. By keeping these style issues in mind when you write your HTML documents, you can make documents that are more portable, functional, and attractive.

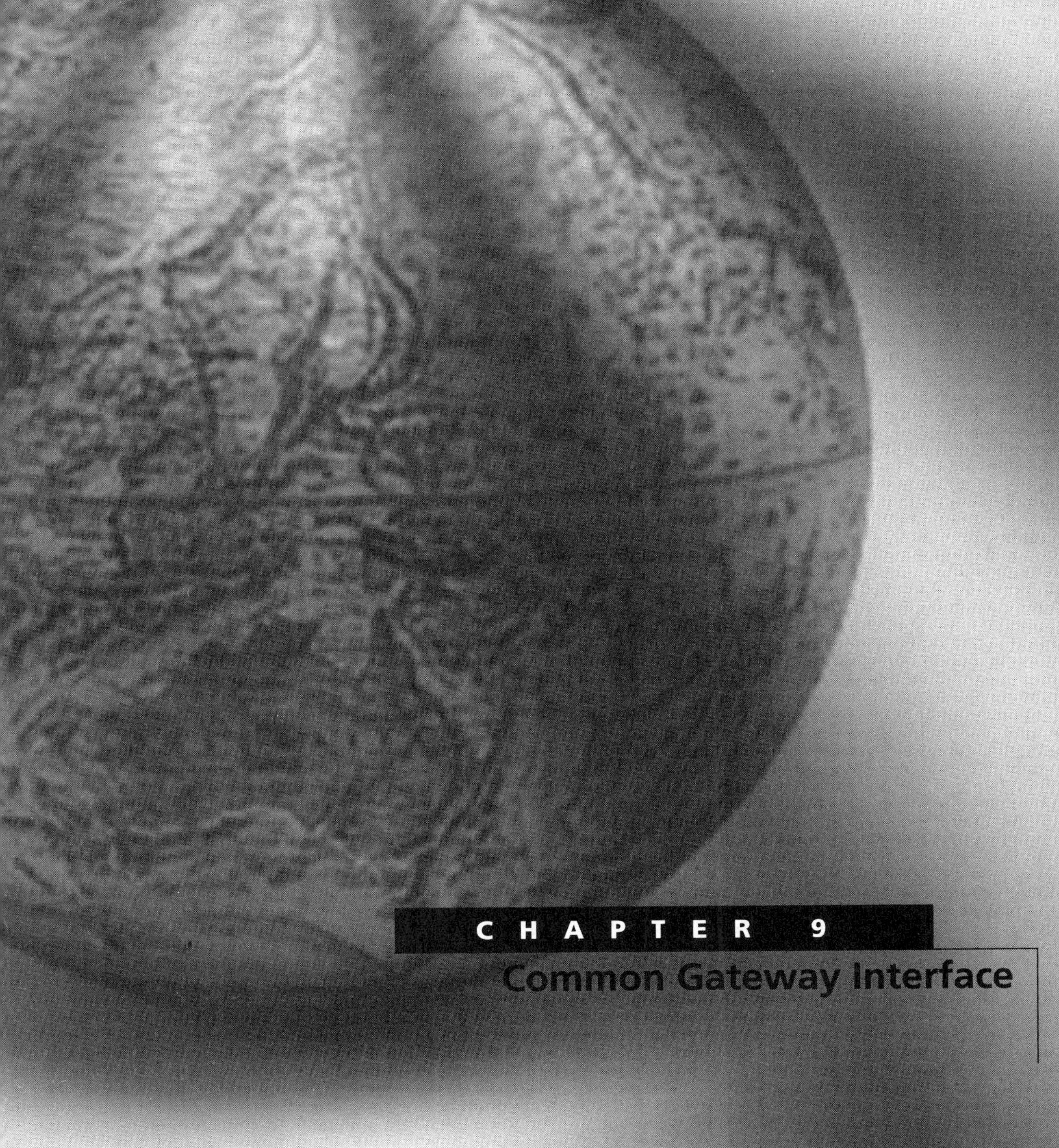

CHAPTER 9
Common Gateway Interface

CHAPTER AT A GLANCE

This chapter provides an in-depth discussion and interpretation of the standard that governs the Common Gateway Interface (CGI). This section makes the distinction between a *standard,* which CGI is, and a *specification,* which CGI is not. We discuss the practical application of CGI scripts and what you need to know in order to use them effectively. We define the headers and environmental variables used in CGI input and output, and provide some tips for debugging CGI scripts. We also talk about the typical uses for CGI scripts, and provide several sample CGI scripts.

REQUISITES

Some familiarity with programming concepts and the perl programming language. In addition, an understanding of the syntax of HTTP responses as specified in Chapters 5 and 6.

MORE DETAIL

Chapter 11 provides a library of useful examples of CGI scripts.

In the early days of the Web, each main server offered its own form of server-side, executable support. This is the functionality that allows a server to call upon an executable program to assist in fulfilling a request. The CERN and NCSA httpd servers supported the use of htbin scripts, and the Plexus server allowed users to integrate their perl scripts directly into the server code. In order to provide a standard interface so that users could write general scripts, NCSA developed version 1.0 of the Common Gateway Interface. A couple of months later, CGI/1.1 emerged with slightly extended functionality.

CGI is a standard, not a specification. Its purpose is to provide a means of passing information between servers and executables so that input from users can be used by the executable programs.

The Common Gateway Interface is not a programming language either. It is simply a standard to which both servers and server-side executables can adhere in order to communicate effectively. As a standard, CGI bears more resemblance to a spoken language with dictionary definitions and grammatical rules. There is no "right" language, and each is as good as the other. What matters is that two people speak the same language so they can understand one another.

When the server and executable need to communicate with one another, only two things need to be agreed upon:

- The way the server passes input to the program
- The way the program passes its output back to the server

As you'll see in a moment, CGI resolves these two issues by defining a standard usage of environment variables.

The CGI standard does not place restrictions on which programming languages may be used to create executables. CGI programs are called CGI "scripts" most of the time because they are often written in scripting languages such as sh, bash, and perl. However, CGI programs may also be written in C, C++, FORTRAN, and Visual Basic, although problems arise with some of these languages, as Section 9.3.4 explains.

Before we describe the environment variables, let's take a look at a client-server communications involving CGI scripts. The diagram in Figure 9-1 shows this communication flow.

Chapters 5 and 6 covered the request and response portions of this interchange in great detail. Now let's take a look at the CGI input and output portions of the interchange.

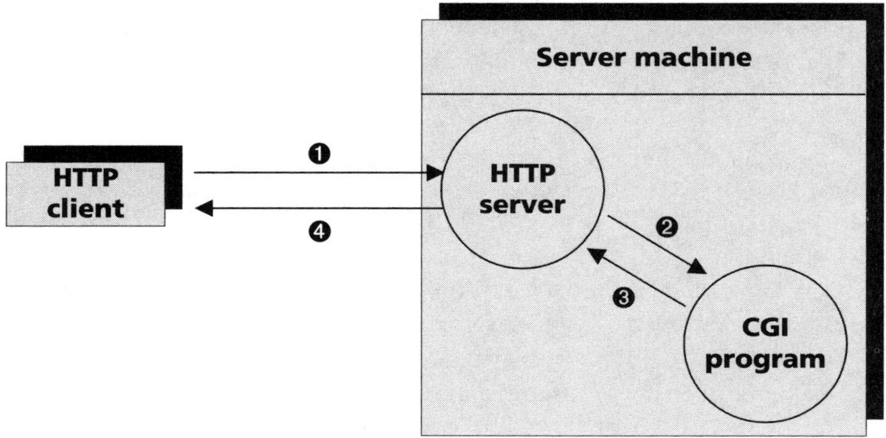

1. The client connects to the HTTP server and makes its request.
2. The server sets several environment variables and runs the CGI program, passing to it whatever input was received with the request (i.e., from data or whatever was in the Entity-Body received from the client).
3. The CGI program passes its results back to the HTTP server after completing its processing.
4. The HTTP server sends its response back to the client.

Figure 9–1 The flow of a client-server communication interchange involving a CGI script

9.1 CGI Input

Before the HTTP server starts up the CGI program, it must set the values of some known environment variables. Setting these values is standard operating procedure whether or not a CGI script is involved. A *variable* is a place in memory that holds a value; a program can access a variable by name. An *environment variable* is a variable that is accessible not only to the program that defines it, but also to all other executables that may be called from the initial program. Therefore, when a server (which is itself a program) sets environment variables and then starts the CGI program, the CGI program also has access to these environment variables.

Lots of programs use environment variables, and you can use them in the programs that you run. CGI uses environment variables to pass information from one process to another, and the standard defines how these variables are to be interpreted. Following is a detailed look at the environment variables that have special meanings under CGI.

NOTE

Some environment variables are used extensively in UNIX programs. Such variables include *TERM, PATH, MANPATH,* and *DISPLAY,* which are used to tell programs where to find programs on users' systems and how to display output for the user. If you want to see all the environment variables in your current environment, use the printenv command.

9.1.1 Defining Environment Variables

A number of environment variables are used by CGI. They include *REQUEST_METHOD, CONTENT_LENGTH, PATH_INFO, PATH_TRANSLATED, SCRIPT_NAME, QUERY_STRING, CONTENT_TYPE, GATEWAY_INTERFACE, SERVER_PROTOCOL, SERVER_SOFTWARE, SERVER_NAME, SERVER_PORT, REMOTE_ADDR, REMOTE_HOST, AUTH_TYPE, REMOTE_USER,* and *REMOTE_IDENT.* Other variables begin with *"HTTP_,"* including *HTTP_USER_AGENT* and *HTTP_REFERER.*

NOTE

The names of environment variables are case-sensitive and are always written entirely in uppercase.

REQUEST_METHOD

The *REQUEST_METHOD* variable contains a string that indicates the method that was used in the client's request. This variable is used by the CGI script to determine where it can find the input data (see Section 9.1.2) and what kind of output is expected. All seven of the defined HTTP methods (GET, POST, HEAD, PUT, DELETE, LINK, and UNLINK) are acceptable to CGI, even though the latter four are seldom, if ever, used.

CONTENT_LENGTH

The *CONTENT_LENGTH* variable specifies the number of data bytes that were submitted with the request. This field is very important when reading in the data from a PUT or POST request (as shown in Listing 9-1 later on).

PATH_INFO

The *PATH_INFO* variable contains the portion of the URI that follows the string that identifies the CGI script being run. This value is often used to pass extra arguments to the program. For example, *PATH_INFO* would be set to **/debug/red/erichard** in the following URL:

http://www.netgen.com/cgi-bin/test-cgi/debug/red/erichard

This variable can be used in whatever way the script wants to use it. Perhaps it can be used as a slash-delimited list of configuration opens for the program. A common use of *PATH_INFO* is to provide the script with a list of option settings that tell the script how to behave. For example, you could indicate that the script should output HTML instead of a GIF, or you could set debugging to on or off. It is up to the script to interpret this string, so there are no limits on what the script can do with this information.

PATH_TRANSLATED

The *PATH_TRANSLATED* variable contains the physical path (i.e., the path in the file system) that corresponds to the portion of the URL in *PATH_INFO*. By using *PATH_TRANSLATED,* it is possible to specify the URL for a file after the URL to the CGI-script, so that the CGI script can then use the contents of that file. For example, in the following URL, *PATH_TRANSLATED* would be something like /usr/local/etc/httpd/homepage.html—the location of the object identified by **/homepage.html**:

http://www.netgen.com/cgi-bin/test-cgi/homepage.html

Because the script has the physical location for this file, it could be used to print out the file or save to the file.

NOTE

We spent a lot of time in Chapter 4 explaining that a URL does not necessarily represent a physical location. And that is true. However, because URLs are so often treated like physical addresses, it is not uncommon for URLs to correspond to physical locations. Therefore, *PATH_TRANSLATED* provides a way for the CGI script to get its hands on this information.

SCRIPT_NAME

The *SCRIPT_NAME* variable contains the portion of the URI that identifies the CGI script being run. For example, in the following URL, *SCRIPT_NAME* is /cgi-bin/test-cgi:

http://www.netgen.com/cgi-bin/test-cgi

The CGI script can use this value to reference itself in URLs that may be part of the output (for example, self-redirections or URLs within documents that it returns).

QUERY_STRING

The *QUERY_STRING* variable contains the searchpart of the URL that was submitted with the request. Often this variable is used to store a list of keywords submitted for a search or the contents of a form submitted via the GET method.

CONTENT_TYPE

The *CONTENT_TYPE* variable contains the MIME Content-Type for any data that was submitted with the request. In cases where data from a form is submitted via the POST method, this value is application/x-www-form-urlencoded, because the contents of the form are encoded according to the URL specifications.

GATEWAY_INTERFACE

The *GATEWAY_INTERFACE* variable contains the version of CGI with which the server complies. The format of this variable is CGI/*version*—for example, CGI/1.0 or CGI/1.1. The variable must be set by the server for every request. As new versions evolve, new variables may be added, and existing variables may take on new meanings. Therefore, CGI programs should always check the value in the *GATEWAY_INTERFACE* variable. Table 9-1 shows versions of main servers and which versions of CGI they support.

SERVER_PROTOCOL

The *SERVER_PROTOCOL* variable contains the name and version of HTTP that the server supports. This variable is just like the HTTP Version field in HTTP Request headers, and it has the same format: HTTP/*version*—for example, HTTP/1.0 or HTTP/0.9. CGI programs should always check the value of this variable to ensure that the HTTP version being used is one that

Table 9–1. Main Server Programs and the CGI Versions They Support

Server Name	Version	CGI/1.0	CGI/1.1
CERN	< 2.15	N	N
	2.15–2.17	Y	N
	> 2.17	Y	Y
NCSA	< 1.0	N	N
	1.0, 1.1	Y	N
	> 1.1	Y	Y
Netsite Communications	Any	Y	Y
Netsite Commerce	Any	Y	Y

is compatible with the needs of your script. If a server only supports HTTP/0.9, for example, Content-Type cannot be used.

SERVER_SOFTWARE

The *SERVER_SOFTWARE* variable contains the name and version of the HTTP server software. This variable is just like the Server response header in HTTP, both functionally and in its format. Like the Server response header, its format is *name/version*. The *SERVER_SOFTWARE* variable must be set by the server for every request, regardless of whether a CGI script is involved. In fact, the variable is rarely used by CGI programs, probably because the differences between the behavior of the various servers is currently not great enough to make it useful.

SERVER_NAME

The *SERVER_NAME* variable contains the hostname or IP address of the server. It can be used if the CGI script needs to return any self-referencing URLs. For the CERN and NCSA servers, the *SERVER_NAME* variable corresponds to the *ServerName* variable set in the configuration files. This variable must be set by the server for every request, regardless of whether a CGI script is involved.

TIP

If your CGI script needs to return a self-referencing URL, it is best to use the *SERVER_NAME* variable. You could hard-code the server name value, but it's generally not a good idea to hard-code any values when a dynamic option is available. By using *SERVER_NAME,* your program remains flexible. Even if you change the name of your site, the CGI script won't fall apart. The whole

point of CGI was to provide scripts that are server-independent, so it is a good idea to make your CGI programs general (as opposed to hard-coding values). That way, they can be used on other machines without major modifications.

SERVER PORT

The *SERVER_PORT* variable contains the port number that the HTTP server is using for connections. This variable should be used in conjunction with the *SERVER_NAME* field for self-redirections.

REMOTE_HOST

The *REMOTE_HOST* variable contains the name of the host that is making the request. It is only set if the server is set to *reverse resolve* the IP address of the client. (See the "Reverse Resolve" sidebar.) If the server cannot reverse-resolve the IP address, then it should not assign a value to the *REMOTE_HOST* environment variable.

REMOTE_ADDR

The *REMOTE_ADDR* variable (see the sidebar) contains the IP address of the host that is making the request (i.e., the client's host machine).

AUTH_TYPE

The *AUTH_TYPE* variable contains the name of the authentication scheme used in the request. It corresponds to the scheme stated in the Authorization header sent with the request. The only currently defined value is Basic. It corresponds to the Basic User Authentication Scheme proposed in the HTTP/1.0 specs.

REMOTE_USER

The *REMOTE_USER* variable contains the name of the user that was provided during the authentication process, if one occurred.

REMOTE_IDENT

The *REMOTE_INDENT* variable contains the name of the user as retrieved from the client's identd server. This variable is set only if the server is configured to contact the remote machine and determine the user initiating the request. The identd server was discussed in Section 3.4.2. As you may remember, it can be used to try to determine the username of the person making a request. Unfortunately, this value should never be trusted.

Reverse Resolve

Whenever a connection is made between two machines, four important pieces of information define the connection: the IP address and port number on the server, and the IP address and port number on the client. As soon as the client connects, the server can discern the IP address and port number of the client because of the way that communication occurs over sockets. It's like the "caller ID" systems that allow you to see the number of the person calling you. However, the IP address doesn't necessarily tell you the name of the machine contacting you—just as with the caller ID system, where you only learn the number of the person calling you, not his or her name.

In order to figure out who is calling you on the phone, you have to get the number from the caller ID system, find a "reverse phone book," and look up the phone number to see who is listed under the number. Similarly, in order to find the name of the machine that is connecting to you, computers have to take the IP address and look it up through a service called Domain Name Service (DNS). This is known as *reverse resolving* the IP address. (*Resolving* is the process of taking a hostname and finding the IP address, which is just like looking up a person's name in a phone book.)

Of course, just as some people have unlisted phone numbers, some machines are not listed by the DNS, and their IP addresses cannot be reverse resolved. The most common reason for not listing a machine is because the machine is behind a firewall. A firewall IP address not listed by the DNS is somewhat like a phone that goes through a PBX system in an office. You would never be able to look up the person who had the number in the phone book; you could only get the number of the main switchboard.

HTTP_ FIELDS

The values in all header fields submitted with a request are saved in environment variables. An *HTTP_* environment variable is created for a header field if it does not correspond to one of the environment variables described thus far. For example, the User-Agent header field value is saved in an environment variable named *HTTP_USER_AGENT.* The Referer header field value is saved in *HTTP_REFERER.* The From and Date header field values are saved in *HTTP_FROM* and *HTTP_DATE,* respectively.

Don't Be Misled by *REMOTE_ADDR*

One of the most interesting things that you can do with the *REMOTE_HOST* and *REMOTE_ADDR* fields is use them to identify and track a single user of your system. As we've said before, unless you go out of your way to get information from each user (by making users submit a password or by using some sort of UID in the URL to keep track of them), there is generally no way to track a single user of your system from request to request.

If you make the assumption, though, that only one person is using a machine at a time, the IP address for that person's machine really does act as a unique ID, since all the requests coming from the same IP address can be assumed to be from the same user. All you have to do now is decide when a user has "left" your site. (No user ever tells you that he or she is no longer looking at your site. You just stop getting connections.) Generally, you determine when users leave your site by coming up with a time threshold and saying, "If I don't receive a request from an address within so many minutes, I will consider that user to have left my site."

Deciding on a time threshold is an effective way of doing cool things that you couldn't otherwise do (like guessing how many users are on your system at any time), but don't rely on your time threshold calculation to be valid. There are a couple reasons why you shouldn't rely on it.

For one thing, the assumption that only one person is using a machine can get you into big trouble. Nearly all UNIX machines are multiuser machines, since more than one user can be logged in and using the machine at a time. Therefore, it is completely possible for two or more people using the same machine to look at your site. And when they do, you have no way of knowing that two, three, or four people are not a single person. The assumption that only one person is using a machine can really get you into trouble when proxy servers and big Internet gateways (like Prodigy) are involved. When lots of people are using a single proxy server or a single machine to make connections to your machine, they are indistinguishable as far as their *REMOTE_ADDR* goes. Remember our Prodigy browser example a while back? We were able to track users because all of them came from a limited subset of machines that Prodigy was using as its Internet gateways. Hundreds of people could be using one of these machines to connect to your site, but they would all be the same person as far as *REMOTE_ADDR* is concerned.

Don't Be Misled by *REMOTE_ADDR* (Continued)

Second, you can't even trust the IP address to tell you who is connecting. When you make a connection to a remote server, it is possible to lie to that server and tell it you are someone else. (This is called *IP spoofing*.) IP spoofing is beyond the scope of the book, but beware of it if you ever depend on IP addresses for authentication.

9.1.2 Putting It All together

With all the different variables corresponding to different parts of the URL and the request, trying to remember where all the parts come from can be pretty confusing. So, here are two examples that show what all these variables mean.

Let's consider a sample form that is being submitted to the URL:

```
http://www.netgen.com/cgi-bin/test-cgi/homepage.html
```

In this form, **/cgi-bin/test-cgi** identifies the CGI script on www.netgen.com that will handle the request. Let's assume that the form contains two fields named "field1" and "field2," and that the user is submitting the form with values of "value1" and "value2," respectively.

The first example uses GET to submit the form. When the GET method is used this way, the server receives the following request:

```
GET /cgi-bin/test-cgi/homepage.html?field1=value1&field2=value2 HTTP/1.0
```

You saw requests similar to this in Chapter 6. This is simply the path portion of the original URL, plus the contents of the form encoded in the searchpart of the URL. Upon receiving this request, the server sets the environment variables as follows:

```
REQUEST_METHOD = GET
CONTENT_LENGTH = 0
SCRIPT_NAME = /cgi-bin/test-cgi
QUERY_STRING = field1=value1&field2=value2
PATH_INFO = /homepage.html
PATH_TRANSLATED = /usr/local/etc/httpd/homepage.html
```

The second example uses POST to submit the form. When the POST method is used this way, the server receives the following request:

```
POST /cgi-bin/test-cgi/homepage.html HTTP/1.0
Content-Type: application/x-www-form-urlencoded
Content-Length: 27

field1=value1&field2=value2
```

This time the input data is passed to the server as an object, which is why *CONTENT_LENGTH* is 27 here but was 0 in the first example. Upon receiving this request, the server sets the environment variables as follows:

```
REQUEST_METHOD = POST
CONTENT_LENGTH = 27
QUERY_STRING = N/A
PATH_INFO = /homepage.html
SCRIPT_NAME = /cgi-bin/test-cgi
PATH_TRANSLATED = /usr/local/etc/httpd/homepage.html
```

Between the *PATH_INFO* and *QUERY_STRING* variables, you have two different means of passing information to a script. Really, there is no difference between the two and you can use them interchangeably. Some people encode information within the path portion of the URL, while others encode the information within the searchpart portion.

9.1.3 Passing Input to the Script

After the server assimilates the client's request headers into its environment variables, it calls the CGI script. The script has to determine where it will find the rest of the data. That data might be a search string encoded into the URL, or it might be data posted from a form. The answer to where the data is located lies in the value of the *REQUEST_METHOD* environment variable. If the request method is GET, the CGI script knows that it should look in the environment variable called *QUERY_STRING*. If the request method is POST, the CGI script knows that the data is in STDIN (standard input), and it checks *CONTENT_LENGTH* to see how much data it should read from STDIN. Figure 9-2 diagrams the process that one must go through to read the data within a CGI program.

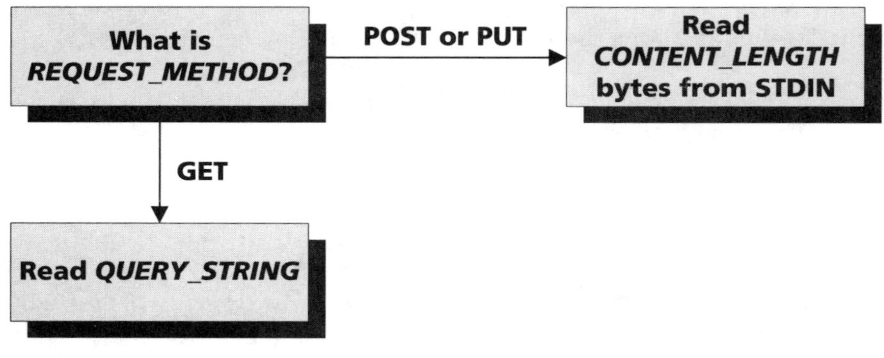

Figure 9–2 Locating the input data for the CGI script

NOTE

STDIN is a file handle, and file handles are used to identify streams of data. Besides standard input, other standard file handles include standard output (STDOUT) and standard error (STDERR).

Listing 9-1 contains sample perl code that can be used at the beginning of any CGI script to read data into a standard variable, regardless of the request method. If you use this code at the beginning of your own CGI scripts, you don't have to code a routine to check the request method being used. Instead, you can access the input data from the *$query* variable we created.

Listing 9–1. **A perl code routine that can be used at the beginning of a CGI script to read data into a standard variable name, regardless of the request method**

```
#!/usr/bin/perl
File Name: parseform.pl

local( $request_method, $content_length, $query_string );

# Grab REQUEST_METHOD< CONTENT_LENGTH, and QUERY_STRING
$request_method = $ENV{ 'REQUEST_METHOD' };
```

```
$content_length = $ENV{ 'CONTENT_LENGTH' };
$query_string   = $ENV{ 'QUERY_STRING' };
# Check if this was a PUT or a POST
if(( $request_method  eq 'POST' ) ||
   ( $request_method  eq 'PUT' ))
{

    # If so, read the right number of bytes off of STDIN
    read( STDIN, $query, $content_length );
}

# Check if this was a GET
elsif ( $request_method  eq 'GET' )
{

    # If so, the data is in QUERY_STRING.
    $query = $query_string;
}
else
{
    # Otherwise, print an error.
    print("Content-Type: text/html\n\n");
    print "<h1>Error: Unacceptable Method</h1>\n";
    print "<hr>\n";
    print "This script does not support the $ENV{'REQUEST_METHOD'}\n";
    print "method for submitting forms.  Please use the POST method.\n";
    exit;
}
```

9.2 CGI Output

Once the CGI script has completed its processing, the script needs to return output to the server—and thus return output indirectly to the client.

Generally, the CGI script produces an object that should be returned to the client. The object is returned as a standard HTTP response including the header fields and the Entity-Body, as described in Chapter 5. Therefore, the CGI script is responsible for returning a series of lines in the format of HTTP headers, followed by a blank line, and then the Entity-Body. As the CGI program outputs these lines to standard output (STDOUT), the server reads the lines, interprets them, and prepares a response to the client. The server computes a Content-Length for the Entity-Body and attaches the appropriate General-Header fields (such as Server and Date).

9.2.1 CGI Headers

CGI defines three special headers—Status, Location, and Content-Type—that are interpreted by the server when returned by a CGI script. After the server interprets the CGI headers, it integrates the information into the appropriate HTTP headers that are a part of the server response.

Location

Instead of returning an object to the server, the CGI script can use the Location CGI header to tell the server one of two things: to send a redirection status to the client, or to retrieve an object from the specified location and return it to the client. What the location header allows the CGI script to do is tell another entity to retrieve an object. In the first case, the script tells the server to provide the client with a URL so that the client can retrieve the object itself. In the second case, the script tells the server to retrieve the object and send it to the client. In both cases, you are using the request to access two different resources. Of course, this is not the purpose for which redirections were originally intended. They are meant to let the user know that a resource has moved, but they can be quite useful this way, too (see the "Success Messages" sidebar).

Following is an example of an HTTP response from a CGI script that returns a Location directive, i.e., a response that indicates that the server should redirect the client to the specified document. This example comes from a CGI script called autopilot.pl that is used to return a random URL from a list of URLs. We will provide the source for this code and an explanation of how it works in Chapter 11.

Here is the CGI output:

```
Location: http://caesar.cs.uiowa.edu/
```

The server interprets this as a redirection. It sends back the appropriate status code and header lines, as follows:

```
HTTP/1.0 302 Found
MIME-Version: 1.0
Server: CERN/3.0pre6
Date: Sunday, 26-Mar-95 21:12:18 GMT
Location: http://caesar.cs.uiowa.edu/
Content-Type: text/html
Content-Length: 386

<HTML>
<HEAD>
<TITLE>Redirection</TITLE>
</HEAD>
<BODY>
<H1>Redirection</H1>
This document can be found
<A HREF="http://caesar.cs.uiowa.edu/">elsewhere.</A><P>
You see this message because your browser doesn't support automatic
redirection handling. <P>
<HR>
<ADDRESS><A HREF="http://info.cern.ch/hypertext/WWW/Daemon/User/
Guide.html">
CERN httpd 3.0pre6</A></ADDRESS>
</BODY>
</HTML>
```

NOTE

As we discussed in Chapter 5, the latest specification introduces the URI response header to replace the Location response header. However, in this example you can see that the CERN server has not yet been updated to match the new specifications.

Success Messages

A CGI script can do one of two things: it can generate output itself or it can send a redirection without generating any real output. One of the more creative uses of redirection is to send the user some sort of "success message" after the CGI script has completed its processing.

For example, suppose you have a CGI script that processes application forms to register users with your system. After reading the input from the server and doing all the necessary processing (adding users to a database, for example), you might want to end by having the script generate a "Thank you for applying" message as output for the response.

Instead of generating an output message, however, your script could return a redirection to a "Thank you for applying" page. There are some distinct advantages to this alternative.

First of all, it's more flexible. You can make changes to the page without having to alter the CGI script. And second, it makes writing the script easier because you no longer need code to generate the output.

The following example specifies that the server retrieve the specified resource itself (in this case, homepage.html) and return it to the client:

```
Location: /homepage.html
```

Content-Type

The Content-Type CGI header is used to specify the Content-Type that the server should return to the client.

Status

The Status CGI header specifies that the server return the specified line as the Status-Line of the response. The Status-Line follows this format:

```
Status: Status_Code Reason
```

where the status codes are the same as those defined in the HTTP/1.0 specifications (discussed in Chapters 5 and 6). For example, the following example shows what happens when autopilot.pl is unable to return a URL (which would happen if autopilot.pl encountered a file error in the list of URLs file).

In this example, the script returns the line `Status: 500 Internal Server Error`. It also returns a Content-Type directive. Here is the output from the CGI script:

```
Status: 500 Internal Server Error
Content-Type: text/html

<html>
<head>
<title>Autopilot Error</title>
</head>
<body>
<h1>Autopilot was unable to retrieve a URL to return.</h1>
</body>
</html>
```

The server interprets this as a status code to return in the response:

```
HTTP/1.0 500 Internal Server Error
MIME-Version: 1.0
Server: CERN/3.0pre6
Date: Sunday, 26-Mar-95 21:14:52 GMT
Content-Type: text/html
Content-Length: 135

<html>
<head>
<title>Autopilot Error</title>
</head>
<body>
<h1>Autopilot was unable to retrieve a URL to return.</h1>
</body>
</html>
```

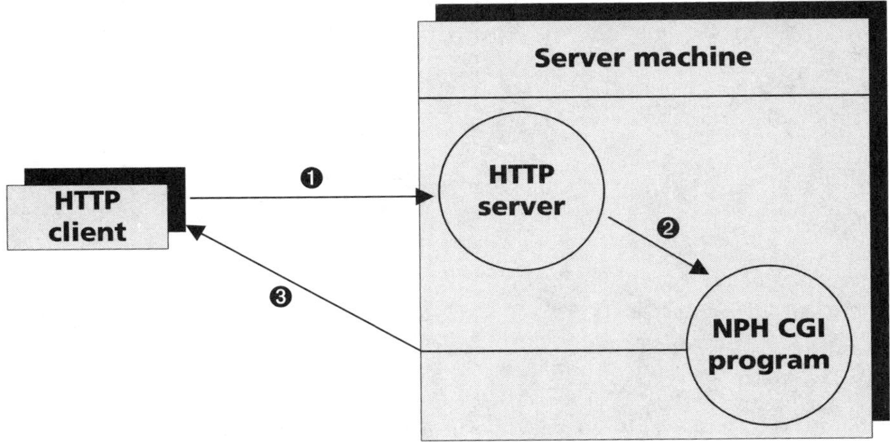

1. The client connects to the HTTP server and makes its request.
2. The server sets several environment variables and runs the NPH CGI program, passing it extra input, if necessary. At this point, the server passes control of all output to the CGI program.
3. After completing its processing, the CGI program passes its results back to the client.

Figure 9–3 The flow of a client-server communication interchange involving an NPH CGI script

9.2.2 NPH Scripts

Sometimes, requiring the server to send the actual response can limit the functionality of the CGI program. Therefore, CGI specifications allow for special type of programs called No-Parse Header (NPH) scripts that allow a CGI program to send responses directly to the client. NPH programs are completely responsible for forming the full HTTP response to the client, including the status codes, header fields, and Entity-Body. Figure 9-3 illustrates the flow of a connection when an NPH script is called.

In order to differentiate NPH scripts from standard CGI scripts, all filenames beginning with *nph-* are considered NPH scripts. (If your name is

Nelson P. Hammar, don't use your initials to name script files unless you are writing NPH scripts!)

Listing 9-2 shows a program that has to be an NPH script in order to work. This example uses the multipart Content-Type. This code produced the "quote of the moment" found in Section 6.1.4.

Listing 9–2. An NPH script using multipart Content-Type

```
#!/usr/bin/perl
$|=1;
#File Name: nph-quote.pl
# Since this is an NPH program, we need to return the Status-Line
# like normal
print("HTTP/1.0 200 OK\r\n");

# We also need to provide the Content-Type for our data
print("Content-type: multipart/x-mixed-replace; boundary=--To-err-is-human-
to-moo-bovine\r\n");

# Now send the CR LF to indicate it is the end of the header information.
print "\r\n";


# Open the file to read the quotes from.
open(QUOTES, "/tmp/quotes");

# Read until you see a blank line.
$/="\n\n";

# Do this for each quote in the file.
while(<QUOTES>)
{

  # Print the boundary string indicating the beginning of the part
  print "--To-err-is-human-to-moo-bovine\r\n";
```

```
    # Return the Content-Type for the part.
    print("Content-type: text/html\r\n");

    # Print a CR LF to indicate it is the end of the header information
    print "\r\n";

    # Print the body of the object
    print("<html>\n");
    print("<head>\n");
    print("<title>Quote of the moment...</title>\n");
    print("</head>\n");
    print("<body>\n");
    print("<h1>Quote of the moment...</h1>\n");
    print("<hr>\r\n");

    # Print out the quote itself
    print $_;

    # Finish off the body
    print("<hr>\r\n");
    print("\r\n");
    print("</body>\n");

    # Wait 10 seconds before starting again.
    sleep(1);
}

# Send the end-of-object boundary string.
print "--To-err-is-human-to-moo-bovine--\r\n";
```

The obvious question is why this has to be an NPH script in order to work. With regular CGI scripts, the server waits patiently until the CGI program has completed its processing. Then once it has received all output from the CGI program, it sends a response to the client. But our sample program is supposed to send each one of the parts every ten seconds. Without an NPH script, the server would not send any of the parts to the client until it had received all the parts from the program. The server would then take the entire response and send it to the client, which would completely ruin the functionality of the program.

9.3 Debugging CGI Scripts

When CGI scripts are called by the server and they don't work, determining what exactly went wrong can be difficult. Here are a few tips that might help.

9.3.1 When in Doubt, Print

It is always a good programming practice to use print statements in your code to help you understand what is happening. As you write your code, constantly be on the lookout for major branches in the flow control, or points where tests occur or variables are set that are important. Whenever you find one of these points, put in a print statement so you know what happened (i.e., so you know which branch the program took, what the result of the test was, and what the variable's value is). Listing 9-3 includes several print statements. When the code runs, it hits each point and prints out a message letting you know what is happening. You can often save a lot of time by analyzing these statements and figuring out where things went wrong. From there, you can backtrack and try to figure out what caused the problem.

Unfortunately, when your script is run by the server, the server tends to capture all messages that are sent to standard error (STDERR), which is a common place to print these debugging messages. In addition, CGI defines the program's standard output as the channel over which all the data is sent back to the server. So unless you are careful here, you can't just send random print statements to standard out (STDOUT) without screwing up the output. Of course, there is a workaround—use HTML comments.

If your CGI program is outputting an HTML document (which is what most scripts are used for), you can use the HTML comment string to send debugging information along without screwing up your output. For example, after you have already printed the Content-Type, you can use the code shown in Listing 9-3 to send hidden debugging information back to the client.

Listing 9–3. CGI script for sending hidden debugging information back to a client

```
#!/usr/bin/perl

local($important_variable);

print "Content-Type: text/html\r\n";
print "\r\n";

# Do some processing here....

# Print a debugging statement
print "<!-- Testing important_variable: $important_variable -->\n";

if ($important_variable)
{
  print "<!-- Test succeeded. -->\n";
  # ...
}
else
{
  print "<!-- Test failed -->\n";
  # ...
}
```

Because all the debugging information is contained within HTML comments, average users don't see any of the information. However, if you tell your browser to show you the raw HTML for the page (most browsers have an option that allows you to view the source for the current page), you can see this debugging information.

Listing 9-4 shows an example of HTML that was generated by our net.Form product. Based on a configurable debugging level, the program embeds large amounts of diagnostic print messages in HTML comments so that users can figure out what is happening.

Listing 9–4. HTML generated by net.Form that includes a lot of diagnostic print messages

```
<title>net.Form Submission</title>
<h1>Error in Form submission</h1>
<!-- SUBMITTED DATA -->
<!--  POST; Reading content from STDIN -->
<!--  Submitted keys and values -->
<!--   field name: netform_version | value: 1.0 -->
<!--   field name: netform_recipient | value: webmaster@netgen.com -->
<!--   field name: netform_success_message | value: http://www.netgen.com/
-->
<!--   field name: netform_config | value: neform_sender EmRe -->
<!--   field name: form_body | value: This is a test -->
<!--   field name: netform_sender | value: erichard -->
<!--   field name: netform_subject | value: netgen.com Comment Gateway -->
<!-- VERSION -->
<!--  Running Version: 1.0 Emulating Version: 1.0. -->
<!-- SUBJECT -->
<!--  Found 'netform_subject' field. -->
<!--  New subject: netgen.com Comment Gateway -->
...
<ul>
<li>The neform_sender field cannot be empty.
</ul>
```

9.3.2 Stick a Content-Type at the Top

One of the problems with the HTML technique we suggested earlier is that until the HTTP Response header is terminated (with the blank line), debugging comments are either ignored (since they aren't valid in the header) or cause an error.

Therefore, it is to your advantage to try to print out all the header information at the beginning of the program so that debugging statements can be used as early as possible. Sometimes, however, you can't finish the header at the beginning. For example, you might have to wait until you have been able to test a set of conditions before you can determine whether to return an error, document, or redirection.

In this case, the best option is to stick in a line specifying a Content-Type of `text/plain` and terminate the header information so that any print statements will be sent to the client. Obviously, this is only a temporary solution while you debug, but at least you are able to see the actual debugging messages that are printed.

9.3.3 Simulate a Request

The second way to test a CGI script is to simulate a request by the Web server and run it yourself. Now that you know about all the variables that the script is going to look for, you can manually set these variables (as if the server had) and then run the program to see what happens.

We'll show you two examples of emulating a request. For our examples, we'll use test-cgi (a simple script that just prints out the values of all the standard CGI environment variables). One example uses GET and the other uses POST.

First you set up the environment variables with the values you want to use:

```
> setenv REQUEST_METHOD 'GET'
> setenv QUERY_STRING 'field1=this%20is%20a%20test'
```

NOTE

This example assumes that the user is using csh or tcsh as their shell. If they are using a shell such as sh or bash, you will need to use a different command to set the environment variables.

Then you run the program and see what the output looks like:

```
> test-cgi

Content-Type: text/plain

CGI/1.0 test script report:
```

```
SERVER_SOFTWARE =
SERVER_NAME =
GATEWAY_INTERFACE =
SERVER_PROTOCOL =
SERVER_PORT =
REQUEST_METHOD = GET
HTTP_ACCEPT =
PATH_INFO =
PATH_TRANSLATED =
SCRIPT_NAME =
QUERY_STRING = field1=this%20is%20a%20test
REMOTE_HOST =
REMOTE_ADDR =
REMOTE_USER =
AUTH_TYPE =
CONTENT_TYPE =
CONTENT_LENGTH =
```

Here is an example of emulating a POST request. Again, you set the environment variables:

```
> setenv REQUEST_METHOD 'POST'
> setenv CONTENT_LENGTH '7'
```

Then you run the program. Because the test-cgi script wants to read seven bytes from STDIN, you type the input after entering the command to run the script. Then it returns its results:

```
> test-cgi
foo=bar

Content-Type: text/plain

CGI/1.0 test script report:
```

```
SERVER_SOFTWARE =
SERVER_NAME =
GATEWAY_INTERFACE =
SERVER_PROTOCOL =
SERVER_PORT =
REQUEST_METHOD = POST
HTTP_ACCEPT =
PATH_INFO =
PATH_TRANSLATED =
SCRIPT_NAME =
QUERY_STRING =
REMOTE_HOST =
REMOTE_ADDR =
REMOTE_USER =
AUTH_TYPE =
CONTENT_TYPE =
CONTENT_LENGTH = 7
```

9.3.4 Hints and Tips

Now we'll tell you about a few weird errors we've encountered. These errors cost us a great deal of debugging time. Debugging is a matter of experience. On our "Hints and Tips on CGI Debugging" page at the netgen.com site, we not only share our experiences with you, but we invite you to share your tips and hints as well. Feel free to use the "In My Experience" input form. We'll add your advice (with your name) to the page.

net.Genesis Debugging Hints & Tips
http://www.netgen.com/book/debug-cgi-hints-and-tips.html

If you are running CERN httpd on a DEC Alpha and experience problems when you use CGI scripts, you're likely encountering some sort of bug in the way that the server handles the output from the scripts. The best solution is to try different server software. Generally, only a portion of the response is sent and the connection closes prematurely. In certain cases, the connection is closed before any response has been sent. Mosaic treats this as an error and informs the user, but Netscape Navigator just returns a blank screen with no error message. The solution is to switch to NCSA's server.

If you are not running CERN httpd on a DEC and one of your scripts always returns an error to Mosaic, a blank screen to Netscape, or partial results to either browser, your script might have an error that causes it to abort before it can send back the entire response. The best thing to do here is run the script manually (as described above) with the same input that is causing the problems to see whether there is an error in the code.

If you are consistently getting an error in Mosaic that says, "Requested document could not be accessed," and/or you are getting a blank screen back in Netscape, the header being sent back by your script might be missing or malformed. The best way to test this error is to telnet into the Web server and make the request. We describe how to do this in Section 6.2. Using this test, you can see exactly what the response looks like and figure out where the problem is.

As we mentioned at the beginning of this chapter, you can write CGI scripts in practically any language. However, not all languages support everything you may want to do. In particular, many shell-scripting languages (like Bourne Shell and C Shell) do not provide a mechanism for reading a known amount of data from standard input. Therefore, these languages can be used to write scripts that handle GET requests, but they cannot be used to handle POST requests at all.

9.4 Typical Uses for CGI Scripts

In addition to creating search programs with CGI scripts, you can create CGI scripts that act as gateways to other protocols and interface with databases. CGI scripts can even handle interaction with clickable image maps and generate documents on-the-fly.

The important thing to recognize is that the CGI program is being run on the server, not on the client's machine. This means that you cannot do certain things, such as make another window pop up on the client's machine. You cannot access the client's disk drive or do anything that requires accessing the client's machine. It also means that if you are doing something that is processor-intensive, the load on your own server machine increases every time a client uses the script.

9.4.1 Gateways to Other Protocols

One of the common uses of CGI scripts is as a gateway to other protocols. Used this way, CGI scripts take an HTTP request, translate it into another pro-

Put the Finger on Someone

Finger is a standard UNIX program that retrieves information about other users. Here's a typical example:

```
> finger devra@netgen.com

[netgen.com]
Login: devra                            Name: Devra Hall
Directory: /home/devra                  Shell: /bin/tcsh
Never logged in.
Plan:
Devra Hall is co-author of "Build a Web Site: A Programmer's Guide".

She is also author of:
o PC World's DOS 6 Handbook
o Teach Yourself Visual Basic
o Teach Yourself Delphi
o The CD-ROM Revolution

She would like to take a very long break after finishing this book, but
she may have to wait until she finishes her two Windows 95 books.
```

tocol, make a request under that protocol, and translate the response back into valid HTTP. CGI scripts are used this way in finger gateways so users can finger other users on a site via the Web, and in mail gateways so users can send mail to people from the Web. (See the sidebar, "Put the Finger on Someone.") Lots of other gateways exist out there, including an interface to zephyr that allows users of the Web to send real-time messages to students who are logged onto machines at MIT.

Listing 9-5 is a sample CGI finger gateway that determines which user to finger based on the *PATH_INFO* environment field.

Listing 9–5. Sample CGI finger gateway

```
#!/usr/bin/perl
#Filename: finger.pl

#Description: Expects PATH_INFO to be a "/" delimited list of usernames
# to finger.  Returns the results of fingering each of these users.

#Grab the username from PATH_INFO
$usernames = $ENV{'PATH_INFO'};

# Remove the initial "/"
$usernames =~ s/^\///;

# Convert this into a list of users
@users = split("/", $usernames);

# Print out the Content-Type header
print "Content-Type: text/plain\r\n";

# End the header
print "\r\n";

# Loop over all the users
foreach $username (@users)
{
    print "Fingering $username\n";
    # Make the finger request
    $result = 'finger $username';

    # Print the results back to the user
    print $result;
    print "\n";
}
```

Here is a finger example using our CGI gateway script from Listing 9-5:

```
GET /cgi/finger.pl/devra@netgen.com/erichard@netgen.com HTTP/1.0

HTTP/1.0 200 Document follows
MIME-Version: 1.0
Server: CERN/3.0pre6
Date: Monday, 27-Mar-95 01:01:16 GMT
Content-Type: text/plain
Content-Length: 777

Fingering devra@netgen.com
[netgen.com]
Login: devra                            Name: Devra Hall
Directory: /home/devra                  Shell: /bin/tcsh
Never logged in.
Plan:
Devra Hall is co-author of "Build a Web Site: A Programmer's Guide".
She is also author of:
o PC World's DOS 6 Handbook
o Teach Yourself Visual Basic
o Teach Yourself Delphi
o The CD-ROM Revolution
She would like to take a very long break after finishing this book, but she
may have to wait until she finishes her two Windows 95 books.

Fingering erichard@netgen.com
[netgen.com]
Login: erichard                         Name: Eric Richard
Directory: /home/erichard               Shell: /bin/tcsh
Office Phone: (617) 267-0793            Home Phone: (617) 225-7602
On since Sun Mar 26 17:20 ((null)) on ttyp0 from CENTAURI.MIT.EDU
No Plan.
```

Figure 9-4 shows how the Mosaic browser renders this response.

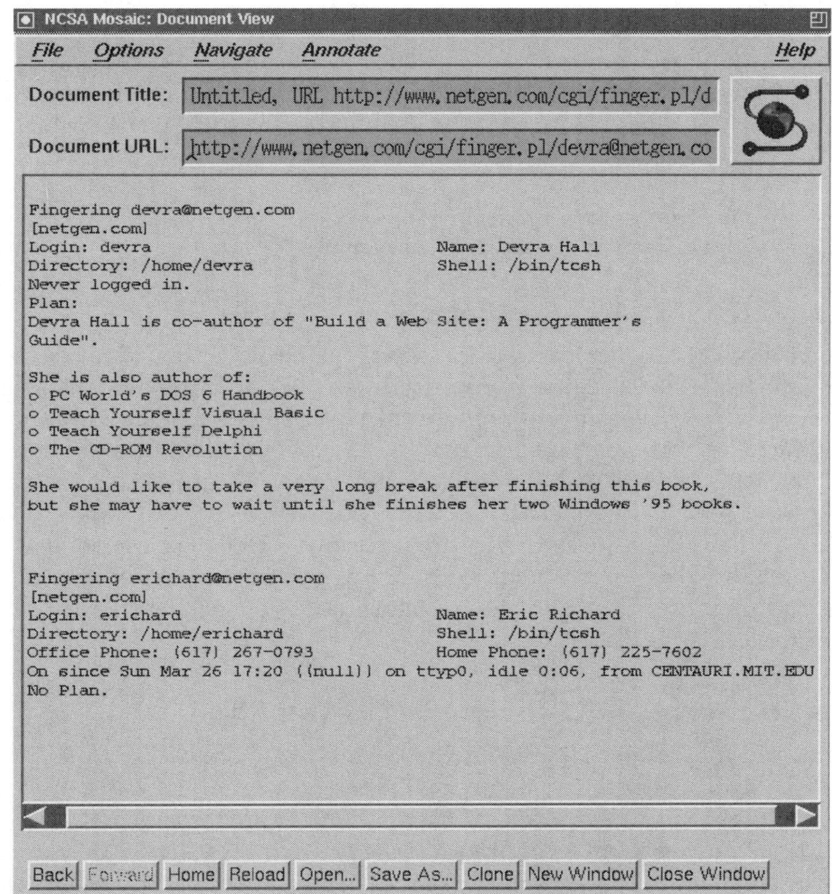
NCSA Mosaic: Document View
File Options Navigate Annotate Help
Document Title: Untitled, URL http://www.netgen.com/cgi/finger.pl/d
Document URL: http://www.netgen.com/cgi/finger.pl/devra@netgen.co
Fingering devra@netgen.com
[netgen.com]
Login: devra Name: Devra Hall
Directory: /home/devra Shell: /bin/tcsh
Never logged in.
Plan:
Devra Hall is co-author of "Build a Web Site: A Programmer's
Guide".
She is also author of:
o PC World's DOS 6 Handbook
o Teach Yourself Visual Basic
o Teach Yourself Delphi
o The CD-ROM Revolution
She would like to take a very long break after finishing this book,
but she may have to wait until she finishes her two Windows '95 books.
Fingering erichard@netgen.com
[netgen.com]
Login: erichard Name: Eric Richard
Directory: /home/erichard Shell: /bin/tcsh
Office Phone: (617) 267-0793 Home Phone: (617) 225-7602
On since Sun Mar 26 17:20 ((null)) on ttyp0, idle 0:06, from CENTAURI.MIT.EDU
No Plan.
Back Forward Home Reload Open... Save As... Clone New Window Close Window

Figure 9–4 A Mosaic rendering of the response from the CGI finger gateway script shown in Listing 9-5

9.4.2 Database Interface

CGI scripts can be used to interface with a local database. For example, suppose you have a huge Oracle database set up on your system and you've been storing information in it for years and years. The best way to make its information available to the rest of the world is to create a CGI script to translate the user's input into a database query and then send back the results to the user.

9.4.3 Search Engines

Lots of sites use CGI scripts to do searches. For example, Wandex is really just a CGI script that takes users' requests and searches a custom-generated database that is compiled by the Wanderer. Lycos and the WebCrawler are also CGI search scripts.

List of Links to Web Search Engines
http://www.netgen.com/book/search-engines.html

9.4.4 Clickable Image Maps

Another class of CGI scripts is used to provide clickable image maps. Any time you see an image on the Web and you can click on different portions of it to go to different resources, some sort of server-side executable is running and doing the necessary processing. When somebody clicks on the picture, the client URL encodes the coordinates into a query string so that they are sent to the server as part of the request. Most of the popular servers take these coordinates and look in a configuration file to determine what URL the coordinates map to. It is up to the script to do whatever processing is necessary to figure out which URL to return to the client and then actually perform that redirection.

9.4.5 Generating Documents On-the-Fly

One of the most powerful uses of CGI scripts is to generate HTML documents or other objects based on user input. For example, based on the interests that a user specifies, a CGI script could search a large database of news feeds and generate a custom newspaper. *The Freshman Fishwrap,* an experimental version of this concept, has been in progress for the past two years at MIT's Media Lab. Members of the MIT community submit topics of interest and personal information. This data is used to generate a personal, on-demand newspaper via the Web.

However, there is no reason to limit yourself to generating HTML documents on-the-fly. You can generate any type of object if you know what you are doing. For example, based on a user's preferences, you could dynamically generate images and return them through a CGI script. As part of the *Fishwrap* project, Mark Hurst has developed software that dynamically generates comic strips by incorporating information about the user into the strip.

This is the wave of the future. The big news agencies are providing MIT with free news feeds for the experimental *Fishwrap* project, which, unfortunately, means that the project is not open to the general public. Fortuntely,

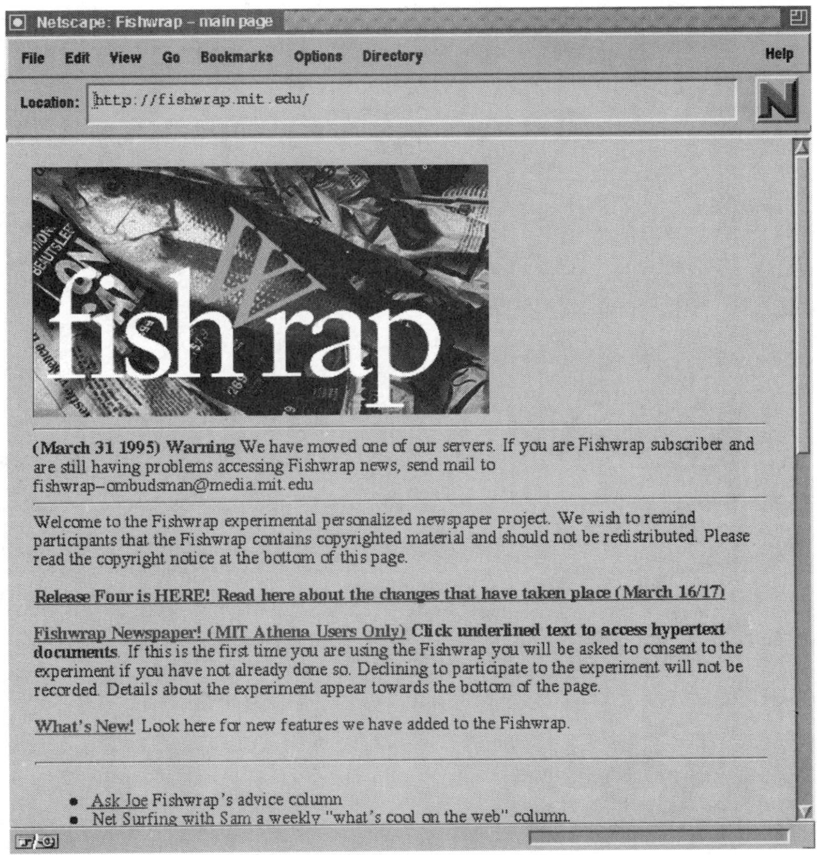

Figure 9-5 *Freshman Fishwrap*

we can show you a page of it (see Figure 9-5). You may also access a top-level page that tells you about the project.

The Freshman Fishwrap
http://www.netgen.com/book/fishwrap.html

PART III
Programming the Web

By this time, you should understand the background of the Web and know why things are the way they are. You should also understand the importance and relevance of the specifications and standards governing the Web, and how to use each to your best advantage.

You are now ready to roll up your sleeves and get ready to work. The chapters in this section take you through the major tasks of setting up and programming a Web site:

- Planning, developing, and maintaining a Web site
- Using CGI scripts to search, maintain state, and automate other functions
- Writing clients to browse, wander, and perform specialized operations
- Programming various server models

Each chapter includes sample program code and discusses practical application and implementation issues.

CHAPTER 10

Designing a Web Site

CHAPTER AT A GLANCE

This chapter presents issues that site administrators need to consider when creating and maintaining a Web site. The popularity of your Web site will depend on a number of issues involving structure, content, and reliability. In this chapter we discuss the need for comprehensive planning and the development of a prototype as a crucial first step. Then, because the ease and efficiency with which users can find information and navigate from topic to topic is important, we discuss how to structure your top-level page and link your documents. We also point out other issues that can affect the popularity of your Web site, such as connection speed, supporting different video configurations, color-friendly GIFs, economizing on images, and other multimedia-related concerns. The last part of this chapter addresses Web site maintenance and includes several sample programs that can help you monitor your site and respond to your users.

REQUISITES

Enough familiarity with HTML 2.0 or 3.0 to write HTML documents as described in Chapter 7 and 8. Some familiarity with programming concepts and the C and/or perl programming languages (some of the code examples include modifications to the CERN and NCSA servers, which are written in C).

MORE DETAIL

Chapter 11 provides a library of useful examples of CGI scripts.

net.Genesis believes that there are three distinct steps to creating a Web site. The first is to plan the site, the second is to determine and implement the content and functionality, and the third is to maintain the system on an ongoing basis. This chapter discusses the three distinct steps to creating a Web site

10.1 Planning a Web Site

Planning is the first phase in creating your own Web site. You begin by developing a prototype. Then, once the prototype has been deemed successful, the next step is to create a detailed design document. The design document outlines your vision for the long-term plan of the site. Once it is completed, you can move to the implementation stage. At this stage, entirely different issues have to be dealt with.

10.1.1 The Prototype

The best way to create a new site is to begin by developing a preliminary prototype. As you develop the prototype, feel free to try many different options to see how they work. The main goal at this stage is to learn, and learning costs little at this stage. As long as you make it clear that your site is under development, you can experiment and try different looks and feels without incurring the wrath of the demanding customer. During this time, you can also apply a much smaller budget to the system so that learning doesn't cost as much, literally. You will learn about presenting graphics and about marketing. Many companies have taken this approach. For example, ESPN developed a beta version of its site months before going online for real. ESPN's goal was to determine what worked and what didn't for its target users, and to determine the interest from corporate sponsors.

It is more important to be able to float ideas than it is to have a complete graphic design. Therefore, take time to come up with new ideas and play with them, even if your ideas aren't fully developed graphically. If you set up your site as a prototype and never change your look, structure, or feel, you will never learn which versions will be most successful. Admittedly, you can strike a perfect combination on the first try, but you are more likely to only get a few pieces right and end up using this learning period to refine the other points.

Think about your long-term vision of the site. This is the time to experiment with specific areas. For example, if the main reason you are setting up a site is to communicate a corporate message and identity, experiment with different home page designs and types of images, graphic designs, layouts, etc., to meet these goals. Look at other sites and evaluate what you see. This is also the time to determine what the focus of the site's content and functionality are.

When you create a live prototype Web site, you get a jump-start on building a user base as well as get valuable user feedback. Planning hardly matters if the design is not attractive or useful to users. The first visitors to your site will help you learn what works and what doesn't.

You can gain information from the user base directly and indirectly. Indirect clues come by looking at the site's usage statistics during this time. You can find out what content users seem most interested in by seeing which information is getting "hit" most often. You'll get excellent feedback for figuring out the focus of the site. (In section 10.3.4, we provide several scripts you can use to obtain this information.)

This is also a good time to be proactive when it comes to eliciting user feedback about your site's structure, content, and look. By emphasizing interaction with users—by locating your feedback forms in a place where users will find them, developing user surveys, and possibly even asking users during this time to register so that you can contact them by e-mail or phone—you can gain a much deeper understanding of what users are thinking.

You want users to come to your site again and again. That means determining what draws users to your site and what keeps them coming back. Dynamic sites tend to have repeat users. A great graphic design at a site is usually not reason enough to visit a site more than once. Interesting content is a powerful draw. The prototype stage is an excellent time to figure out which content draws repeat users.

NOTE

During the prototype phase, it is imperative to make it clear to everybody coming to your site that the content and layout of the site are experimental. Users can go to thousands and thousands of other sites on the Web. If a user spends five minutes at your site and gets frustrated because the site is not developed or because he or she has to register, it is quite conceivable that the user will forget about your site and not come back for months, if ever. But if users understand that your site is a work in progress and that you are actively soliciting their participation and input, they will usually spend a few moments to share their thoughts with you. And they will likely come back to check your progress. You should

give users a hint of what your site will offer in the long run (just a list of what to look forward to is fine) and notification of when they can expect to see it. This is particularly important if you ask users to register at the prototype site but do not plan to continue this for the real release. In this case, make it very clear when you ask users to register that they are registering for the experimental version of the site only.

As you develop the prototype, you will gain many insights to help answer these (and other) questions about the project:

- How should you structure the site?
- What do you need in terms of both capital and human resources to fully implement the site?
- How many technical people, graphic designers, marketing people, and sales people do you need?
- How should the data be laid out within the site?
- How are you going to manage the data on disk? Are you going to use commercial databases to store information or are you going to use a file system?
- How are you going to deal with version control (i.e., how are you going to make sure that no two people edit the same file at the same time)?
- How can you make sure that you are maintaining the structural integrity and stylistic consistency of your site (i.e., how are you going to make sure that you aren't creating dead links as you move documents)?
- How are you going to make sure that all the documents you add fit in conceptually with the rest of your site?

The most important thing to realize is that there are no right answers. The important part is to think about these issues, realize that they are indeed issues, and put a structure in place for dealing with them. It doesn't matter whether you hire a full-time person whose sole job it is to maintain the integrity and consistency of your site or buy a commercial software product to handle this for you. Both options are fine, so long as you plan ahead of time and work the options you choose into your plans for maintaining the site. Depending on the size of the site, maintaining it could take one person a few hours a week or many people forty hours a week. By building a prototype, you will learn the answer to this and other questions.

NOTE

The structure, layout, and design of a site have long-term effects on how it is used. Unless you have enough resources to perform a live overhaul of the site (i.e., change the site while it is still online), you generally wind up building on the structure that is already in place. This is why we advocate setting up a prototype. By the time you go online for real, you need a very stable base, one that supports growth that is in line with your goals. Otherwise, you will wind up spending lots of time and effort fighting against your underlying structure to rectify your mistakes.

10.1.2 The Design Document

After you have experimented with your site, tried different graphic layouts, offered different services, and figured out the internal structure and how to maintain it, it is time to formalize some of these ideas into a design document. This is especially important if you are going to hire contractors to implement your site. When you hand a project off to someone outside, the document needs to be very, very clear about what you want! Think of a design document as a road map for the site's creation. Write down the site's goals and how you are going to achieve them. Also, you should clearly define the project and all of its modules. Personnel allocated to the project must commit to delivering the parts of the project they are responsible for on schedule. For consultants, the design document can serve as the basis for a contract and also as a tool for estimating costs.

One of the important things to realize is that, as time goes by, only a few people will have had an opportunity to learn from the prototype phase. Therefore, it is important not only to document your strategy for the site, but also to document your rationale. You need to explain not only why you chose to implement your site this way, but why you did *not* choose to implement it other ways. Why you didn't take a certain course is often the most valuable information that you can get from the prototype phase—and it is also the information that is most often left out of the design document. If you don't include these sorts of notes, people down the road might wind up spending their time relearning what you learned from the prototype.

When you write the design document, think of the long-term development of the site. Your design document says where people can expect to find certain files (i.e., it should describe the physical structure of your file system, including the purpose for each main directory). It should also say where new files should be placed. It should document all design decisions that have been made—for example, a requirement that all pages adhere to a certain style. You also need to consider technical and customer support, channeling and incorporating feedback, and collateral support, including online sales and traditional marketing.

Again, we want to emphasize that there are few, if any, "right answers." The most important thing is to document are *your* answers so that others can use the design document as a base upon which to build the site.

10.1.3 Implementation

By this phase of the process, you should know what the focus of your site is—the distribution of product information, customer support, or providing a service over the Web. To maintain production quality, your Web site must be stable from both a hardware and software perspective. Your corporate image and reputation will be staked on this site, so it must be the best that it can be. It also goes without saying that many of the graphical and design issues should have been planned and executed by this stage. In the prototype stage, you should have chosen a style that works for your company, and now, as you turn the prototype into a full-fledged production-quality site, you can execute that style.

These are some of the many of the issues raised that should have been thought through and resolved in the design document. But before we move on to discuss the development of the structure and content, we'd like to mention a few other things that you might not have considered.

Getting Value from Your Site

How will your site contribute to your bottom line? This is an important long-term consideration, and obviously an issue that must be thought through from the day you decide to go public. You need to know exactly what your goals are, as well as what your limits are in terms of how much you can pour into this project. Obviously, you must be able to justify the cost of implementing and maintaining a site; otherwise, it makes no sense to create it. In the short-term, you should not expect a great monetary return on your investment, but in this stage you need to determine what role the site will play in the company. There are a number of different models you might want to consider.

NOTE

More likely than not, no site fits perfectly into a single model, but instead resembles one or more model types. These models are presented to give you overall strategies for recovering your costs.

Content providers such as television networks, magazine publishers, and newspaper publishers usually use the advertiser model. These sites provide content at little or no cost to users, but charge advertisers to place images and text in the content. The idea here is basically the same as television or radio, where the cost of providing the service is subsidized by advertisers who buy the right to reach customers over a medium, in this case radio or TV. One example of this sort of site is ESPNET SportsZone (see Figure 10-1). Currently, this site is getting around a half million hits a day, which makes it a pretty valuable resource for sponsors. It should be no surprise that ESPN has sold space on its pages to sponsors. However, the advertising model is only realistic if you get a large number of accesses a day. If you decide to go with this model, it is imperative that you use common sense and not turn your site into a gigantic billboard.

Another way to make money on the Web is to use your site as a channel for selling products. You can create an online ordering system and receive orders via the Web. Depending on the product, this could be an excellent extension to your current sales and marketing efforts. In the selling-products scenario, you need to think about how you will receive payment for your products. Secure credit card transactions are just now becoming a possibility on the Web. To increase the security of online transactions, you can do a number of things, such as calling people back after they order or issuing account numbers and then verifying sales orders through the Web. A large number of "cybermalls" already online follow this model.

Another model is simply to charge for viewing the content. In this case, the provider believes the content is unique and rare enough that consumers will pay for it. It should be emphasized that very few types of information on the Internet are unique enough that users are willing to pay for them. One example of a company that has succeeded in charging users for its content is Encyclopedia Britannica. Unless you have a resource that cannot be found elsewhere and provides a very real value, this model won't succeed on the

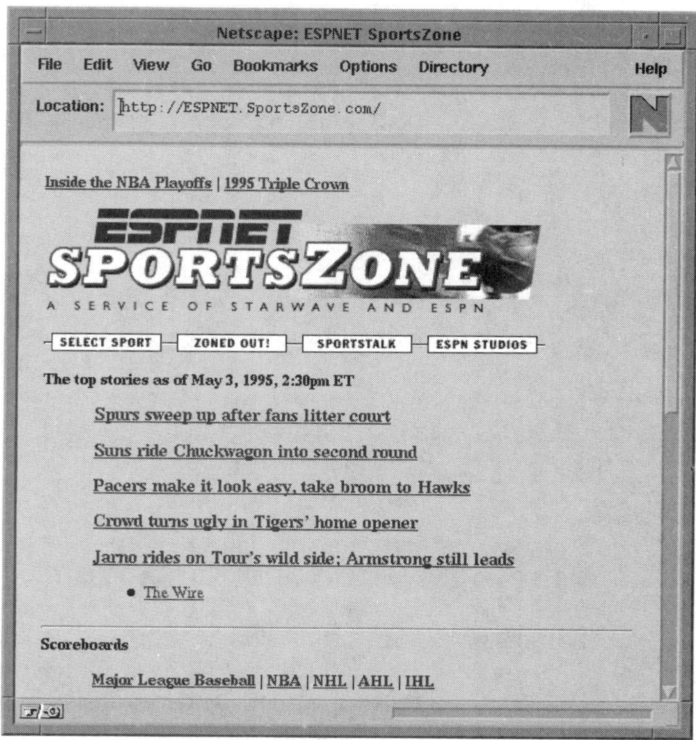

Figure 10–1 The ESPNET SportsZone home page

Web. Many people on the Internet and the Web can put up information, so it is very hard to capture a market that someone else can't undercut by offering the same service for free.

The most popular model for site-generated revenue is the indirect one. In this model, companies simply use their site to disseminate corporate and product information. Such sites are used as a marketing and PR engine for the other activities with which the company is involved.

Internal/External Use

Overall, the focus of most sites is external in nature, but you should consider internal uses as well. For example, sites can be used for internal project management, online company calendars, directory listings, technical resources (unless the resources are proprietary, they can be used externally as well), online training, and product demonstrations. This is one of those areas where you simply need to do a little thinking and determine what right for your company. Does it make sense to use a Web site internally to provide a simple means of distributing information, or are other systems already in place? If such mechanisms don't already exist, this could be a great opportunity to really get a double advantage out of your site.

Infrastructure Support

When your prototype becomes the real thing, full infrastructure support is necessary to keep the site up and running. You have to allocate capital and human resources to support the site. The number of machines, the type of connection, and the amount of money are all factors you must consider during the planning phase. Make plans for handling the various functions, such as usage analysis, site verification, and response to user feedback.

10.2 Developing Content for a Web Site

The popularity of a Web site depends on a number of issues. Structural issues include how easy it is to find information, how easily and efficiently users can navigate from topic to topic, and whether users feel that they understand the structure of the site and where they are within it at any given time. Issues relating to graphics and multimedia include the usefulness of the data and the cost of the data in terms of size and resources. For a site to be successful, users must believe that it has some value for them.

10.2.1 Information Structure

There are no hard and fast rules for organizing data, but there are a few guidelines. The first is to structure the site so that it has both breadth and depth. Don't structure things too flatly or deeply. In order to get at a piece of information, users shouldn't have to click 45 times. However, everything shouldn't be referenced on the top-level page either. You need some sort of cogent, conceptual organization.

Simple Home Page

The second guideline suggests that no matter how a site is organized, you should always provide a top-level page from which users can navigate. For example, even if your site serves a variety of disjointed pieces of information, a top-level page should have pointers to all levels or topics. Most users who visit a site leave remembering only the host name, not the full URL to your other documents. By providing a comprehensive home page, new users can easily see what is available, and returning users can easily find what they are looking for.

NOTE

You will probably want to make your home page available by requesting the / resource from your server. For example, if your server's hostname is www.joe.com, you would want your URL for your top-level page to be http://www.joe.com/. Most servers look for particular files—index.html and welcome.html are two common names—in the server's root directory when such a request is made. Therefore, if you name your home page index.html or welcome.html, you should be set. You'll be making it easier for users who forget the full URL to the pages in your site.

One of the most common architectures is to have a top-level page with a number of conceptually organized subpages. The subpages lead to the real content. This way, the content is about two clicks away from the home page, which is about right. Most users don't want to have to click more than three or four times before they get to the real content of a server.

You need to consider a number of different things when you create the home page. For starters, let's assume that you are creating a home page for a corporation. In this section, we will walk you through creating a commercial-quality home page, and as we do so we'll apply the points discussed in the last few pages. We're focusing on a commercial home page, but there is no reason why our advice can not be used for personal home pages as well.

Companies who create a Web presence need to understand that they are projecting their corporate image to many millions of users around the world. This presents some interesting challenges and opportunities. First, you must clearly identify the purpose of the home page. Is it going to be used for sales and marketing, services, or demos? A clear understanding of your goals will inform the design of your home page. Then, with the site's goals in mind, you need to determine your categories of information.

Let's use net.Genesis as an example here. We are an Internet software development company and we also do some consulting. So the focus of our

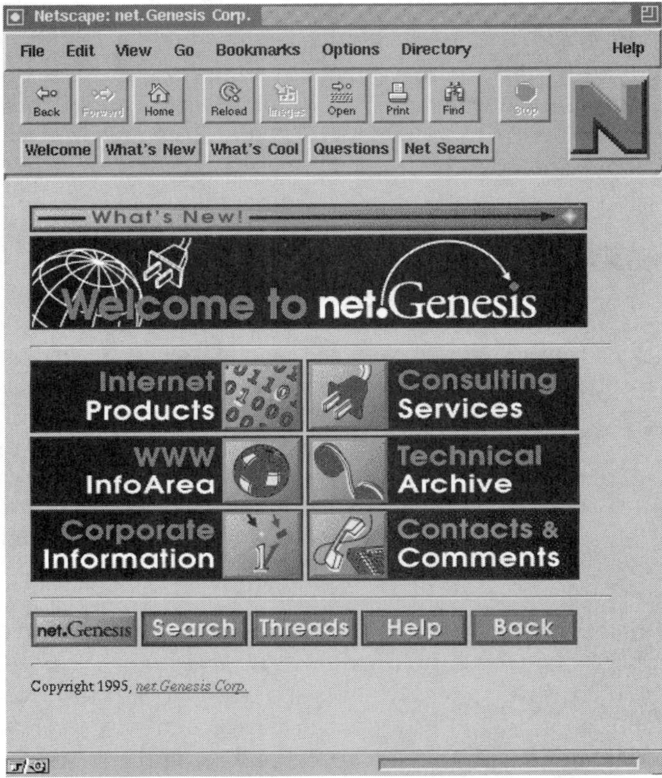

Figure 10–2 The net.Genesis home page, showing our six main categories that provide corporate information or technical resources

Web site is divided between providing corporate information and technical resources. We chose to provide six high-level categories, as follows: Internet Products, Consulting Services, Corporate Info, Contacts and Comments, WWW InfoArea, and Technical Archive, as shown in Figure 10-2.

As you can see, these categories give users a very good, first-level idea of where to find information. Under each of these categories, you can get directly to the information that you are interested in. For example, Figure 10-3 shows the WWW InfoArea page, where a user can access the Comprehensive List of WWW Sites, information about the Growth of the Web, Wandex, and the Sports Information Service.

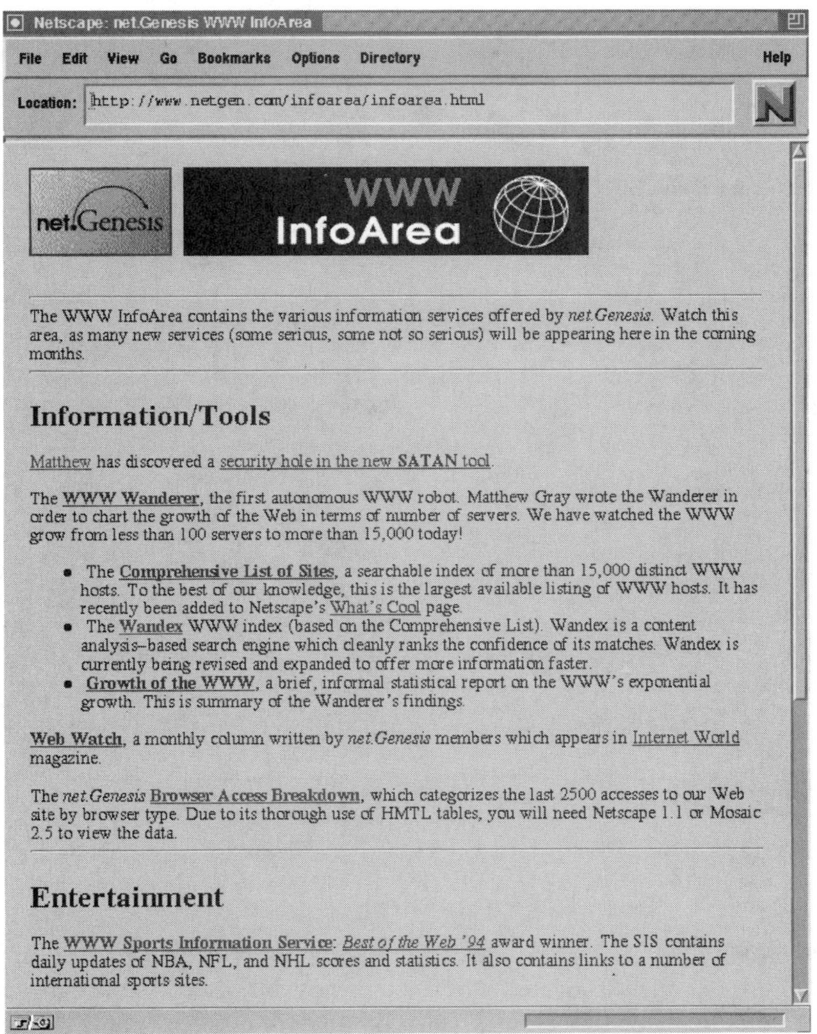

Figure 10-3 The WWW InfoArea page at the net.Genesis site

We're certainly not alone in choosing this structure. Figure 10-4 shows the top-level home page for Sun Microsystems. Sun, too, uses high-level categories to direct users to topics of interest.

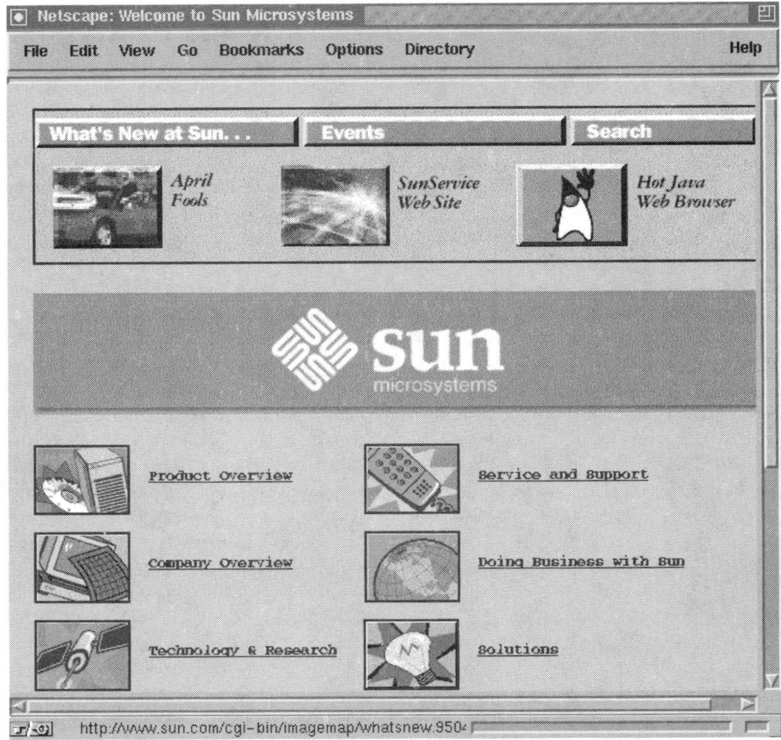

Figure 10–4 The home page for Sun Microsystems, showing its main areas of interest for further exploration

Toolbars

Toolbars, the menus located at the top or bottom of each page with links to major sections of a site, are a great way to maintain consistency throughout a site and also allow users to jump to different sections without much trouble. Toolbars are one of the best ways to give a site much greater depth. By including a toolbar on each page, users always have somewhere to go when they reach the lowest elements in the hierarchical structure. They can use the toolbar to jump to other major areas.

Sites that don't have toolbars are often difficult to navigate, because you can get stuck in a situation where the only way to find more information is to back out to the top level and make a new selection. Users find it annoying to have to back out of things and then go forward again, which is why you should always provide a set of buttons to other popular locations on the server. Tool bars should contain links to the home page, the top level of the current category or section, and other important parts of the system.

If you look back at our net.Genesis home page in Figure 10-2, you'll see a toolbar at the bottom of the page. The toolbar does not correspond to the six high-level categories. Rather, it allows users to jump to popular and useful parts of the site at any time.

Linking

As you plan a site's structure, you must consider links. Links from the toolbar and the home page to the other site pages are only the beginning. You must also consider internal links embedded in your content, as well as external links and reverse links between your site and other sites.

Internal Linking Use the power of hypertext to build strong internal links within your site. When something on a page refers or relates to data elsewhere on your system, create a link to that page. Don't be afraid to use links to cross the walls of the hierarchy you set up on the home page. Whenever we describe a product or service at the net.Genesis site, for example, we include a contact name with an internal link that connects to that person's personal page. Similarly, if a player is mentioned in an article or in a box score in the Sports Information Service, it is nice to have a link to that player's page so users can find out more about him or her.

Remember that one of the greatest strengths of the Web is being able to move from one topic to another, related topic, going as deep as you want. But this is only possible in sites where the links have already been set up. It doesn't help when related pieces of information within a site are not interlinked.

External Links You may also want to include links to outside sites, perhaps lots of outside sites. Including external links has both advantages and disadvantages. External links are what makes the Web a web. If information is out there that relates to the content of your site, users appreciate external links to that information. But users can be fickle, and if the external site you reference does not perform well, the users may blame you. For example, if you have a link to a site in Latvia and the Latvian government collapses and its network goes down, you have no guarantee that the Latvian site is going to stick around. The collapse of a site in Latvia has nothing to do with you and isn't your fault at all, but the users won't know this. After all, the link came from your site. Ghost links often reflect badly on people's perception of your site. Therefore, it is always a good idea to mark your external links in such a way that users know when connections go to places outside of your site. (A simple notation to this effect is sufficient.)

Using Reverse Linking Just as you may include links to outside sites, other sites may include links to your page. When another site points to you, it is often valuable to point back. This is known as *reverse linking*. But how do you know when another site creates a link to yours?

TIP

Reverse links should be explicitly marked, and if you have the resources, you might consider categorizing such links.

Occasionally, you get mail from somebody who says they put a link to your server on one of their pages. Or you just stumble across a link while browsing the Web. However, there is another way to find links to your site. By modifying your server to log a Referer field, you can find out whose pages are referring to the pages on your server. (See Section 10.3.4)

10.2.2 Graphics and Multimedia

The effective integration of multimedia elements—graphics, audio, and video—into a World Wide Web site can be just as important and informative and well-organized content.

Incorporating multimedia into a site can substantially increase its utility as well as its aesthetic appeal. Of course, poorly implemented multimedia can just as easily diminish a site's usefulness. When you deal with multimedia elements, many other issues besides the time delay caused by downloading data must be carefully considered.

Appropriate Size/Format Indicators

It is considered good etiquette to label all large files (larger than approximately 100K) with their data size. This applies to graphics, audio, video, and other large file formats, such as PostScript or DVI files. Because some clients can only accept certain data formats, it is also helpful to provide descriptors or icons that identify what a file is—an image, audio, or video—as well as the data format. This is especially true of very large files. Users get very frustrated when they download 5MB video files only to discover that the files are not in a format that their browsers support.

Graphic Images

Before we get into the specifics of using graphics, we'd like to remind you again that text-based Web clients such as Lynx are still popular. Besides, users with graphical browsers often switch to text-only mode to get documents quicker. If you ignore text-based users, you reduce the value of your Web site. For specific tips about what you can do, see Section 8.3; for other graphics tips, see the "Graphics Tips" sidebar.

Data Formats The most commonly used data format for images on the Web is the CompuServe Graphics Interchange Format (GIF). The GIF format allows for 8-bit color, or a maximum of 256 colors per image. GIF is best suited for "cartoon-like" pictures with large blocks of color. It does not achieve high compression ratios for photographic images that have a high degree of variation. One of the greatest advantages to using GIFs in a site is that most Web browsers allow for inline (embedded) GIFs in documents.

In addition, GIFs have a special feature that allows users to declare a certain color transparent. When transparent GIFs are viewed in browsers that support this feature (e.g., Mosaic and Netscape Navigator), the transparent color is displayed as the background color of the browser. Transparent colors allow you to integrate graphics seamlessly into a document. However, this feature should be used with some care. Most users assume that the background color of the browser is gray or white, but this is not necessarily true. A picture that assumes one of these background colors may be unrecognizable when viewed against a purple or black background. Make sure to test transparent GIFs with a variety of background colors before putting them online.

Another slightly less utilized format on the Web is the Joint Photographic Experts Group (JPEG) format. JPEG was optimized for compression of photographic images and allows for either 8- or 24-bit color. Thus, it achieves high compression ratios on photographic images, and lower ratios on drawings. Thanks to this compression technique, JPEG may produce unwanted fuzzy edges on cartoons or simple graphs. Netscape, new versions of Mosaic, and OmniWeb (a browser for NeXTSTEP) support inline JPEG images. JPEG does not support transparent images.

Graphics Tips from John Kirby, Adion Information Services

In the print world, artists try to retain as much detail and as many colors as possible, but a Web graphic can't be too detailed or colorful because of file size considerations. Often, this means reducing detail and colors as much as possible. Nothing is more annoying than a large GIF that takes an entire coffee break to download. Luckily, most browsers now display the text before downloading the graphics, but a graphic should complement a page, enhance its text, and help the flow of the hyperlinks. This is especially true when using image maps that function as navigational tools. Graphics should enhance the functionality of a Web page rather than get in the way.

Instead of the usual 300, 600, or 1,000 dpi (dots per inch), images should have a maximum of 72 dpi, which is the screen resolution of most monitors. We also recommend a maximum of 256 colors (8-bit) in an image. Most paint programs offer ways to crunch the color map. Some applications allow you to change the color map to bit depths that limit the colors to 128, 64, 32, 16, and even 8. In Adobe Photoshop, this is done by changing to Indexed Color mode. Applications on all platforms allow you to crunch bit depths. Of course, there is a give and take with each image. You may find that 5-bit color just won't do, and 7-bit is the smallest you can go without totally shredding an image's quality.

As for the actual size of the graphic, keep in mind that everyone on the Web is not using the designer's usual 17-inch or larger monitor (remember those Macintosh Color Classics!). Keeping the width down to 8 inches at the very most should allow most monitors to view the graphic in its entirety. We usually try to keep images down to 6- or 7-inches wide. Obviously, the size depends on the graphic itself, but in general a designer should remain conscious of the size of monitors on different platforms. Above all, designers should understand that increased graphic size leads to greater file size and lengthier downloading time. As for height, that again depends on the designer, but the height of a graphic is a little more flexible because the orientation of Web pages is predominantly vertical. In general though, less is better.

Graphics Tips from John Kirby, Adion Information Services (Continued)

Some tricky issues arise when you create graphics for the Web. One problem is trying to deal with images that are only 72 dpi. How to create readable text in these images is a problem. Some effects, like embossing, make text virtually unreadable in some point sizes. At certain resolutions, some small text actually looks better with anti-aliasing off. Experimenting often is really the key, but be prepared to get frustrated. Also, remember that some people don't turn their graphics-loading on, so if there is an important message or link in the image, it should appear in the text as well as the image. Whenever possible, put the text in the Web document itself instead of trying to incorporate it into a graphic.

Sometimes, a transparent GIF can be an especially effective image, where the excessive pixels serve no purpose except to border the graphic, such as company logos and marks. This can also be true of complex graphics that have a simple and somewhat useless background.

Testing images is important. Test your pages by looking at them from different platforms with different browsers. You may be surprised by what a Sun monitor does, for example, to Photoshop Macintosh GIFs. Whenever possible, test the site by accessing the Web through a 9,600- or 14.4-baud modem. This way, you can get a feeling for the user-access spectrum and understand why it's important to keep graphics under control.

The Web is still in its infancy. There are no hard and fast rules and we can expect HTML to change rapidly over the next couple of years. The bottom line for designing Web pages is to experiment and have fun doing it.

XBM-formatted, bit-mapped images are another common type of image on the Web. They do not use compression to store data and only allow for two colors, ON and OFF. The ON color is displayed as the foreground color and the background color is used for OFF. XBM images are inherently transparent. However, because of their compression, two-color GIFs are typically smaller than their equivalent bit-mapped images. While other data formats are available, they are relatively rare on the Web.

Appropriate Element Data Size The amount of data that has to be sent to reproduce an image or video file onscreen is certainly the most important issue to consider, especially when you consider the large number of users on 56Kbps or slower lines. For these users, it can take minutes to receive even a medium-size image, sound, or video file.

To put this in context, a moderate photographic image measuring 4 inches square can take almost a full minute to transfer over a 14.4Kbps line. A photograph is certainly a reasonable graphic element to include, but many users do not have the patience to download it, much less a page that contains several such images.

Browsers are beginning to cater more to the users of slow lines by providing extra functionality. Most browsers allow the user to delay or completely turn off image loading. Several "second-generation" browsers request images simultaneously, or in parallel, which significantly speeds up the retrieval process. These features help, but content providers must carefully watch the size of the images they provide.

A number of techniques exist to reduce the data size of an image. The most obvious way is to reduce the image's total area and make it physically smaller, but this does not necessarily yield a substantial reduction. An important issue to keep in mind when generating images is that different data formats compress images differently. Thus, for a particular image, a JPEG format may be significantly smaller than a GIF, or vice versa.

Another important consideration concerning images is their physical size (i.e., their height and width). The physical size of an image is directly related to its data size, but it is also important to keep the physical size within reasonable limits so that it looks good on most viewers.

Images should be no wider than six inches if they are to fit completely within the windows of most Web browsers. Try to scale or crop banners and other large images to fit within this limit. Most image-processing programs allow you to perform cropping and scaling.

One popular and useful way of reduce the size of the graphics on a page is to use "thumbnail" images as links to the main images. Thumbnail images are very small versions (approximately one inch square) of an image. Thumbnail images have the advantage of being very small (2–5K). In addition, they allow users to decide whether they are interested in retrieving the full image, so they save users additional time.

Reducing the Number of Colors within an Image One means of reducing the size of an image is to reduce the number of colors. Reducing the number of colors can produce substantial savings in data size. By halving the total number of colors, you can reduce file size by 10 to 30 percent. Luckily, users rarely notice a substantial change in the number of colors. And most browsers already limit the number of colors a user can see at a time. Typically, users can only see between 25 and 50 colors on their screens. So reducing the number of image colors provides a more accurate idea of the actual browser display.

On UNIX and DOS-compatible machines, the NetPBM toolkit allows users to reduce the number of colors in a graphic by any amount. Using the NetPBM toolkit, the following command can be used on UNIX machines to create an image "reduced.gif" that uses only forty colors from an image "colors.gif":

```
giftoppm colors.gif | ppmquant 40 | ppmtogif > reduced.gif
```

The NetPBM toolkit is available by anonymous FTP at ftp.cs.ubc.ca in the /ftp/archive/netpbm directory. In addition, most image-processing programs on the Macintosh and PC provide a method for reducing the number of image colors. (John Kirby explains how to use Photoshop to reduce colors in the "Graphics Tips" sidebar.)

Audio/Video

The problem of data size can become significantly worse when you are dealing with audio and video files. A ten-second audio clip of fairly low quality can take more than a minute to download over a 14.4Kbps line. High-quality audio clips—in stereo or at higher sampling rates–are at least double the size of low-quality clips.

Depending on their quality and duration, video clips generally range from hundreds of kilobytes to fifty megabytes or more. Even a few seconds of low-quality video, without audio, can take a long time to download on a 56Kbps line. For videos as short as 30 seconds, you may have to wait minutes even over a full T1 (1.54Mbps) connection. For this reason, audio and video should be used sparingly, and audio and video files should be carefully and appropriately marked so that users know they are dealing with large files.

Large video files can also cause problems for the sites that provide them. Video files are popular with users, and video archive sites have experienced difficulties caused by the tremendous loads generated on their host machines and their network connections.

The best way to reduce the data size of audio and video files is to reduce their quality. For example, changing from stereo to mono sound can yield a cut as large as 50 percent. Lowering the sampling frequency in an audio file, and lowering the frame rate and resolution of a video file can substantially reduce the size of these files.

Similarly, it is important that video and audio clips play less than a minute. On some systems, it is difficult to stop a video or audio file from playing once it is started. Therefore, in addition to keeping the data size of the file down, use shorter clips. That way, users have greater control over what they have to see.

Audio files typically come in either .AU or .WAV formats. Although these two formats are very similar, .WAV files tend to be used more frequently on DOS-compatible machines. Video files come in three main formats: Apple QuickTime, Motion Pictures Expert Group (MPEG), and Intel Video (Indeo). QuickTime and Indeo allow for synchronized sound and video. The playback quality of any format depends very much on the speed of the machine the video is played back on.

Producing Multimedia

High-performance image-editing programs are not absolutely necessary to create useful images. Public-domain programs like Xpaint for UNIX provide the minimal functionality necessary for a beginning user to make simple icons and buttons. For MS-DOS and Macintosh users, a wide variety of paint programs are available. Remember to save files as GIF or JPEG and try to use a small number of colors. For users who do not want to create their graphics, a collection of icons is available at **http://www.netgen.com/book/icons.html**.

Recording audio often requires special hardware (such as a Sound Blaster card on a PC), but is a relatively straightforward process. If possible, save the audio file in one of the following formats: Mu-Law, A-Law, or Wave. Capturing video can be difficult process and often requires special hardware, in addition to large amounts of disk space and memory. The Indeo format seems to be on the rise and is of very good quality. MPEG's major weakness is that it does not offer synchronized audio and video, but the new MPEG-2 standard will fix this. QuickTime is also quite popular for the Macintosh platform.

The most important rule to keep in mind when you integrate multimedia into a site is to always be conscious of users who have slow lines or are using text-based browsers. Make sure to look at your site through several browsers on several platforms before you release any multimedia.

10.3 Maintaining a Web Site

Maintenance is one of the most frequently underestimated and forgotten steps in developing a Web site. Creating the content for a site takes a lot of time, but at least it is a one-time job. Maintenance, on the other hand, is an ongoing, full-time process.

How much effort is needed to maintain a Web site depends on the scale of the site. Maintenance tasks include verifying HTML, checking link integrity, and monitoring the usage of your site's host computer. A simple site consisting of a handful of basic pages can be debugged and properly linked in a short period of time. Problems that arise can be easily noticed and quickly fixed.

For large commercial sites, the most expensive aspect can be the ongoing technical maintenance. Sites that house a large volume of continually changing content and complex forms can be difficult to control and monitor adequately. It is of the utmost importance to provide a stable site that meets users' performance expectations. However, because of the Web's decentralized nature, hyperlinks in documents easily become invalid as sites evolve, as server content is changed, and as servers crash. And a small typo in a link's URL can render the link useless. Thus, server administrators and HTML authors are forced to invest considerable effort in finding and fixing the huge variety of HTML and link-related errors. If such rigorous testing is not performed, site quality can diminish over time.

The first rule is to keep in touch with users and respond to their suggestions and complaints. However, this can be more than a notion.

10.3.1 Being Responsive

Many people don't take into consideration the volume of mail that they may get. If you provide feedback forms and your site is fairly popular, you're going to get a lot of mail. You need a mechanism to respond to that mail. It is a courtesy to respond to, or at least acknowledge, the receipt of e-mail even if hundreds of people are writing to you every week. Automated responses are acceptable, but ideally you should respond to each message. Whatever you do, be sure to fix all the problems that users report.

One of the main reasons for setting up a site is to provide customers with access to your information. Trying to get information to users in a way that they can use it takes on a life of its own, but just as important are the suggestions and questions users have for you. You can either look at their questions and suggestions as a nuisance—it certainly can be a bear dealing with feedback, suggestions, and especially criticism—or as icing on the cake, but the best way to learn and improve a site is to interact with the people who are using your information.

If you are not willing to take the time to handle interaction from users, then there is something wrong with your priorities. If dealing with users is a bother, then you should really question what your goals are for putting up a site. If you are solely putting up a site so you can "establish a presence" on the Internet, realize that you are probably hurting yourself by establishing a negative image for your company.

Being responsive to users' concerns and opinions is almost as important as maintaining the pages that make up your site. No doubt you will get questions that you have no clue what to do with. Some users believe that the people who set up Web sites are omnipotent and can answer the wildest questions. If you put up a site about chip design, for example, you'll get users who assume you know everything there is to know about hard drives, and they will ask you for help.

Over time, you will find that manually responding to e-mail can become a full-time job. You won't get as much mail as President Clinton or Madonna, but on the other hand you won't have a secretary to read and respond to all your mail. You certainly can get bogged down with mail if you don't know how to handle it well.

One of the simplest things that you can do to cut down your workload is establish a list of frequently asked questions (an FAQ file) and make it available online. This way, many users can get their questions answered without having to send you a letter.

Whether or not you have an FAQ, of course, you will still get mail. And lots of that mail can be answered with standard answers to which a few minor modifications are made. When Eric ran the Sports Information Service by himself, he spent six hours on some days replying to mail. And most of his replies were standard "thank you" notes that were easy to type up.

Therefore, in order to alleviate a lot of the redundancy and prune down much of your work, use a form-letter response system. This way, you simply choose from a set of form letters to reply to mail.

The code shown in Listing 10-1 prompts you for certain pieces of information, then it fills out the rest of the letter and mails it for you. Hopefully, such a system can help you reduce the amount of time that you spend writing to the people who visit your site.

The respond.pl program in the listing expects you to have a directory of template files that it can use to send out responses. The first line of each template file contains the description of the file. The second line contains the subject used when the mail is sent. The rest of the template file contains the body of the letter. Both the subject and body can contain variables that the user fills in when prompted by the program. Variables are surrounded by an (: and :). You will find three sample template files in the "Using Templates" sidebar.

You can use this one program for all your responses. Running the program requires one command, followed by a single argument (the name of the user to whom you are writing). The program then prompts you for all the remaining information, including which form template to use.

Listing 10–1. **Respond.pl automates the process for responding to user messages by using predefined template files that prompt you for variable input**

```
#!/usr/bin/perl
#File Name: respond.pl

# Set the location of sendmail
$sm = "/usr/lib/sendmail";

# Set the directory that all your preformatted responses should be in.
$responses_dir = "/tmp/responses";

# Read in the names of all the response files.
opendir(RESPS, $responses_dir) || die "Could not open $responses_dir.\n";
@resps = readdir(RESPS);

# Check to see if the user gave an argument
if ($#ARGV == -1)
{
    print "Usage: $0 recipient\n";
    print "       This will query the user for the response to send to
recipient.\n";
    print "\n";
    exit;
}
```

```
# The first argument to the program should be the name of the person
# to send the response to.
$towho = $ARGV[0];

print("Send response to $towho\n");

$n = 0;
# Loop over the known responses and print the description of the
# response along with a number.
for $r (@resps)
{
    # Ignore . and .. since they aren't really responses
    next if $r eq '.';
    next if $r eq '..';

    # Form the full path name
    $file = "$responses_dir/$r";

    # Keep a counter of the number of files we've read in.
    $n++;

    # Open the file and read in the first line.
    open(FILE, $file) || die "Could not open $file\n";
    $oneline = (<FILE>);
    close(FILE);

    # Create an array of the one-line descriptions.
    $descrip[$n] = $oneline;

    # Remember which response corresponds to which number
    $file[$n] = $file;

    # Print the response number and the description
    print("$n) $oneline");
}
```

```
if ($n == 0)
{
    die "Unable to find any responses in $responses_dir\n";
}


# Ask the user which response to send
while (($which < 1) || ($which > $n))
{
    print "\nPlease chose a number between 1 and $n\n";
    print "Send response \#: > ";
    $which = (<STDIN>);
    chop($which);
    next;
}


# Open the file and read in the text, ignoring the description
open(FILE, $file[$which]) || die "Life sucks: $file[$which] $!";
$firstline = (<FILE>);
$file = "";
while(<FILE>){
    $file .= $_;
}


# Call the subroutine to fill in the response
$out = &fill_in_template($file);

($subject, $body) = split ("\n", $out, 2);

# Send the mail off to the user
open(SM, "|$sm -f$ENV{'USER'} $towho") || die "Could not open sendmail: $!";
print(SM "To: $towho\n");
```

```
print(SM "Subject: $subject\n");
print SM $body;
close(SM);

print("Sent response\n");

# Subroutine designed to take a template and query the user to fill
# in all the blanks.
sub fill_in_template {
    local($temp) = @_;

    $out = $temp;
    print "Here is the template:\n$temp\n";

    # See if there are any remaining template holes.
    while($temp =~ /\(:([^:]*):\)/g){
     $prompt = $1;

     # Ask the user for the value of the field.
     if(!$done{$prompt})
     {
         print("Value for template field \"$prompt\"\n");
         print("-> ");
         $replace{$prompt} = (<STDIN>);
         chop($replace{$prompt});
     }
     $done{$prompt}=1;

     # Make the replacement.
     $out=~s/\(:$prompt:\)/$replace{$prompt}/g;
    }

    # Return the filled in file
    $out; }
```

Using Templates

In order to use these three form template files with the respond.pl script, they should be in the directory /tmp/responses.

1. The Bug Report template:

```
Bug report
(:PROGRAM:) bug-report
Dear (:USER:),

   I wanted to thank you for taking time to notify us about the bug
in (:PROGRAM:).  We certainly do appreciate your help and hope that
you are enjoying the software.  Please let us know if we can be of
assistance in the future.

                              (:SALUTATION:)
                                  Eric Richard
```

2. The User Feedback template:

```
User Feedback
(:TOPIC:)
Dear (:USER:),

   I wanted to thank you for your feedback about (:TOPIC:).  We certainly
do appreciate your comments and hope that you are enjoying our site.
Please let us know if we can be of assistance in the future.

                              (:SALUTATION:)
                                  Eric Richard
```

3. The Product Order template:

```
Product Order
(:TOPIC:)
Dear (:USER:),
```

Using Templates (Continued)

```
     I wanted to thank you for purchasing our (:TOPIC:) product.  We
certainly do appreciate your business and hope that you enjoy
our software. Please let us know if we can be of assistance in
the future.

                                  (:SALUTATION:)
                                     Eric Richard
```

Here's a fictitious example of what happened when we used the respond.pl script to respond to a user (sgprima@aol.com) after the purchase of our net.Form product:

```
> respond sgprima@aol.com

Send response to sgprima@aol.com
1) Bug report
2) User Feedback
3) Product Order

Please chose a number between 1 and 3

Send response #: > 3

Here is the template:
(:TOPIC:)
Dear (:USER:),

   I wanted to thank you for purchasing our (:TOPIC:) product. We
certainly do appreciate your business and hope that you enjoy
our software. Please let us know if we can be of assistance in
the future.

                               (:SALUTATION:),
                                   Eric Richard
```

```
Value for template field "TOPIC"

-> net.Form

Value for template field "USER"

-> Stefan

Value for template field "SALUTATION"

-> Sincerely

Sent response
```

And here is what the script sent to the user:

```
Dear Stefan,

   I wanted to thank you for purchasing our net.Form product. We certainly
do appreciate your business and hope that you enjoy our software. Please let
us know if we can be of assistance in the future.

                              Sincerely,
                                  Eric Richard
```

10.3.2 Verifying HTML

Verifying your HTML means going through and making sure that the HTML on your site is actually valid, that you didn't forget any tags, and that your HTML syntax is correct. Omitting the verification process would be like putting up a page full of text without checking the spelling and grammar. And it may be even worse, because people may not notice typographical errors, but the results of bad or incorrect HTML is usually quite noticeable.

For example, if you forget to close a link element, the rest of your document will be one gigantic link. If you forget to close a bold element, the rest of your document will be bold. If your HTML is invalid, the user's browser will choose how to render it and possibly point out your mistakes. At net.Genesis, we check our HTML by using a product we developed called net.Verify. Your other real option is to hire someone whose job it is to scan a site for errors under different browsers. Some public-domain software packages are available for checking HTML, but most of them are very cryptic in their error reporting and aren't terribly useful on a distributed system like the Web.

10.3.3 Link Integrity

Verifying your link integrity means ensuring that all links on every page in the site lead to a real and viable location. Because the Web is so dynamic and decentralized, things that you're pointing to can move. They can go to another location, their servers can go down, or they can just disappear. This is especially true of student sites. When students graduate, their school accounts often expire and they may no longer be able to maintain their sites. So you must stay vigilant to keep up with the changes. When you're building a site, you must make sure the links that you are constructing all connect to existing locations.

TIP

Many people place "Under Construction" signs on empty pages that have yet to be designed, but we think this is not a good practice. If you don't have something functional on a page yet, don't create a link to it. If you were to go to a site that was under construction and you found five, six, seven links that all led to blank pages or pages that said "Under Construction" and didn't have anything useful on them, you would get very frustrated. Don't do that to the users at your site. Always think like a potential user when creating your site.

By now you may have noticed that all URLs in this book point to some page at netgen.com. In the introduction to the book, we mentioned that many of the services that we are referencing are not ours but that we chose to create a special book page at the net.Genesis site to contain links to those other services. This way, we can maintain the connections for you, and when changes occur we can update the links to point to new URLs long after this book goes to press. Because we use one of our own products (net.Integrity) to verify links, this is not too difficult a task.

10.3.4 Monitoring Usage

All Webmasters should monitor the usage of their sites. This is especially true of commercial sites. Monitoring usage means finding out how many people are accessing a site, which pages are the most interesting, where people are coming from (their hostnames), and more.

If one of your pages is popular, you might want to focus more attention on it and use it to post important notices. If a lot of people use one route to get from the top-level page down to another page, you can use that information to your advantage and customize your site accordingly. Maybe you notice that only a few people are using a particular area of your site, but it's an area that you thought would be especially interesting to many users. It's possible that people aren't aware of that area. In that case, you might post a special notice on your top-level page or some other area with more traffic. By monitoring the usage logs, you get a feeling for how people are using your site and can use that knowledge to improve it.

Monitoring usage means analyzing your log files. Companies that are serious about using this information for marketing reports or internal reports can purchase commercial software tools, like our product, net.Analysis. It provides you with in-depth information about your site's usage. Standard log files provide certain information, such as what pages were accessed, when they were accessed, and what machine the request came from, but you can modify your server source code to gather additional log information. We will show you three monitoring scripts that you can use with standard logs. Then we'll show you how to modify your server and use two additional scripts to gather additional data.

Using Your Standard Server Log

If you are only interested in finding out minimal information from your logs, you can use the script shown in Listing 10-2. It tells you which of your site's pages and scripts are requested the most, and which hosts are accessing your files the most.

Listing 10–2. Analyze.pl, which shows which site page(s) and script(s) are requested the most

```
#!/usr/bin/perl

# File name: analyze.pl



# Set the name of the log file to read in

$log_file = "/tmp/bookcode/access-log";
```

```
# Open the file to read in
open( INPUT, $log_file ) || die "Cannot open $log_file: $!\n";

# Set the size of each tick
$tick_size = 5;

# Set the number of pages to report (i.e., the top 5, 10, 12, etc)
$num_top_requests = 10;

# Set the number of hosts to report (i.e., the top 5, 10, 12, etc)
$num_top_hosts = 10;

# Make it so it will print out lines before a newline
$| = 1;

$line_num = 0;
print "Reading Access Log: ";
while( $current_line = <INPUT> )
{

    if (($line_num % 100)  == 0)
    {
     print ".";
    }
    $line_num++;

    # Check to see if the log is of the standard format
    if($current_line =~ /([^ ]+) ([^ ]+) ([^ ]+) \[([^\]]+)\] \"([^\"]*)\"
([^ ]+) ([^ ]+)/)
    {
     # If so, pick off each of the standard items
     $host = $1;
     $date = $4;
     $request = $5;
```

```
      $status = $6;
      $bytes = $7;

      ($method, $URL, $prot) = split(" ", $request);

      # Increment the number of times the URL has been accessed
      $requests{$URL}++;

      # Increment the number of times the host has made a request
      $hosts{$host}++;
    }
    else
    {
      print(STDERR "Unfamiliar log entry:$current_line\n");
    }
}

print "\n";

print("Top Requests\n");
@topreqs = sort { $requests{$b} <=> $requests{$a}; } keys %requests;
print("------------\n");

for $i (0..$num_top_requests)
{
    printf("%d %-50s\n", $requests{$topreqs[$i]}, $topreqs[$i]);
}
print("\n\n");

print("Top Hosts\n");
@tophosts = sort { $hosts{$b} <=> $hosts{$a}; } keys %hosts;

print("------------\n");
```

```
for $i (0..$num_top_hosts - 1)
{
    printf("%-40s %d\n", $tophosts[$i], $hosts{$tophosts[$i]});
}
print("\n\n");
```

Here is an example of the output we got by running the analyze.pl script shown in Listing 10-2:

```
Reading Access Log: .....
Top Requests
------------
105 /cgi/autopilot.pl
38 /images/wandlogo.gif
36 /cgi/comprehensive
26 /images/clos.gif
22 /images/wandex.gif
20 /~mkgray/autopilot.html
19 /cgi/wandex
17 /cgi/autopilot
17 /sis/sports.html
13 /images/netgen.small.gif

Top Hosts
------------
habanero.lcs.mit.edu                    42
hillres30.cc.purdue.edu                 37
netcom7.netcom.com                      20
vtr21.together.net                      20
204.253.144.130                         16
204.146.73.5                            15
crc3.cris.com                           14
ec68.residence.gatech.edu               13
mac46.debartolo.lab.nd.edu              12
pppd036.inhouse.compuserve.com          11
```

The server-stats.pl program in Listing 10-3 calculates usage statistics for the current day. The program breaks down the statistics by various sections of a site. For example, the Sports Information Service (SIS) is on our Web site. Within SIS, we have three main sections dealing with the NHL, NFL, and NBA. This script also logs the number of total accesses to the site. The reports are generated on our site for internal use every night at approximately midnight.

Listing 10–3. Server-stats.pl, which calculates statistics for the current day's accesses to the HTTP server

```
#!/usr/bin/perl
#  FILE NAME: server-stats.pl
#
#  DESCRIPTION:
#   Calculates statistics for the current day's accesses to the
#   HTTP server

# Tell perl to flush the buffers on every print
$| = 1;

# Set the name of the log file to read in
$log_file = "/netgen/www/servers/cern/httpd-log";

# Open the file to read in
open( INPUT, $log_file ) || die "Cannot open $log_file: $!\n";

# Get today's date
$today = 'date';

# Split the date into its consituent parts
($day_of_week, $month, $day, $time, $tz, $year)  = split (" ", $today);

# Convert it into the format that the server uses
$log_date = sprintf ("%2.2d\/%3s\/%2.2d", $day, $month, $year);
$today = "$month $day, $year";
```

```
print STDERR "Reading log: ";

while(<INPUT>)
{

    # Break the line apart into all of its parts.
    /([^ ]+) ([^ ]+) ([^ ]+) \[([^\]]+)\] \"([^ ]+) ([^ ]+) ([^\"]+)\" ([^
]+) ([^ ]+)/;

    $host = $1; $date = $4; $method = $5; $url = $6; $prot = $7;


    # Print out a . every 1000 lines so you can see the progress.
    if (($current_line++ % 1000) ==  0)
    {
     print STDERR ".";
    }

    # Check to see if the log entry is for today.  If not, skip it.
    if ($date !~ /^$log_date/)
    {
     next;
    }



    # Check to see if the requested document was for a section of
    # the Sports Information Server
    if($url=~/sis/)
    {
     $sis++;

     # Check to see if it was for the NHL
     $nhl++ if ($url=~/NHL/);
```

```
  # Check to see if it was for the NFL
  $nfl++ if ($url=~/NFL/);

  # Check to see if it was for the NBA
  $nba++ if ($url=~/NBA/);
}

# Check to see if the requested document was for the
# Comprehensive List of Sites
elsif ($url=~/comprehensive/)
{
  $compre++;
}

# Check to see if the requested document was for Wandex
elsif ($url=~/wandex/)
{
  $wandex++;
}

# Check to see if the requested document was for the
# Growth of the Web page
elsif ($url =~ /growth/)
{
  $growth++;
}

# Otherwise it is something else.
else
{
  $other++;
}
```

```
    # Check the type of the document accessed
    if (($url =~ /gif$/) ||
     ($url =~ /jpeg$/))
    {
     $pics++;
    }
    elsif ($url =~ /html$/)
    {                 #
     $html++;
    }

    $total_hits++;

}



# Print a header
$title = "Profile of Accesses to the server on $today";
print "\n$title\n";
print "-" x length($title) , "\n";

# Print the number of hits that you got for the day.
print "Total Hits: $total_hits\n\n";

if ($total_hits == 0)
{
    # Exit now so we don't get a divide by zero error later
    exit;
}

# Print out the final report.
print"Area Breakdown:\n";
print("o  SIS: ", int($sis * 100/$total_hits), "%\n");
print("     NFL: ", int(100*$nfl/$sis), "%\n");
```

```
print("     NBA: ", int(100*$nba/$sis), "%\n");
print("     NHL: ", int(100*$nhl/$sis), "%\n");
print("o  Comprehensive list: ", int($compre * 100/$total_hits), "%\n");
print("o  Wandex: ", int($wandex * 100/$total_hits), "%\n");
print("o  Growth page: ", int($growth * 100/$total_hits), "%\n");
print("o  Other stuff: ", int($other* 100/$total_hits), "%\n");

print("\nBy request type:\n");
print("o  GIFs: ", int($pics * 100/$total_hits), "%\n");
print("o  HTML files: ", int($html * 100/$total_hits), "%\n");
```

Here is a sample of the output from the server-stats.pl script:

```
Profile of Accesses to the server on Apr 4, 1995
------------------------------------------------
Total Hits: 98923

Area Breakdown:
o  SIS: 33%
     NFL: 14%
     NBA: 31%
     NHL: 14%
o  Comprehensive list: 13%
o  Wandex: 16%
o  Growth page: 0%
o  Other stuff: 36%

By request type:
o  GIFs: 46%
o  HTML files: 20%
```

In addition, by using the code shown in Listing 10-4, you can generate a histogram showing how the usage of your site varies over the course of a day. Not only are the results pretty spiffy-looking, but you can use this information to determine when your machine and network connection is likely to be heavily loaded and when the load will be light.

Listing 10–4. **Quickhist.pl, which shows how site usage varies over the course of a day**

```
#!/usr/bin/perl
#Program name: quickhist.pl

# Set the name of the log file to read in
$log_file = "/tmp/bookcode/access-log";

# Open the file to read in
open( INPUT, $log_file ) || die "Cannot open $log_file: $!\n";

# Set the size of each tick
$tick_size = 5;

while( $current_line = <INPUT> )
{
    # Look for the time-date stamp
    $current_line =~ /\[([\d]{2}\/...\/[\d]{4}):([\d]{2}):/;

    # Grab the day and hour from this line
    $day = $1;
    $hour = $2;

    # Remember what the last day was that we saw
    $last_day = $day unless $last_day;


    # Check and see if we've changed hours
    if(($hour != $last_hour) && ($hour != $last_hour - 1))
    {
     # Figure out how many ticks to put
        $ticks = '-' x ($count / $tick_size );

     # Print out the entry for the last hour
```

```
        print("$last_day:$last_hour: $ticks $count\n");

        # If we skipped hours (i.e., there were no accesses during that
        # time), print an elipsis.
          print("...\n") if ($hour !=$last_hour + 1);

        # Reinitialize the counter.
          $count = 0;

        # Remember what the last hour was that we saw.
        $last_hour = $hour;
          $last_day = $day;

      }

      # Increment the number of hits for the current hour
      $count++;
}
```

The following is a sample of the output from the quickhist.pl program:

```
24/Mar/1995:00: ----------------------- 1195
24/Mar/1995:01: ------------------ 946
24/Mar/1995:02: ---------------- 842
24/Mar/1995:03: ---------- 505
24/Mar/1995:04: ----------------- 877
24/Mar/1995:05: -------------- 719
24/Mar/1995:06: ------------- 668
24/Mar/1995:07: ------------------ 943
24/Mar/1995:08: -------------------- 1043
24/Mar/1995:09: ------------------------------- 1591
24/Mar/1995:10: ------------------------------------ 1836
24/Mar/1995:11: ------------------------------------------- 2198
24/Mar/1995:12: ------------------------------------------------------ 2732
24/Mar/1995:13: ------------------------------------------------------- 2752
24/Mar/1995:14: ------------------------------------------------------------- 3076
```

```
24/Mar/1995:15: --------------------------------------------------------- 2878
24/Mar/1995:16: --------------------------------------------------- 2582
24/Mar/1995:17: -------------------------------------------- 2237
24/Mar/1995:18: ---------------------------------- 1705
24/Mar/1995:19: ------------------------------ 1527
24/Mar/1995:20: -------------------------- 1338
24/Mar/1995:21: ----------------------- 1195
24/Mar/1995:22: ----------------------- 1182
24/Mar/1995:23: ----------------------- 1177
...
25/Mar/1995:00: ---------------------- 1112
25/Mar/1995:01: --------------------- 1075
25/Mar/1995:02: ------------ 621
25/Mar/1995:03: --------- 476
25/Mar/1995:04: --------- 464
25/Mar/1995:05: -------- 449
25/Mar/1995:06: --------- 475
25/Mar/1995:07: ------------ 610
25/Mar/1995:08: ------------ 643
25/Mar/1995:09: ---------------- 800
25/Mar/1995:10: ---------------------- 1139
25/Mar/1995:11: ----------------------- 1178
25/Mar/1995:12: ---------------------- 1101
25/Mar/1995:13: ---------------------------- 1404
25/Mar/1995:14: ---------------------------- 1419
25/Mar/1995:15: -------------------------- 1312
25/Mar/1995:16: ---------------------- 1149
25/Mar/1995:17: --------------------------- 1396
25/Mar/1995:18: ------------------------ 1232
25/Mar/1995:19: --------------------- 1086
25/Mar/1995:20: -------------------- 1005
25/Mar/1995:21: --------------------- 1089
25/Mar/1995:22: ---------------------- 1124
25/Mar/1995:23: ------------------------- 1298
...
26/Mar/1995:00: ------------------- 981
```

```
26/Mar/1995:01: --------------- 775
26/Mar/1995:02: --------------- 756
26/Mar/1995:03: -------- 422
26/Mar/1995:04: -------- 426
```

Using Your Modified Server Log

For every single connection, all of the standard Web servers provide access log files. These logs show where the connection came from and what document was requested. However, as we mentioned in Chapters 5 and 6, a couple other fields are sent by many browsers—fields such as the User-Agent, Referer, and From fields. These fields can provide useful information as well. But in order to log this information, you have to modify the actual source code to your server and then recompile it.

NOTE

The newest release of the NCSA httpd (version 1.4), contains a mechanism to log the Referer field.

Modifying the CERN server to log the Referer, User-Agent, and From fields actually entails modifications to six different files:

- HTDaemon.c
- HTDaemon.h
- HTLog.c
- HTRequest.c
- HTConfig.c
- HTConfig.h

These files may differ from version to version, but we will provide enough information so that you should be able to make the changes regardless of the version you are using. When you have completed all of the modifications, you must recompile your server source code. When that is done, you can use the referer.pl and browser-breakdown.pl scripts.

Modifying HTDaemon.c Look for the following section (it should be around line 200):

```
/*      Server environment when handling requests
**      -----------------------------------------
*/
```

Directly under this, you'll see a list of variable declarations, including the following:

```
PUBLIC char *          HTWWWAuthenticate      = NULL;
PUBLIC HTAAFailReason HTReason               = HTAA_OK;
PUBLIC char *          HTUserAgent            = NULL;
PUBLIC char *          HTReferer              = NULL;
PUBLIC time_t          HTIfModifiedSince      = 0;
```

Add the following line after HTReferer, and before HTIfModifiedSince:

```
PUBLIC char *          HTFrom                 = NULL;
```

This is the declaration for the variable in which the value in the From field will be stored.

In the function reset_server_env section of the file, you will see the following group of lines:

```
FREE(HTProxyHeaders);
FREE(HTUserAgent);
FREE(HTReferer);
HTIfModifiedSince = 0;
HTReasonLine = NULL;
HTSoc = 0;
```

Right after the line `FREE(HTReferer);`, add the following line:

```
FREE(HTFrom);
```

This frees the memory for the *From* variable when you are done with it.

Modifying HTDaemon.h Look for the section that contains the following list of variable declarations:

```
extern HTAAFailReason HTReason;
extern char *         HTProxyHeaders;
extern char *         HTUserAgent;
extern char *         HTReferer;
extern time_t         HTIfModifiedSince;
```

After the declaration of HTReferer, add the following line:

```
extern char *         HTFrom;
```

This is a declaration of the same *From* variable again.

Modifying HTLog.c Near the beginning of the HTLog.c file, you should see the following lines:

```
PRIVATE FILE *       access_log      = NULL;
PRIVATE FILE *       proxy_log       = NULL;
PRIVATE FILE *       cache_log       = NULL;
PRIVATE FILE *       error_log       = NULL;
```

After the first of these lines, add the following line:

```
PRIVATE FILE *       extra_log       = NULL;
```

This declares the new log file where this extra information will be logged. We create a new log file because we don't want to change the format of the normal log. You never know when you might want to use log-processing software which counts on the log being in Common Log Format, in which case you'd still want your common log to be available.

In the function HTLog_access, you should see the following lines:

```
char * authuser = "-";
char * r_ident = "-";
FILE * log = access_log;

if (cache_hit && out.status_code == 200 && cache_log)
  log = cache_log;
```

After the statement `log = cache_log;`, insert the following line:

```
FILE * elog = extra_log;
```

This makes a copy of the file pointer to the log so that it can be used to print to.

Later in this function, you should see the following lines:

```
fprintf(log, "%s %s %s [%s] \"%s\" %s\n",
        n_pick(HTClientHostName,HTClientHost),
        r_ident, authuser, log_time(), n_noth(HTReqLine), buf);
```

Immediately after this, insert the following:

```
fprintf(elog, "%s (%s) [%s] {%s}-->{%s} <%s>\n",
        n_pick(HTClientHostName, HTClientHost), log_time(),
        HTUserAgent, HTReferer, n_noth(HTReqLine), HTFrom);
```

This is the line that actually writes the information out to the log file.

Later in the HTLog_openAll function, you should find the following lines:

```
/*
 * Open access log file
 */
if (sc.access_log_name) {
    aln = time_escapes(sc.access_log_name);
    access_log = do_open(aln);
    if (access_log) {
        CTRACE(stderr, "Log......... \"%s\" opened\n", aln);
    }
    else {
        HTLog_error2("Can't open log file:", aln);
        flag = NO;
    }
}

 /*
```

```
 * Open proxy access log file
 */
if (sc.proxy_log_name) {
    pln = time_escapes(sc.proxy_log_name);
    proxy_log = do_open(pln);
    if (proxy_log) {
        CTRACE(stderr, "Proxy log... \"%s\" opened\n", pln);
    }
    else {
        HTLog_error2("Can't open proxy access log:", pln);
        flag = NO;
    }
}
```

In between the `Open Access Log` and `Open Proxy Access Log` blocks of code, insert the following:

```
/*
 * Open extra log file
 */
if (sc.extra_log_name) {
  aln = time_escapes(sc.extra_log_name);
  extra_log = do_open(aln);
  if (access_log) {
      CTRACE(stderr, "Extra Log......... \"%s\" opened\n", aln);
  }
  else {
      HTLog_error2("Can't open extra log file:", aln);
       flag = NO;
   }
 }
```

This code actually opens the extra log file.

Modifying HTRequest.c In the HTParseRequest function, you should see the following code:

```
} else if (0==strncasecomp(line, "From", 4)) {

    StrAllocCopy(req->from, HTStrip(p));
    CTRACE(stderr, "From........ %s\n", req->from);

} else if (0==strncasecomp(line, "User-Agent", 10)) {

    hbuf_proxy_cancel_last();
    StrAllocCopy(HTUserAgent, HTStrip(p));
    CTRACE(stderr, "User-Agent.. %s\n", HTUserAgent);
```

Change this line:

```
StrAllocCopy(req->from, HTStrip(p));
```

to the following line:

```
StrAllocCopy(HTFrom, HTStrip(p));
```

This stores the value in the From field in the *HTFrom* variable.

Modifying HTConfig.c In the function HTLoadConfig, you should see the following:

```
conditional statements including:

        } else if (!strncmp(vec[0],"accesslog",9) ||
                   !strcmp(vec[0],"logfile")) {
            sc.access_log_name = tilde_to_home(vec[1]);
            CTRACE(stderr, "AccessLog... %s\n", sc.access_log_name);

         } else if (!strncmp(vec[0],"cacheaccesslog",12)) {
            sc.cache_log_name = tilde_to_home(vec[1]);
            CTRACE(stderr, "Cache log... %s\n", sc.cache_log_name);
```

Between these two statements, enter the following lines:

```
} else if (!strncmp(vec[0],"extralog", 8)) {
   sc.extra_log_name = tilde_to_home(vec[1]);
   CTRACE(stderr, "ExtraLog... %s\n", sc.extra_log_name);
```

This modification allows you to specify the name of the extra log file in the configuration file with the configuration option "extralog."

Modifying HTConfig.h In the `typedef struct _HTServerConfig` declaration you should see the following set of lines.

```
char *     access_log_name;       /* Access log file name          */
char *     proxy_log_name;        /* Proxy access log file name    */
char *     cache_log_name;        /* Cache access log file name    */
```

After the `access_log_name` line, and before `proxy_log_name`, enter the following line:

```
char *     extra_log_name;        /* Extra log file name           */
```

This is the declaration of the variable where the name of the extra log file is stored.

Referer.pl The code shown in Listing 10-5 uses the new log that you created by running your server after making modifications to the source code and recompiling it. The new log captures the Referer field, and referer.pl takes advantage of this new data by going through the log files and generating a list of all the different sites that point to specific pages within the site. This is a very powerful feature for a Web site, since it helps you understand how your site is linked with the Web itself. You can also gain an understanding of what types of other sites are linking to your site, and that can help you understand who comes to your site and why.

Listing 10-5. **Referer.pl, which displays a list of sites that have a link to your site, based on the Referer field in your modified server log**

```
#!/usr/bin/perl
#Filename: referer.pl


# Set the name of the log file to read in
```

```
$log_file = "/tmp/bookcode/extra-log";

# Open the file to read in
open( INPUT, $log_file ) || die "Cannot open $log_file: $!\n";

while( $current_line = <INPUT> )
{
    # Look for the Referer field in between the '{' and '}' and the
    # request right after it.
    $current_line =~ /\{([^\}]+)\}-->\{([^\}]+)\}/;
    $pointer = $1;
    $request = $2;

    # Grab the URL out of the request
    ($method, $url, $protocol) = split (" ", $request);

    # Erase the query string from the requested URL
    $url =~ s/\?.*//;

    # Check to see if the Referer field is blank
    next if $pointer eq "(null)";

    # Keep track of how many documents point to this one.
    # If the document didn't already point to this document,
    # increment the count.
    $pcnt{$url}++ unless $point{$url}=~/$pointer/;

    # Keep track of the total number of unique pages that point to the
    # server.
    $tot++ unless $point{$url}=~/$pointer/;

    # Find out how many times this page was already pointed by the
    # specify document and add one.
    if ($point{$url} =~ /([\d]+) $pointer/)
```

```
    {
     $old_num_hits = $1;
     $new_num_hits = $old_num_hits + 1;
     $point{$url} =~ s/$old_num_hits $pointer/$new_num_hits $pointer/;
    }
    else
    {
     # Otherwise, this is the first hit, so add it.
     $point{$url} .= "1 $pointer\n";
    }

}

# Print a header line
print("Server pointed to by $tot unique other pages\n\n");



# Sort all the documents based on the number of pages pointing to them.
@documents = sort {$pcnt{$b} <=> $pcnt{$a};} keys %point;

for $document (@documents)
{
    # Print the header for the document
    $output_string = "The following $pcnt{$document} pages point to
$document";
    print "$output_string\n";
    print "-" x length($output_string) . "\n";

    # Get an array of all the documents which point to this one
    # and the number of times they refered to it.
    @pointers = split("\n", $point{$document});

    # Sort the documents based on the number of times they were
    # followed.
```

```
    @pointers = sort {$b <=> $a;} @pointers;
    foreach $pointer (@pointers)
    {                   #
     print "$pointer\n";
    }

    print "\n\n";
}
```

The output of the referer.pl script displays the number of sites that point to specific pages at your site and tells you the number of hits that came from those locations. The following is a sample of the output from running this script on a very small portion of the net.Genesis log files:

```
Server pointed to by 48 unique other pages

The following 11 pages point to /cgi/comprehensive
--------------------------------------------------
5 http://home.mcom.com/home/whats-cool.html
3 http://www.mit.edu:8001/people/mkgray/comprehensive.html
3 http://www.clark.net/pub/journalism/awesome.html
2 http://www.netgen.com/cgi/comprehensive
2 http://home.netscape.com/home/whats-cool.html
2 http://www.w3.org/hypertext/WWW/Daemon/User_3.0/
1 http://white.nosc.mil/defense.html
1 http://www.mit.edu:8001/afs/sipb/user/mkgray/ht/compre3.html
1 http://www.cs.cmu.edu:8001/afs/cs.cmu.edu/user/bsy/www/iam.html
1 http://www.secapl.com/cgi-bin/qs
1 http://www.hiram.edu:80/~zoner/

The following 10 pages point to /sis/sports.html
------------------------------------------------
5 http://www.mit.edu:8001/services/sis/sports.html
3 http://zoom.lm.com/
2 http://www.mit.edu:8001/services/sis/NBA/NBA.html
```

```
2 http://www.csbsju.edu/Entertainment/Internetfun.html
2 http://www.yahoo.com/Entertainment/Sports/Basketball/NBA/
1 http://www.w3.org/hypertext/WWW/Daemon/User_3.0/
1 http://www.gnn.com/gnn/wic/sports.10.html
1 http://www.nando.net/newsroom/football/1994/nfl/feat/dal/dal.html
1 http://akebono.stanford.edu/yahoo
1 http://www.southern.edu/

The following 6 pages point to /cgi-bin/wandex/index
----------------------------------------------------
2 http://www.netgen.com/cgi/wandex
2 file:///c:/web/bookmrk1.htm
1 http://netgen.com/cgi-bin/wandex/index?words=BLACK+DOG
1 http://www.cs.cmu.edu:8001/afs/cs.cmu.edu/user/bsy/www/iam.html
1 http://netgen.com/cgi-bin/wandex/index?words=shrimps
1 http://www.netgen.com/cgi/comprehensive

The following 4 pages point to /cgi/wandex
------------------------------------------
2 http://www.mit.edu:8001/cgi/wandex
2 http://www.mit.edu:8001/cgi/wandex/index
1 http://akebono.stanford.edu/yahoo/Reference/Searching_the_Web/
1 http://www.w3.org/hypertext/WWW/Daemon/User_3.0/

The following 3 pages point to /info/growth.html
------------------------------------------------
1 http://www.mit.edu:8001/afs/sipb/user/mkgray/ht/web-growth.html
1 http://web.mit.edu/afs/sipb/user/mkgray/ht/web-growth.html
1 http://www.mit.edu:8001/people/mkgray/web-growth.html

The following 3 pages point to /cgi-bin/wandex/
-----------------------------------------------
2 http://netgen.com/cgi-bin/wandex/
1 http://www.central.surrey.ac.uk/
```

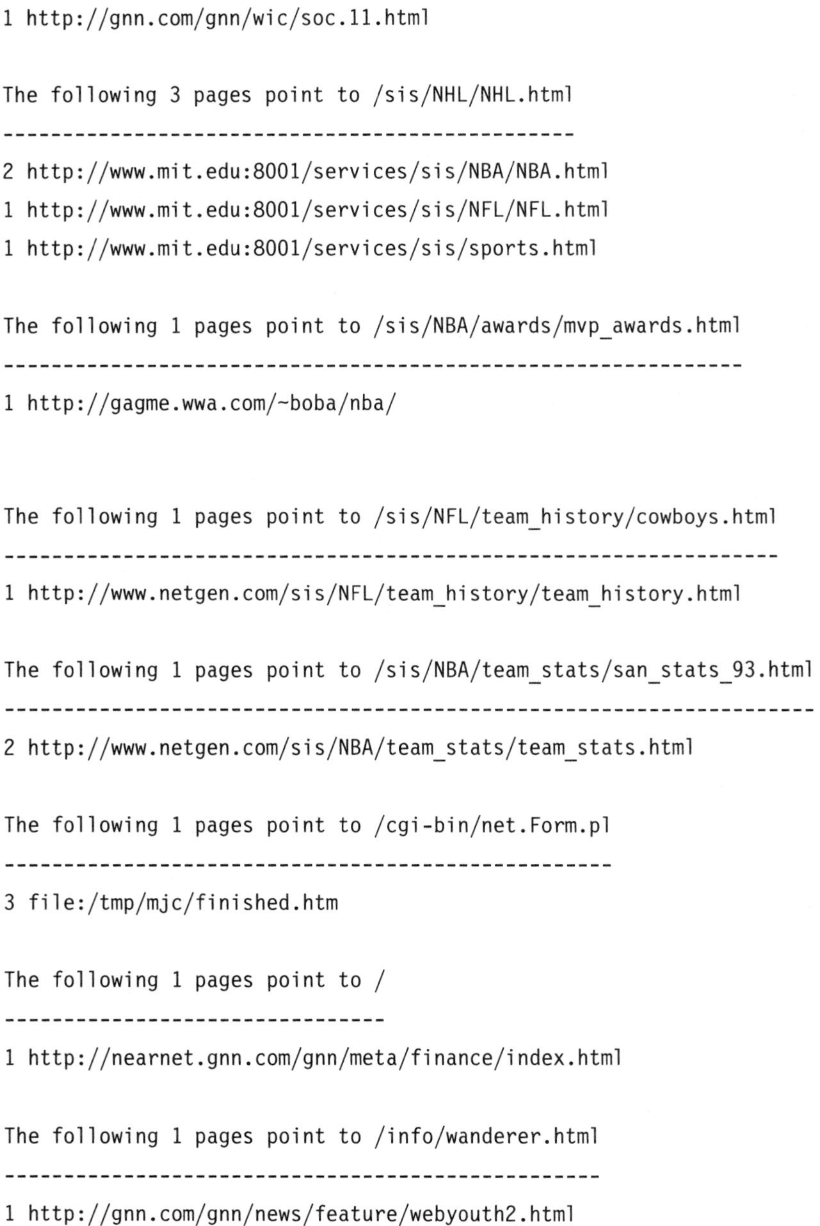

```
1 http://gnn.com/gnn/wic/soc.11.html

The following 3 pages point to /sis/NHL/NHL.html
------------------------------------------------
2 http://www.mit.edu:8001/services/sis/NBA/NBA.html
1 http://www.mit.edu:8001/services/sis/NFL/NFL.html
1 http://www.mit.edu:8001/services/sis/sports.html

The following 1 pages point to /sis/NBA/awards/mvp_awards.html
--------------------------------------------------------------
1 http://gagme.wwa.com/~boba/nba/


The following 1 pages point to /sis/NFL/team_history/cowboys.html
-----------------------------------------------------------------
1 http://www.netgen.com/sis/NFL/team_history/team_history.html

The following 1 pages point to /sis/NBA/team_stats/san_stats_93.html
--------------------------------------------------------------------
2 http://www.netgen.com/sis/NBA/team_stats/team_stats.html

The following 1 pages point to /cgi-bin/net.Form.pl
---------------------------------------------------
3 file:/tmp/mjc/finished.htm

The following 1 pages point to /
--------------------------------
1 http://nearnet.gnn.com/gnn/meta/finance/index.html

The following 1 pages point to /info/wanderer.html
--------------------------------------------------
1 http://gnn.com/gnn/news/feature/webyouth2.html
```

Browser-breakdown.pl Browser-breakdown.pl (shown in Listing 10-6) uses the User-Agent field from the extra-log file to tally the number of hits received from each client.

Listing 10–6. Browser-breakdown.pl, which displays a statistical summary of browsers used to access a site

```
#!/usr/bin/perl
#
#  FILE NAME: browser-breakdown.pl
#
#  DESCRIPTION:
#   Takes the 'extra' log file from the HTTP server and tallies the
#   number of hits from each client.
#

# Set the name of the log file to read in
$log_file = "/tmp/bookcode/extra-log";

# Open the file to read in
open( INPUT, $log_file ) || die "Cannot open $log_file: $!\n";

while( <INPUT> )
{

    # Look for the User-Agent field in between the '[' and ']'
     /\[([^\]]+)\]/;
     $browser_type = $1;

     # Lots of browsers send the version of libwww that they use or
     # a list of proxy servers which they went through to get here.
     # Kill this information

     $browser_type =~ s/libwww\S+//ig;
     $browser_type =~ s/via proxy gateway +[\S]+//g;
```

```
# Delete any trailing spaces
$browser_type =~ s/[\s]+$//g;

# See if the User-Agent field is of the standard format:
# program name / version number
if ($browser_type =~ /^([^\/]+)\/(.*)$/)
{

  # Pick off the program name and version
  $browser_name = $1;
  $browser_version = $2;

  # Some browsers send a version number with their name or have
  # a (tm) in their name.  Kill this stuff.

  $browser_name =~ s/Version [\S]+//gi;
  $browser_name =~ s/\(tm\)//gi;
}

# If the field doesn't match the correct format see if
# we can find the name and the version number.

elsif ($browser_type =~ /^(.+) ([\d]+\.[\d]+.*)/)
{
  # This User-Agent is of the format:
  # MacMosaic 1.2.3

  $browser_name = $1;
  $browser_version = $2;

}

# Else, check and see if no User-Agent was provided
elsif ($browser_type eq "(null)")
```

```
    {
     $browser_name = "Unknown";
    }

    # Otherwise, use the whole value as the browser name
    else
    {
     $browser_name = $browser_type;
    }

    # Convert multiple spaces to a single space and kill any
    # trailing slashes
    $browser_name =~ s/ +/ /g;
    $browser_name =~ s/\/$//;


    # Increment the count on the browser type
    $browser{$browser_name}++;

    # Increment the count on the version of the browser
    $browser_version{"$1\t$2"}++;

    # Increment the number of hits we've gotten
    $total_browsers++;
}

close (INPUT);

# Print a header

print "Browser Name                              Number    Pct of   Cumulative\n";
print "                                           of Acceses Accesses     Pct\n";
```

```
# Sort the list of browsers by their number of accesses.
for $browser_type (sort {$browser{$b} <=>$browser{$a};} keys %browser)
{


    # Every 5 browsers, place a blank line
    if (($browser_count % 5) == 0)
    {
     print "\n";
    }


    # Keep track of how many lines have already been printed
    $browser_count++;


    # Calculate the percentage for this particular browser
    $browser_pct = ($browser{$browser_type} / $total_browsers) * 100;


    # Calculate total number of browsers that have been acounted for.
    $cum_browsers += $browser{$browser_type};


    # Figure out the cumulative percentage for the browsers seen so far
    $browser_cum = ( $cum_browsers / $total_browsers ) * 100;

    # Print the entry for the browser.
    printf ("%-48s %5d    %5.1f      %5.1f\n",
$browser_type,$browser{$browser_type}, $browser_pct, $browser_cum);
}
```

The following is a sample of the output generated by the browser-breakdown.pl script:

Browser Name	Number of Acceses	Pct of Accesses	Cumulative Pct
Mozilla	71	71.0	71.0
Lynx	8	8.0	79.0
NetCruiser	4	4.0	83.0
NCSA Mosaic for the X Window System	3	3.0	86.0
NCSA Mosaic for Windows	3	3.0	89.0
Unknown	3	3.0	92.0
AIR_Mosaic(16bit)	3	3.0	95.0
WinMosaic	2	2.0	97.0
NCSA Mosaic	1	1.0	98.0
NetManage Chameleon Mosaic+	1	1.0	99.0
EI*Net	1	1.0	100.0

10.3.5 Maintaining Style and Currency

It is important to maintain a consistent style and atmosphere throughout the entire site. For example, if you put a toolbar at the bottom of your pages, make sure the toolbar is available throughout the site. And the toolbar itself should be consistent, so that the tools are arranged in the same order from page to page. If you're putting last-updated times at the bottom of one page, put them at the bottom of all pages. If you're signing your pages with the author's name and information about contacting the author, do this at the bottom of all pages so that your site has a consistent look and feel.

At corporate sites, it is important to try to maintain a corporate image throughout the site. This can be achieved by using images with a common theme or look, by using a consistent format for pages, by putting a toolbar on each page, or by putting a graphical banner on each page. By pulling these pieces together, you can establish a corporate image.

If your site is historical, this next point might be irrelevant but, generally speaking, you should update the content in your site on a regular basis. For example, new sports information is available on a daily basis, and it should be available from sports sites as well. If you have a site about biomedical applications, new developments occur less often. Weekly, monthly, quarterly, or even annual updates may be more appropriate. The point is, the more current your content, the more users are likely to (re)visit your site. As your content changes, you need to update indexes and keyword lists at your site.

10.4 General Do's and Don'ts

Here are several helpful do's and don'ts to help you write better HTML. If you keep these ideas in mind when you are creating documents, you can improve the quality of your site.

Provide useful information. Users want useful information. The reason they look at a site is because they are interested in some type of information it has to offer. Users come back to sites that offer useful information. If the information you offer changes and is updated often, people are more likely to come back and see if the information has changed.

Provide significant detail. Because of hypertext and hypermedia, the Web can provide endless amounts of information in a very structured way. For example, let's say an auto company decides to put one of its cars on a Web page. By clicking on different parts of a car image, you learn more about the car. You decide to click on the hood—up comes a picture of the engine. You click again on the transmission—up comes a close-up with a text description. Suppose you could also click on parts and get information from other manufacturers if the parts came from different auto companies. You could keep going deeper and deeper, seeking ever-detailed information. However, if you didn't want to see this much detail, you shouldn't have to look at it.

Structure your site wisely. As we said earlier, you can provide as much information as you want, but the catch is that you need to provide it in a manner that makes it easy to reach. If the most important content you have to offer is buried five layers deep, most people will not have the patience to find it. Give users easy paths to your content and they will visit your site more often.

Solicit user feedback. The Web also presents the opportunity to receive feedback from users. Feedback can be a powerful mechanism for staying in touch with a market and also tapping new markets.

Don't indulge in overhyped advertising. The Net has been generally averse to overhyped advertising. Flashy, in-your-face ads generally turn off the Net population. You need to be careful about how you go about advertising. People on the Net are not against advertising, but they want to be able to retrieve the information themselves. They don't want information shoved in their face.

Don't use extraneous multimedia. Many Net users are on 14.4Kbps dial-up connections and it takes a long time for them to download images, audio, and video. When people don't know that they are downloading a large image, they can get annoyed at having to wait. Multimedia should be used to complement text; it shouldn't completely take it over.

Don't create nonintuitive links. In Section 8.3.3, we warned you about using "Click here" links because they provide very little data to the user. "Click here" links are just a subset of "nonintuitive" links that you should avoid. Whenever you have a link, it should be clear to the user what is behind that link, whether it be another HTML document, graphic, video file, published paper, or other interesting item.

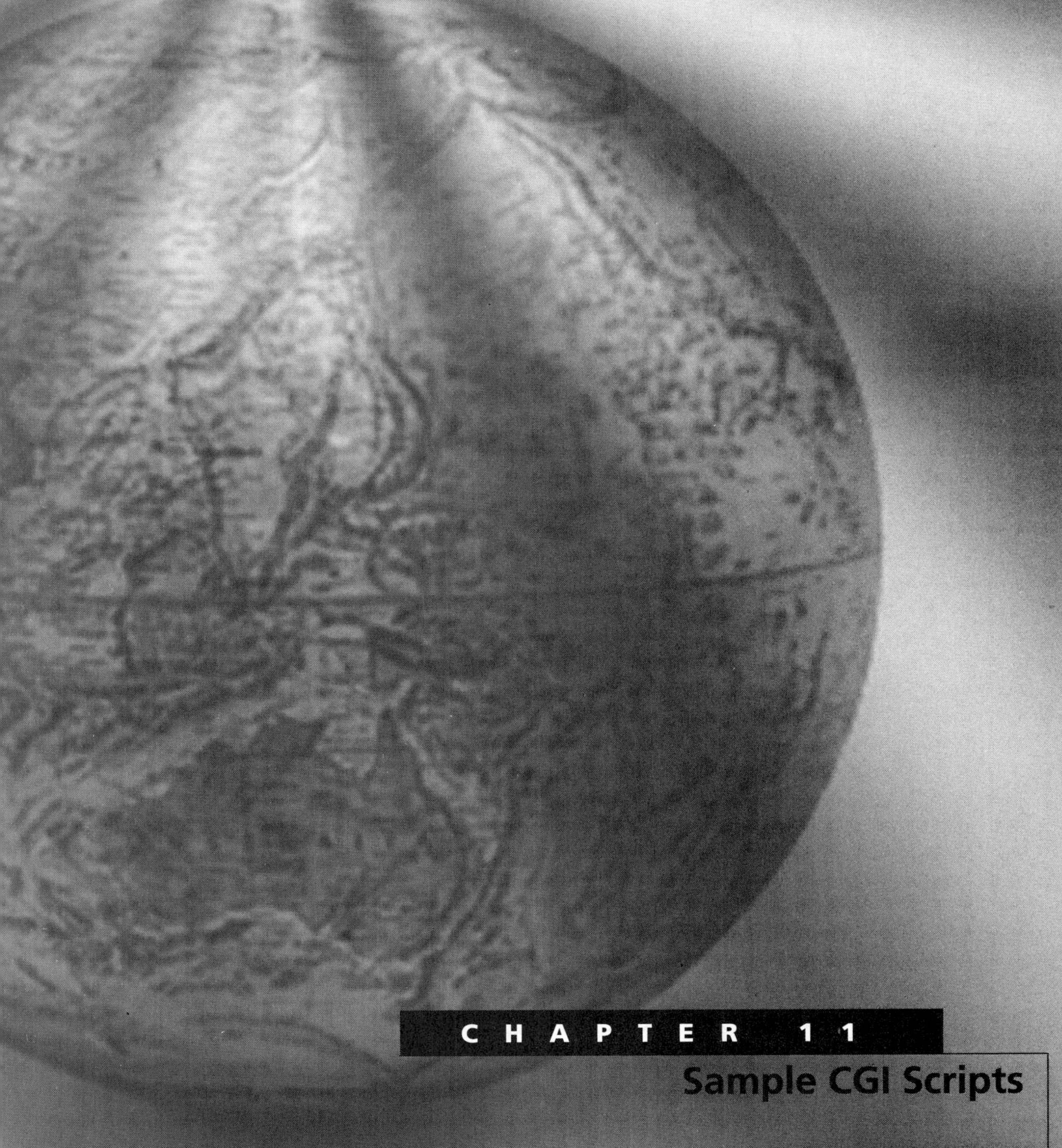

CHAPTER 11
Sample CGI Scripts

CHAPTER AT A GLANCE

This chapter contains seven examples of CGI scripts, each one slightly more advanced than the one before. Examining these scripts will help you understand the types of algorithms and the actual implementation methodology used to create CGI scripts. It should be noted that these scripts are only starting points. Once you understand conceptually what the scripts are trying to accomplish, you can expand their features and functionality. Here you will find scripts for URL parsing, providing basic feedback, searching using grep, maintaining state, monitoring server load, running a basic bulletin board, and forwarding to a random URL.

REQUISITES

Some familiarity with programming concepts and the perl programming language. Understanding of CGI as described in Chapter 9.

CGI scripts can handle all sorts of activities. For example, you can write scripts to display the server load in an HTML document and generate random URLs using Netscape's client pull HTTP extension. Of course, a lot of activities focus on obtaining information from users, including CGI scripts for processing and e-mailing HTML forms. A CGI script can also perform searches, and provide a very basic bulletin board service. One of the most useful functions that a CGI script can provide is maintaining state. But before we present the scripts, let's talk for a moment about perl, the language we've been using to write all these scripts.

11.1 Perl and CGI: Pro and Con

Throughout this book, and especially in these chapters, we chose to write our scripts in perl. But that doesn't mean perl is always the best language for CGI scripting. For the specific cases that we have provided, perl was the best choice. CGI scripting often requires a language that can parse data well and do string manipulation easily and effectively. Perl has advantages and disadvantages, but it is well-suited to many Web-related programming needs.

Perl is compact. What would take a great many lines of code in other languages can often be accomplished in far fewer lines in perl. This is partly due to the fact that perl is a weakly typed language, so perl variables can contain virtually any type of data (strings, integers, floating-point numbers, etc.). Perl also has many native, high-level string processing functions, which makes it relatively easy to do pattern matching and string manipulation. You can read the code without getting bogged down in excessive logistics—whether in variable declarations, memory allocation, or messy string processing.

Perl is also compatible with many platforms. Because perl is maintained and developed at a central location, there are substantially fewer compatibility issues as far as multiple platforms and different versions of the software are concerned. Even C, a program that is meant to be platform-independent, has various functions, such as system calls, that are sensitive to the platform on which the code is being written.

Perl is free, so there aren't different vendor versions to contend with. A perl script that runs on one system is virtually guaranteed to run on another. Perl is widely distributed and available for virtually every variety of UNIX. In addition, perl also runs under DOS, Windows NT, and on Macintosh systems.

NOTE

Perl itself is platform-independent, but you can definitely make system calls that assume particular platform types. Much of the code presented in this book relies on UNIX commands such as sendmail. Because nearly all Web servers are on UNIX platforms, this shouldn't present much of a problem.

However, perl is not always the ideal language for all programming tasks. It was not created with speed in mind, and the code is not compiled before it is run. So perl is not as fast as other languages, such as C. In fact, it's about ten times slower. Therefore, when computational speed is more important than functionality, C is likely a better choice than perl.

In addition, the perl program is larger than sh and ksh, and every time the program is run, the perl interpreter is loaded into memory. Therefore, if a program is going to be run a great many times and is doing something very simple, the Bourne shell or Korn shell may be more appropriate.

Finally, perl does not yet compile down to a binary (this subject has been discussed very much and may be rectified in the future). If you intend to develop commercial software, this is an important consideration because you will be distributing source code to your programs, and people will be able to see and modify that code.

11.2 Parsing Script

In Chapter 4, we talked about encoding data in URLs and showed how values are converted into escape-codes sequences. The following script is useful for dealing with URL-encoded input such as that sent from a form. This utility allows you to decode the URLs that are sent to your server. It "de-escapes" the URL and also takes the key value pairs and puts them in an *associative array* (a set of key-value pairs). For every key in the array, there is exactly one value. For example, we could have an associative array called "foods" where the value for "dog" was "Purina," the value for "cat" was "Friskies," and the value for "Eric" was "Cheeze-Its." It is a one-to-one mapping.

We use this script all the time when we are capturing user input. In fact, all but one of the other scripts in this chapter use this parsing script, parseform.pl. The script is shown in Listing 11-1.

Listing 11–1. **Parseform.pl, which is used to decode data embedded in URLs**

```
# File: parseform.pl
# This subroutine takes a url-encoded string and
# turns it into an associative array.
sub parseform
{
   local($formthing) = @_;

   # Expects something like:
   # foo=wow%21&bar=hello&baz=blah

   # Split the string into each of the key-value pairs
   (@fields) = split('&', $formthing);

   # For each of these key-value pairs, decode the value
   for $field (@fields)
   {

     # Split the key-value pair on the equal sign.
     ($name, $value) = split('=', $f);

     # Change all plus signs to spaces. This is an
     # remnant of ISINDEX
     $value =~ y/\+/ /;

     # Decode the value & removes % escapes.
     $value =~ s/%([\da-f]{1,2})/pack(C,hex($1))/eig;

     # Create the appropriate entry in the
     # associative array lookup
     if(defined $lookup{$name})
```

```
      {
        # If there are multiple values, separate
        # them by newlines
        $lookup{$name} .= "\n".$value;
      }
      else
      {
        $lookup{$name} = $value;
      }
    }

    # Return the associative array
    %lookup;
}

# Always do this for files that you "require"
1;
```

11.3 Basic Feedback Script

Most sites use *feedback scripts* to send the contents of forms via e-mail to site administrators. Feedback scripts are the back-end processors of the data sent by an HTML form. It need only parse the data being sent. After that, it can do something with the data, such as resend it as e-mail or store it in a file.

The code shown in Listing 11-2 serves two functions. First it generates a blank feedback form for the user. Then it processes the information from that form. Basically, this program is recursive in nature. You call it once to get the blank form, and once that form is submitted, the script continues processing.

In order to use this script for your own Web site, you need to set the correct location of parseform.pl (in the `require` statement) and your version of sendmail (change the value of `$sm` to this location). In addition, you need to set `$feedback_recipient` to the e-mail address of the person who should receive the mail, and `$default_sender` to the person that the mail should come from if no sender is specified in the form.

Figures 11-1 through 11-4 show the sequence of events as they occur when running the simple-feedback.pl script.

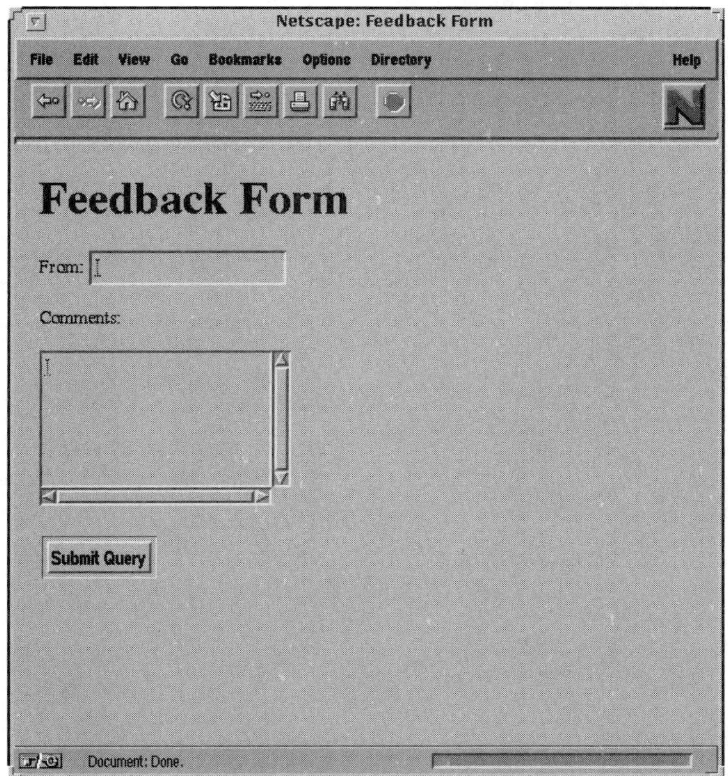

Figure 11–1 When you make a simple request for the feedback script, it returns a blank feedback form that allows you to submit a message.

Listing 11–2. The simple-feedback.pl script, which generates and processes feedback forms

```
#!/usr/bin/perl
# Program Name: simple-feedback.pl

# This uses parseform to decode the data that is read in.
# parseform.pl is included in Chapter 11.
require 'parseform.pl';
```

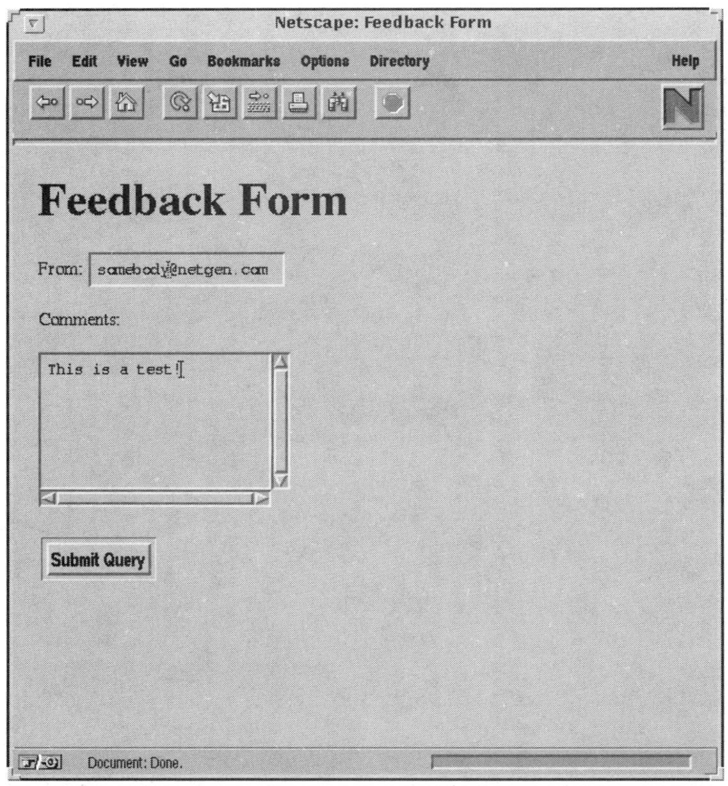

Figure 11–2 Once you fill out this form with your username and comments, you send it back by clicking on the Submit Query button.

```
# Set the location of sendmail for the script to use
$sm = "/usr/lib/sendmail";

# Set the e-mail address of the person to send the mail to,
$feedback_recipient = "erichard\@netgen.com";

# Set the default sender.  If the from field is blank, use
# this value
$default_sender = "erichard\@netgen.com";
```

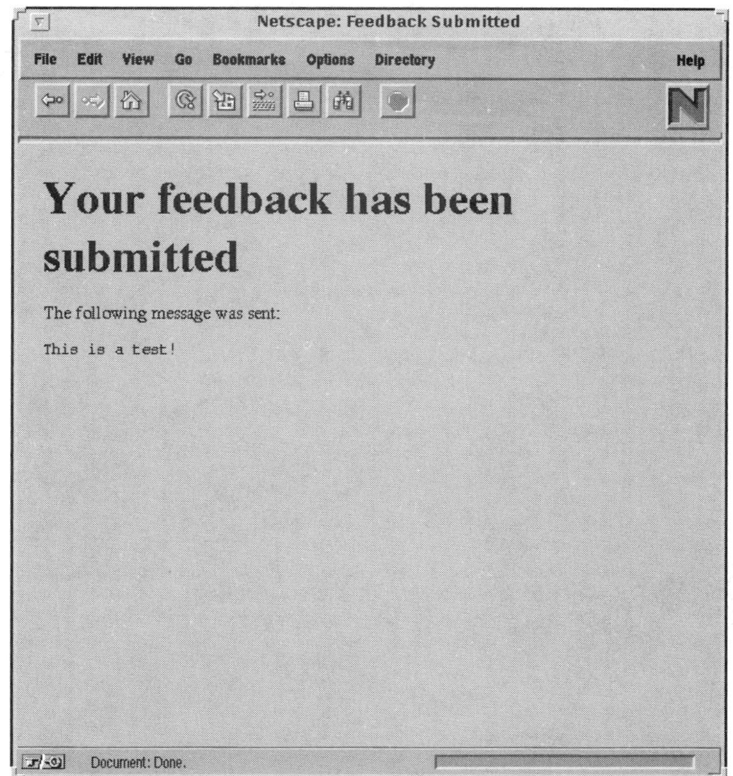

Figure 11–3 When you submit the form, the script generates a reply to let you know that your comments were submitted.

```
# Print the Content-Type of HTML
print "Content-Type: text/html\n";

# print a blank line indicating the end of the header
print "\n";

# Check and see if the POST method was used.  If so, we will
# send the contents to the previously specified user.
if($ENV{"REQUEST_METHOD"} eq "POST")
```

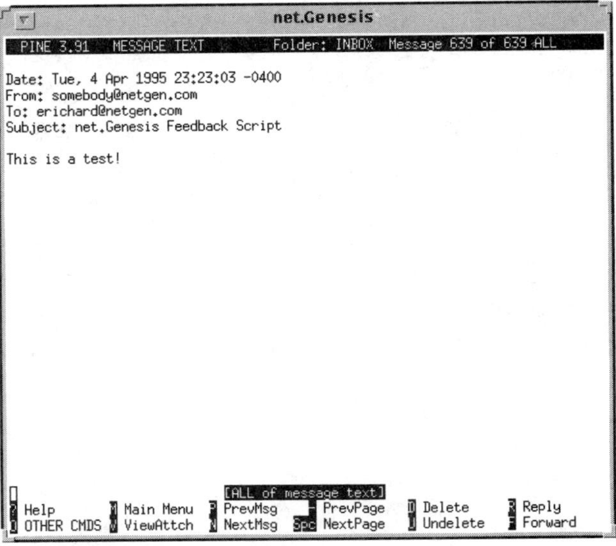

Figure 11–4 The script sends an e-mail message containing the form's comments to the user specified as the recipient in the script.

```
{
  # Read the input off of standard input.
  read(STDIN, $query, $ENV{"CONTENT_LENGTH"});

  # Use parseform to de-escape the data.
  %form = &parseform($query);

  # Look for a special field named "from". If it is found, use
  # it as the sender of the form.
  if ($form{'from'})
  {
    $from = $form{'from'};
  }

  # Otherwise, use the default sender
```

```
   else
   {
     $from = $default_sender;
   }

   # Open a filehandle to sendmail
   open(SM, "|$sm -f$from $feedback_recipient");

   # Print the header lines
   print SM "To: $feedback_recipient\n";
   print SM "Subject: net.Genesis Feedback Script\n";

   # Print a blank line to indicate the beginning of the body.
   print SM "\n";

   # Print the body of the message
   print SM $form{'feedback'};

   # Close the sendmail file handle.
   close(SM);

   # Generate the output to the user.
   print <<EndOfResponse;
<html>
<head>
<title>Feedback Submitted</title>
</head>

<body>
<h1>Your feedback has been submitted</h1>
The following message was sent:
<pre>
$form{'feedback'}
</pre>
```

```
</body>

</html>
EndOfResponse

}

# If another method was used, return a form which can be used to
# submit a comment.
else
{
   print <<EndOfForm;
<html>
<head>
<title>Feedback Form</title>
</head>

<body>
<h1>Feedback Form</h1>
<form method="POST">
From: <input name="from">
<p>
Comments:<p>
<textarea name="feedback" rows=7 cols=24>
</textarea>
<p>
<input type="submit">
</form>
</body>
</html>
EndOfForm
}\
```

11.4 Basic Search Script Using Grep

Here is a simple gateway program that lets you "grep" files for keywords. Grep, a UNIX command, searches a file for a word and then returns all of the lines that contain the word. You can use it as a basic search utility. Matthew uses a variation of the script presented here to perform all queries to Wandex.

If you have a dictionary on disk of HTML-formatted text in which each term is defined on a single line, you could use this script to perform dictionary searches via the Web. If you grepped this file for the word *computer*, for example, you would get a list of all the definitions containing the word *computer*.

The script takes its list of keywords from the *QUERY_STRING* environment variable and uses *PATH_INFO* to specify the name of the file to search. If no file is specified, the script searches the default file. For example, if the script was accessible at **http://www.netgen.com/cgi/grep.pl** and you wanted to search the default file for the word *dog*, you would request the URL **http://www.netgen.com/cgi/grep.pl?dog**. If you wanted to specify that the script should search the file called newindex for the word *dog*, you would request the URL **http://www.netgen.com/cgi/grep.pl/newindex?dog**.

In order to use the script shown in Listing 11-3, you need to specify the correct location for parseform.pl (in the `require` statement) and the location for your version of grep. In addition, you have to set `$database_directory` to be the directory in which to store all the files you want to search. Finally, set `$default_index` to the name of the file (in the directory you just specified) that you want to search if no other filename is provided.

TIP

If you don't know where grep is on your system, try typing which grep **at the prompt.**

Listing 11–3. The cgi-grep.pl script, which uses grep to perform searches

```
#!/usr/bin/perl
# File Name: cgi-grep.pl
# We're going to use parseform.pl. The code for this is included in the CGI
chapter.
require 'parseform.pl';
```

```
# Grab the query string from the environment
$query=$ENV{'QUERY_STRING'};

# Look and see if a database name was supplied
$index=$ENV{'PATH_INFO'};

# Set the location of grep on your server.
$grep = "/usr/bin/grep";

# Set the base directory in which all the databases are located
$database_directory = "/tmp";

# Set the default database to use
$default_database = "index";

# If no database was specified, use the default database
$index = $default_database unless $index;

# Figure out the full file name to the index
$index_file = "$database_directory/$index";

# Print the Content-Type for the data to return
print("Content-Type: text/html\n\r");

# Print a blank line to indicate the end of the header
print "\n\r";

# Print out the basic information common to all results
print "<html>\n";
print "<head>\n";
print "<title>Sample Grep Script</title>\n";
print "</head>\n";
print "<body>\n";
```

```
# Use parseform to figure out the query
%search = &parseform($query);


# Use the 'words' field as the list of words to look for
if($pattern = $search{'words'})
{
   # Change all white space to a single space
   $pattern =~ s/\s+/ /g;

   # Do the search on these words and exit
   &do_search($pattern);
   print "<hr>\n";

   # Print the form out at the bottom of the screen
   &print_form();
}
else
{
   # If no query string is provided, print out the query form.
   &print_form();
}

# Finish off the HTML
print "</body>\n";
print "</html>\n";

# This script performs the actual brunt of the work.
sub do_search
{
   local($pattern) = @_;
   print("<h1>Grep search for $pattern</h1>\n");
```

```
    # Grep the index for the specified word
    $results .= '$grep -i \'$pattern\' $index_file';

    # Print out the results
    print "<ul>\n";
    foreach $result (split ("\n", $results))
    {
      print "<li> $result\n";
    }
  print "</ul>\n";
}

sub print_form
{
    # Print some basic information
    print "<h1>Simple Grep Script</h1>\n";
    print "This allows you to search a file for keywords.\n";

    # Print out the form
    print "<form method=\"GET\">\n";
    print "Search for: <input name=\"words\"><br>\n";
    print "<input type=\"submit\" value=\"Begin Search\">\n";
    print "</form>\n";
}
```

11.5 Maintaining State with a CGI Script

Maintaining some sort of state so you can track a user through your system and remember what the user did previously (i.e., whether the user ordered items in your online stores) is one of the more complex and most useful functions that a CGI script can perform. As we've said many times before, there is no consistent means of identifying users in HTTP, of tracking users, or of maintaining a history of their actions.

One way of getting around this is to assign a *unique identifier* (UID) to each user who comes into your system and then pass that UID around in all the

URLs that the user follows. By doing this, you can write other scripts that use this UID to maintain state (or you can modify the script in this section). In other words, assigning a UID to each user is as good as assigning a name to users, as far as CGI scripts are concerned. The CGI script can then use the UID as a key in a database that stores all the information you need.

As an example, let's say you want to set up an online shopping mall. You need a way to track all the purchases made by each user so that you can bill users when they make purchases. When users first enter your site, you can use the script presented here to assign a UID. Then as users wander through your site, the UID is carried around within the URL. This means that when users submit orders, their UIDs can be submitted as well. And a script would then be able to maintain a database of all the orders made using a particular UID. Finally, when the user is done, the database could be searched to find all the purchases made under that UID.

Sample code for doing this is shown in Listing 11-4. This code is a good start toward providing the functionality you need. You can use this script to append state to existing HTML documents. It uses the *PATH_TRANSLATED* environment variable to determine the location of the document that the user requests. It then takes this document and modifies it by appending a UID to the searchpart of each URL within the document. It also adds a new field to all forms containing the UID. Then it passes the modified document on to the client.

Let's assume that you installed this script and that it is available on your server at the URL **/cgi-bin/state.pl**. In addition, let's say that there is a document on your site located at the URL **/comments/comments.html**. The following URL would lead to the document, though state would not be maintained:

http://yourhost.com/comments/comment.html

In order to access the state-encoded version of this document, you would request the URL like so:

http://yourhost.com/cgi-bin/state.pl/comments/comments.html

Because the only things the script modifies are the links in this document, there are no visible external differences. Both URLs will deliver a document that looks like the one in Figure 11-5. By looking at excerpts of the HTML from the original and modified versions of this page, you can see what the script did.

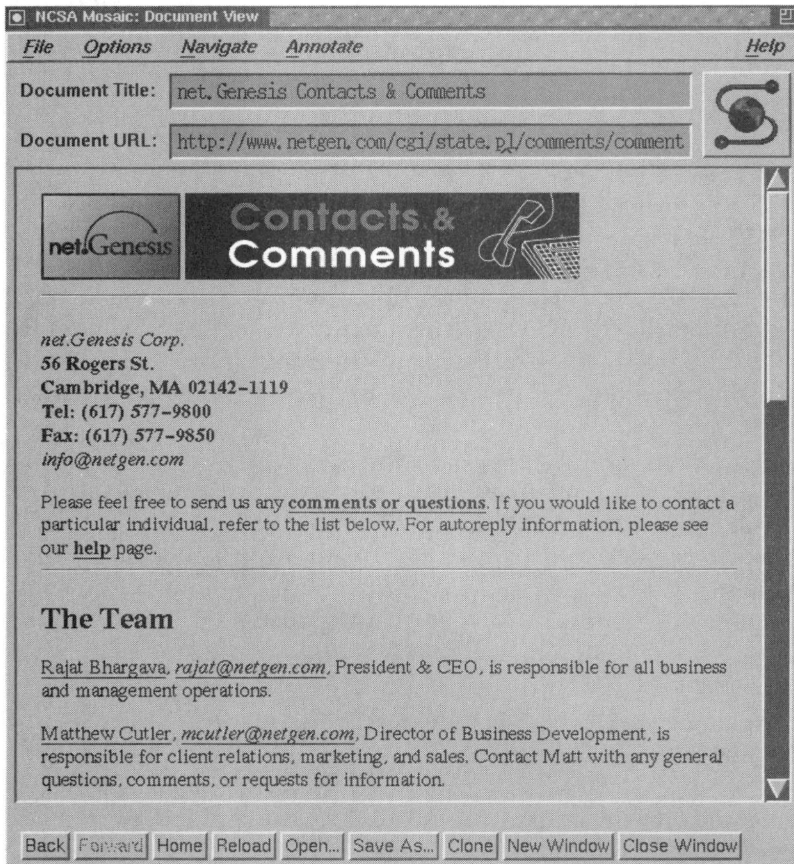

Figure 11-5 The rendered comments.html page looks the same whether you access it directly or through the state.pl script.

Here is an excerpt from **http://www.netgen.com/comments/comments.html**:

```
<p> Please feel free to send us any <a href =
"netgen_comments.html"><strong>comments or questions</strong></a>. If you
would like to contact a particular individual, refer to the list below. For
auto-reply information, please see our <a href = "/
help.html"><strong>help</strong></a> page.
```

```
<hr>
<h1>The Team</h1>
<a href = "/people/rajat.html">Rajat Bhargava</a>, <a href=
"/people/people.email.html"><EM>rajat@netgen.com</EM></a>, President & CEO,
is responsible for all business and management operations.
<p>
```

Compare that to this excerpt from **http://www.netgen.com/cgi/state.pl/comments/comments.html**:

```
<p> Please feel free to send us any
<a href = "netgen_comments.html"><strong>comments or questions</strong></
a>. If you would like to contact a particular individual, refer to the list
below. For auto-reply information, please see our <a href = "/cgi/state.pl/
help.html?uid=10783"><strong>help</strong></a> page.
<hr>
<h1>The Team</h1>
<a href = "/cgi/state.pl/people/rajat.html?uid=10783">Rajat Bhargava</a>,
<a href = "/cgi/state.pl/people/people.email.html?uid=10783">
<EM>rajat@netgen.com</EM></a>, President & CEO, is responsible for all
business and management operations.
<p>
```

NOTE

If you are wondering why the script does not alter the first Anchor (`netgen_comments.html`**) on the second line, it's because it won't modify relative links—i.e., it won't modify links that don't give the full path.**

As you can see, the difference is that when you use the script, the URLs specified within the anchors (i.e., the HREF elements) have a UID attached to the end of them. In addition, the links have been modified so that they point back to the script itself. This means that all documents being pointed to will use this script to maintain state within themselves as well.

If you follow the `rajat@netgen.com` link, it will take you to the net.Genesis Email page shown in Figure 11-6. Again, you can only see the real difference by examining the difference in the HTML between these two pages.

Here is an excerpt from **http://www.netgen.com/people/people.email.html**:

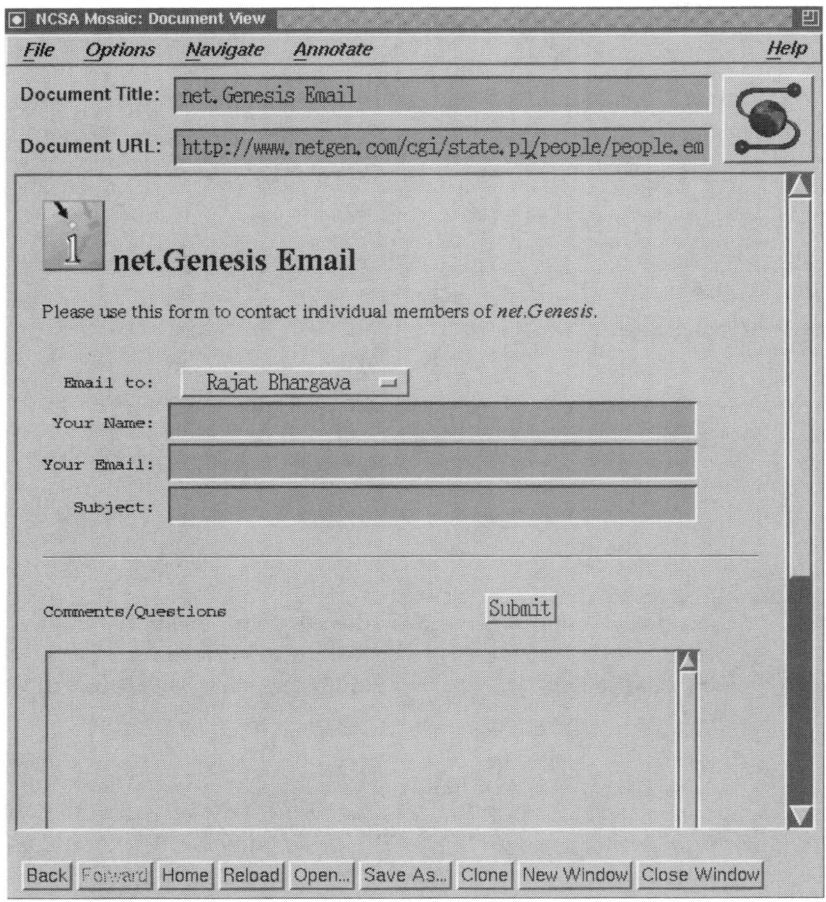

Figure 11-6 The net.Genesis Email page looks the same whether you access it directly or by following a link from a page that was processed by the state.pl script.

```
<title>net.Genesis Email</title>
<h1><img src="/image/other/symbol.gif" alt = "*">
net.Genesis Email</h1>
Please use this form to contact individual members of <em>net.Genesis</em>.
<p>
<form method=POST action=http://www.netgen.com/cgi-bin/net.Form.pl>
```

Here is the same section of code, but from **http://www.netgen.com/cgi/doc_gen.prl/people/people.email.html?uid=10783**:

```
<HTML>
<title>net.Genesis Email</title>

<h1><img src="/image/other/symbol.gif" alt = "*">
net.Genesis Email</h1>
Please use this form to contact individual members of <em>net.Genesis</em>.
<p>
<form method=POST action=http://www.netgen.com/cgi-bin/net.Form.pl>
<input type="hidden" name="uid" value="10783">
```

The important thing to notice here is that the second document contains a hidden form field called uid that contains the value of the UID that was passed in. As we discussed earlier, this allows the script behind the form to use this information, and therein lies the real power of maintaining information.

The script itself is shown in Listing 11-4. The only configuration this script needs is the correct location of parseform.pl in the `require` statement.

Listing 11–4. **State.pl, which attaches a UID to all links in order to track users**

```
#!/usr/bin/perl
# FILE NAME: state.pl

# DESCRIPTION: This script performs the following tasks:
# a) Checks to see if there is a UID attached to the document
# if not it generates one
# b) retrieves the requested document if possible and inserts
# the UID in all links and form actions
```

```
require "parseform.pl";

# Grab the query string
$query_string = $ENV{'QUERY_STRING'};

# Use parseform to split the query string up each of the fields
%form = &parseform($query_string);

# Grab the value, if any, submitted with the 'uid' field
$UID = $form{'uid'};

# Determine the physical path to the document that the user
# requested.
$requested_file = $ENV{'PATH_TRANSLATED'};

# Determine the URL for this script.
$script_URL = $ENV{'SCRIPT_NAME'};

# Print the header so we can send back a document
print "Content-Type: text/html\n";
print "\n";
print "<HTML>\n";

#print "Fetching $requested_file\n";
#print "Script URL: $script_URL\n";

# Call check_uid to see if the UID is valid or generate a new
# one and print any warning mesages
$UID = &check_uid($UID);

# Attach the UID to all of the links and forms in the file and
# print the results back to the user.
print (&attach_state($requested_file, "uid=$UID"));
```

```
# This routine is responsible for taking an HTML file and
# finding all the links and appending the state information on
# to each link.
sub attach_state
{
   # Grab the name of the file to return and the string to
   # append to the end of each URL
   local($filename, $state) = @_;

   # Check and see if the file is readable.
   open(INPUT, "<$filename") || die "Error! Could not access the
      requested URL!\n";

   # Read in the entire file
   undef $/;
   ($data = <INPUT>) || "Error reading file.\n";

   # Now go through the file, attaching state to all the links
   # Look for all Anchor Elements
  while ($data =~ /<(([\s]*a[\s]+href[\s]*=\s*\")([^\"]*)\")/ig)
  {
     $anchor = $1;
     $pre_URL = $2;
     $URL = $3;

     # Make sure the URL doesn't specify a server name
     next if ($URL =~ /^http:/);

     # The script can't handle relative links, so make sure
     # that that the URL isn't relative.
     next if ($URL !~ /^\//);

     # The script can only handle links to other HTML documents
     # so make sure the URL is for an HTML document
     next if ($URL !~ /\.html?$/);
```

```
#Check and see if there already is a query_string
if ($URL =~ /\?(.)*/)
{
   # Add the state onto the end
   $new_URL = $URL . "\&$state";

   # If the new URL doesn't already go to this script, make
   # it use it.
   $new_URL = $script_URL . $new_URL;

   # Create the new anchor
   $new_anchor = $pre_URL . $new_URL . '"';
   # print " New Anchor: $new_anchor\n";
}
# Otherwise create a query string
else
{
  # Add the state onto the end
  $new_URL = $URL . "?$state";

  # If the new URL doesn't already go to this script, make
  # it use it.
  $new_URL = $script_URL . $new_URL;

  # Create the new anchor
  $new_anchor = $pre_URL . $new_URL . '"';
}

#Substitute the new anchor for the old one
$data =~ s/$anchor/$new_anchor/g;
}
```

```
   # Make sure to carry the state around in all forms as well
   if ($data =~ /(<[\s]*form[^>]*>)/)
   {
     $form = $1;
     $new_form = "$form\n<input type=\"hidden\" name=\"uid\" ".
       "value=\"$UID\">";
     $data =~ s/$form/$new_form/ig;
   }

   # Return the modified file
   $data;
}

sub check_uid
{
   local ($key);

   # Grab the UID which was passed in
   local($UID) = @_;

   # Only make a new UID when there isn't one passed in
   if ($UID eq "")
   {
     # if there is no UID attached get one
     $UID=&get_new_UID();
   }

   return($UID);
};


# Generates a new UID for the user
sub get_new_UID
```

```
{
# Use the PID for the current process as the new UID
$new_UID = $$;
return ($new_UID);
}
```

11.6 Monitoring the Server Load

In this part of the chapter, we present a simple, user-independent script that you can use to monitor the load on the server. This script tells you how many accesses per second your Web server is receiving, as well as the processor and memory loads that your machine is under. *Processor load* is the number of jobs your processor is trying to take care of at one time, and *memory load* is how much of your system's memory is currently occupied by the jobs that are running.

This is another gateway script. It provides users with a means of accessing information that isn't available directly through HTTP. The request gets converted into system calls, and the results are reformatted into HTML. Figure 11-7 shows sample output obtained by running the load.pl script shown in Listing 11-5.

Listing 11–5. Load.pl, which monitors server load

```
#!/usr/bin/perl
# File Name: load.pl

require "parseform.pl";

# Set the name of the log file to read in
$log_file = "/tmp/access-log";

# Set the name of the server.  This is just used for pretty
# printing.
$server_name = "net.Genesis";

# Set the location of the uptime command
$uptime = "/usr/bin/uptime";
```

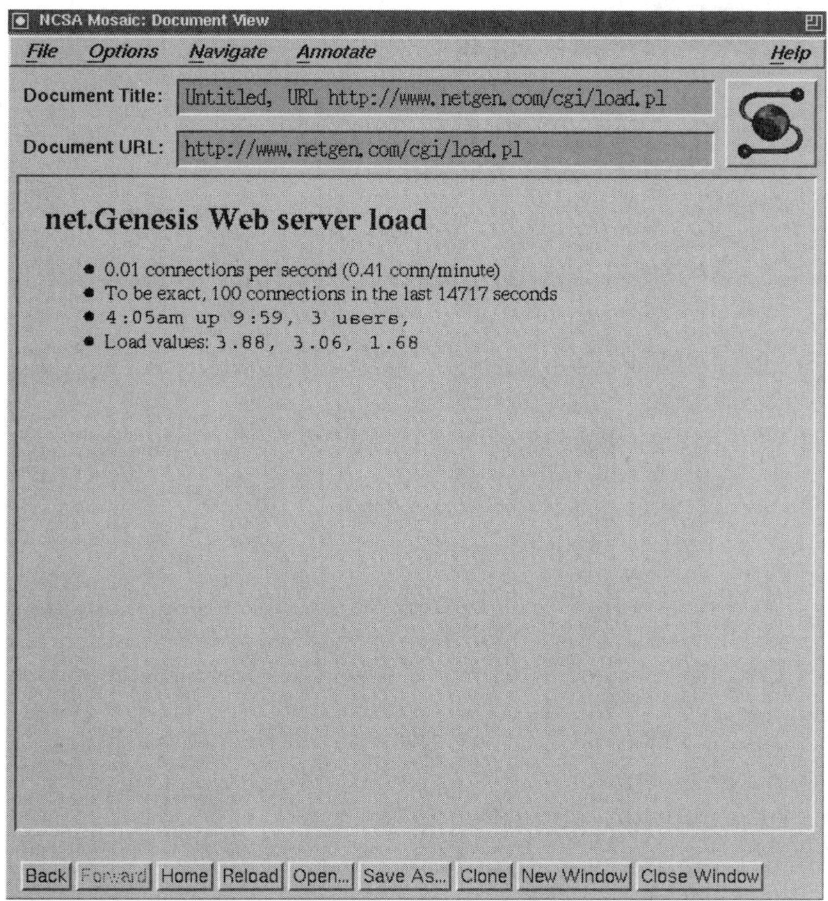

Figure 11–7 Output from load.pl, a script that monitors the load on the server

```
# Set the location of the tail command
$tail = "/usr/bin/tail";

# Set the default number of hits to use as the data
$default_num_hits = 100;
```

```
# Grab the query string
$query_string = $ENV{'QUERY_STRING'};

# Use parseform to split the query string up each of the fields
%form = &parseform($query_string);

# Grab the value, if any, submitted with the 'num_hits' field
$num_hits = $form{'num_hits'};

# Set num_hits to the default value if no other value was
# provided
$num_hits = $default_num_hits unless ($num_hits);

# Grab the last n hits from the access log
$lastblock =  '$tail -$num_hits $log_file';

# Find out what time it is now
($nowsec, $nowmin, $nowhour, @rest) = localtime(time);

# Find out what time the first hit from the data occurred at
$lastblock =~ /\[\d+\/...\/\d\d\d\d:(\d\d):(\d\d):(\d\d)/;
$hour = $1; $min = $2; $sec = $3;
$# = '%.2g';

# If the current hour is less than the first hit's hour, assume
# that we are on the next day and check the difference.
# Note:  This means that the script will not produce the right
# value when the first hit occurred more than a day ago.
$nowhour += 24 if $hour > $nowhour;

# Figure out the number of seconds past midnight that the
# first hit occurred.
$time = $hour*3600+$min*60+$sec;
```

```
# Similarly, figure out the number of seconds past midnight
# that it is now.
$nowtime = $nowhour*3600+$nowmin*60+$nowsec;

# Figure out the difference between these two.
$diff = $nowtime-$time;

# Compute the number of connections per second and connections
# per minute for the last n accesses
$connpersec = $num_hits / $diff;
$connpermin = $connpersec*60;

# Print out the header
print("Content-type: text/html\n");
print("\n");
print("<h1>$server_name Web server load</h1>\n");
print("<ul>\n");

# Print out the number of connections per second and connections
# per minute.
printf("<li>%.2f connections per second (%.2f conn/minute)\n",
$connpersec, $connpermin);
print("<li>To be exact, $num_hits connections in the last $diff seconds\n");

# Get the current system stats
$uptime = '$uptime';
($uptime1, $uptime2) = split(/load average: /, $uptime);

# Print out these statistics
print("<li><tt>$uptime1</tt>\n");
print("<li>Load values: <tt>$uptime2</tt>\n");

# Finish off the document
print("</ul>\n");
```

```
print("</body>\n");
print("</html>\n");
```

The code looks for a field called num_hits in the query string to specify the number of Web server accesses that you want to calculate your access numbers across. If this value is not provided, the value of the variable *$default_num_hits* is used.

To use this code, you need to provide the correct location of parseform.pl in the `require` statement. You must also specify the location of the uptime and tail commands on your system by changing the values of the *$uptime* and *$tail* variables to reflect these locations. (Uptime is a standard UNIX command that provides system information, including the load on the processor and on memory. Tail returns the last *n* lines of a file, where the user specifies *n*.) You need to set *$log_file* to the location of your server's access log file and *$server_name* to the name of your machine. Finally, you need to set *$default_num_hits* to the default number of Web server accesses on which you want to base your calculations. The script only reads in this specified number of lines from your logs (say, for example, the last thousand lines). Then it calculates statistics based on those thousand lines.

You can also integrate the load.pl script with the quickhist.pl code shown in Listing 10-4. Figure 11-8 shows the result of such an integration.

11.7 Bulletin Board Script

Yet another use for CGI scripts is to create online discussion groups so people can post messages for everyone in the group to see. The following script implements a very simple version of these groups. It provides a single bulletin board to which users can append their messages. In addition, the script provides a clear functionality that allows any user to clear the entire contents of the board to date. We also show you which lines to comment-out if you do not want this functionality.

In order to run the script shown in Listing 11-6, you need to set the correct location for your version of parseform.pl in the require statement. You also have to tell the script where to look for the file that contains all the data for the bulletin board. If this file does not exist, the script will attempt to create it, but in order to do this it needs write permissions on the directory where the file resides. For a sample of what the bulletin board looks like, see Figure 11-9.

Listing 11–6. **Board.pl, which provides a single bulletin board to which users can append messages**

```
#!/usr/bin/perl
# File name: board.pl

# This is included elsewhere in the chapter require
require 'parseform.pl';
```

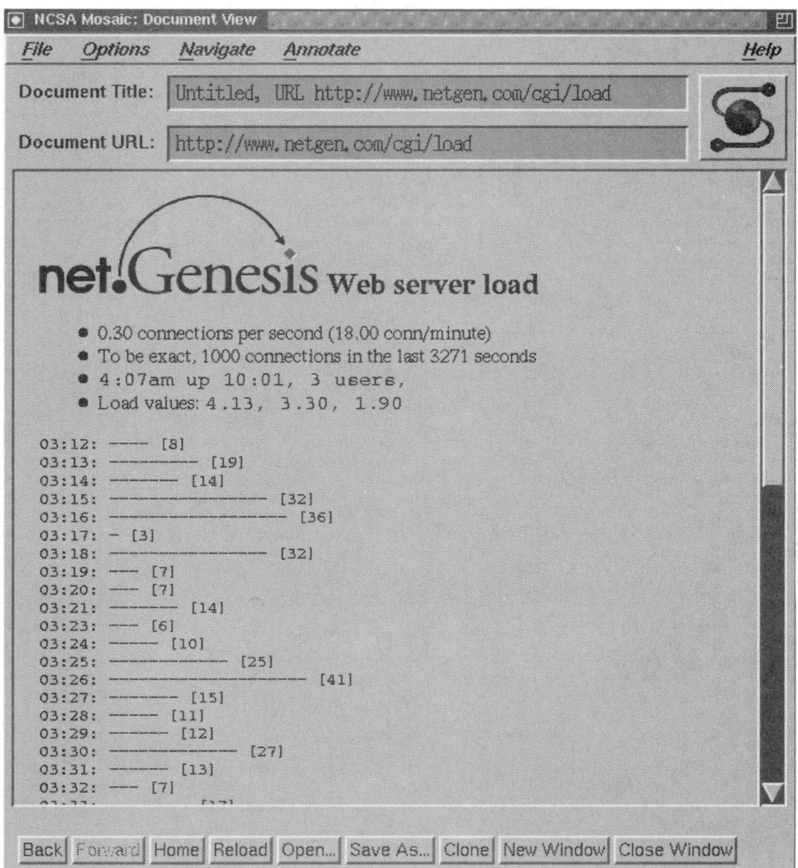

Figure 11–8 You can integrate the load.pl and quickhist.pl scripts to obtain results such as those shown here.

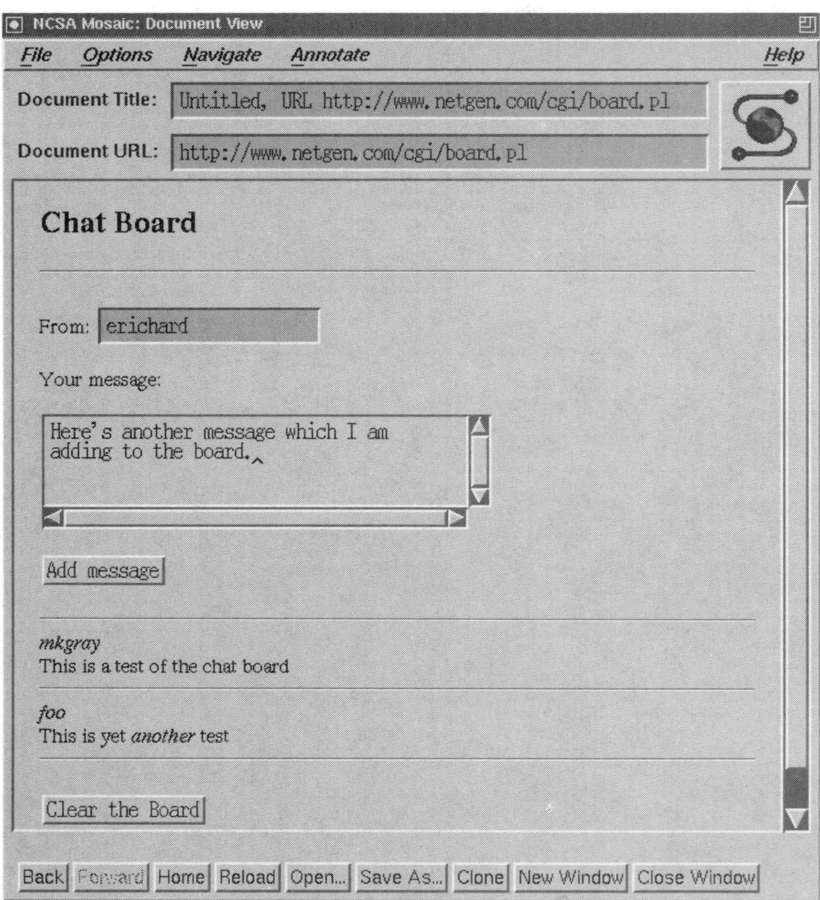

Figure 11–9 A sample discussion board created using board.pl

```
# Set the location of the file that will save the conversation
$boardfile = "/tmp/whiteboard";

# Print the header
print("Content-type: text/html\r\n");
print("\r\n");
```

```
# Check and see if a new message was posted to the system
if($ENV{'REQUEST_METHOD'} eq "POST")
{
   # If so, read in the right amount of data from standard
   # input
   read(STDIN, $data, $ENV{'CONTENT_LENGTH'});

   # Use parseform to split the data into fields
   %form = &parseform($data);

   # If the user submitted a field named  clear', erase the
   # current conversation. If you do not want to give the user
   # this power, comment out the next 6 lines of code.
   if($form{'clear'})
   {
     unlink($boardfile);
     &board_cleared;
     exit;
   }

   # Otherwise, append the new posting to the conversation.
   open(BOARD, ">>$boardfile") ||
     print "Error adding to conversation: $!";

   # Print some formatting information in the file
   print(BOARD "<hr>\n");

   # Use the 'from' field to specify who the message is from
   print(BOARD "<em>$form{'from'}</em><br>\n");

   # Add the 'message' field as the contents of the message
   print(BOARD "$form{'message'}");
```

```
   # Close the file so the changes get written out
   close(BOARD);

   # Send back the new board
   &view_board;
}

# If a new message isn't being posted, then just show the current
# board.
else
{
   &view_board;
}

# This subroutine displays the current board.
sub view_board
{
   print("<h1>Chat Board</h1>\n");
   print("<hr>\n");

   # Insert a form for users to add to the board.
   print("<form method=POST>\n");
   print("From: <input name=\"from\"><p>\n");
   print("Your message:<p>\n");
   print("<textarea rows=4 cols=40name=\"message\">\n";
   print("</textarea>\n");
   print("<p><input type=submit value=\"Add message\">\n");
   print("</form>\n");

   # Display the current contents of the board
   open(BOARD, "$boardfile");
   while(<BOARD>)
   {
     print;
   }
```

```
    close(BOARD);

    # Make a separate form which is used to clear the board. If you did
    # not give the user power to clear the board, comment out the next 5
    # lines.
    print("<hr>\n");
    print("<form method=POST>\n");
    print "<input type=hidden name=clear value=1>\n";
    print "<input type=submit value=\"Clear the Board\">\n";
    print "</form>\n";

}

# Print a message out saying the board has been cleared
sub board_cleared
{
    print("<h1>The Board has been cleared</h1>\n");
    print("<hr>\n");
    &view_board;
}
```

11.8 Random URL Forwarder

Compared to the other scripts in this chapter, this next program isn't terribly functional, since it doesn't perform any real services to a site. But it is pretty amusing. This script takes a file containing a list of URLs and randomly selects a URL to which it redirects the client. If the value in the User-Agent field indicates that the client happens to be Netscape Navigator 1.1 or higher, it uses the *client pull* feature to make the browser ask for another URL every ten seconds.

NOTE

The client pull feature is a new Netscape Navigator feature. It allows a server to specify that the client remake a request to a document after a certain amount of time has elapsed. In our example, the server sends back the Refresh header, which tells the client to reload the URL every ten seconds.

In order to use the script shown in Listing 11-7, you need to tell it where to find the list of URLs (change the value of the *$filename* variable to reflect this). You also need to tell how many lines are in the file (change the *$num_lines* variable).

TIP

It is possible to use the wc command in the script so that it automatically determines the number of lines in the file. However, this would slow the script down substantially for large lists, so we chose not to do that.

Listing 11–7. Autopilot.pl, which randomly selects URLs from a list in a specified file

```
#!/usr/bin/perl
# Filename: autopilot.pl

# Set a variable to the file name of the file with the
# list of URLs
$filename = "/tmp/urllist";

# Set a variable to the number of lines in the file.
# Our file has 7250 lines in it.
$num_lines = 7250;

# Figure out the browser type for the client
$client_type = $ENV{'HTTP_USER_AGENT'};
# Break the client type into the program name and the version
# number.
$client_type =~ /^([^\/]*)\/([\d\.]*)/;
$client_program = $1;
$client_version = $2;


# Initialize the random seed (don't worry about this)
srand;
```

```
# Find a random variable between 0 and the number of lines in
# the file. This will be the line of the file that we return.
$which_line = int( rand( $num_lines ) );
# Open the file that has the list of URLs. Check to make sure it
# opened properly.
if (open (LIST, $filename))
{
# The file opened fine.  Now find the line corresponding to
# $which_line.
# In order to do this, set up a loop to read in $which_line
# lines.
while( $current_line = <LIST> )
     {
        $line_no++;
        if ($line_no == $which_line)
          {
              last;
          }

     }



        if ($line_no <  $which_line)
     {
        &return_error();
     }


# Once we get to the end, close the file.
close(LIST);
# $current_line should now contain the last line read.
# If the client is Netscape 1.1 or higher, tell the client
# to make the request every 10 seconds.
if (($client_program eq "Mozilla") && ($client_version >= 1.1))
```

```
  {
     print("Refresh: 10; URL=http://www.netgen.com/cgi/autopilot.pl\n");
  }

# Regardless of the browser type being used, return a
# redirection
print ("Location: $current_line");
# Send the blank line to end the response.
print "\n";
exit;
}

&return_error();
sub return_error
{

# If there was an error, return an error status code.
print "Status: 500 Internal Server Error\n";
# Return a Content Type along with the error.
print "Content-Type: text/html\n";
# Print the blank line to end the response;
print "\n";
# Print an error message
print "<html>\n";
print "<head>\n";
print "<title>Autopilot Error</title>\n";
print "</head>\n";
print "<body>\n";
print "<h1>Autopilot was unable to retrieve a URL to return.</h1>\n";
print "</body>\n";
print "</html>\n";
}
exit;
```

As you can see, CGI scripts can really add a tremendous amount of power to any Web site. They allow you to break free of the restrictions imposed by the server software and allow you the full functionality of general programming languages. The examples in this chapter only touch upon what is possible with CGI scripts. By understanding the CGI specifications, you can use CGI scripts to fill in many of the gaps left by the implementations of HTTP.

CHAPTER 12

Writing a Client

CHAPTER AT A GLANCE

In this chapter we define various types of clients and discuss why you might want to program your own. Besides describing implementation considerations, we cover the general design principles of writing a client, and talk at some length about wanderers and methods of traversing the Web. This chapter ends with the code for our Niftiness Agent, a specialized agent client that you can use to retrieve documents and generate statistical information based on those documents.

REQUISITES

Detailed understanding of HTTP/1.0 as described in Chapters 5 & 6.

Familiarity with HTML as described in Chapters 7 & 8.

Experience with programming concepts and the perl programming language.

Understanding of UNIX sockets.

Now that you understand the technical details of HTML, HTTP, and URLs, you might want to write your own HTTP client. Lots of people write their own clients to perform a variety of functions on different platforms. The most common reason to write a client or modify an existing one is to create your own user interface with new functionality or behavior. For example, you could write a client to use the PUT and DELETE methods or write one to have a completely different user interface. If you simply want to add new functionality or create a new user interface, your best option is to modify the source code of an existing client. This way, you don't have to redo everything that the client already does. NCSA Mosaic, Lynx, and TkWWW are a couple of the browsers for which the source code is available.

NOTE

NCSA Mosaic may have special licensing agreements regarding obtaining source code.

Another common reason for writing your own client is to design a very specialized client to perform a particular task. For example, Matthew's World Wide Web Wanderer was originally designed to traverse the Web in a systematic fashion in order to determine the size of the Web. Since then, the Wanderer has been modified to index the Web for the Wandex database and generate the Comprehensive List of Sites. In these cases, it makes a lot more sense to develop your own client than to try to extend a preexisting client, since so much of what has already been written would be unnecessary.

12.1 Types of Clients

Before you begin thinking about writing a new client, you need to know what type of client you need. Browsers, robots, spiders, wanderers, and specialized agents are all different types of clients.

12.1.1 Client vs. Browser

All browsers are clients, but not all clients are browsers. A *client* is a program that communicates with servers in order to make requests and retrieve files over the Web. The Wanderer (by Matthew Gray) is a client, not a browser. *Browsers* are a class of clients that provide a user interface so that users can traverse the Web by following links from place to place. They take the results of a request and display the data onscreen. Lynx is an example of a text-based browser. Netscape and Mosaic are examples of browsers with graphical user interfaces.

12.1.2 Robots, Spiders, and Wanderers

Robots, spiders, and *wanderers* are synonymous. All three traverse the Web by automatically following links from one page to another. The key word here is "automatically." These programs were not intended for use by typical users who want to retrieve individual documents from the Web. Wanderers are designed to do complete (or mostly complete) traversals of a set of documents. In contexts outside of this book, the terms *robot* and *spider* are used to characterize the clients that we call *wanderers*. In this book, however, these terms imply a client that traverses the Web thoroughly.

12.1.3 Specialized Agents

Specialized agents are clients that have highly specific purposes. Some have highly utilitarian functions, such as HTML verification, checking link integrity, and retrieving for translation into another format. Other agents serve more frivolous purposes, such as measuring distances between documents, doing textual analysis of documents, and generating local caches. It is often possible to combine a specialized agent with a wanderer to build a specialized agent that automatically traverses a set of documents.

12.1.4 Hybrids

In actuality, many clients combine the functionality of the browsers, wanderers, and specialized agents. We refer to these as *hybrid clients*. For example, in Section 12.5 we show you an example of a specialized agent/browser combination whose purpose is not to display documents, but to analyze HTML documents and report on them. In one sense, our agent/browser is definitely a specialized agent. On the other hand, on each page it provides you with a list of links in the document and allows you to select one of those links. In that sense, it is a browser.

12.2 Implementation Considerations

When implementing a browser or other client, there are three main considerations: what functionality you want to provide, how you can speed up the performance of your client, and what the medium for your client's output should be.

12.2.1 Functionality

One of the major issues that you must consider when designing a client is what functionality you want it to have. The first question is whether you want your client to be a wanderer, a browser, a specialized agent, or some hybrid. While this obviously defines much of the scope of your client, there are still many features that you must think about. The level of your client's functionality will determine the difficulty of your project. If you are fortunate, you may be able to find source code from other clients that implement similar functionality.

One of the original features of the Wanderer was storing the URL for the *parent* (the document that points to it) of each document it found. Because it stored URLs, it was theoretically possible for the Wanderer to generate the full path from the top document to any child document and generate a full topology of the Web. In practice, however, traversing this tree was more time-consuming than any other step of the Wanderer's process. Later versions of the Wanderer were revised to store complete ancestor lists. The point here is that this was a feature that had not been implemented before, and many issues had to be resolved simply through trial and error. If you want to provide a certain functionality, find out first if it has ever been implemented before—and, if so, how. You will then have a gauge of how complex and involved it is to add this functionality.

12.2.2 Speeding Up Performance

You need to consider overall speed when writing a client. Unless you are careful, you might slow down the browser by adding lots of functionality and a nice graphical interface. If the browser is too slow, it isn't really useful for users. It is critical for people to feel that the browser is fast and can be used effectively. When you are writing a wanderer, speed is important so that the traversal can be completed as quickly as possible. Ideally, none of the client's functionality should be slower than the time it takes to connect and make a request. If there is to be a bottleneck, it should be in making the connection and transferring the data. Then users can always improve the speed of the client by upgrading the speed of their network connection.

There are many ways to help improve the speed of a client. The first, and most obvious, is to identify the bottlenecks in your program. If a client is spending a majority of its time rendering images, then trying to speed up the HTML-rendering functionality is not likely to increase speed. In that case, you should focus on the image-rendering process instead. One of the easiest ways to find where bottlenecks occur in code is to keep track of the time that the browser enters and exits each major piece of code in the system. For example, your program could print a message when it begins to make the request and another when it has finished. By examining the pieces of code that take the longest to execute, you can determine whether the code can be optimized.

One way to speed up requests is to issue parallel requests. Instead of requesting one document at a time from a server, the client requests all the documents it needs at one time. When a client makes serial requests, the time it takes to download all objects is the sum of the time it takes to download each object. When a client makes a parallel request, however, the time needed for downloading all objects is the same as the maximum of the download times for each object. Figure 12-1 illustrates this difference.

Whether you make serial or parallel requests, you still have to transfer the exact same amount of data. So how can parallel requests speed things up? The answer lies in the fact that the actual time to transfer a document might not be the major time sink. Instead, more time might be spent resolving the hostname or waiting for the server to process the request before it returns a response. In both of these cases, parallel requests speed up the process because all of the waiting occurs simultaneously. Some browsers, including Netscape, are beginning to use parallel requests to retrieve all inline images for a document.

Another way to improve client speed is to cache-request documents and then use the If-Modified-Since field to re-retrieve the document *only* if it has been modified since the local copy was last saved. The If-Modified-Since header is relatively new. Most popular clients implement caching by doing a HEAD request, looking at the Last-Modified time, and then doing a GET if necessary. The If-Modified-Since field boils this down to a single call.

TIP

It is possible for a client to get hung up and wait indefinitely for a server to respond. In order to avoid this, you should code time-outs that tell the client to return an error if the server doesn't respond within a specified amount of time. (The error should be something along the lines of "Requested document not available.")

A more unusual approach is to have the client "pre-fetch" all of the children for a current page. In other words, while you read a document, your browser is busy retrieving all of the linked documents so that they are

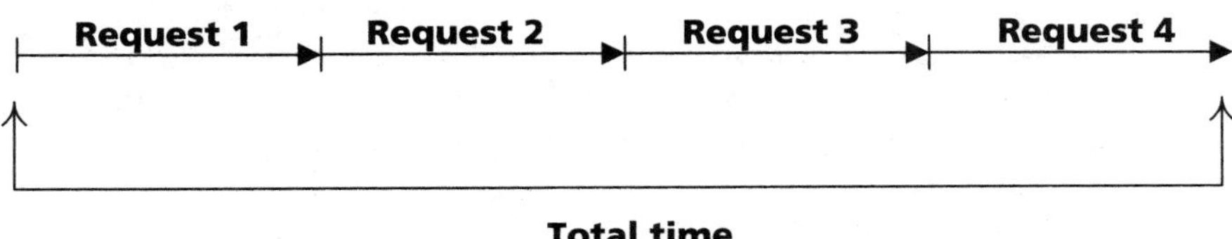

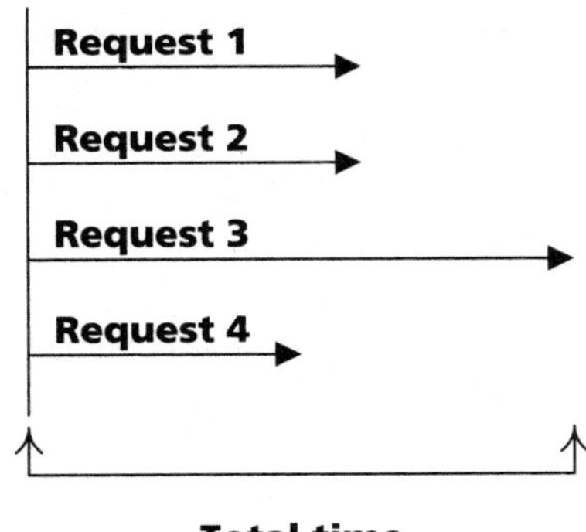

Figure 12-1 The download time for serial requests (top) is the sum of each request's download time. The download time for a parallel request (bottom) is the maximum of the download times for each request.

available when you select one of the links. The disadvantage of pre-fetching, of course, is that you may not view all the pages that are retrieved, thereby taking up network resources and CPU time unnecessarily. This approach has not been implemented in any of the popular clients, but it may be an acceptable trade-off.

NOTE

Such a trade-off may be acceptable under certain situations. If your network resources are expendable (probably true if you are on a T1 line, but not if you are on a 14.4 line), the trade-off might be worthwhile. It may also be worth it if your users spend at least five to ten seconds on each page before going to the next one. That gives the browser enough time to pre-fetch the other documents.

These features can add significantly to the complexity of your software and, in so doing, take you longer to implement, but they are issues that you should consider when implementing a client.

12.2.3 Output Media

As we mentioned in Section 7.2, you should not write HTML code with only one browser in mind, because there are so many browsers available. Indeed, one of HTML's design goals is to be medium-independent. Specifically, at the start of Chapter 7 we quoted HTML 3.0 specifications, pointing out that HTML is "designed to allow rendering on a very wide range of devices from clunky teletypes to terminals, DOS, Windows, Macs, and high-end workstations, as well as nonvisual media such as speech and Braille." In other words, one of HTML's design goals is to be able to mark up text that can be rendered appropriately on any client or medium. For all intents and purposes, it shouldn't matter if an HTML document is being rendered onscreen or into speech, or even into an interpretive dance.

Currently, the only real browsers are either text-based or graphics-based, but don't restrict yourself to thinking about browsers in this limited fashion. Obviously, the interpretive dance idea is a bit extreme, but only because it is beyond what seems reasonable as a means of expressing HTML, not because it isn't technically possible. Rendering an HTML document into speech is already technologically feasible.

Therefore, when you are writing a client, you need to think about how it should render HTML, i.e., exactly how to render each HTML element. For example, the Strong element might be spoken with a louder voice, or might be danced with exaggerated motions in our two examples.

NOTE

While the HTML 3.0 specs mention rendering HTML into voice, they never mention rendering it into interpretive dance. Nonetheless, there really are no limitations on what media can be used to render it.

12.3 Design Modules

When you are designing your client, you'll need code to handle three types of functionalities: HTTP data retrieval, data processing, and the user interface. That means your client program should have at least three code modules, one to handle each of the three functional areas.

12.3.1 HTTP Data Retrieval

All clients need code to handle data retrieval via HTTP. In Section 6.3, we presented a simple script, http_get.pl, which took a machine name, a partial URI, and a port number and proceeded to retrieve the resource. You could build upon that script to write your client. Once you understand network programming and HTTP, the HTTP handling routine isn't technically difficult. There are, however, a few issues to address.

If you are trying to optimize your client's performance, you might consider making this module a separate process that communicates with the main client via sockets. It is common to write small programs whose sole job it is to make HTTP requests and receive the responses. These programs are commonly called *fetcher daemons*. By making this a separate process, you can spend your time fine-tuning this module to produce a quick, lightweight program that does exactly what you need it to do. This architecture is especially useful if you are going to be issuing parallel requests, because then it is easy to ask each fetcher daemon to make a separate request. Depending on how many requests you want your client to be able to make and how quickly you want your client to process requests, you can use several fetcher daemons to make all requests in parallel.

12.3.2 Data Processing

Data-processing functions can range from GIF-rendering programs to code that determines how HTML elements should be rendered. Data-processing modules get their input from the HTTP module and make requests to the HTTP module. For example, the data-processing module makes requests to the HTTP module to retrieve inline images in an HTML document.

The data-processing module also can be used to do content analysis. For example, you could use it to analyze HTML documents to see if they comply with the HTML specifications or to determine some quantitative measure of how marked-up they are. You can also use a data-processing module for tasks that are not limited to HTML documents, such as indexing the content of objects and spell-checking.

In summary, data-processing modules are used to process the data retrieved by the HTTP module before passing it off to the user interface module.

12.3.3 User Interface

It is pretty clear that a client wouldn't be useful if it didn't have some output format (display/reporting) or provide a means for the user to control what the client is doing (interaction). You provide the means of interaction between the user and the client in the user interface module.

Displaying/Reporting

One of the important functions of the user interface module is displaying information back to the user (for example, displaying a rendered version of retrieved objects) and telling the user what information was retrieved.

In the case of browsers, the display portion of the code takes the document with its rendering instructions from the data-processing module and displays it to the user. Display actions include building a window and all the graphical elements necessary to display the object in a GUI, displaying the formatted text within a text-based user interface, outputting the data through a voice synthesizer for audio-based browsers, and dumping a PostScript file to a printer.

For wanderers and specialized agents, the display code is responsible for generating the report and providing reports to the user. If you are using a specialized agent to do HTML verification, it could consist of a formatted list of errors saved to a file. The Wanderer outputs a list of all the sites it visits and an index for each site to a file. Obviously, the content that your wanderer or agent outputs depends very much on the actual function of the program. But no matter its functionality, it is critical for users to get the information that they need in a usable format. For example, an agent designed to report how many times a company's name is mentioned in a list of pages should have a display that makes it easy to find that information in the report. People should not have to search through pages and pages of output to find the information they need.

Data should also be presented in a way that makes sense to users. If your code is designed to check HTML documents for errors, the error reports should clearly identify the problem, the location of the problem, and a solution. If you write a great client that finds every error in a document but generates baffling error messages, it won't be very useful.

Interaction

The second part of the user interface deals with how the user controls the client. This can involve how the user navigates the Web and requests resources, to how the user defines the scope of a wanderer's search. A lot of issues revolve around making the interaction between the user and client easier. For example, if you are writing a browser, you need to provide a way for users to indicate that they want to follow a link. Browsers do this in different ways. In Mosaic, you click on a highlighted piece of text. In Lynx, you press the cursor keys to move on top of the text and then hit the Enter key. In the LineMode Browser, you use the keyboard to type in a number corresponding to the link. You could provide some other mechanism, such as speech. The question, of course, is how can the user best navigate the Web and request specific resources.

If you are writing a wanderer or specialized agent, fewer issues are involved because there is substantially less interaction between the user and client. However, you still have to decide what aspects of the wanderer or specialized agent's behavior should be controlled by the user, and by what mechanism the user is to direct the client's behavior. For example, you may need a way for the user to define the scope of a wanderer's search.

Regardless of what type of client you are writing, a lot of thought has to go into the means of interaction between the user and the client. Providing a usable, intuitive interface is just as important as providing usable, understandable output. No matter what features you have "under the hood," people won't use your client if they can't figure out how to use it.

12.4 Robots, Spiders, and Wanderers

You should be warned that writing a browser can often be a time-consuming process. Since there are so many interesting things you can do with a simple wanderer, you may be tempted to play around and write your own.

There are a number of reasons to write a wanderer. First and foremost is the original reason wanderers were created—to measure the Web. Another reason is to generate indexes of portions of the Web, such as those generated by Wandex and the Web Crawler. Other purposes include searching for specific content or mapping the topology of the Web. You can also use a wanderer or specialized agent to generate reports on the average transfer times for documents and the distribution of different Content-Types on the Web (i.e., how many GIFs are available compared to TIFFs or HTML documents). And these are just a few of the things you can do with wanderers.

If you write a wanderer of your own, write a responsible program that does not adversely affect other sites or your network. Carefully considering design issues will not only help you write responsible programs, but will also help you avoid common mistakes.

12.4.1 Traversal Search Methods

When you write a wanderer, you must first decide how you want it to traverse the Web. In other words, you must decide which documents to retrieve and in what order to retrieve them. Related to this is the issue of how to discover new documents and know when documents have changed (so you can update information you store that reflects updates). The first main issue is defining the *scope* of your wanderer's search and what documents your wanderer should be looking at.

The most common technique for defining a wanderer's scope is to have a list of *starting points*. You provide this list to the wanderer and it follows the links from these pages to find new documents. Basically, you are providing the wanderer with the URLs for the top documents of various subsections of the Web that you want to search. Usually, you also specify limitations on how deep the wander should travel from these starting points. A common technique is to place limits on how many levels from the starting point the wanderer can go. Once it gets to a page that is at the limit, it does not follow the links on that page. These limitations are like a leash that restricts how far out the wanderer can go but not how wide the search from the starting point can be.

Providing a *restrict list* is another way of limiting a wanderer's search. A restrict list usually specifies a set of regular expressions that restrict which URLs the wanderer can follow. When the wanderer finds a link to follow, it finds out if the referenced document is on the restrict list. If it is on the list, it follows the link; but if it is not on the list, it does not follow the link. In this way, you can see to it that the wanderer searches only one or more specified sites or subsets of a site. Think of building a fence around your property to restrict where your dog can go. The fence is not defined in terms of a distance from a central point, but instead is defined functionally.

Once the scope of the search has been defined and you have a few starting points, you have to figure how the wanderer is going to get from document to document. Once it retrieves one document, which document does it go to next? There are many search methods, each with its advantages and disadvantages. If you are looking for more information about search methods or explanations about searches, any book on algorithms should have more details.

A *depth-first search* is one of the simplest search algorithms. In a depth-first search, you try to get to the *leaf nodes* of the structure you are searching. In math terms, leaf nodes are the nodes of a tree that does not have any children. In Web terms, leaf nodes are documents that do not contain any links. When you are at a document, you choose one link and then perform a depth-first search on the document being linked to. You are done with the search of the document when no other links are there to follow. The key concept is to completely explore a single link before exploring the remaining links, if there are any.

If you were using a browser, a depth-first search would be the same as constantly following links on pages until you can't go any further, then backing up one page and following another link on that page. Depth-first searches are usually a bad idea when it comes to Web wandering, because the Web has some fairly deep structures. Once you get into one, you may never get out. In particular, a program can get stuck in infinitely deep trees created by CGI scripts. This happens when you encounter a CGI script that generates a document with a link back to the CGI, which then generates a new document. When a wanderer finds one of these infinite trees, it gets stuck because it keeps trying to get to the leaf nodes that don't exist.

There are ways to avoid infinite structures. One of the simplest is to have your wanderer recognize from the URLs of the documents that it is exploring when it is in a very deep structure. The URLs in an infinite structure tend to look the same. Usually, they are all the same except for small derivations in the last portion of the searchpath or maybe derivations in the query string. Since they tend to look the same, you can try to build heuristics into a wanderer which recognize infinite-structure URLs. The original Wanderer used a depth-first search. Matthew came up with such an algorithm and termed it "boredom" because it appeared as if the Wanderer got bored when it went too deep into a structure.

Another method of avoiding infinite structures is to use a *breadth-first search*. In a breadth-first search, you explore everything at one level before exploring the next level. On a page with three links on it, for example, you follow one and process that document without following any of the document's links, then you back up and follow the second link, process that document, back up again, follow the third link and process that document, and so on. Once all the links on one level have been followed, you can start exploring the links in the documents you just retrieved. This guarantees getting all the shallow things first. If you encounter a deep branch that goes all the way off into infinity, you won't get bogged down in it.

A breadth-first search also has the advantage of enabling you to find the shortest path between two documents. If you start at document A and use a breadth-first search to find document B, you can be assured that the first path you find between A and B is the shortest path. Breadth-first searching is usually the best way to implement wanderers, because it is easy to implement and has most of the desired functionality. On the other hand, if you are trying to traverse a specific site or set of documents that are deeply nested, it takes a long time for a breadth-first search to reach the deep documents. That is the disadvantage of breadth-first searches.

Just as a depth-first search can get caught by an infinitely deep structure, a breadth-first search can get caught by an infinitely broad structure. But in terms of the Web, infinitely broad structures are easy to get around because they imply infinitely long HTML documents. In order to detect such a document, a Wanderer should place a limit on the amount of data that it can read in for a single document. This way, you can't ever get an "infinitely long" HTML document.

12.4.2 Conscientious Use of Resources

Another really important concept to consider when you write a client is making sure that the client is conscientious about its use of resources. A client takes up memory and processor speed on the machine running it. In addition, because the client uses a network to retrieve documents, it takes up some bandwidth on the network connection. Finally, because the client makes requests to other servers, it uses the server's processor, memory, and network resources. Depending on how fast you can write your client (using parallel requests and fetcher daemons to produce tens of requests per second), it is very possible to cripple a server by saturating its load, memory, and network resources.

Even if the server does not crash because of the load, you can tie up the machine so that it no longer can perform tasks until the load diminishes. Doing this to someone else's server without their permission is unacceptable. Bombarding a machine with requests so it cannot function is called *spamming*. It is also called a "denial of service attack." It is very possible to cripple a server simply by designing a fast wanderer. Therefore, in order to design a responsible wanderer, it is important to take all these issues into consideration. You may even have to limit the performance of your client so you don't abuse the resources on your machine or the servers your client contacts.

NOTE

As a point of reference, we found in our testing that a Sparc-5 with 24MB of memory running NCSA httpd could handle more than a thousand connections per minute if the network connection was not the limiting factor. However, this number of connections put the machine under an extreme load. It was not useful for anything else and couldn't effectively serve any processor-intensive requests (i.e., requests that call CGI scripts).

You can do a couple things to make a wanderer more responsible. First, you can limit how often the robot makes requests from a single site per minute. This prevents the wanderer from spamming any sites, regardless of how fast it is. Of course, the wanderer may have to sit idle for some portion of each minute, but that is the way it has to be. Better for a wanderer to take extra time to complete a traversal than for it to irritate site administrators.

It is also advisable to make use of the HEAD method or the If-Modified-Since header with the GET method to determine the document's Content-Type and see whether the document has changed since the last time you retrieved it. If your wanderer has no use for images, use the HEAD method to make sure that you don't request any images. This really helps conserve bandwidth when you need to transfer data.

Besides these suggestions, there is a proposal to create a standard known as the "Robot Exclusion Principle." With this standard, site administrators can define which robots are allowed to access their sites and which documents they are allowed to access. The idea is for every site to provide a standard resource, **/robots.txt**, that every robot looks for before it makes queries. This file would specify whether or not the robot could make further requests. The Robot Exclusion Principle is detailed at Martijn Koster's home page site. We suggest that wanderers conform to the Robot Exclusion Principle. We also suggest that site administrators only restrict robots that have proven to be irresponsible. Plenty of very useful wanderers are out there, and it would be a shame to restrict all of them from doing their jobs.

Robot Exclusion Principle
http://www.netgen.com/book/robots

12.5 Specialized Agent Example: Niftiness Agent

In Chapter 6, we presented a very simple client for retrieving documents and viewing their raw data. In this section, we show you how to build on that code to create a specialized agent that retrieves documents and generates statistical information based on those documents. For each document, nifty.pl (see Listing 12-1) returns information about the length of the document, how many links it contains, and how many images it has. Based on these numbers, it calculates a "niftiness number" for the document. From experience, we've seen that a niftiness number does a reasonable job of quantifying the look and feel of documents on the Web. That is, documents that have close niftiness numbers tend to look and feel similar. We don't contend that this number is an actual measure of the quality of a document; it is simply an interesting example of what you can do with a specialized agent.

The nifty.pl code shown in Listing 12-1 calls upon three other code modules and an example showing the output of the niftiness agent: user_interface.pl (see Listing 12-2), http_get.pl (see Listing 6-4), and analyze-html.pl (see Listing 12-3).

Listing 12–1. **Nifty.pl, which returns statistical information about documents**

```
#!/usr/bin/perl
# File Name: nifty.pl

# This is the main program, but it simply calls on all the other programs
require 'analyze-html.pl';
require 'http_get.pl';
require 'user_interface.pl';

# Run the main program.
&run_user_interface();
```

Listing 12–2. **User_interface.pl, which handles all the user interaction**

```
# File Name: user_interface.pl

sub run_user_interface
```

```
{
    $next_URL = &find_starting_URL();

    while (1)
    {
     &fulfill_request($next_URL);
     $next_URL = &prompt_user();
     $next_URL = &handle_response($next_URL);
    }
}

sub find_starting_URL
{

    # Allow the user to specify the first document to retrieve
    # on the command line.
    if($ARGV[0])
    {
     return $ARGV[0];
    }

    # Otherwise use the WWW_HOME environment variable
    elsif($ENV{'WWW_HOME'})
    {
     return $ENV{'WWW_HOME'};
    }

    # Otherwise default to the netgen home page
    else
    {
     return ("http://www.netgen.com/");
    }
}
```

```
sub fulfill_request
{
    # The URL to retrieve is passed as input.
    local($url) = @_;

    # Keep track of where you've been
    push(@url_history, $url);

    # Initialize variables
    $head = "";
    $body = "";

    # Print a message out.
    print("Fulfilling $url...\n");

    # Fetch the document
    ($head, $body) = &get_document($url);

    # If there was an error, just return
    if ($head eq "0")
    {
     return;
    }

    # Check and see if a Content-Type was returned
    if ($head =~ /Content-Type:\s*(.+)/i)
    {
     $type = $1;

     # If so, display it
     &display($type, $url, $body);
    }

    # Otherwise display an unknown type
```

```
    else
    {
     &display("unknown", $url, $body, $url);
    }
}

sub get_document
{
    local($url) = @_;

    # Pick off the parts of the URL
    ($protocol, $host, $port, $path) = &process_url($url);

    # If the protocol isn't HTTP, return an error
    if ($protocol  !~ /http/i)
    {
     print "Nifty can only retrieve documents via HTTP.\n";
     return 0;

    }

    # If a host was specified, grab the document
    if($host)
    {
     ($head, $body) = &HTTP_get($host, $port, $path);
     ($head, $body);
    }

    # Otherwise, return an error
    else
    {
     return (0);
    }
}
```

```
sub display
{
    local($type, $url, $body) = @_;

    if($type eq 'text/html')
    {
     &display_html_document($url, $body);
    }

    else
    {
     print "Can not display $type document type\n";
    }

}

sub display_html_document
{
    # The URL and body to the document are passed
    # as arguments
    local($url, $body) = @_;

    # Clear the page
    print 'clear';

    # Print the URL for the document
    print("URL: $url\n\n");

    # Grab the title for the document and print it.
    $title = &get_title($body);
    print(&underline("Title: \"$title\"\"$title\""));

    # Find all the links in the document and print out
    # how many there are
```

```
@links=();
@links = &get_links($body);
$nlinks = $#links+1;
print("Document contains $nlinks links\n");

# Find all the heading elements
$nheadings = ($body =~ s/<h\d/<h\d/gi);
print("Document contains $nheadings headings\n");

# Find all the images in the document and print out
# how many there are.
$nimages = ($body =~ s/<img/<img/gi);
print("Document contains $nimages images\n");

# Calculate the niftiness
$nifty = 60 * $nlinks + 40 * $nimages + 30 * $nheadings;
print "Niftiness: $nifty\n";

print("\n\n");

# Print the list of links
print(&underline("List of Links"));
for $linkn (0..$#links)
{
 $link = $links[$linkn];

 # Come up with the full URL for relative URLs
 $realurl = &relative_url($url, $link);

 # Update the array
 $links[$linkn] = $realurl;

 print("$linkn) $realurl\n");
}
```

```
    print("Type the number of a URL to visit it\n");
    print("Type \"g URL\" to go to a specified URL\n");
    print "Type \"b\" to go back a URL\n\n";
}


# Print out a prompt for the user and read in the response
sub prompt_user
{
    local($answer);

    print("--> ");
    chop($answer = (<STDIN>));
    $answer;
}

# Interpret the user's response
sub handle_response
{
    local($response) = @_;

    # Grab the command and any options to the command
    ($c, @opts) = split(' ', $response);

    # If the command was "g", then go to the specified URL
    if($c eq "g")
    {
     return($opts[0]);
    }

    # If the command was "b", then go back to the last URL
    elsif ($c eq "b")
```

```
    {
     pop(@url_history);
     $new_url = pop(@url_history);
     print "Fulfilling request: $new_url\n";
     return($new_url);
    }

    # If the user specified a number, return the specified link
    elsif($c !~ /\D/)
    {
     return(&relative_url($url, $links[$c]));
    }
}

# Underline a piece of text
sub underline {
    local($_) = @_;

    @unders=();
    split;
    for $w (@_)
    {
     push(@unders, "-" x length($w));
    }
    $l1 = join(" ", @_);
    $l2 = join(" ", @unders);
    "$l1\n$l2\n";
}

1;
```

Listing 12–3. **Analyze-html.pl, which handles all the HTML processing**

```
# File Name: analyze-html.pl

sub process_url {
    # Returns protocol, site, port, path
    local($url) = @_;

    #

    print" Processing: $url...\n";


    # Pick apart the CISS URL format
    if ($url =~ /([^:]+):\/\/([^\/]+)(\/.*)/)
    {
     $proto = $1;
     $siteport = $2;
     $path = $3;

     print "URL: $url\n";
     print "Proto: $proto Siteport: $siteport Path: $path\n";
     $port = 0;
     ($site, $port) = split(':', $siteport);

     # If no port was specified, pick it off.
     if(!$port)
     {
         $site = $siteport;

         if ($proto =~ /http/i)
         {
          $port = 80;
         }
     }
```

```
        # Split the path into its elements
        @path = split ("/", $path);

        # Change all the .. and . portions of the URL
        $pn = 0;
        for (@path)
        {
            if($_ eq '..')
            {
             splice(@path, $pn-1, 3);
             $pn -=2;
            }
            if($_ eq '.')
            {
             splice(@path, $pn, 1);
             $pn -=1;
            }
            $pn++;
        }
        $path = '/'.join('/', @path);

        ($proto, $site, $port, $path);
    }
}

# Find the title in the given HTML document
sub get_title
{
    # Pass the document in as an argument
    local($document) = @_;

    $*=1;
    # Remove all the new line characters so the string
    # is easier to search
```

```
        $document =~ s/\n/ /g;

        # See if the document has a title element
        if($document =~ /<title>/i)
        {
         $title = $';
         $title =~ /<\/title>/i;
         $title = $';
        }

        # If not send back "No Title"
        else
        {
         $title="No Title";
        }

        return ($title);
    }

    # Find all the links in the document
    sub get_links
    {
        # Pass the document in as an argument
        local($document) = @_;

        # Initialize the list of anchors
        @anchs = ();

        # Delete all the new lines to make the document
        # easier to search
        $document =~ s/\n/ /g;

        undef $known;
```

```
    # Find all of the links within the document
    while (($document =~ /<a\s+[^>]*href\s*=\s*\"([^\"]+)\"[^>]*>/ig) ||
        ($document =~ /<a\s+[^>]*href\s*=\s*([^\"\'\s]+)[^>]*>/ig))

    {
     if (!$known{$1})
     {
         push(@anchs, $1);
         $known{$1} = "yes";
     }
    }

    # Return the array
    return(@anchs);
}

# Convert a relative link into a real link
sub relative_url
{
    # Take the current document's URL and the relative URL
    # as arguments
    local($current, $rellink) = @_;

    # Use $url to store the new full URL
    local($url);

    # If the URL is full just use it.
    if($rellink =~ /:\/\//)
    {
        $url = $rellink;
    }

    # Otherwise if the URL begins with a /, just append
    # the scheme, hostname, and port
```

```
    elsif ($rellink =~ /^\//)
    {
     # Find the scheme, hostname, and port of the current
     # document
       $current =~ /^[^:]+:\/\/[^\/]+/;

     # Form the new URL
       $url = $&.$rellink;
    }
    # Otherwise, form the full URL based on the current URL's path
    else
    {
        (@parts) = split(/\//, $current);
        $np = ($current=~/\/$/) ? $#parts : $#parts-1;
        $url = join('/', (@parts[0..$np], $rellink));
    }
    $url;
}

1;
```

The following is a sample of the output you get when you run nifty.pl and fetch two pages:

```
> nifty.pl
Fulfilling http://www.netgen.com/...
Processing: http://www.netgen.com/...
URL: http://www.netgen.com/
Proto: http Siteport: www.netgen.com Path: /
creating socket to www.netgen.com:80...
binding...
connecting...
connected.
returning with new filehandle chatsymbol000001
```

```
URL: http://www.netgen.com/

Title: " net.Genesis Corporation Home Page "
------ - ----------- ----------- ---- ---- -
Document contains 12 links
Document contains 0 headings
Document contains 13 images
Niftiness: 1240


List of Links
---- -- -----
0) http://www.netgen.com/whatsnew/whatsnew.html
1) http://www.netgen.com/corpinfo/corpinfo.html
2) http://www.netgen.com/products/products.html
3) http://www.netgen.com/consult/consult.html
4) http://www.netgen.com/infoarea/infoarea.html
5) http://www.netgen.com/archive/archive.html
6) http://www.netgen.com/comments/comments.html
7) http://www.netgen.com/
8) http://www.netgen.com/search.html
9) http://www.netgen.com/cgi/netgen-thread
10) http://www.netgen.com/help.html
11) http://www.netgen.com/help.html
Type the number of a URL to visit it
Type "g URL" to go to a specified URL
Type "b" to go back a URL

--> 1

Fulfilling http://www.netgen.com/corpinfo/corpinfo.html...
Processing: http://www.netgen.com/corpinfo/corpinfo.html...
URL: http://www.netgen.com/corpinfo/corpinfo.html
Proto: http Siteport: www.netgen.com Path: /corpinfo/corpinfo.html
```

```
creating socket to www.netgen.com:80...
binding...
connecting...
connected.
returning with new filehandle chatsymbol000002

URL: http://www.netgen.com/corpinfo/corpinfo.html

Title: " net.Genesis Corporate Information "
------ - ----------- --------- ----------- -
Document contains 7 links
Document contains 1 headings
Document contains 7 images
Niftiness: 730


List of Links
---- -- -----
0) http://www.netgen.com/people/bfeld.html
1) http://www.netgen.com/people/rajat.html
2) http://www.netgen.com/people/mcutler.html
3) http://www.netgen.com/people/erichard.html
4) http://www.netgen.com/people/mkgray.html
5) http://www.netgen.com/people/nanette.html
6) http://www.netgen.com/people/nanette.email.html
Type the number of a URL to visit it
Type "g URL" to go to a specified URL
Type "b" to go back a URL

-->
```

Writing a client can be great fun. However, you have to approach it with caution. Make sure that throughout your design and implementation you are being conscientious of the resources being made available to you. Unfortunately, it doesn't take too much—either through simple naïveté or genuine maliciousness—to turn a simple client/wanderer into a "Web hammer" (as Matthew calls them) that will bring down sites or render them useless. So long as you are thinking about these issues, writing a client can be extremely educational and useful as well. Just as CGI allows you to fill in the holes left by servers, writing your own server will allow you to get the exact functionality that you want out of your browser.

CHAPTER 13

Writing an HTTP Server

CHAPTER AT A GLANCE

This chapter is about HTTP servers: what they are and how you can write them. We define and describe three server models (blocking, multiplexing, and forking), and provide you with sample code for each model. We also show you how to provide additional capabilities such as proxy and caching services. You will find that once you have the basic server code in place, a few modifications are all you need to create other models or add functionality.

If you're wondering why you would ever want to write your own server, there are three reasons that come immediately to mind:

- **To add functionality.** There are many things a server can do that might not have been coded into your existing server program.
- **To speed things up.** You might want to alter how the server works so that you can speed it up. You can do this either by optimizing the server for your site, based on specific information about how your site will be used, or you can make general performance improvements, which would improve the speed regardless of the site it was used on. We will show you several examples of how you can improve the performance of servers in general.
- **To port your server to a new platform.** It is possible that you might want to make an existing server available on a currently unsupported platform. (We don't go into any detail about porting to new platforms.)

REQUISITES

Detailed understanding of HTTP/1.0 as described in Chapters 5 and 6.

Experience with programming concepts of the perl programming language.

Understanding of UNIX sockets.

Writing a server of your own is pretty difficult to do unless you really understand HTTP and sockets. But it's worth it to have your own server. Throughout this book, we've discussed how current implementations of HTTP servers handle different features. We've given you hints as well as concrete examples of things that servers can do, but don't do by default. Well, here is your chance to have a server that does all of these things. Do you think content negotiation is a useful feature but don't want to have to use a CGI script to implement it? It sounds like a great feature to have in a server. Maybe you want to use the PUT and POST methods as they were originally intended. Or maybe you just want your server to automatically track its own usage and do its own log analysis, instead of having to run programs on the logs to generate these reports. All of these things are possible when you understand HTTP.

Unless you are bold and adventurous, don't write your own Web server from scratch. Instead, get the source code to one of the existing servers (the source code for both the CERN and NCSA HTTP servers are available), and extend it to handle these new features. There are a couple of big advantages of doing this:

- You begin with a debugged system that already takes care of all the basic functionality of a Web server. You can focus on making only the changes you want and not having to bother with the rest of the code.
- The CERN httpd is built on top of a library of code called libwww that handles many of the general features needed to implement Web clients and servers. You gain an advantage by using this library, because the library itself evolves to keep up with the standards and you only have to upgrade to the new library to keep your code up to date.
- Both the CERN httpd and NCSA httpd code are in the public domain. You can take this source code, modify it however you like, redistribute it, and charge for your version of the software.

On the other hand, there are some definite disadvantages to modifying preexisting code:

- When you modify preexisting code, you must understand how it works before you can make the existing tools do what you want them to do. This is not an easy task with a large set of code, no matter how many comments the code contains. Unfortunately, the NCSA httpd and CERN httpd source code are particularly difficult to understand. Regardless of how many changes you want to make, you have to spend a lot of time just trying to figure out what needs changing.

- If your primary interest is fully understanding HTTP and experimenting with real applications, it is probably easier to start on a smaller scale with code that you understand completely. This way, you can focus on experimenting instead of figuring out how to fit your changes into a preexisting framework.
- If you plan to make significant modifications to the code, you might be better off starting from scratch. Existing servers are usually designed around a set of assumptions about how the server will be used. If you need to change major design elements, you will find it hard to work your changes into a system that wasn't designed to do what you want it to do.

In this chapter, we present a series of code samples to help you understand the issues involved in writing an HTTP server. The code presented here is flexible and easy to understand. You can extend and experiment with it. We will show you three server models: blocking, forking, multiplexing. By reading the embedded comments, you should be able to understand everything you need to know to modify the program. In fact, we will show you simple changes that drastically alter the functional behavior of the code. You don't always have to make major modifications to have a major impact. (The accompanying sidebar offers definitions of the terms that we use repeatedly in the code.)

13.1 Server Models: Handling Connections

As we discussed in Chapters 5 and 6, HTTP involves a four-step process: open connection, request, response, and close connection. What we didn't mention is that there are many different ways for the server to handle all of the connections and requests that it gets. If a server was only getting one connection at a time and was given enough time to respond to the client and close the connection before the next connection came, there would be no reason to have different server models. However, nearly every site out there receives multiple requests, at least at some point during the day, so there needs to be a way of dealing with multiple requests. Different server models deal with multiple connections in different ways. In terms of performance, they deal with very light loads in virtually the same way, but under higher loads the performance of a server depends very much on which model it is using to process requests.

Some Code Terminology

Following are definitions of the terms we use in the code in this chapter.

- **file handle:** The name the system uses to identify each file. For every file handle there is a corresponding file number.
- **file number:** A positive integer associated with every file handle you have open in a program. The positive integer uniquely defines the file handle.
- **bitstring:** A sequence of 1 and 0 characters. For example, 01001001 is a bitstring in which the 0 character is 0, the first character is 1, the second and third characters are 0, etc. In the context of our code, we will use bitstrings to keep track of information about the different files that are currently open. We do this by associating each file number with its respective character in the string. For example, if bitstrings were being used to indicate which files had data to be read, the example we gave above (01001001) would mean that the files corresponding to numbers 1, 4, and 7 would have data to be read in (because those files have the value 1 in the bitstring), while the others would not.
- **bitmask:** Very similar to a bitstring. It contains the exact same data, but in a more compact format. A bitmask is a sequence of bits. On standard operating systems, there are at least 8 bits per character, which means that the example above used $8 \times 8 = 64$ bits to store this data. Since bitstrings can only contain 1 and 0 characters, it is trivial to transform a bitstring into a bitmask. The above bitstring, 01001001, would translate into a single byte of data (8 bits) whose binary representation is 01001001. Just to emphasize the difference here, if you tried to print out the bitmask version of a character, you would only see one character, ASCII 73. All the same data is here, but it is in a much more compressed format. In our code, therefore, we use bitmasks to actually store and pass around data. We convert bitmasks to bitstrings only when we need to deal with data in a more manageable format.

In order to explain the differences between the server models, we are going to revisit the "this guy" model of client-server interactions that we brought up in Chapter 2. If you remember, "this guy" is a server in the model. Much like a bank teller, this guy waits for clients to come to him and make requests. It is this guy's job to listen to requests and fulfill them. The difference between the models is how this guy deals with multiple clients who make requests at the same time.

The *blocking model* is the simplest model. Under this model, this guy gets a connection, listens to the client, and leaves the window to take care of the client's request. If any other clients come up to the window during this time, they have to wait for this guy to finish with the first client to be served. This model is the most similar to what happens in the real world. As you can probably guess, if this guy can't serve the client requests quickly enough a line of clients waiting to be served forms. In addition, just like in the real world, if clients have to wait in line too long, they give up. In computer terms, the client will "time-out with an error." The typical time that clients wait before timing out is 60 seconds. Obviously, this method is not very useful for servers that expect high loads, and that is why none of the major HTTP servers use the blocking model.

The *multiplexing model* is a little more complicated. It starts out the same as the blocking model: a client comes up to this guy, makes a request, and this guy attempts to fill the request. However, unlike the blocking model, this guy attempts to help new clients who come to the window as well as clients he's already helping. Basically, this guy does a little bit of work for the first client, a little for the second, then goes back to the first and continues like this until one of the jobs is done. The multiplexing model has roots in every day life. It is what happens when several people ask you to do things for them and you try to do all of them at the same time. This model does allow the server to handle multiple connections at one time, but as the load increases, it takes longer and longer for each connection to be completed, because the server is trying to do so many other things at once. Because time is usually of the essence, this method isn't used much either.

The *forking model* is a little more complicated. In this model, a client comes to this guy, but before the client can make a request, this guy makes a copy of himself in order to handle the new request. The clone then goes off, handles the request, and gives the response back to the client. After the clone has handled the request, it disappears. In this model, the sole job of this guy is to make copies of himself to handle each incoming connection. In case you've never tried, making a copy of oneself is not a fast process. Under heavy loads, the server can get slowed down by having to make so many copies of itself.

Besides, computer memory can become a limited resource when many copies of the server are all in existence at the same time. Imagine this guy and all his clones in a room of finite size. If there are too many clones, the room gets overcrowded. Fortunately, computers have a way of dealing with this: virtual memory. Although the computer may have a limited amount of physical memory—typically between 8 and 64MB of RAM—it can store the data for processes on disk when the physical memory gets full. However, once a process is swapped out—that is, stored on disk—it can't make any progress until it gets swapped back in. Going back to our example, we can think of virtual memory as a back room that copies can go into if the main room gets too full. However, when the copies are back there, they can't do any work.

The forking model is one of the most popular models used by HTTP servers. Both CERN httpd and NCSA httpd use the forking model. If you are running a forking server, memory becomes a major resource—the more memory, the better. The server shouldn't be swapping in and out of memory all the time, because it slows things down too much. In an ideal world, the server should never swap in and out.

The *process pool* is the most complex of the four models. It was designed to make up for some of the weaknesses of the forking model. When a process pool server starts up, the first thing it does is create a bunch of fetcher children to help it fulfill requests. Basically, this is like this guy asking a bunch of his friends to come help out by doing some work for him. The friends either know how to do everything that this guy does or they can just know how to do very specific tasks. In other words, unlike in the forking model, the friends don't have to be full copies of this guy. The advantage here is you can create small processes that handle specialized jobs very quickly. For example, if you know that your server performs large numbers of file accesses, you can create small and fast fetcher children to handle file access.

Another big difference between the process pool model and the forking model is that the fetcher children can remain around for the life of the server. Unlike the forking model, time is not spent creating a new clone for each new request. After all the children have been created, this guy begins accepting connections. When a client makes a request of a process pool server, this guy handles the request and assigns processes to its fetcher children, when appropriate. NCSA's httpd 1.4 and Netscape Netsite use the process pool model and reports performance gains under high loads because of it.

13.1.1 Blocking Server

Since the simplest of the servers is the blocking server, we will start there. You can use the code shown in Listing 13-1 as a library to implement a functional blocking HTTP server. This code is meant to be used as a package within another block of code (we'll get to that shortly). It takes care of all of the requests and calls a routine `handle_request` to write the response out to the client. In other words, you can use this piece of code to do a lot of the low-level HTTP handling when you are writing your own server.

NOTE

A *library, or package,* is a predefined piece of code that you can use when you are writing your own programs. In other words, it is one or more functions that you can make calls to from your code. Libraries or packages can't stand on their own (i.e., you can't *run* a library or package). Instead, parts of them get used by other programs.

Listing 13–1. **Blocking HTTP server library**

```
#!/usr/bin/perl
# File name: nghttpd.pl
# Description: A blocking model of the nghttpd server package

# Declare this to be a package called 'nghttpd'
package nghttpd;

# First we set some initial variables.  These definitions will
# take place when the main program requires this file.

# We'll use $nghttp_debug to determine if we should print out
# messages as the code runs.  This value can be changed by
# an argument to nghttp.

$nghttp_debug = 0;

# Make I/O unbuffered.  This means that every time you print
# it will automatically write the string to the file.  Usually
# the string will only be written out after you send a newline
# character.  We will be using this multiple times throughout
# this code.
```

```
$|=1;

# Pick an initial file handle.  Successive file handles will be
# NGAAB, NGAAC, etc.  This variable could have been chosen to be
# anything.

$fh = 'NGAAA';

# Set a couple response codes.  These will be returned by the
# handle_connection routine when it is done to indicate what
# should happen with the connection.

$CLOSE_CONNECTION = 17;
$KEEP_OPEN = 22;

# Set a time-out parameter. This specifies how many seconds the
# connection should remain open if handle_connection does not
# explicitly say what it should do.

$TIMEOUT = 60;

# This is the main body of the Web server.  It makes a call back
# to a function called main'handle_connection (the main' can be
# left out if the function is defined in the main module of the
# code anyway) which is responsible for actually doing anything
# with the request.  This handles multiple simultaneous incoming
# connections and passes the results onto the handle_connection
# routine for processing and then closes connections.

sub nghttpd
{
    # It takes one argument, the port number it should run on
    local($port, $debug_flag) = @_;
```

```
# We need to use perl socket libraries throughout this code.
# All code which uses sockets must require this library.
require 'sys/socket.ph';

# If the user provided a $debug_flag, change $nghttp_debug.
$nghttp_debug = $debug_flag if ($debug_flag ne "");

# This is the packing template for a socket. Don't worry
# about what this means and don't change it.  You need to do
# this anytime you are using sockets.
$sockaddr = 'S n a4 x8';

# Get the protocol number for TCP and get the port number
# if a port was given by name.  Don't worry about
# what this means and don't change it.  You need to do this
# anytime you are using TCP.
($name, $aliases, $proto) = getprotobyname('tcp');

# If the argument passed into the routine is a number, use
# it as the port number to listen on.
if ($port =~ /^\d+/)
{
 $port_num = $port;
}

# If the argument passed into the routine was a word, assume
# that it is the name of a service, so look it up and find
# the port number. For example, you could specify 'http' as
# the protocol and it would look up that string in
# /etc/services and determine that the standard port to
# listen on is port 80.

elsif ($port =~ /^\w+$/)
```

```
{
 ($name, $aliases, $port_num) = getservbyname($port, 'tcp');
}


# If the port number still isn't defined, default to the
# HTTP port.

($name, $aliases, $port_num) = getservbyname('http', 'tcp')
 unless ($port_num);

# Make the local packed socket structure.  Don't worry about
# what this means and don't change it.  You need to do this
# anytime you are using sockets.

$this = pack($sockaddr, &AF_INET, $port_num, "\0\0\0\0");

# Make the socket and start listening for connections.
# Don't worry about what this means and don't change it.
# You need to do this anytime you are using TCP.

socket(S, &AF_INET, &SOCK_STREAM, $proto) ||
  die "socket: $!";
bind(S, $this) || die "bind: $!";
listen(S,5) || die "connect: $!";

# Make the socket unbuffered.  Look at the top of the file
# to see what this means.
select(S); $| = 1; select(STDOUT);

# Grab the file number for the socket we are listening on.
$socket_fileno = fileno(S);
```

```
# We are going to use the variable $read_mask to indicate
# which files we should be listening to for data.  We
# initialize this
# bitmask to have the bit for the socket we are listening
# set to 1.  All the other bits are 0.

vec($read_mask, $socket_fileno, 1) = 1;

# Get this thing started
print("net.Genesis HTTPD stub started on port
  $port_num...\n");
print("Printing turned on.\n") if ($nghttp_debug);

while(1)
{

  # We are going to use the bitmask $pending_mask to indicate
  # all of the files on which there is actual data to read.
  # We initialize this to be all of the files which we are
  # are paying attention to (remember, that is $read_mask).

  $pending_mask = $read_mask;

  # Select is used to find out which files have data to be
  # read.  Select takes a bitmask telling it what file numbers
  # we should be looking at and modifies it to indicate which
  # of those file numbers have data to read.  Therefore,
  # $pending_mask will get modified by select.  In addition,
  # select takes another variable which indicates a time-out.
  # If select doesn't find any files which have data to be
  # read, it will wait many seconds before it returns an
  # empty bitmask in the hope that new data will come in.
  # In this case, we set the timeout to 1/10 of a second.
  # Select returns the number of files which have data to be read.
```

```
$nfound = select($pending_mask, undef, undef, .1);

# If $nfound is non-zero, it means that there are files
# which have data to be read in.  So, lets handle them
if($nfound)
{
    # Check $pending_mask to see if there is data to be
    # read from the socket itself.  If there is, that means
    # that there is a new connection which needs to be
    # accepted, so take care of that. Since this is a
    # blocking server we handle the connection completely
    # before handling any others by the end of the body,
    # the connection will have be completely handled and
    # closed.

    if(vec ($pending_mask, $socket_fileno, 1))
    {
      # This will create a new file which
      # will be used to handle this connection.
      $conn = &accept_new_connection;

      # Read all the data from the connection
      $done_reading = 0;
      while ($done_reading == 0)
      {
         $done_reading =
            &handle_readable_connection($conn);
      }
      # Write all the data out to the connection
      $done_writing = 0;
      while ($done_writing == 0)
      {
        $done_writing = &handle_writable_connection($conn);
      }
```

```
            }

        }

      }
}


sub handle_writable_connection
{
    # This routine is called whenever there is a connection
    # which can be written to.  Mostly we just send this off to
    # the handle_connection routine.
    # The routine takes a single argument: the file number that
    # needs to be handled.
    local($conn) = @_;

    # Hand it off to the handle_connection routine, telling them
    # what the request was, when it was, and where it was from,
    # and what the file handle is.  We get back some status from
    # this routine.
    $status = &main'handle_connection
                        ("nghttp'".$filehandle[$conn],
                         $connection_request[$conn],
                         $connection_time[$conn],
                         $connection_remoteaddr[$conn]);

    # Check the status, see we are supposed to close the
    # connection now. If so, close it.
    if($status == $CLOSE_CONNECTION)
    {
        &close_connection($conn);
        return(1);
    }
```

```
    # Maybe we're explicitly supposed to keep it open.
    elsif($status == $KEEP_OPEN)
    {
     # Don't do anything
    }

    # handle_connection didn't return a known status code.
    # Therefore, we'll check and see how long this connection
    # has been open and if it's been open too long we'll assume
    # they meant to close it or perhaps they already closed it
    # themselves.  This is mostly just a safeguard against
    # handle_connection routines which don't
    # return the correct codes.

    else
    {
     # See what time it is now.
     $now = time();

     # See if the connection has been open longer than $TIMEOUT
     if(($now - $connection_time[$conn]) > $TIMEOUT)
     {
         # If so, close the connection and clean up.
         &close_connection($conn);
            return(1);

     }
    }
    return(0);
}

sub close_connection
{
    # Close the connection, clean up the bitmasks, and unset the
    # filehandle
```

```
    # The routine takes a single argument: the file number that
    # needs to be closed
    local($conn) = @_;

    # We no longer need to pay attention to this file for
    # writing, so set that bit to zero in $write_mask
    vec($write_mask,$conn,1) = 0;

    # We can close the connection.  (Close takes a file handle
    # though, so we grab that from our associative array
    close($filehandle[$conn]);

    # Erase the entry from our associative array since we don't
    # need it any more.
    $filehandle[$conn]='';
}

sub handle_readable_connection
{
    # This routine is called whenever there is a connection
    # which has data to be handled.

    # The connection that we have to read from is passed in
    local($conn) = @_;

    # First check and see if this connection has been open too
    # long.   If so, close it.

    # See what time it is now.
    $now = time();

    # See if the connection has been open longer than $TIMEOUT
    if(($now - $connection_time[$conn]) > $TIMEOUT)
```

```
{
   # If so, stop reading.
   &complete_request_on_connection($conn);
   # Print out some debugging info
   print "Read on connection $conn timed out.\n";

   return(1);
}


# In most current servers, data is read off of the socket
# one byte at a time, until it sees a double CRLF at which
# point it knows it has the full request and anything that
# comes after it is part of the data of a post. This is
# horribly slow, so, I read 512 bytes at a time.

# This causes the "problem" that the data of a post request
# is going to be read in as well, and I need a way of knowing
# when it is so I do what anyone would, and that is look at
# the content length header.

# This of course means if you want to implement a fully
# featured and CGI-compliant Web server in the
# handle_connection routine (which is completely doable)
# then you would have to parse out the data portion of POST
# requests and send it to the standard input of the CGI
# scripts manually instead of just duping the file handle
# onto STDIN.  No big loss, though.  Cope.

# Also note that this only handles HTTP/1.0 connections.
# HTTP/0.9 will end up waiting for ever.  This is a bug.
# Cope.
```

```
# Read the data off the file into $outtemp.  Try to read up
# to 512 bytes. $nbread will be the number of bytes that we
# actually read.
$nbread = read($filehandle[$conn], $outtemp, 512);

# Add whatever we get to the request so far
$connection_request[$conn] .= $outtemp;

print "  So far seen:\n[$connection_request[$conn]]\n";
# Check if we received a double CRLF.  Actually check for
# double LF too, since some clients are broken and we want
# to be tolerant.
if($connection_request[$conn] =~ /\r?\n\r?\n/)
{

 # The data is anything that comes after the double CRLF
 $data = $';

 # Check if the header has a content length in it.  If so
 # then we should make sure we read that much.
 if($connection_request[$conn] =~ /Content-length: (.+)/i)
 {
     $len = $1;

     print "  Looking for $len bytes of data.\n";
     print "  Read " . length($data) . " so far\n";

     # If we have as much as it says we should, let's
     # go into what we do once we have a complete request
     if(length($data) >= $len)
     {
      $data = substr($data, 0, $len);
```

```
            # We've read in all the data we need to, so clean up.
            &complete_request_on_connection($conn);
            return(1);
          }
        }
        # OK, no content length, and double CRLFs, that's a
        # complete request
        else
        {
          # We've read in all the data we need to, so clean up.
          &complete_request_on_connection($conn);
          return(1);
        }
      }

    return(0);
}

sub complete_request_on_connection
{
    # Cool, we have a complete request.  This means we no longer
    # care about reading from the connection, but are ready to
    # write to it. Adjust the bitmasks accordingly.

    # The file number for the connection that we are using is
    # passed in.
    local($conn) = @_;

    # We are finished reading from this file, so we no longer to
    # pay attention to whether there is data coming in or not.
    # So, flip that bit in $read_mask
    vec($read_mask, $conn, 1) = 0;
```

```
    # But we now need to check and see if the connection is
    # writable. So, flip that bit in $write_mask
    vec($write_mask, $conn, 1) = 1;

    # Print some debugging information if nghttp_debug is on.
    if ($nghttp_debug)
    {
     $header = "Request Received from
       $connection_remoteaddr[$conn]\n";
     print "$header\n";
     print "-" x length($header) . "\n";
     print $connection_request[$conn];
     print "\n";
    }


}

sub accept_new_connection
{


    # This routine is called whenever there is a new connection
    # which needs to be accepted.

    # The file number for the connection is passed in
    local($conn);

    # Accept the connection and set $thisfh to the filehandle of
    # the new file.
    $addr = accept($thisfh = &new_filehandle, S);

    # Make it unbuffered.  Do you sense a theme?
    select($thisfh); $|=1; select(STDOUT);
```

```
# Now we have a new connection, we need to save some
# information about it.

# Find the file number for the new file handle and save that
$conn = fileno($thisfh);

# Now that we have a new connection, we need to pay
# attention to it to see if there is any data to be read.
# So, set the appropriate bits on $read_mask
vec($read_mask, $conn, 1) = 1;

# Ok, let's find out where this connection came from.  Don't
# worry about how it does this.
($af,$port_num,$inetaddr) = unpack($sockaddr, $addr);
($hostname, $aliases, $addrtype,$length, @addrs) =
 gethostbyaddr($inetaddr,2);

# Set some parameters about the connection

# Save the time that the current connection was accepted.
$connection_time[$conn] = time();

# Store the file handle in the array
$filehandle[$conn]=$thisfh;

# Save the remote address of the client for the connection
$remote_addr= $hostname ? $hostname:join('.', @addrs);
$connection_remoteaddr[$conn] = $remote_addr;

# Initialize the request to null. It will be filled in as
# the data is received.
$connection_request[$conn] = '';
```

```
    # Print out some information if the debug flag is on
    if ($nghttp_debug)
    {
     $header = "Connection \#$conn";
     print "$header\n";
     print "-" x length($header) . "\n"; #
     print ("  Received request from $remote_addr.\n");
     print("  Using file handle: $thisfh\n");
     print("\n");
    }

   return($conn);
}



sub new_filehandle
{
    # Get a new filehandle.  Perl autoincrement of a string
    # changes NGAAA to NGAAB to NGAAC etc.  Handy, huh?

    $fh++;
}

# Return 1, 'cuz packages should.
1;
```

In order to write a server based on the code in Listing 13-1, you need to require nghttpd.pl and provide a `handle_connection` routine to write data out for each connection. Listing 13-2 shows an example that can be used for any of the server models presented here.

Listing 13–2. **Simple server using the nghttpd package**

```
#!/usr/bin/perl
# File Name: quicktest.pl
```

```
# We are going to use our code package to do all the socket
# stuff.  Change the file name here if you want to use one of
# the other server models.
require 'nghttpd.pl';

# Call the main routine in the package so that it will open the
# connection and begin listening to the port.  Allow the user
# to specify the port number that the server should run on and
# whether debugging statements should be turned on.
&nghttp'nghttpd($ARGV[0], $ARGV[1]);

sub handle_connection
{
    # After the nghttpd routine has read in the entire request
    # and the connection can be written to, it calls this
    # routine.  This routine then writes out whatever it needs
    # to the file.

    # The program takes the following variables:
    #   $fh:   The file handle for the connection
    #   $req:  The request made by the client
    #   $time: The time the connection was made
    #   $addr: The address of the client
    local($fh, $req, $time, $addr) = @_;

    # Make the file unbuffered. This means that each time you
    # use a print statement, it will write to the file
    # immediately as opposed to buffering it until a newline is
    # sent
    select($fh); $|=1;

    # Grab the request line.  This should always be the first
    # line in the request.
    $request_line = $req;
```

```
$request_line =~ /^(.*)/;
$request_line =~ $1;

($method, $URI, $method) = split (" ", $request_line);

# We will use the flag $lookup_result to see if
# we need to perform the actual request.
$lookup_result = 1;

# Look up the URI in our associative array cache and see
# if the result is already known.  If it is, check to
# see if it is expired.  In this case,
if (($cache{$URI}) &&
    ($expire_time{$URI} > time()))
{
   # Hopefully, we'll be able to just use this value.
   $lookup_result = 0;
}

# Check and see if the "Pragma: no-cache" header was
# received.  If so, it means we can't use the cached
# value
if ($req =~ /Pragma:\s*no-cache/i)
{
  $lookup_result = 1;
}

print "Content-Type: text/plain\r\n";
print "Server: net.Genesis Book Caching HTTPD/1.0\r\n";
print "\r\n";

# If $lookup_result is zero, we can just use the cached
# result.
if (!$lookup_result)
```

```
    {
       print $cache{$URI};
    }
    # Otherwise, look it up
    else
    {
       # Find the file and read its contents in.
       open (INPUT, $URI);
       $data = <INPUT>;

       # Send that data out as the body.
       print $data;

       # Update the cache
       $cache{$URI} = $data;

       # Set the data to expire in 10 minutes
       $expire_time{$URI} = time() + 600;
    }

    # We are done, so close the connection.
    return($nghttp'CLOSE_CONNECTION);
}
```

Remember, if you are running your server on any port less than 1024, you have to be logged in as root. If you are not logged in as root, the program will not be able to bind to the port and will return an error.

In order to run the blocking server, invoke the following command. The first argument is the port you wish to run the server on; use a second, nonzero argument if you want debugging mode on. For example, doing the following on the machine test.netgen.com starts the blocking server running on port 8001 with debugging turned on:

```
quicktest.pl 8001 1
```

Now that you are running the blocking server, you can see how this model can create problems. To observe this, telnet into your newly run server by specifying the name of the machine that you ran it on and the port. To connect to our server from the example above, invoke this command:

```
telnet test.netgen.com 8001
```

If you are running your server with debugging mode on, some information will print out verifying your connection. Now pull up a Web browser (like Lynx or Mosaic) and specify a URL to access your server. In our example, we would use **http://test.netgen.com:8001/**. This causes your browser to try to request the document from the server. However, because we are using a blocking server, it can't even make the connection until the first connection is done (or it times-out). To see this happen, hit Enter twice in your telnet window. The server interprets that as the end of the request and responds to it. As soon as the connection is closed, the server can handle the request from your browser.

13.1.2 Multiplexing Server

The blocking model is far from ideal when it comes to handling multiple connections. The multiplexing model is much more useful under high loads. By modifying portions of the blocking model server, we can transform it into a multiplexing server.

The only portion of the code that needs to be modified is the `while` loop in the nghttpd routine. Listing 13-3 shows the new loop. Notice how it handles the requests and responses differently. In the blocking server code, the server waits until `handle_readable_connection` and `handle_writable_connection` are both completely finished before trying to deal with a different connection. In this case, the server reads a little bit off each open connection and writes a little to each connection. In this way, it handles all open connections at once.

Listing 13–3. Code for multiplexing nghttpd package

```
while(1)
    {

      # We are going to use the bitmask $pending_mask to indicate
      # all of the files on which there is actual data to read.
      # We initialize this to be all of the files which we are
      # are paying attention to (remember, that is $read_mask).
```

```
$pending_mask = $read_mask;

# Select is used to find out which files have data to be
# read.  Select takes a bitmask telling it what file numbers
# we should be looking at and modifies it to indicate which
# of those file numbers have data to read.  Therefore,
# $pending_mask will get modified by select.  In addition,
# select takes another variable which indicates a time-out.
# If select doesn't find any files which have data to be
# read, it will wait many seconds before it returns an
# empty bitmask in the hopes that new data will come in.
# In this case, we set the timeout to 1/10 of a second.
# Select returns the number of files which have data to be read.

$nfound = select($pending_mask, undef, undef, .1);

# If $nfound is non-zero, it means that there are files
# which have data to be read in.  So, lets handle them
if($nfound)
{
    # Check $pending_mask to see if there is data to be
    # read from the socket itself.  If there is, that means
    # that there is a new connection which needs to be
    # accepted, so take care of that. Since this is a
    # blocking server we handle the connection completely
    # before handling any others by the end of the body,
    # the connection will have be completely handled and
    # closed.

    if(vec ($pending_mask, $socket_fileno, 1))
    {
     # This will create a new file which
     # will be used to handle this connection.
     &accept_new_connection;
```

```
          # Now that we've created a new file to deal with
          # the data, we can turn off the bit for the socket.
          vec($pending_mask, $socket_fileno, 1) = 0;
        }

    }

    # Generate a bitstring, $pending_bits, from $pending_mask
    $pending_bits = unpack("b*", $pending_mask);

    # Walk down the bitstring, looking for every "1" in the
    # string.  This represents a file which has data to be
    # read in.  For each of these files, call
    # handle_readable_connection.

    $idx = 0;
    while(($idx = index($pending_bits, "1", $idx+1)) != -1)
    {
        &handle_readable_connection($idx);
    }



    # We are going to use the bitmask $ready_mask to indicate
    # all of the files which can be written to. We initialize
    # this to be all of the files which we are paying
    # attention to for writing (that is what $write_mask is).

    $ready_mask = $write_mask;

    # Use select to determine which files can be written to.

    $nfound = select(undef, $ready_mask, undef, .1);
```

```
    # If $nfound is non-zero, it means that there are files
    # which can be written to.  So, lets handle them
    if($nfound)
    {
        # Generate a bitstring, $ready_bits, from $ready_mask
        $ready_bits = unpack("b*", $ready_mask);

        # Deal with each of the writable connections.
        $idx = 0;
        while(($idx = index($ready_bits, "1", $idx+1)) != -1)
        {
         &handle_writable_connection($idx);
        }
    }

   }
```

If you perform the same test as you did before (by telnetting in and using your browser to make a request), you will see that both connections are handled at the same time.

13.1.3 Forking Server

With only a few minor modifications to the blocking server code, you can write a forking server. The only portion of the code that needs to be modified is the `while` loop in the nghttpd routine. Listing 13-4 shows the new loop. In this code, you can see that instead of having the main program handle the reading and writing, we fork and have a child process take care of the connection. We also have put in some code to clean up after all the forked children, since a forking server creates a little mess in memory.

Listing 13–4. **Code for forking nghttpd package**

```
while(1)
   {

    # We are going to use the bitmask $pending_mask to indicate
    # all of the files on which there is actual data to read.
```

```
# We initialize this to be all of the files which we are
# are paying attention to (remember, that is $read_mask).

$pending_mask = $read_mask;

# Select is used to find out which files have data to be
# read.  Select takes a bitmask telling it what file numbers
# we should be looking at and modifies it to indicate which
# of those file numbers have data to read.  Therefore,
# $pending_mask will get modified by select.  In addition,
# select takes another variable which indicates a time-out.
# If select doesn't find any files which have data to be
# read, it will wait many seconds before it returns an
# empty bitmask in the hopes that new data will come in.
# In this case, we set the timeout to 1/10 of a second.
# Select returns the number of files which have data to be read.

$nfound = select($pending_mask, undef, undef, .1);

# If $nfound is non-zero, it means that there are files
# which have data to be read in.  So, lets handle them
if($nfound)
{
    # Check $pending_mask to see if there is data to be
    # read from the socket itself.  If there is, that means
    # that there is a new connection which needs to be
    # accepted, so take care of that. Since this is a
    # blocking server we handle the connection completely
    # before handling any others by the end of the body,
    # the connection will have be completely handled and
    # closed.


    if(vec ($pending_mask, $socket_fileno, 1))
```

```
{

  # This is where we actually perform the fork.
  # fork causes a copy of the process to be made and
  # returns different values to each of the processes
  # fork returns 0 to the child (the result of the
  # fork). fork returns the pid of the child to the
  # parent (the original process).

  $child_pid = fork();

  # If the $child_pid is non-zero, then this is the
  # parent.
  if ($child_pid)
  {
      print "Forked process $child_pid to handle new
        connection.\n";

      # Fork is a little messy though.  At some point
      # you have to clean up after your children (just
      # like real-life, eh?).  So, keep track of how
      # many children you have.
      $num_children++;

      # The parent process will now continue on its way
      # waiting for new connections and handling them.

  }

  # Otherwise, this is the child.
  else
  {
     $conn = &accept_new_connection;
```

```
            # Read everything necessary off the connection
            $done_reading = 0;
            while ($done_reading == 0)
            {
               $done_reading =
                 &handle_readable_connection($conn);
            }
            # Write whatever is necessary to the connection
            $done_writing = 0;
            while ($done_writing == 0)
            {
                $done_writing =
                  &handle_writable_connection($conn);
            }

            # Kill the child process once it is done
            exit;
        }

      }

}

# We need to check and see if we have too many children
# that we haven't cleaned up after.  If so, then do the
# clean up now. The numbers we use (10 and 6) are completely
# arbitrary.
if ($num_children > 10)
{
   while ($num_children > 6)
   {
      # wait is the function that is used to clean up after
      # children.  It waits until one of the children dies
      # and then returns.  If one of the children has
```

```
            # already died, it returns immediately.
            wait();
            $num_children--;
        }
    }
}
```

As the code says, whenever you have a forking server you need to do some cleanup. The standard function to call for this is `wait`. When a child process dies (i.e., when the process is completed), the kernel must be notified so that it can officially kill off the process. Until that happens, the completed child process is considered a *zombie* and continues to take up memory. In order to clean out the zombie and free your resources, the parent process issues a `wait` command. This serves to block (that is, it does not return) until the kernel officially kills off a zombie.

If a zombie already exists when `wait` is called, the response is immediate. If, however, there is no zombie, the parent process waits until a child process dies. During the time that `wait` is blocking, no new connections can be made. Obviously, if any real percentage of the time is being spent blocking, this can cause a problem. Our solution is to hold off issuing a `wait` command until there are more than ten child processes in existence. The hope is that by the time ten children have accumulated, at least some of them will have already become zombies when `wait` is called, in which case `wait` will return instantaneously.

Another option is to use a *nonblocking wait.* In this case, `wait` returns immediately, regardless of whether any children have died. However, in order to do a nonblocking wait in perl, you have to require sys/wait.ph, which depends on a lot of other system header files being in place and properly installed. If they are not all properly installed, you cannot do this. NCSA and CERN httpd (both of which are written in C) use nonblocking waits.

13.2 Providing Additional Capabilities

You might choose to add plenty of additional pieces of functionality on top of a basic server. You should be able to add these capabilities by modifying the `handle_connection` routine. Here is a list of things that you might want to do:

- Provide a proxy server
- Provide a caching server
- Encrypt some or all of the data being sent by the server
- Provide a server that does automatic content negotiation

We will provide examples for the first two to show how you could implement these extensions.

13.2.1 Proxy Server

In Section 4.2.6 and elsewhere we discussed proxy servers and their uses. Here we show you how to use the nghttpd package to implement a proxy server. Most proxy servers are used on firewalls to make requests on behalf of the client, but they can also be used to modify the documents that they retrieve, as shown in the next example. In particular, this server checks whether the retrieved object is an HTML document. If it is, the server removes all of the Image elements and replaces them with values for their ALT attributes, if they are provided. This makes retrieving documents faster because the browser does not retrieve any images. This same functionality can be achieved in most browsers by turning off image loading, but many browsers do not automatically use the ALT attribute even when image loading is turned off. After the server has made the modifications, it forwards the modified version of the document to the client.

This server was built on top of the nghttpd package by modifying the quicktest.pl file presented in Listing 13-2. It also calls for the nifty.pl script from Chapter 12. Listing 13-5 shows the revised code, yielding our "ALTifier" proxy server.

Listing 13–5. **Sample "ALTifier" proxy server code**

```
#!/usr/bin/perl
# File Name: altifier.pl

require 'nghttpd.pl';
require 'nifty.pl'

# Call the main routine in the package so that it will open the
# connection and begin listening to the port.  Allow the user
# to specify the port number that the server should run on and
```

```
# whether debugging statements should be turned on.
&nghttp'nghttpd($ARGV[0], $ARGV[1]);

sub handle_connection
{
    # After the nghttpd routine has read in the entire request
    # and the connection can be written to, it calls this
    # routine.  This routine then writes out whatever it needs
    # to the file.

    # The program takes the following variables:
    #   $fh:   The file handle for the connection
    #   $req:  The request made by the client
    #   $time: The time the connection was made
    #   $addr: The address of the client
    local($fh, $req, $time, $addr) = @_;

    # Make the file unbuffered. This means that each time you
    # use a print statement, it will write to the file
    # immediately as opposed to buffering it until a newline is
    # sent
    select($fh); $|=1;

    # Grab the request line.  This should always be the first
    # line in the request.
    $request_line = $req;
    $request_line =~ /^(.*)/;
    $request_line =~ $1;

    # Grab the method and the URI and possibly the protocol and
    # version.
    ($method, $URI, $protocol) = split (" ", $request_line);
```

```
        # If the method was not GET, return an error
        if ($method !~ /GET/i)
        {
           print "HTTP/1.0 405 Method Not Allowed\r\n";
           print "Allow: GET\r\n";
           print "\r\n";

           # Close the connection after sending this
           return(nghttpd'CLOSE_CONNECTION);
        }

        # Use the get_url function from the previous chapter
        # to fetch the contents of the specified URI
        ($headers, $body) = &get_document($URI);

        # Call the adjust function to modify the data received.
        # It is the responsibility of adjust to correctly modify
        # the header to reflect any changes to the body (for example
        # changing the Content-Length header to match the modified
        # data.
        ($headers, $body) = &adjust($headers, $body);


        # Send the modified header and body to the client
        print "$headers\r\n";
        print $body;

        # Finally, return a CLOSE_CONNECTION status so the
        # connection will be closed.
        return(nghttpd'CLOSE_CONNECTION);
    }

    # This function is used to modify the data being sent back to
    # the client.
    sub adjust
```

```
{
    # The routine gets two arguments corresponding to the
    # current headers and body of the response
    local($headers, $body)=@_;

    # This will only modify HTML documents
    if ($headers =~ /Content-Type: text\/html/i)
    {
       # Find all of the Image elements in the body
       while ($body =~ /(<\s*img[^>]>)/ig)
       {
          $element = $1;

          # See if the ALT attribute was provided
          if (($element =~ /alt\s*=\s*\"([^\"]*)\"/i)||
              ($element =~ /alt\s*=\s*([\S]+)/i))
          {
             $alt_value = $1;

             # If so, replace the entire element with the
             # value of the ALT attribute
             $body =~ s/$element/ $alt_value /g;
          }

          # Otherwise, replace the element with "[IMAGE]"
          else
          {
             $body =~ s/$element/ [Image] /g;
          }
       }

       # We probably modified the length of the data, so update
       # that.
```

```
        $new_length = length($body);

        # If the Content-Length was already provided, modify it.
        if ($headers =~ /(Content-Length:.*/i)
        {
           $headers =~ s/$1/Content-Length: $new_length/g;
        }
        # Otherwise, add the header
        else
        {
           $headers .= "Content-Length: $new_length\r\n";
        }
    }

    # Finally, return the modified headers and body
    return ($headers,$text);
}
```

13.2.2 Caching Server

One other feature that you can easily add to the server is caching. By caching requests, you speed up the performance of the server. One of the issues that we deal with in our implementation is how long to keep a cached value around before it expires. We've decided to have all items in the cache expire after ten minutes. If a value was cached more than ten minutes ago, the value needs to be looked up again. In order to make a caching server, you can modify the quicktest.pl code as shown in Listing 13-6.

Listing 13–6. **Sample caching server code**

```
#!/usr/bin/perl
# File Name: ngcache.pl

# We are going to use our code package to do all the socket
# stuff.
require 'nghttpd.pl';
```

```
# Call the main routine in the package so that it will open the
# connection and begin listening to the port.  Allow the user
# to specify the port number that the server should run on and
# whether debugging statements should be turned on.
&nghttp'nghttpd($ARGV[0], $ARGV[1]);

sub handle_connection
{
    # After the nghttpd routine has read in the entire request
    # and the connection can be written to, it calls this
    # routine.  This routine then writes out whatever it needs
    # to the file.

    # The program takes the following variables:
    #   $fh:   The file handle for the connection
    #   $req:  The request made by the client
    #   $time: The time the connection was made
    #   $addr: The address of the client
    local($fh, $req, $time, $addr) = @_;

    # Make the file unbuffered. This means that each time you
    # use a print statement, it will write to the file
    # immediately as opposed to buffering it until a newline is
    # sent
    select($fh); $|=1;

    # Grab the request line.  This should always be the first
    # line in the request.
    $request_line = $req;
    $request_line =~ /^(.*)/;
    $request_line =~ $1;

    ($method, $URI, $method) = split (" ", $request_line);
```

```
# We will use the flag $lookup_result to see if
# we need to perform the actual request.
$lookup_result = 1;

# Look up the URI in our associative array cache and see
# if the result is already known.  If it is, check to
# see if it is expired.  In this case,
if (($cache{$URI}) &&
     ($expire_time{$URI} > time()))
{
   # Hopefully we'll be able to just use this value.
   $lookup_result = 0;
}

# Check and see if the "Pragma: no-cache" header was
# received.  If so, it means we can't use the cached
# value
if ($req =~ /Pragma:\s*no-cache/i)
{
  $lookup_result = 1;
}

print "Content-Type: text/plain\r\n";
print "Server: net.Genesis Book Caching HTTPD/1.0\r\n";
print "\r\n";

# If $lookup_result is zero, we can just use the cached
# result.
if (!$lookup_result)
{
   print $cache{$URI};
}
# Otherwise, look it up
else
```

```
    {
        # Find the file and read its contents in.
        open (INPUT, $URI);
        $data = <INPUT>;

        # Send that data out as the body.
        print $data;

        # Update the cache
        $cache{$URI} = $data;

        # Set the data to expire in 10 minutes
        $expire_time{$URI} = time() + 600;
    }

    # We are done, so close the connection.
    return($nghttp'CLOSE_CONNECTION);
}
```

As we said in the beginning, these examples were provided to help you grasp what is needed to write a server. Now that you have a foundation to build on, you can either take this code and extend it as you see fit, or you can really get into the NCSA and CERN HTTP servers and try to understand what is going on. Existing servers could use a lot of improvements. Making changes can be a real challenge if you are up to it.

PART IV

Appendixes

In this last section you can find three specification documents:

- RFC 1738—Uniform Resource Locators (Appendix A)
- HTTP/1.0 Internet Draft (Appendix B)
- HTML 2.0 Internet Draft (Appendix C)

These three specs are reprinted without alteration, with kind permission from the Internet Engineering Task Force and their respective authors. We have annotated each document to indicate changes from a previous version and cross-reference relevant sections in this book. We have also provided you with tips for safely working around a limitation. Our comments are in italics so that you should not confuse them with the actual specification documents themselves.

APPENDIX A

Uniform Resource Locators (URLs)

Network Working Group
Request for Comments: 1738
Category: Standards Track

T. Berners-Lee
CERN
L. Masinter
Xerox Corporation
M. McCahill
University of Minnesota
Editors
December 1994

Status of This Memo

This document specifies an Internet standards track protocol for the Internet community, and requests discussion and suggestions for improvements. Please refer to the current edition of the "Internet Official Protocol Standards" (STD 1) for the standardization state and status of this protocol. Distribution of this memo is unlimited.

Abstract

This document specifies a Uniform Resource Locator (URL), the syntax and semantics of formalized information for location and access of resources via the Internet.

1. Introduction

This document describes the syntax and semantics for a compact string representation for a resource available via the Internet. These strings are called "Uniform Resource Locators" (URLs).

The specification is derived from concepts introduced by the World- Wide Web global information initiative, whose use of such objects dates from 1990 and is described in "Universal Resource Identifiers in WWW", RFC 1630. The specification of URLs is designed to meet the requirements laid out in "Functional Requirements for Internet Resource Locators" [12].

This document was written by the URI working group of the Internet Engineering Task Force. Comments may be addressed to the editors, or to the URI-WG <uri@bunyip.com>. Discussions of the group are archived at <URL:http://www.acl.lanl.gov/URI/archive/uri-archive.index.html>

2. General URL Syntax

Just as there are many different methods of access to resources, there are several schemes for describing the location of such resources.

The generic syntax for URLs provides a framework for new schemes to be established using protocols other than those defined in this document.

URLs are used to `locate' resources, by providing an abstract identification of the resource location. Having located a resource, a system may perform a variety of operations on the resource, as might be characterized by such words as `access', `update', `replace', `find attributes'. In general, only the `access' method needs to be specified for any URL scheme.

2.1. The Main Parts of URLs

A full BNF description of the URL syntax is given in Section 5.

In general, URLs are written as follows:

```
        <scheme>:<scheme-specific-part>
```

A URL contains the name of the scheme being used (<scheme>) followed by a colon and then a string (the <scheme-specific-part>) whose interpretation depends on the scheme.

Scheme names consist of a sequence of characters. The lower case letters "a"--"z", digits, and the characters plus ("+"), period ("."), and hyphen ("-") are allowed. For resiliency, programs interpreting URLs should treat upper case letters as equivalent to lower case in scheme names (e.g., allow "HTTP" as well as "http").

2.2. URL Character Encoding Issues

URLs are sequences of characters, i.e., letters, digits, and special characters. A URLs may be represented in a variety of ways: e.g., ink on paper, or a sequence of octets in a coded character set. The interpretation of a URL depends only on the identity of the characters used.

In most URL schemes, the sequences of characters in different parts of a URL are used to represent sequences of octets used in Internet protocols. For example, in the ftp scheme, the host name, directory name and file names are such sequences of octets, represented by parts of the URL. Within those parts, an octet may be represented by the chararacter which has that octet as its code within the US-ASCII [20] coded character set.

In addition, octets may be encoded by a character triplet consisting of the character "%" followed by the two hexadecimal digits (from "0123456789ABCDEF") which forming the hexadecimal value of the octet. (The characters "abcdef" may also be used in hexadecimal encodings.)

Octets must be encoded if they have no corresponding graphic character within the US-ASCII coded character set, if the use of the corresponding character is unsafe, or if the corresponding character is reserved for some other interpretation within the particular URL scheme.

No corresponding graphic US-ASCII:

URLs are written only with the graphic printable characters of the US-ASCII coded character set. The octets 80-FF hexadecimal are not used in US-ASCII, and the octets 00-1F and 7F hexadecimal represent control characters; these must be encoded.

Unsafe:

Characters can be unsafe for a number of reasons. The space character is unsafe because significant spaces may disappear and insignificant spaces may be introduced when URLs are transcribed or typeset or subjected to the treatment of word-processing programs. The characters "<" and ">" are unsafe because they are used as the delimiters around URLs in free text; the quote mark (""") is used to delimit URLs in some systems. The character "#" is unsafe and should always be encoded because it is used in World Wide Web and in other systems to delimit a URL from a fragment/anchor identifier that might follow it. The character "%" is unsafe because it is used for encodings of other characters. Other characters are unsafe because gateways and other transport agents are known to sometimes modify such characters. These characters are "{", "}", "|", "\", "^", "~", "[", "]", and "`".

See Table 4-1 for a listing of several commonly escaped sequences and their meanings.

All unsafe characters must always be encoded within a URL. For example, the character "#" must be encoded within URLs even in systems that do not normally deal with fragment or anchor identifiers, so that if the URL is copied into another system that does use them, it will not be necessary to change the URL encoding.

Reserved:

Many URL schemes reserve certain characters for a special meaning: their appearance in the scheme-specific part of the URL has a designated semantics. If the character corresponding to an octet is reserved in a scheme, the octet must be encoded. The characters ";", "/", "?", ":", "@", "=" and "&" are the characters which may be reserved for special meaning within a scheme. No other characters may be reserved within a scheme.

See Table 4-3 for the common meanings of many reserved characters.

Usually a URL has the same interpretation when an octet is represented by a character and when it encoded. However, this is not true for reserved characters: encoding a character reserved for a particular scheme may change the semantics of a URL.

Thus, only alphanumerics, the special characters "$-_.+!*'(),", and reserved characters used for their reserved purposes may be used unencoded within a URL.

On the other hand, characters that are not required to be encoded (including alphanumerics) may be encoded within the scheme-specific part of a URL, as long as they are not being used for a reserved purpose.

2.3 Hierarchical Schemes and Relative Links

In some cases, URLs are used to locate resources that contain pointers to other resources. In some cases, those pointers are represented as relative links where the expression of the location of the second resource is in terms of "in the same place as this one except with the following relative path". Relative links are not described in this document. However, the use of relative links depends on the original URL containing a hierarchical structure against which the relative link is based.

See Section 4.2.1, "The Power of Relative URLs," for a description of how to use relative URLs.

Some URL schemes (such as the ftp, http, and file schemes) contain names that can be considered hierarchical; the components of the hierarchy are separated by "/".

See Section 4.2.5, "URL Mapping," for a discussion of the meaning of hierarchical HTTP URLs.

3. Specific Schemes

The mapping for some existing standard and experimental protocols is outlined in the BNF syntax definition. Notes on particular protocols follow. The schemes covered are:

```
ftp        File Transfer protocol
http       Hypertext Transfer Protocol
gopher     The Gopher protocol
mailto     Electronic mail address
news       USENET news
nntp       USENET news using NNTP access
telnet     Reference to interactive sessions
wais       Wide Area Information Servers
file       Host-specific file names
prospero   Prospero Directory Service
```

See Table 4-2 for a list of these schemes, along with the default values for each scheme.

Other schemes may be specified by future specifications. Section 4 of this document describes how new schemes may be registered, and lists some scheme names that are under development.

3.1. Common Internet Scheme Syntax

While the syntax for the rest of the URL may vary depending on the particular scheme selected, URL schemes that involve the direct use of an IP-based protocol to a specified host on the Internet use a common syntax for the scheme-specific data:

```
//<user>:<password>@<host>:<port>/<url-path>
```

Some or all of the parts "<user>:<password>@", ":<password>", ":<port>", and "/<url-path>" may be excluded. The scheme specific data start with a double slash

"//" to indicate that it complies with the common Internet scheme syntax. The different components obey the following rules:

- user — An optional user name. Some schemes (e.g., ftp) allow the specification of a user name.
- password — An optional password. If present, it follows the user name separated from it by a colon.

The user name (and password), if present, are followed by a commercial at-sign "@". Within the user and password field, any ":", "@", or "/" must be encoded.

Note that an empty user name or password is different than no user name or password; there is no way to specify a password without specifying a user name. E.g., <URL:ftp://@host.com/> has an empty user name and no password, <URL:ftp://host.com/> has no user name, while <URL:ftp://foo:@host.com/> has a user name of "foo" and an empty password.

- host — The fully qualified domain name of a network host, or its IP address as a set of four decimal digit groups separated by ".". Fully qualified domain names take the form as described in Section 3.5 of RFC 1034 [13] and Section 2.1 of RFC 1123 [5]: a sequence of domain labels separated by ".", each domain label starting and ending with an alphanumerical character and possibly also containing "-" characters. The rightmost domain label will never start with a digit, though, which syntactically distinguishes all domain names from the IP addresses.
- port — The port number to connect to. Most schemes designate protocols that have a default port number. Another port number may optionally be supplied, in decimal, separated from the host by a colon. If the port is omitted, the colon is as well.
- url-path — The rest of the locator consists of data specific to the scheme, and is known as the "url-path". It supplies the details of how the specified resource can be accessed. Note that the "/" between the host (or port) and the url-path is NOT part of the url-path.

The url-path syntax depends on the scheme being used, as does the manner in which it is interpreted.

3.2. FTP

The FTP URL scheme is used to designate files and directories on Internet hosts accessible using the FTP protocol (RFC959).

See Section 4.1.2, "FTP," for a description of the FTP scheme.

A FTP URL follow the syntax described in Section 3.1. If :<port> is omitted, the port defaults to 21.

3.2.1. FTP Name and Password

A user name and password may be supplied; they are used in the ftp "USER" and "PASS" commands after first making the connection to the FTP server. If no user name or password is supplied and one is requested by the FTP server, the conventions for "anonymous" FTP are to be used, as follows:

The user name "anonymous" is supplied.

The password is supplied as the Internet e-mail address of the end user accessing the resource.

If the URL supplies a user name but no password, and the remote server requests a password, the program interpreting the FTP URL should request one from the user.

3.2.2. FTP url-path

The url-path of a FTP URL has the following syntax:

```
<cwd1>/<cwd2>/.../<cwdN>/<name>;type=<typecode>
```

Where <cwd1> through <cwdN> and <name> are (possibly encoded) strings and <typecode> is one of the characters "a", "i", or "d". The part ";type=<typecode>" may be omitted. The <cwdx> and <name> parts may be empty. The whole url-path may be omitted, including the "/" delimiting it from the prefix containing user, password, host, and port.

The url-path is interpreted as a series of FTP commands as follows:

Each of the <cwd> elements is to be supplied, sequentially, as the argument to a CWD (change working directory) command.

If the typecode is "d", perform a NLST (name list) command with <name> as the argument, and interpret the results as a file directory listing.

Otherwise, perform a TYPE command with <typecode> as the argument, and then access the file whose name is <name> (for example, using the RETR command.)

Within a name or CWD component, the characters "/" and ";" are reserved and must be encoded. The components are decoded prior to their use in the FTP protocol. In particular, if the appropriate FTP sequence to access a particular file requires supplying a string containing a "/" as an argument to a CWD or RETR command, it is necessary to encode each "/".

For example, the URL <URL:ftp://myname@host.dom/%2Fetc/motd> is interpreted by FTP-ing to "host.dom", logging in as "myname" (prompting for a password if it is asked for), and then executing "CWD /etc" and then "RETR motd". This has a different meaning from <URL:ftp://myname@host.dom/etc/motd> which would "CWD etc" and then "RETR motd"; the initial "CWD" might be executed relative to the default directory for "myname". On the other hand, <URL:ftp://myname@host.dom//etc/motd>, would "CWD " with a null argument, then "CWD etc", and then "RETR motd".

FTP URLs may also be used for other operations; for example, it is possible to update a file on a remote file server, or infer information about it from the directory listings. The mechanism for doing so is not spelled out here.

3.2.3. FTP Typecode is Optional

The entire ;type=<typecode> part of a FTP URL is optional. If it is omitted, the client program interpreting the URL must guess the appropriate mode to use. In general, the data content type of a file can only be guessed from the name, e.g., from the suffix of the name; the appropriate type code to be used for transfer of the file can then be deduced from the data content of the file.

3.2.4 Hierarchy

For some file systems, the "/" used to denote the hierarchical structure of the URL corresponds to the delimiter used to construct a file name hierarchy, and thus, the filename will look similar to the URL path. This does NOT mean that the URL is a Unix filename.

3.2.5. Optimization

Clients accessing resources via FTP may employ additional heuristics to optimize the interaction. For some FTP servers, for example, it may be reasonable to keep the control connection open while accessing multiple URLs from the same server. However, there is no common hierarchical model to the FTP protocol, so if a directory change command has been given, it is impossible in general to deduce what sequence should be given to navigate to another directory for a second retrieval, if the paths are different. The only reliable algorithm is to disconnect and reestablish the control connection.

3.3. HTTP

The HTTP URL scheme is used to designate Internet resources accessible using HTTP (HyperText Transfer Protocol).

The HTTP scheme is discussed in Section 4.1.3, "HTTP."

The HTTP protocol is specified elsewhere. This specification only describes the syntax of HTTP URLs.

An HTTP URL takes the form:

```
http://<host>:<port>/<path>?<searchpart>
```

where <host> and <port> are as described in Section 3.1. If :<port> is omitted, the port defaults to 80. No user name or password is allowed. <path> is an HTTP selector, and <searchpart> is a query string. The <path> is optional, as is the <searchpart> and its preceding "?". If neither <path> nor <searchpart> is present, the "/" may also be omitted.

Within the <path> and <searchpart> components, "/", ";", "?" are reserved. The "/" character may be used within HTTP to designate a hierarchical structure.

3.4. Gopher

The Gopher URL scheme is used to designate Internet resources accessible using the Gopher protocol.

The Gopher scheme is discussed in Section 4.1.4, "Gopher."

The base Gopher protocol is described in RFC 1436 and supports items and collections of items (directories). The Gopher+ protocol is a set of upward compatible extensions to the base Gopher protocol and is described in [2].

Gopher+ supports associating arbitrary sets of attributes and alternate data representations with Gopher items. Gopher URLs accommodate both Gopher and Gopher+ items and item attributes.

3.4.1. Gopher URL syntax

A Gopher URL takes the form:

```
gopher://<host>:<port>/<gopher-path>
```

where <gopher-path> is one of

```
<gophertype><selector>

<gophertype><selector>%09<search>

<gophertype><selector>%09<search>%09<gopher+_string>
```

If :<port> is omitted, the port defaults to 70. <gophertype> is a single-character field to denote the Gopher type of the resource to which the URL refers. The entire <gopher-path> may also be empty, in which case the delimiting "/" is also optional and the <gophertype> defaults to "1".

<selector> is the Gopher selector string. In the Gopher protocol, Gopher selector strings are a sequence of octets which may contain any octets except 09 hexadecimal (US-ASCII HT or tab) 0A hexadecimal (US-ASCII character LF), and 0D (US-ASCII character CR).

Gopher clients specify which item to retrieve by sending the Gopher selector string to a Gopher server.

Within the <gopher-path>, no characters are reserved.

Note that some Gopher <selector> strings begin with a copy of the <gophertype> character, in which case that character will occur twice consecutively. The Gopher selector string may be an empty string; this is how Gopher clients refer to the top-level directory on a Gopher server.

3.4.2 Specifying URLs for Gopher Search Engines

If the URL refers to a search to be submitted to a Gopher search engine, the selector is followed by an encoded tab (%09) and the search string. To submit a search to a Gopher search engine, the Gopher client sends the <selector> string (after decoding), a tab, and the search string to the Gopher server.

3.4.3 URL syntax for Gopher+ items

URLs for Gopher+ items have a second encoded tab (%09) and a Gopher+ string. Note that in this case, the %09<search> string must be supplied, although the <search> element may be the empty string.

The <gopher+_string> is used to represent information required for retrieval of the Gopher+ item. Gopher+ items may have alternate views, arbitrary sets of attributes, and may have electronic forms associated with them.

To retrieve the data associated with a Gopher+ URL, a client will connect to the server and send the Gopher selector, followed by a tab and the search string (which may be empty), followed by a tab and the Gopher+ commands.

3.4.4 Default Gopher+ data representation

When a Gopher server returns a directory listing to a client, the Gopher+ items are tagged with either a "+" (denoting Gopher+ items) or a "?" (denoting Gopher+ items which have a +ASK form associated with them). A Gopher URL with a Gopher+ string consisting of only a "+" refers to the default view (data representation) of the item while a Gopher+ string containing only a "?" refer to an item with a Gopher electronic form associated with it.

3.4.5 Gopher+ items with electronic forms

Gopher+ items which have a +ASK associated with them (i.e. Gopher+ items tagged with a "?") require the client to fetch the item's +ASK attribute to get the form definition, and then ask the user to fill out the form and return the user's responses along with the selector string to retrieve the item. Gopher+ clients know how to do this but depend on the "?" tag in the Gopher+ item description to know when to handle this case. The "?" is used in the Gopher+ string to be consistent with Gopher+ protocol's use of this symbol.

3.4.6 Gopher+ item attribute collections

To refer to the Gopher+ attributes of an item, the Gopher URL's Gopher+ string consists of "!" or "$". "!" refers to the all of a Gopher+ item's attributes. "$" refers to all the item attributes for all items in a Gopher directory.

3.4.7 Referring to specific Gopher+ attributes

To refer to specific attributes, the URL's gopher+_string is "!<attribute_name>" or "$<attribute_name>". For example, to refer to the attribute containing the abstract of an item, the gopher+_string would be "!+ABSTRACT".

To refer to several attributes, the gopher+_string consists of the attribute names separated by coded spaces. For example, "!+ABSTRACT%20+SMELL" refers to the +ABSTRACT and +SMELL attributes of an item.

3.4.8 URL syntax for Gopher+ alternate views

Gopher+ allows for optional alternate data representations (alternate views) of items. To retrieve a Gopher+ alternate view, a Gopher+ client sends the appropriate view and language identifier (found in the item's +VIEW attribute). To refer to a specific Gopher+ alternate view, the URL's Gopher+ string would be in the form:

```
+<view_name>%20<language_name>
```

For example, a Gopher+ string of "+application/postscript%20Es_ES" refers to the Spanish language postscript alternate view of a Gopher+ item.

3.4.9 URL syntax for Gopher+ electronic forms

The gopher+_string for a URL that refers to an item referenced by a Gopher+ electronic form (an ASK block) filled out with specific values is a coded version of what the client sends to the server. The gopher+_string is of the form:

```
+%091%0D%0A+-
1%0D%0A<ask_item1_value>%0D%0A<ask_item2_value>%0D%0A.%0D%0A
```

To retrieve this item, the Gopher client sends:

```
<a_gopher_selector><tab>+<tab>1<cr><lf>
+-1<cr><lf>
<ask_item1_value><cr><lf>
<ask_item2_value><cr><lf>
.<cr><lf>
```

to the Gopher server.

3.5. Mailto

The mailto URL scheme is used to designate the Internet mailing address of an individual or service. No additional information other than an Internet mailing address is present or implied.

The mailto scheme is discussed in Section 4.1.5, "Mailto."

A mailto URL takes the form:

```
mailto:<rfc822-addr-spec>
```

where <rfc822-addr-spec> is (the encoding of an) addr-spec, as specified in RFC 822 [6]. Within mailto URLs, there are no reserved characters.

Note that the percent sign ("%") is commonly used within RFC 822 addresses and must be encoded.

Unlike many URLs, the mailto scheme does not represent a data object to be accessed directly; there is no sense in which it designates an object. It has a different use than the message/external-body type in MIME.

3.6. News

The news URL scheme is used to refer to either news groups or individual articles of USENET news, as specified in RFC 1036.

The news scheme is discussed in Section 4.1.6, "News and NNTP."

A news URL takes one of two forms:

```
news:<newsgroup-name>
news:<message-id>
```

A <newsgroup-name> is a period-delimited hierarchical name, such as "comp.infosystems.www.misc". A <message-id> corresponds to the Message-ID of section 2.1.5 of RFC 1036, without the enclosing "<" and ">"; it takes the form <unique>@<full_domain_name>. A message identifier may be distinguished from a news group name by the presence of the commercial at "@" character. No additional characters are reserved within the components of a news URL.

If <newsgroup-name> is "*" (as in <URL:news:*>), it is used to refer to "all available news groups".

The news URLs are unusual in that by themselves, they do not contain sufficient information to locate a single resource, but, rather, are location-independent.

3.7. NNTP

The nntp URL scheme is an alternative method of referencing news articles, useful for specifying news articles from NNTP servers (RFC 977).

The NNTP scheme is discussed in Section 4.1.6, "News and NNTP."

A nntp URL take the form:

```
nntp://<host>:<port>/<newsgroup-name>/<article-number>
```

where <host> and <port> are as described in Section 3.1. If :<port> is omitted, the port defaults to 119.

The <newsgroup-name> is the name of the group, while the <article- number> is the numeric id of the article within that newsgroup.

Note that while nntp: URLs specify a unique location for the article resource, most NNTP servers currently on the Internet today are configured only to allow access from local clients, and thus nntp URLs do not designate globally accessible resources. Thus, the news: form of URL is preferred as a way of identifying news articles.

3.8. Telnet

The Telnet URL scheme is used to designate interactive services that may be accessed by the Telnet protocol.

The telnet protocol is discussed in Section 4.1.7, "Telnet."

A telnet URL takes the form:

```
telnet://<user>:<password>@<host>:<port>/
```

as specified in Section 3.1. The final "/" character may be omitted. If :<port> is omitted, the port defaults to 23. The :<password> can be omitted, as well as the whole <user>:<password> part.

This URL does not designate a data object, but rather an interactive service. Remote interactive services vary widely in the means by which they allow remote logins; in practice, the <user> and <password> supplied are advisory only: clients accessing a telnet URL merely advise the user of the suggested username and password.

3.9. WAIS

The WAIS URL scheme is used to designate WAIS databases, searches, or individual documents available from a WAIS database. WAIS is described in [7]. The WAIS protocol is described in RFC 1625 [17]; Although the WAIS protocol is based on Z39.50-1988, the WAIS URL scheme is not intended for use with arbitrary Z39.50 services.

The WAIS scheme is discussed in Section 4.1.8, "WAIS."

A WAIS URL takes one of the following forms:

```
wais://<host>:<port>/<database>

wais://<host>:<port>/<database>?<search>

wais://<host>:<port>/<database>/<wtype>/<wpath>
```

where <host> and <port> are as described in Section 3.1. If :<port> is omitted, the port defaults to 210. The first form designates a WAIS database that is available for searching. The second form designates a particular search. <database> is the name of the WAIS database being queried.

The third form designates a particular document within a WAIS database to be retrieved. In this form <wtype> is the WAIS designation of the type of the object. Many WAIS implementations require that a client know the "type" of an object prior to retrieval, the type being returned along with the internal object identifier in the search response. The <wtype> is included in the URL in order to allow the client interpreting the URL adequate information to actually retrieve the document.

The <wpath> of a WAIS URL consists of the WAIS document-id, encoded as necessary using the method described in Section 2.2. The WAIS document-id should be treated opaquely; it may only be decomposed by the server that issued it.

3.10 Files

The file URL scheme is used to designate files accessible on a particular host computer. This scheme, unlike most other URL schemes, does not designate a resource that is universally accessible over the Internet.

The file scheme is discussed in Section 4.1.9, "File."

A file URL takes the form:

```
file://<host>/<path>
```

where <host> is the fully qualified domain name of the system on which the <path> is accessible, and <path> is a hierarchical directory path of the form <directory>/<directory>/.../<name>.

For example, a VMS file

```
DISK$USER:[MY.NOTES]NOTE123456.TXT
```

might become

```
<URL:file://vms.host.edu/disk$user/my/notes/note12345.txt>
```

As a special case, <host> can be the string "localhost" or the empty string; this is interpreted as `the machine from which the URL is being interpreted'.

The file URL scheme is unusual in that it does not specify an Internet protocol or access method for such files; as such, its utility in network protocols between hosts is limited.

3.11 Prospero

The Prospero URL scheme is used to designate resources that are accessed via the Prospero Directory Service. The Prospero protocol is described elsewhere [14].

The Prospero scheme is discussed in Section 4.1.10, "Prospero."

A prospero URLs takes the form:

prospero://<host>:<port>/<hsoname>;<field>=<value>

where <host> and <port> are as described in Section 3.1. If :<port> is omitted, the port defaults to 1525. No username or password is allowed.

The <hsoname> is the host-specific object name in the Prospero protocol, suitably encoded. This name is opaque and interpreted by the Prospero server. The semicolon ";" is reserved and may not appear without quoting in the <hsoname>.

Prospero URLs are interpreted by contacting a Prospero directory server on the specified host and port to determine appropriate access methods for a resource, which might themselves be represented as different URLs. External Prospero links are represented as URLs of the underlying access method and are not represented as Prospero URLs.

Note that a slash "/" may appear in the <hsoname> without quoting and no significance may be assumed by the application. Though slashes may indicate hierarchical structure on the server, such structure is not guaranteed. Note that many <hsoname>s begin with a slash, in which case the host or port will be followed by a double slash: the slash from the URL syntax, followed by the initial slash from the <hsoname>. (E.g., <URL:prospero://host.dom//pros/name> designates a <hsoname> of "/pros/name".)

In addition, after the <hsoname>, optional fields and values associated with a Prospero link may be specified as part of the URL. When present, each field/value pair is separated from each other and from the rest of the URL by a ";" (semicolon). The name of the field and its value are separated by a "=" (equal sign). If present, these fields serve to identify the target of the URL. For example, the OBJECT-VERSION field can be specified to identify a specific version of an object.

4. Registration of New Schemes

A new scheme may be introduced by defining a mapping onto a conforming URL syntax, using a new prefix. URLs for experimental schemes may be used by mutual agreement between parties. Scheme names starting with the characters "x-" are reserved for experimental purposes.

The Internet Assigned Numbers Authority (IANA) will maintain a registry of URL schemes. Any submission of a new URL scheme must include a definition of an algorithm for accessing of resources within that scheme and the syntax for representing such a scheme.

URL schemes must have demonstrable utility and operability. One way to provide such a demonstration is via a gateway which provides objects in the new scheme for clients using an existing protocol. If the new scheme does not locate resources that are data objects, the properties of names in the new space must be clearly defined.

New schemes should try to follow the same syntactic conventions of existing schemes, where appropriate. It is likewise recommended that, where a protocol allows for retrieval by URL, that the client software have provision for being configured to use specific gateway locators for indirect access through new naming schemes.

The following scheme have been proposed at various times, but this document does not define their syntax or use at this time. It is suggested that IANA reserve their scheme names for future definition:

```
afs          Andrew File System global file names.
mid          Message identifiers for electronic mail.
cid          Content identifiers for MIME body parts.
nfs          Network File System (NFS) file names.
tn3270       Interactive 3270 emulation sessions.
mailserver   Access to data available from mail servers.
z39.50       Access to ANSI Z39.50 services.
```

5. BNF for Specific URL Schemes

This is a BNF-like description of the Uniform Resource Locator syntax, using the conventions of RFC822, except that "|" is used to designate alternatives, and brackets [] are used around optional or repeated elements. Briefly, literals are quoted with "", optional elements are enclosed in [brackets], and elements may be preceded with <n>* to designate n or more repetitions of the following element; n defaults to 0.

```
; The generic form of a URL is:

      genericurl     = scheme ":" schemepart

; Specific predefined schemes are defined here; new schemes

; may be registered with IANA

      url            = httpurl | ftpurl | newsurl |
                       nntpurl | telneturl | gopherurl |
                       waisurl | mailtourl | fileurl |
                       prosperourl | otherurl

; new schemes follow the general syntax

      otherurl       = genericurl

; the scheme is in lower case; interpreters should use case-ignore

      scheme         = 1*[ lowalpha | digit | "+" | "-" | "." ]
      schemepart     = *xchar | ip-schemepart

; URL schemeparts for ip based protocols:

      ip-schemepart  = "//" login [ "/" urlpath ]
      login          = [ user [ ":" password ] "@" ] hostport
      hostport       = host [ ":" port ]
      host           = hostname | hostnumber
      hostname       = *[ domainlabel "." ] toplabel
      domainlabel    = alphadigit | alphadigit *[ alphadigit | "-" ] alphadigit
      toplabel       = alpha | alpha *[ alphadigit | "-" ] alphadigit
      alphadigit     = alpha | digit
      hostnumber     = digits "." digits "." digits "." digits
```

```
      port            = digits
      user            = *[ uchar | ";" | "?" | "&" | "=" ]
      password        = *[ uchar | ";" | "?" | "&" | "=" ]
      urlpath         = *xchar    ; depends on protocol see section 3.1

; The predefined schemes:

; FTP (see also RFC959)

      ftpurl          = "ftp://" login [ "/" fpath [ ";type=" ftptype ]]
      fpath           = fsegment *[ "/" fsegment ]
      fsegment        = *[ uchar | "?" | ":" | "@" | "&" | "=" ]
      ftptype         = "A" | "I" | "D" | "a" | "i" | "d"

; FILE

      fileurl         = "file://" [ host | "localhost" ] "/" fpath

; HTTP

      httpurl         = "http://" hostport [ "/" hpath [ "?" search ]]
      hpath           = hsegment *[ "/" hsegment ]
      hsegment        = *[ uchar | ";" | ":" | "@" | "&" | "=" ]
      search          = *[ uchar | ";" | ":" | "@" | "&" | "=" ]

; GOPHER (see also RFC1436)

      gopherurl       = "gopher://" hostport [ / [ gtype [ selector
                        [ "%09" search [ "%09" gopher+_string ] ] ] ] ]
      gtype           = xchar
      selector        = *xchar
      gopher+_string = *xchar

; MAILTO (see also RFC822)

      mailtourl       = "mailto:" encoded822addr
      encoded822addr = 1*xchar               ; further defined in RFC822

; NEWS (see also RFC1036)

      newsurl         = "news:" grouppart
      grouppart       = "*" | group | article
      group           = alpha *[ alpha | digit | "-" | "." | "+" | "_" ]
      article        = 1*[ uchar | ";" | "/" | "?" | ":" | "&" | "=" ] "@" host

; NNTP (see also RFC977)

      nntpurl         = "nntp://" hostport "/" group [ "/" digits ]

; TELNET

      telneturl       = "telnet://" login [ "/" ]

; WAIS (see also RFC1625)

      waisurl         = waisdatabase | waisindex | waisdoc
      waisdatabase    = "wais://" hostport "/" database
      waisindex       = "wais://" hostport "/" database "?" search
      waisdoc         = "wais://" hostport "/" database "/" wtype "/" wpath
      database        = *uchar
```

```
        wtype           = *uchar
        wpath           = *uchar

; PROSPERO

        prosperourl     = "prospero://" hostport "/" ppath *[ fieldspec ]
        ppath           = psegment *[ "/" psegment ]
        psegment        = *[ uchar | "?" | ":" | "@" | "&" | "=" ]
        fieldspec       = ";" fieldname "=" fieldvalue
        fieldname       = *[ uchar | "?" | ":" | "@" | "&" ]
        fieldvalue      = *[ uchar | "?" | ":" | "@" | "&" ]

; Miscellaneous definitions

        lowalpha        = "a" | "b" | "c" | "d" | "e" | "f" | "g" | "h" |
                          "i" | "j" | "k" | "l" | "m" | "n" | "o" | "p" |
                          "q" | "r" | "s" | "t" | "u" | "v" | "w" | "x" |
                          "y" | "z"
        hialpha         = "A" | "B" | "C" | "D" | "E" | "F" | "G" | "H" | "I" |
                          "J" | "K" | "L" | "M" | "N" | "O" | "P" | "Q" | "R" |
                          "S" | "T" | "U" | "V" | "W" | "X" | "Y" | "Z"
        alpha           = lowalpha | hialpha
        digit           = "0" | "1" | "2" | "3" | "4" | "5" | "6" | "7" |
                          "8" | "9"
        safe            = "$" | "-" | "_" | "." | "+"
        extra           = "!" | "*" | "'" | "(" | ")" | ","
        national        = "{" | "}" | "|" | "\" | "^" | "~" | "[" | "]" | "`"
        punctuation     = "<" | ">" | "#" | "%" | <">

        reserved        = ";" | "/" | "?" | ":" | "@" | "&" | "="
        hex             = digit | "A" | "B" | "C" | "D" | "E" | "F" |
                          "a" | "b" | "c" | "d" | "e" | "f"
        escape          = "%" hex hex

        unreserved      = alpha | digit | safe | extra
        uchar           = unreserved | escape
        xchar           = unreserved | reserved | escape
        digits          = 1*digit
```

6. Security Considerations

The URL scheme does not in itself pose a security threat. Users should beware that there is no general guarantee that a URL which at one time points to a given object continues to do so, and does not even at some later time point to a different object due to the movement of objects on servers.

A URL-related security threat is that it is sometimes possible to construct a URL such that an attempt to perform a harmless idempotent operation such as the retrieval of the object will in fact cause a possibly damaging remote operation to occur. The unsafe URL is typically constructed by specifying a port number other than that reserved for the network protocol in question. The client unwittingly contacts a server which is in fact running a different protocol. The content of the URL contains instructions which when interpreted according to this other protocol cause an unexpected operation. An example has been the use of gopher URLs to cause a rude message to be sent via a SMTP server. Caution should be used when using any URL which specifies a port number other than the default for the protocol, especially when it is a number within the reserved space.

Care should be taken when URLs contain embedded encoded delimiters for a given protocol (for example, CR and LF characters for telnet protocols) that these are not unencoded before transmission. This would violate the protocol but could be used to simulate an extra operation or parameter, again causing an unexpected and possible harmful remote operation to be performed.

The use of URLs containing passwords that should be secret is clearly unwise.

7. Acknowledgements

This paper builds on the basic WWW design (RFC 1630) and much discussion of these issues by many people on the network. The discussion was particularly stimulated by articles by Clifford Lynch, Brewster Kahle [10] and Wengyik Yeong [18]. Contributions from John Curran, Clifford Neuman, Ed Vielmetti and later the IETF URL BOF and URI working group were incorporated.

Most recently, careful readings and comments by Dan Connolly, Ned Freed, Roy Fielding, Guido van Rossum, Michael Dolan, Bert Bos, John Kunze, Olle Jarnefors, Peter Svanberg and many others have helped refine this RFC.

APPENDIX: Recommendations for URLs in Context

URIs, including URLs, are intended to be transmitted through protocols which provide a context for their interpretation.

In some cases, it will be necessary to distinguish URLs from other possible data structures in a syntactic structure. In this case, is recommended that URLs be preceeded with a prefix consisting of the characters "URL:". For example, this prefix may be used to distinguish URLs from other kinds of URIs.

In addition, there are many occasions when URLs are included in other kinds of text; examples include electronic mail, USENET news messages, or printed on paper. In such cases, it is convenient to have a separate syntactic wrapper that delimits the URL and separates it from the rest of the text, and in particular from punctuation marks that might be mistaken for part of the URL. For this purpose, is recommended that angle brackets ("<" and ">"), along with the prefix "URL:", be used to delimit the boundaries of the URL. This wrapper does not form part of the URL and should not be used in contexts in which delimiters are already specified.

In the case where a fragment/anchor identifier is associated with a URL (following a "#"), the identifier would be placed within the brackets as well.

In some cases, extra whitespace (spaces, linebreaks, tabs, etc.) may need to be added to break long URLs across lines. The whitespace should be ignored when extracting the URL.

No whitespace should be introduced after a hyphen ("-") character. Because some typesetters and printers may (erroneously) introduce a hyphen at the end of line when breaking a line, the interpreter of a URL containing a line break immediately after a hyphen should ignore all unencoded whitespace around the line break, and should be aware that the hyphen may or may not actually be part of the URL.

Examples:

Yes, Jim, I found it under <URL:ftp://info.cern.ch/pub/www/doc;
type=d> but you can probably pick it up from <URL:ftp://ds.in
ternic.net/rfc>. Note the warning in <URL:http://ds.internic.
net/instructions/overview.html#WARNING>.

References

[1] Anklesaria, F., McCahill, M., Lindner, P., Johnson, D., Torrey, D., and B. Alberti, "The Internet Gopher Protocol (a distributed document search and retrieval protocol)", RFC 1436, University of Minnesota, March 1993. <URL:ftp://ds.internic.net/rfc/rfc1436.txt;type=a>

[2] Anklesaria, F., Lindner, P., McCahill, M., Torrey, D., Johnson, D., and B. Alberti, "Gopher+: Upward compatible enhancements to the Internet Gopher protocol", University of Minnesota, July 1993. <URL:ftp://boombox.micro.umn.edu/pub/gopher/gopher_protocol/Gopher+/Gopher+.txt>

[3] Berners-Lee, T., "Universal Resource Identifiers in WWW: A Unifying Syntax for the Expression of Names and Addresses of Objects on the Network as used in the World-Wide Web", RFC 1630, CERN, June 1994. <URL:ftp://ds.internic.net/rfc/rfc1630.txt>

[4] Berners-Lee, T., "Hypertext Transfer Protocol (HTTP)", CERN, November 1993. <URL:ftp://info.cern.ch/pub/www/doc/http-spec.txt.Z>

[5] Braden, R., Editor, "Requirements for Internet Hosts -- Application and Support", STD 3, RFC 1123, IETF, October 1989. <URL:ftp://ds.internic.net/rfc/rfc1123.txt>

[6] Crocker, D. "Standard for the Format of ARPA Internet Text essages", STD 11, RFC 822, UDEL, April 1982. URL:ftp://ds.internic.net/rfc/rfc822.txt>

[7] Davis, F., Kahle, B., Morris, H., Salem, J., Shen, T., Wang, R., Sui, J., and M. Grinbaum, "WAIS Interface Protocol Prototype Functional Specification", (v1.5), Thinking Machines Corporation, April 1990. <URL:ftp://quake.think.com/pub/wais/doc/protspec.txt>

[8] Horton, M. and R. Adams, "Standard For Interchange of USENET Messages", RFC 1036, AT&T Bell Laboratories, Center for Seismic Studies, December 1987. <URL:ftp://ds.internic.net/rfc/rfc1036.txt>

[9] Huitema, C., "Naming: Strategies and Techniques", Computer Networks and ISDN Systems 23 (1991) 107-110.

[10] Kahle, B., "Document Identifiers, or International Standard Book Numbers for the Electronic Age", 1991. <URL:ftp://quake.think.com/pub/wais/doc/doc-ids.txt>

[11] Kantor, B. and P. Lapsley, "Network News Transfer Protocol: A Proposed Standard for the Stream-Based Transmission of News", RFC 977, UC San Diego & UC Berkeley, February 1986. <URL:ftp://ds.internic.net/rfc/rfc977.txt>

[12] Kunze, J., "Functional Requirements for Internet Resource Locators", Work in Progress, December 1994. <URL:ftp://ds.internic.net/internet-drafts/draft-ietf-uri-irl-fun-req-02.txt>

[13] Mockapetris, P., "Domain Names - Concepts and Facilities", STD 13, RFC 1034, USC/Information Sciences Institute, November 1987. <URL:ftp://ds.internic.net/rfc/rfc1034.txt>

[14] Neuman, B., and S. Augart, "The Prospero Protocol", USC/Information Sciences Institute, June 1993. <URL:ftp://prospero.isi.edu/pub/prospero/doc/prospero-protocol.PS.Z>

[15] Postel, J. and J. Reynolds, "File Transfer Protocol (FTP)", STD 9, RFC 959, USC/Information Sciences Institute, October 1985. <URL:ftp://ds.internic.net/rfc/rfc959.txt>

[16] Sollins, K. and L. Masinter, "Functional Requirements for Uniform Resource Names", RFC 1737, MIT/LCS, Xerox Corporation, December 1994. <URL:ftp://ds.internic.net/rfc/rfc1737.txt>

[17] St. Pierre, M, Fullton, J., Gamiel, K., Goldman, J., Kahle, B., Kunze, J., Morris, H., and F. Schiettecatte, "WAIS over Z39.50-1988", RFC 1625, WAIS, Inc., CNIDR, Thinking Machines Corp., UC Berkeley, FS Consulting, June 1994. <URL:ftp://ds.internic.net/rfc/rfc1625.txt>

[18] Yeong, W. "Towards Networked Information Retrieval", Technical report 91-06-25-01, Performance Systems International, Inc. <URL:ftp://uu.psi.com/wp/nir.txt>, June 1991.

[19] Yeong, W., "Representing Public Archives in the Directory", Work in Progress, November 1991.

[20] "Coded Character Set -- 7-bit American Standard Code for Information Interchange", ANSI X3.4-1986.

Editors' Addresses

Tim Berners-Lee

World-Wide Web project

CERN

1211 Geneva 23

Switzerland

Phone: +41 (22)767 3755

Fax: +41 (22)767 7155

EMail: timbl@info.cern.ch

Larry Masinter

Xerox PARC

3333 Coyote Hill Road

Palo Alto, CA 94034

Phone: (415) 812-4365

Fax: (415) 812-4333

EMail: masinter@parc.xerox.com

Mark McCahill

Computer and Information Services

University of Minnesota

Room 152 Shepherd Labs

100 Union Street SE

Minneapolis, MN 55455

Phone: (612) 625 1300

EMail: mpm@boombox.micro.umn.edu

A P P E N D I X B

Hypertext Transfer Protocol—HTTP/1.0[1]

HTTP Working Group T. Berners-Lee
INTERNET-DRAFT R. T. Fielding
<draft-ietf-http-v10-spec-00.txt> H. Frystyk Nielsen
Expires September 8, 1995 March 8, 1995

Status of This Memo

This document is an Internet-Draft. Internet-Drafts are working documents of the Internet Engineering Task Force (IETF), its areas, and its working groups. Note that other groups may also distribute working documents as Internet-Drafts.

Internet-Drafts are draft documents valid for a maximum of six months and may be updated, replaced, or obsoleted by other documents at any time. It is inappropriate to use Internet-Drafts as reference material or to cite them other than as "work in progress".

To learn the current status of any Internet-Draft, please check the "1id-abstracts.txt" listing contained in the Internet-Drafts Shadow Directories on ftp.is.co.za (Africa), nic.nordu.net (Europe), munnari.oz.au (Pacific Rim), ds.internic.net (US East Coast), or ftp.isi.edu (US West Coast).

Distribution of this document is unlimited. Please send comments to the HTTP working group at <http-wg@cuckoo.hpl.hp.com>. Discussions of the working group are archived at <URL:http://www.ics.uci.edu/pub/ietf/http/>. General discussions about HTTP and the applications which use HTTP should take place on the <www-talk@info.cern.ch> mailing list.

Abstract

The Hypertext Transfer Protocol (HTTP) is an application-level protocol with the lightness and speed necessary for distributed, collaborative, hypermedia

1. Note: This draft will expire. See **http://www.netgen.com/book/http-spec** for information on the current state of this protocol.

information systems. It is a generic, stateless, object-oriented protocol which can be used for many tasks, such as name servers and distributed object management systems, through extension of its request methods (commands). A feature of HTTP is the typing and negotiation of data representation, allowing systems to be built independently of the data being transferred.

HTTP has been in use by the World-Wide Web global information initiative since 1990. This specification reflects preferred usage of the protocol referred to as "HTTP/1.0", and is compatible with the most commonly used HTTP server and client programs implemented prior to November 1994.

Table of Contents

1. Introduction

1.1 Purpose

The Hypertext Transfer Protocol (HTTP) is an application-level protocol with the lightness and speed necessary for distributed, collaborative, hypermedia information systems. HTTP has been in use by the World-Wide Web global information initiative since 1990. This specification reflects preferred usage of the protocol referred to as "HTTP/1.0". This specification does not necessarily reflect the "current practice" of any single HTTP server or client implementation. It does, however, seek to remain compatible with existing implementations wherever possible, and should be considered the reference for future implementations of HTTP/1.0.

Practical information systems require more functionality than simple retrieval, including search, front-end update, and annotation. HTTP/1.0 allows an open-ended set of methods to be used to indicate the purpose of a request. It builds on the discipline of reference provided by the Universal Resource Identifier (URI) [3], as a location (URL) [5] or name (URN), for indicating the resource on which a method is to be applied. Messages are passed in a format similar to that used by Internet Mail [8] and the Multipurpose Internet Mail Extensions (MIME) [6].

HTTP/1.0 is also used for communication between user agents and various gateways, allowing hypermedia access to existing Internet protocols like SMTP [14], NNTP [12], FTP [16], Gopher [2], and WAIS [9]. HTTP/1.0 is designed to allow such gateways, via proxy servers, without any loss of the data conveyed by those earlier protocols.

1.2 Overall Operation

The HTTP protocol is based on a request/response paradigm. A requesting program (termed a client) establishes a connection with a receiving program (termed a server) and sends a request to the server in the form of a request method, URI, and protocol version, followed by a MIME-like message containing request modifiers, client information, and possible body content. The server responds with a status line (including its protocol version and a success or error code), followed by a MIME-like message containing server information, entity metainformation, and possible body content. It should be noted that a given program may be capable of being both a client and a server; our use of those terms refers only to the role being performed by the program during a particular connection, rather than to the program's purpose in general.

On the Internet, the communication generally takes place over a TCP/IP connection. The default port is TCP 80 [17], but other ports can be used. This does not preclude the HTTP/1.0 protocol from being implemented on top of any other protocol on the Internet, or on other networks. The mapping of the HTTP/1.0 request and response structures onto the transport data units of the protocol in question is outside the scope of this specification.

For most implementations, the connection is established by the client prior to each request and closed by the server after sending the response. However, this is not a feature of the protocol and is not required by this specification. Both clients and servers must be capable of handling cases where either party closes the connection prematurely, due to user action, automated time-out, or program failure. In any case, the closing of the connection by either or both parties always terminates the current request, regardless of its status.

1.3 Terminology

This specification uses a number of terms to refer to the roles played by participants in, and objects of, the HTTP communication.

connection — A virtual circuit established between two parties for the purpose of communication.

message — A structured sequence of octets transmitted via the connection as the basic component of communication.

request — An HTTP request message (as defined in Section 5).

response — An HTTP response message (as defined in Section 6).

resource — A network data object or service which can be identified by a URI.

entity — A particular representation or rendition of a resource that may be enclosed within a request or response message. An entity consists of metainformation (in the form of entity headers) and content (in the form of an entity body).

One of the major semantic changes between this version of the specifications and previous versions was the change from calling the data sent in HTTP transactions the "Entity." Previously, this portion of the request or response was called the "Object." Therefore, the portion of the header describing this data is now called the "Entity-Header" and the data itself is called the "Entity-Body."

client — A program that establishes connections for the purpose of sending requests.

user agent — The client program which is closest to the user and which initiates requests at their behest.

server — A program that accepts connections in order to service requests by sending back responses.

origin server — The server on which a given resource resides or is to be created.

proxy — An intermediary program which acts as both a server and a client for the purpose of forwarding requests. Proxies are often used to act as a portal through a network firewall. A proxy server accepts requests from other clients and services them either internally or by passing them (with possible translation) on to other servers. A caching proxy is a proxy server with a local cache of server responses -- some requested resources can be serviced from the cache rather than from the origin server. Some proxy servers also act as origin servers.

See Section 4.2.6: "Proxy Servers and Gateways," for a discussion of caching and proxy servers.

gateway — A proxy which services HTTP requests by translation into protocols other than HTTP. The reply sent from the remote server to the gateway is likewise translated into HTTP before being forwarded to the user agent.

Section 4.2.6 also contains a discussion about the differences between a gateway and a proxy.

2. Notational Conventions and Generic Grammar

2.1 Augmented BNF

All of the mechanisms specified in this document are described in both prose and an augmented Backus-Naur Form (BNF) similar to that used by RFC 822 [8]. Implementors will need to be familiar with the notation in order to understand this specification. The augmented BNF includes the following constructs:

name = definition

The name of a rule is simply the name itself (without any enclosing "<" and ">") and is separated from its definition by the equal character "=". Whitespace is only significant in that indentation of continuation lines is used to indicate a rule definition that spans more than one line. Certain basic rules are in uppercase, such as SP, LWS, HTAB, CRLF, DIGIT, ALPHA, etc. Angle brackets are used within definitions whenever their presence will facilitate discerning the use of rule names.

"literal"

Quotation marks surround literal text. Unless stated otherwise, the text is case-insensitive.

rule1 | rule2

Elements separated by a bar ("I") are alternatives, e.g. "yes | no" will accept yes or no.

(rule1 rule2)

Elements enclosed in parentheses are treated as a single element. Thus,"(elem (foo | bar) elem)" allows the token sequences "elem foo elem" and "elem bar elem".

*rule

The character "*" preceding an element indicates repetition. The full form is "<n>*<m>element" indicating at least <n> and at most <m> occurrences of element. Default values are 0 and infinity so that "*(element)" allows any number, including zero; "1*element" requires at least one; and "1*2element" allows one or two.

[rule]

Square brackets enclose optional elements; "[foo bar]" is equivalent to "*1(foo bar)".

N rule

Specific repetition: "<n>(element)" is equivalent to "<n>*<n>(element)"; that is, exactly <n> occurrences of (element). Thus 2DIGIT is a 2-digit number, and 3ALPHA is a string of three alphabetic characters.

#rule

A construct "#" is defined, similar to "*", for defining lists of elements. The full form is "<n>#<m>element" indicating at least <n> and at most <m> elements, each separated by one or more commas (",") and optional linear whitespace (LWS). This makes the usual form of lists very easy; a rule such as "(*LWS element *(*LWS "," *LWS element))" can be shown as "1#element". Wherever this construct is used, null elements are allowed, but do not contribute to the count of elements present. That is, "(element), , (element)" is permitted, but counts as only two elements. Therefore, where at least one element is required, at least one non-null element must be present. Default values are 0 and infinity so that "#(element)" allows any number, including zero; "1#element" requires at least one; and "1#2element" allows one or two.

; comment

A semi-colon, set off some distance to the right of rule text, starts a comment that continues to the end of line. This is a simple way of including useful notes in parallel with the specifications.

implied *LWS

The grammar described by this specification is word-based. Except where noted otherwise, zero or more linear whitespace (LWS) can be included between any two words (token or quoted-string) without changing the interpretation of a field. However, applications should attempt to follow "common form" when generating HTTP constructs, since there exist some implementations that fail to accept anything beyond the common forms.

2.2 Basic Rules

The following rules are used throughout this specification to describe basic parsing constructs. The US-ASCII character set is defined by [18].

```
OCTET          = <any 8-bit character>
CHAR           = <any US-ASCII character (octets 0 - 127)>
UPALPHA        = <any US-ASCII uppercase letter "A".."Z">
LOALPHA        = <any US-ASCII lowercase letter "a".."z">
ALPHA          = UPALPHA | LOALPHA
DIGIT          = <any US-ASCII digit "0".."9">
CTL            = <any US-ASCII control character (octets 0 -
                 31) and DEL (127)>
CR             = <US-ASCII CR, carriage return (13)>
LF             = <US-ASCII LF, linefeed (10)>
SP             = <US-ASCII SP, space (32)>
HTAB           = <US-ASCII HT, horizontal-tab (9)>
<">            = <US-ASCII double-quote mark>
```

HTTP/1.0 defines the octet sequence CR LF as the end-of-line marker for all protocol elements except the Entity-Body (see Appendix C for tolerant applications). The end-of-line marker for an Entity-Body is defined by its associated media type, as described in Section 8.1.

```
CRLF           = CR LF
```

HTTP/1.0 headers can be folded onto multiple lines if the continuation lines begin with linear whitespace characters. All linear whitespace (including folding) has the same semantics as SP.

```
LWS            = [CRLF] 1*( SP | HTAB )
```

Many HTTP/1.0 header field values consist of words separated by LWS or special characters. These special characters must be in a quoted string to be used within a parameter value.

```
word                    = token | quoted-string
token                   = 1*<any CHAR except CTLs or tspecials>
tspecials               = "(" | ")" | "<" | ">" | "@" | "," | ";" |
                          ":" | "\" | <"> | "/" | "[" | "]" | "?" | "="
                          | SP | HTAB
```

A string of text is parsed as a single word if it is quoted using double-quote marks or angle brackets.

```
quoted-string           = ( <"> *(qdtext) <"> ) | ( "<" *(qatext) ">" )
qdtext                  = <any CHAR except <"> and CTLs, but including
                          LWS>
qatext                  = <any CHAR except "<", ">", and CTLs, but
                          including LWS>
```

The text rule is only used for descriptive field contents. Words of *text may contain characters from character sets other than US-ASCII only when encoded according to the rules of RFC 1522 [13].

```
text                    = <any OCTET except CTLs, but including LWS>
```

3. Protocol Parameters

3.1 HTTP Version

HTTP uses a "<major>.<minor>" numbering scheme to indicate versions of the protocol. The protocol versioning policy is intended to allow the sender to indicate the format of a message and its capacity for understanding further HTTP communication, rather than the features obtained via that communication. No change is made to the version number for the addition of message components which do not affect communication behavior or which only add to extensible field values. The <minor> number is incremented when the changes made to the protocol add features which do not change the general message parsing algorithm, but which may add to the message semantics and imply additional capabilities of the sender. The <major> number is incremented when the format of a message within the protocol is changed.

The version of an HTTP message is indicated by an HTTP-Version field in the first line of the message. If the protocol version is not specified, the recipient must assume that the message is in the simple HTTP/0.9 format.

```
HTTP-Version            = "HTTP" "/" 1*DIGIT "." 1*DIGIT
```

Note that the major and minor numbers should be treated as separate integers and that each may be incremented higher than a single digit. Thus, HTTP/2.4 is a lower version than HTTP/2.13, which in turn is lower than HTTP/12.3. Leading zeroes should be ignored by recipients and never generated by senders.

This document defines both the 0.9 and 1.0 versions of the HTTP protocol. Applications sending Full-Request or Full-Response messages, as defined by this specification, must include an HTTP-Version of "HTTP/1.0".

HTTP servers are required to be able to recognize the format of the Request-Line for all lower-version requests, understand requests with a format within one major number of their native version (i.e. <major1> and <major>), and respond appropriately with a message within the same <major> protocol number (even if the response is simply an error message). HTTP clients are required to be able to recognize the format of the Status-Line for all lower-version responses and understand responses with a format within one major number of their request version. The following hypothetical example illustrates the required behavior.

* A valid HTTP/3.5 request is received and the server's native protocol version is

* Less than 3.0: it should attempt to understand the request and respond (possibly with an error) in its native format;

* Major number of 3: It should understand the request and respond in its native format;

* Major number of 4: It should understand the request and respond with a version 3 message;

* Major number higher than 4: It should attempt to understand the request and respond (possibly with an error) with a version 3 message;

* User agent receives a response to an HTTP/3.5 request, and the response version is

* Less than 2.0: It should attempt to understand the response and unobtrusively warn the user of the version mismatch;

* 2.0--3.4: It should understand the response and be aware that its request may not have been fully understood by the server;

* 3.5 or higher 3: It should understand the response and can assume that the server understood all aspects of the request if the response does not indicate an error;

* 4.0 or higher: It should attempt to understand the response and unobtrusively warn the user of the version mismatch.

Proxies must be careful in forwarding requests that are received in a format different than that of the proxy's native version. Since the protocol version indicates the protocol capability of the sender, a proxy must never send a message with a version indicator which is greater than its native version; if a higher version request is received, the proxy must either downgrade the request version or respond with an error. Requests with a version lower than that of the proxy's native format may be upgraded by the proxy before being forwarded; the proxy's response to that request must follow the normal server requirements.

3.2 Universal Resource Identifiers

This section is To-Be-Specified. It will contain a brief description of URIs as defined by RFC 1630, including mention of the allowed characters and the hex encoding, and provide a full definition of the http URL scheme.

```
URI                = <As defined in RFC 1630>
```

All URI protocol elements must be encoded using the escaping scheme described in RFC 1630 [3].

See **http://www.netgen.com/book** *for the full text of RFC 1630.*

3.3 Date/Time Formats

3.3.1 Full Date

HTTP/1.0 applications have historically allowed three different formats for the representation of date/time stamps:

```
Sun, 06 Nov 1994 08:49:37 GMT    ; RFC 822, updated by RFC 1123
Sunday, 06-Nov-94 08:49:37 GMT   ; RFC 850, obsoleted by RFC 1036
Sun Nov  6 08:49:37 1994         ; ANSI C's asctime() format
```

The first format is preferred as an Internet standard and represents a fixed-length subset of that defined by RFC 1123 [7] (an update to RFC 822 [8]). The second format is in common use, but is based on the obsolete RFC 850 [11] date format and lacks a four-digit year. HTTP/1.0 clients and servers must accept all three formats, though they should never generate the third (asctime) format. Future clients and servers must only generate the RFC 1123 format for representing date/time stamps in HTTP/1.0 requests and responses.

All HTTP/1.0 date/time stamps must be represented in Universal Time (UT), also known as Greenwich Mean Time (GMT), without exception. This is indicated in the first two formats by the inclusion of "GMT" as the three-letter abbreviation for time zone, and should be assumed when reading the asctime format.

```
HTTP-date      = rfc1123-date | rfc850-date | asctime-date

rfc1123-date   = wkday "," SP date1 SP time SP "GMT"
rfc850-date    = weekday "," SP date2 SP time SP "GMT"
asctime-date   = wkday SP date3 SP time SP 4DIGIT

date1          = 2DIGIT SP month SP 4DIGIT
                 ; day month year (e.g. 02 Jun 1982)

date2          = 2DIGIT "-" month "-" 2DIGIT
                 ; day-month-year (e.g. 02-Jun-82)

date3          = month SP ( 2DIGIT | ( SP 1DIGIT ))
                 ; month day (e.g. Jun  2)

time           = 2DIGIT ":" 2DIGIT ":" 2DIGIT
                 ; 00:00:00 - 23:59:59

wkday          = "Mon" | "Tue" | "Wed"
               | "Thu" | "Fri" | "Sat" | "Sun"
```

```
weekday        = "Monday" | "Tuesday" | "Wednesday"
               | "Thursday" | "Friday" | "Saturday" |
               "Sunday"

month          = "Jan" | "Feb" | "Mar" | "Apr"
               | "May" | "Jun" | "Jul" | "Aug"
               | "Sep" | "Oct" | "Nov" | "Dec"
```

Comments and/or extra LWS are not permitted inside an HTTP-date value generated by a conformant application. However, recipients of date values should be robust in accepting date values that may have been generated by non-HTTP applications (as is sometimes the case when retrieving or posting messages via gateways to SMTP or NNTP).

Note: HTTP/1.0 requirements for the date/time stamp format apply only to their usage within the protocol stream. Clients and servers are not required to use these formats for user presentation, request logging, etc.

3.3.2 Delta Seconds

Some HTTP header fields allow a time value to be specified as an integer number of seconds (represented in decimal) after the time that the message was received. This format should only be used to represent short time periods or periods that cannot start until receipt of the message.

```
delta-seconds  = 1*DIGIT
```

4. HTTP Message

4.1 Message Types

HTTP messages consist of requests from client to server and responses from server to client.

```
HTTP-message   = Simple-Request           ; HTTP/0.9 messages
               | Simple-Response
               | Full-Request             ; HTTP/1.0 messages
               | Full-Response
```

Full-Request and Full-Response use the generic message format of RFC 822 [8] for transferring entities. Both messages may include optional header fields (a.k.a. "headers") and an entity body. The entity body is separated from the headers by a null line (i.e., a line with nothing preceding the CRLF).

```
Full-Request   = Request-Line              ; Section 5.1
                 *( General-Header         ; Section 4.3
                  | Request-Header         ; Section 5.4
                  | Entity-Header )        ; Section 7.1
                 CRLF
                 [ Entity-Body ]           ; Section 7.2

Full-Response  = Status-Line               ; Section 6.1
                 *( General-Header         ; Section 4.3
                  | Response-Header        ; Section 6.3
                  | Entity-Header )        ; Section 7.1
```

```
                    CRLF
                    [ Entity-Body ]          ; Section 7.2
```

Simple-Request and Simple-Response do not allow the use of any header information and are limited to a single request method (GET).

```
Simple-Request         = "GET" SP Request-URI CRLF

Simple-Response        = [ Entity-Body ]
```

Use of the Simple-Request format is discouraged because it prevents the client from using content negotiation and the server from identifying the media type of the returned entity.

4.2 Message Headers

HTTP header fields, which include General-Header (Section 4.3), Request-Header (Section 5.4), Response-Header (Section 6.3), and Entity-Header (Section 7.1) fields, follow the same generic format as that given in Section 3.1 of RFC 822 [8]. Each header field consists of a name followed by a colon (":") and the field value. The field value may be preceded by any amount of LWS, though a single SP is preferred. Header fields can be extended over multiple lines by preceding each extra line with at least one LWS.

```
HTTP-header            = field-name ":" [ field-value ] CRLF

field-name             = 1*<any CHAR, excluding CTLs, SP, and ":">
field-value            = *( field-content | comment | LWS )

field-content          = <the OCTETs making up the field-value and
                         consisting of either *text or combinations of
                         token, tspecials, and quoted-string>
```

The order in which header fields are received is not significant. However, it is considered "good practice" to send General-Header fields first, followed by Request-Header or Response-Header fields prior to the Entity-Header fields. Comments can be included in HTTP header fields by surrounding the comment text with parentheses.

```
comment                = "(" *( ctext | comment ) ")"
ctext                  = <any text excluding "(" and ")">
```

Note: Use of comments within HTTP headers is generally discouraged, since they are rarely seen by human eyes and hence only increase network traffic. However, they may be useful for messages posted or retrieved via NNTP and SMTP gateways.

4.3 General Message Header Fields

There are a few header fields which have general applicability for both request and response messages, but which do not apply to the communicating parties or the entity being transferred. Although none of the General-Header fields are required, they are all strongly recommended where their use is appropriate, and should be understood by all future HTTP/1.0 clients and servers. These headers apply only to the message being transmitted.

General message header fields are discussed in Section 5.1.6, "Meta-information."

```
General-Header          = Date
                        | Forwarded
                        | Message-ID
                        | MIME-Version
                        | extension-header
```

Although additional general header fields may be implemented via the extension mechanism, applications which do not recognize those fields should treat them as Entity-Header fields.

4.3.1 Date

The Date header represents the date and time at which the message was originated, having the same semantics as orig-date in RFC 822. The field value is an HTTP-date, as described in Section 3.3.

```
Date                    = "Date" ":" HTTP-date
```

An example is

```
Date: Tue, 15 Nov 1994 08:12:31 GMT
```

If a message is received via direct connection with the user agent (in the case of requests) or the origin server (in the case of responses), then the default date can be assumed to be the current date at the receiving end. However, since the date--as it is believed by the origin--is important for evaluating cached responses, origin servers should always include a Date header. Clients should only send a Date header field in messages that include an entity body, as in the case of the PUT and POST requests, and even then it is optional. A received message which does not have a Date header field should be assigned one by the receiver if and only if the message will be cached by that receiver or gatewayed via a protocol which requires a Date.

Only one Date header field is allowed per message. In theory, the date should represent the moment just before the status/request-line is generated (i.e. the time at which the originator made the determination of what the request/response should be). In practice, the date can be generated at any time during the message origination without affecting its semantic value.

Note: An earlier version of this document incorrectly specified that this field should contain the creation date of the enclosed Entity-Body. This has been changed to reflect actual (and proper) usage.

4.3.2 Forwarded

The Forwarded header is to be used by proxies to indicate the intermediate steps between the user agent and the server (on requests) and between the origin server and the client (on responses). It is analogous to the "Received" field of RFC 822 and is intended to be used for tracing transport problems and avoiding request loops.

```
Forwarded               = "Forwarded" ":" "by" URI [ "(" product ")" ]
                          [ "for" FQDN ]

FQDN                    = <Fully-Qualified Domain Name>
```

For example, a message could be sent from a client on ptsun00.cern.ch to a server at www.ics.uci.edu port 80, via an intermediate HTTP proxy at info.cern.ch port 8000. The request received by the server at www.ics.uci.edu would then have the following Forwarded header field:

```
Forwarded: by http://info.cern.ch:8000/ for ptsun00.cern.ch
```

Multiple Forwarded header fields are allowed and should represent each proxy that has forwarded the message. It is strongly recommended that proxies used as a portal through a network firewall do not, by default, send out information about the internal hosts within the firewall region. This information should only be propagated if explicitly enabled. If not enabled, the for token and FQDN should not be included in the field value.

4.3.3 Message-ID

The Message-ID field in HTTP is identical to that used by Internet Mail and USENET messages, as defined in [11]. That is, it gives the message a single, unique identifier which can be used for identifying the message (not its contents) for "much longer" than the expected lifetime of that message.

```
Message-ID          = "Message-ID" ":" "<" addr-spec ">"
addr-spec           = <as defined in RFC 822 [8]>
```

Although it is not required, the addr-spec format typically used within a Message-ID consists of a string that is unique at the originator's machine, followed by the required "@" character and the fully-qualified domain name of that machine. An example is

```
Message-ID: <9411151630.4256@info.cern.ch>
```

which is composed using the time, date and process-ID on the host info.cern.ch. However, this is only one of many possible methods for generating a unique Message-ID and recipients of a message should consider the entire value opaque.

The Message-ID field is normally not generated by HTTP applications and is never required. It should only be generated by a gateway application when the message is being posted to some other protocol that desires a Message-ID. HTTP responses should only include a Message-ID header field when the entity being transferred already has one assigned to it (as in the case of resources that were originally posted via Internet Mail or USENET).

4.3.4 MIME-Version

HTTP is not a MIME-conformant protocol. However, HTTP/1.0 messages may include a single MIME-Version header field to indicate what version of the MIME protocol was used to construct the message. Use of the MIME-Version header field should indicate that the message is in full compliance with the MIME protocol (as defined in [6]). Unfortunately, current versions of HTTP/1.0 clients and servers use this field indiscriminately, and thus receivers must not take it for granted that the message is indeed in full compliance with MIME. Gateways are responsible for ensuring this compliance (where possible) when exporting HTTP messages to strict MIME environments. Future HTTP/1.0 applications must only use MIME-Version when the message is intended to be MIME-conformant.

```
MIME-Version        = "MIME-Version" ":" 1*DIGIT "." 1*DIGIT
```

MIME version "1.0" is the default for use in HTTP/1.0. However, HTTP/1.0 message parsing and semantics are defined by this document and not the MIME specification.

5. Request

A request message from a client to a server includes, within the first line of that message, the method to be applied to the resource requested, the identifier of the resource, and the protocol version in use. For backwards compatibility with the more limited HTTP/0.9 protocol, there are two valid formats for an HTTP request:

```
Request             = Simple-Request | Full-Request

Simple-Request      = "GET" SP Request-URI CRLF

Full-Request        = Request-Line              ; Section 5.1
                      *( General-Header         ; Section 4.3
                      |  Request-Header         ; Section 5.4
                      |  Entity-Header )        ; Section 7.1
                      CRLF
                      [ Entity-Body ]           ; Section 7.2
```

If an HTTP/1.0 server receives a Simple-Request, it must respond with an HTTP/0.9 Simple-Response. An HTTP/1.0 client capable of receiving a Full-Response should never generate a Simple-Request.

5.1 Request-Line

The Request-Line begins with a method token, followed by the Request-URI and the protocol version, and ending with CRLF. The elements are separated by SP characters. No CR or LF are allowed except in the final CRLF sequence.

```
Request-Line        = Method SP Request-URI SP HTTP-Version CRLF
```

Note that the difference between a Simple-Request and the Request-Line of a Full-Request is the presence of the HTTP-Version field.

5.2 Method

The Method token indicates the method to be performed on the resource identified by the Request-URI. The method is case-sensitive and extensible.

```
Method              = "GET" | "HEAD" | "PUT" | "POST"
                    | "DELETE" | "LINK" | "UNLINK"
                    | extension-method

extension-method    = token
```

For a description of how each of these methods is currently implemented in HTTP servers, see Section 6.1.1, "Request Methods."

The list of methods acceptable by a specific resource can be specified in an "Allow" Entity-Header (Section 7.1.1). However, the client is always notified through the return code of the response whether a method is currently allowed on a specific resource, as this can change dynamically. Servers should return the status code "405 Method Not Allowed" if the method is known by the server but not allowed for the requested resource, and "501 Not Implemented" if the method is unknown or not implemented by the server.

The set of common methods for HTTP/1.0 is described below. Although this set can be easily expanded, additional methods cannot be assumed to share the same semantics for separately extended clients and servers. In order to maintain compatibility, the semantic definition for extension methods should be registered with the IANA [17].

5.2.1 GET

The GET method means retrieve whatever information (in the form of an entity) is identified by the Request-URI. If the Request-URI refers to a data-producing process, it is the produced data which shall be returned as the entity in the response and not the source text of the process (unless that text happens to be the output of the process).

The semantics of the GET method changes to a "conditional GET" if the request message includes an If-Modified-Since header field. A conditional GET method requests that the identified resource be transferred only if it has been modified since the date given by the If-Modified-Since header. The algorithm for determining this includes the following cases:

a) If the request would normally result in anything other than a "200 OK" status, or if the passed If-Modified-Since date is invalid, the response is exactly the same as for a normal GET.

b) If the resource has been modified since the If-Modified-Since date, the response is exactly the same as for a normal GET.

c) If the resource has not been modified since the If-Modified-Since date, the server shall return a "304 Not Modified" response.

The conditional GET method is intended to reduce network usage by allowing cached entities to be refreshed without requiring multiple requests or transferring unnecessary data.

For examples of using the If-Modified-Since header in GET method requests, see the "If-Modified-Since" section in Section 6.1.2, "Request Fields."

5.2.2 HEAD

The HEAD method is identical to GET except that the server must not return any Entity-Body in the response. The metainformation contained in the HTTP headers in response to a HEAD request should be identical to the information sent in response to a GET request. This method can be used for obtaining metainformation about the resource identified by the Request-URI without transferring the Entity-Body itself. This method is often used for testing hypertext links for validity, accessibility, and recent modification.

There is no "conditional HEAD" requests analogous to the conditional GET. If an If-Modified-Since header field is included with a HEAD request, it should be ignored.

For examples of using the HEAD method and results from each of the main servers, see Section 6.1.1, "Request Methods."

5.2.3 POST

The POST method is used to request that the destination server accept the entity enclosed in the request as a new subordinate of the resource identified by the Request-URI in the Request-Line. POST is designed to allow a uniform method to cover the following functions:

* Annotation of existing resources;
* Posting a message to a bulletin board, newsgroup, mailing list, or similar group of articles;
* Providing a block of data (usually a form) to a data-handling process;
* Extending a database through an append operation.

As is discussed in Section 6.1.1, "Request Methods," currently the most common use of the POST method is for data processing.

The actual function performed by the POST method is determined by the server and is usually dependent on the Request-URI. The posted entity is considered to be subordinate to that URI in the same way that a file is subordinate to a directory containing it, a news article is subordinate to a newsgroup to which it is posted, or a record is subordinate to a database.

The client can suggest a URI for identifying the new resource by including a URI-header field in the request. However, the server should treat that URI as advisory only and may store the entity under a different URI or without any URI.

The client may apply relationships between the new resource and other existing resources by including Link header fields, as described in Section 7.1.10. The server may use the Link information to perform other operations as a result of the new resource being added. For example, lists and indexes might be updated. However, no mandatory operation is imposed on the origin server. The origin server may also generate its own or additional links to other resources.

A successful POST does not require that the entity be created as a resource on the origin server or made accessible for future reference. That is, the action performed by the POST method might not result in a resource that can be identified by a URI. In this case, either "200 OK" or "204 No Content" is the appropriate response status, depending on whether or not the response includes an entity that describes the result.

If a resource has been created on the origin server, the response should be "201 Created" and contain the allocated URI, all applicable Link header fields, and an entity (preferably of type "text/html") which describes the status of the request and refers to the new resource.

5.2.4 PUT

The PUT method requests that the enclosed entity be stored under the supplied Request-URI. If the Request-URI refers to an already existing resource, the enclosed entity should be considered a modified version of the one residing on the origin server. If the Request-URI does not point to an existing resource, and that URI is capable of being defined as a new resource by the requesting user agent, the origin server can create the resource with that URI. If a new resource is created, the origin server must inform the user agent via the "201 Created" response. If an existing resource is modified, the "200 OK" response should be sent to indicate successful completion of the request. If the resource could not be created or modified with the Request-URI, an appropriate error response should be given that reflects the nature of the problem.

The fundamental difference between the POST and PUT requests is reflected in the different meaning of the Request-URI. The URI in a POST request identifies the resource that will handle the enclosed entity as an appendage. That resource may be a data-accepting process, a gateway to some other protocol, or a separate entity that accepts annotations. In contrast, the URI in a PUT request identifies the entity enclosed with the request. The requestor of a PUT knows what URI is intended and the receiver must not attempt to apply the request to some other resource. If the receiver desires that the request be applied to a different URI, it must send a "301 Moved Permanently" response; the requestor may then make its own decision regarding whether or not to redirect the request.

The client can create or modify relationships between the enclosed entity and other existing resources by including Link header fields, as described in Section 7.1.10. As with POST, the server may use the Link information to perform other operations as a result of the request. However, no mandatory operation is imposed on the origin server. The origin server may generate its own or additional links to other resources.

The actual method for determining how the resource is placed, and what happens to its predecessor, is defined entirely by the origin server. If version control is implemented by the origin server, the Version and Derived-From header fields should be used to help identify and control revisions to a resource.

For examples of PUT method requests to each of the major servers, see Section 6.1.1, "Request Methods."

5.2.5 DELETE

The DELETE method requests that the origin server delete the resource identified by the Request-URI. This method may be overridden by human intervention (or other means) on the origin server. The client cannot be guaranteed that the operation has been carried out, even if the status code returned from the origin server indicates that the action has been completed successfully. However, the server should not indicate success unless, at the time the response is given, it intends to delete the resource or move it to an inaccessible location.

A successful response should be "200 OK" (if the response includes an entity describing the status), "202 Accepted" (if the action has not yet been enacted), or "204 No Content" (if the response is OK but does not include an entity).

For examples of DELETE method requests to each of the major servers, see Section 6.1.1, "Request Methods."

5.2.6 LINK

The LINK method establishes one or more Link relationships between the existing resource identified by the Request-URI and other existing resources. The difference between LINK and other methods allowing links to be established between resources is that the LINK method does not allow any Entity-Body to be sent in the request and does not result in the creation of new resources.

See the definition of the Link object header in Section 5.1.6, "Meta-information," for a description of the valid Link relationships which can be established between resources.

5.2.7 UNLINK

The UNLINK method removes one or more Link relationships from the existing resource identified by the Request-URI. These relationships may have been established using the LINK method or by any other method supporting the Link header. The removal of a link to a resource does not imply that the resource ceases to exist or becomes inaccessible for future references.

5.3 Request-URI

The Request-URI is a Universal Resource Identifier (Section 3.2) and identifies the resource upon which to apply the request.

```
Request-URI              = URI
```

Unless the server is being used as a proxy, a partial URI shall be given with the assumptions of the scheme (http) and hostname:port (the server's address) being obvious. That is, if the full URI looks like

```
http://info.cern.ch/hypertext/WWW/TheProject.html
```

then the corresponding partial URI in the Simple-Request or Full-Request is

```
/hypertext/WWW/TheProject.html
```

If the client is sending the request through a proxy, the absolute form of the URI (including scheme and server address) must be used. A proxy must be able to recognize all of its server names, including any aliases, local variations, and the numeric IP address.

5.4 Request Header Fields

The request header fields allow the client to pass additional information about the request (and about the client itself) to the server. All header fields are optional and conform to the generic HTTP-header syntax.

```
Request-Header           = Accept
                         | Accept-Charset
                         | Accept-Encoding
                         | Accept-Language
                         | Authorization
                         | From
                         | If-Modified-Since
                         | Pragma
                         | Referer
                         | User-Agent
                         | extension-header
```

Although additional request header fields may be implemented via the extension mechanism, applications which do not recognize those fields should treat them as Entity-Header fields.

For a description of each of these request header fields, see "Request Headers" in Section 5.2.2, "Make a Request."

5.4.1 Accept

The Accept header field can be used to indicate a list of media ranges which are acceptable as a response to the request. The asterisk "*" character is used to group media types into ranges, with "*/*" indicating all media types and "type/*" indicating all subtypes of that type. The set of ranges given by the client should represent what types are acceptable given the context of the request. The Accept field should only be used when the request is specifically limited to a set of desired types (as in the case of a request for an in-line image), to indicate qualitative preferences for specific media types, or to indicate acceptance of unusual media types.

See Section 6.1.2, "Request Fields," for a list of the common Accept headers which each of the major browsers support. This includes a code sample which implements the Content-Negotiation algorithm by using the Accept header.

The field may be folded onto several lines and more than one occurrence of the field is allowed (with the semantics being the same as if all the entries had been in one field value).

```
Accept          = "Accept" ":" 1#(
                  media-range
                  [ ";" "q" "=" ( "0" | "1" | float ) ]
                  [ ";" "mxb" "=" 1*DIGIT ] )

media-range     = ( "*/*"
                |   ( type "/" "*" )
                |   ( type "/" subtype )
                ) *( ";" parameter )

float           = < ANSI-C floating point text representa-
                tion,
                where (0.0 < float < 1.0) >
```

The parameter q is used to indicate the quality factor, which represents the user's preference for that range of media types, and the parameter mxb gives the maximum acceptable size of the Entity-Body (in decimal number of octets) for that range of media types. Section 9 describes the content negotiation algorithm which makes use of these values. If at least one Accept header is present, a quality factor of 0 is equivalent to not sending an Accept header field containing that media-type or set of media-types. The default values are: q=1 and mxb=undefined (i.e. infinity).

The example

```
Accept: audio/*; q=0.2, audio/basic
```

should verbally be interpreted as "if you have audio/basic, send it; otherwise send me any audio type."

If no Accept header is present, then it is assumed that the client accepts all media types with quality factor 1. This is equivalent to the client sending the following accept header field:

```
Accept: */*; q=1
```

or

```
Accept: */*
```

A more elaborate example is

```
Accept: text/plain; q=0.5, text/html,
  text/x-dvi; q=0.8; mxb=100000, text/x-c
```

Verbally, this would be interpreted as "text/html and text/x-c are the preferred media types, but if they do not exist then send the Entity-Body in text/x-dvi if the entity is less than 100000 bytes, otherwise send text/plain".

Note: In earlier versions of this document, the mxs parameter defined the maximum acceptable delay in seconds before the response would arrive. This has been removed as the server has no means of obtaining a useful reference value. However, this does not prevent the client from internally measuring the response time and optimizing the Accept header field accordingly.

It must be emphasized that this field should only be used when it is necessary to restrict the response media types to a subset of those possible, to indicate the acceptance of unusual media types, or when the user has been permitted to specify qualitative values for ranges of media types. If no quality factors have been set by the user, and the context of the request is such that the user agent is capable of saving the entity to a file if the received media type is unknown, then the only appropriate value for Accept is "*/*" and the list of unusual types. Whether or not a particular media type is deemed "unusual" should be a configurable aspect of the user agent.

5.4.2 Accept-Charset

The Accept-Charset header field can be used to indicate a list of preferred character sets other than the default US-ASCII and ISO-8859-1. This field allows clients capable of understanding more comprehensive or special-purpose character sets to signal that capability to a server which is capable of representing documents in those character sets.

A code sample that implements the Content Negotiation algorithm is available in Section 6.1.2, "Request Fields." This code could be easily modified to support the Accept-Charset header field.

```
Accept-Charset          = "Accept-Charset" ":" 1#charset
```

Character set values are described in Section 8.3. An example is

```
Accept-Charset: iso-8859-5, unicode-1-1
```

The value of this field should not include "US-ASCII" or "ISO-8859-1", since those values are always assumed by default. If a resource is only available in a character set other than the defaults, and that character set is not listed in the Accept-Charset field, it is only acceptable for the server to send the entity if the character set can be identified by an appropriate charset parameter on the media type or within the format of the media type itself.

Note: User agents are not required to be able to render the characters associated with the ISO-8859-1 character set. However, they must be able to interpret their meaning to whatever extent is required to properly handle messages in that character set..

5.4.3 Accept-Encoding

The Accept-Encoding header field is similar to Accept, but lists the encoding-mechanisms and transfer-encoding values which are acceptable in the response.

A code sample which implements the Content Negotiation algorithm is available in Section 6.1.2, "Request Fields." This code could be easily modified to support the Accept-Encoding header field.

```
Accept-Encoding        = "Accept-Encoding" ":"
                         1#( encoding-mechanism | transfer-encoding )
```

An example of its use is

```
Accept-Encoding: compress, base64, gzip, quoted-printable
```

The field value should never include the identity transfer-encoding values ("7bit", "8bit", and "binary") since they actually represent "no encoding." If no Accept-Encoding field is present in a request, it must be assumed that the client does not accept any encoding-mechanism and only the identity transfer-encodings.

5.4.4 Accept-Language

The Accept-Language header field is similar to Accept, but lists the set of natural languages that are preferred as a response to the request.

A code sample that implements the Content Negotiation algorithm is available in Section 6.1.2, "Request Fields." This code could be easily modified to support the Accept-Language header field. See* http://www.netgen.com/book *for RFC 1766, which describes the syntax of the language types.

```
Accept-Language        = "Accept-Language" ":" 1#language-tag
```

The language-tag is described in Section 8.2. Languages are listed in the order of their preference to the user. For example,

```
Accept-Language: dk, en-gb
```

would mean: "Send me a Danish version if you have it; else a British English version."

If the server cannot fulfill the request with one or more of the languages given, or if the languages only represent a subset of a multi-linguistic Entity-Body, it is acceptable to serve the request in an unspecified language.

Note: As intelligibility is highly dependent on the individual user, it is recommended that client applications make the choice of linguistic preference available to the user.

5.4.5 Authorization

A user agent that wishes to authenticate itself with a server (usually, but not necessarily, after receiving a "401 Unauthorized" response), may do so by including an Authorization header field with the request. The Authorization field value consists of credentials containing the authentication information of the user agent for the realm of the resource being requested.

See Section 6.1.3, "The Response: Status Codes," for an example of a request which uses the Authorization header and the Basic Access Authentication Scheme to provide a username and password to a site.

```
Authorization          = "Authorization" ":" credentials
```

HTTP access authentication is described in Section 10. If a request is authenticated and a realm specified, the same credentials should be valid for all other requests within this realm.

5.4.6 From

The From header field, if given, should contain an Internet e-mail address for the human user who controls the requesting user agent. The address should be machine-usable, as defined by addr-spec in RFC 822:

See Section 6.1.2, "Request Fields," for a list of the browsers which currently send the From field.

```
From                        = "From" ":" addr-spec
```

An example is:

```
From: webmaster@w3.org
```

This header field may be used for logging purposes and as a means for identifying the source of invalid or unwanted requests. It should not be used as an insecure form of access protection. The interpretation of this field is that the request is being performed on behalf of the person given, who accepts responsibility for the method performed. In particular, robot agents should include this header so that the person responsible for running the robot can be contacted if problems occur on the receiving end.

The Internet e-mail address in this field does not have to correspond to the Internet host which issued the request. (For example, when a request is passed through a proxy, then the original issuer's address should be used). The address should, if possible, be a valid Internet e-mail address, whether or not it is in fact an Internet e-mail address or the Internet e-mail representation of an address on some other mail system.

Note: The client should not send the From header field without the user's approval, as it may conflict with the user's privacy interests or their site's security policy. It is strongly recommended that the user be able to disable, enable, and modify the value of this field at any time prior to a request.

5.4.7 If-Modified-Since

The If-Modified-Since header field is used with the GET method to make it conditional: if the requested resource has not been modified since the time specified in this field, a copy of the resource will not be returned from the server; instead, a "304 Not Modified" response will be returned without any Entity-Body.

For examples of using the If-Modified-Since header in GET method requests, see the "If-Modified-Since" section in Section 6.1.2, "Request Fields."

```
If-Modified-Since       = "If-Modified-Since" ":" HTTP-date
```

An example of the field is:

```
If-Modified-Since: Sat, 29 Oct 1994 19:43:31 GMT
```

The purpose of this feature is to allow efficient updates of local cache information with a minimum amount of transaction overhead. The same functionality can be obtained, though with much greater overhead, by issuing a HEAD request and following it with a GET request if the server indicates that the entity has been modified.

5.4.8 Pragma

The Pragma header field is used to specify directives that must be applied to all servers along the request chain (where relevant). The directives typically specify behavior that prevents intermediate proxies from changing the nature of the request. Although multiple pragma directives can be listed as part of the request, HTTP/1.0 only defines semantics for the "no-cache" directive.

```
Pragma               = "Pragma" ":" 1#pragma-directive

pragma-directive     = "no-cache" | extension-pragma
                       extension-pragma = token
```

When the "no-cache" directive is present, a caching proxy must forward the request toward the origin server even if it has a cached copy of what is being requested. This allows a client to insist upon receiving an authoritative response to its request. It also allows a client to refresh a cached copy which has become corrupted or is known to be stale.

Pragmas must be passed through by a proxy even when they have significance to that proxy. This is necessary in cases when the request has to go through many proxies, and the pragma may affect all of them. It is not possible to specify a pragma for a specific proxy; however, any pragma-directive not relevant to a gateway or proxy should be ignored.

5.4.9 Referer

The Referer field allows the client to specify, for the server's benefit, the address (URI) of the document (or element within the document) from which the Request-URI was obtained. This allows a server to generate lists of back-links to documents, for interest, logging, optimized caching, etc. It also allows obsolete or mistyped links to be traced for maintenance. The format of the field is:

See Section 6.1.2, "Request Fields," for a list of the browsers which currently send the Referer field as well as a sample use for the field.

```
Referer              = "Referer" ":" URI
```

Example:

```
        Referer: http://info.cern.ch/hypertext/DataSources/Overview.html
```

If a partial URI is given, it should be interpreted relative to the Request-URI.

Note: Because the source of a link may be considered private information or may reveal an otherwise secure information source, it is strongly recommended that the user be able to select whether or not the Referer field is sent. For example, a browser client could have a toggle switch for browsing openly/ anonymously, which would respectively enable/disable the sending of Referer and From information.

5.4.10 User-Agent

The User-Agent field contains information about the user agent originating the request. This is for statistical purposes, the tracing of protocol violations, and automated recognition of user agents for the sake of tailoring responses to avoid particular user agent limitations. Although it is not required, user agents should always include this field with requests. The field can contain multiple tokens specifying the product name, with an optional slash and version designator, and other products which form a significant part of the user agent. By convention, the products are listed in order of their significance for identifying the application.

See Section 6.1.2, "Request Fields" for a list of the User-Agent values sent by different browsers as well as a code sample showing how this information can be used.

```
User-Agent          = "User-Agent" ":" 1*( product )

product             = token ["/" product-version]
product-version     = token
```

Example:

```
User-Agent: CERN-LineMode/2.15 libwww/2.17b3
```

Product tokens should be short and to the point -- use of this field for advertizing or other non-essential information is explicitly deprecated and will be considered as non-conformance to the protocol. Although any token character may appear in a product-version, this token should only be used for a version identifier (i.e., successive versions of the same product should only differ in the product-version portion of the product value). The User-Agent field may include additional information within comments that are not part of the value of the field.

Note: Some current proxy applications append their product information to the list in the User-Agent field. This is no longer recommended, since it makes machine interpretation of these fields ambiguous. Instead, proxies should use the Forwarded header described in Section 4.3.2.

6. Response

After receiving and interpreting a request message, a server responds in the form of an HTTP response message.

```
Response      = Simple-Response | Full-Response

Simple-Response     = [ Entity-Body ]

Full-Response       = Status-Line              ; Section 6.1
                      *( General-Header        ; Section 4.3
                      |  Response-Header       ; Section 6.3
                      |  Entity-Header )       ; Section 7.1
                      CRLF
                      [ Entity-Body ]          ; Section 7.2
```

A Simple-Response should only be sent in response to an HTTP/0.9 Simple-Request or if the server only supports the more limited HTTP/0.9 protocol. If a client sends an HTTP/1.0 Full-Request and receives a response that does not begin with a Status-Line, it should assume that the response is a Simple-Response and parse it accordingly. Note that the Simple-Response consists only of the entity body and is terminated by the server closing the connection.

6.1 Status-Line

The first line of a Full-Response message is the Status-Line, consisting of the protocol version followed by a numeric status code and its associated textual phrase, with each element separated by SP characters. No CR or LF is allowed except in the final CRLF sequence.

```
Status-Line            = HTTP-Version SP Status-Code SP Reason-
                         Phrase CRLF
```

Since a status line always begins with the protocol version's

```
"HTTP/" 1*DIGIT "." 1*DIGIT
```

(e.g. "HTTP/1.0"), the presence of that expression is considered sufficient to differentiate a Full-Response from a Simple-Response. Although the Simple-Response format may allow such an expression to occur at the beginning of an entity body (and thus cause a misinterpretation of the message if it was given in response to a Full-Request), the likelihood of such an occurrence is negligible.

6.2 Status Codes and Reason Phrases

The Status-Code element is a 3-digit integer result code of the attempt to understand and satisfy the request. The Reason-Phrase is intended to give a short textual description of the Status-Code. The Status-Code is intended for use by automata and the Reason-Phrase is intended for the human user. The client is not required to examine or display the Reason-Phrase.

The first digit of the Status-Code defines the class of response. The last two digits do not have any categorization role. There are 5 values for the first digit:

* 1xx: Informational - Not used, but reserved for future use

* 2xx: Success - The action was successfully received, understood, and accepted.

* 3xx: Redirection - Further action must be taken in order to complete the request

* 4xx: Client Error - The request contains bad syntax or cannot be fulfilled

* 5xx: Server Error - The server failed to fulfill an apparently valid request

The individual values of the numeric status codes defined for HTTP/1.0, and an example set of corresponding Reason-Phrase's, are presented below. The reason phrases listed here are only recommended -- they may be replaced by local equivalents without affecting the protocol.

```
Status-Code            = "200"   ; OK
                       | "201"   ; Created
                       | "202"   ; Accepted
                       | "203"   ; Provisional Information
```

```
                        | "204"   ; No Content
                        | "300"   ; Multiple Choices
                        | "301"   ; Moved Permanently
                        | "302"   ; Moved Temporarily
                        | "303"   ; Method
                        | "304"   ; Not Modified
                        | "400"   ; Bad Request
                        | "401"   ; Unauthorized
                        | "402"   ; Payment Required
                        | "403"   ; Forbidden
                        | "404"   ; Not Found
                        | "405"   ; Method Not Allowed
                        | "406"   ; None Acceptable
                        | "407"   ; Proxy Authentication Required
                        | "408"   ; Request Timeout
                        | "409"   ; Conflict
                        | "410"   ; Gone
                        | "500"   ; Internal Server Error
                        | "501"   ; Not Implemented
                        | "502"   ; Bad Gateway
                        | "503"   ; Service Unavailable
                        | "504"   ; Gateway Timeout
                        | extension-code

extension-code          = 3DIGIT

Reason-Phrase           = token *( SP token )
```

HTTP status codes are extensible and should be registered with the IANA. HTTP applications are not required to understand the meaning of all registered status codes, though such understanding is obviously desirable. However, applications are required to understand the class of any status code (as indicated by the first digit) and to treat the response as being equivalent to the x00 status code of that class. For example, if an unknown status code of 421 is received by the client, it can safely assume that there was something wrong with its request and treat the response as if it had received a 400 status code. In such cases, user agents are encouraged to present the entity returned with the response to the user, since that entity is likely to include human-readable information which will explain the unusual status.

Each Status-Code is described below, including a description of which method(s) it can follow and any metainformation required in the response.

6.2.1 Successful 2xx

This class of status codes indicates that the client's request was successfully received, understood, and accepted.

200 OK

* Following: any method

* Required headers: none

The request has been fulfilled and an entity corresponding to the requested resource is being sent in the response. If the HEAD method was used, the response should only contain the Entity-Header information and no Entity-Body.

201 Created

* Following: any method that may request a new resource be created

* Required headers: URI-header

The request has been fulfilled and resulted in a new resource being created. The newly created resource can be referenced by the URI(s) returned in the URI-header field of the response. The origin server is encouraged, but not obliged, to actually create the resource before using this Status-Code. If the action cannot be carried out immediately, or within a clearly defined timeframe, the server should respond with "202 Accepted" instead.

Of the methods defined by this specification, only PUT and POST can create a resource.

202 Accepted

* Following: any method

* Required headers: none

The request has been accepted for processing, but the processing has not been completed. The request may or may not eventually be acted upon, as it may be disallowed when processing actually takes place. There is no facility for re-sending a status code from an asynchronous operation such as this.

The "202 Accepted" response is intentionally non-committal. Its purpose is to allow a server to accept a request for some other process (perhaps a batch-oriented process that is only run once per day) without requiring that the user agent's connection to the server persist until the process is completed. The entity returned with this response should include an indication of the request's current status and either a pointer to a status monitor or some estimate of when the user can expect the request to be enacted.

203 Provisional Information

* Following: GET, HEAD

* Required headers: none

The returned metainformation in the Entity-Header is not the definitive set as available from the origin server, but is gathered from a local or a third-party copy. The set presented may be a subset or superset of the original version. For example, including local annotation information about the resource may result in a superset of the metainformation known by the origin server.

204 No Content

* Following: any method

* Required headers: none

The server has fulfilled the request but there is no new information to send back. If the client is a user agent, it should not change its document view. This response is primarily intended to allow input for scripts or other actions to take place without causing a change to the user agent's current document view.

6.2.2 Redirection 3xx

This class of status code indicates that further action needs to be taken by the client in order to fulfill the request. The action required can sometimes be carried out by the client without interaction with the user, but it is strongly recommended that this only takes place if the method used in the request is idempotent (GET or HEAD).

300 Multiple Choices

* Following: any method

* Required headers: none

The requested resource is available at one or more locations and a preferred location could not be determined via content negotiation. Unless it was a HEAD request, the response must include an entity containing a formatted list of resource characteristics and locations from which the user agent can choose the one most appropriate. The entity format is specified by the media type given in the Content-Type header field. Depending upon the format and the capabilities of the user agent, selection of the most appropriate choice may be performed automatically.

301 Moved Permanently

* Following: any method

* Required headers: URI-header, Location

The requested resource has been assigned a new permanent URI and any future references to this resource must be done using the returned URI. Clients with link editing capabilities are encouraged to automatically relink references to the Request-URI to the new reference returned by the server, where possible.

It is possible for the server to send this status code in response to a request using the PUT, POST, or DELETE methods. However, as this might change the conditions under which the request was issued, the user agent must not automatically redirect the request unless it can be confirmed by the user.

302 Moved Temporarily

* Following: any method

* Required headers: URI-header, Location

The requested resource resides temporarily under a different URI. Since the redirection may be altered on occasion, the client should on future requests from the user continue to use the original Request-URI and not the URI returned in the URI-header field and Location fields.

It is possible for the server to send this status code in response to a request using the PUT, POST, or DELETE methods. However, as this might change the conditions under which the request was issued, the user agent must not automatically redirect the request unless it can be confirmed by the user.

303 Method

This code is obsolete.

304 Not Modified

* Following: conditional GET

* Required headers: none

If the client has performed a conditional GET request and access is allowed, but the document has not been modified since the date and time specified in the If-Modified-Since field, the server shall respond with this status code and not send an Entity-Body to the client. Header fields contained in the response should only include information which is relevant to cache managers and which may have changed independently of the entity's Last-Modified date. Examples of relevant header fields include: Date, Server, and Expires.

6.2.3 Client Error 4xx

The 4xx class of status codes is intended for cases in which the client seems to have erred. If the client has not completed the request when a 4xx code is received, it should immediately cease sending data to the server. Except when responding to a HEAD request, the server is encouraged to include an entity containing an explanation of the error situation, and whether it is a temporary or permanent condition. These status codes are applicable to any request method.

400 Bad Request

The request had bad syntax or was inherently impossible to be satisfied. The client is discouraged from repeating the request without modifications.

401 Unauthorized

* Required headers: WWW-Authenticate

The request requires user authentication. The response must include a WWW-Authenticate header field (Section 6.3.4) containing a challenge applicable to the requested resource. The client may repeat the request with a suitable Authorization header field. HTTP access authentication is explained in Section 10.

402 Payment Required

This code is not currently supported, but is reserved for future use.

403 Forbidden

The request is forbidden because of some reason that remains unknown to the client. Authorization will not help and the request should not be repeated. This status code can be used if the server does not want to make public why the request cannot be fulfilled.

404 Not Found

The server has not found anything matching the Request-URI. No indication is given of whether the condition is temporary or permanent. If the server does not wish to make this information available to the client, the status code "403 Forbidden" can be used instead. The "410 Gone" status code should be used if the server knows (through some internally configurable method) that an old resource is permanently unavailable and has no forwarding address.

405 Method Not Allowed

* Required headers: Allow

The method specified in the Request-Line is not allowed for the resource identified by the Request-URI. The response must include an Allow header containing a list of valid method's for the requested resource.

406 None Acceptable

* Required headers: Content-*, where applicable to the Request-URI

The server has found a resource matching the Request-URI, but not one that satisfies the conditions identified by the Accept and Accept-Encoding request headers. The response must include (when applicable) the Content-Type, Content-Encoding, and Content-Language of the resource, and is encouraged to include the resource's complete metainformation. No Entity-Body can be included in the response.

407 Proxy Authentication Required

This code is reserved for future use. It is similar to "401 Unauthorized", but indicates that the client must first authenticate itself with the proxy. HTTP/1.0 does not provide a means for proxy authentication -- this feature will be available in future versions.

408 Request Timeout

The client did not produce a request within the time that the server was prepared to wait. The client may repeat the request without modifications at any later time.

409 Conflict

The request could not be completed due to a conflict with the current state of the resource. This code is only allowed in situations where it is expected that the user may be able to resolve the conflict and resubmit the request. The response body should include enough information for the user to recognize the source of the conflict. Ideally, the response entity would include enough information for the user (or user-agent) to fix the problem; however, that may not be possible and is not required.

Conflicts are most likely to occur in response to a PUT request. If versioning is being used and the entity being PUT includes changes to a resource which conflict with those made by an earlier (third-party) request, the server may use the "409 Conflict" response to indicate that it can't complete the PUT. In this case, the response entity may contain a list of the differences between the two versions.

410 Gone

The requested resource is no longer available at the server and no forwarding address is known. This condition should be considered permanent. Clients with link editing capabilities are encouraged to delete references to the Request-URI (after user approval). If the server does not know (or has no facility to determine) whether or not the condition is permanent, the status code "404 Not Found" can be used instead.

The "410 Gone" response is primarily intended to assist the task of web maintenance by notifying the recipient that the resource is intentionally unavailable and that the server owners desire that remote links to that resource be removed. Such an event is common for limited-time, promotional services and for resources belonging to individuals no longer working at the server's site. It is not necessary to mark all permanently unavailable resources as "gone" or to keep the mark for any length of time -- that is left to the discretion of the server owner.

6.2.4 Server Errors 5xx

Response status codes beginning with the digit "5" indicate cases in which the server is aware that it has erred or is incapable of performing the request. If the client has not completed the request when a 5xx code is received, it should immediately cease sending data to the server. Except when responding to a HEAD request, the server is encouraged to include an entity containing an explanation of the error situation, and whether it is a temporary or permanent condition. These response codes are applicable to any request method and there are no required header fields.

500 Internal Server Error

The server encountered an unexpected condition which prevented it from fulfilling the request.

501 Not Implemented

The server does not support the functionality required to fulfill the request. This is the appropriate response when the server does not recognize the request method and is not capable of supporting it for any resource.

502 Bad Gateway

The server received an invalid response from the gateway or upstream server it accessed in attempting to complete the request.

503 Service Unavailable

The server is currently unable to handle the request due to a temporary overloading or maintenance of the server. The implication is that this is a temporary condition which will be alleviated after some delay. If known, the length of the delay may be indicated in a Retry-After header. If no Retry-After is given, the client should handle the response as it would a "500 Internal Server Error".

Note: The presence of the 503 status code does not imply that a server must use it when becoming overloaded. Some servers may wish to simply refuse the connection.

504 Gateway Timeout

The server did not receive a timely response from the gateway or upstream server it accessed in attempting to complete the request.

6.3 Response Header Fields

The response header fields allow the server to pass additional information about the response which cannot be placed in the Status-Line. These header fields are not intended to give information about an Entity-Body returned in the response, but about the server itself.

```
    Response-Header         = Public
                            | Retry-After
                            | Server
                            | WWW-Authenticate
                            | extension-header
```

Although additional response header fields may be implemented via the extension mechanism, applications which do not recognize those fields should treat them as Entity-Header fields.

6.3.1 Public

The Public header field lists the set of non-standard methods supported by the server. The purpose of this field is strictly to inform the recipient of the capabilities of the server regarding unusual methods. The methods listed may or may not be applicable to the Request-URI; the Allow header field (Section 7.1.1) should be used to indicate methods allowed for a particular URI. This does not prevent a client from trying other methods. The field value should not include the methods predefined for HTTP/1.0 in Section 5.2.

```
    Public                  = "Public" ":" 1#method
```

Example of use:

```
        Public: OPTIONS, MGET, MHEAD
```

This header field applies only to the current connection. If the response passes through a proxy, the proxy must either remove the Public header field or replace it with one applicable to its own capabilities.

6.3.2 Retry-After

The Retry-After header field can be used with "503 Service Unavailable" to indicate how long the service is expected to be unavailable to the requesting client. The value of this field can be either an full HTTP-date or an integer number of seconds (in decimal) after the time of the response.

```
    Retry-After             = "Retry-After" ":" ( HTTP-date | delta-
                              seconds )
```

Two examples of its use are

```
        Retry-After: Wed, 14 Dec 1994 18:22:54 GMT
        Retry-After: 120
```

In the latter example, the delay is 2 minutes.

6.3.3 Server

The Server header field contains information about the software being used by the origin server program handling the request. The field is analogous to the User-Agent field and has the following format:

```
Server                 = "Server" ":" 1*( product )
```

Example:

```
Server: CERN/3.0 libwww/2.17
```

If the response is being forwarded through a proxy, the proxy application must not add its data to the product list. Instead, it should include a Forwarded field, as described in Section 4.3.2.

6.3.4 WWW-Authenticate

The WWW-Authenticate header field must be included as part of a "401 Unauthorized" response. The field value consists of a challenge that indicates the authentication scheme and parameters applicable to the Request-URI.

```
WWW-Authenticate       = "WWW-Authenticate" ":" challenge
```

The HTTP access authentication process is described in Section 10.

7. Entity

Full-Request and Full-Response messages may transfer an entity within some requests and responses. An entity consists of Entity-Header fields and (usually) an Entity-Body. In this section, both sender and recipient refer to either the client or the server, depending on who sends and who receives the entity.

7.1 Entity Header Fields

This section specifies the format and semantics of the Entity-Header fields. Entity-Header fields define optional metainformation about the Entity-Body or, if no body is present, about the resource identified by the request.

```
Entity-Header          = Allow
                       | Content-Encoding
                       | Content-Language
                       | Content-Length
                       | Content-Transfer-Encoding
                       | Content-Type
                       | Derived-From
                       | Expires
                       | Last-Modified
                       | Link
                       | Location
                       | Title
                       | URI-header
                       | Version
                       | extension-header

extension-header       = HTTP-header
```

Each entity header field is explained in the subsections below. Other header fields are allowed but cannot be assumed to be recognizable by the recipient. Unknown header fields should be ignored by the recipient and forwarded by proxies.

Note: It has been proposed that any HTML metainformation element (allowed within the <HEAD> element of a document) be a valid candidate for an HTTP entity header. This document defines two header fields, Link and Title, which are both examples of this. Base will be used in future versions of HTTP.

7.1.1 Allow

The Allow header field lists the set of methods supported by the resource identified by the Request-URI. The purpose of this field is strictly to inform the recipient of valid methods associated with the resource; it must be present in a response with status code "405 Method Not Allowed".

```
Allow                = "Allow" ":" 1#method
```

Example of use:

```
Allow: GET, HEAD, PUT
```

This does not prevent a client from trying other methods. However, it is recommended that the indications given by this field be followed. This field has no default value; if left undefined, the set of allowed methods is defined by the origin server at the time of each request.

If a response passes through a proxy which does not understand one or more of the methods indicated in the Allow header, the proxy must not modify the Allow header; the user agent may have other means of communicating with the origin server.

7.1.2 Content-Encoding

The Content-Encoding header field is used as a modifier to the media-type. When present, its value indicates what additional encoding mechanism has been applied to the resource, and thus what decoding mechanism must be applied in order to obtain the media-type referenced by the Content-Type header field. The Content-Encoding is primarily used to allow a document to be compressed without losing the identity of its underlying media type.

```
Content-Encoding     = "Content-Encoding" ":" encoding-mechanism
```

Encoding mechanisms are defined in Section 8.4. An example of its use is

```
Content-Encoding: gzip
```

The Content-Encoding is a characteristic of the resource identified by the Request-URI. Typically, the resource is stored with this encoding and is only decoded before rendering or analogous usage.

7.1.3 Content-Language

The Content-Language field describes the natural language(s) of the intended audience for the enclosed entity. Note that this may not be equivalent to all the languages used within the entity.

```
Content-Language     = "Content-Language" ":" 1#language-tag
```

Language tags are defined in Section 8.2. The primary purpose of Content-Language is to allow a selective consumer to identify and differentiate resources according to the consumer's own preferred language. Thus, if the body content is intended only for a Danish audience, the appropriate field is

```
Content-Language: dk
```

If no Content-Language is specified, the default is that the content is intended for all language audiences. This may mean that the sender does not consider it to be specific to any natural language, or that the sender does not know for which language it is intended.

Multiple languages may be listed for content that is intended for multiple audiences. For example, a rendition of the "Treaty of Waitangi," presented simultaneously in the original Maori and English versions, would call for

```
Content-Language: mi, en
```

However, just because multiple languages are present within an entity does not mean that it is intended for multiple linguistic audiences. An example would be a beginner's language primer, such as "A First Lesson in Latin," which is clearly intended to be used by an English audience. In this case, the Content-Language should only include "en".

Content-Language may be applied to any media type --it should not be considered limited to textual documents.

7.1.4 Content-Length

The Content-Length header field indicates the size of the Entity-Body (in decimal number of octets) sent to the recipient or, in the case of the HEAD method, the size of the Entity-Body that would have been sent had the request been a GET.

This header is important for a client to know how much data to read in. See Section 6.3, "Sample Code for Creating a Full Request," for the subroutine which uses this field to read data from servers.

```
Content-Length         = "Content-Length" ":" 1*DIGIT
```

An example is

```
Content-Length: 3495
```

Although it is not required, applications are strongly encouraged to use this field to indicate the size of the Entity-Body to be transferred, regardless of the media type of the entity.

Any Content-Length greater than or equal to zero is a valid value. Section 7.2.2 describes how to determine the length of an Entity-Body if a Content-Length is not given.

Note: The meaning of this field is significantly different from the corresponding definition in MIME, where it is an optional field used within the "message/external-body" content-type. In HTTP, it should be used whenever the entity's length can be determined prior to being transferred.

7.1.5 Content-Transfer-Encoding

The Content-Transfer-Encoding (CTE) header indicates what (if any) type of transformation has been applied to the entity in order to safely transfer it between the sender and the recipient. This differs from the Content-Encoding in that the CTE is a property of the message, not of the original resource.

```
Content-Transfer-Encoding = "Content-Transfer-Encoding" ":" transfer-
                            encoding
```

Transfer encodings are defined in Section 8.5. Because all HTTP transactions take place on an 8-bit clean connection, the default Content-Transfer-Encoding for all messages is binary. However, HTTP may be used to transfer MIME messages which already have a defined CTE. An example is:

```
Content-Transfer-Encoding: quoted-printable
```

Many older HTTP/1.0 applications do not understand the Content-Transfer-Encoding header. However, since it may appear in any MIME message (i.e. entities retrieved via a gateway to a MIME-conformant protocol), future HTTP/1.0 applications are required to understand it upon receipt. Gateways are the only HTTP applications that would generate a CTE.

7.1.6 Content-Type

The Content-Type header field indicates the media type of the Entity-Body sent to the recipient or, in the case of the HEAD method, the media type that would have been sent had the request been a GET.

See the sidebar on MIME (Multipurpose Internet Mail Extensions) in Section 5.1.6, "Meta-information," for a list of the commonly used Content-Types. Also see Section 6.1.4, "Object: Content-Type," for a sample of how servers generally determine the Content-Type of a file from its extensions.

```
Content-Type          = "Content-Type" ":" media-type
```

Media types are defined in Section 8.1. An example of the field is

```
Content-Type: text/html; charset=ISO-8859-4
```

The Content-Type header field has no default value. Further discussion of methods for identifying the media type of an entity is provided in Section 7.2.1.

7.1.7 Derived-From

The Derived-From header field can be used to indicate the version tag of the resource from which the enclosed entity was derived before modifications were made by the sender. This field is used to help manage the process of merging successive changes to a resource, particularly when such changes are being made in parallel and from multiple sources.

```
Derived-From          = "Derived-From" ":" version-tag
```

An example use of the field is:

```
Derived-From: 2.1.1
```

A longer example of version control is included in Appendix C. The Derived-From field is required for PUT requests if the entity being put was previously retrieved from the same URI and a Version header was included with the entity when it was last retrieved.

7.1.8 Expires

The Expires field gives the date/time after which the entity should be considered stale. This allows information providers to suggest the volatility of the resource. Caching clients (including proxies) must not cache this copy of the resource beyond the date given, unless its status has been updated by a later check of the origin server. The presence of an Expires field does not imply that the original resource will change or cease to exist at, before, or after that time. However, information providers that know (or even suspect) that a resource will change by a certain date are strongly encouraged to include an Expires header with that date. The format is an absolute date and time as defined by HTTP-date in Section 3.3.

```
Expires                = "Expires" ":" HTTP-date
```

An example of its use is

```
Expires: Thu, 01 Dec 1994 16:00:00 GMT
```

The Expires field has no default value. If the date given is equal to or earlier than the value of the Date header, the recipient must not cache the enclosed entity. If a resource is dynamic by nature, as is the case with many data-producing processes, copies of that resource should be given an appropriate Expires value which reflects that dynamism.

The Expires field cannot be used to force a user agent to refresh its display or reload a resource; its semantics apply only to caching mechanisms, and such mechanisms need only check a resource's expiration status when a new request for that resource is initiated.

Note: Applications are encouraged to be tolerant of bad or misinformed implementations of the Expires header. In particular, recipients may wish to recognize a delta-seconds value (any decimal integer) as representing the number of seconds after receipt of the message that its contents should be considered expired. Likewise, a value of zero (0) or an invalid date format may be considered equivalent to an "expires immediately." Although these values are not legitimate for HTTP/1.0, a robust implementation is always desirable.

7.1.9 Last-Modified

The Last-Modified header field indicates the date and time at which the sender believes the resource was last modified. The exact semantics of this field are defined in terms of how the receiver should interpret it: if the receiver has a copy of this resource which is older than the date given by the Last-Modified field, that copy should be considered stale.

```
Last-Modified          = "Last-Modified" ":" HTTP-date
```

An example of its use is

```
Last-Modified: Tue, 15 Nov 1994 12:45:26 GMT
```

The exact meaning of this header field depends on the implementation of the sender and the nature of the original resource. For files, it may be just the file system last-mod date. For entities with dynamically included parts, it may be the most recent of the set of last-mod dates of its component parts. For database gateways, it may be the last-update timestamp of the record. For virtual objects, it may be the last time the internal state changed. In any case, the recipient should only know (and care) about the result -- whatever gets stuck in the Last-Modified field --and not worry about how that result was obtained.

7.1.10 Link

The Link header provides a means for describing a relationship between the entity and some other resource. An entity may include multiple Link values. Links at the metainformation level typically indicate relationships like hierarchical structure and navigation paths. The Link field is semantically equivalent to the <LINK> element in HTML [4].

See the definition of the Link object header in Section 5.1.6, "Meta-information," for a list of the different Link relationships which exist, and descriptions of each.

```
Link              = "Link" ":" 1#("<" URI ">"
                    [ ";" "rel" "=" relation ]
                    [ ";" "rev" "=" relation ]
                    [ ";" "title" "=" quoted-string ] )

relation          = sgml-name

sgml-name         = ALPHA *( ALPHA | DIGIT | "." | "-" )
```

Relation values are not case-sensitive and may be extended within the constraints of the sgmlname syntax. There are no predefined link relationship values for HTTP/1.0. The title parameter may be used to label the destination of a link such that it can be used as identification within a human-readable menu. Examples of usage include:

```
Link: <http://www.cern.ch/TheBook/chapter2>; rel="Previous"

Link: <mailto:timbl@w3.org>; rev="Made"; title="Tim Berners-Lee"
```

The first example indicates that the entity is previous to chapter2 in a logical navigation path. The second indicates that the publisher of the resource is identified by the given e-mail address.

7.1.11 Location

The Location header field is an earlier form of the URI-header and is considered obsolete. However, HTTP/1.0 applications should continue to support the Location header in order to properly interface with older applications. The purpose of Location is identical to that of the URI-header, except that no variants can be specified and only one absolute location URL is allowed.

See Section 9.2.1, "CGI Headers," for an example of redirection using the Location header field.

```
Location          = "Location" ":" URI
```

An example is

```
Location: http://info.cern.ch/hypertext/WWW/NewLocation.html
```

7.1.12 Title

The Title header field indicates the title of the entity

```
Title             = "Title" ":" *text
```

An example of the field is

```
Title: Hypertext Transfer Protocol -- HTTP/1.0
```

This field is to be considered isomorphic with the <TITLE> element in HTML [4].

7.1.13 URI

The URI-header field may contain one or more Universal Resource Identifiers (URIs) by which the resource origin of the entity can be identified. There is no guarantee that the resource can be accessed using the URI(s) specified. This field is required for the 201, 301, and 302 response messages, and may be included in any message that contains resource metainformation.

```
URI-header          = "URI" ":" 1#( "<" URI ">" [ ";" vary ] )

vary                = "vary" "=" <"> 1#vary-dimension <">
vary-dimension      = "type" | "language" | "version" | "encoding"
                    | "charset" | "user-agent" | extension-vary

extension-vary      = token
```

Any URI specified in this field can be either absolute or relative to the URI given in the Request-Line. The URI-header improves upon the Location header field described in Section 7.1.11. For backwards compatibility with older clients, servers are encouraged to include both header fields in 301 and 302 responses.

The URI-header may also be used by a client performing a POST request to suggest a URI for the new entity. Whether or not the suggested URI is used is entirely up to the server to decide. In any case, the server's response must include the actual URI(s) of the new resource if one is successfully created (status 201).

If a URI refers to a set of variants, then the dimensions of that variance must be given with a vary parameter. One example is:

```
URI:<http://info.cern.ch/hypertext/WWW/TheProject.multi>;
vary="type,language"
```

which indicates that the URI covers a group of entities that vary in media type and natural language. A request for that URI will result in a response that depends upon the client's request headers for Accept and Accept-Language. Similar dimensions exist for the Accept-Encoding, Accept-Charset, Version, and User-Agent header fields, as demonstrated in the following example.

```
URI:<TheProject.ps>;vary="encoding,version",
<TheProject.html>;vary="user-agent,charset,version"
```

The vary parameter has an important effect on cache management, particularly for caching proxies which service a diverse set of user agents. Since the response to one user agent may differ from the response to a second user agent if the two agents have differing request profiles, a caching proxy must keep track of the content metainformation for resources with varying dimensions. Thus, the vary parameter tells the caching proxy what entity headers must be part of the key for caching that URI. When the caching proxy gets a request for that URI, it must forward the request toward the origin server if the request profile includes a variant dimension that has not already been cached.

7.1.14 Version

The Version field defines the version tag associated with a rendition of an evolving entity. Together with the Derived-From field described in Section 7.1.7, it allows a group of people to work simultaneously on the creation of a work as an iterative process. The field should be used to allow evolution of a particular work along a single path. It should not be used to indicate derived works or renditions in different representations.

```
Version             = "Version" ":" version-tag

version-tag         = token | quoted-string
```

Examples of the Version field include:

```
Version: 2.1.2

Version: "Fred 19950116-12:26:48"

Version: 2.5a4-omega7
```

The version tag should be considered opaque to all parties but the origin server. A user agent can request a particular version of an entity by including its tag in a Version header as part of the request. Similarly, a user agent may suggest a value for the version of an entity transferred via a PUT or POST request. However, only the origin server can reliably assign or increment the version tag of an entity.

7.2 Entity Body

The entity-body (if any) sent with an HTTP/1.0 request or response is in a format and encoding defined by the Entity-Header fields.

```
Entity-Body         = *OCTET
```

An entity-body is included with a request message only when the request method calls for one. This specification defines two request methods, "POST" and "PUT", that allow an entity-body. In general, the presence of an entity-body in a request is signaled by the inclusion of a Content-Length and/or Content-Transfer-Encoding header field in the request message headers.

Note: Most current implementations of the POST and PUT methods require a valid Content-Length header field. This can cause problems for some systems that do not know the size of the entity-body before transmission. Experimental implementations (and future versions of HTTP) may use a packetized Content-Transfer-Encoding to obviate the need for a Content-Length.

For response messages, whether or not an entity-body is included with a message is dependent on both the request method and the response code. All responses to the HEAD request method must not include a body, even though the presence of Content header fields may lead one to believe they should. Similarly, the responses "204 No Content", "304 Not Modified", and "406 None Acceptable" must not include a body.

7.2.1 Type

When an Entity-Body is included with a message, the data type of that body is determined via the header fields Content-Type, Content-Encoding, and Content-Transfer-Encoding. These define a three-layer, ordered encoding model:

```
entity-body <-
Content-Transfer-Encoding( Content-Encoding( Content-Type ) )
```

The default for both encodings is none (i.e., the identity function). A Content-Type specifies the media type of the underlying data. A Content-Encoding may be used to indicate an additional encoding mechanism applied to the type (usually for the purpose of data compression) that is a property of the resource requested. A Content-Transfer-Encoding may be applied by a transport agent to ensure safe and/or proper transfer of the message. Note that the Content-Transfer-Encoding is a property of the message, not of the resource.

The Content-Type header field has no default value. If and only if the media type is not given by a Content-Type header (as is always the case for Simple-Response messages), the receiver may attempt to guess the media type via inspection of its content and/or the name extension(s) of the URL used to access the resource. If the media type remains unknown, the receiver should treat it as type "application/octet-stream".

7.2.2 Length

When an Entity-Body is included with a message, the length of that body may be determined in one of several ways. If a Content-Length header field is present, its value in bytes (number of octets) represents the length of the Entity-Body. Otherwise, the body length is determined by the Content-Type (for types with an explicit end-of-body delimiter), the Content-Transfer-Encoding (for packetized encodings), or the closing of the connection by the server. Note that the latter cannot be used to indicate the end of a request body, since it leaves no possibility for the server to send back a response.

Note: Some older servers supply an invalid Content-Length when sending a document that contains server-side includes dynamically inserted into the data stream. It must be emphasized that this will not be tolerated by future versions of HTTP. Unless the client knows that it is receiving a response from a compliant server, it should not depend on the Content-Length value being correct.

8. Content Parameters

8.1 Media Types

HTTP uses Internet Media Types [15], formerly referred to as MIME Content-Types [6], in order to provide open and extensible data typing and type negotiation. For mail applications, where there is no type negotiation between sender and receiver, it is reasonable to put strict limits on the set of allowed media types. With HTTP, however, user agents can identify acceptable media types as part of the connection, and thus are allowed more freedom in the use of non-registered types. The following grammar for media types is a superset of that for MIME because it does not restrict itself to the official IANA and x-token types.

```
media-type          = type "/" subtype *( ";" parameter )
type                = token
subtype             = token
```

Parameters may follow the type/subtype in the form of attribute/value pairs.

```
parameter           = attribute "=" value
attribute           = token
value               = token | quoted-string
```

The type, subtype, and parameter attribute names are not case-sensitive. Parameter values may or may not be case-sensitive, depending on the semantics of the parameter name. No LWS is allowed between the type and subtype, nor between an attribute and its value.

If a given media-type value has been registered by the IANA, any use of that value must be indicative of the registered data format. Although HTTP allows the use of non-registered media types, such usage must not conflict with the IANA registry. Data providers are strongly encouraged to register their media types with IANA via the procedures outlined in RFC 1590 [15].

All media-type's registered by IANA must be preferred over extension tokens. However, HTTP does not limit conforming applications to the use of officially registered media types, nor does it encourage the use of an "x-" prefix for unofficial types outside of explicitly short experimental use between consenting applications.

8.1.1 Canonicalization and Text Defaults

Media types are registered in a canonical form. In general, entity bodies transferred via HTTP must be represented in the appropriate canonical form prior to transmission. If the body has been encoded via a Content-Encoding and/or Content-Transfer-Encoding, the data must be in canonical form prior to that encoding. However, HTTP modifies the canonical form requirements for media of primary type "text" and for "application" types consisting of text-like records.

HTTP redefines the canonical form of text media to allow multiple octet sequences to indicate a text line break. In addition to the preferred form of CRLF, HTTP applications must accept a bare CR or LF alone as representing a single line break in text media. Furthermore, if the text media is represented in a character set which does not use octets 13 and 10 for CR and LF respectively (as is the case for some multi-byte character sets), HTTP allows the use of whatever octet sequence(s) is defined by that character set to represent the equivalent of CRLF, bare CR, and bare LF. It is assumed that any recipient capable of using such a character set will know the appropriate octet sequence for representing line breaks within that character set.

Note: This interpretation of line breaks applies only to the contents of an Entity-Body and only after any Content-Transfer-Encoding and/or Content-Encoding has been removed. All other HTTP constructs use CRLF exclusively to indicate a line break. Encoding mechanisms define their own line break requirements.

A recipient of an HTTP text entity should translate the received entity line breaks to the local line break conventions before saving the entity external to the application and its cache; whether this translation takes place immediately upon receipt of the entity, or only when prompted by the user, is entirely up to the individual application.

HTTP also redefines the default character set for text media in an entity body. If a textual media type defines a charset parameter with a registered default value of "US-ASCII", HTTP changes the default to be "ISO-8859-1". Since the character set ISO-8859-1 [19] is a superset of USASCII [18], this has no effect upon the interpretation of entity bodies which only contain octets within the US-ASCII set (0 - 127). The presence of a charset parameter value in a Content-Type header field overrides the default.

HTTP does not require that the character set of an entity body be labelled as the lowest common denominator of the character codes used within a document.

8.1.2 Multipart Types

MIME provides for a number of "multipart" types -- encapsulations of several entities within a single message's Entity-Body. The multipart types registered by IANA [17] do not have any special meaning for HTTP/1.0, though user agents may need to understand each type in order to correctly interpret the purpose of each body-part. Ideally, an HTTP user agent should follow the same or similar behavior as a MIME user agent does upon receipt of a multipart type.

See Section 6.1.4, "Object: Content-Type," for an example of using Multipart types to return multiple objects in a response.

As in MIME [6], all multipart types share a common syntax and must include a boundary parameter as part of the media type value. The message body is itself a protocol element and must therefore use only CRLF to represent line breaks between body-parts. Unlike in MIME, multipart body-parts may contain HTTP header fields which are significant to the meaning of that part.

A URI-header field (Section 7.1.13) should be included in the body-part for each enclosed entity that can be identified by a URI.

8.2 Language Tags

A language tag identifies a natural language spoken, written, or otherwise conveyed by human beings for communication of information to other human beings. Computer languages are explicitly excluded. The HTTP/1.0 protocol uses language tags within the Accept-Language and Content-Language header fields.

The syntax and registry of HTTP language tags is the same as that defined by RFC 1766 [1]. In summary, a language tag is composed of 1 or more parts: A primary language tag and a (possibly empty) series of subtags:

```
language-tag        = primary-tag *( "-" subtag )

primary-tag         = 1*8ALPHA
subtag              = 1*8ALPHA
```

Whitespace is not allowed within the tag and all tags are to be treated as case insensitive. The namespace of language tags is administered by the IANA. Example tags include:

```
en, en-US, en-cockney, i-cherokee, x-pig-latin
```

where any two-letter primary-tag is an ISO 639 language abbreviation and any two-letter initial subtag is an ISO 3166 country code.

Note: Earlier versions of this document specified an incomplete language tag, where values were limited to ISO 639 language abbreviations with an optional ISO 3166 country code appended after an underscore ("_") or slash ("/") character. This format was abandoned in favor of the recently proposed standard for Internet protocols.

8.3 Character Sets

HTTP uses the same definition of the term "character set" as that described for MIME:

The term "character set" is used in this document to refer to a method used with one or more tables to convert a sequence of octets into a sequence of characters. Note that unconditional conversion in the other direction is not required, in that not all characters may be available in a given character set and a character set may provide more than one sequence of octets to represent a particular character. This definition is intended to allow various kinds of character encodings, from simple single-table mappings such as US-ASCII to complex table switching methods such as those that use ISO 2022's techniques. However, the definition associated with a MIME character set name must fully specify the mapping to be performed from octets to characters. In particular, use of external profiling information to determine the exact mapping is not permitted.

Character sets are identified by case-insensitive tokens. The complete set of allowed charset values are defined by the IANA Character Set registry [17]. However, because that registry does not define a single, consistent token for each character set, we define here the preferred names for those character sets most likely to be used with HTTP entities. This set of charset values includes those registered by RFC 1521 [6] -- the US-ASCII [18] and ISO8859 [19] character sets -- and other character set names specifically recommended for use within MIME charset parameters.

```
charset          = "US-ASCII"
                 | "ISO-8859-1" | "ISO-8859-2" | "ISO-8859-3"
                 | "ISO-8859-4" | "ISO-8859-5" | "ISO-8859-6"
                 | "ISO-8859-7" | "ISO-8859-8" | "ISO-8859-9"
                 | "ISO-2022-JP" | "ISO-2022-JP-2" | "ISO-
                 2022-KR"
                 | "UNICODE-1-1" | "UNICODE-1-1-UTF-7" | "UNI-
                 CODE-1-1-UTF-8"
                 | token
```

Although HTTP allows an arbitrary token to be used as a character set value, any token that has a predefined value within the IANA Character Set registry [17] must represent the character set defined by that registry. Applications are encouraged, but not required, to limit their use of character sets to those defined by the IANA registry.

8.4 Encoding Mechanisms

Encoding mechanism values are used to indicate an encoding transformation that has been or can be applied to a resource. Encoding mechanisms are primarily used to allow a document to be compressed or encrypted without losing the identity of its underlying media type. Typically, the resource is stored with this encoding and is only decoded before rendering or analogous usage.

```
encoding-mechanism    = "gzip" | "compress" | token
```

Note: For historical reasons, HTTP/1.0 applications should consider "x-gzip" and "x-compress" to be equivalent to "gzip" and "compress", respectively.

All encoding-mechanism values are case-insensitive. HTTP/1.0 uses encoding-mechanism values in the Accept-Encoding (Section 5.4.3) and Content-Encoding (Section 7.1.2) header fields. Although the value describes the encoding-mechanism, what is more important is that it indicates what decoding mechanism will be required to remove the encoding. Note that a single program may be capable of decoding multiple encoding-mechanism formats. Two values are defined by this specification:

gzip An encoding format produced by the file compression program "gzip" (GNU zip) developed by Jean-loup Gailly. This format is typically a Lempel-Ziv coding (LZ77) with a 32 bit CRC. Gzip is available from the GNU project at <URL:ftp://prep.ai.mit.edu/pub/gnu/>.

compress The encoding format produced by the file compression program "compress". This format is an adaptive Lempel-Ziv-Welch coding (LZW).

8.5 Transfer Encodings

Transfer encoding values are used to indicate an encoding transformation that has been, can be, or may need to be applied to an Entity-Body in order to ensure safe transport through the network. Transfer encodings are only used with entities destined for or retrieved from MIME-conformant systems, and thus will rarely occur in an HTTP/1.0 message. This differs from an encoding-mechanism in that the transfer encoding is a property of the message, not of the original resource.

```
transfer-encoding    = "binary" | "8bit" | "7bit"
                     | "quoted-printable" | "base64"
                     | token
```

All transfer-encoding values are case-insensitive. HTTP/1.0 uses transfer-encoding values in the Accept-Encoding (Section 5.4.3) and Content-Transfer-Encoding (Section 7.1.5) header fields.

The values "7bit", "8bit", and "binary" are used to indicate that no transfer encoding has been performed. Instead, they describe the sort of encoding that might be needed for transmission through an unsafe transport system. Binary indicates that the body may contain any set of octets. 8bit adds the restrictions that CR and LF characters only occur as part of CRLF line separators, all lines are short (less than 1000 octets), and no NULs (octet 0) are present. 7bit adds a further restriction that all octets are 7-bit US-ASCII characters.

The "quoted-printable" and "base64" values indicate that the associated encoding (as defined in MIME [6]) has been applied to the body. These encodings consist entirely of 7-bit US-ASCII characters.

9. Content Negotiation

Content negotiation is an optional feature of the HTTP protocol. It is designed to allow for preemptive selection of a preferred content representation, within a single request-response round-trip, and without intervention from the user. However, this may not always be desirable for the user and is sometimes unnecessary for the content provider. Implementors are encouraged to provide mechanisms whereby the amount of preemptive content negotiation, and the parameters of that negotiation, are configurable by the user and server maintainer.

See Section 6.1.2, "Request Fields," for a sample piece of code which fully implements the Content Negotiation algorithm, along with several examples of the results of different requests to the server.

The first step in the negotiation algorithm is for the server to determine whether or not there are any content variants for the requested resource. Content variants may be in the form of multiple preexisting entities or a set of dynamic conversion filters. If there are no variant forms of the resource, the "negotiation" is limited to whether or not that single media type is acceptable under the constraints given by the Accept request header field (if any).

If variants are available, those variants that are completely unacceptable should be removed from consideration first. Unacceptable variants include those with a Content-Encoding not listed in an Accept-Encoding field, those with a character subset (other than the default ISO-8859-1) not listed in an Accept-Charset field, and those with a media type not within any of the media ranges of an explicitly constrained Accept field (or listed with a zero quality parameter).

If no acceptable variants remain at this point, the server should respond with a "406 None Acceptable" response message. If more than one variant remains, and at least one has a Content-Language within those listed by an Accept-Language field, any variants which do not match the language constraint are removed from further consideration.

If multiple choices still remain, the selection is further winnowed by calculating and comparing the relative quality of the available media types. The calculated weights are normalized to a real number in the range 0 through 1, where 0 is the minimum and 1 the maximum value. The following parameters are included in the calculation:

q The quality factor chosen by the user agent (and configurable by the user) that represents the desirability of that media type. In this case, desirability is usually a measure of the clients ability to faithfully represent the contents of that media type to the user. The value is in the range [0,1], where the default value is 1.

qs The quality factor, as chosen by the server (via some unspecified mechanism), to represent the relative quality of a particular variant representation of the source. For example, a picture originally in JPEG form would have a lower qs when translated to the XBM format, and much lower qs when translated to an ASCII-art representation. Note, however, that this is a function of the source -- an original piece of ASCII-art may degrade in quality if it is captured in JPEG form. The qs value has the same range and default as q.

mxb The maximum number of bytes in the Entity-Body accepted by the client. The default value is mxb=undefined (i.e. infinity).

bs The actual number of bytes in the Entity-Body for a particular source representation. This should equal the value sent as Content-Length. The default value is 0.

The discrete mapping function is defined as:

```
                              { if mxb=undefined, then (qs * q) }
      Q(q,qs,mxb,bs)          = { if mxb >= bs,      then (qs * q) }
                              { if mxb <  bs,      then 0        }
```

The variants with a maximal value for the Q function represent the preferred representation(s) of the entity. If multiple representations exist for a single media type (as would be the case if they only varied by Content-Encoding), then the smallest representation (lowest bs) is preferred.

Finally, there may still be multiple choices available to the user. If so, the server may either choose one (possibly at random) from those available and respond with "200 OK", or it may respond with "300 Multiple Choices" and include an entity describing the choices. In the latter case, the entity should either be of type "text/html' (such that the user can choose from among the choices by following an exact link) or of some type that would allow the user agent to perform the selection automatically (no such type is available at the time of this writing).

The "300 Multiple Choices" response can be given even if the server does not perform any winnowing of the representation choices via the content negotiation algorithm described above. Furthermore, it may include choices that were not considered as part of the negotiation algorithm and resources that may be located at other servers.

10. Access Authentication

HTTP provides a simple challenge-response authorization mechanism which may be used by a server to challenge a client request and by a client to provide authentication information. The mechanism uses an extensible token to identify the authentication scheme, followed by a comma-separated list of attribute-value pairs which carry the parameters necessary for achieving authentication via that scheme.

```
      auth-scheme          = "Basic" | token

      auth-param           = token "=" quoted-string
```

The "401 Unauthorized" response message is used by an origin server to challenge the authorization of a user agent. This response must include a WWW-Authenticate header field containing the challenge applicable to the requested resource.

```
      challenge            = auth-scheme 1*LWS realm [ "," 1#auth-param ]
```

```
realm                     = "Realm" "=" quoted-string
```

The realm attribute is required for all access authentication schemes which issue a challenge. The realm value, in combination with the root URL of the server being accessed, defines the authorization space. These realms allow the protected resources on a server to be partitioned into a set of authorization spaces, each with its own authentication scheme and/or database. The realm value is a string, generally assigned by the origin server, which may have additional semantics specific to the authentication scheme.

A user agent that wishes to authenticate itself with a server (usually, but not necessarily, after receiving a 401 response), may do so by including an Authorization header field with the request. The Authorization field value consists of credentials containing the authentication information of the user agent for the realm of the resource being requested.

```
credentials          = auth-scheme [ 1*LWS encoded-cookie ] #auth-param

encoded-cookie       = 1*<any CHAR except CTLs or tspecials, but
                       including "=" and "/">
```

The domain over which credentials can be automatically applied by a user agent is determined by the authorization space. If a request is authenticated, the credentials can be reused for all other requests within that authorization space for a period of time determined by the authentication scheme, parameters, and/or user preference.

The HTTP protocol does not restrict applications to this simple challenge-response mechanism for access authentication. Additional mechanisms may be used at the transport level, via message encapsulation, and/or with additional header fields specifying authentication information. However, these additional mechanisms are not defined by this specification.

Proxies must be completely transparent regarding user agent access authentication. That is, they must forward the WWW-Authenticate and Authorization headers untouched. HTTP/1.0 does not provide a means for a client to be authenticated with a proxy -- this feature will be available in future versions of HTTP.

Note: The names Proxy-Authenticate and Proxy-Authorization have been suggested as headers, analogous to WWW-Authenticate and Authorization, but applying only to the immediate connection with a proxy.

10.1 Basic Authentication Scheme

The basic authentication scheme is based on the model that the client must authenticate itself with a user-ID and a password for each realm. The realm value should be considered an opaque string which can only be compared for equality with other realms. The server will service the request only if it can validate the user-ID and password for the domain of the Request-URI.

See Section 6.1.3, "The Response: Status Codes," for an example of a request and response using the Basic Access Authentication Scheme. In addition, see Section 5.3.1, "S-HTTP Extensions," for a description of another authentication method which has been proposed.

```
basic-challenge           = "Basic" SP realm
```

The client sends the user-ID and password (separated by a single colon ":" character) within a base64 [6] encoded-cookie in the credentials.

```
basic-credentials    = "Basic" SP basic-cookie

basic-cookie         = <base64 encoding of userid-password>

userid-password      = [ token ] ":" *text
```

There are no optional authentication parameters for the basic scheme. For example, if the user agent wishes to send the user-ID "Aladdin" and password "open sesame", it would use the following header field:

```
Authorization: Basic QWxhZGRpbjpvcGVuIHNlc2FtZQ==
```

The basic authentication scheme is a non-secure method of filtering unauthorized access to resources on an HTTP server. It is based on the assumption that the connection between the client and the server can be regarded as a trusted carrier. As this is not generally true on an open network, the basic authentication scheme should be used accordingly. In spite of this, clients are strongly encouraged to implement the scheme in order to communicate with servers that use it.

11. Security Considerations

This section is meant to inform application developers, information providers, and users of the security limitations in HTTP/1.0 as described by this document. The discussion does not include definitive solutions to the problems revealed, though it does make some suggestions for reducing security risks.

11.1 Authentication of Clients

As mentioned in Section 10.1, the Basic authentication scheme is not considered to be a secure method of user authentication, nor does it prevent the Entity-Body from being transmitted in clear text across the physical network used as the carrier. HTTP/1.0 does not prevent additional authentication schemes and encryption mechanisms to be employed to increase security.

11.2 Idempotent Methods

The writers of client software should be aware that the software represents the user in their interactions over the net, and should be careful to allow the user to be aware of any actions they may take which may have an unexpected significance to themselves or others.

In particular, the convention has been established that the GET and HEAD methods should never have the significance of taking an action. The link "click here to subscribe"--causing the reading of a special "magic" document--is open to abuse by others making a link "click here to see a pretty picture." These methods should be considered "safe" and should not have side effects. This allows the client software to represent other methods (such as POST, PUT and DELETE) in a special way, so that the user is aware of the fact that an action is being requested.

11.3 Abuse of Server Log Information

A server is in the position to save personal data about a user's requests which may identify their reading patterns or subjects of interest. This information is clearly confidential in nature and its handling may be constrained by law in certain countries. People using the HTTP protocol to provide data are responsible for ensuring that such material is not distributed without the permission of any individuals that are identifiable by the published results.

Two header fields are worth special mention in this context: Referer and From. The Referer field allows reading patterns to be studied and reverse links drawn. Although it can be very useful, its power can be abused if user details are not separated from the information contained in the Referer. Even when the personal information has been removed, the Referer field may have indicated a secure document's URI, whose revelation itself would be a breach of security.

The information sent in the From field might conflict with the user's privacy interests or their site's security policy, and hence it should not be transmitted without the user being able to disable, enable, and modify the contents of the field. The user must be able to set the active contents of this field within a user preference or application defaults configuration.

We suggest, though do not require, that a convenient toggle interface be provided for the user to enable or disable the sending of From and Referer information.

12. Acknowledgments

This specification makes heavy use of the augmented BNF and generic constructs defined by David H. Crocker for RFC 822 [8]. Similarly, it reuses many of the definitions provided by Nathaniel Borenstein and Ned Freed for MIME [6]. We hope that their inclusion in this specification will help reduce past confusion over the relationship between HTTP/1.0 and Internet mail.

The HTTP protocol has evolved considerably over the past three years. It has benefited from a large and active developer community-- the many people who have participated on the www-talk mailing list-- and it is that community which has been most responsible for the success of HTTP and of the World-Wide Web in general. Marc Andreessen, Robert Cailliau, Daniel W. Connolly, Bob Denny, Phillip M. Hallam-Baker, Haringkon W. Lie, Ari Luotonen, Rob McCool, Dave Raggett, Tony Sanders, and Marc VanHeyningen deserve special recognition for their efforts in defining aspects of the protocol for early versions of this specification.

This document has benefited greatly from the comments of all those participating in the HTTPWG. In addition to those already mentioned, the following individuals have contributed to this specification:

Gary Adams	Harald Tveit Alvestrand
Keith Ball	Brian Behlendorf
Paul Burchard	Maurizio Codogno
Mike Cowlishaw	Michael A. Dolan
John Franks	Alex Hopmann

Bob Jernigan
Martijn Koster
Dave Kristol
Daniel LaLiberte
Albert Lunde
John C. Mallery
Larry Masinter
Mitra
Gavin Nicol
Marc Salomon
Chuck Shotton
Eric W. Sink
Simon E. Spero

13. References

[1] H. T. Alvestrand. "Tags for the identification of languages." RFC 1766, UNINETT, March 1995.

[2] F. Anklesaria, M. McCahill, P. Lindner, D. Johnson, D. Torrey, and B. Alberti. "The Internet Gopher Protocol: A distributed document search and retrieval protocol." RFC 1436, University of Minnesota, March 1993.

[3] T. Berners-Lee. "Universal Resource Identifiers in WWW: A Unifying Syntax for the Expression of Names and Addresses of Objects on the Network as used in the World-Wide Web." RFC 1630, CERN, June 1994.

[4] T. Berners-Lee and D. Connolly. "HyperText Markup Language Specification - 2.0." Work in Progress (draft-ietf-html-spec- 01.txt), CERN, HaL Computer Systems, February 1995.

[5] T. Berners-Lee, L. Masinter, and M. McCahill. "Uniform Resource Locators (URL)." RFC 1738, CERN, Xerox PARC, University of Minnesota, October 1994.

[6] N. Borenstein and N. Freed. "MIME (Multipurpose Internet Mail Extensions) Part One: Mechanisms for Specifying and Describing the Format of Internet Message Bodies." RFC 1521, Bellcore, Innosoft, September 1993.

[7] R. Braden. "Requirements for Internet hosts - application and support." STD 3, RFC 1123, IETF, October 1989.

[8] D. H. Crocker. "Standard for the Format of ARPA Internet Text Messages." STD 11, RFC 822, UDEL, August 1982.

[9] F. Davis, B. Kahle, H. Morris, J. Salem, T. Shen, R. Wang, J. Sui, and M. Grinbaum. "WAIS Interface Protocol Prototype Functional Specification." (v1.5), Thinking Machines Corporation, April 1990.

[10] R. T. Fielding. "Relative Uniform Resource Locators." Work in Progress (draft-ietf-uri-relative-url-05.txt), UC Irvine, January 1995.

[11] M. Horton and R. Adams. "Standard for interchange of USENET messages." RFC 1036 (Obsoletes RFC 850), AT&T Bell Laboratories, Center for Seismic Studies, December 1987.

[12] B. Kantor and P. Lapsley. "Network News Transfer Protocol: A Proposed Standard for the Stream-Based Transmission of News." RFC 977, UC San Diego, UC Berkeley, February 1986.

[13] K. Moore. "MIME (Multipurpose Internet Mail Extensions) Part Two: Message Header Extensions for Non-ASCII Text." RFC 1522, University of Tennessee, September 1993.

[14] J. Postel. "Simple Mail Transfer Protocol." STD 10, RFC 821, USC/ISI, August 1982.

[15] J. Postel. "Media Type Registration Procedure." RFC 1590, USC/ISI, March 1994.

[16] J. Postel and J. K. Reynolds. "File Transfer Protocol (FTP)." STD 9, RFC 959, USC/ISI, October 1985.

[17] J. Reynolds and J. Postel. "Assigned Numbers." STD 2, RFC 1700, USC/ISI, October 1994.

[18] US-ASCII. Coded Character Set - 7-Bit American Standard Code for Information Interchange. Standard ANSI X3.4-1986, ANSI, 1986.

[19] ISO-8859. International Standard -- Information Processing -- 8-bit Single-Byte Coded Graphic Character Sets -- Part 1: Latin Alphabet No. 1, ISO 8859-1:1987. Part 2: Latin alphabet No. 2, ISO 8859-2, 1987. Part 3: Latin alphabet No. 3, ISO 8859-3, 1988. Part 4: Latin alphabet No. 4, ISO 8859-4, 1988. Part 5: Latin/Cyrillic alphabet, ISO 8859-5, 1988. Part 6: Latin/Arabic alphabet, ISO 8859-6, 1987. Part 7: Latin/Greek alphabet, ISO 8859-7, 1987. Part 8: Latin/Hebrew alphabet, ISO 8859-8, 1988. Part 9: Latin alphabet No. 5, ISO 8859-9, 1990.

14. Authors' Addresses

Tim Berners-Lee
Director, W3 Consortium
MIT Laboratory for Computer Science
545 Technology Square
Cambridge, MA 02139, U.S.A.
Tel: +1 (617) 253 9670
Fax: +1 (617) 258 8682
Email: timbl@w3.org

Roy T. Fielding
Department of Information and Computer Science
University of California
Irvine, CA 92717-3425, U.S.A.

Tel: +1 (714) 824-4049
Fax: +1 (714) 824-4056
Email: fielding@ics.uci.edu

Henrik Frystyk Nielsen
World-Wide Web Project
CERN
1211 Geneva 23, Switzerland
Tel: +41 (22) 767 8265
Fax: +41 (22) 767 8730
Email: frystyk@w3.org

Appendices

These appendices are provided for informational reasons only -- they do not form a part of the HTTP/1.0 specification.

A. Internet Media Type message/http

In addition to defining the HTTP/1.0 protocol, this document serves as the specification for the Internet media type "message/http". The following is to be registered with IANA [15].

Media Type name:	message
Media subtype name:	http
Required parameters:	none
Optional parameters:	version, type
version:	The HTTP-Version number of the enclosed message (e.g. "1.0"). If not present, the version can be determined from the first line of the body.
type:	The message type -- "request" or "response". If not present, the type can be determined from the first line of the body.
Encoding considerations:	only "7bit", "8bit", or "binary" are permitted
Security considerations:	none

B. Minimum Compliance

Early reviews of this specification have indicated the need for a statement of the minimum requirements for an implementation to be considered in compliance with HTTP/1.0. This section will be written soon.

Note: The primary difficulty in determining a standard for minimum compliance rests in the fact that HTTP is a flexible protocol which can be used for many purposes. The requirements for special purpose applications often differ from those of general purpose applications.

B.1 Servers

Servers have a special responsibility for being honest when generating their responses to requesting clients. The Status-Code sent in the Status-Line must correspond to the actual action taken by the server. This is especially the case when the method used in the request is one of PUT, POST, DELETE, LINK, and UNLINK. If a Status-Code of 200 is returned, the client must be able to assume that the action has been carried out. If the server is not able to fulfill the requested action immediately, the correct status code to use is "202 Accepted".

The methods GET and HEAD must be supported by all general-purpose servers. Servers which provide Last-Modified dates for resources must also support the conditional GET method.

C. Tolerant Applications

While it may be appropriate for testing applications to verify full conformance to this specification, it is recommended that operational applications be tolerant of deviations. This appendix mentions the most important topics where tolerance is recommended.

C.1 Request-Line, Status-Line, and Header Fields

Clients should be tolerant in parsing the Status-Line and servers tolerant when parsing the Request-Line. In particular, they should accept any amount of SP and HTAB characters between fields, even though only a single SP is specified.

The line terminator for HTTP-header fields should be the sequence CRLF. However, we recommend that applications, when parsing such headers, recognize a single LF as a line terminator and ignore the leading CR.

We recommend that servers allocate URIs free of "variant" characters (characters whose representation differs in some of the national variant character sets), punctuation characters, and spaces. This makes URIs easier to handle by humans when the need arises (such as for debugging or transmission through non hypertext systems).

D. Relationship to MIME

HTTP/1.0 reuses many of the constructs defined for Internet Mail (RFC 822 [8]) and the Multipurpose Internet Mail Extensions (MIME [6]) to allow entities to be transmitted in an open variety of representations and with extensible mechanisms. However, HTTP is not a MIME-conforming application. HTTP's performance requirements differ substantially from those of Internet mail. Since it is not limited by the restrictions of existing mail protocols and gateways, HTTP does not obey some of the constraints imposed by RFC 822 and MIME for mail transport.

This appendix describes specific areas where HTTP differs from MIME. Gateways to MIME-compliant protocols must be aware of these differences and provide the appropriate conversions where necessary. No conversion should be necessary for a MIME-conforming entity to be transferred using HTTP.

D.1 Conversion to Canonical Form

MIME requires that an entity be converted to canonical form prior to being transferred, as described in Appendix G of RFC 1521 [6]. Although HTTP does require media types to be transferred in canonical form, it changes the definition of "canonical form" for text-based media types as described in Section 8.1.1.

D.1.1 Representation of Line Breaks

MIME requires that the canonical form of any text type represent line breaks as CRLF and forbids the use of CR or LF outside of line break sequences. Since HTTP allows CRLF, bare CR, and bare LF (or the octet sequence(s) to which they would be translated for the given character set) to indicate a line break within text content, recipients of an HTTP message cannot rely upon receiving MIME-canonical line breaks in text.

Where it is possible, a gateway from HTTP to a MIME-conformant protocol should translate all line breaks within text/* media types to the MIME canonical form of CRLF. However, this may be complicated by the presence of a Content-Encoding and by the fact that HTTP allows the use of some character sets which do not use octets 13 and 10 to represent CR and LF (as is the case for some multi-byte character sets).

D.1.2 Default Character Set

MIME requires that all subtypes of the top-level Content-Type "text" have a default character set of US-ASCII [18]. In contrast, HTTP defines the default character set for "text" to be ISO88591 [19] (a superset of US-ASCII). Therefore, if a text/* media type given in the Content-Type header field does not already include an explicit charset parameter, the parameter

```
;charset="iso-8859-1"
```

should be added by the gateway if the entity contains any octets greater than 127.

D.2 Default Content-Transfer-Encoding

The default Content-Transfer-Encoding (CTE) for all MIME messages is "7bit". In contrast, HTTP defines the default CTE to be "binary". Therefore, if an entity does not include an explicit CTE header field, the gateway should apply either the "quoted-printable" or "base64" transfer encodings and add the appropriate Content-Transfer-Encoding field. At a minimum, the explicit CTE field of

```
Content-Transfer-Encoding: binary
```

should be added by the gateway if it is unwilling to apply a mail-safe encoding.

D.3 Introduction of Content-Encoding

MIME does not include any concept equivalent to HTTP's Content-Encoding header field. Since this acts as a modifier on the media type, gateways to MIME-conformant protocols should either change the value of the Content-Type header field or decode the Entity-Body before forwarding the message.

Note: Some experimental applications of Content-Type for Internet mail have used a media-type parameter of ";conversions=<encoding-mechanisms>" to perform an equivalent function as Content-Encoding. However, this parameter is not part of the MIME specification at the time of this writing.

E. Example of Version Control

This appendix gives an example on how the Entity-Header fields Version and Derived-From can be used to apply version control to the creation and parallel development of a work. In order to simplify the example, only two user agents (A and B) are considered together with an origin server S.

* A sends a POST request to S, including the header "Version: 1.0" and an entity
* S replies "201 Created" to A, including the header "Version: 1.0" and a URI-header which should be used for future references
* A starts editing the entity
* B sends a GET request to S
* S replies "200 OK" to B, including the entity with a header "Version: 1.0"
* B starts editing the entity
* B sends a PUT request to S, including the entity and a header "Derived-From: 1.0"
* S replies "204 No Content" to B, including a header "Version: 1.1" but no entity
* A sends a PUT request to S, including the entity and a header "Derived-From: 1.0"
* S replies "409 Conflict" to A, including "Version: 1.1" and the list of problems with merging A's changes to 1.0 with those already applied for B and version 1.1
* A merges B's changes with its own, possibly with help from the user of A
* A sends a PUT request to S including the entity and the header "Derived-From: 1.1"
* S replies "204 No Content" to A, including the header "Version: 1.2" but no entity

The example can be expanded to any number of involved user agents, though the likelihood of conflicts and the difficulty of resolving them may increase.

A p p e n d i x C

Hypertext Markup Language Specification Version 2.0[1]

INTERNET DRAFT **February 8, 1995**

Expires in six months

Hypertext Markup Language Specification - 2.0

<draft-ietf-html-spec-01.txt>

Status of This Memo

This document is an Internet draft. Internet drafts are working documents of the Internet Engineering Task Force (IETF), its areas, and its working groups. Note that other groups may also distribute working documents as Internet drafts.

Internet drafts are draft documents valid for a maximum of six months and may be updated, replaced, or obsoleted by other documents at any time. It is inappropriate to use Internet drafts as reference material or to cite them other than as "work in progress."

To learn the current status of any Internet-Draft, please check the "1id-abstracts.txt" listing contained in the Internet- Drafts Shadow Directories on ftp.is.co.za (Africa), nic.nordu.net (Europe), munnari.oz.au (Pacific Rim), ds.internic.net (US East Coast), or ftp.isi.edu (US West Coast).

Distribution of this document is unlimited. Please send comments to the HTML working group (HTML-WG) of the Internet Engineering Task Force (IETF) at <html-wg@oclc.org>. Discussions of the group are archived at URL: http://www.acl.lanl.gov/HTML_WG/archives.html.

According to Tim Berners-Lee, the HTML specifications are currently in the final stages of editing and should become an RFC in the near future.

Abstract

The HyperText Markup Language (HTML) is a simple markup language used to create hypertext documents that are portable from one platform to another. HTML docu-

1. Note: This draft will expire. See **http://www.w3.org/hypertext/WWW/MarkUp** for information on the current state of this protocol.

ments are SGML documents with generic semantics that are appropriate for representing information from a wide range of applications. HTML markup can represent hypertext news, mail, documentation, and hypermedia; menus of options; database query results; simple structured documents with in-lined graphics; and hypertext views of existing bodies of information.

HTML has been in use by the World Wide Web (WWW) global information initiative since 1990. This specification roughly corresponds to the capabilities of HTML in common use prior to June 1994. It is defined as an application of ISO Standard 8879:1986 Information Processing Text and Office Systems; Standard Generalized Markup Language (SGML).

The "text/html; version=2.0" Internet Media Type (RFC 1590) and MIME Content Type (RFC 1521) is defined by this specification.

Contents

1. Overview of HTML Specification

This chapter is a summary of the HTML specification. See Section 2. for the complete specification.

HTML describes the structure and organization of a document. It only suggests appropriate presentations of the document when processed.

In HTML documents, tags define the start and end of headings, paragraphs, lists, character highlighting and links. Most HTML elements are identified in a document as a start tag, which gives the element name and attributes, followed by the content, followed by the end tag. Start tags are delimited by < and >, and end tags are delimited by </ and >.

Example:

```
<H1>This is a heading</H1>
```

Every HTML document starts with a HTML document identifier which contains two sections, a head and a body. The head contains HTML elements which describe the documents title, usage and relationship with other documents. The body contains other HTML elements with the entire text and graphics of the document.

This overview briefly describes the syntax of HTML elements and provides an example HTML document.

NOTE: The term "HTML user agent" is used in this document to describe applications that are used with HTML documents.

1.1 HTML Elements

1.1.1 Document Structure Elements

HTML Identifier

```
<HTML> ... </HTML>
```

The HTML identifier defines the document as containing HTML elements. It contains only the Head and Body elements.

Head

```
<HEAD> ... </HEAD>
```

The Head element contains HTML elements that describe the documents title, usage and relationship with other documents.

See Section 7.3.1 for more information on the Head element.

Body

```
<BODY> ... </BODY>
```

The Body element contains the text and its associated HTML elements of the document.

See Section 7.3.1 for more information on the Body element.

Example of Document Structure Elements

```
<HTML>
<HEAD>
<TITLE>The Document's Title</TITLE>
</HEAD>
<BODY>
The document's text.
</BODY>
```

1.1.2 Anchor Element

Anchor

```
<A> ... </A>
```

An anchor specifies a link to another location (<A HREF>) or the value to use when linking to this location from another location (<A NAME>):

```
See <A HREF="http://www.hal.com/">HaL</A>'s information for more
details.
<A NAME="B">Section B</A> describes...
...
See <A HREF="#B">Section B</A> for more information.
```

See Section 7.3.3 for more information on the Anchor element. See Sections 8.3.2 and 8.3.3 for tips on how to avoid making common mistakes with the Anchor element.

1.1.3 Block Formatting Elements

HTML 3.0 adds the Division and Horizonal Tab elements. See Section 7.4.2 for more information on each of these.

For more information on any of the HTML 2.0 block formatting elements, see Section 7.3.4.

Address

```
<ADDRESS> ... </ADDRESS>
<ADDRESS>
Newsletter editor<BR>
J.R. Brown<BR>
JimquickPost News, Jumquick, CT 01234<BR>
Tel (123) 456 7890
</ADDRESS>
```

Body

```
<BODY> ... </BODY>
```

Place the <BODY> and </BODY> tags above and below the body of the text (not including the head) of your HTML document.

Blockquote

```
<BLOCKQUOTE>... </BLOCKQUOTE>
I think it ends
<BLOCKQUOTE>
<P>Soft you now, the fair Ophelia. Nymph, in thy
orisons, be all my sins remembered.
</BLOCKQUOTE>
but I am not sure.
```

Head

```
<HEAD> ... </HEAD>
```

Every HTML document must have a head, which provides a title. Example:

```
<HTML>
<HEAD>
<TITLE>Introduction to HTML</TITLE>
</HEAD>
```

Headings

```
<H1>This is a first level heading</H1>
<P>There are six levels of headings.
<H2>Second level heading</H2>
<P>This text appears under the second level heading
```

Horizontal Rule

HTML 3.0 allows the Horizontal Rule element to take an SRC attribute specifying an image to use for the rule.

```
<HR>
```

Inserts a horizontal rule that spans the width of the document. Example:

```
<HR>
<ADDRESS>February 8, 1995, CERN</ADDRESS>
</BODY>
```

HTML Identifier

```
<HTML> ... </HTML>
```

An HTML document begins with an <HTML> tag and ends with the </HTML> tag.

Line Break

```
<BR>
```

Forces a line break:

```
Name<BR>
Street address<BR>
City, State Zip
```

Paragraph

```
<P> ... </P>
<H1>This Heading Precedes the Paragraph</H1>
<P>This is the text of the first paragraph.
<P>This is the text of the second paragraph. Although
you do not need to start paragraphs on new lines,
maintaining this convention facilitates document
maintenance.
<P>This is the text of a third paragraph.
```

Preformatted Text

```
<PRE> ... </PRE>
<PRE WIDTH="80">
This is an example of preformatted text.
</PRE>
```

Title

```
<TITLE> ... </TITLE>
<TITLE>Title of document</TITLE>
```

1.1.4 List Elements

See Section 7.3.5 for more information on the various list elements.

HTML 3.0 introduces the List Header element which specifies a title for a list. See Section 7.4.3 for more information on this element.

Definition List

```
<DL> ... <DT>term<DD>definition... </DL>
<DL>
```

```
<DT>Term<DD>This is the first definition.
<DT>Term<DD>This is the second definition.
</DL>
```

Directory List

```
<DIR> ... <LI>List item... </DIR>
<DIR>
<LI>A-H<LI>I-M
<LI>M-R<LI>S-Z
</DIR>
```

HTML 3.0 makes this element obsolete by extending the functionality of the Unordered List element.

Menu List

```
<MENU> ... <LI>List item... </MENU>
<MENU>
<LI>First item in the list.
<LI>Second item in the list.
<LI>Third item in the list.
</MENU>
```

HTML 3.0 makes this element obsolete by extending the functionality of the Unordered List element.

Ordered List

HTML 3.0 adds new attributes (CONTINUE, COMPACT, and SEQNUM) to allow for more specific formatting of lists.

```
<OL> ... <LI>List item... </OL>
<OL>
<LI>Click the Web button to open the Open the URL
window.
<LI>Enter the URL number in the text field of the Open
URL window. The Web document you specified is displayed.
<LI>Click highlighted text to move from one link to
another.
</OL>
```

Unordered List

HTML 3.0 adds new attributes (COMPACT, DINGBAT, PLAIN, and WRAP) to allow for more specific formatting of lists.

```
<UL> ... <LI>List item... </UL>
<UL>
<LI>This is the first item in the list.
<LI>This is the second item in the list.
<LI>This is the third item in the list.
</UL>
```

1.1.5 Information Type and Character Formatting Elements

See 7.3.6 for information on HTML 2.0 information type elements and Section 7.3.7 for the HTML 2.0 character formatting elements.

HTML 3.0 adds the following new information type elements: Definition, Quotation, Language, Author, Person, Acronym, Abbreviation, Inserted Text, Deleted Text, Admonishment, and Footnote. See Section 7.4.3 for more information on these elements.

HTML 3.0 adds the following new character formatting elements: Strikethrough, Big Print, Small Print, Subscript, and Superscript. See Section 7.4.4 for more information on these elements.

Bold

<B> ... </B>

Suggests the rendering of the text in boldface. If boldface is not available, alternative mapping is allowed.

Citation

<CITE> ... </CITE>

Specifies a citation; typically rendered as italic.

Code

<CODE> ... </CODE>

Indicates an inline example of code; typically rendered as monospaced.. Do not confuse with the <PRE> tag.

Emphasis

<EM> ... </EM>

Provides typographic emphasis; typically rendered as italics.

Italics

<I> ... </I>

Suggests the rendering of text in italic font, or slanted if italic is not available.

Keyboard

<KBD> ... </KBD>

Indicates text typed by a user; typically rendered as monospaced.

Sample

<SAMP> ... </SAMP>

Indicates a sequence of literal characters; typically rendered as monospaced..

Strong

<STRONG> ... </STRONG>

Provides strong typographic emphasis; typically rendered as bold.

Typetype

```
<TT> ... </TT>
```

Specifies that the text be rendered in fixed-width font.

Variable

```
<VAR> ... </VAR>
```

Indicates a variable name; typically rendered as italic.

1.1.6 Image Element

HTML 3.0 adds the Figure element, which provides much greater formatting control over images. In addition, HTML 3.0 adds the Credit, Caption, and Figure Overlay elements to improve the functionality of inlined images. See Section 7.4.6 for more information on these elements.

Image

```
<IMG>
```

Inserts the referenced graphic image into the document at the location where the element occurs.

Example:

```
<IMG SRC ="triangle.gif" ALT="Warning:"> Be sure to read
these instructions.
```

1.1.7 Form Elements

For more information on the HTML 2.0 form elements, see Section 7.3.9.

Form

```
<FORM> ... </FORM>
```

The Form element contains nested elements (described below) which define user input controls and allows descriptive text to be displayed when the document is processed.

Input

```
<INPUT>
```

Takes these attributes: ALIGN, MAXLENGTH, NAME, SIZE, SRC, TYPE, VALUE. The type attribute can define these field types: CHECKBOX, HIDDEN, IMAGE, PASSWORD, RADIO, RESET, SUBMIT, TEXT.

HTML 3.0 adds several new input types including ranges, files, and "scribble." See Section 7.3.9 for more information on these new input types.

Example:

```
<FORM METHOD="POST" action="http://www.hal.com/sample">
<P>Your name: <INPUT NAME="name" SIZE="48">
<P>Male <INPUT NAME="gender" TYPE=RADIO VALUE="male">
```

```
<P>Female <INPUT NAME="gender" TYPE=RADIO
VALUE="female">
</FORM>
```

Option

```
<OPTION>
```

The Option element can only occur within a Select element. It represents one choice.

HTML 3.0 extends the functionality of the Option element to allow users to define client-side image maps with text support. See Section 7.3.9 for more information on this functionality.

Select

```
<SELECT NAME="..." > ... </SELECT>
```

Select provides a list of choices.

```
<SELECT NAME="flavor">
<OPTION>Vanilla
<OPTION>Strawberry
<OPTION>Rum and Raisin
<OPTION>Peach and Orange
</SELECT>
```

Textarea

```
<TEXTAREA> ... </TEXTAREA>
```

Textarea defines a multi-line text entry input control. It contains the initial text contents of the control.

```
<TEXTAREA NAME="address" ROWS=64 COLS=6>
HaL Computer Systems
1314 Dell Avenue
Campbell California 95008
</TEXTAREA>
```

1.1.8 Character Data in HTML

Representing Graphic Characters in HTML

Because of the way special characters are used in marking up HTML text, character strings are used to represent the less than (<) and greater than (>) symbols and the ampersand (&) as shown in Section 2.17.1.

Representing Special Characters in HTML

HTML inherits both from SGML and from MIME in its description of characters and character sets. The result is a small amount of duplication of function: there are multiple ways to code characters in HTML.

HTML documents are encoded in some character encoding; the character encoding may be specified, for example, by the "charset" parameter associated with the "text/html" media type. Independent of the character encoding used, HTML also allows references to any of the ISO Latin-1 alphabet, using the names in the table ISO Latin-1 Character Representations, which is derived from ISO Standard 8879:1986//ENTITIES Added Latin 1//EN. For details, see 2.17.2.

1.2 Example HTML Document

```
<HTML>
<HEAD>
<TITLE>Structural Example</TITLE>
</HEAD>
<BODY>
<H1>First Header</H1>
<P>This is a paragraph in the example HTML file.
Keep in mind that the title does not appear in the
document text, but that the header (defined by H1) does.
<UL>
<LI>First item in an unordered list.
<LI>Second item in an unordered list.
</UL>
<P>This is an additional paragraph. Technically, end
tags are not required for paragraphs, although they are
allowed. You can include character highlighting in a paragraph.
<I>This sentence of the paragraph is in italics.</I>
<IMG SRC ="triangle.gif" alt="Warning:"> Be sure to read
these instructions.
</BODY>
</HTML>
```

2. HTML Specification

HTML has been in use by the World Wide Web (WWW) global information initiative since 1990. This specification corresponds to the legitimate capabilities of HTML in common use prior to June 1994. It is defined as an application of ISO Standard 8879:1986: Standard Generalized Markup Language (SGML). This specification is proposed as the Internet Media Type (RFC 1590) and MIME Content Type (RFC 1521) called "text/html", or "text/html; version=2.0".

This specification also includes:

0 5.1 SGML Declaration for HTML

0 5.1.1 Sample SGML Open Style Entity Catalog for HTML

0 5.2 HTML DTD

This specification is currently available on the World Wide Web at URL: http://www.hal.com/%7Econnolly/html-spec Please send comments to the discussion list at: html- wg@oclc.org

2.1 Levels of Conformance

Version 2.0 of the HTML specification introduces forms for user input of information, and adds a distinction between levels of conformance:

Level 0
Indicates the minimum conformance level. When writing Level 0 documents, authors can be confident that the rendering at different sites will reflect their intent.

Level 1
Includes Level 0 features plus features such as highlighting and images.

Level 2
Includes all Level 0 and Level 1 features, plus forms. Features of higher levels, such as tables, figures, and mathematical formulae, are under discussion and are described as proposed where mentioned.

2.2 Undefined Tag and Attribute Names

An accepted networking principle is to be conservative in that which one produces, and liberal in that which one accepts. HTML user agents should be liberal except when verifying code. HTML generators should generate strictly conforming HTML.

The behavior of HTML user agents reading HTML documents and discovering tag or attribute names which they do not understand should be to behave as though, in the case of a tag, the whole tag had not been there but its content had, or in the case of an attribute, that the attribute had not been present.

2.3 Deprecated and Recommended Sections in DTDs

In Section 5., optional "deprecated" and "recommended" sections are used. Conformance with this specification is defined with these sections disabled. In the liberal spirit of Section 2.2, HTML user agents reading HTML documents should accept syntax corresponding to the specification with "deprecated" turned on. HTML user agents generating HTML may in the spirit of conservation, generate documents that conform to the specification with the "recommended" sections turned on.

2.4 HTML as an Internet Media Type

This (and upward compatible specifications) define the Internet Media Type (RFC 1590) and MIME Content Type (RFC 1521) called "text/html".

The type "text/html" accepts the following parameters:

Level
The level parameter specifies the feature set used in the document. The level is an integer number, implying that any features of same or lower level may be present in the document. Levels 0, 1 and 2 are defined by this specification.

Version
To help avoid future compatibility problems, the version parameter may be used to give the version number of the specification to which the document conforms. The version number appears at the front of this document and within the public identifier for the SGML DTD. This specification defines version 2.0.

Charset

The charset parameter (as defined in section 7.1.1 of RFC 1521) may be used with the text/html to specify the encoding used to represent the HTML document as a sequence of bytes. Normally, text/* media types specify a default value of US-ASCII for the charset parameter. However, for text/html, if the byte stream contains data that is not in the 7-bit US-ASCII set, the HTML interpreting agent should assume a default charset of ISO-8859-1.

When an HTML document is encoded using US-ASCII, the mechanisms of numeric character references (see Section 2.16.2) and character entity references (see Section 2.16.3) may be used to encode additional characters from ISO-8859-1.

Other values for the charset parameter are not defined in this specification, but may be specified in future levels or versions of HTML.

It is envisioned that HTML will use the charset parameter to allow support for non-Latin characters such as Greek, Arabic, Hebrew, Japanese, rather than relying on any SGML mechanism for doing so.

2.5 Understanding HTML and SGML

HTML is an application of ISO Standard 8879:1986 - Standard Generalized Markup Language (SGML). SGML is a system for defining structured document types, and markup languages to represent instances of those document types. The SGML declaration for HTML is given in Section 5.1. It is implicit among HTML user agents.

If the HTML specification and SGML standard conflict, the SGML standard is definitive.

Every SGML document has three parts:

SGML declaration

Binds SGML processing quantities and syntax token names to specific values. For example, the SGML declaration in the HTML DTD specifies that the string that opens an end tag is </ and the maximum length of a name is 72 characters.

Prologue

Includes one or more document type declarations, which specify the element types, element relationships and attributes.

Instance

Contains the data and markup of the document.

HTML refers to the document type as well as the markup language for representing instances of that document type.

2.6 Working with Structured Text

An HTML document is like a text file, except that some of the characters are markup. Markup (tags) define the structure of the document.

To identify information as HTML, each HTML document should start with the prologue:

```
<!DOCTYPE HTML PUBLIC "-//IETF//DTD HTML//EN//2.0">
```

NOTE: If the body of a text/html body part does not begin with a document type declaration, an HTML user agent should infer the above document type declaration.

HTML documents should also contain an <HTML> tag at the beginning of the file, after the prologue, and an </HTML> tag at the end. Within those tags, an HTML document is organized as a head and a body, much like memo or a mail message. Within the head, you can specify the title and other information about the document. Within the body, you can structure text into paragraphs and lists as well as highlighting phrases and creating links. You do this using HTML elements.

NOTE: Technically, the start and end tags for HTML, Head, and Body elements are omissible; however, this is not recommended since the head/ body structure allows an implementation to determine certain properties of a document, such as the title, without parsing the entire document.

2.6.1 HTML Elements

In HTML documents, tags define the start and end of headings, paragraphs, lists, character highlighting and links. Most HTML elements are identified in a document as a start tag, which gives the element name and attributes, followed by the content, followed by the end tag. Start tags are delimited by < and >, and end tags are delimited by </ and >.

Example:

```
<H1>This is a Heading</H1>
```

Some elements only have a start tag without an end tag. For example, to create a line break, you use the <BR> tag. Additionally, the end tags of some other elements, such as Paragraph (<P>), List Item (<LI>), Definition Term (<DT>), and Definition Description (<DD>) elements, may be omitted.

The content of an element is a sequence of characters and nested elements. Some elements, such as anchors, cannot be nested. Anchors and character highlighting may be put inside other constructs.

NOTE: The SGML declaration for HTML specifies SHORTTAG YES, which means that there are other valid syntaxes for tags, such as NET tags, <EM/.../; empty start tags, <>; and empty end tags, </>. Until support for these idioms is widely deployed, their use is strongly discouraged.

2.6.2 Names

A name consists of a letter followed by up to 71 letters, digits, periods, or hyphens. Element names are not case sensitive, but entity names are. For example, <BLOCKQUOTE>, <BlockQuote>, and <blockquote> are equivalent, whereas & is different from &.

In a start tag, the element name must immediately follow the tag open delimiter <.

2.6.3 Attributes

In a start tag, white space and attributes are allowed between the element name and the closing delimiter. An attribute typically consists of an attribute name, an equal sign, and a value (although some attributes may be just a value). White space is allowed around the equal sign.

The value of the attribute may be either:

0 A string literal, delimited by single quotes or double quotes and not containing any occurrences of the delimiting character.

0 A name token (a sequence of letters, digits, periods, or hyphens)

In this example, A is the element name, HREF is the attribute name, and http://host/dir/file.html is the attribute value:

```
<A HREF="http://host/dir/file.html">
```

NOTE: Some non-SGML implementations consider any occurrence of the > character to signal the end of a tag. For compatibility with such implementations, when > appears in an attribute value, you may want to represent it with an entity or numeric character reference (see Section 2.17.1), such as:

```
<IMG SRC="eq1.jpg" alt="a &#62; b">
```

To put quotes inside of quotes, you may use the character representation " as in:

```
<IMG SRC="image.jpg" alt="First &quot;real&quot; example">
```

The length of an attribute value is limited to 1024 characters after replacing entity and numeric character references.

NOTE: Some non-SGML implementations allow any character except space or > in a name token. Attributes values must be quoted only if they don't satisfy the syntax for a name token.

Attributes with a declared value of NAME, such as ISMAP and COMPACT, may be written using a minimized syntax. The markup:

```
<UL COMPACT="compact">
```

can be written using a minimized syntax:

```
<UL COMPACT>
```

NOTE: Some non-SGML implementations only understand the minimized syntax.

2.6.4 Special Characters

Characters that are used to represent markup (such as ampersand (&), lesser (<) and greater (>)) should themselves be represented by markup, using either entity or numeric character references. For more information, see Section 2.16.

2.6.5 Comments

To include comments in an HTML document that will be ignored by the HTML user agent, surround them with <!-- and -->. After the comment delimiter, all text up to the next occurrence of --> is ignored. Hence comments cannot be nested. White space is allowed between the closing -- and >, but not between the opening <! and --.

See Section 8.4.4 for tips on using the HTML comment string.

For example:

```
<HEAD>
<TITLE>HTML Guide: Recommended Usage</TITLE>
<!-- Id: Text.html,v 1.6 1994/04/25 17:33:48 connolly Exp -->
</HEAD>
```

NOTE: Some historical HTML user agents incorrectly consider a > sign to terminate a comment.

2.7 The Head Element and Related Elements

See Section 7.3.2 for information on each of the head elements.

HTML 3.0 adds the following three head elements to increase the user's ability to control a page's layout: Banner, Range, and Style. See Section 7.4.1 for information on each of these elements.

Only certain elements are allowed in the head of an HTML document. Elements that may be included in the head of a document are:

2.7.1 Head

```
<HEAD> ... </HEAD>
```

Level 0

The head of an HTML document is an unordered collection of information about the document. It requires the Title element between <HEAD> and </HEAD> tags in this format:

```
<HEAD>
<TITLE>Introduction to HTML</TITLE>
</HEAD>
```

2.7.2 Base

Level 0

The Base element allows the URL of the document itself to be recorded in situations in which the document may be read out of context. URLs within the document may be in a "partial" form relative to this base address.

Where the base address is not specified, the HTML user agent uses the URL it used to access the document to resolve any relative URLs.

The Base element has one attribute, HREF, which identifies the URL.

2.7.3 Isindex

Level 0

The Isindex element tells the HTML user agent that the document is an index document. As well as reading it, the reader may use a keyword search.

The document can be queried with a keyword search by adding a question mark to the end of the document address, followed by a list of keywords separated by plus signs.

NOTE: The Isindex element is usually generated automatically by a server. If added manually to an HTML document, the HTML user agent assumes that the server can handle a search on the document. To use the Isindex element, the server must have a search engine that supports this element.

2.7.4 Link
Level 1

The Link element indicates a relationship between the document and some other object. A document may have any number of Link elements.

The Link element is empty (does not have a closing tag), but takes the same attributes as the Anchor element.

Typical uses are to indicate authorship, related indexes and glossaries, older or more recent versions, etc. Links can indicate a static tree structure in which the document was authored by pointing to a "parent" and "next" and "previous" document, for example.

Servers may also allow links to be added by those who do not have the right to alter the body of a document.

2.7.5 Nextid
Level 0

The Nextid element is a parameter read by and generated by text editing software to create unique identifiers. This tag takes a single attribute which is the next document-wide alpha-numeric identifier to be allocated of the form z123:

```
<NEXTID N=Z27>
```

When modifying a document, existing anchor identifiers should not be reused, as these identifiers may be referenced by other documents. Human writers of HTML usually use mnemonic alphabetical identifiers.

HTML user agents may ignore the Nextid element. Support for the Nextid element does not impact HTML user agents in any way.

2.7.6 Title

```
<TITLE> ... </TITLE>
```

Level 0

Every HTML document must contain a Title element. The title should identify the contents of the document in a global context, and may be used in a history lists and as a label for the window displaying the document. Unlike headings, titles are not typically rendered in the text of a document itself.

The Title element must occur within the head of the document, and may not contain anchors, paragraph tags, or highlighting. Only one title is allowed in a document.

NOTE: The length of a title is not limited; however, long titles may be truncated in some applications. To minimize this possibility, titles should be fewer than 64 characters. Also keep in mind that a short title, such as Introduction, may be meaningless out of context. An example of a meaningful title might be "Introduction to HTML Elements."

2.7.7 Meta
Level 1

The Meta element is used within the Head element to embed document meta-information not defined by other HTML elements. Such information can be extracted by servers/clients for use in identifying, indexing, and cataloging specialized document meta-information.

Although it is generally preferable to use named elements that have well-defined semantics for each type of meta-information, such as a title, this element is provided for situations where strict SGML parsing is necessary and the local DTD is not extensible.

In addition, HTTP servers can read the content of the document head to generate response headers corresponding to any elements defining a value for the attribute HTTP- EQUIV. This provides document authors a mechanism (not necessarily the preferred one) for identifying information that should be included in the response headers for an HTTP request.

Attributes of the Meta element:

HTTP-EQUIV

This attribute binds the element to an HTTP response header. If the semantics of the HTTP response header named by this attribute is known, then the contents can be processed based on a well-defined syntactic mapping whether or not the DTD includes anything about it. HTTP header names are not case sensitive. If not present, the NAME attribute should be used to identify this meta- information and it should not be used within an HTTP response header.

NAME

Meta-information name. If the NAME attribute is not present, the name can be assumed equal to the value of HTTP-EQUIV.

CONTENT

The meta-information content to be associated with the given name and/or HTTP response header.

Examples

If the document contains:

```
<META HTTP-EQUIV="Expires" CONTENT="Tue, 04 Dec 1993 21:29:02 GMT">
<META HTTP-EQUIV="Keywords" CONTENT="Fred, Barney">
<META HTTP-EQUIV="Reply-to" content="fielding@ics.uci.edu (Roy Field-
ing)">
Expires: Tue, 04 Dec 1993 21:29:02 GMT
Keywords: Fred, Barney
Reply-to: fielding@ics.uci.edu (Roy Fielding)
```

When the HTTP-EQUIV attribute is not present, the server should not generate an HTTP response header for this meta-information; e.g.,

```
<META NAME="IndexType" CONTENT="Service">
```

Do not use the Meta element to define information that should be associated with an existing HTML element.

Example of an inappropriate use of the Meta element:

```
<META NAME="Title" CONTENT="The Etymology of Dunsel">
```

Do not name an HTTP-EQUIV equal to a response header that should typically only be generated by the HTTP server. Some inappropriate names are "Server", "Date", and "Last-modified". Whether a name is inappropriate depends on the particular server implementation. It is recommended that servers ignore any Meta elements that specify HTTP-equivalents equal (case-insensitively) to their own reserved response headers.

2.8 The Body Element and Related Elements

The following elements may be included in the body of an HTML document:

2.8.1 Body

```
<BODY> ... </BODY>
```

Level 0

The Body element identifies the body component of an HTML document. Specifically, the body of a document may contain links, text, and formatting information within <BODY> and </BODY> tags.

2.8.2 Address

```
<ADDRESS> ... </ADDRESS>
```

Level 0

The Address element specifies such information as address, signature and authorship, often at the top or bottom of a document.

Typically, an Address is rendered in an italic typeface and may be indented. The Address element implies a paragraph break before and after.

Example of use:

```
<ADDRESS>
Newsletter editor<BR>
J.R. Brown<BR>
JimquickPost News, Jumquick, CT 01234<BR>
Tel (123) 456 7890
</ADDRESS>
```

2.8.3 Anchor

<A> ... </A>

Level 0

An anchor is a marked text that is the start and/or destination of a hypertext link. Anchor elements are defined by the <A> tag. The <A> tag accepts several attributes, but either the NAME or HREF attribute is required.

Attributes of the <A> tag:

HREF

Level 0

If the HREF attribute is present, the text between the opening and closing anchor tags becomes hypertext. If this hypertext is selected by readers, they are moved to another document, or to a different location in the current document, whose network address is defined by the value of the HREF attribute.

Example:

```
See <A HREF="http://www.hal.com/">HaL</A>'s information for more
details.
```

In this example, selecting "HaL" takes the reader to a document at http://www.hal.com. The format of the network address is specified in the URI specification for print readers.

With the HREF attribute, the form HREF="#identifier" can refer to another anchor in the same document.

Example:

```
The <A HREF="document.html#glossary">glossary</A>
```

defines terms used in this document.

In this example, selecting "glossary" takes the reader to another anchor (i.e., <A NAME="glossary">Glossary</A>) in the same document (document.html). The NAME attribute is described below. If the anchor is in another document, the HREF attribute may be relative to the document's address or the specified base address (see 2.7.2 Base).

NAME

Level 0

If present, the NAME attribute allows the anchor to be the target of a link. The value of the NAME attribute is an identifier for the anchor. Identifiers are arbitrary strings but must be unique within the HTML document.

Example of use:

```
<A NAME="coffee">Coffee</A> is an example of ...
          ...
An example of this is <A HREF="#coffee">coffee</A>.
```

Another document can then make a reference explicitly to this anchor by putting the identifier after the address, separated by a hash sign:

```
<A NAME="drinks.html#coffee">
```

TITLE

Level 1

The TITLE attribute is informational only. If present, the TITLE attribute should provide the title of the document whose address is given by the HREF attribute.

The TITLE attribute is useful for at least two reasons. The HTML user agent may display the title of the document prior to retrieving it, for example, as a margin note or on a small box while the mouse is over the anchor, or while the document is being loaded. Another reason is that documents that are not marked up text, such as graphics, plain text and Gopher menus, do not have titles. The TITLE attribute can be used to provide a title to such documents. When using the TITLE attribute, the title should be valid and unique for the destination document.

REL

Level 1

The REL attribute gives the relationship(s) described by the hypertext link from the anchor to the target. The value is a comma-separated list of relationship values. Values and their semantics will be registered by the HTML registration authority. The default relationship if none other is given is void. The REL attribute is only used when the HREF attribute is present.

REV

Level 1

The REV attribute is the same as the REL attribute, but the semantics of the link type are in the reverse direction. A link from A to B with REL="X" expresses the same relationship as a link from B to A with REV="X". An anchor may have both REL and REV attributes.

URN

Level 1

If present, the URN attribute specifies a uniform resource name (URN) for a target document. The format of URNs is under discussion (1994) by various working groups of the Internet Engineering Task Force.

METHODS

The METHODS attributes of anchors and links provide information about the functions that the user may perform on an object. These are more accurately given by the HTTP protocol when it is used, but it may, for similar reasons as for the TITLE attribute, be useful to include the information in advance in the link. For example, the HTML user agent may chose a different rendering as a function of the methods allowed; for example, something that is searchable may get a different icon.

The value of the METHODS attribute is a comma separated list of HTTP methods supported by the object for public use.

See also: 2.7.4 Link

2.8.4 Blockquote

```
<BLOCKQUOTE> ... </BLOCKQUOTE>
```

Level 0

The Blockquote element is used to contain text quoted from another source.

A typical rendering might be a slight extra left and right indent, and/or italic font. The Blockquote element causes a paragraph break, and typically provides space above and below the quote.

Single-font rendition may reflect the quotation style of Internet mail by putting a vertical line of graphic characters, such as the greater than symbol (>), in the left margin.

Example of use:

```
I think the poem ends
<BLOCKQUOTE>
<P>Soft you now, the fair Ophelia. Nymph,
in thy orisons, be all my sins remembered.
</BLOCKQUOTE>
but I am not sure.
```

2.8.5 Headings

```
<H1> ... </H1> through <H6> ... </H6>
```

Level 0

HTML defines six levels of heading. A Heading element implies all the font changes, paragraph breaks before and after, and white space necessary to render the heading.

The highest level of headings is H1, followed by H2 ... H6.

Example of use:

```
<H1>This is a heading</H1>
Here is some text
<H2>Second level heading</H2>

Here is some more text.
```

Te rendering of headings is determined by the HTML user agent, but typical renderings are:

```
<H1> ... </H1>
```

Bold, very-large font, centered. One or two blank lines above and below.

```
<H2> ... </H2>
```

Bold, large font, flush-left. One or two blank lines above and below.

```
<H3> ... </H3>
```

Italic, large font, slightly indented from the left margin. One or two blank lines above and below.

```
<H4> ... </H4>
```

Bold, normal font, indented more than H3. One blank line above and below.

```
<H5> ... </H5>
```

Italic, normal font, indented as H4. One blank line above.

```
<H6> ... </H6>
```

Bold, indented same as normal text, more than H5. One blank line above.

Although heading levels can be skipped (for example, from H1 to H3), this practice is discouraged as skipping heading levels may produce unpredictable results when generating other representations from HTML.

2.9 Overview of Character-Level Elements

Level 2 (all elements)

Character-level elements are used to specify either the logical meaning or the physical appearance of marked text without causing a paragraph break. Like most other elements, character-level elements include both opening and closing tags. Only the characters between the tags are affected:

```
This is <EM>emphasized</EM> text.
```

Character-level tags may be ignored by minimal HTML applications.

Character-level tags are interpreted from left to right as they appear in the flow of text. Level 1 HTML user agents must render highlighted text distinctly from plain text. Additionally, EM content must be rendered as distinct from STRONG content, and B content must rendered as distinct from I content.

Character-level elements may be nested within the content of other character-level elements; however, HTML user agents are not required to render nested character- level elements distinctly from non-nested elements:

```
plain <B>bold <I>italic</I></B>
```

may the rendered the same as

```
plain <B>bold </B><I>italic</I>
```

Note that typical renderings for information type elements vary between applications. If a specific rendering is necessary, for example, when referring to a specific text attribute as in "The italic parts are mandatory", a formating element can be used to ensure that the intended rendered is used where possible.

2.10 Information Type Elements

Note that different information type elements may be rendered in the same way.

2.10.1 Citation

```
<CITE>...</CITE>
```

The Citation element specifies a citation; typically rendered as italics.

2.10.2 Code

```
<CODE> ... </CODE>
```

The Code element indicates an example of code; typically rendered as monospaced . Do not confuse with the Preformatted Text element.

2.10.3 Emphasis

```
<EM> ... </EM>
```

The Emphasis element indicates typographic emphasis, typically rendered as italics.

2.10.4 Keyboard

<KBD> ... </KBD>

The Keyboard element indicates text typed by a user; typically rendered as monospaced. It might commonly be used in an instruction manual.

2.10.5 Sample

<SAMP> ... </SAMP>

The Sample element indicates a sequence of literal characters; typically rendered as monospaced.

2.10.6 Strong

<STRONG> ... </STRONG>

The Strong element indicates strong typographic emphasis, typically rendered in bold.

2.10.7 Variable

<VAR> ... </VAR>

The Variable element indicates a variable name; typically rendered as italic.

2.11 Character Format Elements

Character format elements are used to specify the format of marked text. Example of use:

2.11.1 Bold

<B> ... </B>

The Bold element specifies that the text should be rendered in boldface, where available. Otherwise, alternative mapping is allowed.

2.11.2 Italic

<I> ... </I>

The Italic element specifies that the text should be rendered in italic font, where available. Otherwise, alternative mapping is allowed.

2.11.3 Teletype

<TT> ... </TT>

The Teletype element specifies that the text should be rendered in fixed-width typewriter font.

2.12 Image Element

```
<IMG>
```

Level 0

The Image element is used to incorporate in-line graphics (typically icons or small graphics) into an HTML document. This element cannot be used for embedding other HTML text.

HTML user agents that cannot render in-line images ignore the Image element unless it contains the ALT attribute. Note that some HTML user agents can render linked graphics but not in-line graphics. If a graphic is essential, you may want to create a link to it rather than to put it in-line. If the graphic is not essential, then the Image element is appropriate.

The Image element, which is empty (no closing tag), has these attributes:

ALIGN
The ALIGN attribute accepts the values TOP or MIDDLE or BOTTOM, which specifies if the following line of text is aligned with the top, middle, or bottom of the graphic.

ALT
Optional text as an alternative to the graphic for rendering in non-graphical environments. Alternate text should be provided whenever the graphic is not rendered. Alternate text is mandatory for Level 0 documents. Example of use:

```
<IMG SRC="triangle.gif" ALT="Warning:"> Be sure to read
these instructions.
```

ISMAP
The ISMAP (is map) attribute identifies an image as an image map. Image maps are graphics in which certain regions are mapped to URLs. By clicking on different regions, different resources can be accessed from the same graphic. Example of use:

```
<A HREF="http://machine/htbin/imagemap/sample">
<IMG SRC="sample.gif" ISMAP>
</A>
```

SRC
The value of the SRC attribute is the URL of the document to be embedded; only images can be embedded, not HTML text. Its syntax is the same as that of the HREF attribute of the <A> tag. SRC is mandatory. Image elements are allowed within anchors.

Example of use:

```
<IMG SRC ="triangle.gif">Be sure to read these
instructions.
```

2.13 List Elements

HTML supports several types of lists, all of which may be nested.

2.13.1 Definition List

```
<DL> ... </DL>
```

Level 0

A definition list is a list of terms and corresponding definitions. Definition lists are typically formatted with the term flush-left and the definition, formatted paragraph style, indented after the term.

Example of use:

```
<DL>
<DT>Term<DD>This is the definition of the first term.
<DT>Term<DD>This is the definition of the second term.
</DL>
```

If the DT term does not fit in the DT column (one third of the display area), it may be extended across the page with the DD section moved to the next line, or it may be wrapped onto successive lines of the left hand column.

Single occurrences of a <DT> tag without a subsequent <DD> tag are allowed, and have the same significance as if the <DD> tag had been present with no text.

The opening list tag must be <DL> and must be immediately followed by the first term (<DT>).

The definition list type can take the COMPACT attribute, which suggests that a compact rendering be used, because the list items are small and/or the entire list is large.

Unless you provide the COMPACT attribute, the HTML user agent may leave white space between successive DT, DD pairs.The COMPACT attribute may also reduce the width of the left-hand (DT) column.

If using the COMPACT attribute, the opening list tag must be <DL COMPACT>, which must be immediately followed by the first <DT> tag:

```
<DL COMPACT>
<DT>Term<DD>This is the first definition in compact format.
<DT>Term<DD>This is the second definition in compact format.
</DL>
```

2.13.2 Directory List

```
<DIR> ... </DIR>
```

Level 0

A Directory List element is used to present a list of items containing up to 20 characters each. Items in a directory list may be arranged in columns, typically 24 characters wide. If the HTML user agent can optimize the column width as function of the widths of individual elements, so much the better.

A directory list must begin with the <DIR> tag which is immediately followed by a <LI> (list item) tag:

```
<DIR>
<LI>A-H<LI>I-M
<LI>M-R<LI>S-Z
</DIR>
```

2.13.3 Menu List

```
<MENU> ... </MENU>
```

Level 0

A menu list is a list of items with typically one line per item. The menu list style is more compact than the style of an unordered list.

A menu list must begin with a <MENU> tag which is immediately followed by a <LI> (list item) tag:

```
<MENU>
<LI>First item in the list.
<LI>Second item in the list.
<LI>Third item in the list.
</MENU>
```

2.13.4 Ordered List

```
<OL> ... </OL>
```

Level 0

The Ordered List element is used to present a numbered list of items, sorted by sequence or order of importance.

An ordered list must begin with the <OL> tag which is immediately followed by a <LI> (list item) tag:

```
<OL>
<LI>Click the Web button to open the Open the URL window.
<LI>Enter the URL number in the text field of the Open URL
window. The Web document you specified is displayed.
<LI>Click highlighted text to move from one link to another.
</OL>
```

The Ordered List element can take the COMPACT attribute, which suggests that a compact rendering be used.

2.13.5 Unordered List

```
<UL> ... </UL>
```

Level 0

The Unordered List element is used to present a list of items which is typically separated by white space and/or marked by bullets.

An unordered list must begin with the <UL> tag which is immediately followed by a <LI> (list item) tag:

```
<UL>
<LI>First list item
<LI>Second list item
<LI>Third list item
</UL>
```

2.14 Other Elements

2.14.1 Paragraph

```
<P>
```

Level 0

The Paragraph element indicates a paragraph. The exact indentation, leading, etc. of a paragraph is not defined and may be a function of other tags, style sheets, etc.

Typically, paragraphs are surrounded by a vertical space of one line or half a line. This is typically not the case within the Address element and or is never the case within the Preformatted Text element. With some HTML user agents, the first line in a paragraph is indented.

Example of use:

```
<H1>This Heading Precedes the Paragraph</H1>
<P>This is the text of the first paragraph.
<P>This is the text of the second paragraph. Although you
do not need to start paragraphs on new lines, maintaining
this convention facilitates document maintenance.
<P>This is the text of a third paragraph.
```

2.14.2 Preformatted Text

```
<PRE> ... </PRE>
```

Level 0

The Preformatted Text element presents blocks of text in fixed-width font, and so is suitable for text that has been formatted on screen.

The <PRE> tag may be used with the optional WIDTH attribute, which is a Level 1 feature. The WIDTH attribute specifies the maximum number of characters for a line and allows the HTML user agent to select a suitable font and indentation. If the WIDTH attribute is not present, a width of 80 characters is assumed. Where the WIDTH attribute is supported, widths of 40, 80 and 132 characters should be presented optimally, with other widths being rounded up. Within preformatted text:

- 0 Line breaks within the text are rendered as a move to the beginning of the next line.
- 0 The <P> tag should not be used. If found, it should be rendered as a move to the beginning of the next line.
- 0 Anchor elements and character highlighting elements may be used.
- 0 Elements that define paragraph formatting (headings, address, etc.) must not be used.
- 0 The horizontal tab character (encoded in US-ASCII and ISO-8859-1 as decimal 9) must be interpreted as the smallest positive nonzero number of spaces which will leave the number of characters so far on the line as a multiple of 8. Its use is not recommended however.

NOTE: References to the "beginning of a new line" do not imply that the renderer is forbidden from using a constant left indent for rendering preformatted text. The left indent may be constrained by the width required.

Example of use:

```
<PRE WIDTH="80">
This is an example line.
</PRE>
```

NOTE: Within a Preformatted Text element, the constraint that the rendering must be on a fixed horizontal character pitch may limit or prevent the ability of the HTML user agent to render highlighting elements specially.

2.14.3 Line Break

```
<BR>
```

Level 0

The Line Break element specifies that a new line must be started at the given point. A new line indents the same as that of line-wrapped text.

Example of use:

```
<P>
Pease porridge hot<BR>
Pease porridge cold<BR>
Pease porridge in the pot<BR>
Nine days old.
```

2.14.4 Horizontal Rule

```
<HR>
```

Level 0

A Horizontal Rule element is a divider between sections of text such as a full width horizontal rule or equivalent graphic.

Example of use:

```
<HR>
<ADDRESS>February 8, 1995, CERN</ADDRESS>
</BODY>
```

2.15 Form Elements

Forms are created by placing input fields within paragraphs, preformatted/literal text, and lists. This gives considerable flexibility in designing the layout of forms.

The following elements (all are HTML 2 features) are used to create forms:

FORM
A form within a document.

INPUT
One input field.

OPTION
One option within a Select element.

SELECT
A selection from a finite set of options.

TEXTAREA
A multi-line input field.

Each variable field is defined by an Input, Textarea, or Option element and must have an NAME attribute to identify its value in the data returned when the form is submitted.

Example of use (a questionnaire form):

```
<H1>Sample Questionnaire</H1>
<P>Please fill out this questionnaire:
<FORM METHOD="POST" ACTION="http://www.hal.com/sample">
<P>Your name: <INPUT NAME="name" size="48">
<P>Male <INPUT NAME="gender" TYPE=RADIO VALUE="male">
<P>Female <INPUT NAME="gender" TYPE=RADIO VALUE="female">
<P>Number in family: <INPUT NAME="family" TYPE=text>
<P>Cities in which you maintain a residence:
<UL>
<LI>Kent <INPUT NAME="city" TYPE=checkbox VALUE="kent">
<LI>Miami <INPUT NAME="city" TYPE=checkbox VALUE="miami">
<LI>Other <TEXTAREA NAME="other" cols=48 rows=4></textarea>
</UL>
Nickname: <INPUT NAME="nickname" SIZE="42">
<P>Thank you for responding to this questionnaire.
<P><INPUT TYPE=SUBMIT> <INPUT TYPE=RESET>
</FORM>
```

In the example above, the <P> and <UL> tags have been used to lay out the text and input fields. The HTML user agent is responsible for handling which field will currently get keyboard input.

Many platforms have existing conventions for forms, for example, using Tab and Shift keys to move the keyboard focus forwards and backwards between fields, and using the Enter key to submit the form. In the example, the SUBMIT and RESET buttons are specified explicitly with special purpose fields. The SUBMIT button is used to e- mail the form or send its contents to the server as specified by the ACTION attribute, while RESET resets the fields to their initial values. When the form consists of a single text field, it may be appropriate to leave such buttons out and rely on the Enter key.

The Input element is used for a large variety of types of input fields.

To let users enter more than one line of text, use the Textarea element.

2.15.1 Representing Choices

The radio button and checkbox types of input field can be used to specify multiple choice forms in which every alternative is visible as part of the form. An alternative is to use the Select element which is typically rendered in a more compact fashion as a pull down combo list.

2.15.2 Form

<FORM> ... </FORM>

Level 2

The Form element is used to delimit a data input form. There can be several forms in a single document, but the Form element can't be nested.

The ACTION attribute is a URL specifying the location to which the contents of the form is submitted to elicit a response. If the ACTION attribute is missing, the URL of the document itself is assumed. The way data is submitted varies with the access protocol of the URL, and with the values of the METHOD and ENCTYPE attributes.

In general:

- the METHOD attribute selects variations in the protocol.
- the ENCTYPE attribute specifies the format of the submitted data in case the protocol does not impose a format itself.

The Level 2 specification defines and requires support for the HTTP access protocol only.

When the ACTION attribute is set to an HTTP URL, the METHOD attribute must be set to an HTTP method as defined by the HTTP method specification in the IETF draft HTTP standard. The default METHOD is GET, although for many applications, the POST method may be preferred. With the post method, the ENCTYPE attribute is a MIME type specifying the format of the posted data; by default, is application/x-www-form-urlencoded.

Under any protocol, the submitted contents of the form logically consist of name/value pairs. The names are usually equal to the NAME attributes of the various interactive elements in the form.

NOTE: The names are not guaranteed to be unique keys, nor are the names of form elements required to be distinct. The values encode the user's input to the corresponding interactive elements. Elements capable of displaying a textual or numerical value will return a name/value pair even when they receive no explicit user input.

2.15.3 Input

<INPUT>

Level 2

The Input element represents a field whose contents may be edited by the user.

Attributes of the Input element:

ALIGN

Vertical alignment of the image. For use only with TYPE=IMAGE in HTML level 2. The possible values are exactly the same as for the ALIGN attribute of the image element.

CHECKED

Indicates that a checkbox or radio button is selected. Unselected checkboxes and radio buttons do not return name/value pairs when the form is submitted.

MAXLENGTH

Indicates the maximum number of characters that can be entered into a text field. This can be greater than specified by the SIZE attribute, in which case the field will scroll appropriately. The default number of characters is unlimited.

NAME

Symbolic name used when transferring the form's contents. The NAME attribute is required for most input types and is normally used to provide a unique identifier for a field, or for a logically related group of fields.

SIZE

Specifies the size or precision of the field according to its type. For example, to specify a field with a visible width of 24 characters:

```
INPUT TYPE=text SIZE="24"
```

SRC

A URL or URN specifying an image. For use only with TYPE=IMAGE in HTML Level 2.

TYPE

Defines the type of data the field accepts. Defaults to free text. Several types of fields can be defined with the type attribute:

CHECKBOX

Used for simple Boolean attributes, or for attributes that can take multiple values at the same time. The latter is represented by a number of checkbox fields each of which has the same name. Each selected checkbox generates a separate name/value pair in the submitted data, even if this results in duplicate names. The default value for checkboxes is "on".

HIDDEN

No field is presented to the user, but the content of the field is sent with the submitted form. This value may be used to transmit state information about client/server interaction.

IMAGE

An image field upon which you can click with a pointing device, causing the form to be immediately submitted. The coordinates of the selected point are measured in pixel units from the upper-left corner of the image, and are returned (along with the other contents of the form) in two name/value pairs. The x-coordinate is submitted under the name of the field with .x appended, and the y- coordinate is submitted under the name of the field with .y appended. Any VALUE attribute is ignored. The image itself is specified by the SRC attribute, exactly as for the Image element.

NOTE: In a future version of the HTML specification, the IMAGE functionality may be folded into an enhanced SUBMIT field.

PASSWORD is the same as the TEXT attribute, except that text is not displayed as it is entered.

RADIO is used for attributes that accept a single value from a set of alternatives. Each radio button field in the group should be given the same name. Only the selected radio button in the group generates a name/value pair in the submitted data. Radio buttons require an explicit VALUE attribute.

RESET is a button that when pressed resets the form's fields to their specified initial values. The label to be displayed on the button may be specified just as for the SUBMIT button.

SUBMIT is a button that when pressed submits the form. You can use the VALUE attribute to provide a non- editable label to be displayed on the button. The default label is application-specific. If a SUBMIT button is pressed in order to submit the form, and that button has a NAME attribute specified, then that button contributes a name/value pair to the submitted data. Otherwise, a SUBMIT button makes no contribution to the submitted data.

TEXT is used for a single line text entry fields. Use in conjunction with the SIZE and MAXLENGTH attributes. Use the Textarea element for text fields which can accept multiple lines.

VALUE

The initial displayed value of the field, if it displays a textual or numerical value; or the value to be returned when the field is selected, if it displays a Boolean value. This attribute is required for radio buttons.

2.15.4 Option

<OPTION>

Level 2

The Option element can only occur within a Select element. It represents one choice, and can take these attributes:

DISABLED

Proposed.

SELECTED

Indicates that this option is initially selected.

VALUE

When present indicates the value to be returned if this option is chosen. The returned value defaults to the contents of the Option element.

The contents of the Option element is presented to the user to represent the option. It is used as a returned value if the VALUE attribute is not present.

2.15.5 Select

```
<SELECT NAME=... > ... </SELECT>
```

Level 2

The Select element allows the user to chose one of a set of alternatives described by textual labels. Every alternative is represented by the Option element.

Attributes are:

ERROR

Proposed.

MULTIPLE

The MULTIPLE attribute is needed when users are allowed to make several selections, e.g. <SELECT MULTIPLE>.

NAME

Specifies the name that will submitted as a name/value pair.

SIZE

Specifies the number of visible items. If this is greater than one, then the resulting form control will be a list.

The Select element is typically rendered as a pull down or pop-up list. For example:

```
<SELECT NAME="flavor">
<OPTION>Vanilla
<OPTION>Strawberry
<OPTION>Rum and Raisin
<OPTION>Peach and Orange
</SELECT>
```

If no option is initially marked as selected, then the first item listed is selected.

2.15.6 Text Area

```
<TEXTAREA> ... </TEXTAREA>
```

Level 2

The Textarea element lets users enter more than one line of text. For example:

```
<TEXTAREA NAME="address" ROWS=64 COLS=6>
HaL Computer Systems
1315 Dell Avenue
Campbell, California 95008
</TEXTAREA>
```

The text up to the end tag (</TEXTAREA>) is used to initialize the field's value. This end tag is always required even if the field is initially blank. When submitting a form, lines in a TEXTAREA should be terminated using CR/LF.

In a typical rendering, the ROWS and COLS attributes determine the visible dimension of the field in characters. The field is rendered in a fixed-width font. HTML user agents should allow text to extend beyond these limits by scrolling as needed.

NOTE: In the initial design for forms, multi-line text fields were supported by the Input element with TYPE=TEXT. Unfortunately, this causes problems for fields with long text values. SGML's default (Reference Quantity Set) limits the length of attribute literals to only 240 characters. The HTML 2.0 SGML declaration increases the limit to 1024 characters.

2.16 Character Data

Level 0

The characters between HTML tags represent text. A HTML document (including tags and text) is encoded using the coded character set specified by the "charset" parameter of the "text/html" media type. For levels defined in this specification, the "charset" parameter is restricted to "US-ASCII" or "ISO-8859-1". ISO-8859-1 encodes a set of characters known as Latin Alphabet No. 1, or simply Latin-1. Latin-1 includes characters from most Western European languages, as well as a number of control characters. Latin-1 also includes a non-breaking space, a soft hyphen indicator, 93 graphical characters, 8 unassigned characters, and 25 control characters.

Because non-breaking space and soft hyphen indicator are not recognized and interpreted by all HTML user agents, their use is discouraged.

There are 58 character positions occupied by control characters. See Section 2.16.2 for details on the interpretation of control characters.

Because certain special characters are subject to interpretation and special processing, information providers and HTML user agent implementors should follow the guidelines in Section 2.16.1.

In addition, HTML provides character entity references (see Section 2.17.2) and numerical character references (see Section 2.17.3) to facilitate the entry and interpretation of characters by name and by numerical position.

Because certain characters will be interpreted as markup, they must be represented by entity references as described in Section 2.16.3 and Section 2.16.4.

2.16.1 Special Characters

Certain characters have special meaning in HTML documents. There are two printing characters which may be interpreted by an HTML application to have an effect of the format of the text:

Space

- 0 Interpreted as a word space (place where a line can be broken) in all contexts except the Preformatted Text element.
- 0 Interpreted as a nonbreaking space within the Preformatted Text element.

Hyphen

0 Interpreted as a hyphen glyph in all contexts

0 Interpreted as a potential word space by hyphenation engine

2.16.2 Control Characters

Control characters are non-printable characters that are typically used for communication and device control, as format effectors, and as information separators.

In SGML applications, the use of control characters is limited in order to maximize the chance of successful interchange over heterogenous networks and operating systems. In HTML, only three control characters are used: Horizontal Tab (HT, encoded as 9 decimal in US-ASCII and ISO-8859-1), Carriage Return, and Line Feed.

Horizontal Tab is interpreted as a word space in all contexts except preformatted text. Within preformatted text, the tab should be interpreted to shift the horizontal column position to the next position which is a multiple of 8 on the same line; that is, col := (col+8) mod 8.

Carriage Return and Line Feed are conventionally used to represent end of line. For Internet Media Types defined as "text/*", the sequence CR LF is used to represent an end of line. In practice, text/html documents are frequently represented and transmitted using an end of line convention that depends on the conventions of the source of the document; frequently, that representation consists of CR only, LF only, or CR LF combination. In HTML, end of line in any of its variations is interpreted as a word space in all contexts except preformatted text. Within preformatted text, HTML interpreting agents should expect to treat any of the three common representations of end-of-line as starting a new line.

2.16.3 Numeric Character References

In addition to any mechanism by which characters may be represented by the encoding of the HTML document, it is possible to explicitly reference the printing characters of the ISO-8859-1 character encoding using a numeric character reference. See Section 2.17.1 for a list of the characters, their names and input syntax.

0 Two reasons for using a numeric character reference:

0 the keyboard does not provide a key for the character, such as on U.S. keyboards which do not provide European characters

0 the character may be interpreted as SGML coding, such as the ampersand (&), double quotes ("), the lesser (<) and greater (>) characters

Numeric character references are represented in an HTML document as SGML entities whose name is number sign (#) followed by a numeral from 32-126 and 161-255. The HTML DTD includes a numeric character for each of the printing characters of the ISO-8859-1 encoding, so that one may reference them by number if it is inconvenient to enter them directly:

0 the ampersand (&), double quotes ("), lesser (<) and greater (>) characters

2.16.4 Character Entities

In addition, many of the Latin alphabet No. 1 set of printing characters may be represented within the text of an HTML document by a character entity. See 2.17.2 for a list of the characters, names, input syntax, and descriptions. See 5.2.1 for the SGML entity definitions of "Added Latin 1 for HTML".

Two reasons for using a character entity:

- the keyboard does not provide a key for the character, such as on U.S. keyboards which do not provide European characters
- the character may be interpreted as SGML coding, such as the ampersand (&), double quotes ("), the lesser (<) and greater (>) characters

A character entity is represented in an HTML document as an SGML entity whose name is defined in the HTML DTD. The HTML DTD includes a character entity for each of the SGML markup characters and for each of the printing characters in the upper half of Latin-1, so that one may reference them by name if it is inconvenient to enter them directly:

- the ampersand (&), double quotes ("), lesser (<) and greater (>) characters

  Kurt Gödel was a famous logician and mathematician.

NOTE: To ensure that a string of characters is not interpreted as markup, represent all occurrences of <, >, and & by character or entity references.

NOTE: There are SGML features, CDATA and RCDATA, to allow most <, >, and & characters to be entered without the use of entity or character references. Because these features tend to be used and implemented inconsistently, and because they require 8-bit characters to represent non-ASCII characters, they are not used in this version of the HTML DTD. An earlier HTML specification included an Example element (<XMP>) whose syntax is not expressible in SGML. No markup was recognized inside of the Example element except the </XMP> end tag. While HTML user agents are encouraged to support this idiom, its use is deprecated.

2.17 Character Entity Sets

The following entity names are used in HTML, always prefixed by ampersand (&) and followed by a semicolon as shown.

They represent particular graphic characters which have special meanings in places in the markup, or may not be part of the character set available to the writer.

2.17.1 Numeric and Special Graphic Entities

The following table lists each of the supported characters specified in the Numeric and Special Graphic entity set, along with its name, syntax for use, and description. This list is derived from ISO Standard 8879:1986//ENTITIES Numeric and Special Graphic//EN however HTML does not provide support for the entire entity set. Only the entities listed below are supported.

Table C–1. Numeric and Special Graphic Entities

GLYPH	NAME	SYNTAX	DESCRIPTION
<	lt	<	Less than sign
>	gt	>	Greater than sign
&	amp	&	Ampersand
"	quot	"	Double quote sign

2.17.2 ISO Latin 1 Character Entities

The following table lists each of the characters specified in the Added Latin 1 entity set, along with its name, syntax for use, and description. This list is derived from ISO Standard 8879:1986//ENTITIES Added Latin 1//EN. HTML supports the entire entity set.

Table C–2. ISO Latin 1 Character Entities

NAME	SYNTAX	DESCRIPTION
Aacute	Á	Capital A, acute accent
Agrave	À	Capital A, grave accent
Acirc	Â	Capital A, circumflex accent
Atilde	Ã	Capital A, tilde
Aring	Å	Capital A, ring
Auml	Ä	Capital A, dieresis or umlaut mark
AElig	Æ	Capital AE dipthong (ligature)
Ccedil	Ç	Capital C, cedilla
Eacute	É	Capital E, acute accent
Egrave	È	Capital E, grave accent
Ecirc	Ê	Capital E, circumflex accent
Euml	Ë	Capital E, dieresis or umlaut mark
Iacute	Í	Capital I, acute accent
Igrave	Ì	Capital I, grave accent
Icirc	Î	Capital I, circumflex accent
Iuml	Ï	Capital I, dieresis or umlaut mark
ETH	Ð	Capital Eth, Icelandic
Ntilde	Ñ	Capital N, tilde
Oacute	Ó	Capital O, acute accent
Ograve	Ò	Capital O, grave accent
Ocirc	Ô	Capital O, circumflex accent
Otilde	Õ	Capital O, tilde
Ouml	Ö	Capital O, dieresis or umlaut mark
Oslash	Ø	Capital O, slash
Uacute	Ú	Capital U, acute accent
Ugrave	Ù	Capital U, grave accent

Table C–2. ISO Latin 1 Character Entities (Continued)

NAME	SYNTAX	DESCRIPTION
Ucirc	Û	Capital U, circumflex accent
Uuml	Ü	Capital U, dieresis or umlaut mark
Yacute	Ý	Capital Y, acute accent
THORN	Þ	Capital THORN, Icelandic
szlig	ß	Small sharp s, German (sz ligature)
aacute	á	Small a, acute accent
agrave	à	Small a, grave accent
acirc	â	Small a, circumflex accent
atilde	ã	Small a, tilde
aring	å	Small a, ring
auml	ä	Small a, dieresis or umlaut mark
aelig	æ	Small ae dipthong (ligature)
ccedil	ç	Small c, cedilla
eacute	é	Small e, acute accent
egrave	è	Small e, grave accent
ecirc	ê	Small e, circumflex accent
euml	ë	Small e, dieresis or umlaut mark
iacute	í	Small i, acute accent
igrave	ì	Small i, grave accent
icirc	î	Small i, circumflex accent
iuml	ï	Small i, dieresis or umlaut mark
eth	ð	Small eth, Icelandic
ntilde	ñ	Small n, tilde
oacute	ó	Small o, acute accent
ograve	ò	Small o, grave accent
ocirc	ô	Small o, circumflex accent
otilde	õ	Small o, tilde
ouml	ö	Small o, dieresis or umlaut mark
oslash	ø	Small o, slash
uacute	ú	Small u, acute accent
ugrave	ù	Small u, grave accent
ucirc	û	Small u, circumflex accent
uuml	ü	Small u, dieresis or umlaut mark
yacute	ý	Small y, acute accent
thorn	þ	Small thorn, Icelandic
yuml	ÿ	Small y, dieresis or umlaut mark

2.17.3 Numerical Character References

This list, sorted numerically, is derived from ISO-8859-1 8-bit single-byte coded graphic character set:

Table C–3. Numerical Character References

REFERENCE	DESCRIPTION
� -	Unused
	Horizontal tab
Line feed
-	Unused
	Space
!	Exclamation mark
"	Quotation mark
#	Number sign
$	Dollar sign
%	Percent sign
&	Ampersand
'	Apostrophe
(	Left parenthesis
)	Right parenthesis
*	Asterisk
+	Plus sign
,	Comma
-	Hyphen
.	Period (fullstop)
/	Solidus (slash)
0 - 9	Digits 0-9
:	Colon
;	Semi-colon
<	Less than
=	Equals aign
>	Greater than
?	Question mark
@	Commercial at
A - Z	Letters A-Z
[	Left square bracket
\	Reverse solidus (backslash)
]	Right square bracket
^	Caret
_	Horizontal bar
`	Acute accent
a - z	Letters a-z
{	Left curly brace
		Vertical bar
}	Right curly brace
~	Tilde

Table C–3. Numerical Character References (Continued)

REFERENCE	DESCRIPTION
-	Unused
¡	Inverted exclamation
¢	Cent sign
£	Pound sterling
¤	General currency sign
¥	Yen sign
¦	Broken vertical bar
§	Section sign
¨	Umlaut (dieresis)
©	Copyright
ª	Feminine ordinal
«	Left angle quote, guillemotleft
¬	Not sign
	Soft hyphen
®	Registered trademark
¯	Macron accent
°	Degree sign
±	Plus or minus
²	Superscript two
³	Superscript three
´	Acute accent
µ	Micro sign
¶	Paragraph sign
·	Middle dot
¸	Cedilla
¹	Superscript one
º	Masculine ordinal
»	Right angle quote, guillemotright
¼	Fraction one-fourth
½	Fraction one-half
¾	Fraction three-fourths
¿	Inverted question mark
À	Capital A, acute accent
Á	Capital A, grave accent
Â	Capital A, circumflex accent
Ã	Capital A, tilde
Ä	Capital A, ring
Å	Capital A, dieresis or umlaut mark
Æ	Capital AE dipthong (ligature)
Ç	Capital C, cedilla

Table C–3. Numerical Character References (Continued)

REFERENCE	DESCRIPTION
È	Capital E, acute accent
É	Capital E, grave accent
Ê	Capital E, circumflex accent
Ë	Capital E, dieresis or umlaut mark
Ì	Capital I, acute accent
Í	Capital I, grave accent
Î	Capital I, circumflex accent
Ï	Capital I, dieresis or umlaut mark
Ð	Capital Eth, Icelandic
Ñ	Capital N, tilde
Ò	Capital O, acute accent
Ó	Capital O, grave accent
Ô	Capital O, circumflex accent
Õ	Capital O, tilde
Ö	Capital O, dieresis or umlaut mark
×	Multiply sign
Ø	Capital O, slash
Ù	Capital U, acute accent
Ú	Capital U, grave accent
Û	Capital U, circumflex accent
Ü	Capital U, dieresis or umlaut mark
Ý	Capital Y, acute accent
Þ	Capital THORN, Icelandic
ß	Small sharp s, German (sz ligature)
à	Small a, acute accent
á	Small a, grave accent
â	Small a, circumflex accent
ã	Small a, tilde
ä	Small a, dieresis or umlaut mark
å	Small a, ring
æ	Small ae dipthong (ligature)
ç	Small c, cedilla
è	Small e, acute accent
é	Small e, grave accent
ê	Small e, circumflex accent
ë	Small e, dieresis or umlaut mark
ì	Small i, acute accent
í	Small i, grave accent
î	Small i, circumflex accent

Table C–3. Numerical Character References (Continued)

REFERENCE	DESCRIPTION
ï	Small i, dieresis or umlaut mark
ð	Small eth, Icelandic
ñ	Small n, tilde
ò	Small o, acute accent
ó	Small o, grave accent
ô	Small o, circumflex accent
õ	Small o, tilde
ö	Small o, dieresis or umlaut mark
÷	Division sign
ø	Small o, slash
ù	Small u, acute accent
ú	Small u, grave accent
û	Small u, circumflex accent
ü	Small u, dieresis or umlaut mark
ý	Small y, acute accent
þ	Small thorn, Icelandic
ÿ	Small y, dieresis or umlaut mark

3. Security Considerations

Anchors, embedded images, and all other elements which contain URIs as parameters may cause the URI to be dereferenced in response to user input. In this case, the security considerations of the URI specification apply.

Documents may be constructed whose visible contents mislead the reader to follow a link to unsuitable or offensive material.

4. Obsolete and Proposed Features

4.1 Obsolete Features

This section describes elements that are no longer part of HTML. Client implementors should implement these obsolete elements for compatibility with previous versions of the HTML specification.

4.1.1 Comment

The Comment element is used to delimit unneeded text and comments. The Comment element has been introduced in some HTML applications but should be replaced by the SGML comment feature in new HTML user agents (see Section 2.6.5).

4.1.2 Highlighted Phrase

The Highlighted Phrase element (<HP>) should be ignored if not implemented. This element has been replaced by more meaningful elements (see Section 2.9).

Example of use:

```
<HP1>first highlighted phrase</HP1>non
highlighted text<HP2>second highlighted
phrase</HP2> etc.
```

4.1.3 Plain Text

```
<PLAINTEXT>
```

The Plain Text element is used to terminates the HTML entity and to indicate that what follows is not SGML which does not require parsing. Instead, an old HTTP convention specified that what followed was an ASCII (MIME "text/plain") body. Its presence is an optimization. There is no closing tag.

Example of use:

```
<PLAINTEXT>
0001 This is line one of a long listing
0002 file from <ANY@HOST.INC.COM> which is sent
```

4.1.4 Example and Listing

```
<XMP> ... </XMP> and <LISTING> ... </LISTING>
```

The Example element and Listing element have been replaced by the Preformatted Text element.

These styles allow text of fixed-width characters to be embedded absolutely as is into the document. The syntax is:

```
<LISTING>
...
</LISTING>
```

or

```
<XMP>
...
</XMP>
```

The text between these tags is typically rendered in a monospaced font so that any formatting done by character spacing on successive lines will be maintained.

Between the opening and closing tags:

0 The text may contain any ISO Latin-1 printable characters, expect for the end tag opener. The Example and Listing elements have historically used specifications which do not conform to SGML. Specifically, the text may contain ISO Latin printable characters, including the tag opener, as long it they does not contain the closing tag in full.

0 SGML does not support this form. HTML user agents may vary on how they interpret other tags within Example and Listing elements.

0 Line boundaries within the text are rendered as a move to the beginning of the next line, except for one immediately following a start tag or immediately preceding an end tag.

0 The horizontal tab character must be interpreted as the smallest positive nonzero number of spaces which will leave the number of characters so far on the line as a multiple of 8. Its use is not recommended.

0 The Listing element is rendered so that at least 132 characters fit on a line. The Example element is rendered to that at least 80 characters fit on a line but is otherwise identical to the Listing element.

4.2 Proposed Features

This section describes proposed HTML elements and entities that are not currently supported under HTML Levels 0, 1, or 2, but may be supported in the future.

4.2.1 Defining Instance

<DFN> ... </DFN>

The Defining Instance element indicates the defining instance of a term. The typical rendering is bold or bold italic. This element is not widely supported.

4.2.2 Special Characters

To indicate special characters, HTML uses entity or numeric representations. Additional character presentations are proposed:

Table C–4. Special Characters

CHARACTER	REPRESENTATION
Non-breaking space	
Soft-hyphen	
Registered	®
Copyright	©

4.2.3 Strike

<STRIKE> ... </STRIKE>

The Strike element is proposed to indicate strikethrough, a font style in which a horizontal line appears through characters. This element is not widely supported.

4.2.4 Underline

<U> ... </U>

The Underline element is proposed to indicate that the text should be rendered as underlined. This proposed tag is not supported by all HTML user agents.

Example of use:

```
The text <U>shown here</U> is rendered in the document
as underlined.
```

5. HTML Document Type Definitions

5.1 SGML Declaration for HTML

This is the SGML Declaration for HyperText Markup Language (HTML) as used by the World Wide Web (WWW) application:

```
<!SGML  "ISO 8879:1986"
--
SGML Declaration for HyperText Markup Language (HTML).

--

CHARSET
        BASESET  "ISO 646:1983//CHARSET
                  International Reference Version
                  (IRV)//ESC 2/5 4/0"
        DESCSET  0   9   UNUSED
                 9   2   9
                 11  2   UNUSED
                 13  1   13
                 14  18  UNUSED
                 32  95  32
                 127 1   UNUSED
    BASESET   "ISO Registration Number 100//CHARSET
               ECMA-94 Right Part of
               Latin Alphabet Nr. 1//ESC 2/13 4/1"

        DESCSET  128  32   UNUSED
                 160  96    32

CAPACITY        SGMLREF
               TOTALCAP        150000
               GRPCAP          150000

SCOPE    DOCUMENT
SYNTAX
        SHUNCHAR CONTROLS 0 1 2 3 4 5 6 7 8 9 10 11 12 13 14 15 16
 17 18 19 20 21 22 23 24 25 26 27 28 29 30 31 127
        BASESET  "ISO 646:1983//CHARSET
                  International Reference Version
                  (IRV)//ESC 2/5 4/0"
        DESCSET  0 128 0
        FUNCTION
  RE          13
                 RS          10
                 SPACE       32
                 TAB SEPCHAR  9

        NAMING   LCNMSTRT ""
                 UCNMSTRT ""
```

```
                  LCNMCHAR ".-"
                  UCNMCHAR ".-"
                  NAMECASE GENERAL YES
                           ENTITY  NO
         DELIM    GENERAL  SGMLREF
                  SHORTREF SGMLREF
         NAMES    SGMLREF
         QUANTITY SGMLREF
                  ATTSPLEN 2100
                  LITLEN   1024
                  NAMELEN  72    -- somewhat arbitrary; taken from
                                internet line length conventions --
                  PILEN    1024
                  TAGLEN   2100

FEATURES
 MINIMIZE
   DATATAG  NO
   OMITTAG  YES
   RANK     NO
   SHORTTAG YES
 LINK
   SIMPLE   NO
   IMPLICIT NO
   EXPLICIT NO
 OTHER
   CONCUR   NO
   SUBDOC   NO
   FORMAL   YES
 APPINFO    "SDA"  -- conforming SGML Document Access application
    --
>
<!--
$Id: html.decl,v 1.13 1995/02/08 08:29:33 connolly Exp $

Author: Daniel W. Connolly <connolly@hal.com>

See also: http://www.hal.com/%7Econnolly/html-spec
  http://info.cern.ch/hypertext/WWW/MarkUp/MarkUp.html
-->
```

5.1.1 Sample SGML Open Style Entity Catalog for HTML

The SGML standard describes an "entity manager" as the portion or component of an SGML system that maps SGML entities into the actual storage model (e.g., the file system). The standard itself does not define a particular mapping methodology or notation.

To assist the interoperability among various SGML tools and systems, the SGML Open consortium has passed a technical resolution that defines a format for an application-independent entity catalog that maps external identifiers and/or entity names to file names.

Each entry in the catalog associates a storage object identifier (such as a file name) with information about the external entity that appears in the SGML document. In addition to entries that associate public identifiers, a catalog entry can associate an entity name with a storage object indentifier. For example, the following are possible catalog entries:

```
PUBLIC "ISO 8879:1986//ENTITIES Added Latin 1//EN" "iso-lat1.gml"
PUBLIC "-//ACME DTD Writers//DTD General Report//EN" report.dtd
ENTITY "graph1" "graphics\graph1.cgm"
```

In particular, the following shows entries relevant to HTML.

```
           -- catalog: SGML Open style entity catalog for HTML --
           -- $Id: catalog,v 1.1 1994/10/07 21:35:07 connolly Exp $ --
           -- Ways to refer to Level 2: most general to most specific --
PUBLIC  "-//IETF//DTD HTML//EN"                  html.dtd
PUBLIC  "-//IETF//DTD HTML//EN//2.0"             html.dtd
PUBLIC  "-//IETF//DTD HTML Level 2//EN"          html.dtd
PUBLIC  "-//IETF//DTD HTML Level 2//EN//2.0"     html.dtd

           -- Ways to refer to Level 1: most general to most specific --
PUBLIC  "-//IETF//DTD HTML Level 1//EN"          html-1.dtd
PUBLIC  "-//IETF//DTD HTML Level 1//EN//2.0"     html-1.dtd

           -- Ways to refer to Level 0: most general to most specific --
PUBLIC  "-//IETF//DTD HTML Level 0//EN"          html-0.dtd
PUBLIC  "-//IETF//DTD HTML Level 0//EN//2.0"     html-0.dtd


           -- ISO latin 1 entity set for HTML --
PUBLIC  "-//IETF//ENTITIES Added Latin 1//EN"    ISOlat1.sgml
```

5.2 HTML DTD

This is the Document Type Definition for the HyperText Markup Language (HTML DTD):

```
<!--    html.dtd

           Document Type Definition for the HyperText Markup Language
  (HTML DTD)

$Id: html.dtd,v 1.24 1995/02/06 21:28:45 connolly Exp $

Author: Daniel W. Connolly <connolly@hal.com>
See Also: html.decl, html-0.dtd, html-1.dtd
  http://www.hal.com/%7Econnolly/html-spec/index.html
  http://info.cern.ch/hypertext/WWW/MarkUp2/MarkUp.html
-->

<!ENTITY % HTML.Version
        "-//IETF//DTD HTML 2.0//EN"

        -- Typical usage:
```

```
            <!DOCTYPE HTML PUBLIC "-//IETF//DTD HTML//EN">
            <html>
            ...
            </html>
        --
        >


<!-============= Feature Test Entities ========================-->

<!ENTITY % HTML.Recommended "IGNORE"
-- Certain features of the language are necessary for
   compatibility with widespread usage, but they may
   compromise the structural integrity of a document.
   This feature test entity enables a more prescriptive
   document type definition that eliminates
   those features.
-->

<![ %HTML.Recommended [
        <!ENTITY % HTML.Deprecated "IGNORE">
]]>

<!ENTITY % HTML.Deprecated "INCLUDE"
-- Certain features of the language are necessary for
   compatibility with earlier versions of the specification,
   but they tend to be used an implemented inconsistently,
   and their use is deprecated. This feature test entity
   enables a document type definition that eliminates
   these features.
-->

<!ENTITY % HTML.Highlighting "INCLUDE"
-- Use this feature test entity to validate that a
   document uses no highlighting tags, which may be
   ignored on minimal implementations.
-->

<!ENTITY % HTML.Forms "INCLUDE"
        -- Use this feature test entity to validate that a document
           contains no forms, which may not be supported in minimal
           implementations
        -->

<!-============== Imported Names ===============================-->

<!ENTITY % Content-Type "CDATA"
        -- meaning an internet media type
           (aka MIME content type, as per RFC1521)
        -->
```

```
<!ENTITY % HTTP-Method "GET | POST"
        -- as per HTTP specification, in progress
        -->

<!ENTITY % URI "CDATA"
        -- The term URI means a CDATA attribute
           whose value is a Uniform Resource Identifier,
           as defined by
"Universal Resource Identifiers" by Tim Berners-Lee
aka RFC 1630

Note that CDATA attributes are limited by the LITLEN
capacity (1024 in the current version of html.decl),
so that URIs in HTML have a bounded length.

        -->


<!--========== DTD "Macros" =====================-->

<!ENTITY % heading "H1|H2|H3|H4|H5|H6">

<!ENTITY % list " UL | OL | DIR | MENU " >


<!--======= Character mnemonic entities =================-->

<!ENTITY % ISOlat1 PUBLIC
 "ISO 8879-1986//ENTITIES Added Latin 1//EN//HTML">
%ISOlat1;

<!ENTITY amp CDATA "&#38;"     -- ampersand          -->
<!ENTITY gt CDATA "&#62;"      -- greater than       -->
<!ENTITY lt CDATA "&#60;"      -- less than          -->
<!ENTITY quot CDATA "&#34;"    -- double quote       -->


<!--========== SGML Document Access (SDA) Parameter Entities =====-->

<!-- HTML 2.0 contains SGML Document Access (SDA) fixed attributes
in support of easy transformation to the International Committee
for Accessible Document Design (ICADD) DTD
 "-//EC-USA-CDA/ICADD//DTD ICADD22//EN".
ICADD applications are designed to support usable access to
structured information by print-impaired individuals through
Braille, large print and voice synthesis.  For more information on
SDA & ICADD:
        - ISO 12083:1993, Annex A.8, Facilities for Braille,
  large print and computer voice
        - ICADD ListServ
```

```
  <ICADD%ASUACAD.BITNET@ARIZVM1.ccit.arizona.edu>
       - Usenet news group bit.listserv.easi
       - Recording for the Blind, +1 800 221 4792
-->

<!ENTITY % SDAFORM  "SDAFORM  CDATA  #FIXED"
  -- one to one mapping        -->
<!ENTITY % SDARULE  "SDARULE  CDATA  #FIXED"
  -- context-sensitive mapping -->
<!ENTITY % SDAPREF  "SDAPREF  CDATA  #FIXED"
  -- generated text prefix     -->
<!ENTITY % SDASUFF  "SDASUFF  CDATA  #FIXED"
  -- generated text suffix     -->
<!ENTITY % SDASUSP  "SDASUSP  NAME   #FIXED"
  -- suspend transform process -->


<!--========== Text Markup =====================-->

<![ %HTML.Highlighting [

<!ENTITY % font " TT | B | I ">

<!ENTITY % phrase "EM | STRONG | CODE | SAMP | KBD | VAR | CITE ">

<!ENTITY % text "#PCDATA | A | IMG | BR | %phrase | %font">

<!ELEMENT (%font;|%phrase) - - (%text)*>
<!ATTLIST ( TT | CODE | SAMP | KBD | VAR )
       %SDAFORM; "Lit"
       >
<!ATTLIST ( B | STRONG )
       %SDAFORM; "B"
       >
<!ATTLIST ( I | EM | CITE )
       %SDAFORM; "It"
       >

<!-- <TT>       Typewriter text                       -->
<!-- <B>        Bold text                             -->
<!-- <I>        Italic text                           -->

<!-- <EM>       Emphasized phrase                     -->
<!-- <STRONG>   Strong emphais                        -->
<!-- <CODE>     Source code phrase                    -->
<!-- <SAMP>     Sample text or characters             -->
<!-- <KBD>      Keyboard phrase, e.g. user input      -->
<!-- <VAR>      Variable phrase or substituable       -->
<!-- <CITE>     Name or title of cited work           -->
```

```
<!ENTITY % pre.content "#PCDATA | A | HR | BR | %font | %phrase">

]]>

<!ENTITY % text "#PCDATA | A | IMG | BR">

<!ELEMENT BR    - O EMPTY>
<!ATTLIST BR
       %SDAPREF; "&#RE;"
       >

<!-- <BR>       Line break      -->


<!--========== Link Markup ======================-->

<![ %HTML.Recommended [
       <!ENTITY % linkName "ID">
]]>

<!ENTITY % linkName "CDATA">

<!ENTITY % linkType "NAME"
       -- a list of these will be specified at a later date -->

<!ENTITY % linkExtraAttributes
       "REL %linkType #IMPLIED
       REV %linkType #IMPLIED
       URN CDATA #IMPLIED
       TITLE CDATA #IMPLIED
       METHODS NAMES #IMPLIED
       ">

<![ %HTML.Recommended [
       <!ENTITY % A.content   "(%text)*"
       -- <H1><a name="xxx">Heading</a></H1>
               is preferred to
          <a name="xxx"><H1>Heading</H1></a>
       -->
]]>

<!ENTITY % A.content   "(%heading|%text)*">

<!ELEMENT A     - - %A.content -(A)>
<!ATTLIST A
       HREF %URI #IMPLIED
       NAME %linkName #IMPLIED
       %linkExtraAttributes;
       %SDAPREF; "<Anchor: #AttList>"
       >
```

```
<!-- <A>Anchor; source/destination of link-->
<!-- <A NAME="...">Name of this anchor-->
<!-- <A HREF="...">Address of link destination-->
<!-- <A URN="...">Permanent address of destination-->
<!-- <A REL=...>Relationship to destination-->
<!-- <A REV=...>Relationship of destination to this -->
<!-- <A TITLE="...">Title of destination (advisory) -->
<!-- <A METHODS="...">Operations on destination (advisory)-->


<!--========== Images ===========================-->

<!ELEMENT IMG    - O EMPTY>
<!ATTLIST IMG
       SRC %URI;  #REQUIRED
       ALT CDATA #IMPLIED
       ALIGN (top|middle|bottom) #IMPLIED
       ISMAP (ISMAP) #IMPLIED
       %SDAPREF; "<Fig><?SDATrans Img: #AttList>#AttVal(Alt)</Fig>"
       >

<!-- <IMG>              Image; icon, glyph or illustration      -->
<!-- <IMG SRC="...">    Address of image object                 -->
<!-- <IMG ALT="...">    Textual alternative                     -->
<!-- <IMG ALIGN=...>    Position relative to text               -->
<!-- <IMG ISMAP>        Each pixel can be a link                -->

<!--========== Paragraphs=======================-->

<!ELEMENT P      - O (%text)*>
<!ATTLIST P
       %SDAFORM; "Para"
       >

<!-- <P>        Paragraph       -->


<!--========== Headings, Titles, Sections ================-->

<!ELEMENT HR     - O EMPTY>
<!ATTLIST HR
       %SDAPREF; "&#RE;&#RE;"
       >

<!-- <HR>       Horizontal rule -->

<!ELEMENT ( %heading )  - -  (%text;)*>
<!ATTLIST H1
       %SDAFORM; "H1"
       >
```

```
<!ATTLIST H2
        %SDAFORM; "H2"
        >
<!ATTLIST H3
        %SDAFORM; "H3"
        >
<!ATTLIST H4
        %SDAFORM; "H4"
        >
<!ATTLIST H5
        %SDAFORM; "H5"
        >
<!ATTLIST H6
        %SDAFORM; "H6"
        >

<!-- <H1>       Heading, level 1 -->
<!-- <H2>       Heading, level 2 -->
<!-- <H3>       Heading, level 3 -->
<!-- <H4>       Heading, level 4 -->
<!-- <H5>       Heading, level 5 -->
<!-- <H6>       Heading, level 6 -->


<!--========== Text Flows =====================-->

<![ %HTML.Forms [
        <!ENTITY % block.forms "BLOCKQUOTE | FORM | ISINDEX">
]]>

<!ENTITY % block.forms "BLOCKQUOTE">

<![ %HTML.Deprecated [
        <!ENTITY % preformatted "PRE | XMP | LISTING">
]]>

<!ENTITY % preformatted "PRE">

<!ENTITY % block "P | %list | DL
        | %preformatted
        | %block.forms">

<!ENTITY % flow "(%text|%block)*">

<!ENTITY % pre.content "#PCDATA | A | HR | BR">
<!ELEMENT PRE - - (%pre.content)*>
<!ATTLIST PRE
        WIDTH NUMBER #implied
        %SDAFORM; "Lit"
        >
```

```
<!-- <PRE>                   Preformatted text              -->
<!-- <PRE WIDTH=...>         Maximum characters per line    -->

<![ %HTML.Deprecated [

<!ENTITY % literal "CDATA"
        -- historical, non-conforming parsing mode where
           the only markup signal is the end tag
           in full
        -->

<!ELEMENT (XMP|LISTING) - -  %literal>
<!ATTLIST XMP
        %SDAFORM; "Lit"
        %SDAPREF; "Example:&#RE;"
        >
<!ATTLIST LISTING
        %SDAFORM; "Lit"
        %SDAPREF; "Listing:&#RE;"
        >

<!-- <XMP>                   Example section          -->
<!-- <LISTING>               Computer listing         -->

<!ELEMENT PLAINTEXT - O %literal>
<!-- <PLAINTEXT>             Plain text passage       -->

<!ATTLIST PLAINTEXT
        %SDAFORM; "Lit"
        >
]]>


<!--========== Lists ==================-->

<!ELEMENT DL    - -  (DT | DD)+>
<!ATTLIST DL
        COMPACT (COMPACT) #IMPLIED
        %SDAFORM; "List"
        %SDAPREF; "Definition List:"
        >

<!ELEMENT DT    - O (%text)*>
<!ATTLIST DT
        %SDAFORM; "Term"
        >

<!ELEMENT DD    - O %flow>
<!ATTLIST DD
        %SDAFORM; "LItem"
```

```
>

<!-- <DL>                 Definition list, or glossary    -->
<!-- <DL COMPACT>         Compact style list              -->
<!-- <DT>                 Term in definition list         -->
<!-- <DD>                 Definition of term              -->

<!ELEMENT (OL|UL) - -  (LI)+>
<!ATTLIST OL
       COMPACT (COMPACT) #IMPLIED
       %SDAFORM; "List"
       >
<!ATTLIST UL
       COMPACT (COMPACT) #IMPLIED
       %SDAFORM; "List"
       >
<!-- <UL>                 Unordered list                  -->
<!-- <UL COMPACT>         Compact list style              -->
<!-- <OL>                 Ordered, or numbered list       -->
<!-- <OL COMPACT>         Compact list style              -->


<!ELEMENT (DIR|MENU) - -  (LI)+ -(%block)>
<!ATTLIST DIR
       COMPACT (COMPACT) #IMPLIED
       %SDAFORM; "List"
       %SDAPREF; "<LHead>Directory</LHead>"
       >
<!ATTLIST MENU
       COMPACT (COMPACT) #IMPLIED
       %SDAFORM; "List"
       %SDAPREF; "<LHead>Menu</LHead>"
       >

<!-- <DIR>                Directory list                  -->
<!-- <DIR COMPACT>        Compact list style              -->
<!-- <MENU>               Menu list                       -->
<!-- <MENU COMPACT>       Compact list style              -->

<!ELEMENT LI     - O %flow>
<!ATTLIST LI
       %SDAFORM; "LItem"
       >

<!-- <LI>                 List item                       -->

<!--========== Document Body ===================-->

<![ %HTML.Recommended [
<!ENTITY % body.content "(%heading|%block|HR|ADDRESS|IMG)*"
```

```
-- <h1>Heading</h1>
   <p>Text ...
is preferred to
   <h1>Heading</h1>
   Text ...
-->
]]>

<!ENTITY % body.content "(%heading | %text | %block |
              HR | ADDRESS)*">

<!ELEMENT BODY O O  %body.content>

<!-- <BODY>     Document body   -->

<!ELEMENT BLOCKQUOTE - - %body.content>
<!ATTLIST BLOCKQUOTE
       %SDAFORM; "BQ"
       >

<!-- <BLOCKQUOTE>       Quoted passage  -->

<!ELEMENT ADDRESS - - (%text|P)*>
<!ATTLIST  ADDRESS
       %SDAFORM; "Lit"
       %SDAPREF; "Address:&#RE;"
       >

<!-- <ADDRESS>Address, signature, or byline-->


<!--======= Forms ====================-->

<![ %HTML.Forms [

<!ELEMENT FORM - - %body.content -(FORM) +(INPUT|SELECT|TEXTAREA)>
<!ATTLIST FORM
       ACTION %URI #IMPLIED
       METHOD (%HTTP-Method) GET
       ENCTYPE %Content-Type; "application/x-www-form-urlencoded"
       %SDAPREF; "<Para>Form:</Para>"
       %SDASUFF; "<Para>Form End.</Para>"
       >

<!-- <FORM>                     Fill-out or data-entry form     -->
<!-- <FORM ACTION="...">        Address for completed form      -->
<!-- <FORM METHOD=...>          Method of submitting form       -->
<!-- <FORM ENCTYPE="...">       Representation of form data     -->
```

```
<!ENTITY % InputType "(TEXT | PASSWORD | CHECKBOX |
                       RADIO | SUBMIT | RESET |
                       IMAGE | HIDDEN )">
<!ELEMENT INPUT - O EMPTY>
<!ATTLIST INPUT
TYPE %InputType TEXT
NAME CDATA #IMPLIED
VALUE CDATA #IMPLIED
SRC %URI #IMPLIED
CHECKED (CHECKED) #IMPLIED
SIZE CDATA #IMPLIED
MAXLENGTH NUMBER #IMPLIED
ALIGN (top|middle|bottom) #IMPLIED
       %SDAPREF; "Input: "
>

<!-- <INPUT>Form input datum-->
<!-- <INPUT TYPE=...>Type of input interaction-->
<!-- <INPUT NAME=...>Name of form datum-->
<!-- <INPUT VALUE="...">Default/initial/selected value-->
<!-- <INPUT SRC="...">Address of image-->
<!-- <INPUT CHECKED>Initial state is "on"-->
<!-- <INPUT SIZE=...>Field size hint-->
<!-- <INPUT MAXLENGTH=...>Data length maximum-->
<!-- <INPUT ALIGN=...>Image alignment-->

<!ELEMENT SELECT - - (OPTION+) -(INPUT|SELECT|TEXTAREA)>
<!ATTLIST SELECT
       NAME CDATA #REQUIRED
       SIZE NUMBER #IMPLIED
       MULTIPLE (MULTIPLE) #IMPLIED
       %SDAFORM; "List"
       %SDAPREF;
       "<LHead>Select #AttVal(Multiple)</LHead>"
>

<!-- <SELECT>Selection of option(s)-->
<!-- <SELECT NAME=...>Name of form datum-->
<!-- <SELECT SIZE=...>Options displayed at a time-->
<!-- <SELECT MULTIPLE>Multiple selections allowed-->

<!ELEMENT OPTION - O (#PCDATA)*>
<!ATTLIST OPTION
       SELECTED (SELECTED) #IMPLIED
       VALUE CDATA #IMPLIED
       %SDAFORM; "LItem"
       %SDAPREF;
       "Option: #AttVal(Value) #AttVal(Selected)"
>
```

```
<!-- <OPTION>A selection option-->
<!-- <OPTION SELECTED>Initial state-->
<!-- <OPTION VALUE="...">Form datum value for this option-->

<!ELEMENT TEXTAREA - - (#PCDATA)* -(INPUT|SELECT|TEXTAREA)>
<!ATTLIST TEXTAREA
       NAME CDATA #REQUIRED
       ROWS NUMBER #REQUIRED
       COLS NUMBER #REQUIRED
       %SDAFORM; "Para"
       %SDAPREF; "Input Text -- #AttVal(Name): "
       >

<!-- <TEXTAREA>An area for text input-->
<!-- <TEXTAREA NAME=...>Name of form datum-->
<!-- <TEXTAREA ROWS=...>Height of area-->
<!-- <TEXTAREA COLS=...>Width of area-->

]]>


<!--======= Document Head ======================-->

<![ %HTML.Recommended [
<!ENTITY % head.extra "META* & LINK*">
]]>

<!ENTITY % head.extra "NEXTID? & META* & LINK*">

<!ENTITY % head.content "TITLE & ISINDEX? & BASE? &
       (%head.extra)">

<!ELEMENT HEAD O O  (%head.content)>

<!-- <HEAD>     Document head   -->

<!ELEMENT TITLE - -  (#PCDATA)*>
<!ATTLIST TITLE
       %SDAFORM; "Ti"    >

<!-- <TITLE>    Title of document -->

<!ELEMENT LINK - O EMPTY>
<!ATTLIST LINK
       HREF %URI #REQUIRED
       %linkExtraAttributes;
       %SDAPREF; "Linked to : #AttVal (TITLE) (URN) (HREF)>"    >

<!-- <LINK>Link from this document-->
<!-- <LINK HREF="...">Address of link destination-->
```

```
<!-- <LINK URN="...">Lasting name of destination-->
<!-- <LINK REL=...>Relationship to destination-->
<!-- <LINK REV=...>Relationship of destination to this -->
<!-- <LINK TITLE="...">Title of destination (advisory) -->
<!-- <LINK METHODS="..."> Operations allowed (advisory)-->

<!ELEMENT ISINDEX - O EMPTY>
<!ATTLIST ISINDEX
       %SDAPREF;
  "<Para>[Document is indexed/searchable.]</Para>">

<!-- <ISINDEX>          Document is a searchable index          -->

<!ELEMENT BASE - O EMPTY>
<!ATTLIST BASE
       HREF %URI; #REQUIRED     >

<!-- <BASE>             Base context document                   -->
<!-- <BASE HREF="...">  Address for this document               -->

<!ELEMENT NEXTID - O EMPTY>
<!ATTLIST NEXTID
       N %linkName #REQUIRED     >

<!-- <NEXTID>Next ID to use for link name-->
<!-- <NEXTID N=...>Next ID to use for link name-->

<!ELEMENT META - O EMPTY>
<!ATTLIST META
       HTTP-EQUIV  NAME    #IMPLIED
       NAME        NAME    #IMPLIED
       CONTENT     CDATA   #REQUIRED    >


<!-- <META>                      Generic Metainformation        -->
<!-- <META HTTP-EQUIV=...>       HTTP response header name      -->
<!-- <META HTTP-EQUIV=...>       Metainformation name           -->
<!-- <META CONTENT="...">        Associated information         -->

<!--======= Document Structure ==================-->

<![ %HTML.Deprecated [
       <!ENTITY % html.content "HEAD, BODY, PLAINTEXT?">
]]>
<!ENTITY % html.content "HEAD, BODY">

<!ELEMENT HTML O O  (%html.content)>
<!ENTITY % version.attr "VERSION CDATA #FIXED '%HTML.Version;'">
```

```
<!ATTLIST HTML
        %version.attr;
        %SDAFORM; "Book"
        >

<!-- <HTML>HTML Document-->
```

5.2.1 ISO Latin 1 Definitions for HTML

```
<!-- (C) International Organization for Standardization 1986
    Permission to copy in any form is granted for use with
    conforming SGML systems and applications as defined in
    ISO 8879:1986, provided this notice is included in all copies.
-->
<!-- Character entity set. Typical invocation:
    <!ENTITY % ISOlat1 PUBLIC
      "-//IETF//ENTITIES Added Latin 1 for HTML//EN">
    %ISOlat1;
-->
<!-- Modified for use in HTML
  $Id: ISOlat1.sgml,v 1.1 1994/09/24 14:06:34 connolly Exp $ -->
<!ENTITY AElig  CDATA "&#198;" -- capital AE diphthong (ligature) -->
<!ENTITY Aacute CDATA "&#193;" -- capital A, acute accent -->
<!ENTITY Acirc  CDATA "&#194;" -- capital A, circumflex accent -->
<!ENTITY Agrave CDATA "&#192;" -- capital A, grave accent -->
<!ENTITY Aring  CDATA "&#197;" -- capital A, ring -->
<!ENTITY Atilde CDATA "&#195;" -- capital A, tilde -->
<!ENTITY Auml   CDATA "&#196;" -- capital A, dieresis or umlaut mark -
->
<!ENTITY Ccedil CDATA "&#199;" -- capital C, cedilla -->
<!ENTITY ETH    CDATA "&#208;" -- capital Eth, Icelandic -->
<!ENTITY Eacute CDATA "&#201;" -- capital E, acute accent -->
<!ENTITY Ecirc  CDATA "&#202;" -- capital E, circumflex accent -->
<!ENTITY Egrave CDATA "&#200;" -- capital E, grave accent -->
<!ENTITY Euml   CDATA "&#203;" -- capital E, dieresis or umlaut mark -
->
<!ENTITY Iacute CDATA "&#205;" -- capital I, acute accent -->
<!ENTITY Icirc  CDATA "&#206;" -- capital I, circumflex accent -->
<!ENTITY Igrave CDATA "&#204;" -- capital I, grave accent -->
<!ENTITY Iuml   CDATA "&#207;" -- capital I, dieresis or umlaut mark -
->
<!ENTITY Ntilde CDATA "&#209;" -- capital N, tilde -->
<!ENTITY Oacute CDATA "&#211;" -- capital O, acute accent -->
<!ENTITY Ocirc  CDATA "&#212;" -- capital O, circumflex accent -->
<!ENTITY Ograve CDATA "&#210;" -- capital O, grave accent -->
<!ENTITY Oslash CDATA "&#216;" -- capital O, slash -->
<!ENTITY Otilde CDATA "&#213;" -- capital O, tilde -->
<!ENTITY Ouml   CDATA "&#214;" -- capital O, dieresis or umlaut mark -
->
```

```
<!ENTITY THORN  CDATA "&#222;" -- capital THORN, Icelandic -->
<!ENTITY Uacute CDATA "&#218;" -- capital U, acute accent -->
<!ENTITY Ucirc  CDATA "&#219;" -- capital U, circumflex accent -->
<!ENTITY Ugrave CDATA "&#217;" -- capital U, grave accent -->
<!ENTITY Uuml   CDATA "&#220;" -- capital U, dieresis or umlaut mark -
->
<!ENTITY Yacute CDATA "&#221;" -- capital Y, acute accent -->
<!ENTITY aacute CDATA "&#225;" -- small a, acute accent -->
<!ENTITY acirc  CDATA "&#226;" -- small a, circumflex accent -->
<!ENTITY aelig  CDATA "&#230;" -- small ae diphthong (ligature) -->
<!ENTITY agrave CDATA "&#224;" -- small a, grave accent -->
<!ENTITY aring  CDATA "&#229;" -- small a, ring -->
<!ENTITY atilde CDATA "&#227;" -- small a, tilde -->
<!ENTITY auml   CDATA "&#228;" -- small a, dieresis or umlaut mark -->
<!ENTITY ccedil CDATA "&#231;" -- small c, cedilla -->
<!ENTITY eacute CDATA "&#233;" -- small e, acute accent -->
<!ENTITY ecirc  CDATA "&#234;" -- small e, circumflex accent -->
<!ENTITY egrave CDATA "&#232;" -- small e, grave accent -->
<!ENTITY eth    CDATA "&#240;" -- small eth, Icelandic -->
<!ENTITY euml   CDATA "&#235;" -- small e, dieresis or umlaut mark -->
<!ENTITY iacute CDATA "&#237;" -- small i, acute accent -->
<!ENTITY icirc  CDATA "&#238;" -- small i, circumflex accent -->
<!ENTITY igrave CDATA "&#236;" -- small i, grave accent -->
<!ENTITY iuml   CDATA "&#239;" -- small i, dieresis or umlaut mark -->
<!ENTITY ntilde CDATA "&#241;" -- small n, tilde -->
<!ENTITY oacute CDATA "&#243;" -- small o, acute accent -->
<!ENTITY ocirc  CDATA "&#244;" -- small o, circumflex accent -->
<!ENTITY ograve CDATA "&#242;" -- small o, grave accent -->
<!ENTITY oslash CDATA "&#248;" -- small o, slash -->
<!ENTITY otilde CDATA "&#245;" -- small o, tilde -->
<!ENTITY ouml   CDATA "&#246;" -- small o, dieresis or umlaut mark -->
<!ENTITY szlig  CDATA "&#223;" -- small sharp s, German(sz ligature)-->
<!ENTITY thorn  CDATA "&#254;" -- small thorn, Icelandic -->
<!ENTITY uacute CDATA "&#250;" -- small u, acute accent -->
<!ENTITY ucirc  CDATA "&#251;" -- small u, circumflex accent -->
<!ENTITY ugrave CDATA "&#249;" -- small u, grave accent -->
<!ENTITY uuml   CDATA "&#252;" -- small u, dieresis or umlaut mark -->
<!ENTITY yacute CDATA "&#253;" -- small y, acute accent -->
<!ENTITY yuml   CDATA "&#255;" -- small y, dieresis or umlaut mark -->
```

5.3 HTML Level 0 DTD

This is the Document Type Definition for the HyperText Markup Language as used by minimally conforming World Wide Web applications (HTML Level 0 DTD):

```
<!--html-0.dtd

        Document Type Definition for the HyperText Markup Language as
used by minimally conforming World Wide Web applications
(HTML Level 0 DTD).
```

```
$Id: html-0.dtd,v 1.11 1995/01/28 05:59:32 connolly Exp $

Author: Daniel W. Connolly <connolly@hal.com>
See Also: http://www.hal.com/%7Econnolly/html-spec/index.html
  http://info.cern.ch/hypertext/WWW/MarkUp2/MarkUp.html
-->

<!ENTITY % HTML.Version
"-//IETF//DTD HTML 2.0 Level 0//EN"
-- public identifier for "minimal conformance" version          --
-- Typical usage:

           <!DOCTYPE HTML PUBLIC
"-//IETF//DTD HTML Level 0//EN">
    <html>
    ...
    </html>
--
>

<!-- Feature Test Entities -->

<!ENTITY % HTML.Highlighting "IGNORE">
<!ENTITY % HTML.Forms "IGNORE">

<!ENTITY % head.extra " ">
<!ENTITY % linkExtraAttributes " ">

<!ENTITY % html PUBLIC "-//IETF//DTD HTML 2.0//EN">
%html;
```

5.4 HTML Level 1 DTD

This is the Document Type Definition for the HyperText Markup Language with Level 1 Extensions (HTML Level 1 DTD):

```
<!--html-1.dtd

      Document Type Definition for the HyperText Markup Language
with Level 1 Extensions(HTML Level 1 DTD).

$Id: html-1.dtd,v 1.6 1994/11/30 23:45:26 connolly Exp $

Author: Daniel W. Connolly <connolly@hal.com>
See Also: http://www.hal.com/%7Econnolly/html-spec/index.html
  http://info.cern.ch/hypertext/WWW/MarkUp2/MarkUp.html
-->

<!ENTITY % HTML.Version
"-//IETF//DTD HTML 2.0 Level 1//EN"
```

```
        -- Typical usage:

            <!DOCTYPE HTML PUBLIC
"-//IETF//DTD HTML Level 1//EN">
    <html>
    ...
    </html>
--
>

<!-- Feature Test Entities -->
<!ENTITY % HTML.Forms "IGNORE">

<!ENTITY % html PUBLIC "-//IETF//DTD HTML 2.0//EN">
%html;
```

6. Glossary

The HTML specification uses these words with precise meanings:

attribute A syntactical component of an HTML element which is often used to specify a characteristic quality of an element, other than type or content.

document type definition (DTD) A DTD is a collection of declarations (entity, element, attribute, link, map, etc.) in SGML syntax that defines the components and structures available for a class (type) of documents.

element A component of the hierarchical structure defined by the document type definition; it is identified in a document instance by descriptive markup, usually a start-tag and an end-tag.

HTML HyperText Markup Language.

HTML user agent Any tool used with HTML documents.

HTML document A collection of information represented as a sequence of characters. An HTML document consists of data characters and markup. In particular, the markup describes a structure conforming to the HTML document type definition.

HTTP A generic stateless object-oriented protocol, which may be used for many similar tasks by extending the commands, or "methods", used. For example, you might use HTTP for name servers and distributed object-oriented systems, With HTTP, the negotiation of data representation allows systems to be built independent of the development of new representations. For more information see: http://info.cern.ch/hypertext/WWW/Protocols/HTTP/HTTP2.html

(document) instance The document itself including the actual content with the actual markup. Can be a single document or part of a document instance set that follows the DTD.

markup Text added to the data of a document to convey information about it. There are four different kinds of markup: descriptive markup (tags), references, markup declarations, and processing instructions.

Multipurpose Internet Mail Extensions (MIME) An extension to Internet email which provides the ability to transfer non-textual data, such as graphics, audio and fax. It is defined in RFC 1341.

representation The encoding of information for interchange. For example, HTML is a representation of hypertext.

rendering Formatting and presenting information.

SGML Standard Generalized Markup Language is a data encoding that allows the information in documents to be shared - either by other document publishing systems or by applications for electronic delivery, configuration management, database management, inventory control, etc. Defined in ISO 8879:1986 Information Processing Text and Office Systems; Standard Generalized Markup Language (SGML).

SGMLS An SGML parser by James Clark, jjc@jclark.com, derived from the ARCSGML parser materials which were written by Charles F. Goldfarb. The source is available at ftp.ifi.uio.no/pub/SGML/SGMLS.

tag Descriptive markup. There are two kinds of tags; start- tags and end-tags.

URI Universal Resource Identifiers (URIs) is the name for a generic WWW identifier. The URI specification simply defines the syntax for encoding arbitrary naming or addressing schemes, and has a list of such schemes. See also: http://info.cern.ch/hypertext/WWW/Addressing/Addressing.html

WWW A hypertext-based, distributed information system created by researchers at CERN in Switzerland. Users may create, edit or browse hypertext documents. The clients and servers are freely available.See also: http://info.cern.ch/hypertext/WWW/TheProject.html

6.1 Imperatives

may The implementation is not obliged to follow this in any way.

must If this is not followed, the implementation does not conform to this specification.

shall If this is not followed, the implementation does not conform to this specification.

should If this is not followed, though the implementation officially conforms to the specification, undesirable results may occur in practice.

typical Typical rendering is described for many elements. This is not a mandatory part of the specification but is given as guidance for designers and to help explain the uses for which the elements were intended.

7. References

The HTML specification cites these works:

HTTP HTTP: A Protocol for Networked Information. This document is available at http://info.cern.ch/hypertext/WWW/Protocols/HTTP/HTTP2.h tml.

MIME N. Borenstein, N. Freed, MIME (Multipurpose Internet Mail Extensions) Part One: Mechanisms for Specifying and Describing the Format of Internet Message

Bodies, 09/23/1993. (Pages=81) (Format=.txt, .ps) (Obsoletes RFC1341) (Updated by RFC1590).

SGML ISO Standard 8879:1986 Information Processing Text and Office Systems; Standard Generalized Markup Language (SGML).

SGMLS An SGML parser by James Clark, jjc@jclark.com, derived from the ARCSGML parser materials which were written by Charles F. Goldfarb. The source is available at ftp.ifi.uio.no/pub/SGML/SGMLS.

URI Universal Resource Identifiers. Available by anonymous FTP as Postscript (info.cern.ch/pub/www/doc/url.ps) or text (info.cern.ch/pub/www/doc/url.txt)

WWW The World Wide Web , a global information initiative. For bootstrap information, telnet info.cern.ch or find documents by ftp://info.cern.ch/pub/www/doc.

8. Acknowledgments

The HTML document type was designed by Tim Berners-Lee at CERN as part of the 1990 World Wide Web project. In 1992, Dan Connolly wrote the HTML Document Type Definition (DTD) and a brief HTML specification.

Since 1993, a wide variety of Internet participants have contributed to the evolution of HTML, which has included the addition of in-line images introduced by the NCSA Mosaic software for WWW. Dave Raggett played an important role in deriving the FORMS material from the HTML+ specification.

Dan Connolly and Karen Olson Muldrow rewrote the HTML Specification in 1994.

Special thanks to the many people who have contributed to this specification:

- Terry Allen; O'Reilly & Associates; terry@ora.com
- Marc Andreessen; Netscape Communications Corp; marca@mcom.com
- Paul Burchard; The Geometry Center, University of Minnesota; burchard@geom.umn.edu
- James Clark; jjc@jclark.com
- Daniel W. Connolly; HaL Computer Systems; connolly@hal.com
- Roy Fielding; University of California, Irvine; fielding@ics.uci.edu
- Peter Flynn; University College Cork, Ireland; pflynn@www.ucc.ie
- Jay Glicksman; Enterprise Integration Technology; jay@eit.com
- Paul Grosso; ArborText, Inc.; paul@arbortext.com
- Eduardo Gutentag; Sun Microsystems; eduardo@Eng.Sun.com
- Bill Hefley; Software Engineering Institute, Carnegie Mellon University; weh@sei.cmu.edu
- Chung-Jen Ho; Xerox Corporation; cho@xsoft.xerox.com
- Mike Knezovich; Spyglass, Inc.; mike@spyglass.com
- Tim Berners-Lee; CERN; timbl@info.cern.ch
- Tom Magliery; NCSA; mag@ncsa.uiuc.edu
- Murray Maloney; Toronto Development Centre, The Santa Cruz Operation (SCO); murray@sco.com

- 0 Larry Masinter; Xerox Palo Alto Research Center; masinter@parc.xerox.com
- 0 Karen Olson Muldrow; HaL Computer Systems; karen@hal.com
- 0 Bill Perry, Spry, Inc., wmperry@spry.com
- 0 Dave Raggett, Hewlett Packard, dsr@hplb.hpl.hp.com
- 0 E. Corprew Reed; Cold Spring Harbor Laboratory; corp@cshl.org
- 0 Yuri Rubinsky; SoftQuad, Inc.; yuri@sq.com
- 0 Eric Schieler; Spyglass, Inc.; eschieler@spyglass.com
- 0 James L. Seidman; Spyglass, Inc.; jim@spyglass.com
- 0 Eric W. Sink; Spyglass, Inc.; eric@spyglass.com
- 0 Stuart Weibel; OCLC Office of Research; weibel@oclc.org
- 0 Chris Wilson; Spry, Inc.; cwilson@spry.com

9. Authors' Addresses

Tim Berners-Lee
timbl@quag.lcs.mit.edu

Daniel W. Connolly
Hal Software Systems
3006A Longhorn Blvd.
Austin, TX 78758
phone: (512) 834-9962 extension 5010
fax: (512) 823-9963
URL: http://www.hal.com/~connolly
email: connolly@hal.com

Glossary

A

AFS (Andrew File System) A distributed file system developed at Carnegie Mellon University. It is more advanced than its more common counterpart, *NFS,* and requires a license to use it. It is marketed by Transarc and will soon be replaced by *DFS.*

agent/specialized agent Sort of like James Bond, but different. A program that processes or seeks out information on behalf of a user. For example, mail agents are generally used to automatically filter incoming mail for a user. With regards to the Web, we discuss specialized agents in Chapter 12.

anonymous FTP A method of logging in to an FTP server with the name "anonymous" or "ftp" and using your e-mail address as the password. This allows anyone to log in and download files, and is common for sites that are trying to make information available to everybody.

associative array A data type in perl that consists of a set of key-value pairs, where there is a single mapping between a key and its value (i.e., you cannot have duplicate keys although you can have duplicate values). Often used to do very simple, yet efficient lookup tables in perl. For example, you could have an associative array, *last_name,* which maps the key *Eric* to the value *Richard.*

Athena MIT's campus-wide computing environment.

B

breadth-first search A method of traversing a tree in which all the nodes at a single level are searched before any nodes on the next level are searched, guaranteeing that the first path found between two points is the shortest path possible.

browser/Web browser Software programs that allow you to retrieve documents on the Web and follow links from document to document.

C

CERN Conseil Européen pour la Recherche Nucléaire (European Laboratory for Particle Physics), the birthplace of the Web. Tim Berners-Lee worked at CERN when he came up with the original proposals for the Web, and CERN was the testing ground for many of the original Web protocols. In addition, CERN wrote one of the major HTTP servers—the CERN httpd.

CGI (Common Gateway Interface) The standard used to define the mechanism by which HTTP servers communicate with server-side executables. CGI/1.0 has been replaced by CGI/1.1, which allows for slightly greater flexibility.

D

daemon One of Satan's minions. Also, a UNIX process that waits for system events to occur and responds to them. For example, an HTTP server—like the NCSA httpd or CERN httpd—is a daemon waiting to respond to requests from the outside world. Other standard daemons include fingerd (the finger daemon), lpd (the print-spool daemon), ftpd (the FTP server daemon), and inetd (the super-daemon that listens on multiple ports and starts up other daemons when necessary). *Daemon* can also be spelled *demon,* although techies tend to prefer the former spelling. See also *fetcher daemon.*

DFS (Distributed File System) A distributed file system developed by Transarc as the successor to AFS.

DNS (Domain Name Service) The means of translating between hostnames and IP addresses. It is the computer equivalent of a telephone book. Whenever you have a hostname, like netgen.com, DNS provides the means of looking up that name and finding the machine's IP address.

DIPB (Distributed Information Processing Board) A more interesting (and possibly more appropriate) name for MIT's SIPB. The name change has been proposed numerous times, but has not yet been accepted.

document An object of a specific type as identified by the server so the client will know how to handle/display it.

DTD (Document Type Definition) An ugly, heinous way of describing in gory detail the grammar of a language. Often confused with another, equally dangerous material, DDT. For example, the HTML 3.0 DTD defines, in tremendous detail, exactly which elements are allowed within others, what attributes are required, etc.

F

fetcher daemon Sort of like a "gofer" (*not* Gopher), but more demonic. A small program which is part of a larger program that listens for requests from the main program and then makes a request on behalf of the main program. Because these programs are small, they can be highly specialized and tuned to achieve high performance. In Chapter 12 we explain how a client could use fetcher daemons to make many requests at a time.

firewall A security measure used to protect computers on a local network from outside accesses. This is achieved by making a single gateway between the network and the outside world through which all the packets have to travel. This gateway is then configured to allow only certain types of accesses. For example, it is possible to configure a firewall to allow only outside accesses on ports 21 (FTP) and 23 (telnet) and refuse all other connections. It is also possible to forbid accesses from certain outside IP addresses; however, this really isn't that secure since it is always possible to spoof your IP address (see *IP spoofing*).

G

gateway A computer or router connected to two networks which allows data to get from one network to the other.

Gopher A means of accessing distributed information on the Internet. The most immediate precursor to the Web.

H

host A machine on a network. Also the person who greets you at a party.

Hot Java A browser by Sun Microsystems which allows for the downloading and running of miniature applications written in a language called Java.

HTML (Hypertext Markup Language) The principal language used to define documents on the World Wide Web. HTML is a markup language which allows for the creation of hypertext links between related documents or objects.

HTTP (Hypertext Transfer Protocol) The principal protocol used to transfer data on the Web. HTTP provides certain advantages over previous protocols, like FTP, because it allows more meta-information to be translated with the data being sent.

httpd The Hypertext Transfer Protocol daemon.

I

IETF (Internet Engineering Task Force) The organization principally responsible for the definition of most standards on the Internet.

Internet The global network of networks that has become infamous as the "Information Superhighway." It's sort of like a bowl of soup and a car, but different.

IP (Internet Protocol) The standard protocol used to transfer data from machine to machine on the Internet. IP provides for a certain amount of reliability that other standards (see *UDP*) don't provide, although this comes at the cost of a greater overhead (i.e., slower speed).

IP address The numeric address that identifies a particular computer on the Internet. IP addresses consist of four octets that uniquely identify a computer. Just like a phone number is used to determine how to route a phone call, a computer's IP address is used to route packets to it (see *multihosting*).

IP spoofing Sending packets that claim to be from another computer. Whenever a packet is sent from one machine to another, the packet contains the IP address for both the recipient and the sender. However, it is possible for the sender to put down any address it wants. Therefore, it is very insecure to use the IP address of the sender for any security purposes (for example, if it is being used to restrict accesses through a firewall or authenticate a user). IP spoofing is not nice.

ISP (Internet Service Provider) A company that provides customers connections to the Internet. Generally ISPs offer connections at speeds anywhere between 14.4 kbps to full T1 connections.

J

Java A "safe" version of C++ used by Hot Java. "Safe" means limiting what the user can do to a set of operations so that they cannot do any damage to the local system.

K

kludging Doing something that is technically possible, though it wasn't the intended feature of the program. Also known as "hacking."

L

leaf nodes The nodes in a tree which don't have any children. In Web terms, these are the documents which do not contain any links.

library A place with lots of books or, alternatively, a place with lots of code. Specifically, a predefined piece of code that you can use when you are writing your own program. One or more functions that you can make calls to from your code. Libraries can't stand on their own (i.e., you can't run a library or package); instead, parts of them get used by other programs. See also *package*.

Linux A free UNIX operating system for the x86 chipset developed by Linus Torvalds. (Pronounced like "linnucks.")

M

mirror site A site which makes a regular, complete copy of the contents of another site. This is generally done to reduce the load on a popular site. For example, Digital Equipment Corporation (DEC) provides mirror of O'Reilly's Global Network Navigator to reduce the load that GNN receives.

MIT (Massachusetts Institute of Technology) Home of the *SIBP* and *W3C,* and alma mater of net.Genesis. Often confused with "Montana Institute for Trucking" or "Must Increase Tuition." We hope it means "Millionaires in Training."

Mosaic The graphical Web browser written at NCSA which is really responsible for the popularity of the Web.

Mozilla According to the Netscape Navigator README file, this is the pronunciation of the word "Netscape." Also refers to the Godzilla-like creature that is Netscape's mascot. Its origin is probably a cross between the words "Mosaic" and "Godzilla."

multihosting A way of *kludging* your computer to accept packets addressed to multiple IP addresses. By detecting which IP address the packet was intended for, it is possible to simulate multiple servers on a single machine.

multitasking Working on multiple jobs at once. Sort of like walking and chewing gum at the same time, but less complicated.

N

name server A computer running DNS that manages Internet domain names and numeric IP addresses.

Netscape A company founded by Jim Clark and Marc Andreesen. The company has produced both servers and browsers for the commercial market, including the currently most popular browser, Netscape Navigator (commonly just called "Netscape").

NFS (Network File System) The most widely used distributed file system. It is standard on most UNIX machines and does not require a license to use. NFS clients and servers are also available for Windows and Windows NT machines.

P

package Something you get in the mail. Also, the perl term for a *library.*

packet lossage The phenomenon of data on a network not making it from the origin to the destination within an accepted amount of time. When packets are lost, they have to be resent, which slows down communication.

packet sniffing Reading packets on a network that are not intended for you. Because of the way the Ethernet protocol works, it is possible to configure your machine so that it listens for packets that are intended for someone else, or that are from other computers on your same local network. By doing this, you can watch any text they are sending "in the clear" (i.e., unencrypted). This is one of the easiest ways to get passwords—simply set up a packet-sniffing program and watch for users to send their name and password in the clear.

perl (Practical Extraction and Report Language) An interpreted language written by Larry Wall that is great for string manipulation and parsing tasks. Many CGI scripts are written in perl since it is so easy to use. Also known as Pathologically Eclectic Rubbish Lister.

ping A standard UNIX command that sends packets to a machine and looks for a response. You can use ping to determine whether another machine is connected to the network. In addition, ping can be used to obtain performance statistics about the network between two machines.

PPP A protocol that allows for routing of any protocol (e.g., IP, AppleTalk, Novell NetWare, etc.) over a serial line (modem). By setting up a PPP connection from your machine, it is possible to use all the standard network related utilities (FTP, telnet, etc.) even though you are only connected to the rest of the world via a modem.

preemptive multitasking The means for deciding which process gets the system's attention at any given moment, at which time the system can choose to take the control from one process and give it to another. UNIX, Windows 95, OS/2, and Windows NT use preemptive multitasking. However DOS, Windows 3.1, and System 7 do not support this sharing attitude. Therefore, when one process gains control it will continue to maintain control until its task is completed or it chooses to relinquish control. Thus, when a program gets out of control and crashes, it is impossible to regain control of your computer without rebooting it. With preemptive multitasking, it is possible simply to kill off the offending process and move on.

processor load A measure of the number of jobs your processor is trying to take care of at one time. A load of 1.0 is equivalent to saying that your processor has exactly one job at every clock cycle. Loads lower than 1.0 indicate that processor time is being spent idle. Processor loads above 1.0 signify that your processor has more to do than it can currently handle.

protected memory Sort of like a repressed memory, but different. In computing, some operating systems like UNIX prevent processes from accessing the memory which is being used by other processes. This means that no single process can write over the memory space that another process is using. Other operating systems such as DOS and System 7 do not enforce this constraint, violating system integrity or causing the infamous GPF errors that Windows 3.1 users hate so much. (Windows 95 is not supposed to have this problem.)

proxy server A server that makes a request on behalf of a client instead of the client doing it directly. This is often required in the case of a firewalled network, where the proxy server sits on both the Internet and the secure internal network. A user on the secure internal network cannot make a request directly to the outside world, so it asks the proxy server, which requests the document on its behalf.

R

router A computer that decides which path the Internet traffic will take to reach its destination. A router can also filter network packets to restrict traffic in or out of its local network.

S

SATAN (System Administrator's Tool for Analyzing Networks) A security tool that many people worried about much more than they needed to. Still, a useful tool.

sendmail A standard UNIX program that handles e-mail. It is notorious for being confusing to set up and therefore has been the cause of many security concerns. In fact, the Internet Worm exploited a common configuration error in sendmail to gain access to remote machines.

server load A measure of how many accesses a Web server is receiving. Commonly measured in hits per second.

SGML (Standard Generalized Markup Language) A language that is used to define markup languages. For example, the HTML 2.0 and 3.0 specifications define HTML in a SGML grammar.

S-HTTP (Secure Hypertext Transfer Protocol) One of the evolving standards on the Web that allows for secure transactions.

SIPB (Student Information Processing Board) A volunteer student computer service organization at MIT (maintainers of **http://www.mit.edu:8001**).

site A service offered by a single HTTP server listening to a single port. By this definition, all the resources available at www.netgen.com on port 80 are a site. This definition breaks down for a number of reasons, however. It is possible to have multiple machines serving a single site (for example, the NCSA site uses multiple machines to handle their load). It is also possible to have multiple conceptual sites served from a single machine. For example, on the net.Genesis server, we provide net.Genesis corporate information as well as the Sports Information Service. Conceptually, these are two different entities and could be described as two separate sites. The meaning of *site* is probably best described as a coherent/unified set of internally interlinked pages and objects.

SLIP A method of speaking IP over a serial line. Not as cool, useful, generic, or in vogue as PPP.

SMTP (Simple Mail Transport Protocol) The protocol by which real e-mail is transferred. Often this is what people are talking about when they say "Internet e-mail."

spamming Bombarding a machine with requests in order to hamper its ability to function properly.

SSL (Secure Sockets Layer) Netscape's proposed standard for secure transactions. Involves full end-to-end encryption of all sockets communication.

T

TBL Tim Berners-Lee, founder of the Web.

TCP (Transmission Control Protocol) A network protocol for sequenced packet delivery.

U

UDP (Unreliable Datagram Protocol) A transport layer protocol (like *TCP*) designed to ensure that packets get from their source to their destination. Unlike TCP, however, UDP is connectionless and does not ensure that packets will arrive at their destination in any order.

UNIX Men who at a young age have undergone surgery to remove—uh, never mind. Also a widely used operating system developed at AT&T's Bell Labs, refined at Berkeley, and various other places. It doesn't stand for anything.

URI (Universal Resource Identifier) An identification scheme for Internet resources that encompasses URLs and URNs.

URL (Uniform Resource Locator) A means of identifying the exact location of a particular resource on the Internet.

URN (Uniform Resource Name) A naming scheme for resources on the Internet that can be used to map a particular name to one or more resources (much like a hostname can map to one or more IP addresses).

W

World Wide Web The distributed, multimedia network of hypertext documents designed by Tim Berners-Lee of CERN.

W3C World Wide Web Consortium. A global standards body charged with furthering the progress and development of the Web.

Wandex A Web search engine maintained and constantly updated by net.Genesis. It is a content-based search engine, which analyzes the contents of documents it indexes.

INDEX

B

C

D

E

F

G

H

I

J

K

L

O

P

Q

R

S

T

U

Y

Other Prima Computer Books

The CD-ROM Revolution	24.95
Internet After Hours	19.95
Free Electronic Networks	24.95
The Software Developer's Complete Legal Companion (with 3½" disk)	39.95
CompuServe Information Manager for Windows: The Complete Membership Kit & Handbook (with two 3½" disks)	34.95
Internet for Windows: America Online Edition	19.95
Cruising America Online	19.95
The USENET Navigator Kit	24.95
Interactive Internet: The Insider's Guide to MUDs, MOOs, and IRC	19.95
The Warp Book: Your Definitive Guide to Installing and Using OS/2 v3	24.95
Paradox for Windows Essential Power Programming (with 3½" disk)	39.95
Thom Duncan's Guide to NetWare Shareware (with 3½" disk)	29.95
Visual Basic for Applications Revealed!	27.95
The Slightly Skewed Computer Dictionary	8.95
Create Wealth with Quicken, Second Edition	19.95
Microsoft Office in Concert, Professional Edition	27.95